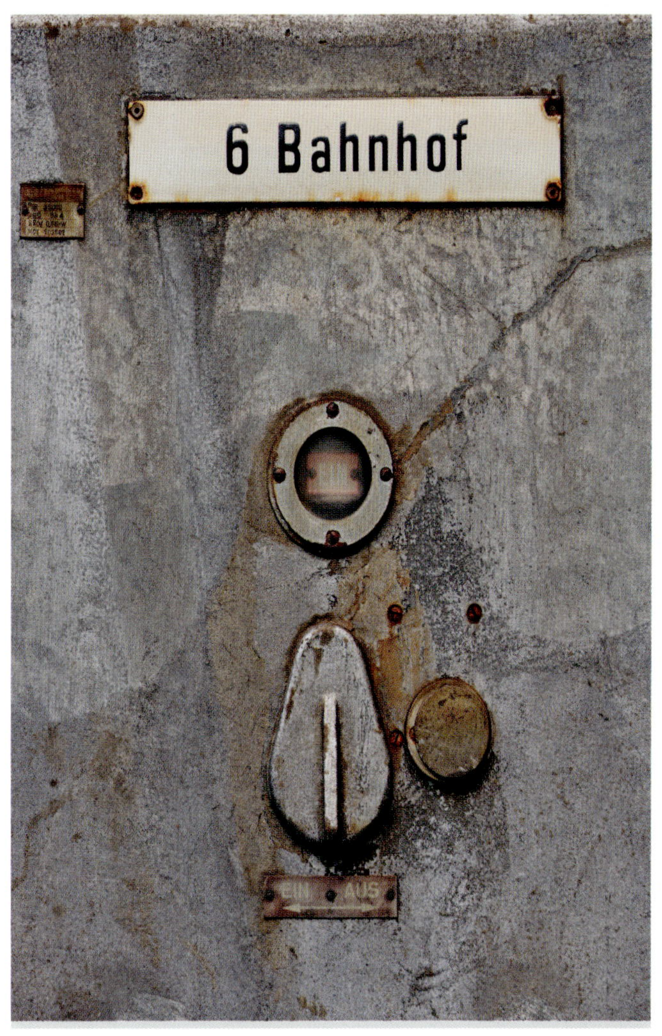

Tom Waits
"Down There by the Train"

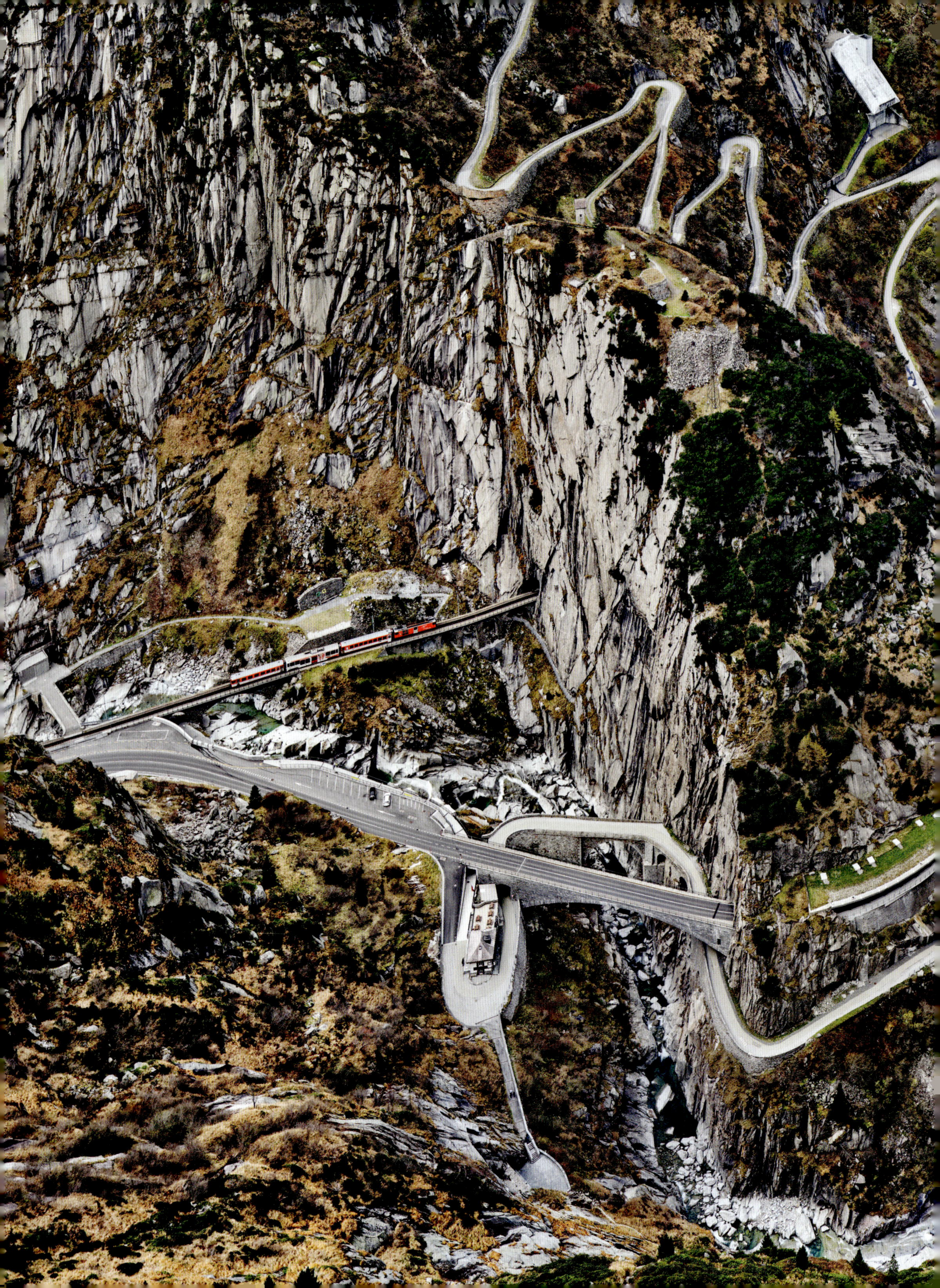

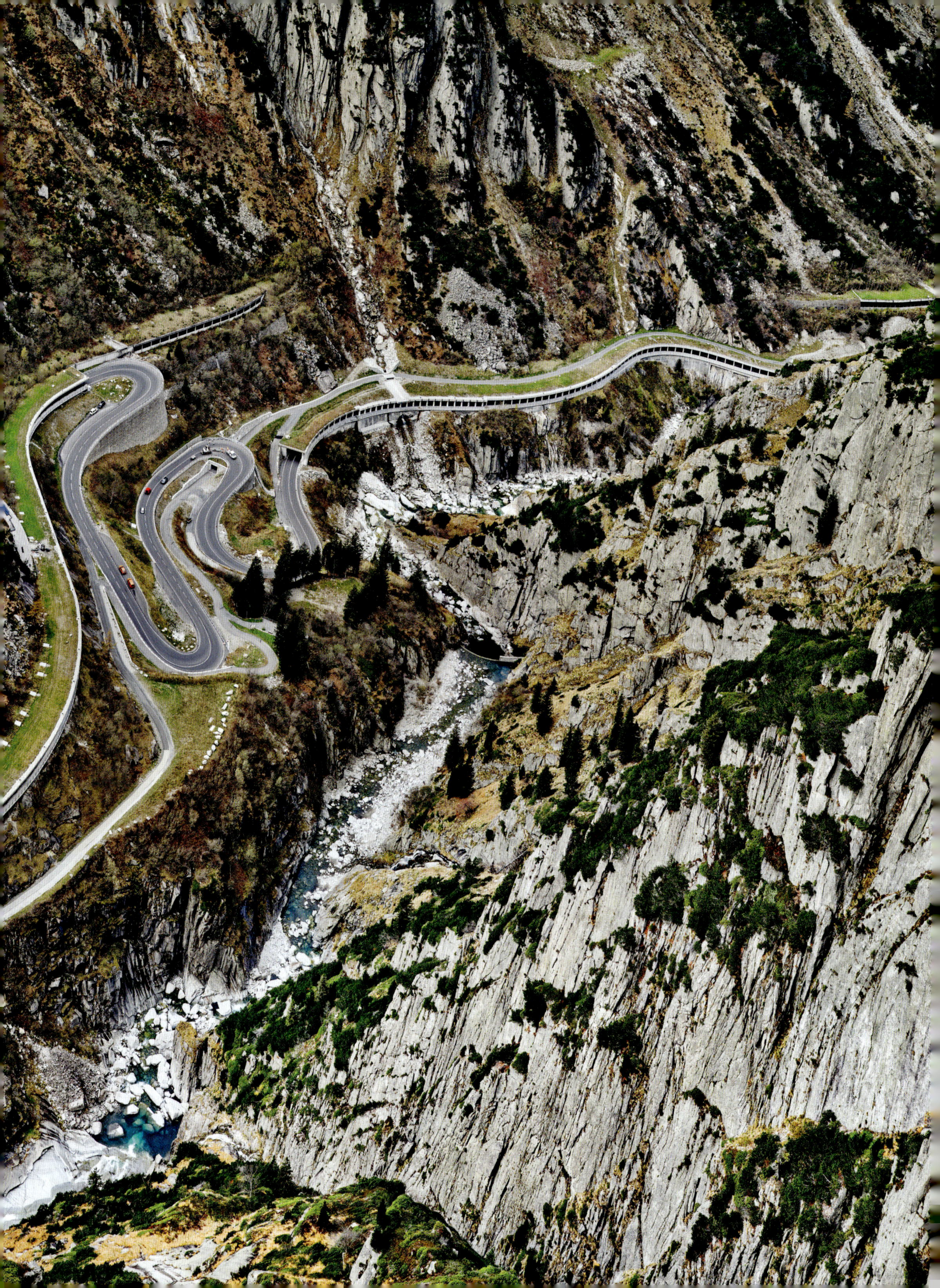

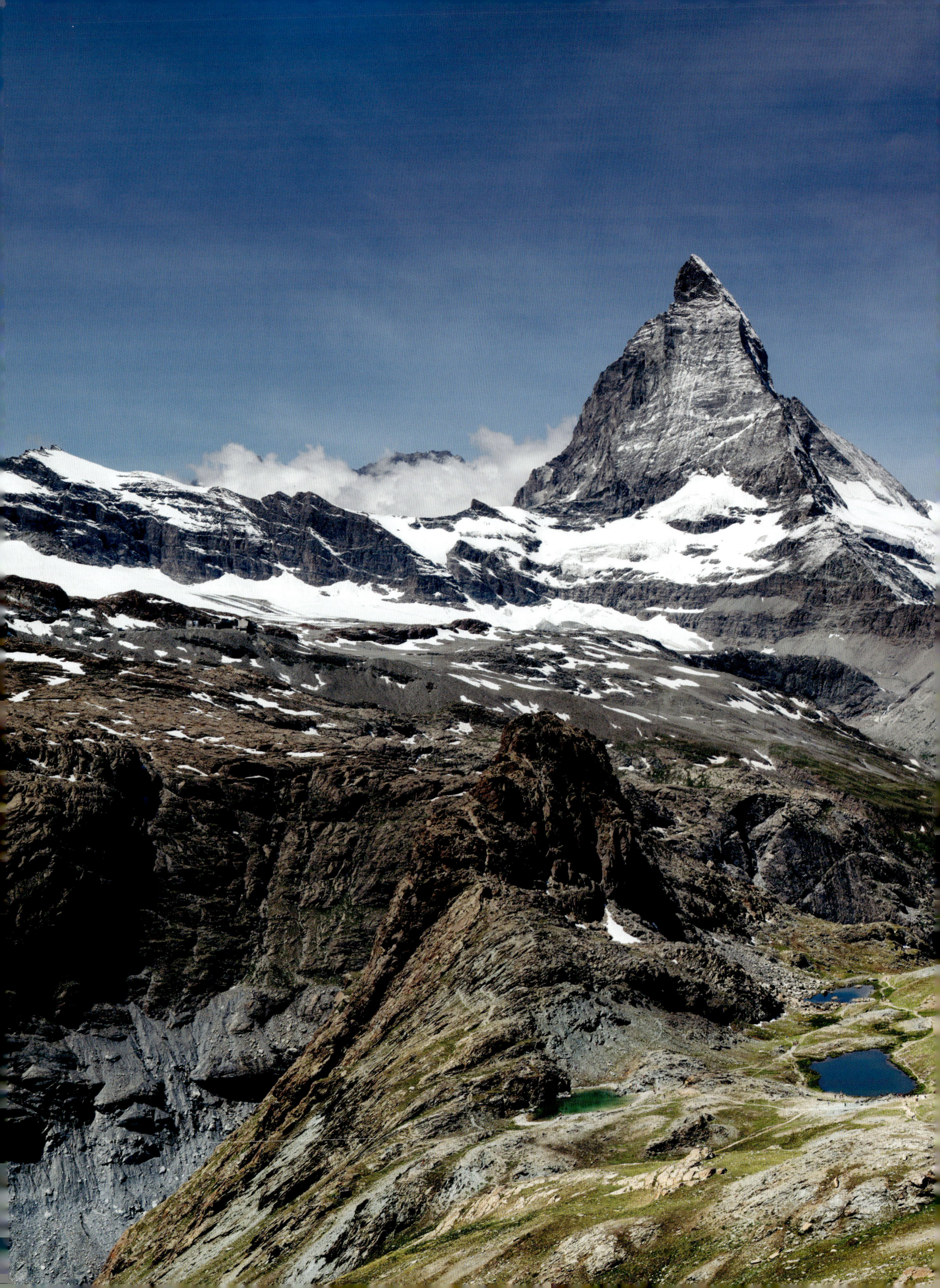

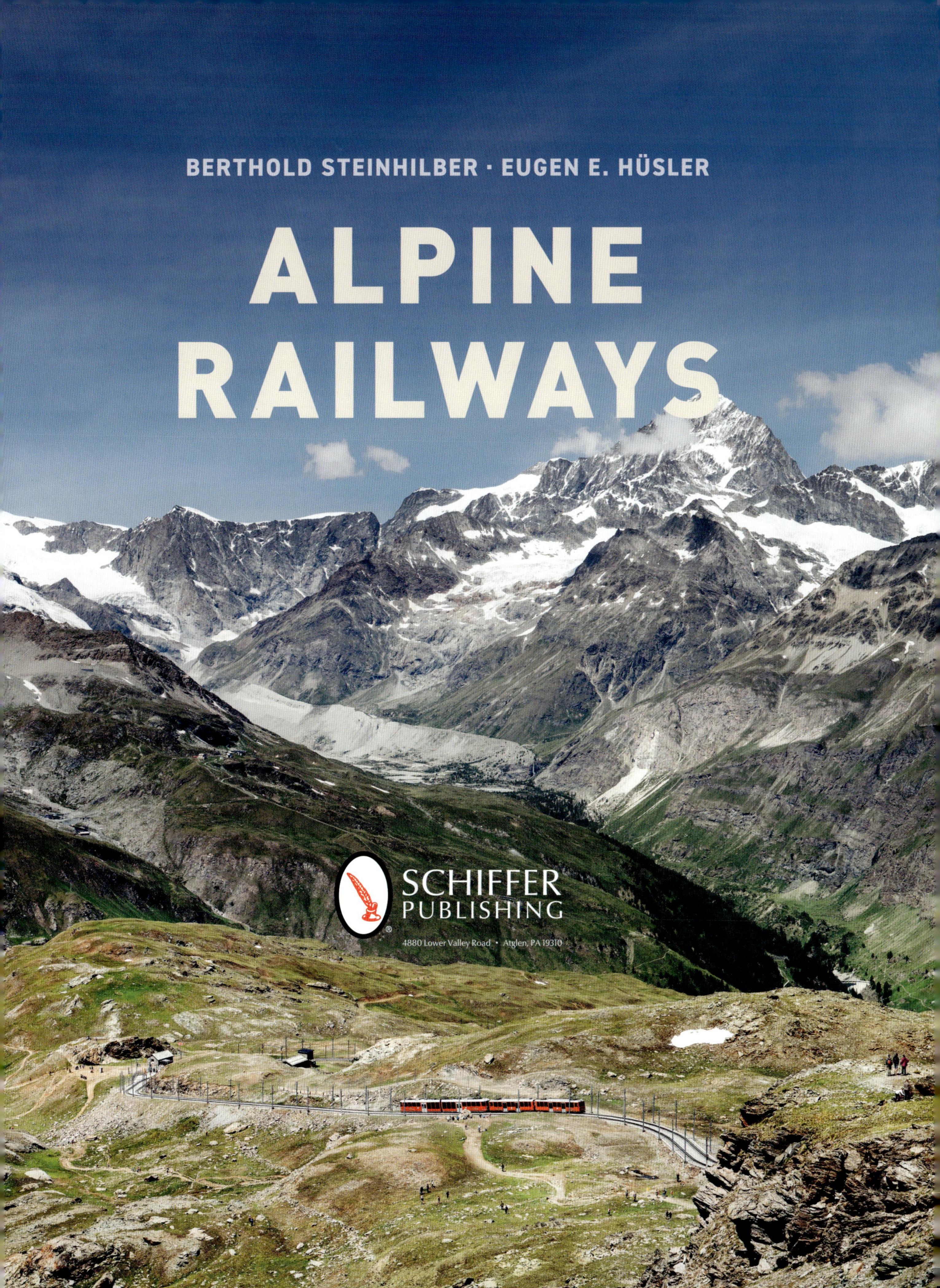

BERTHOLD STEINHILBER · EUGEN E. HÜSLER
ALPINE RAILWAYS
SCHIFFER PUBLISHING
4880 Lower Valley Road · Atglen, PA 19310

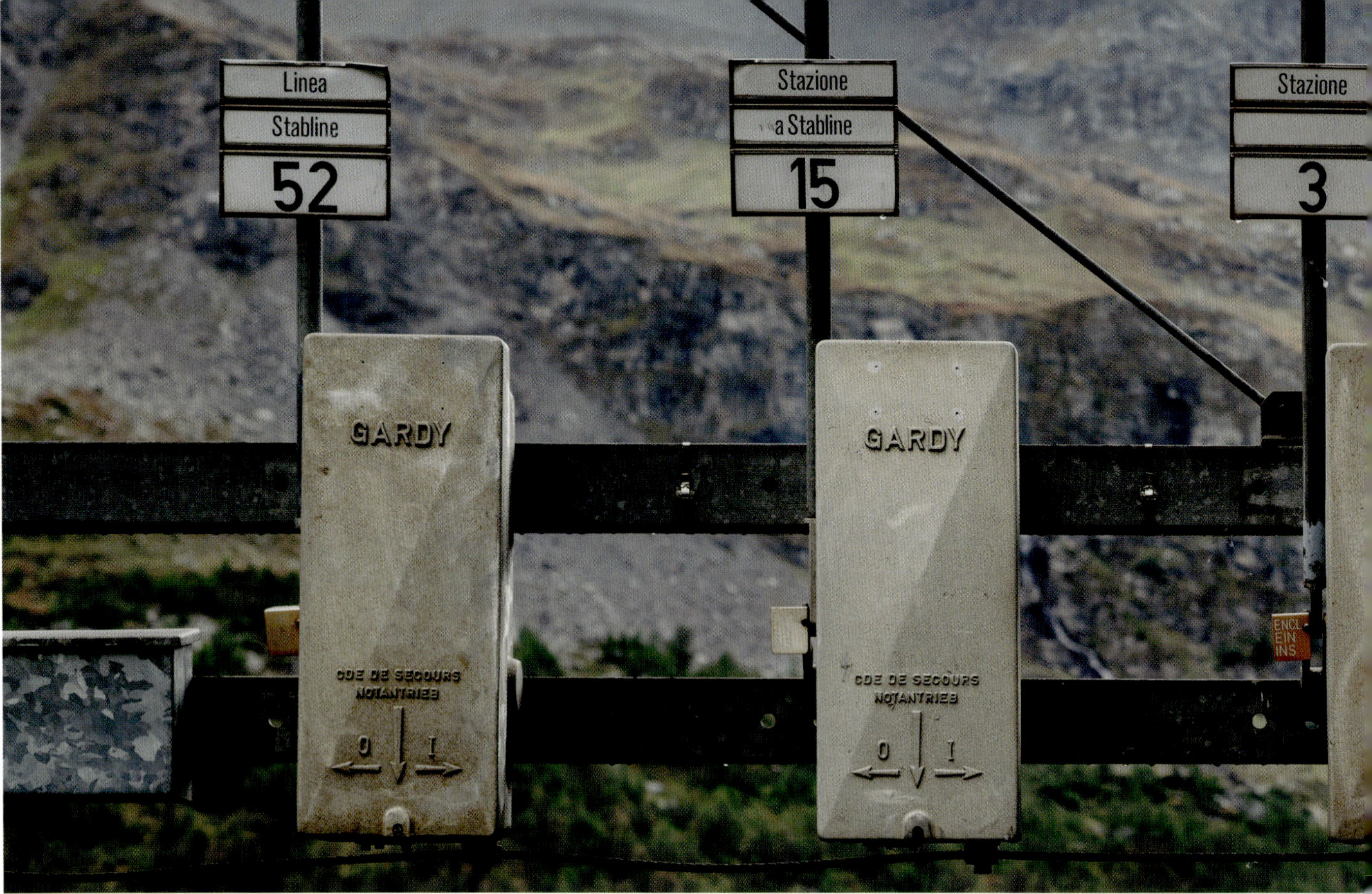

CONTENTS

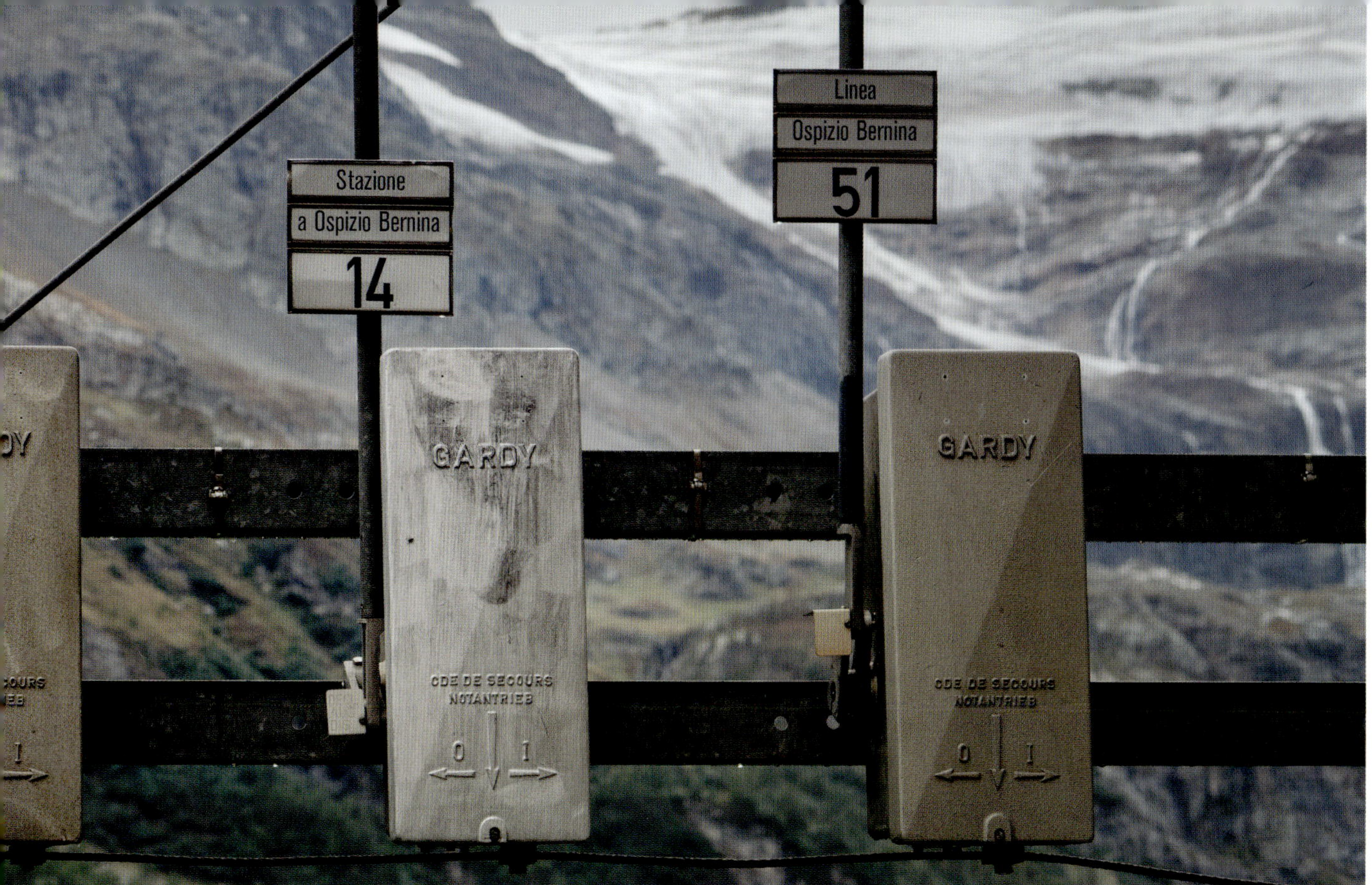

Stazione
a Ospizio Bernina
14
Linea
Ospizio Bernina
51
GARDY
GARDY
CDE DE SECOURS
NOTANTRIEB
0   1
CDE DE SECOURS
NOTANTRIEB
0   1

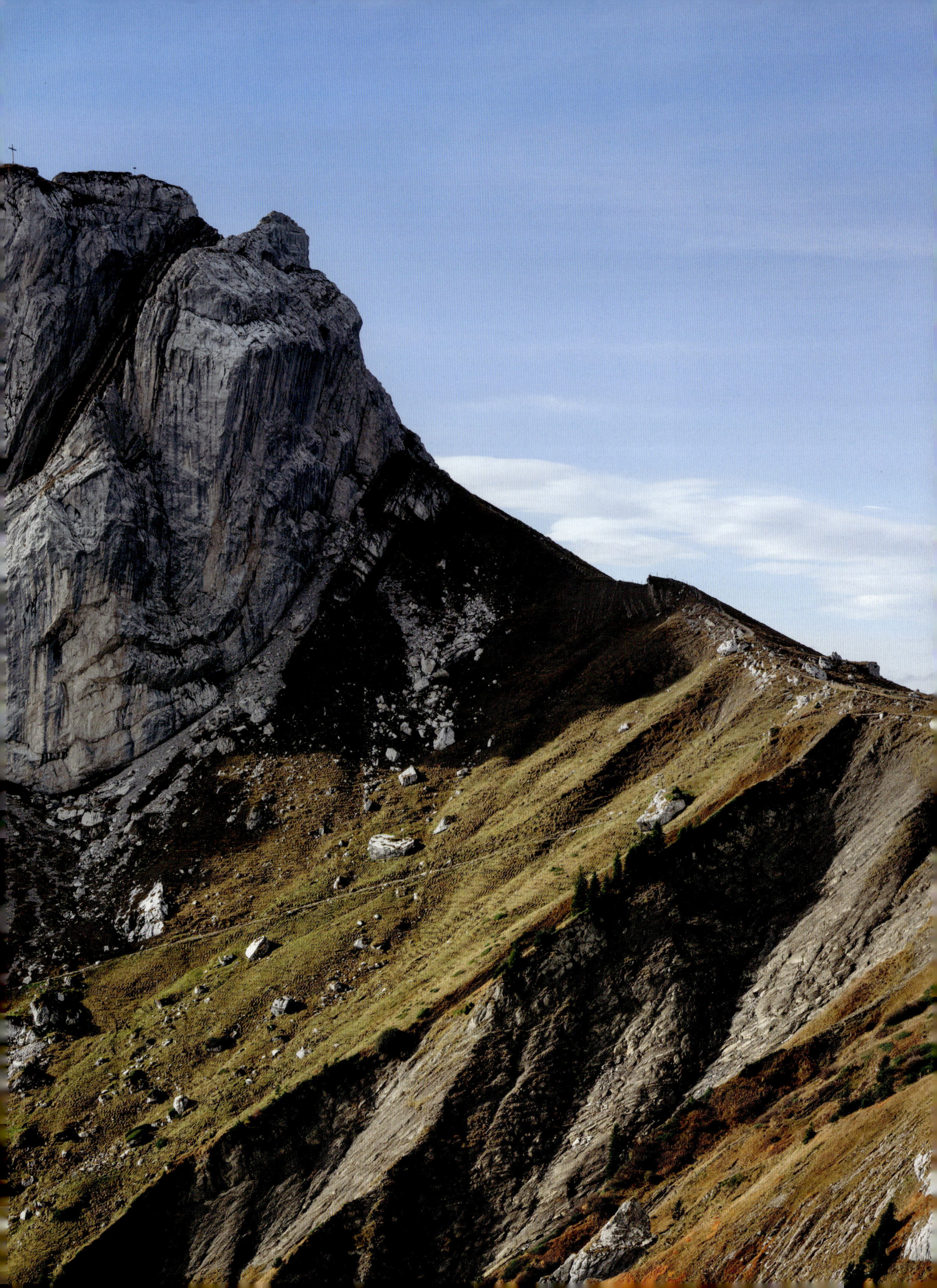

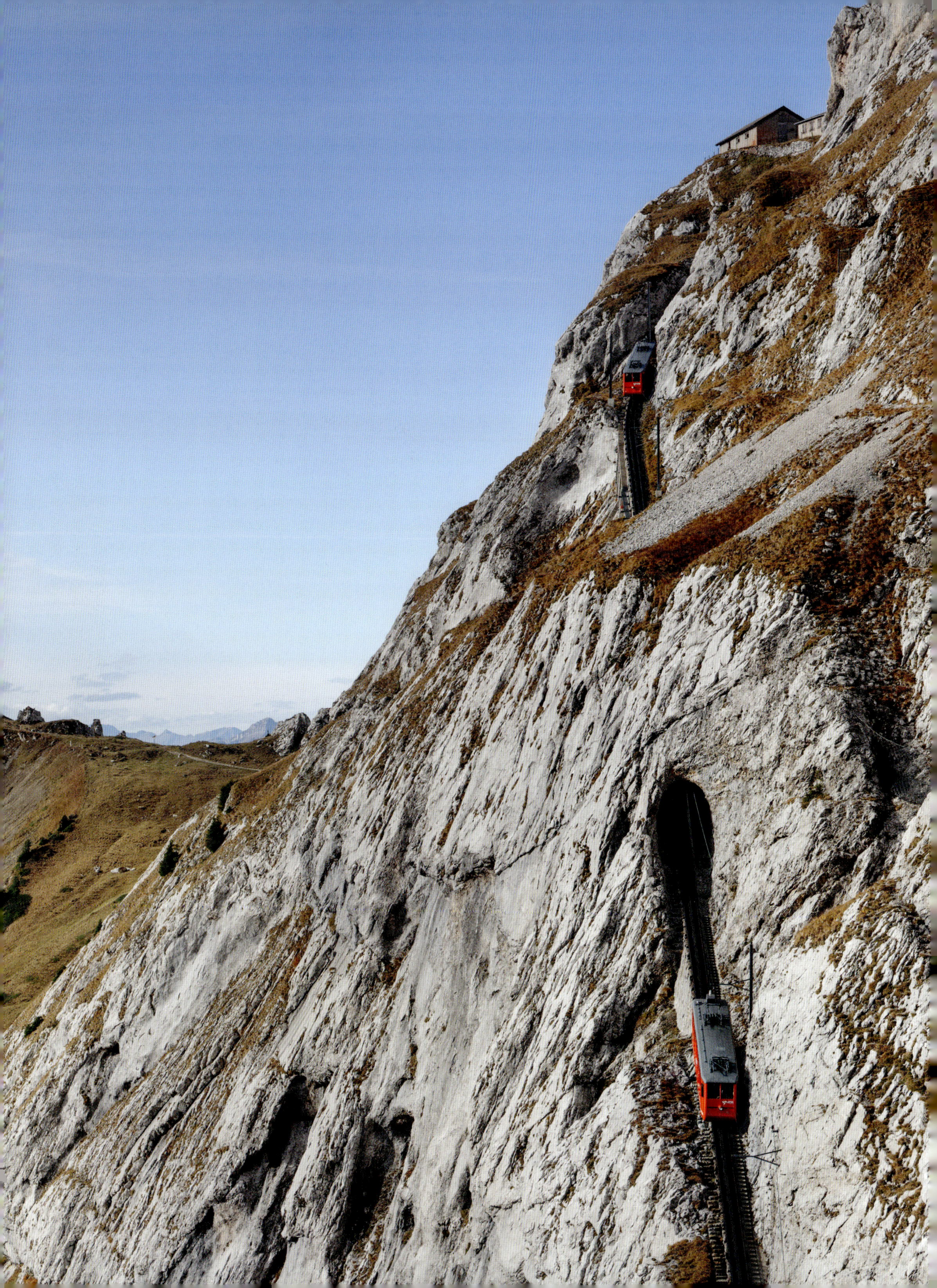

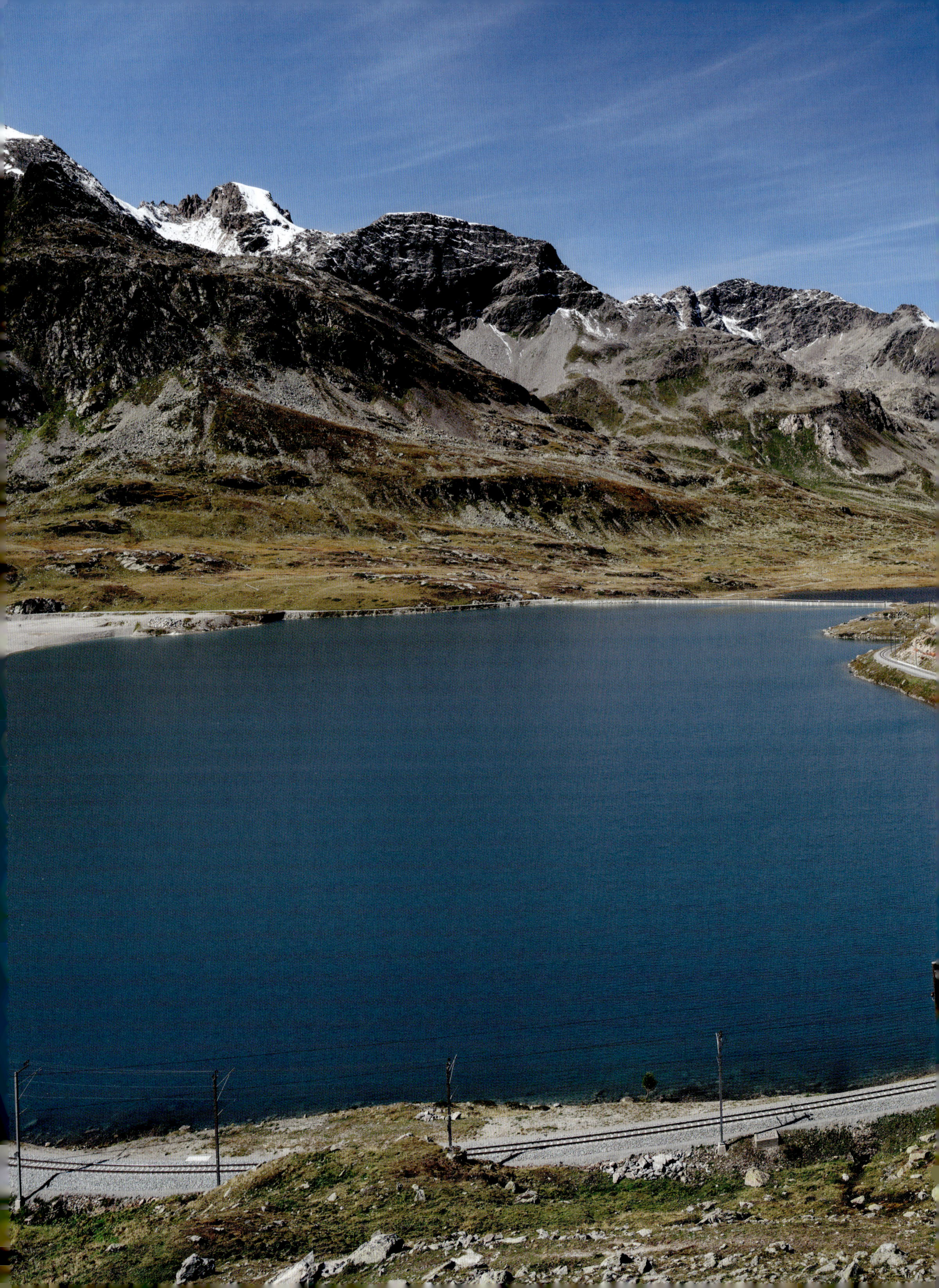

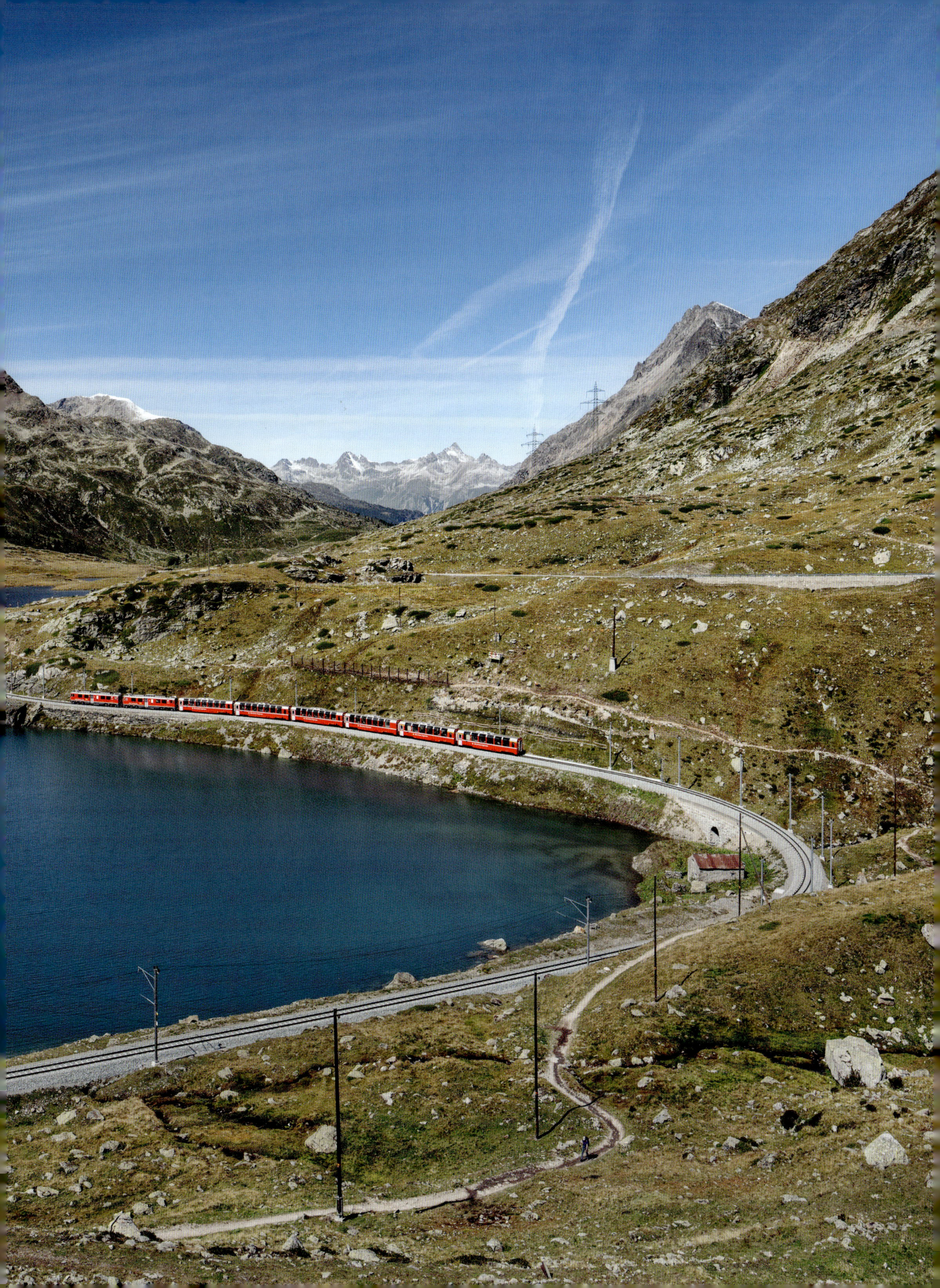

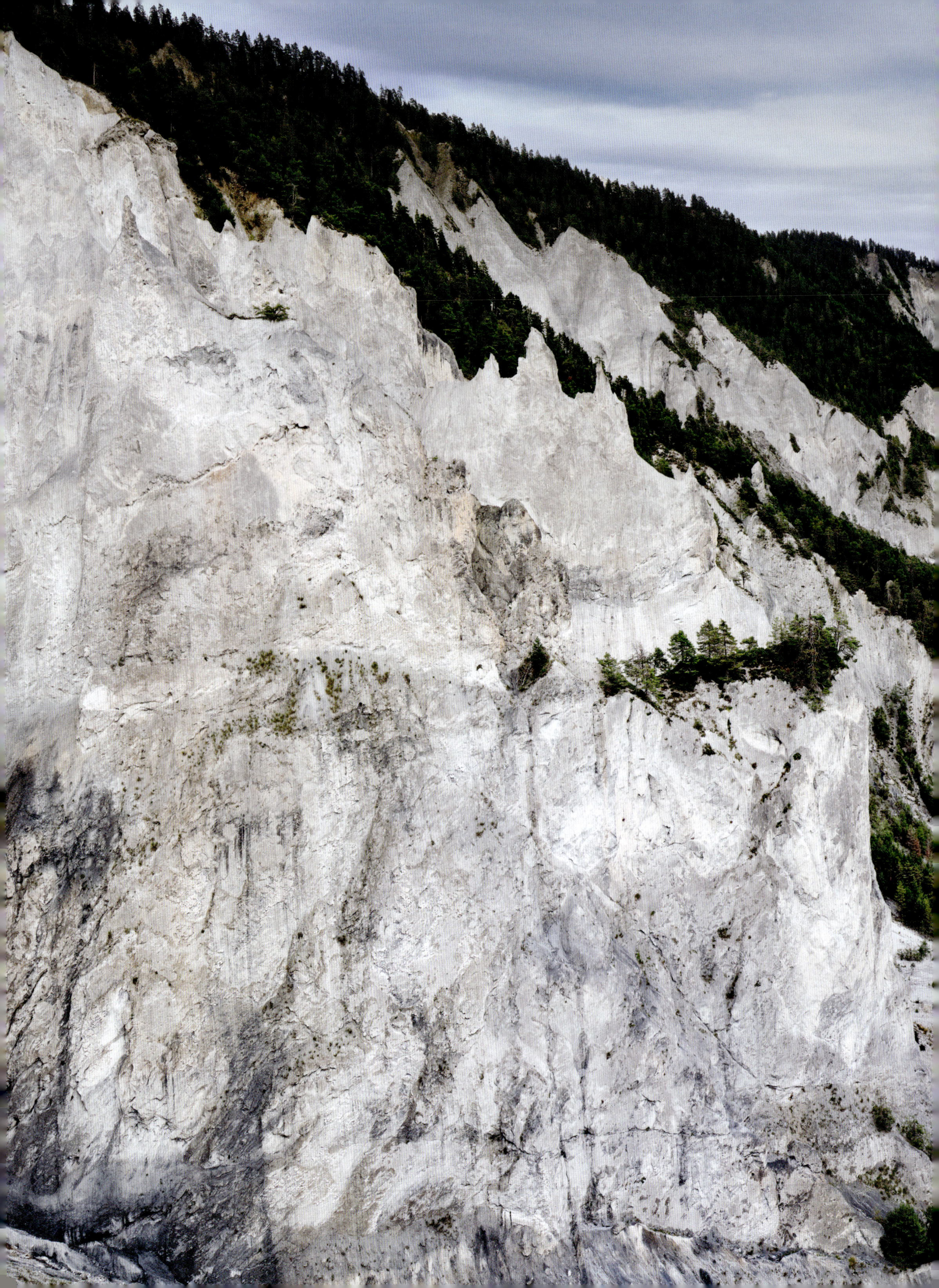

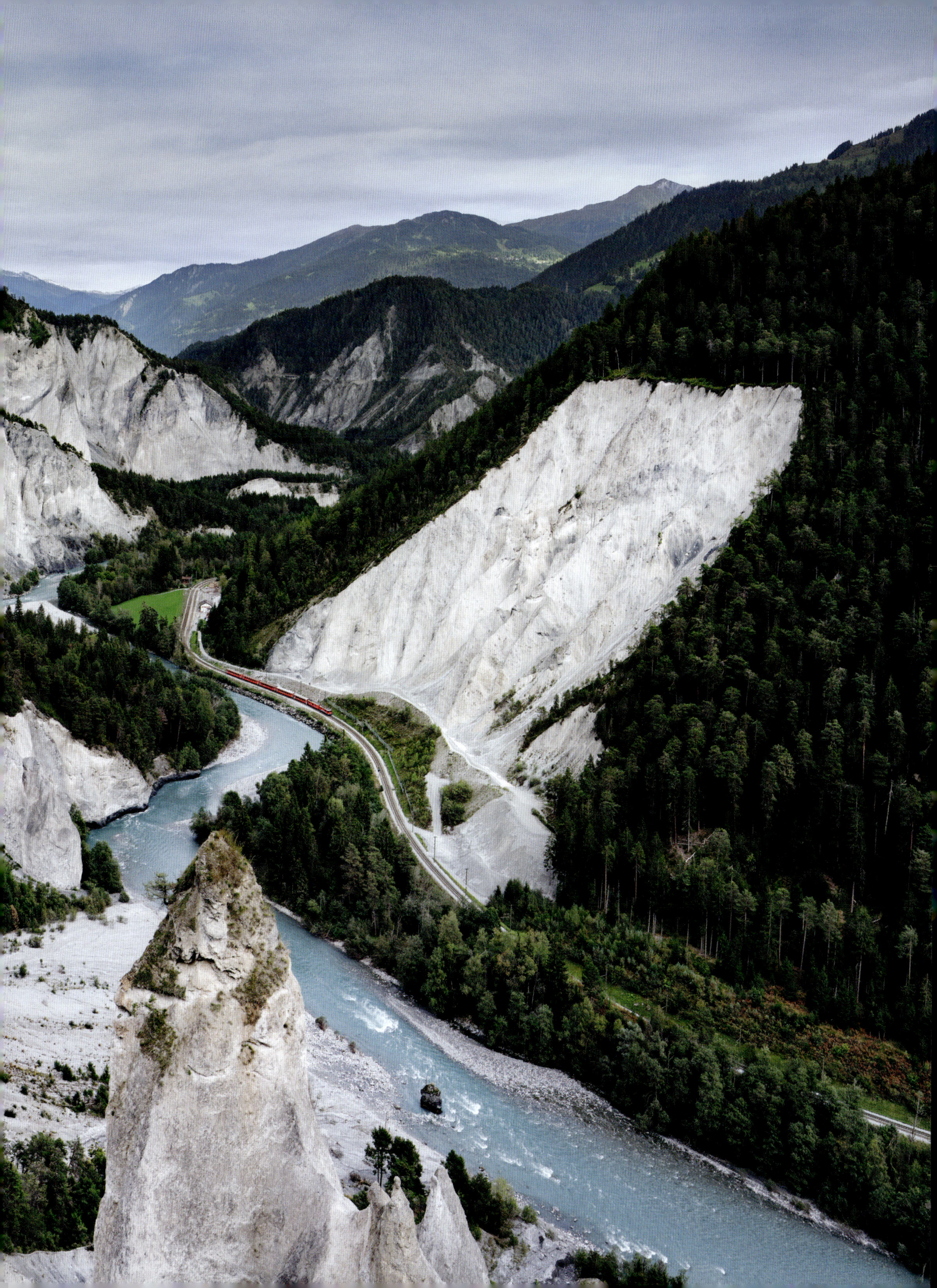

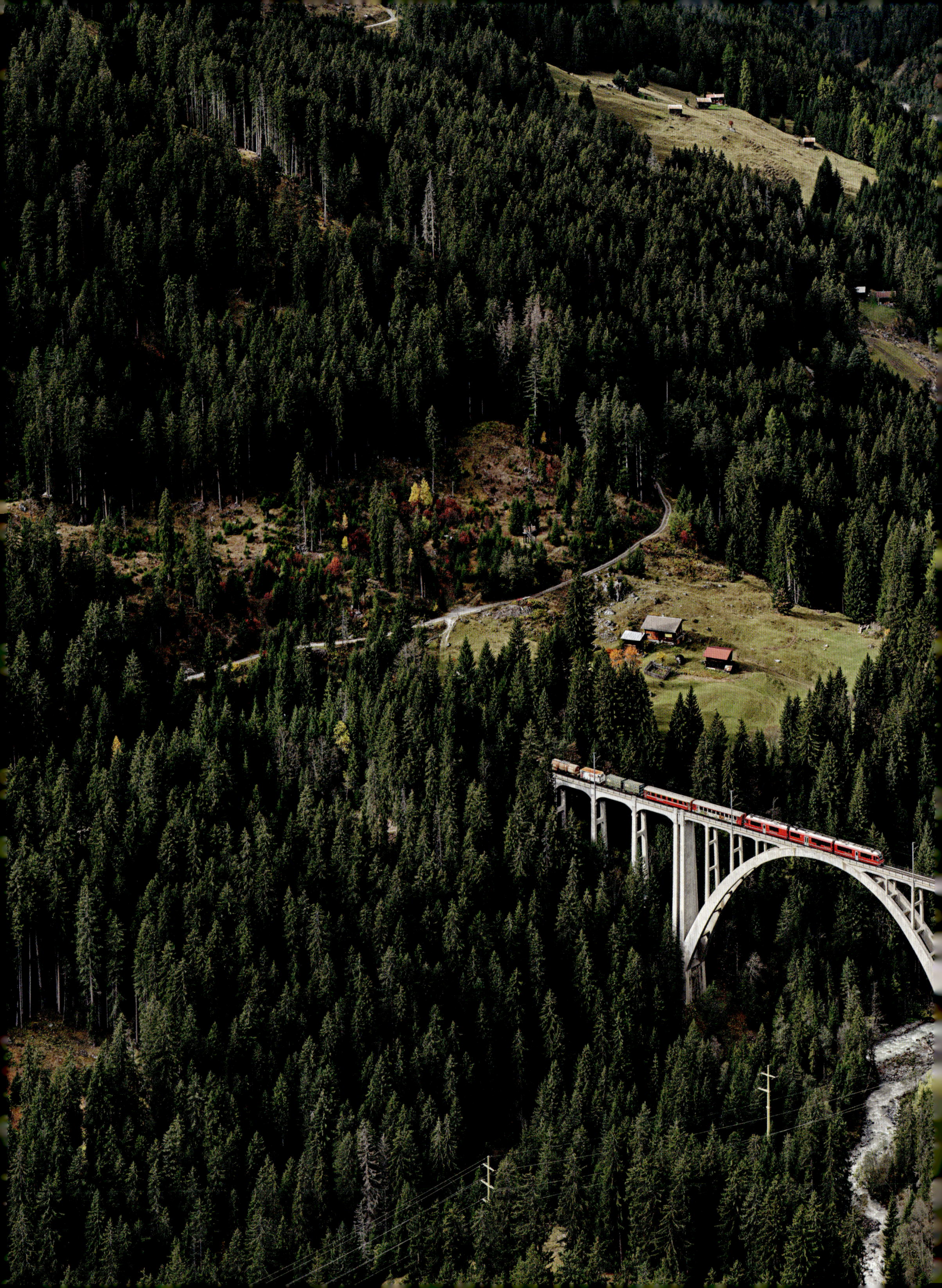

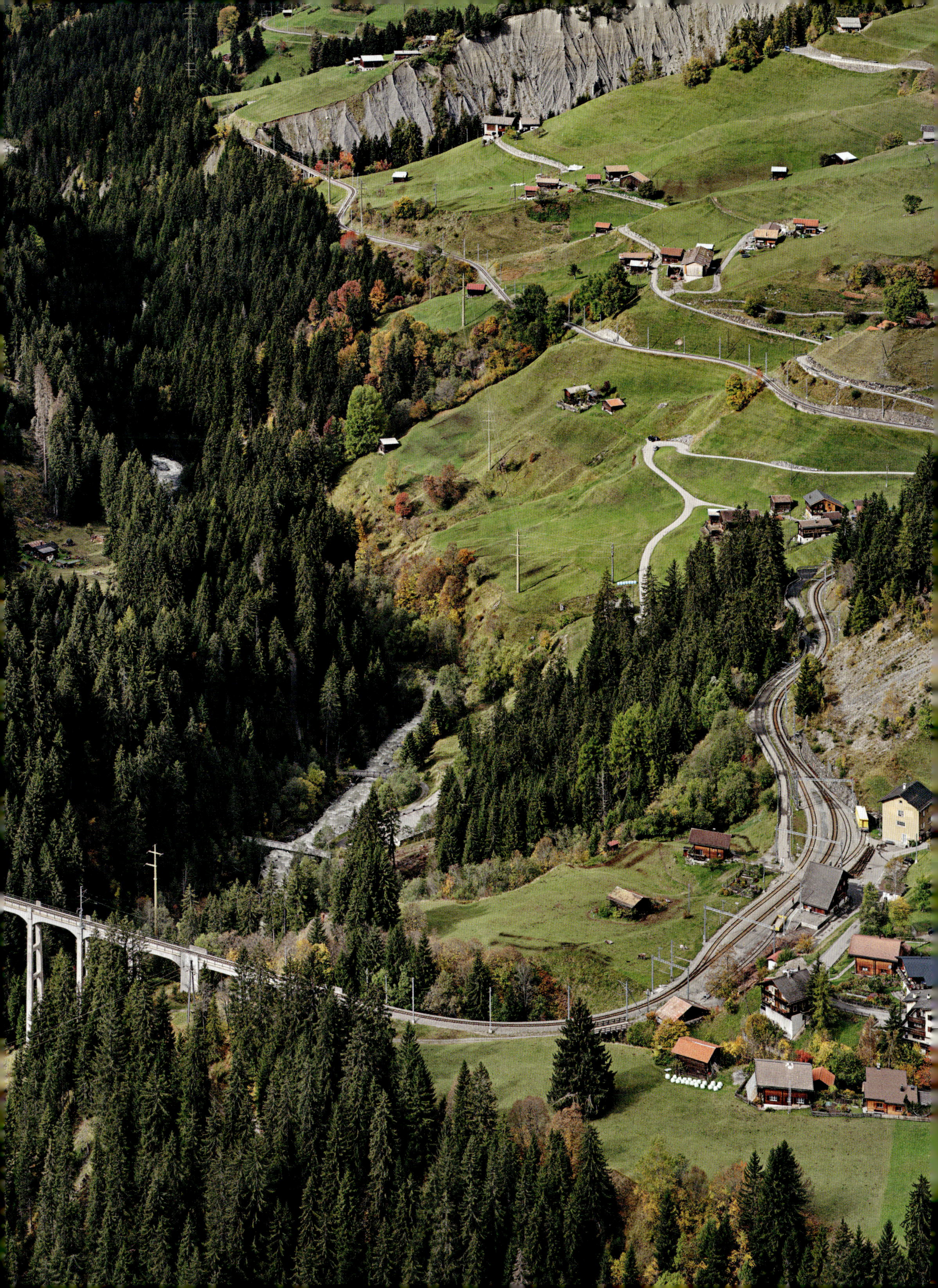

EMERGED FROM THE MOUNTAINS—THE HISTORY OF THE ALPINE RAILWAYS

Long ago—when televisions were not yet in color and the Adriatic beaches were the most popular vacation destination for Germans—model trains from Märklin, Fleischmann, and company were undisputedly at the top of wish lists for boys. Technology was fascinating, and it came as no surprise when these popular toys emerged with steam engines. Even little Eugene was able to observe practical demonstrations in physics during playtime: Steam creates energy, and energy creates movement. The excess pressure coming from the evaporated water drives one wheel forward—and shows the way of industrialization. A truly revolutionary discovery!

Christoph Bernoulli found the right words when in his *Handbuch der Dampfmaschinen-Lehre* (*Handbook of Steam Engines*), published in 1833, he wrote, "What the invention of printing has become for our intellectual culture, for the advancement of science and enlightenment, the steam engine may become, perhaps very shortly, for human industrial activity, for the increase and spread of wealth and material goods." How true! Soon after, the first steam engines made their way to the oceans (until 1889 with additional supporting sails), and on dry land the triumph of the railways could not be stopped. People and goods now traveled quicker and more comfortably throughout Europe. That stimulated the economy, which in turn brought growing prosperity. Just as Mr. Bernoulli predicted.

Then the railways came to the Alps. In 1854, way in the east, the first mountain railways based on the plans of Carl von Ghega went into operation on the Semmering. Shortly after, in the western part of the Alpine range, Germain Sommeiller provided free travel through the mountains from France to Italy with the Mont Cenis Tunnel.

SOME SWISS HISTORY

And what about Switzerland, today the railway country par excellence? In the first half of the nineteenth century, Switzerland was characterized by the conflicts between (rich) cities and the (poor) rural population. The economic, cultural, and religious tensions ultimately erupted in a civil war (1847). It ended with a devastating defeat of the rural, Catholic, conservative party and brought the country to a new, liberally characterized state.

The motto now was progress. And a new branch of industry, for which trains were to prove to be a real blessing, also would contribute to this: tourism. The rampant enthusiasm for nature helped turn rural farming regions into popular tourist destinations. This is how the forbidding Alpine peaks turned into a solid basis for tourism. Streets and hostels were built in the Bernese Oberland on the large lakes. And above all, there were railways. This was how one could comfortably travel from Paris to Lake Geneva or from Berlin to Lucerne and take delight in all the mountains. However, the only way up to the top was on foot.

Until the engineer Niklaus Riggenbach had a dazzling idea: a rack and a pinion. The pinion would be installed between the rails, the rack would be driven by the steam engine, and both would be connected. This allowed even extreme gradients to be safely overcome. The proof that this method worked flawlessly was delivered by Riggenbach right at the most well-known scenic mountain in the country: on the Rigi. On May 21, 1871, the first train puffed its way from Vitznau up to Rigi Kulm on the cogwheel railway. It was a moment for the history books; the conquest of Alpine peaks through technology could begin. Mountain landscapes could be experienced comfortably.

A true construction boom seized the Swiss mountains. Groups of workers arrived, paths were blasted free, and tracks were laid, and this way, many scenic mountains and peaks got a hotel right away. The traveling public of the Belle Époque era valued luxury. On the Rigi, lodging could be found at the Grandhotel Schreiber, above Lake Geneva in the Palace Hôtel near Montreux, or in St. Moritz in Badrutt's Palace.

Meanwhile the engineers were eyeing the really high peaks, the ones over 4,000 meters (13,123 feet), also referred to as "four-thousanders." Their plans became even bolder, practically utopian. Not even the Matterhorn was left out, but Xaver Imfeld's plans failed due to the bitter resistance of the mountaineering community. And so, it remained with the Gornergrat Railway, whose mountain station was already over 3,000 meters (9,842 feet) above sea level. And this railway had one unbeatable advantage over the (planned) Matterhorn Railway: the wonderful view over the most beautiful mountain in the Alps.

EDISON AND THE ELECTRIFICATION OF THE WORLD

In 1880 a lightbulb went on, quite literally, thanks to Thomas Edison's groundbreaking invention. For many years prior, engineers had already experimented with electrical motors, with the Scotsman Robert Davidson's locomotive even reaching a speed of 4 (!) miles per hour in a test run between Edinburgh and Glasgow in 1842, without any charge. A three-axle car belonging to the American Charles Grafton Page also had already reached 31 kilometers per hour (19 miles per hour). However, the test drive was not really a success, since the batteries, weighing several tons, ended up dying. The new technology first became practical through an external power source, which eliminated the need to install huge batteries on a train. At the Exposition Internationale d'Électricité in Paris, the first exposition of its kind in the world (1881), Siemens introduced the first overhead contact line: a breakthrough. As early as 1893, the people of Zermatt were able to celebrate a Swiss premiere: the opening of the first electrically powered cogwheel railway.

Electricity instead of steam. This was especially welcomed in Switzerland, for very mundane reasons. The country had only a few minable coal deposits, and the extra demand had to be met through imports. On the other hand, the conditions for generating electricity through hydropower were optimal. Already in 1873, the first (electric) lights in St. Moritz had been turned on—in the Kulm Hotel. The output of the mini hydroelectric power station was 7 kilowatts. But it was perfectly adequate to light the splendid dining room . . .

In a veritable feat that put a heavy strain on state finances, the Imperial and Royal monarchy built its "new Alpine railways" in the east of the Alpine range: approximately 250 miles (400 kilometers) long, with many structures such as tunnels in the High Tauern, the Pyhrn, Karawanks, the Bohinj Valley, and the Wechsel. With the (late) opening of the Tauern Tunnel, construction was completed in 1908. An extra historical remark: At the 1.5-mile-long (2.5-kilometer-long) Hartberg Tunnel near Mönichkirchen in the Wechsel, Hitler set up his headquarters during the Yugoslavia campaign, which lasted only two weeks in the spring of 1941. The train was positioned in such a way that it could be pushed into the tunnel in the event of an air raid.

Almost simultaneously with the "new" Austrian Alpine railways, construction began farther west, in Grisons. The initiator of the first mountain route was Willem Jan Holsboer, a Dutchman who sought healing for his wife (with a lung condition) in the Swiss Alps and later had a spa house built in Davos. In 1890 the Prättigau Line was opened. A few years later, it became part of the newly founded Rhaetian Railway (RhB). The RhB, with its almost 250-mile (400-kilometer) route network, remained absolutely unrivaled for a long time, which definitely did not hurt the balance sheets. Until 1925, cars on Grisons' streets were namely forbidden . . .

WAR—ALSO IN THE ALPS

With the eruption of World War I, tourism in the Alps collapsed, and Europe's youths died a senseless death in the trenches. The Alps were also not spared from the inferno. Fierce fighting raged along the "impossible" front line, stretching from the Ortler to the Isonzo (Soča) River. The railroad gained a new, very different purpose: It allowed supplies to be quickly transported and replenished at the front line. The Bohinj Railway, which was used to bring soldiers and materials to the Isonzo, gained somber notoriety. The twelve battles in the backcountry of Gorizia, on the southeastern edge of the Alps, were among the costliest in World War I. There were also struggles in the Dolomites, as well as immense losses from avalanches during winter. After Italy's declaration of war (1915), the Imperial and Royal troops built several field railways to the front, such as to Wolkenstein in Gröden, to Schluderbach, and to the Fiemme Valley. Then the second world catastrophe left the continent in ruins. Only Switzerland was spared. However, during the war, Switzerland had to permit the transport of armaments on the Gotthard route between Nazi Germany and Italy. This was agreed in the state treaty of 1909, which the Confederation had entered into with the neighboring nations.

Half a century later, another agreement had far greater consequences for Europe: the Marshall Plan. It secured new markets for the United States and gave the ailing countries a brilliant economic upswing. Soon the first packed "Beetles" traveled over the Brenne to "Bella Italia."

The car—it was impossible to ignore—replaced the train as the most popular mode of transportation. The new currency was horsepower; instead of a ticket for one trip, one got a driver's license for life. The government worked diligently to help—the surge of cars rolled over increasingly wider streets. Many railways were shut down, in the Alps as well. This impacted Italy and France above all. In Lombardy, it meant the end to most regional trains. In Austria, the Salzkammergut Railway was shut down in 1957, among others. Some routes have been preserved as railway museums and are now maintained and operated through private initiatives. The most well-known example is the old Furka Steam Railway, which chugs its way back over the pass as a steam train during the summer—much to the delight of countless fans.

THE LONGEST ALPINE TUNNEL AND A VISION

Switzerland lived up to its reputation as a railway country; it held on to (with very few exceptions) its dense rail network resolutely—above all in the New Railway Link through the Alps (NRLA) and here in the Gotthard Base Tunnel. With the breaking of ground in this project, a new chapter in railway history was opened. A 35-mile-long (57-kilometer-long) tunnel between Erstfeld and Bodio removed the Alps as a traffic obstacle once and for all. "Clear view to the Mediterranean" was the chant of defiant students in Zurich

twenty years earlier. Engineers turned this dream into reality in their own way—and with very different goals. On June 1, 2016, at the opening of the tunnel, the president of the Swiss Confederation, Johann Schneider, remarked, "Today is a historic day for our country: With the Gotthard Base Tunnel we are completing the project of the century—a work in which several generations have been involved, from the first sketch up until the planning and construction of the tunnel. That fills me with pride, but also with humility. After all, it cannot be taken for granted that projects like this will succeed. . . . With the Gotthard Base Tunnel, we are bringing people and economies together—and with this project of the century we are building on the pioneering achievements of our ancestors! The Gotthard Base Tunnel, which we celebrate today, is the longest construction project of its kind in the world. And a strong signal beyond our national borders: In Switzerland and in Europe, revolutionary achievements are still possible. The twenty-first century can also be a European one!"

Who would want to disagree with this good man? The story of the railway is still being written. Even in the Alps.

OLD FURKA STEAM RAILWAY

Between green meadows and old snow, the route of the old Furka Steam Railway climbs up the high mountain valley of Furkareuss to the 6,148-foot-long (1,874-meter-long) summit tunnel under the pass of the same name. ▽ ▽

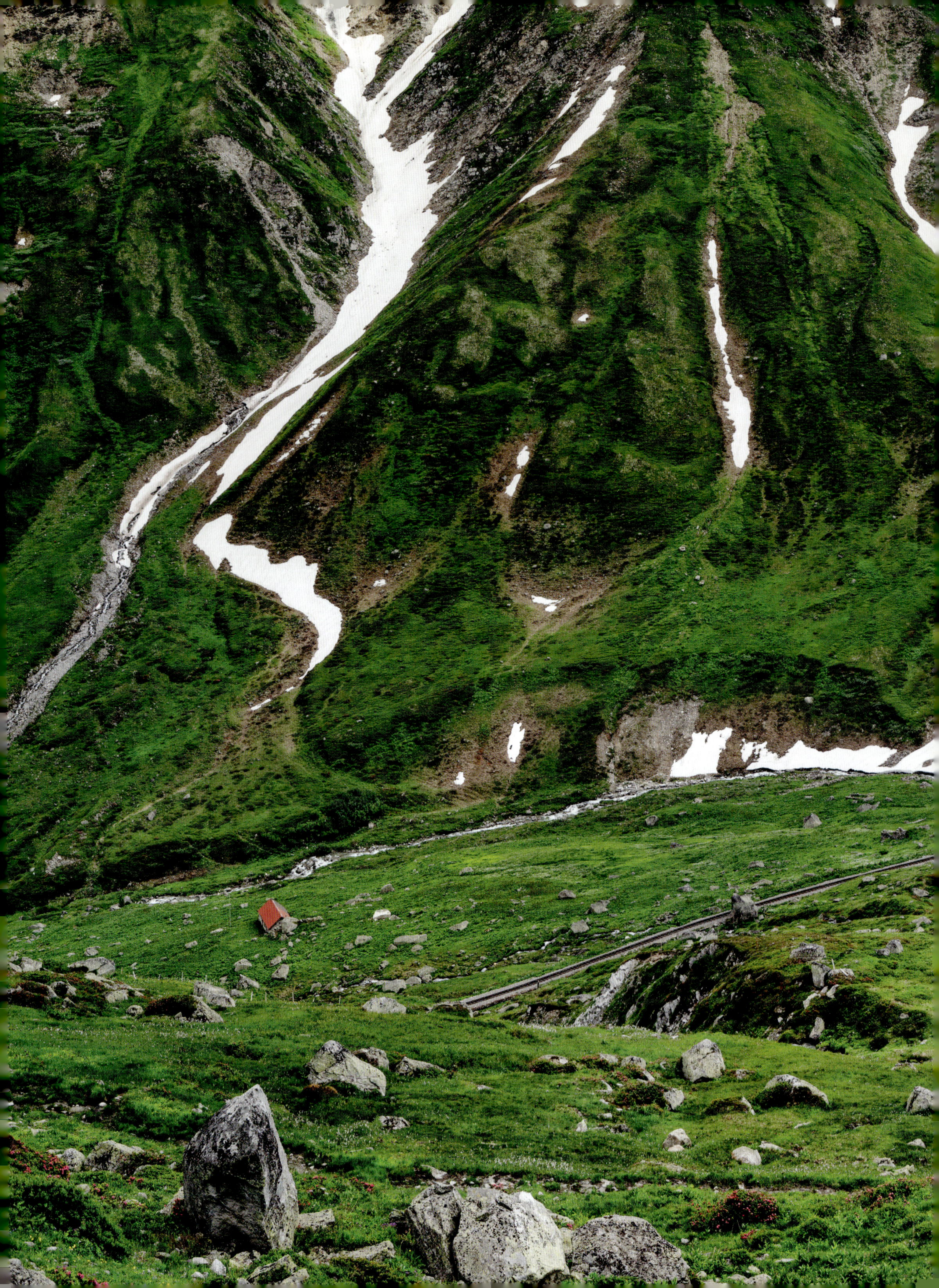

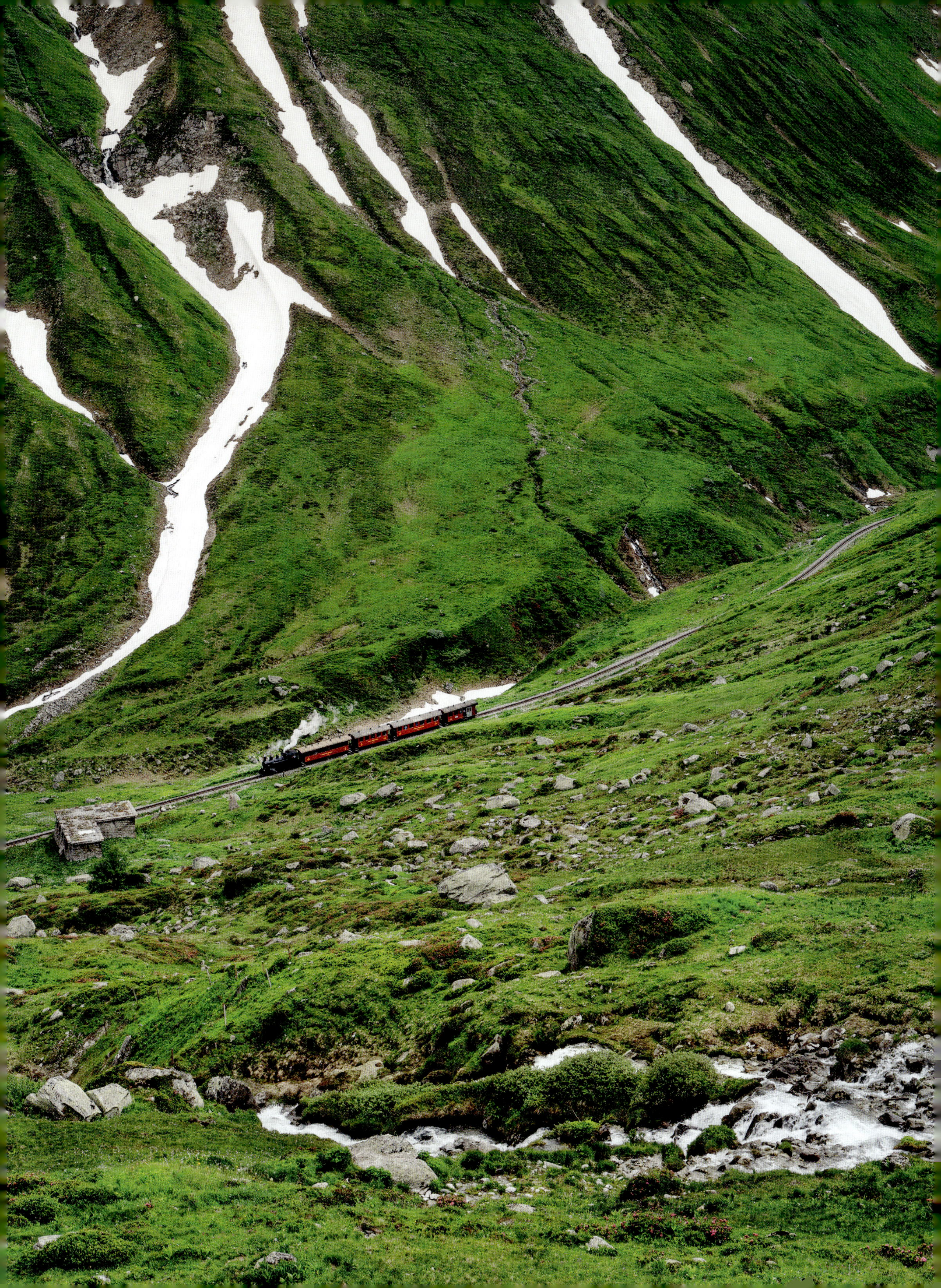

THE SOUTHWESTERN ALPS

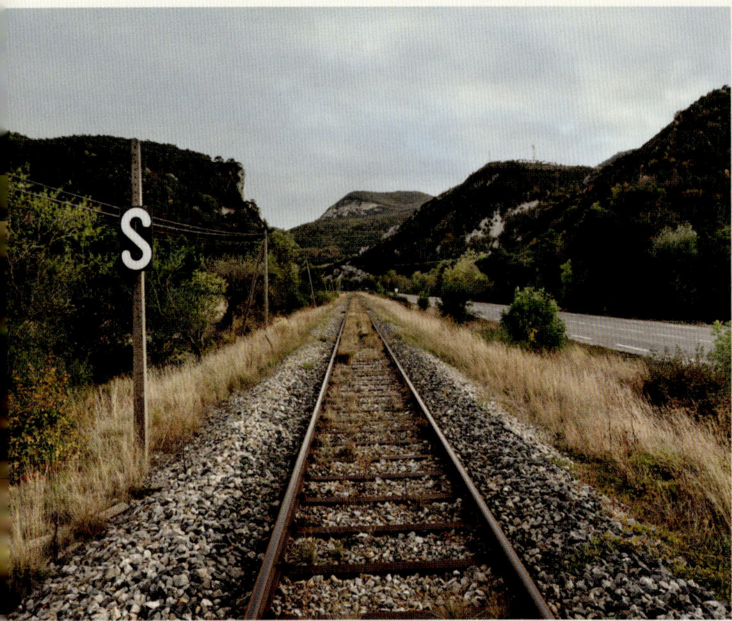

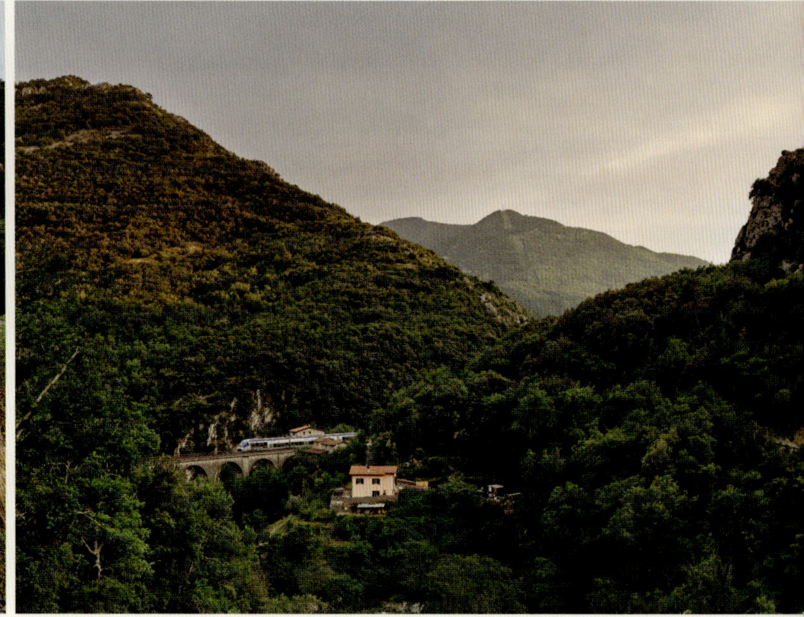

FROM THE MEDITERRANEAN TO MONT BLANC, THE "ROOF OF THE ALPS"

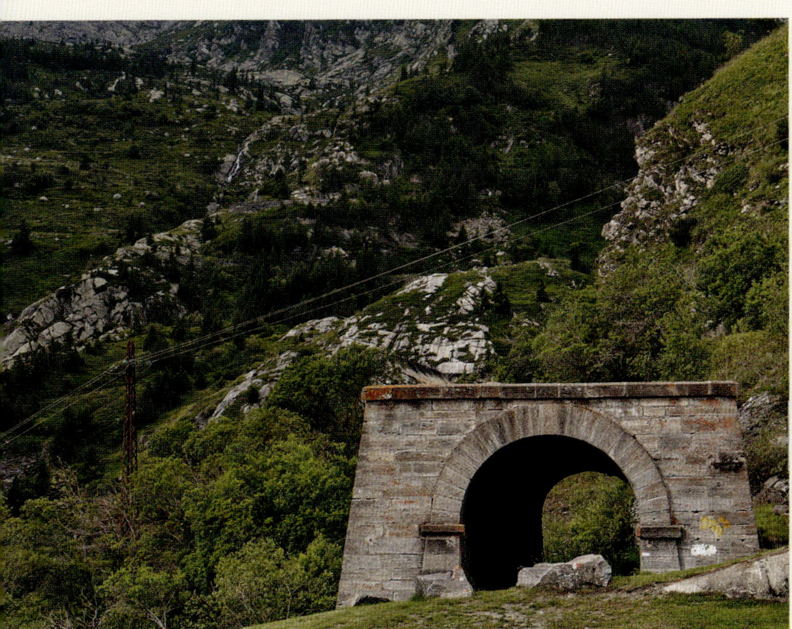
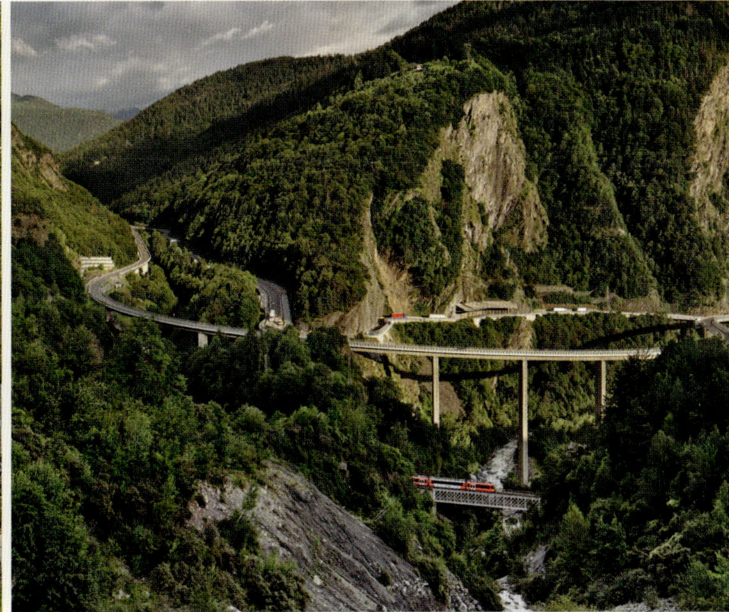

Since the fall of the Kingdom of Savoy (Sardinia), the main ridge of the Alps in the southwest has formed not only a geographical but also a political border. This is also reflected in the transportation network. The only railway connection between France and Italy is the one at Mont Cenis. Curiously enough, its construction began during the Savoy era. Even the Tenda Line, the most spectacular mountain route west of Switzerland, became a political pawn in its more than hundred-year history and was shut down for many years.

THE MOST BEAUTIFUL, CURVY MERRY-GO-ROUND THROUGH THE MARITIME ALPS

Railway lines tend to represent threads throughout history. In them you find story after story, some exciting and others absurd. A classic example of this can be found in the story of the *Tenda Line*, which survived both economic crises and world wars. Luckily.

Whoever looks down from the Tenda Pass—6,138 feet (1,871 meters)—to the Roya Valley will see, for one, what looks like a snake: the old military route with its sixty-four serpentine curves, which today is a popular cycling route. The other, the iron serpent, is not so easy to spot in the rugged gorge, which is flanked by craggy rocks on either side. This is because it runs across long distances in the mountain. In general: The entire route forms a sequence of viaducts and tunnels, some with 180-degree turns, three even taking a full rotation. Comparatively it makes the well-known Gotthard Line look like a high-speed train route.

Almost more unbelievable than the winding line itself is the history of the railway. Two world wars with changing alliances, a world economic crisis, shifting borders, political squabbles—all of these impeded the construction of this one-of-a-kind route in the Alps. Exactly eight decades lie between the start of the summit tunnel in Colle di Tenda (1899) and its most recent reopening. In between, it was expanded and dismantled, and (partially) electrified; the branch line to Nice was built, and bridges were blown up—those from Saorge were blown up a total of three times in World War II! The line was threatened with closure several times—the fact that it is still running today is akin to a (modern) fairy tale. And the railway should stay

in operation. Local residents have been fighting for this for a long time, especially in the Roya Valley. During the last two hundred years, the valley belonged to the County of Nice and then the Duchy of Savoy, making it part of the Kingdom of Savoy-Sardinia. Once Savoy fell to France in 1860, the communities at the upper reaches of Roya remained with the newly founded Kingdom of Italy. This was supposedly because the king valued the region for its hunting in particular. In 1940, Mussolini had a mighty (border) railway station built in Saint-Dalmas-de-Tende in the neobaroque style. It still stands today as a "white elephant" next to the tracks, over which only a few trains roll each day. A missed opportunity?

A RISKY ENDEAVOR

The construction was always a risk, for several reasons. Not only was the region regarded as politically unstable, but it was also geologically and morphologically demanding—quite a challenge for the engineers. In addition, the demand for such a railway was probably overestimated: Because of this, its impact remained regional. Additionally, tourism in the area has always been concentrated on the Ligurian coast and the Côte d'Azur.

From left: South of Saint-Julien-en-Beauchêne, the streets and railway lines run parallel to each other and straight through the Val Buëch-Méouge; the Bassèra Viaduct of the Tenda Line, between Breil-sur-Roya and Sospel; old gallery of the Mont-Cenis Postal Railway; and Mont-Blanc Express in the Arve Valley near Chedde, with the nearly 1-mile-long (1.5-kilometer-long) Égratz Viaduct of the expressway to the Mont-Blanc Tunnel above.

>> The real voyage of discovery consists not in seeking new lands but seeing with new eyes. <<

Marcel Proust (1871–1922)

The Maritime Alps were (and continue to be) backcountry, retreat areas and hiking regions. They do not provide the best conditions for such a demanding technical project, where very steep gradients had to be overcome: 3,281 feet (1,000 meters) in altitude between the Mediterranean Coast and the tunnel entrance under the Col de Tende—and that was using standard gauge and adhesion traction. The steepest gradient is 2.5 percent. There are eighty-three tunnels and ten larger viaducts on the main line between Cúneo and Ventimiglia. A ride on the Tenda Line is quite an experience—and a marvel in railway engineering!

ANCIENT ARTWORKS

The Vallée des Merveilles offers wonders of a different kind. Hidden a short distance west of Tende, it is at the foot of Mont Bégo and is famous for its prehistoric rock carvings. To date, more than 40,000 engravings have been discovered and cataloged; the oldest are believed to date back to around 3000 BC and were made with stone tools.

A hike of just under three hours leads from Lac des Mesches (access from Saint-Dalmas-de-Tende) to the Refuge des Merveilles (6,926 feet / 2,111 meters). You can stay overnight in the hut; guided tours of the rock art on Mont Bégo are offered. A visit to the Musée des Merveilles in Tende is also recommended.

TENDA LINE

In Breil-sur-Roya, the Tenda Line splits. The French line goes to Nice through two long tunnels. On the outskirts of L'Escarène, it crosses the flat valley floor on a 738-foot-long (225-meter-long) arched viaduct. ▽ ▽

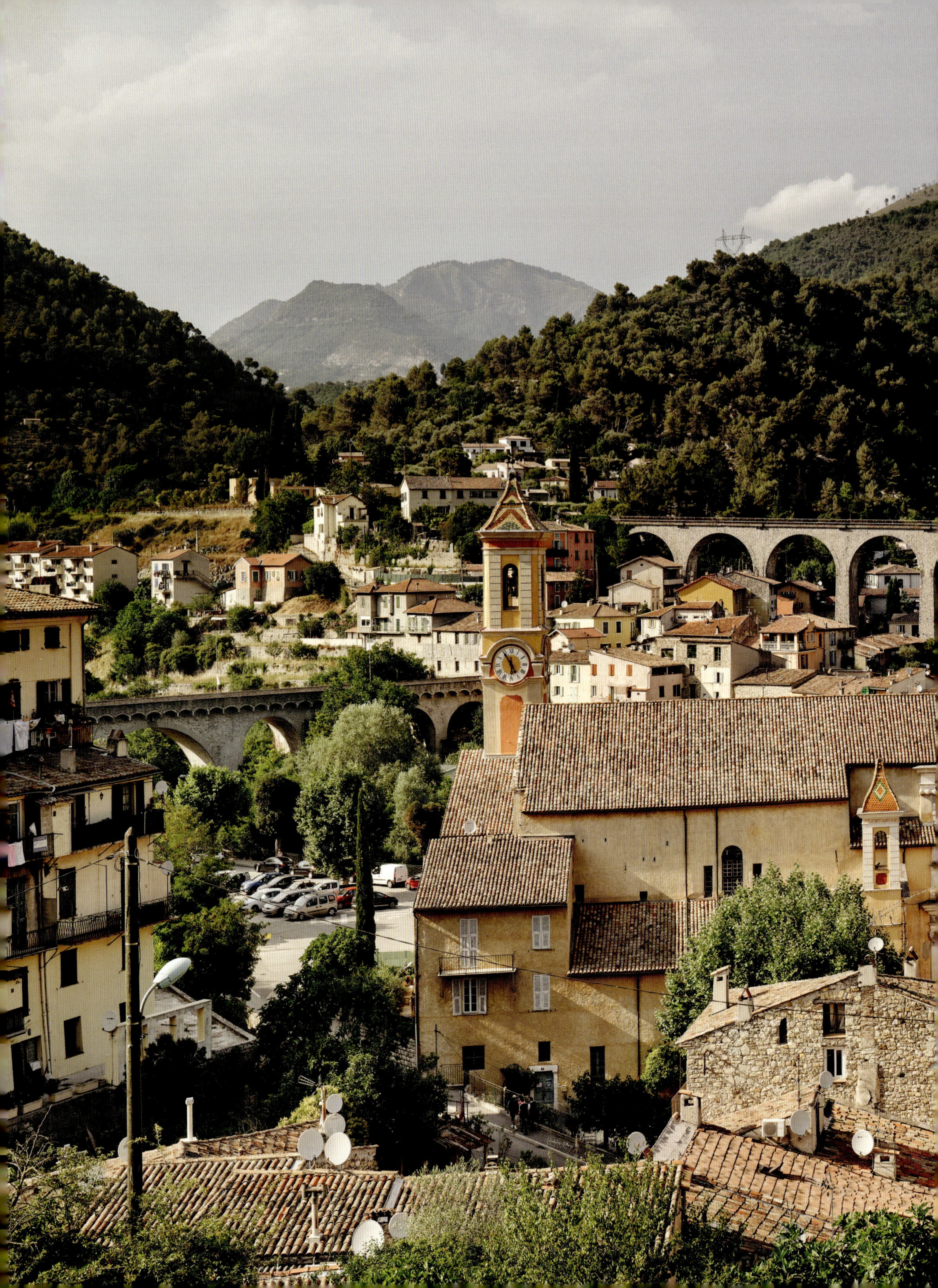

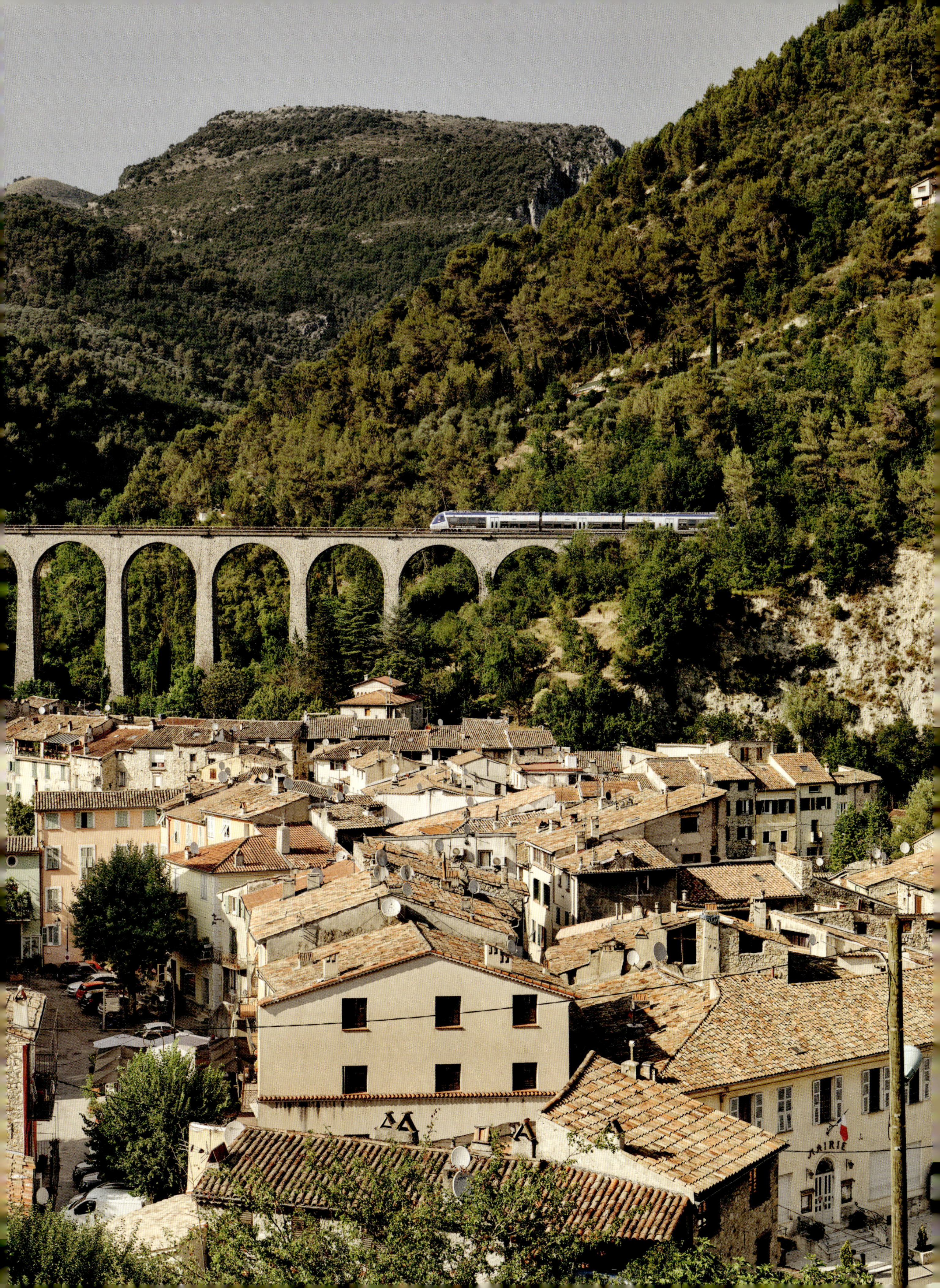

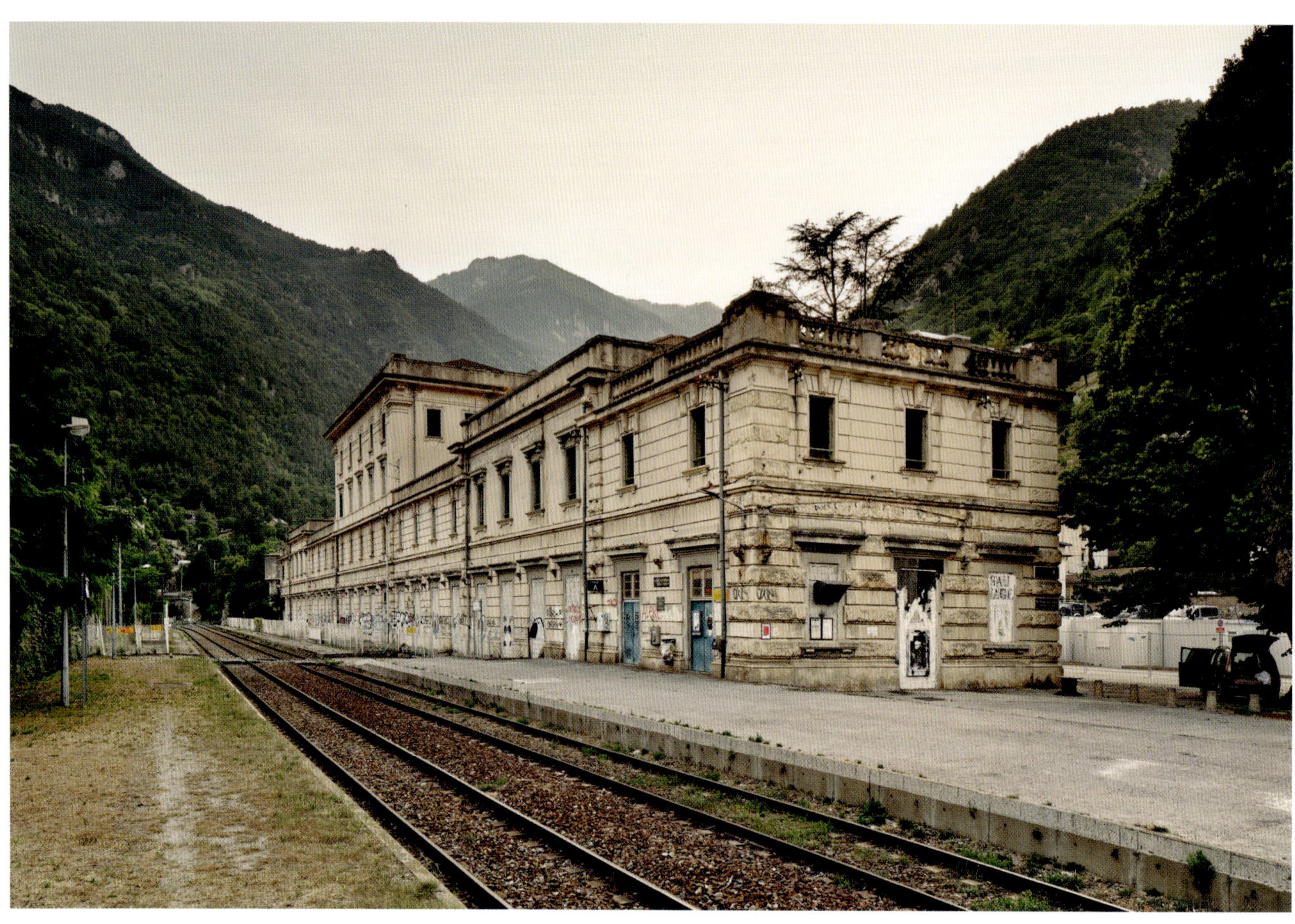

A monument to Fascist megalomania: Mussolini's Saint-Dalmas-de-Tende
train station. In the 1930s, the upper Roya Valley still belonged to Italy. △

An original construction supports the Viaduc du Caï, which stands
perpendicular to the bridge and is anchored in the stones over the
Bévera stream. During World War II, the viaduct was destroyed and first
rebuilt in 1962, using reinforced concrete. ▷

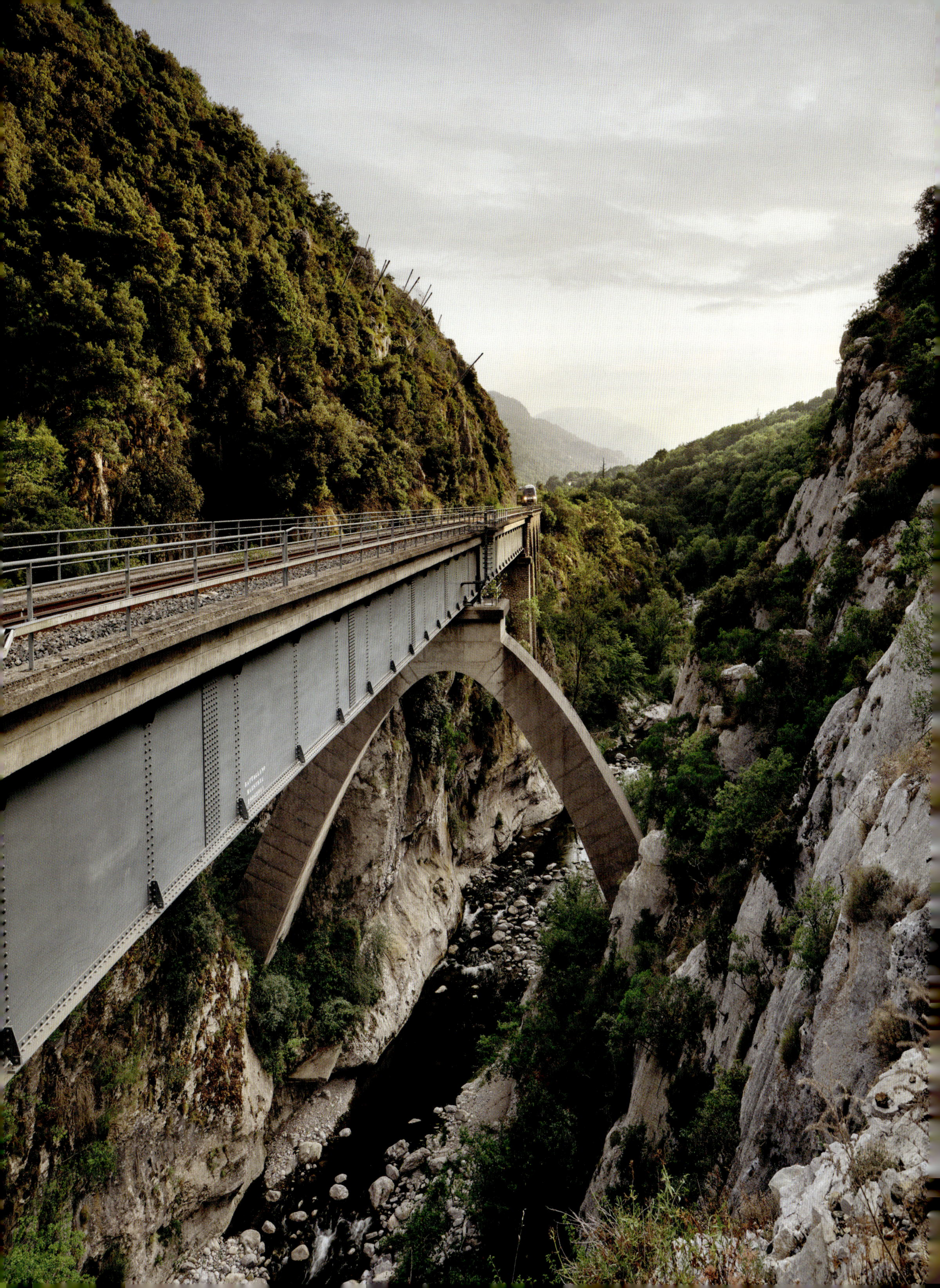

Wrung out of the rocky terrain:
the Tenda Line route in the
Roya Gorge. Falling rocks are a
constant danger here. A network
of wires strung across masts
along the route allows all signals
to immediately be stopped in the
event of damage.

The Tenda Line often overcomes
major differences in altitude by
using a spiral tunnel on difficult
terrain, including in the Gorges
de Berghe between Fontan and
Saint-Dalmas-de-Tende. The
Berghe spiral tunnel connects
directly to the Scarassoui Viaduct.
▽ ▽

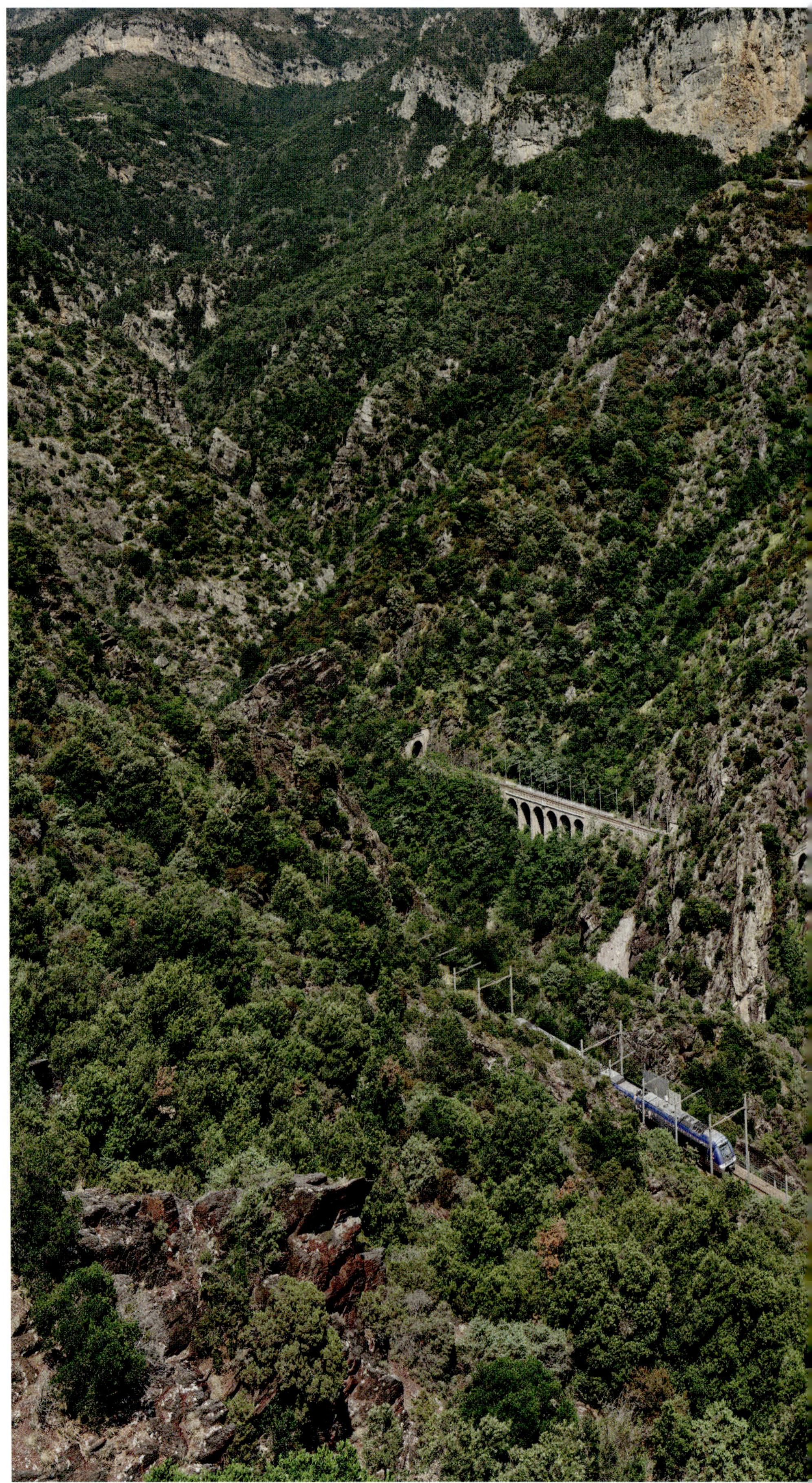

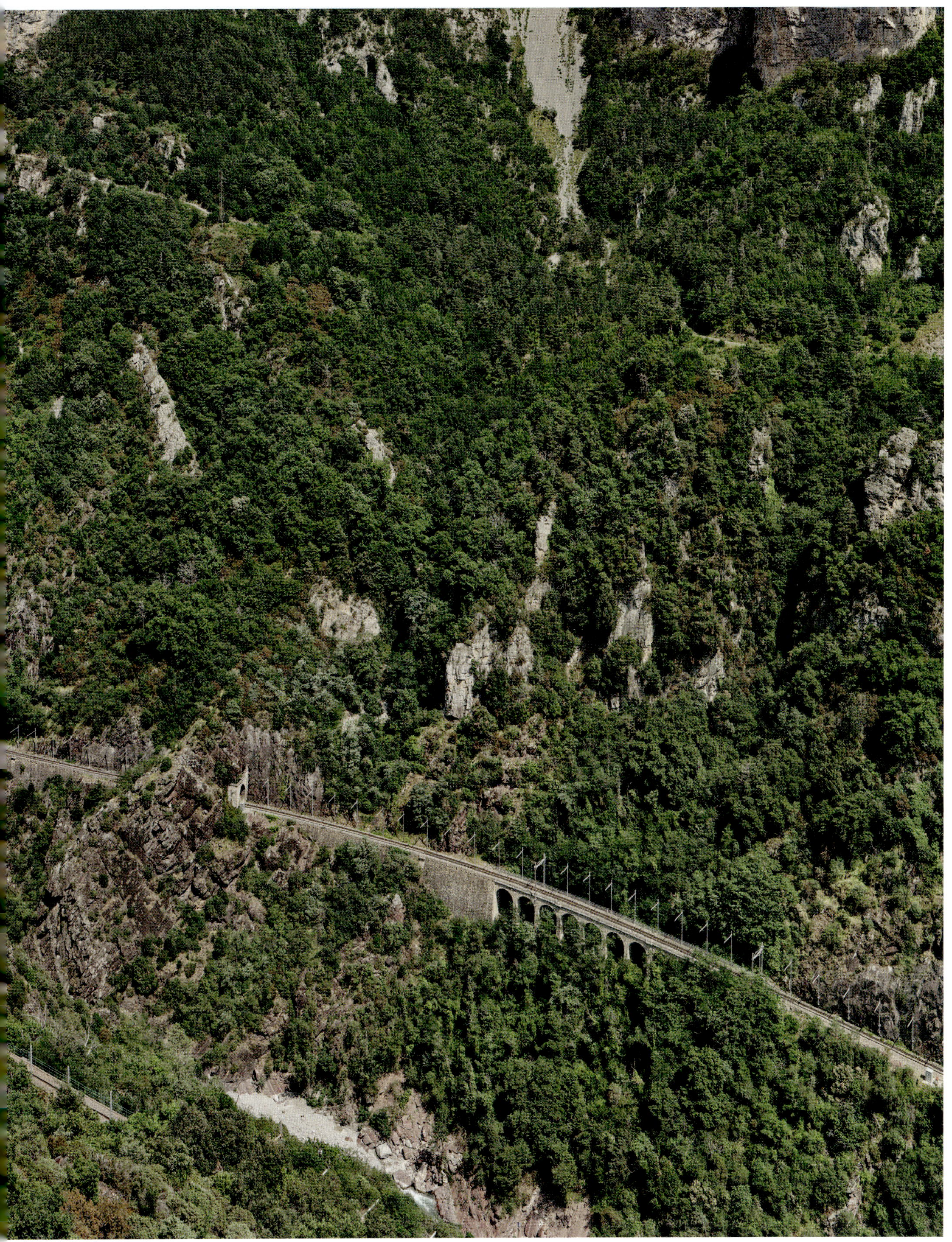

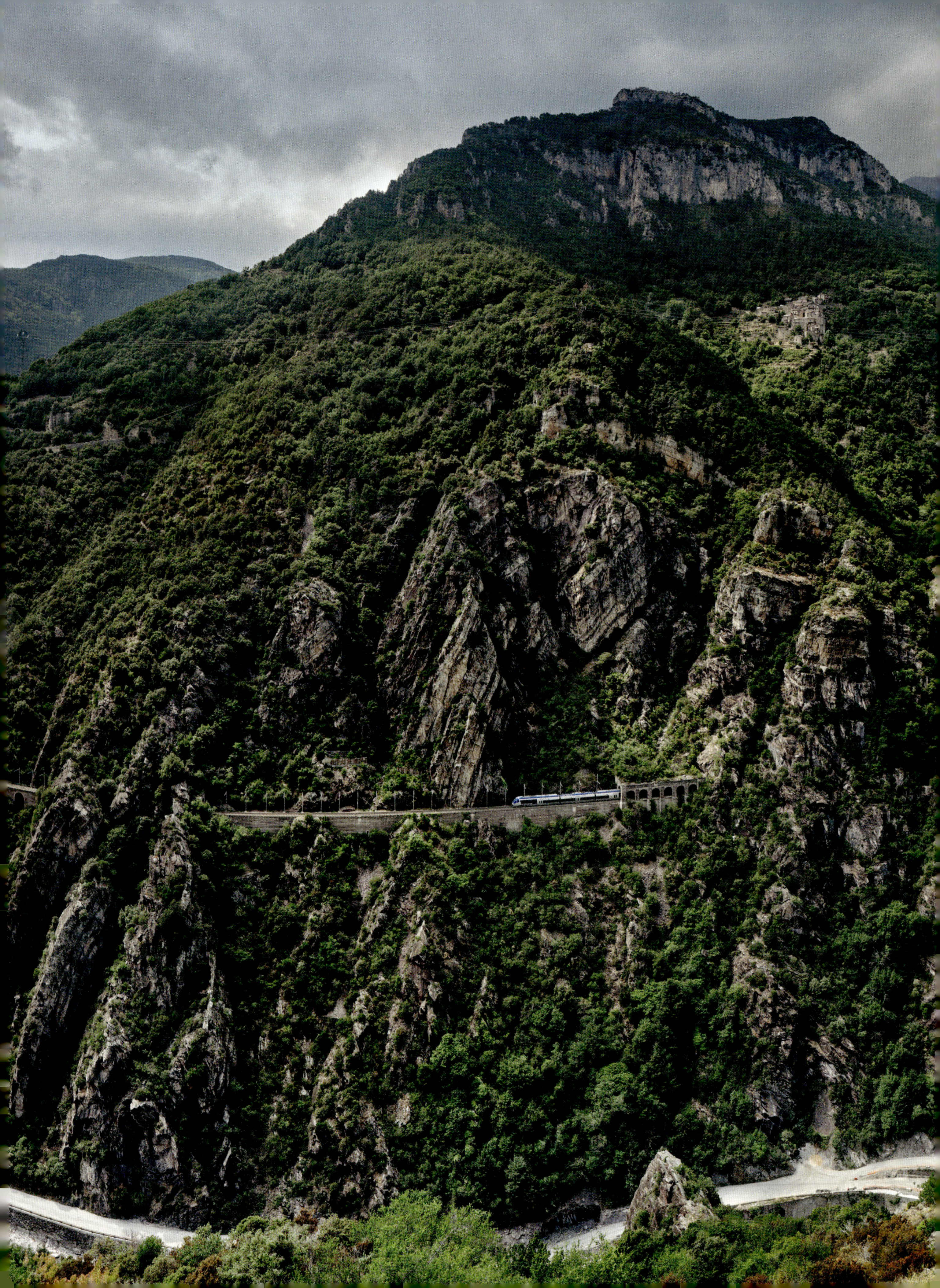

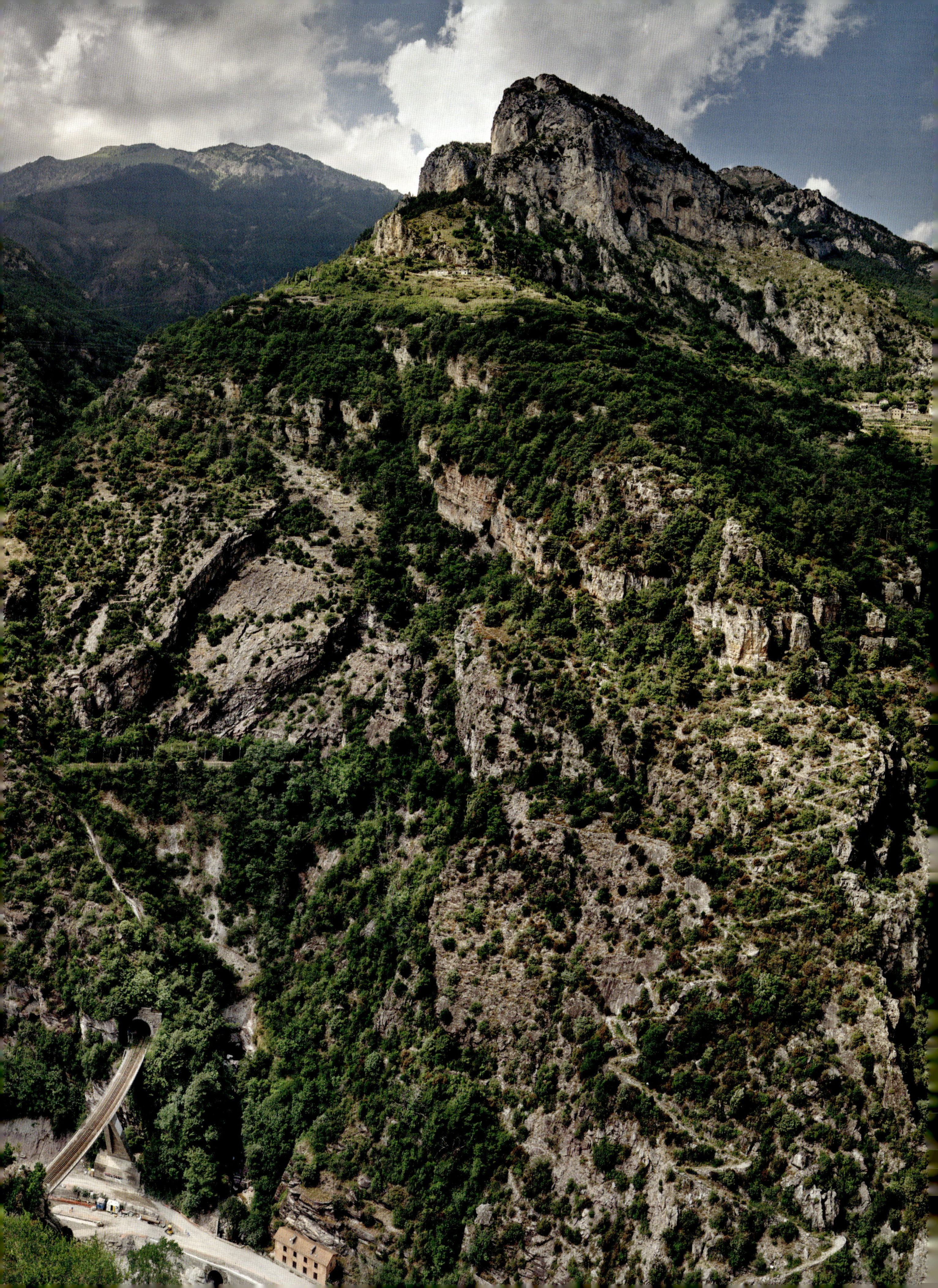

PROVINCIAL LIGHT AND LANDSCAPES

You can hardly travel to the magical world of Haute Provence in a more beautiful (and comfortable) way than with the Train des Pignes. *What a contrast between the Côte d'Azur and the "forgotten" valleys of the backcountry!*

Backcountry. An ambivalent term. Some may think of regions in which progress has been forgotten—on the other hand, it promises city-weary contemporaries a sought-after break. Peace at last, farewell to the hustle and bustle. Nice is loud, Grasse smells, Roquesteron is boring, Castellane waits for Napoleon. And Digne? It is the capital city of lavender, whose purple, blooming fields have become synonymous with the provincial mountains. In the observatory on Mont Chiran, one can look up into space or down to bottomless depths at the edge of the Verdon Gorge. And then there is the incomparable light of Provence, to which many painters felt irresistibly attracted two centuries ago. A magical world on the southwestern edge of the Alps or the simple home of "backcountry" folk?

In order to discover the land behind the Côte, one must board the Train des Pignes in Nice. It is said that the journey was so leisurely that one could gather pine cones during the ride. That might be an exaggeration, but this train is not an express. Luckily. Soon the mountains approach, and the stones to the right and left become more rugged. The Var is extremely tame, rippling in its wide riverbed. However, things can go differently, which was proven by this Alpine river in the fall of 2020. A stop in Puget-Théniers, no one gets on, and the train proceeds. Entrevaux, a cluster of closely built houses, dozes in the morning sun in the shadow of its

citadel. In 1690 the "Sun King," Louis XIV, commissioned the architect to the imperial court, Vauban, to fortify the square: At that point, the border to the county of Nice ran only a few kilometers downstream.

THE CAPITAL CITY OF LAVENDER

Annot—another picturesque, sleepy spot. Here the train turns into the Vaïre Valley. Near Fugeret, the train gains altitude with a loop that includes a spiral tunnel, only to disappear behind Méailles in the longest out of a total of twenty-three tunnels along the 93-mile (150-kilometer) route. After 11,342 feet (3,457 meters), the train reappears in the daylight in the Verdon Valley. In Barrême, the Train des Pignes meets the Route Napoléon. In 1815 the emperor's goal was to return to power in Paris—but this train's route ends after about three hours in Digne, which lies on the lower reaches of the Bléone and since 1988 has been adorned with the les Bains addition.

The area is famous for its lavender. One central location is south of Digne, on the expansive plateau around Valensole. Flowering time is from mid-May to early August. Another unforgettable experience in the quiet backcountry of the Côte d'Azur.

Old walls "between the valleys" (Entrevaux). The picturesque spot, guarded by Vauban's citadel, is a stop on the Ligne des Pignes.

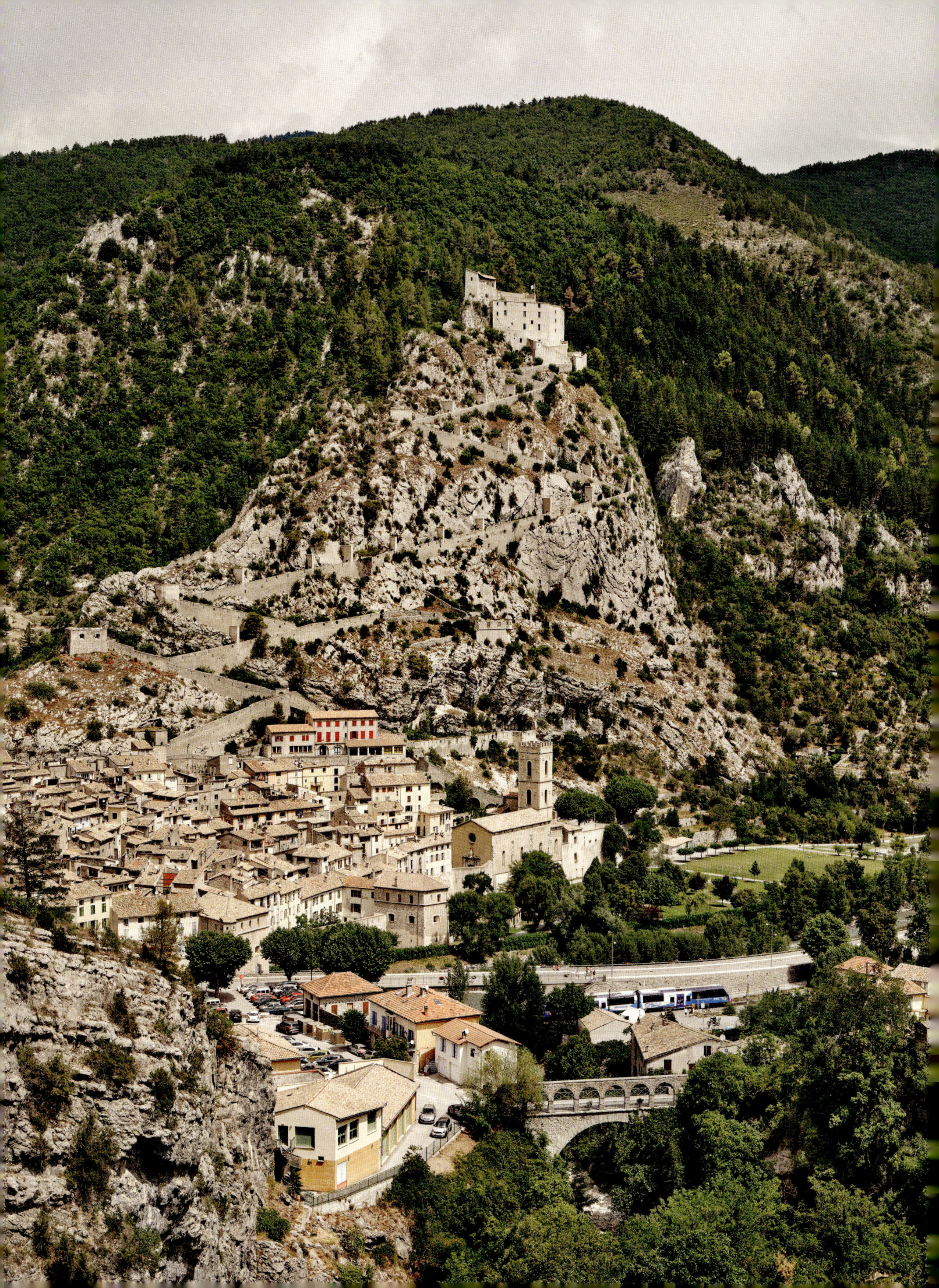

TRAIN DES PIGNES

The La Tinée train station stands
as an example of many old
stations along the route that
are not in operation but are still
preserved (museum), such as La
Tinée with its large water reservoir.
On the lower reaches of the Var,
the river has dug a deep gorge.

Railway romance à la française.
During the summer, a historical
steam train runs on the Ligne
des Pignes, from Puget-Théniers
to Annot or Le Fugeret and back.
In the picture, the train is running
across the La Donne Viaduct
near Annot—you can almost
smell it! ▽ ▽

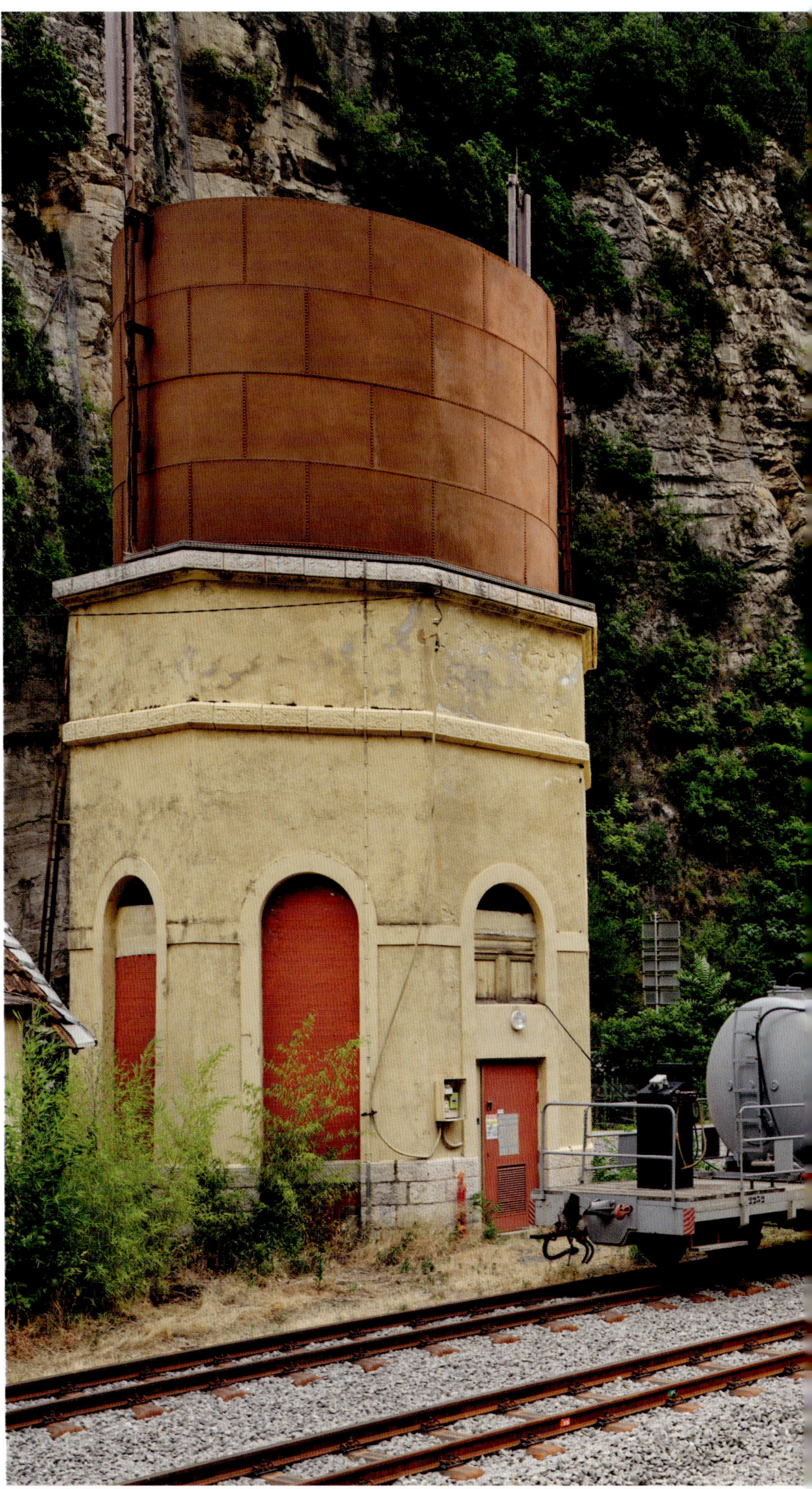

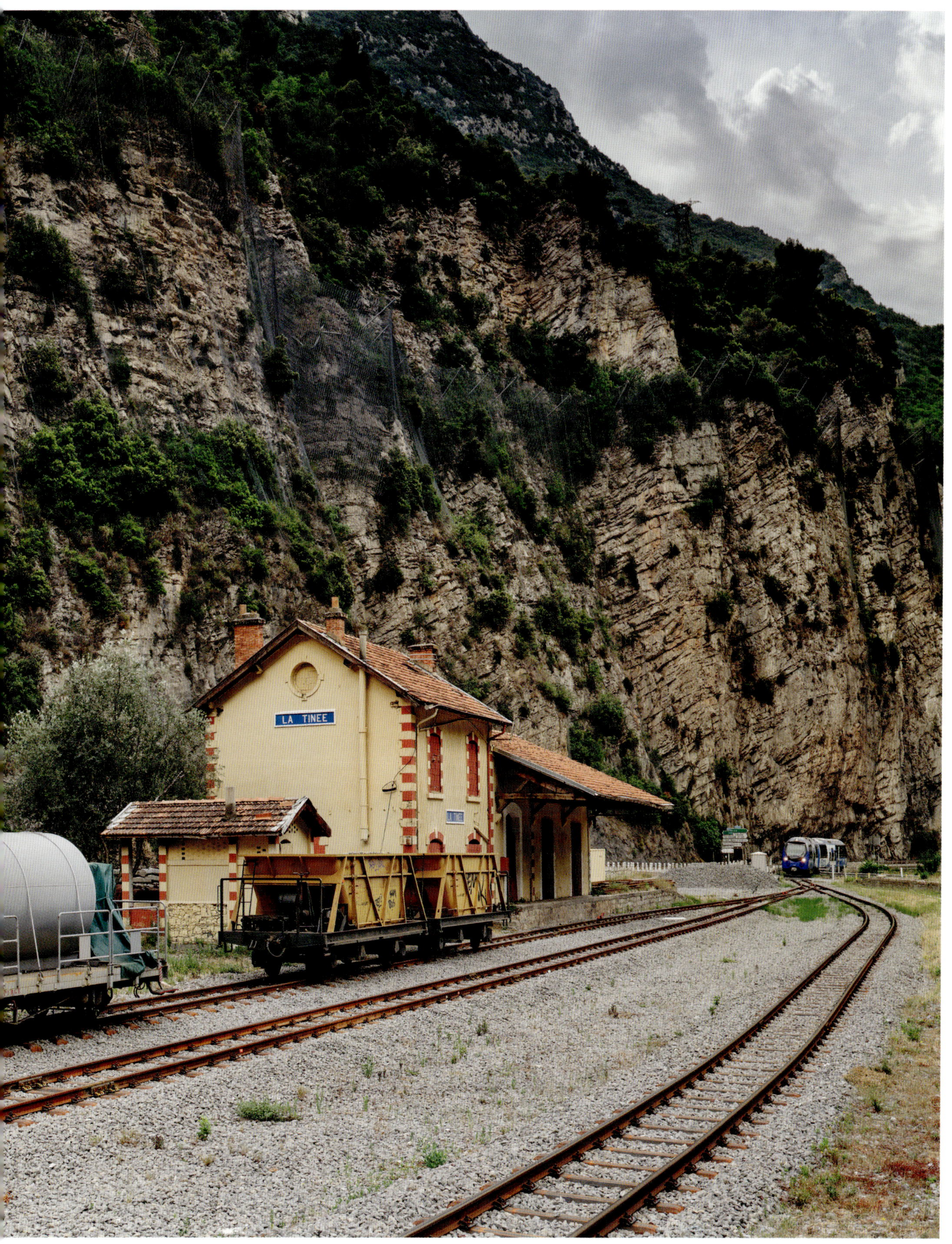

LA TINÉE

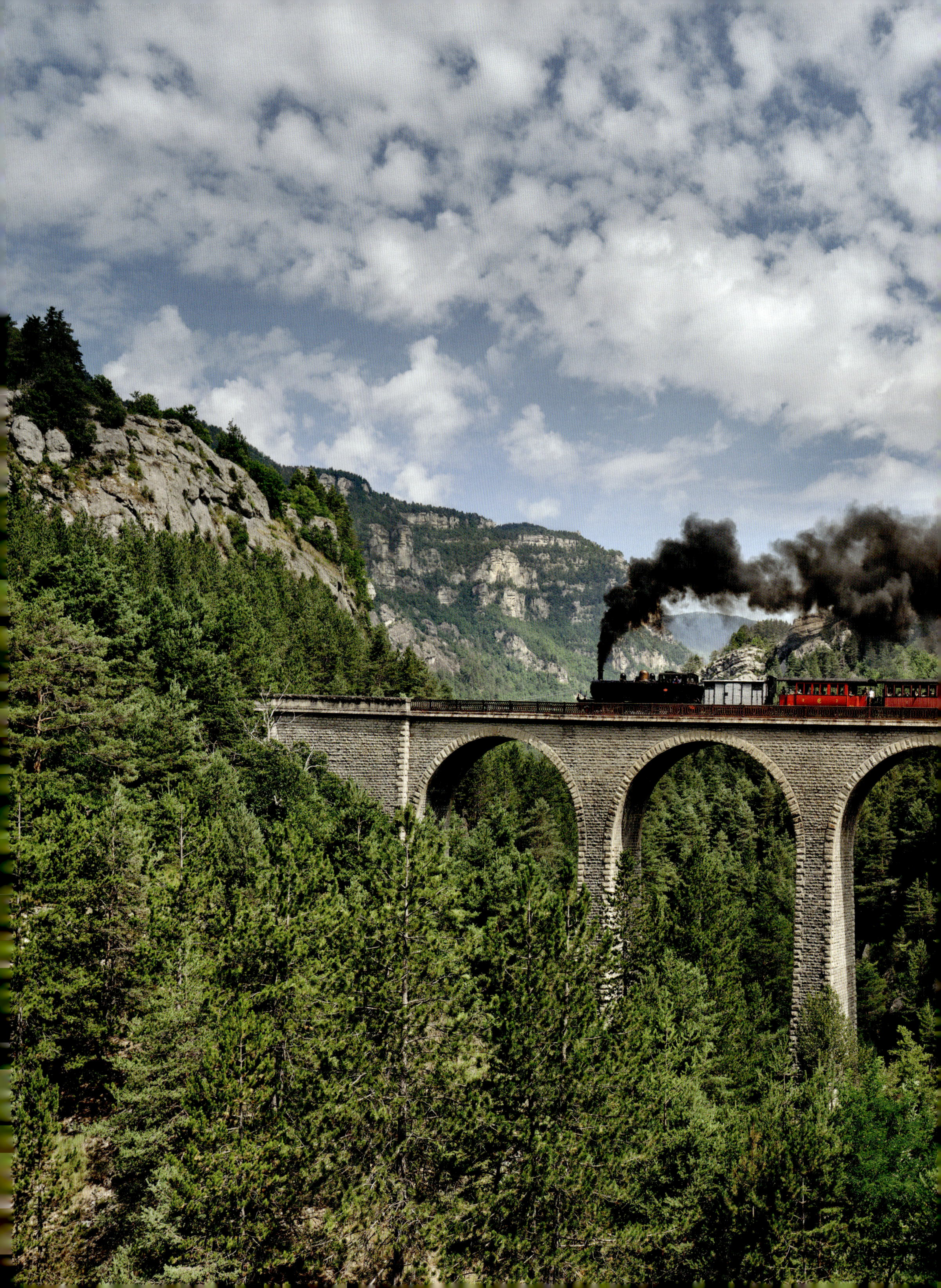

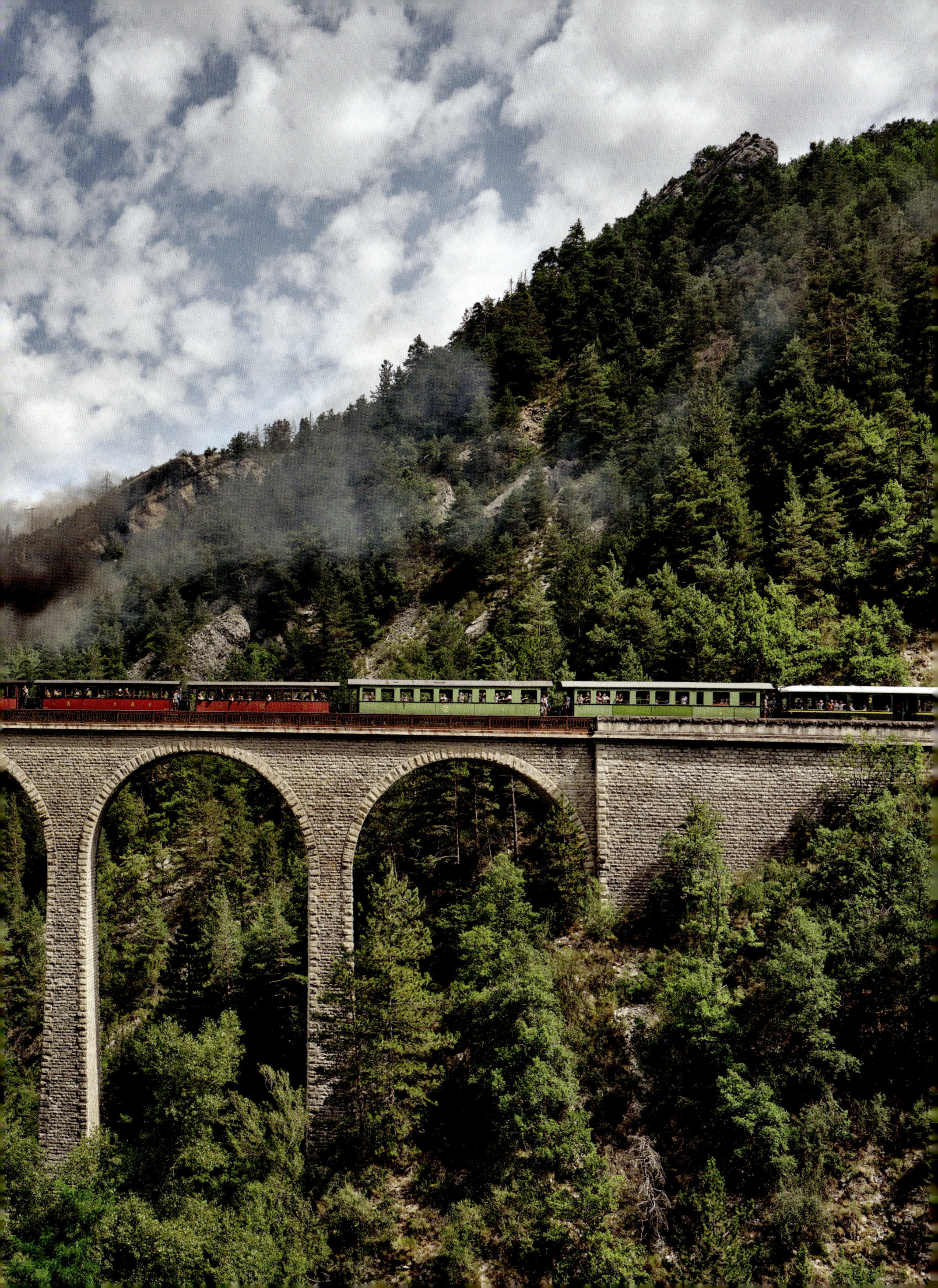

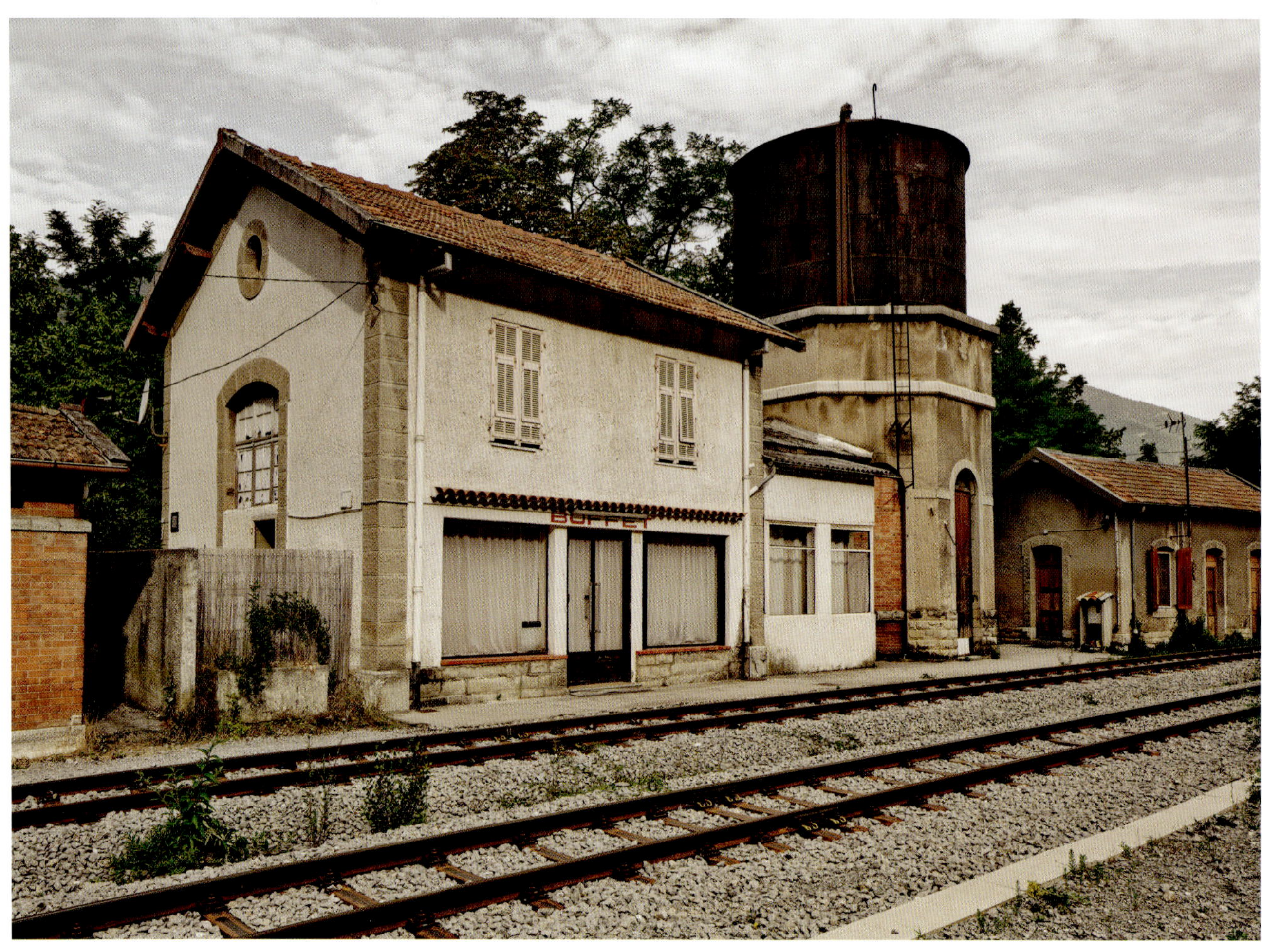

TRAIN DES PIGNES

How about a café or a génépi? Even
if it doesn't necessarily look like it, the
old train station in Annot has a small
restaurant. À votre santé!

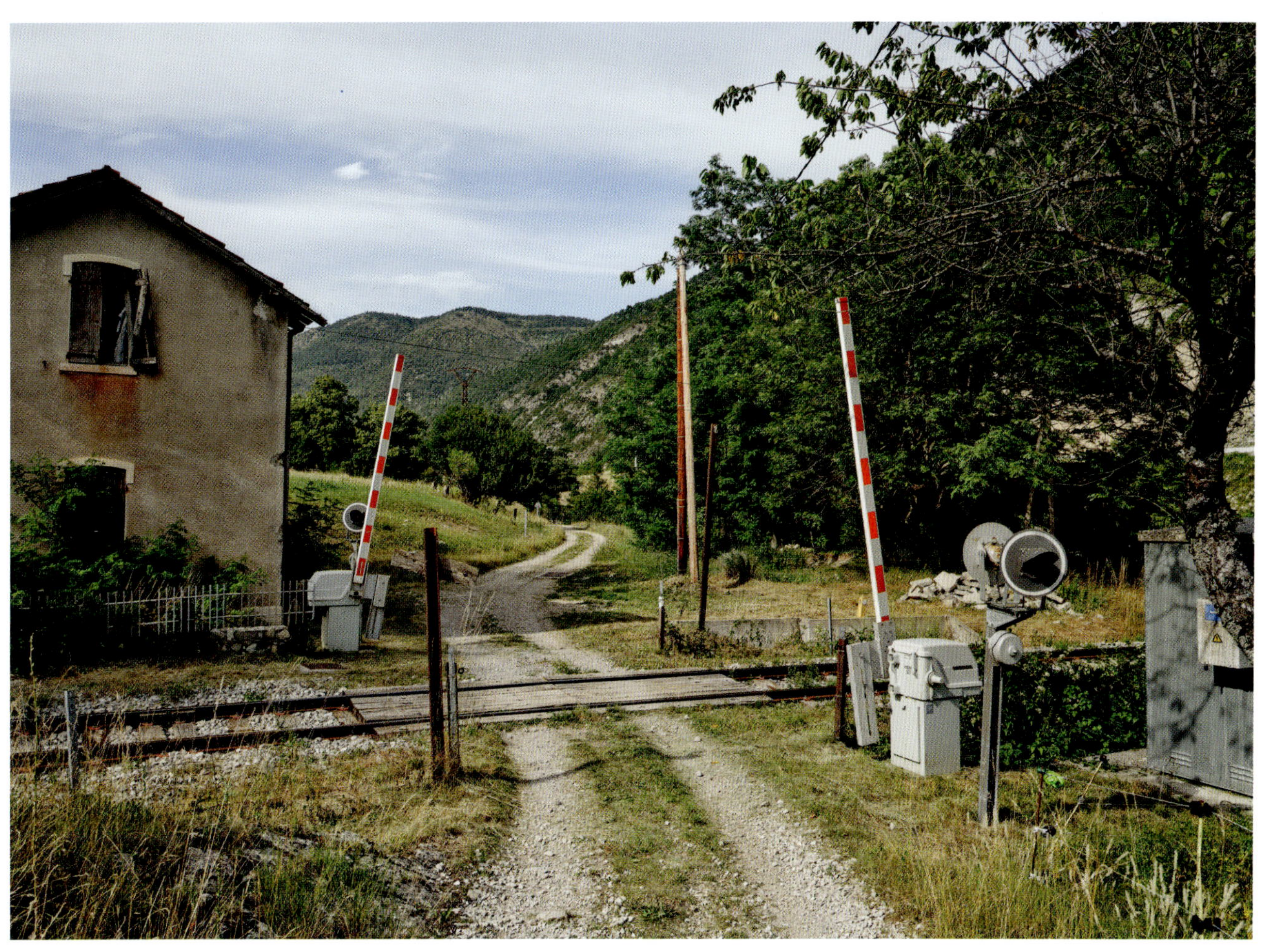

TRAIN DES PIGNES

The signalman's hut has long been abandoned—the barrier near Thorame-Haute is raised and lowered automatically. Progress embedded in a nostalgic backdrop, reminiscent of the good old days.

Perched high above the valley on a rocky terrace near Méailles, the Train des Pignes crosses two large arched bridges: the Maouna Viaduct (646 feet / 197 meters) and the Guillaumasse Viaduct (397 feet / 121 meters). ▽ ▽

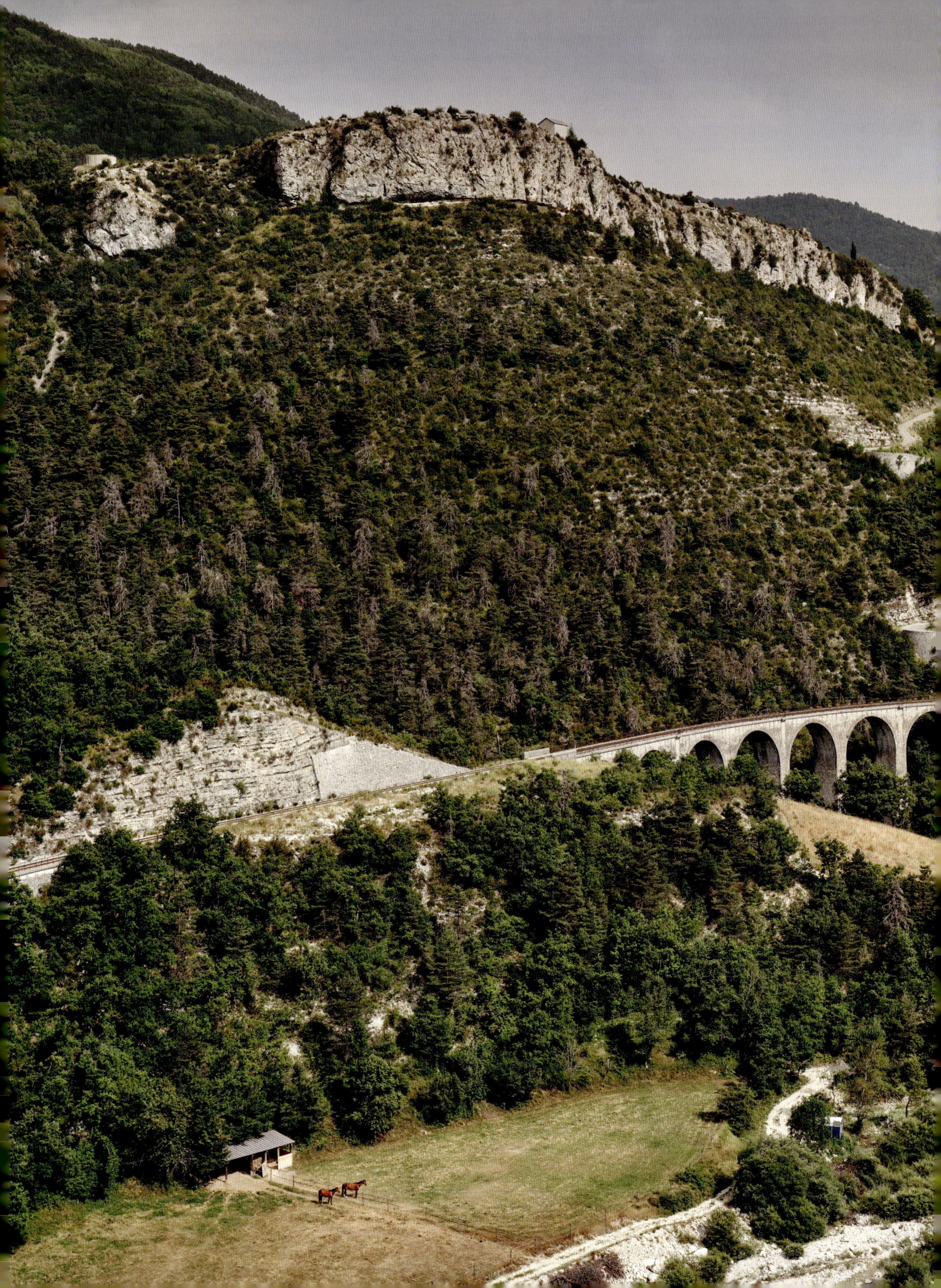

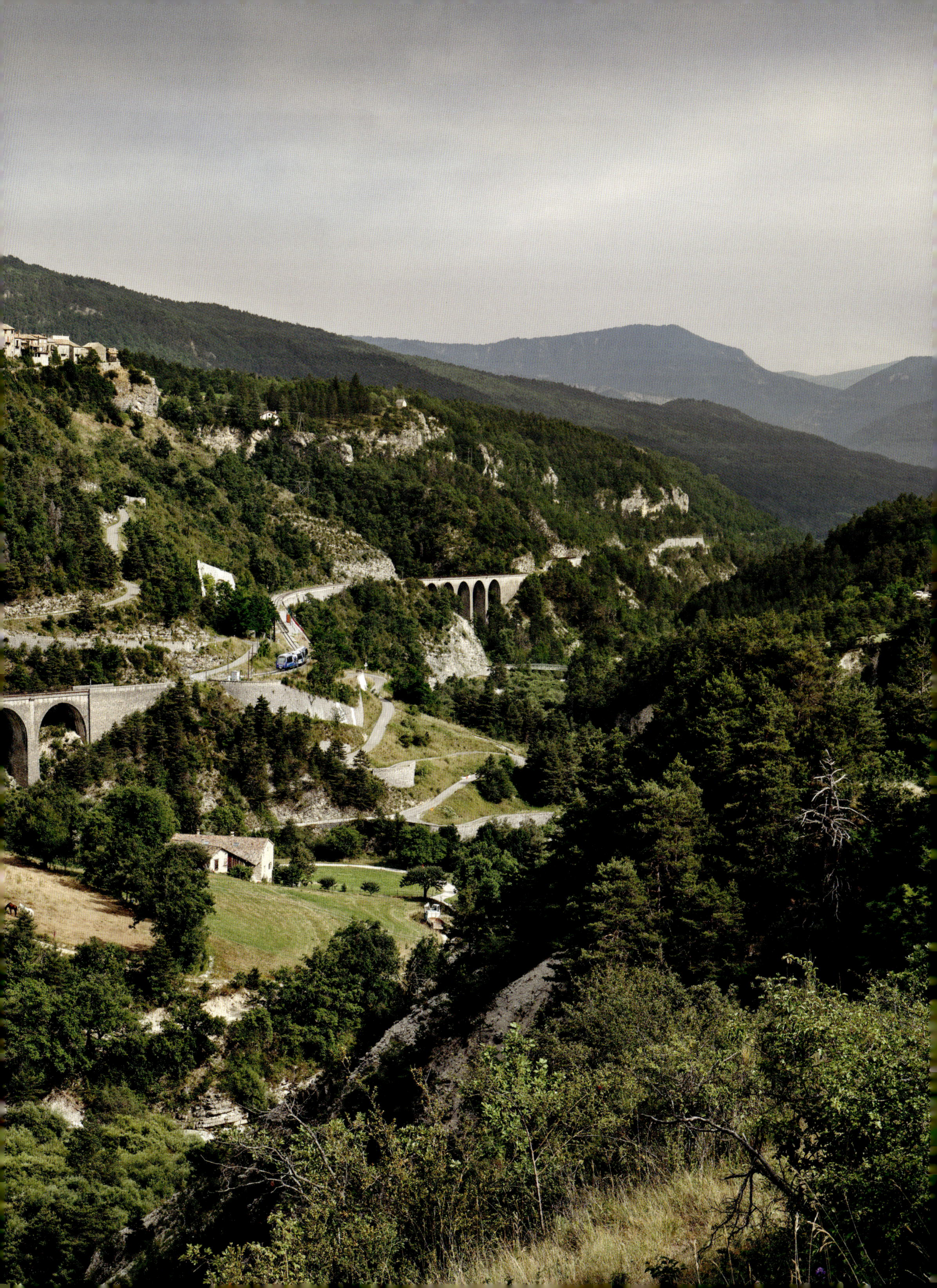

THREE HUNDRED DAYS OF SUNSHINE AND A FOUR-THOUSANDER

Grenoble is the economic hub of the French Alps, while Briançon is its historic center. The *Ligne des Alpes* and its continuation through the upper Durance Valley connects the two cities. The *Little Train of La Mure* recalls the mining in the Grenoble backcountry.

The old, fortified town of Briançon is just 6 miles (10 kilometers) from the Italian border—just a stone's throw away. Paris, the hub of the Grande Nation, is decidedly farther—about 310 miles (500 kilometers) as the crow flies. Looking from Paris's Quai d'Orsay, Briançon is far away, in the *banlieue* of the country, so to speak. That explains, perhaps, why a train ride from Grenoble via Gap into the high Durance Valley feels like an eternity, between four and eight hours. In the same amount of time, a well-trained racing cyclist can make it easily over the Col du Lautaret (1.3 miles / 2,058 meters) to Briançon. We're taking the low-speed train, monsieur!

STRUCTURES ALONG THE ALPINE ROUTE

However, there is one advantage to the long train ride. Whoever has time and is willing to spend it will enjoy at leisure the sights along the route: the unbelievable Mont Aiguille rock tower near the outskirts of the Vercours Massif; the Serre-Ponçon Reservoir; the Vauben Fortress of Mont Dauphin; the Massif des Écrins, whose highest peak towers over 13,123 feet (4,000 meters); and, like something out of a Tolkien novel, Briançon with its narrow alleyways and large fortress walls. Railway fanatics are impressed by the many viaducts on the first section of track; for example, at Vif (Croset), Clelles (Orbanne), or Lus-la-Croix Haute (Fauries).

After passing through Gap, which has had a railway connection since 1875, the Lac de Serre-Ponçon comes into view. A 2,067-foot-long (630-meter-long) earth dam has been blocking the nearly 10-square-mile (25-square-kilometer) stretch of water in the Durance Valley since 1961. About 1,500 people needed to be relocated before the streets and the tracks could be built leading to Briançon. The lake serves both to produce energy and to protect the lower reaches of the Durance from flooding. When the water is low, the 984-foot-long (300-meter-long) Chanteloube Viaduct emerges. It was a part of the never completed rail line to Barcelonnette (construction started in 1909 and was abandoned in 1941).

The ride ends in Briançon Gare: the Alpine city that draws visitors with its three hundred days of sunshine. The first train arrived in the year 1884. There were both economic and political reasons for not continuing the line into Piemont. During the time when trains already rattled through the 7.5-mile-long (12-kilometer-long) tunnel between Mondane and Bardoneccia, the French and Italians could not agree on a route: Col de Montgenevre or Col de l'Échelle?

A direct connection with the Piedmont metropolis of Turin or a connection to the Savoy railway network via the Cénis Tunnel? In addition to the (expensive) tunnel styles—using the Mont Cenis as a model—a cogwheel railway using the Fell system (see page 57) was considered. A connection between Boùrg-d'Oisans and Briançon via the Col du Lautaret got stuck in the planning stage as well.

FROM INDUSTRIAL RAILWAYS TO MUSEUMS

The railway industry opened new possibilities not only for the transportation of people but also for the transportation of goods. In order to make the transport of coal from the mines in La Mure near Grenoble more profitable, it was decided to construct a factory train. The challenging terrain did not make it easy for the engineers: The 18.6-mile-long (30-kilometer-long) route includes six large viaducts and eighteen tunnels. In 1888, after six years of construction, the Chemin de Fer de La Mure went into operation. The electrification of the line began by 1903, with the first locomotive—Le Drac, named after the region's main river—featuring 500 horsepower and pulling twenty empty wagons uphill. Its four motors were driven with a direct-current system developed by the Swiss engineer René Thury. In 1912 the whole route was electrified—the first in the world!

Railway history. In 1988, anthracite mining ended in La Mure. The "little train" ran awhile longer with rolling stock that came from old Swiss stockpiles. Then a landslide brought it to its end. Almost. After a few years, the people in Trièves remembered the coal railway and recognized its historical and cultural significance—and its tourist potential. With a considerable financial effort, the line was partially renovated; in 2021, about 9.3 miles (15 kilometers) from La Mure to Belvédère via the Monteynard Reservoir could be put back into operation.

UNFINISHED

Originally, La Mure should not have been the last station. A continuation of the railway into the Champsur and then down into Gap was planned. However, it was never finished—only the segment to Corps went into operation, and that for only ten years. Some striking viaducts have remained, which are used today for roads. The imposing Buzon Viaduct stands above Gap as a white giant among the landscape—a popular photo op and a stone monument to unfulfilled dreams.

The Thoranne Viaduct spans the gorge in Eau Grosse in an elegant arch. The structure is one of many in the scenically delightful stretch from Grenoble to Col de la Croix Haute (3,858 feet / 1,176 meters). ▽ ▽

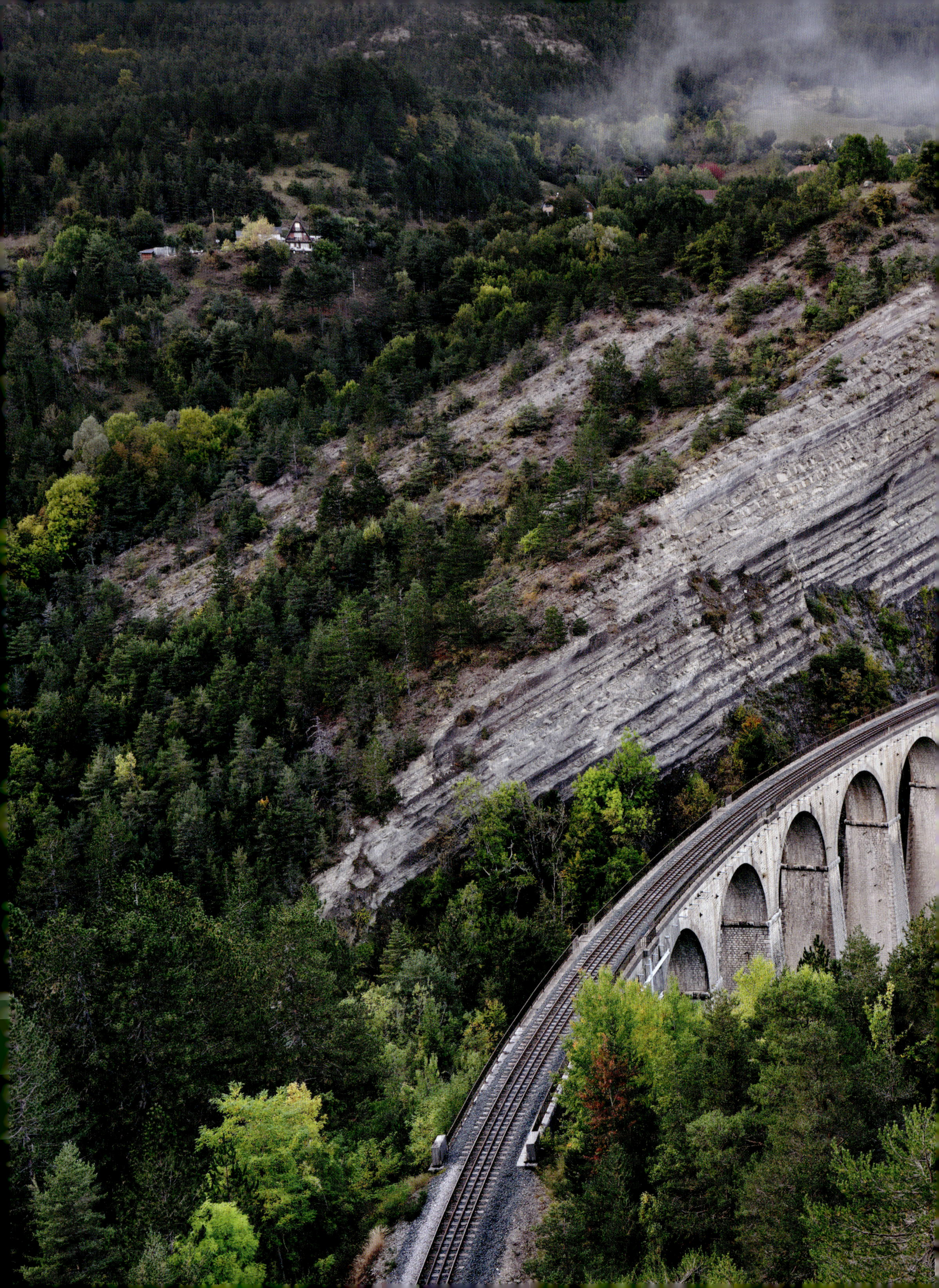

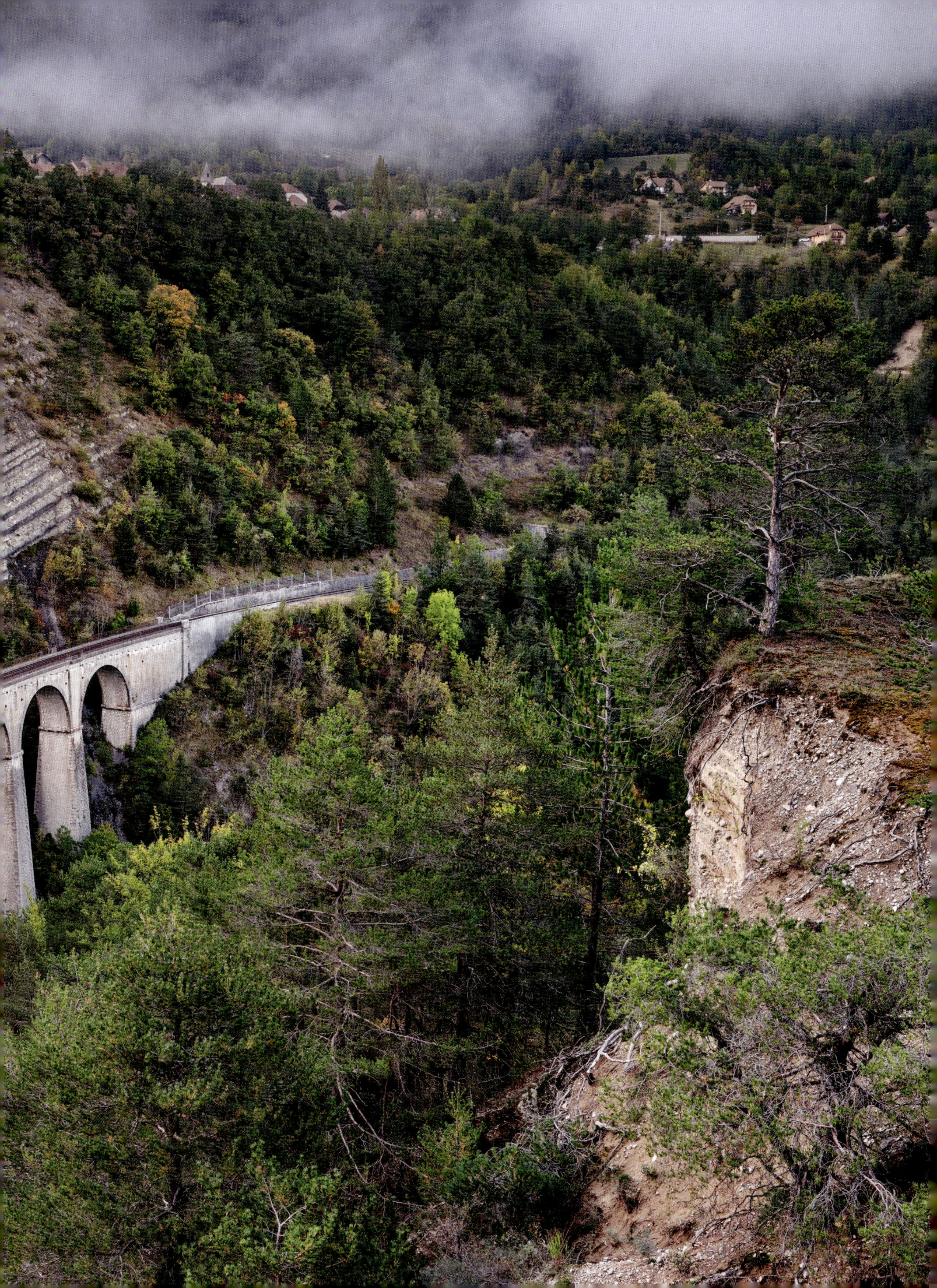

LIGNE DES ALPES

An absolute eye-catcher along the
Ligne des Alpes is Mont Aiguille
(6,847 feet / 2,087 meters). The
crest, which is completely isolated
from the main ridge of the Vercors,
was climbed for the first time in the
year 1492, by order of the French
king Charles VIII. Incredible!

From the Col de la Croix Haute,
the Ligne des Alpes gently
descends through friendly park-
land to Lus-la-Croix-Haute. In the
center is the Fauries Viaduct; on
the horizon, the rugged rockheads
of Tête de Vachères, Tête de la
Plainie, and Tête de Garnesier.
▽ ▽

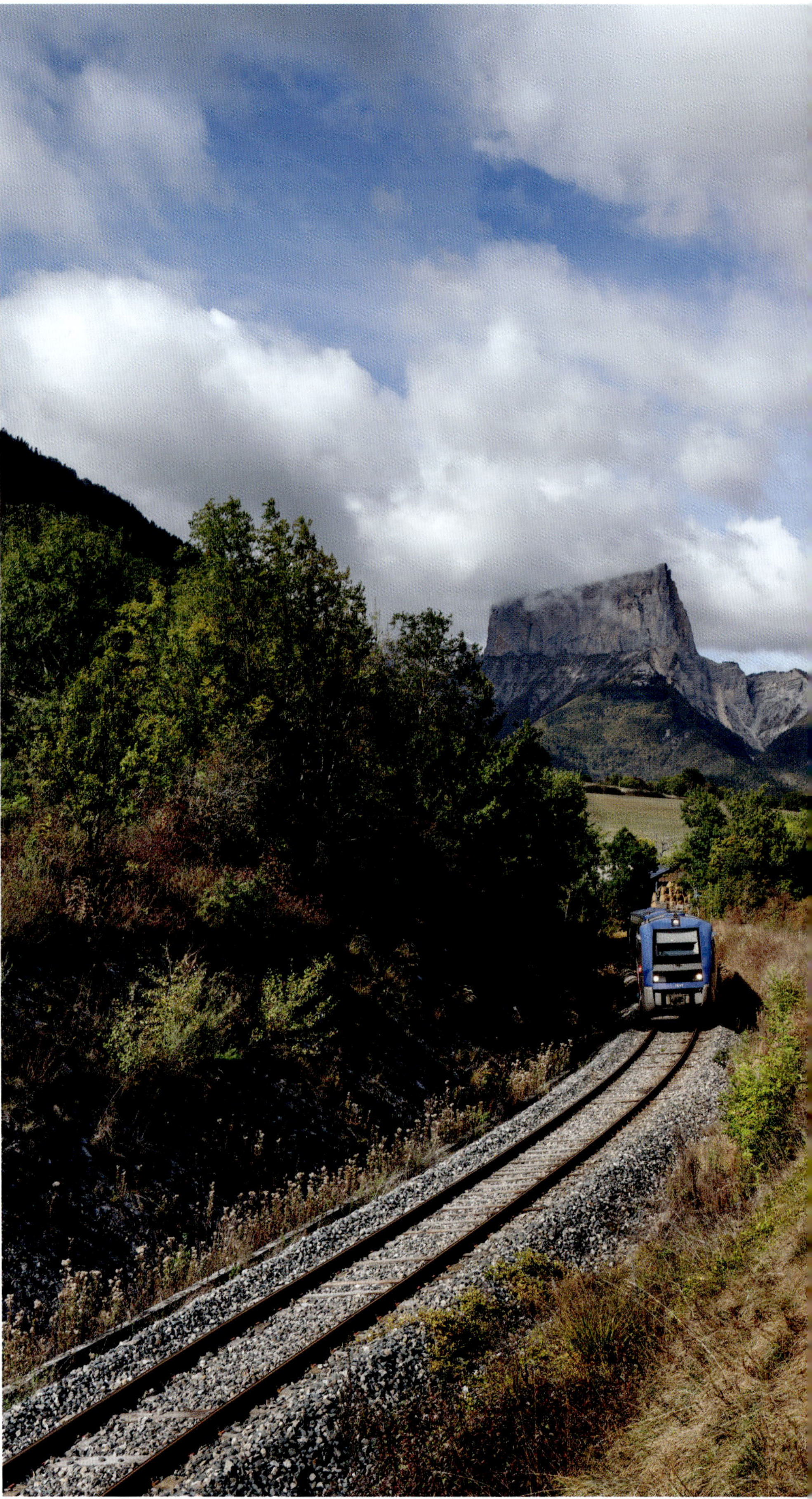

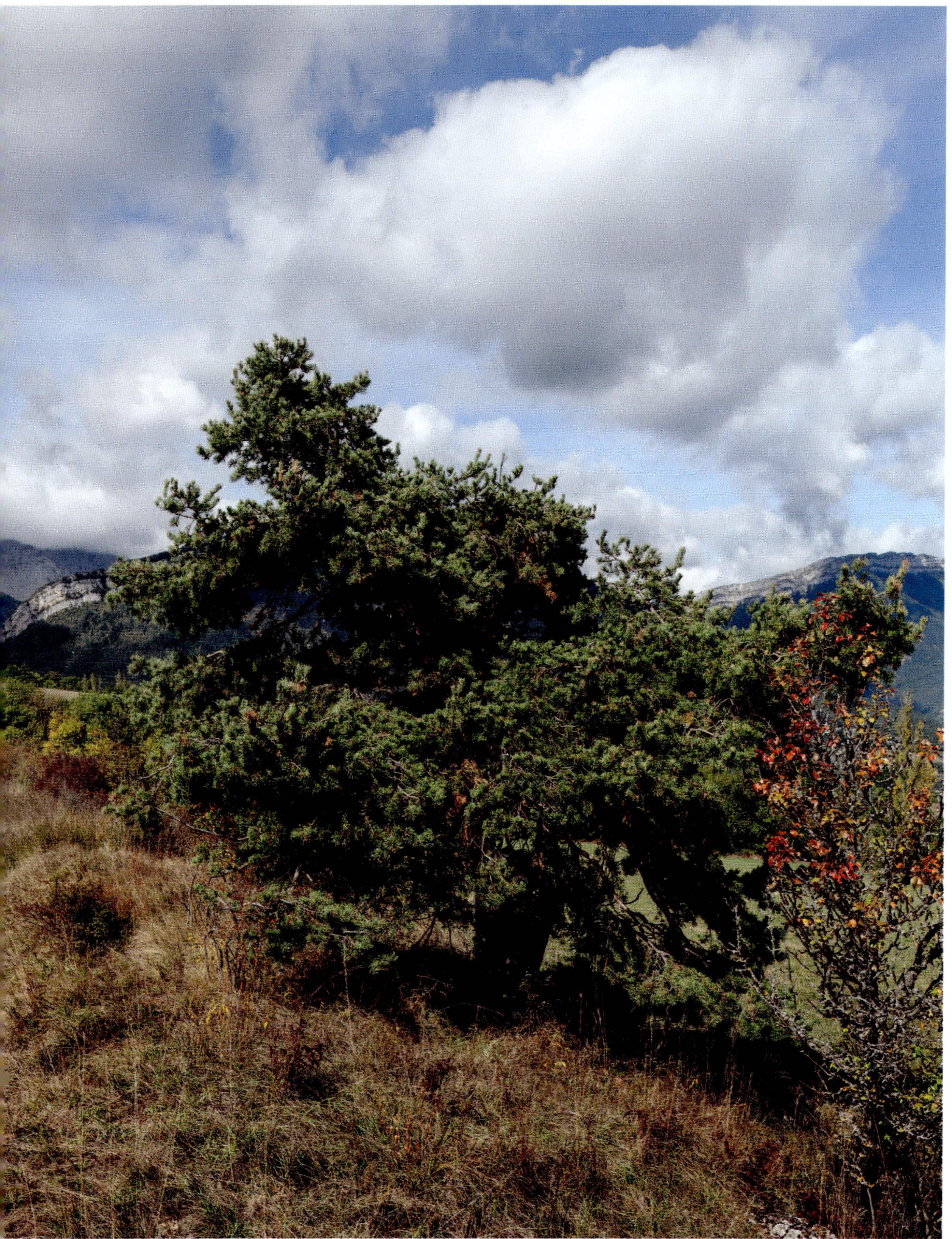

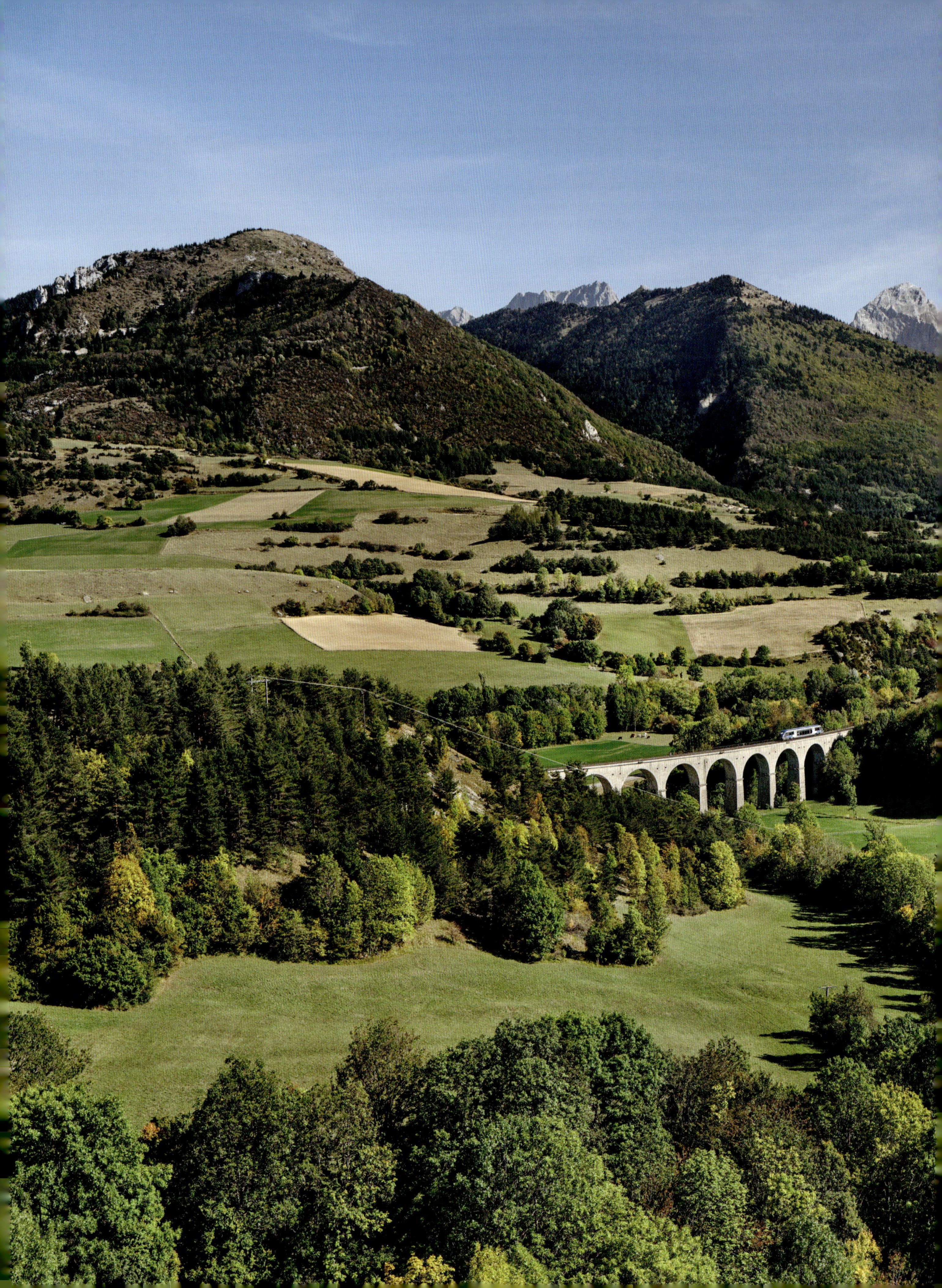

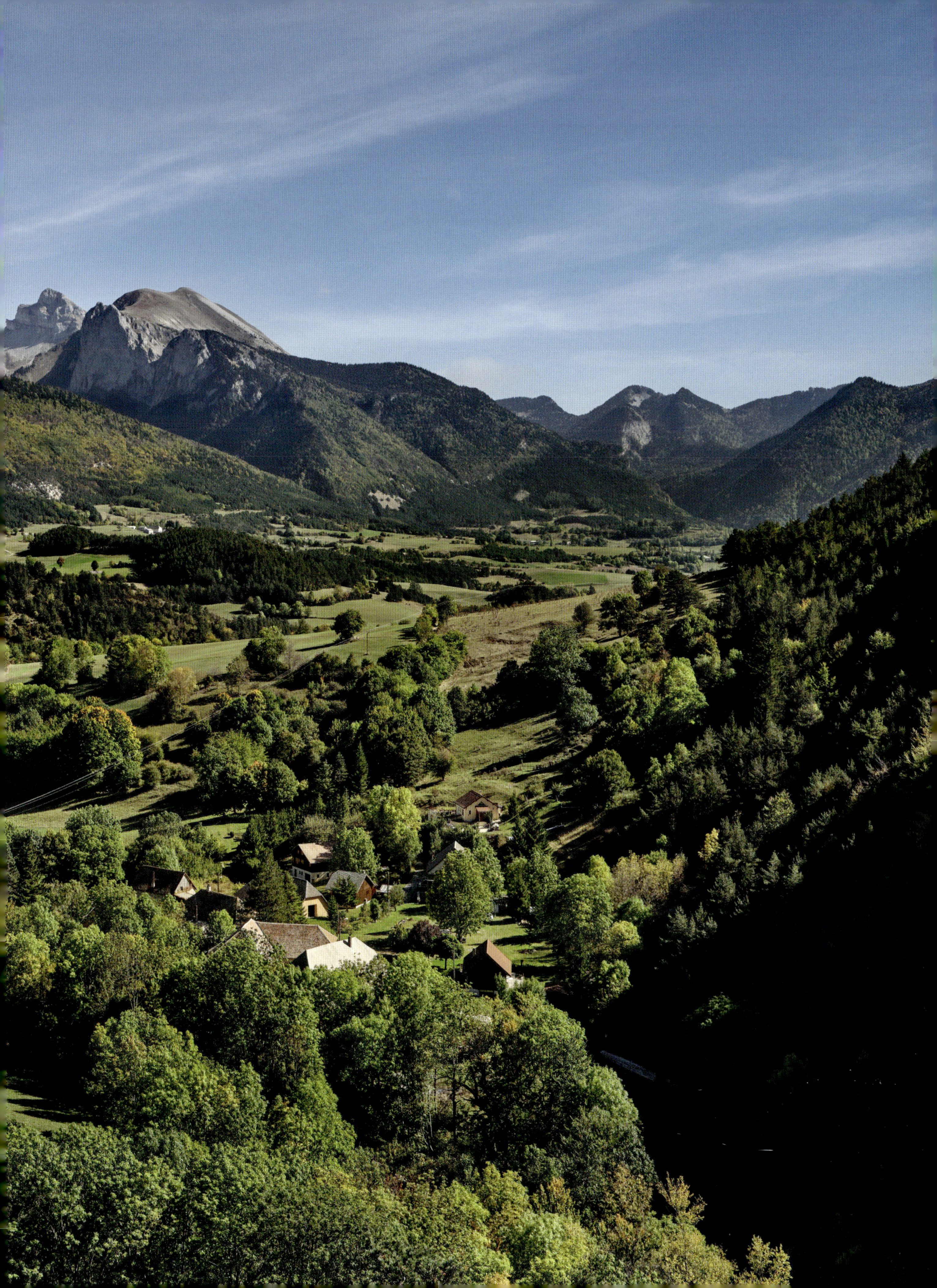

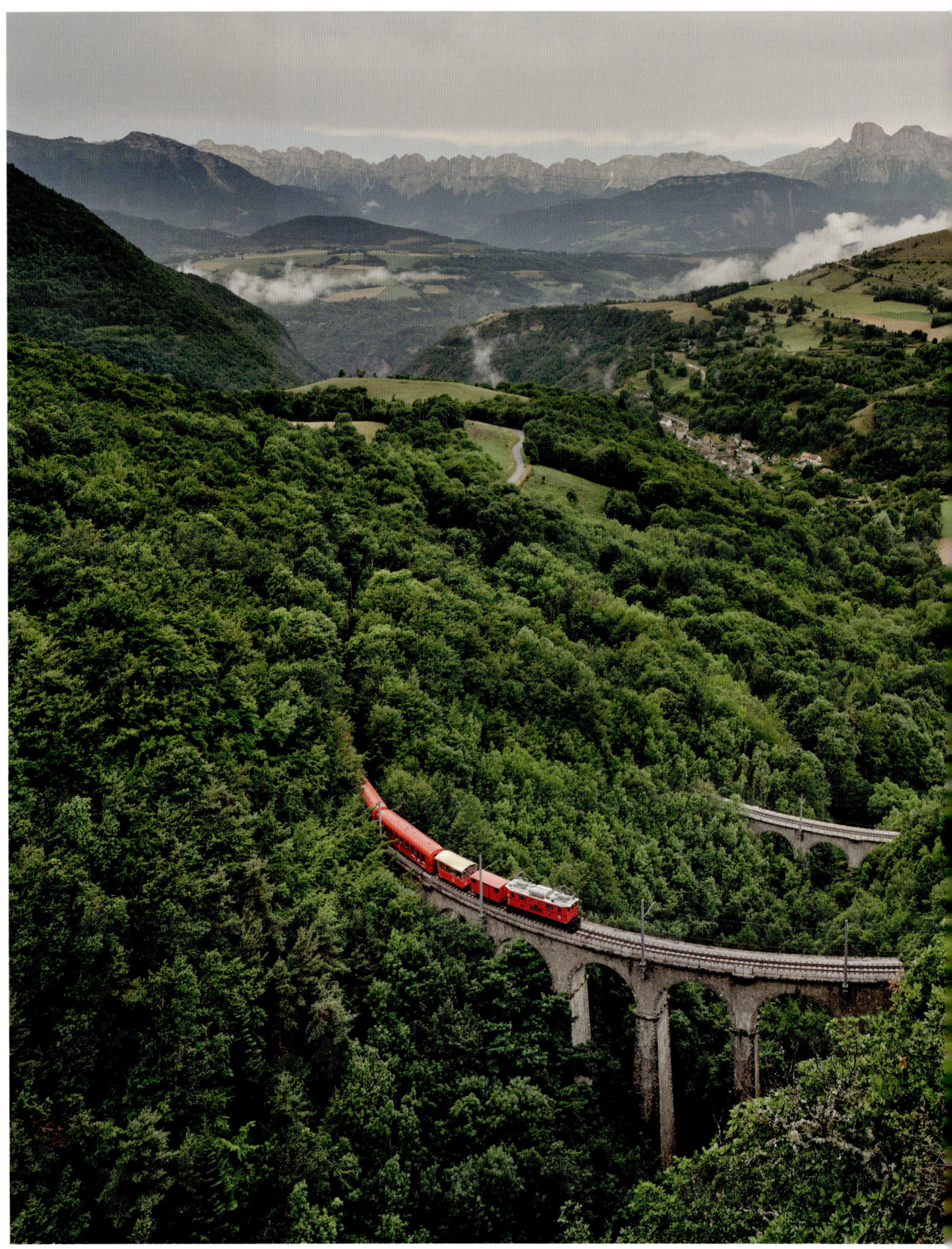

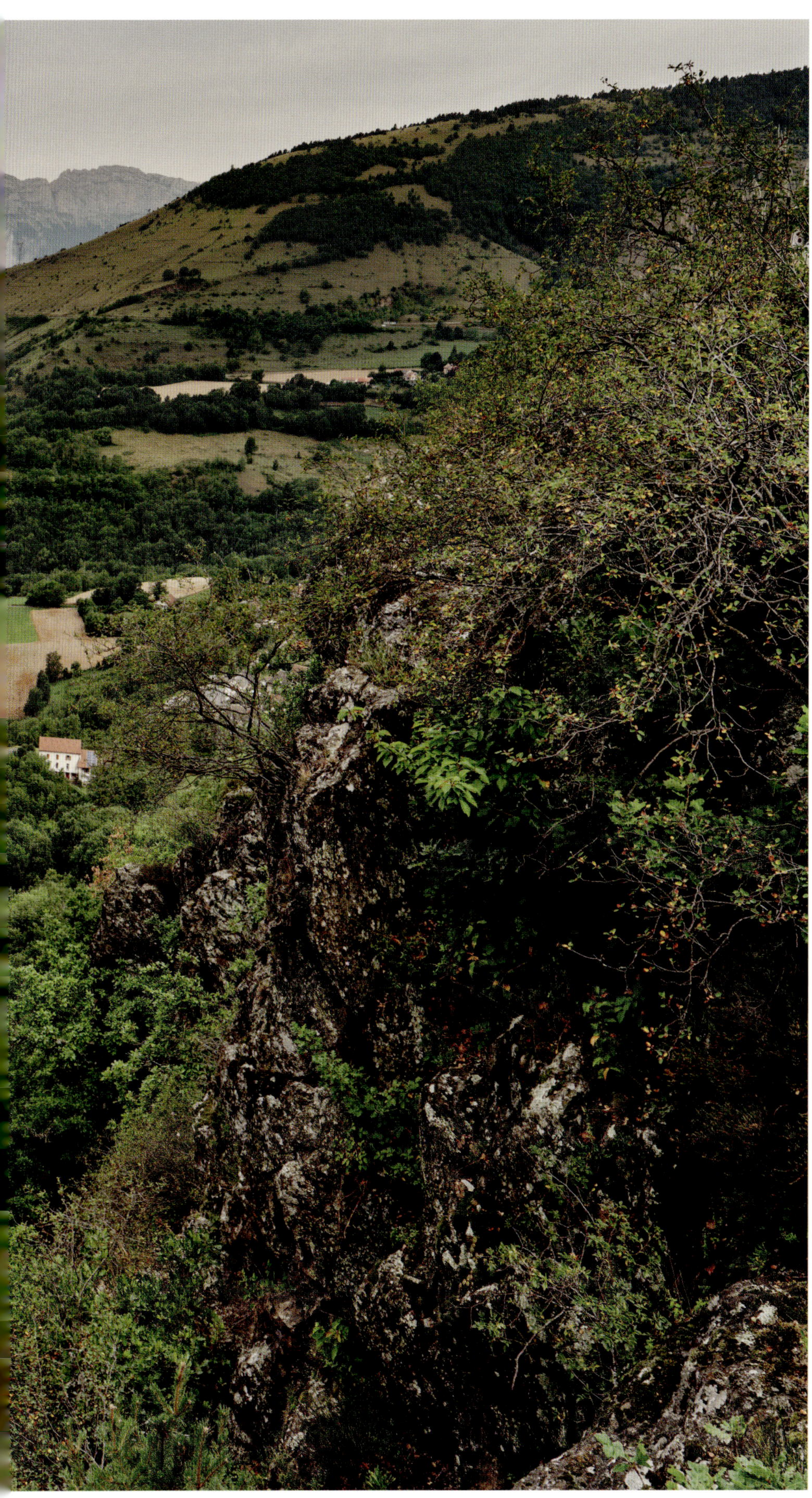

THE LITTLE TRAIN OF LA MURE

The little train climbs the plateaus
of La Mure over two wide loops.
In the forefront are both Loulla
Viaducts; on the horizon, the main
ridge of the Vercours with the two
sister mountains: to the left the
Grande Soeur Agathe (7,162 feet /
2,183 meters), to the right—slightly
less prominent—the Petite Soeur
Sophie (7,093 feet / 2,162 meters).

Built out of one of the most difficult
terrains: the former factory train to
La Mure. It was buried by a landslide in 2010 (*left in the picture*) and
is now in operation as a museum
train from La Mure to the Quai des
Grands Balcons (with a restaurant
and observation deck). The view of
Lac de Monteynard is unique, which
is dammed a little farther down by
a 502-foot-high (153-meter-high)
concrete wall. ▽ ▽

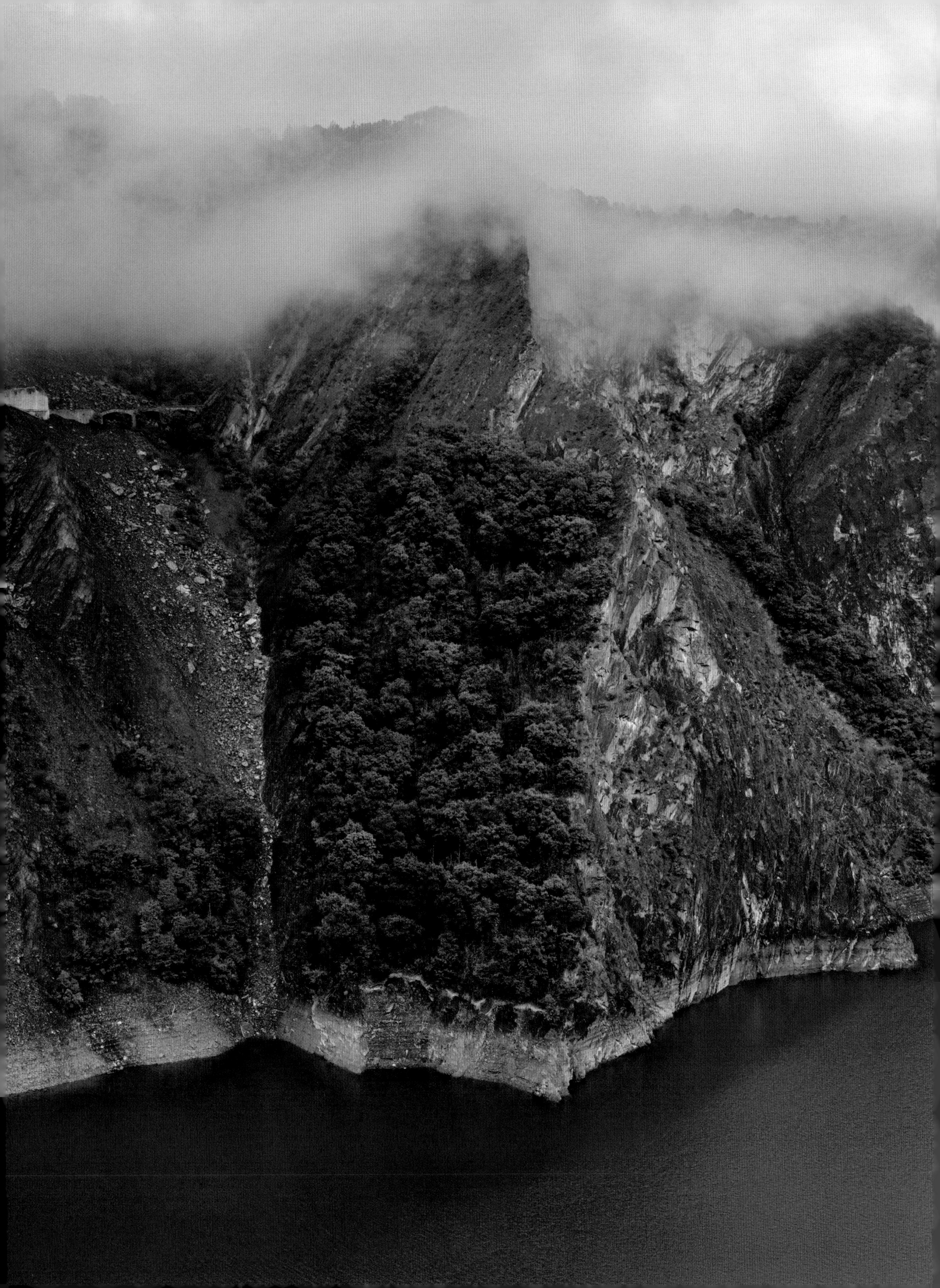

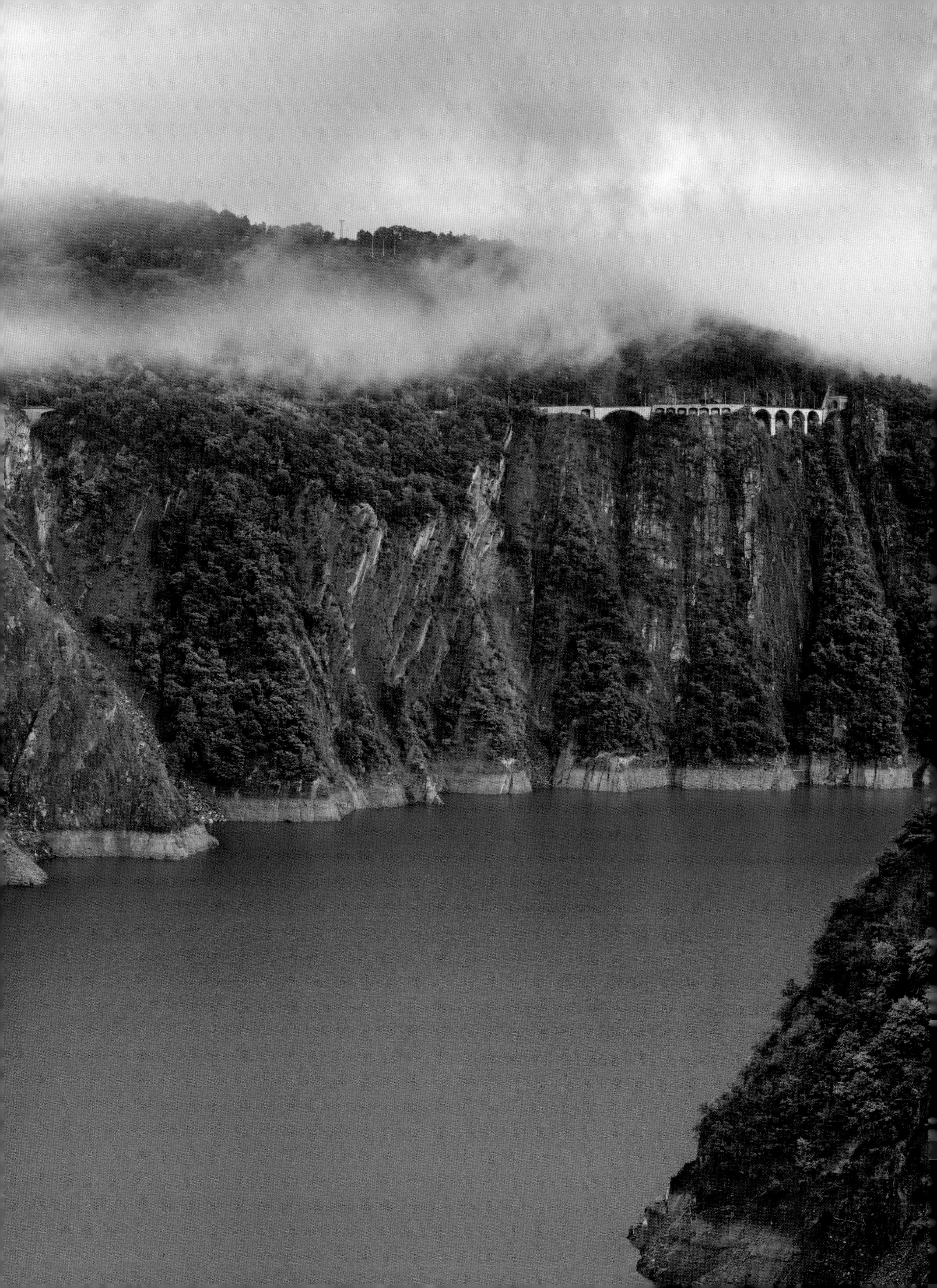

THE FIRST MASSIVE BREAKTHROUGH THROUGH THE ALPS

In the nineteenth century, engineering history was made at Mont Cenis, two thousand years after Hannibal's legendary Alpine crossing, which probably took place here. First, the English built a postal railway over the pass; a little later, the first big railway tunnel, the Mont-Cenis Tunnel, under the Col du Fréjus was opened.

Whoever sees Switzerland as the birthplace of railways (which many do) is only partially right. This is due to the fact that the first large railway tunnel was not built at Gotthard, but instead far in the west of the Alps, between Maurienne and the Susa Valley. A government that no longer exists was responsible for this pioneering feat: the Duchy of Savoy, later the Kingdom of Savoy-Sardinia. Responsible for the planning and construction was Germain Sommeiller, who was born in 1815 in Saint-Jeoire, east of Geneva, so a true Savoyard. Apparently, he was a man of vision, because his railway line ran not over the Alps but *through* the mountain. The Mont-Cenis Tunnel was planned to be 7.6 miles (12.2 kilometers) long, an almost foolhardy undertaking for its time. It was calculated—based on the state of technology in the middle of the nineteenth century—to have a construction time of at least thirty years.

THROUGH THE MOUNTAIN BY TRAIN

But things would happen differently. Sommeiller, a well-educated engineer, made use of new technical innovations; instead of gunpowder and hand tools, he used modern jackhammers and dynamite. Because of this, the construction time decreased dramatically; already in 1870, only thirteen years after the start, the first locomotive steamed through the tunnel! The impossible became a reality, the mountain "conquered."

A new age began in the Alpine region with this railway, and the region was changed politically during the construction of the tunnel. The quaint Kingdom of Savoy-Sardinia disappeared off the map, split between France and the newly formed country of Italy. Vittorio Emanuele II from the House of Savoy sat on the throne in Rome as the first Italian king on March 14, 1861. The railway tunnel at the Col du Fréjus, which was originally projected and begun to be a line within Savoy, now connected France and Italy.

THE POSTAL RAILWAY

Another Alpine railway was built but soon lost to history: the postal train over the Col du Mont Cenis (6,834 feet / 2,083 meters). The project was conceived in London, at that time the hub of the world (and world power). A well-functioning communication network with their distant colonies, such as India, was important to the Brits. The only postal route was via ship, which of course took time. A much quicker way was through a new mode of transportation: the train. And the rail network in Europe was expanding rapidly. Even the Alps were no longer an insurmountable obstacle. Around 1890—according to the planning—was the expected opening of the first massive rail tunnel. But for the Brits and their postal route to India, this time frame was decidedly too long. As a result, they tasked themselves with the construction of a small cogwheel railway. The system developed by the British engineer John Barraclough Fell, with a third track, enabled ascents up to 8.8 percent—ideal for surmounting great differences in height. After a very short construction of only two years, the small postal railway went into operation in 1868. However, its time was short lived, because three years later the Mont-Cenis Tunnel between Modane and Bardonecchia was opened.

A MUSEUM IN NEW ZEALAND

Advances in technology had taken over the Mont-Cenis Railway—and one train overtook the other. Now people and mail traveled much faster, in the tunnel of Monsieur Sommeiller. Mr. Fell built a few more small mountain trains in distant New Zealand (which at that time was still a part of the British Empire). The Kiwis thanked him with a monument on their southern island: the Fell Railway Museum. In this museum, visitors can marvel at the world's only surviving steam engine of the Fell system.

>> The time will come when people will travel in stages moved by steam engines, from city to city, almost as fast as birds fly—fifteen or twenty miles an hour. <<

Oliver Evans (1755–1819),
American inventor

MONT-CENIS RAILWAY

Near Exilles, the Fréjus Line runs
along the imposing fortress of the
same name. It was built in the nineteenth century by the Savoyards,
after Napoleon had had the previous
construction demolished. During the
reign of Louis XIV, a secret prisoner
dwelled within the old castle: the "man
in the iron mask." Persistent rumors
claim that this man could have been
the monarch's twin brother.

MONT-CENIS POSTAL RAILWAY

The snakelike curves of the Mont-
Cenis Street below the large dam.
Clearly visible is the route of the
Fell Postal Railway, which operated
at the pass for three years from
1868 until 1871. ▽ ▽

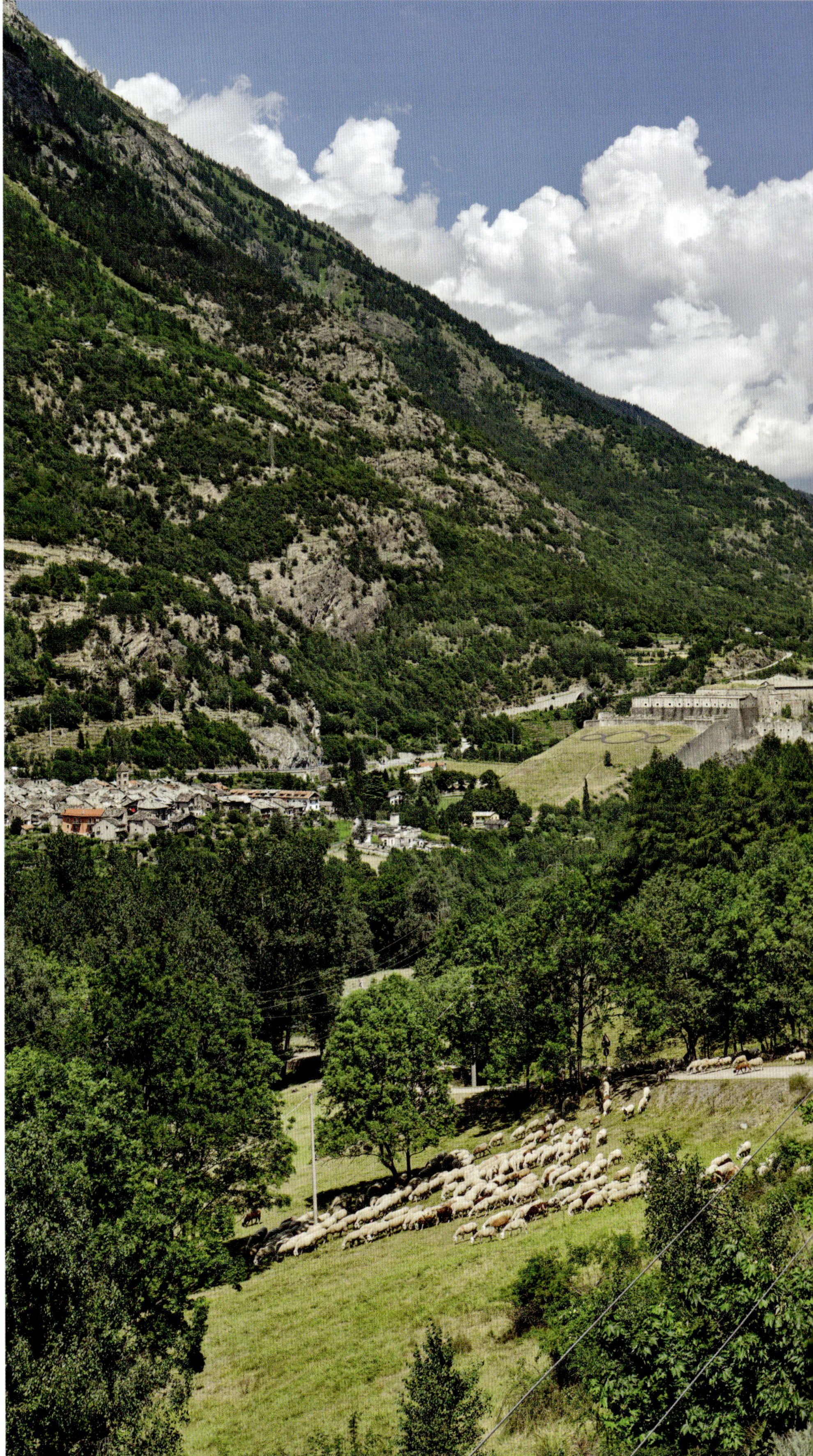

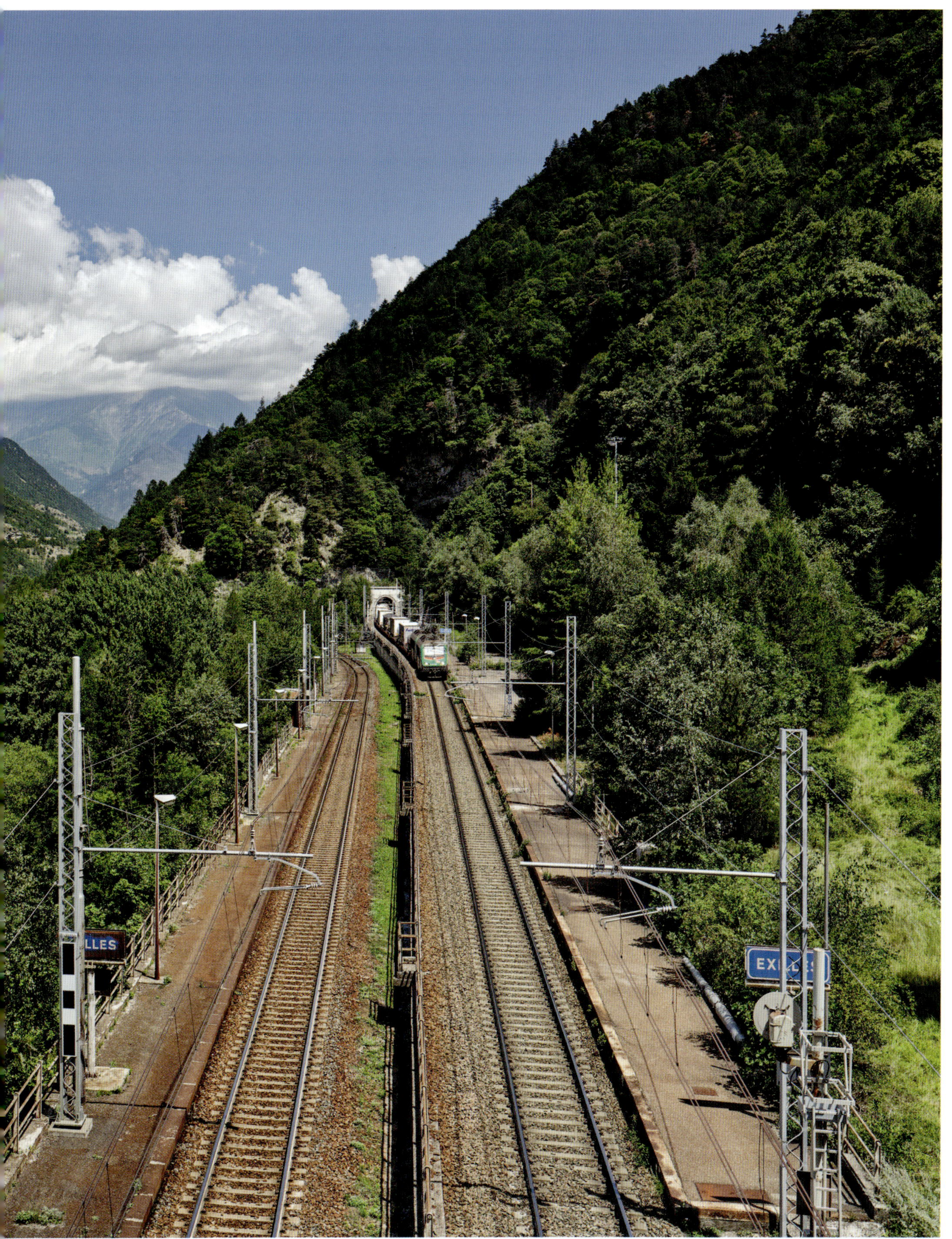

LLES
EXILLES

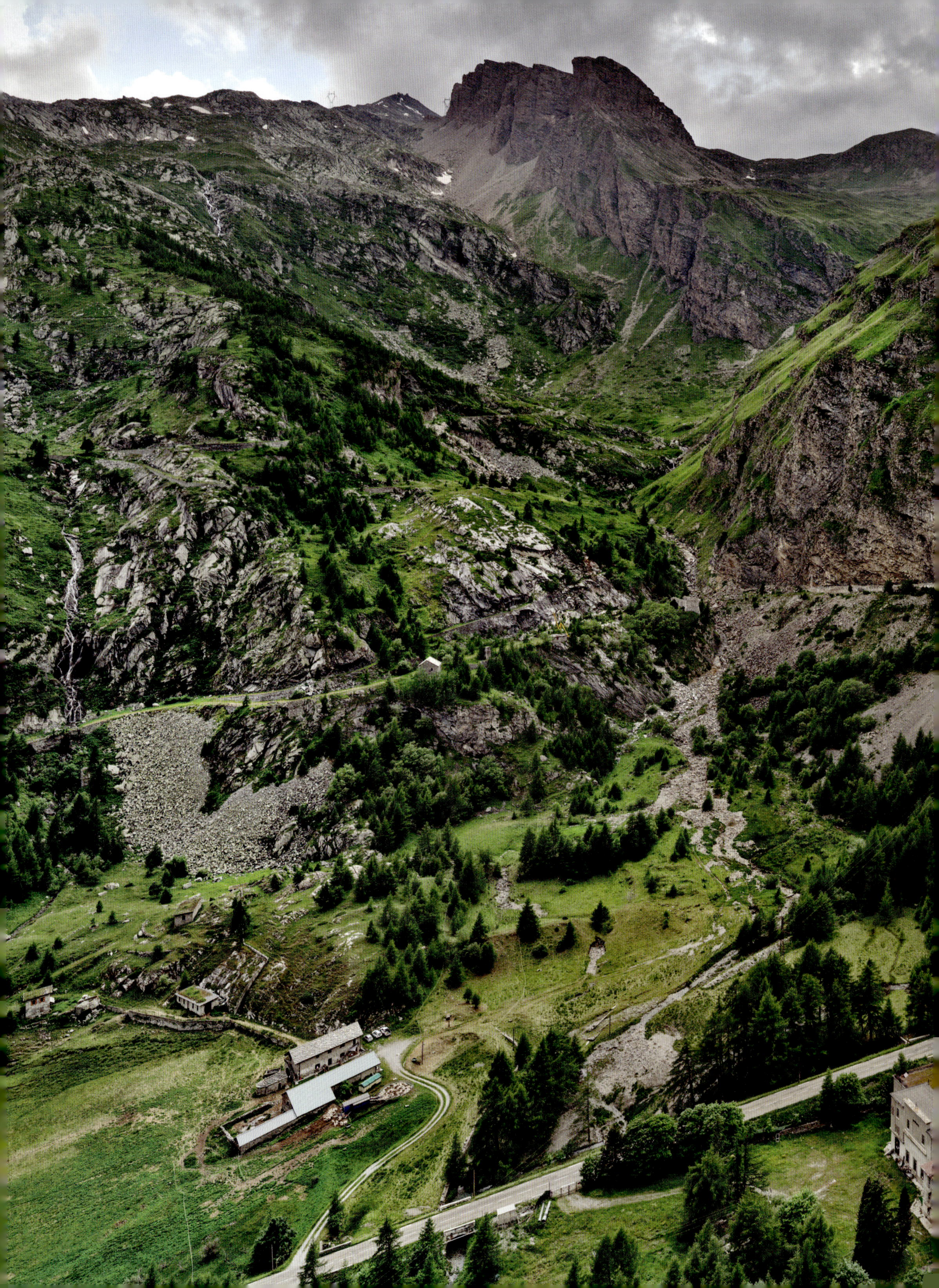

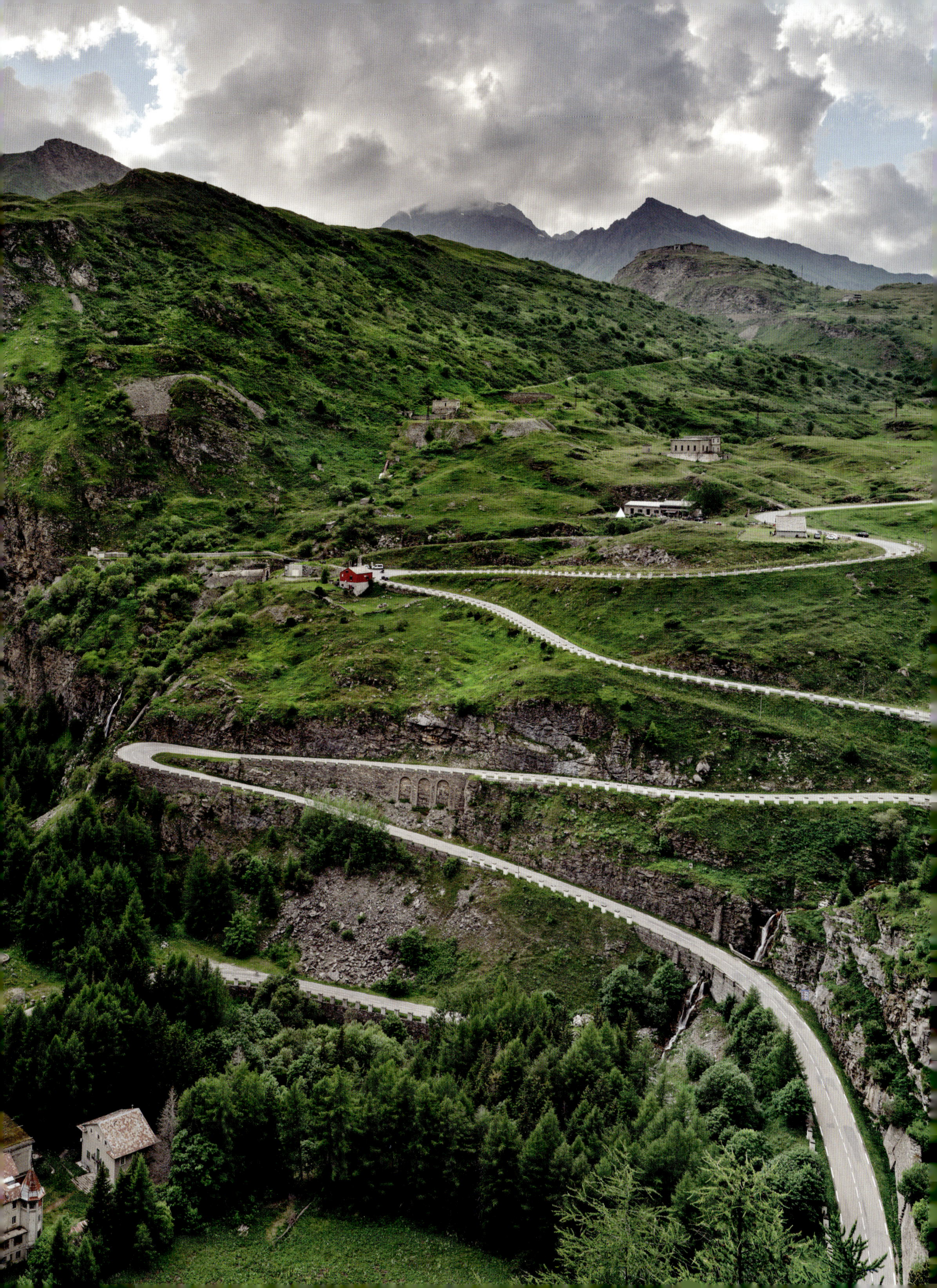

MONT-BLANC EXPRESS

IN THE SHADOW OF THE "WHITE GIANT"

On the way from Lower Valais to Chamonix on the *Mont-Blanc Express*, you come pretty close to the tallest mountain in the Alps, even closer if you do an excursion to *Montenvers* or *Nid d-Aigle.* However, the most beautiful view of the white giant can be found at the *Parc d'Attractions* in Emosson.

Mont-Blanc Express. An extremely effective promotional name. After all, Mont Blanc is number one among all Alpine peaks, higher than all other mountains between Vienna and Nice. It's only logical that the transit line from Martigny to Chamonix and continuing to Saint-Gervais-les-Bains has the mountain in its name. But watch out: If you're not careful (and sitting on the correct side of the train), you won't see the 15,781-foot-high (4,810-meter-high) snow-covered peak at all, neither at the southern entrance of the tunnel under the Col des Montets nor in Chamonix. This is because the "white giant" hides discreetly behind his smaller counterparts. And they steal the show when it comes to this train journey.

Rugged granite peaks pierce the sky, led by the Aiguille Verte, the Drus, and the Aiguille du Midi; behind it, a snow-covered, gently curved ridge peers into the grand picture: the "Roof of Europe." Incidentally, it has not yet been clarified if the highest peak in the Alps is in French territory or if it is a border summit between Italy and France. The case is currently with the UN.

UP TO THE PARC D'ATTRACTIONS

The mountain doesn't care about this detail, and neither do the travelers on the Mont-Blanc Express. They enjoy the two-hour ride from the Rhone Valley of Valais into the Arve Valley of Savoy. The start is already spectacular. After a steep stretch and a winding tunnel, the route leads high above the wild Trient Gorge over bridges and through galleries and tunnels into the valley. The second-to-last stop before the French border is the small town of Le Châtelard, well known by railway fanatics for its Parc d'Attractions. It consists essentially of two funicular railways and a narrow-gauge line, on which a steam train from 1911 with the cute name "Liseli" is occasionally used.

The lower of the two funicular railways was the steepest two-cabin funicular railway in Europe (87 percent incline) until the opening of the new Schwyz–Stoos funicular (2017). The trip to the dammed Lac d'Emosson offers not only a historic railway experience but also beautiful landscapes, including a magnificent view of Mont Blanc. A five-hour hike will lead you to the footprints of earlier archosaurs, which were discovered not far from the Lac du Vieux Emosson. Their estimated age: 240 million years old.

TO THE SEA OF ICE ON THE CHEMIN DE FER DU MONTENVERS

The Mont-Blanc Express passes by the watershed between Trient and Arve through the tunnel under the Col des Montets (4,793 feet / 1,461 meters). In Chamonix, there are two ways to cool down during the summer: a stop at the nearest ice cream shop or a ride up to Montenvers with the cogwheel railway, called the Chemin de fer du Montenvers. Goete took the same journey during his trip to Switzerland in 1779, but by foot, of course. He wrote this down in his diary: "What a dedication to this spectacle of ice!" It's understandable that this privy councillor was impressed. At that point, the tongue of the Mer de Glace hung down almost to the green soil of the Arve Valley, and from it a cool breeze blew to the nearest viewing tower. Today, you must climb about 656 feet (200 meters) to get to the ice (cable car, stairs). And that ice is still hidden under a thick layer of rock debris as well. Mer de Glace? Each year, mountain guides from the Alpine city give everyone goose bumps as they dig out the man-made ice grotto in the living glacier.

Only a few years after Goethe's visit in Chamonix did the first men stand on the top of Mont Blanc: After their two-day climb, Jacques Balmat and Michel-Gabriel Paccard hoisted a flag at the summit on August 8, 1786, that could be seen with binoculars from Chamonix. Chapeau!

Once technology allowed the highest mountains to be conquered, railway builders also began to focus on Mont Blanc, as previously was the case with the Matterhorn and the Jungfrau in the Swiss Alps. Two projects were competing at the "White Mountain," with starting points in Les Houches and Saint-Gervais-les-Bains. The latter project partly came to fruition before the outbreak of World War I and is still in operation today as the Tramway du Mont Blanc. The end station of the 7.8-mile-long (12.5-kilometer-long) cogwheel railway (with an incline up to 25 percent) is not the summit but a viewing tower at about half the height: Le Nid d'Aigle (7,782 feet / 2,372 meters). This is the starting point of the most frequented ascent up the "Roof of Europe" via the Dôme du Gouter and the northwestern ridge. Each year about twenty thousand (!) mountaineers start the climb, including many beginners. Because of this, Mont Blanc not only is the highest mountain in the Alps but also tends to lead in the statistics when it comes to accidents. A sad record.

MONT-BLANC EXPRESS

The Mont-Blanc Express overcomes the height difference
between the floor of the Rhone
Valley and Salvan by using a rack
with inclines of up to 20 percent.
Electricity is delivered to the trains
by using a rail affixed to the side
of the track (*to the right in this
picture*). The planned conversion
to an overhead line, which was
actually mandatory for safety
reasons, failed because the tunnel
cross section was too small.

The villages of the lower Trient
Valley lie among sunny hillside
terraces above the rugged gorge.
Le Trétien is the exception, with
houses that literally cling to the
sloping forest ridge in the area
between the Triège and Trient
Gorges. ▽ ▽

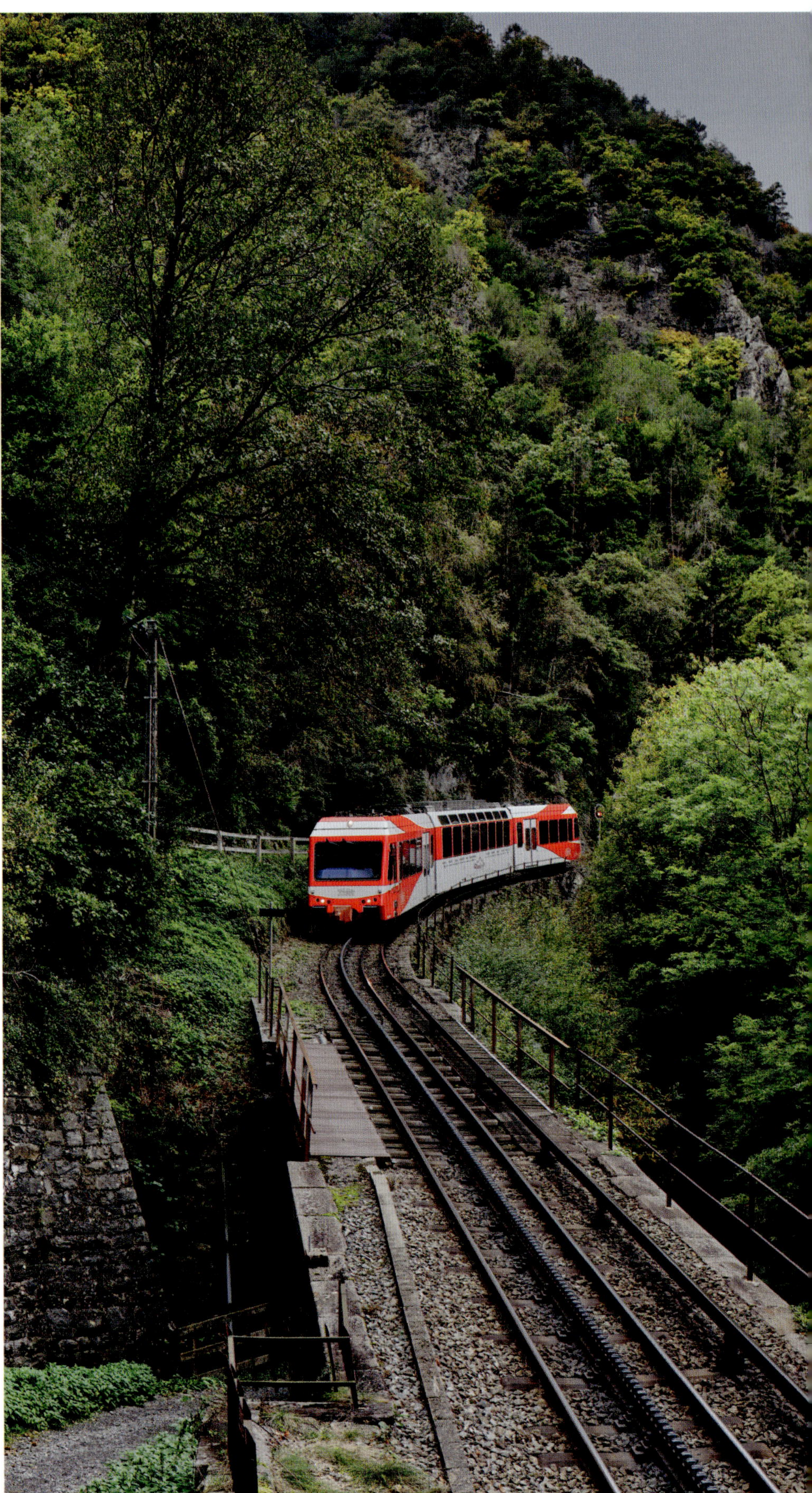

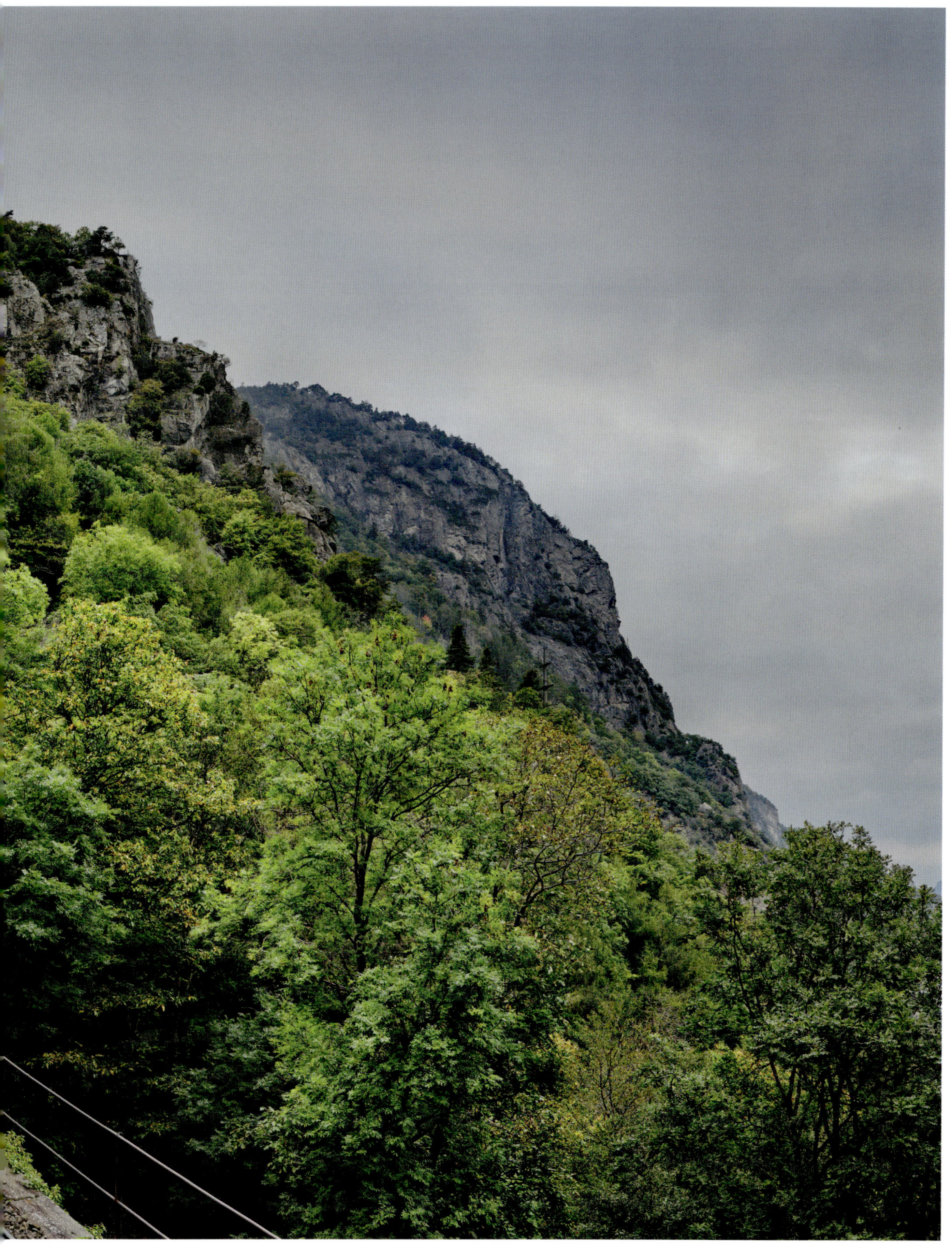

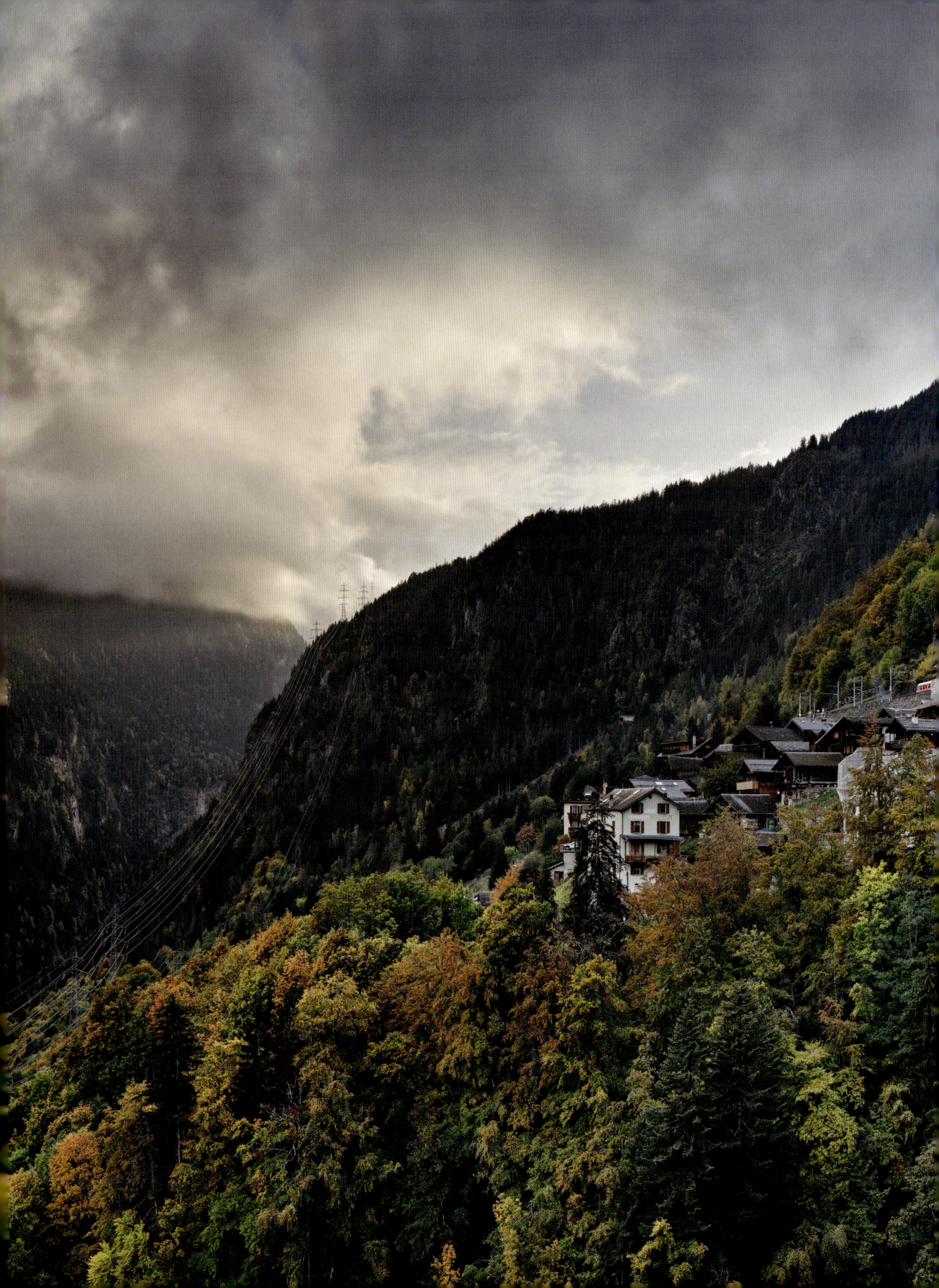

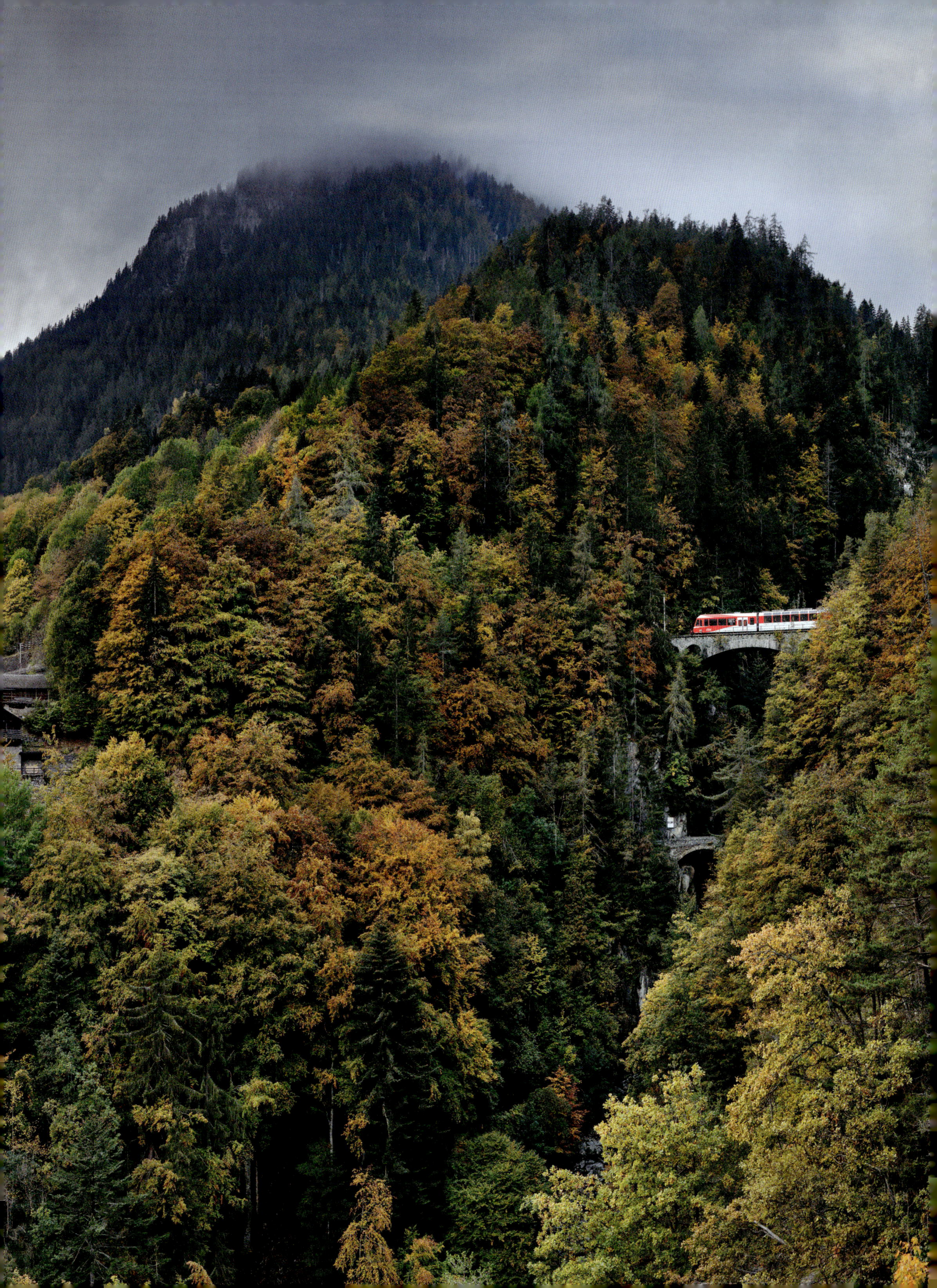

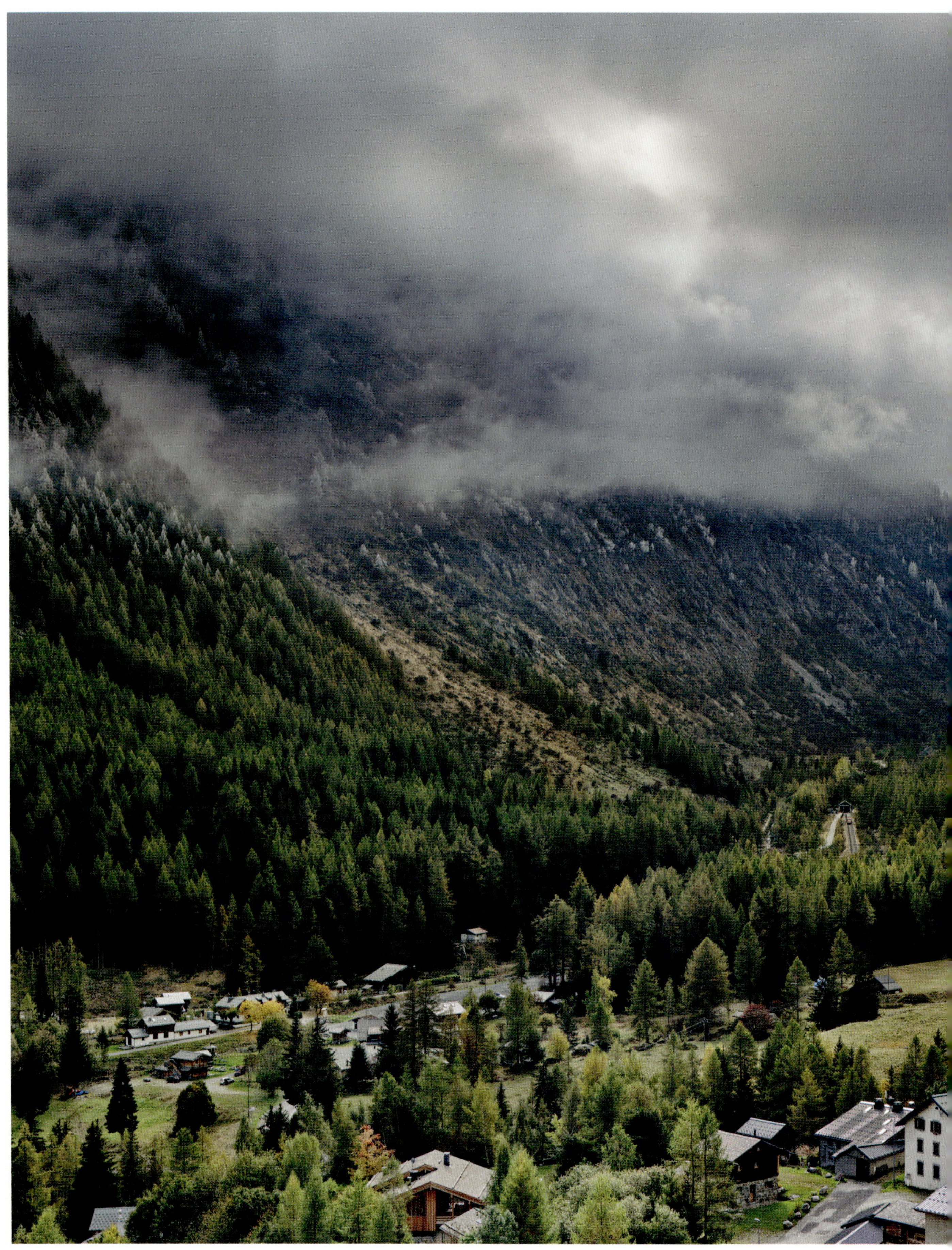

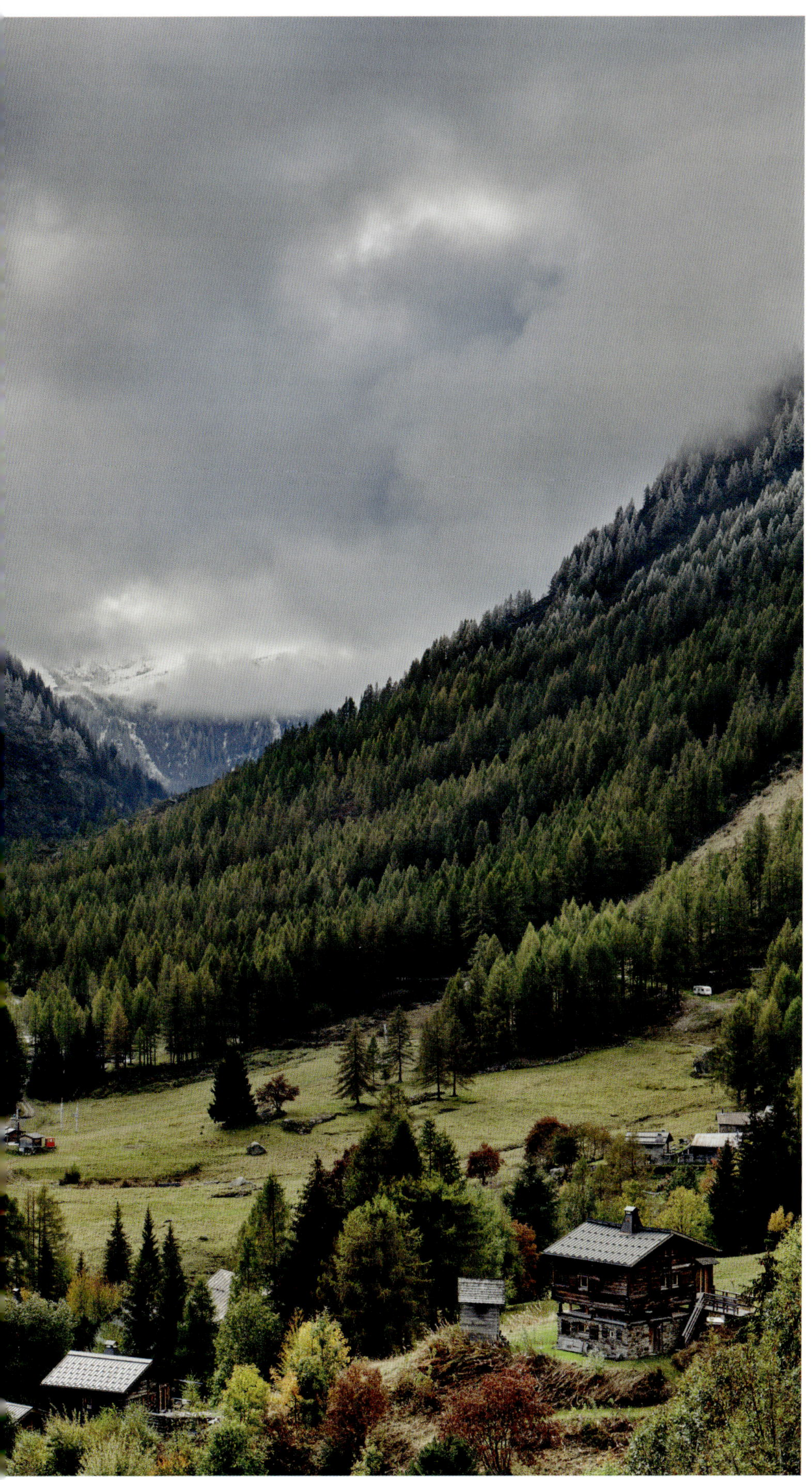

MONT-BLANC EXPRESS

The Col des Montets (4,793 feet /
1,461 meters) is the watershed
between the Eau Noire and
the Arve. The railway passes
under it through a 6,112-foot-
long (1,863-meter-long) tunnel
between Vallorcine (*see picture*)
and Argentiere.

Near Les Houches the Mont-
Blanc Express crosses the Arve
high up on the Sainte-Marie
Viaduct. ▽ ▽

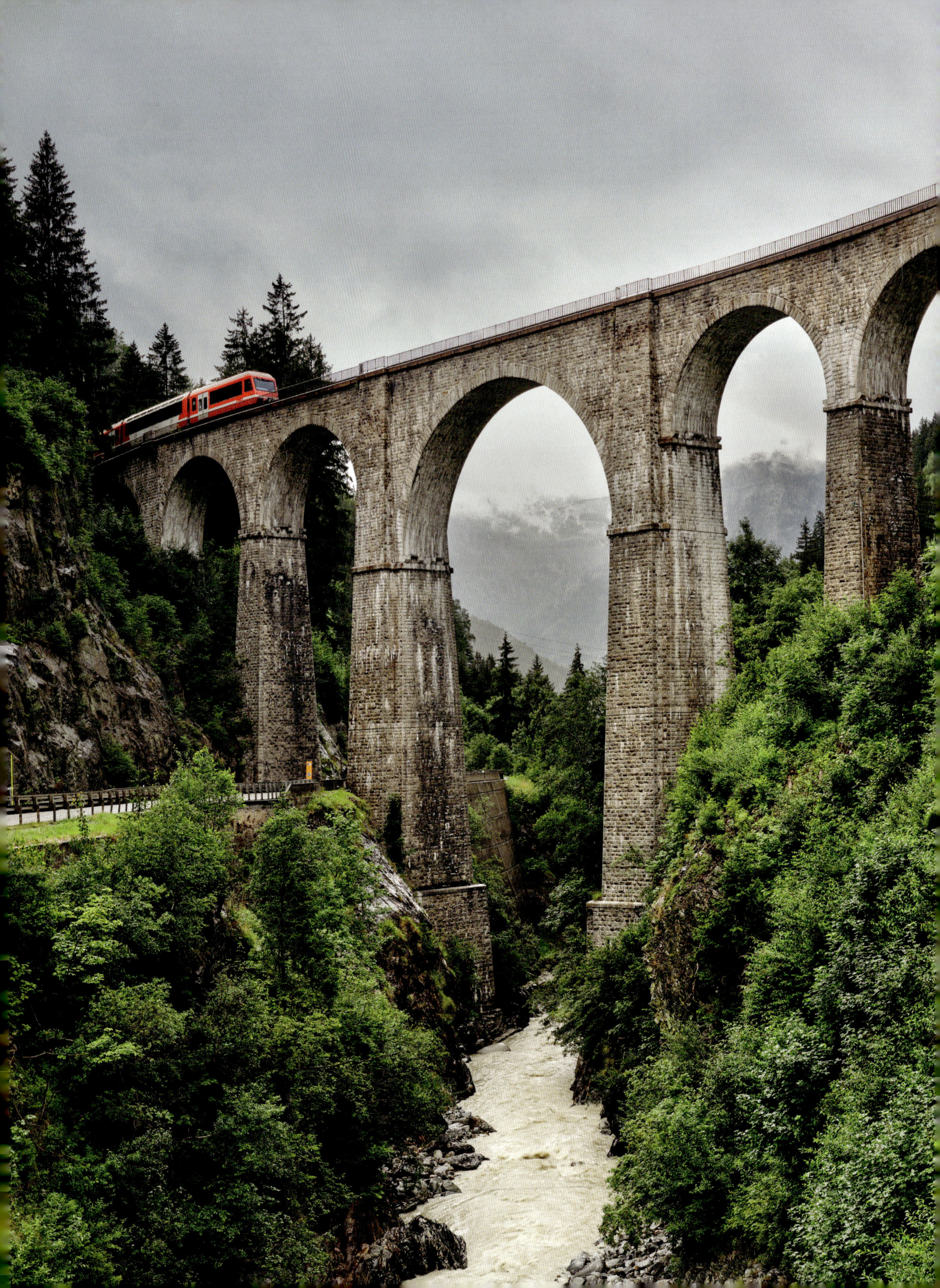

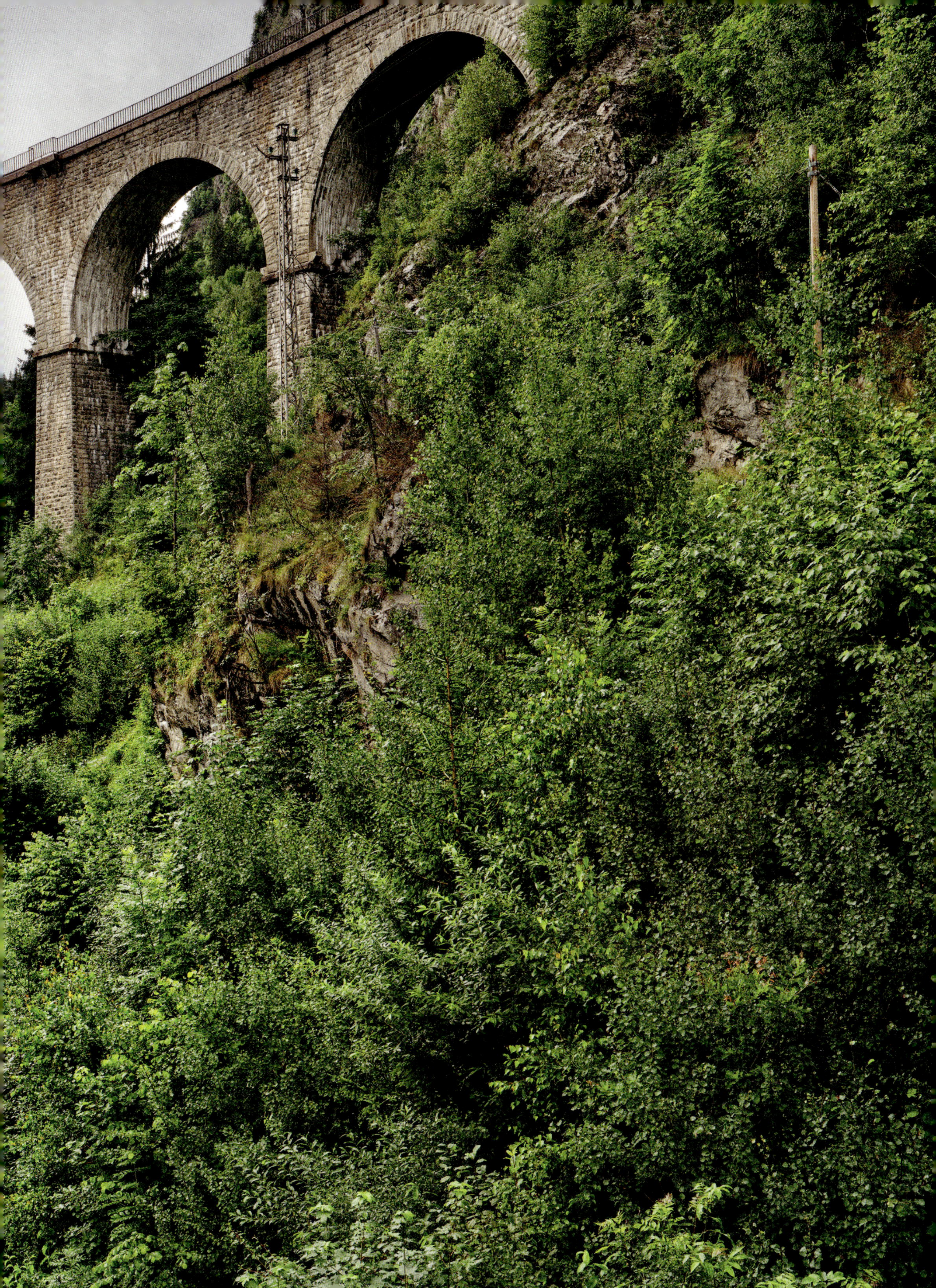

MONT-BLANC EXPRESS

Larches and birches line the route
of the Mont-Blanc Express on its
way up to the tunnel under the Col
des Montets.

CHEMIN DE FER DU
MONTENVERS

Montenvers Station (6253 feet /
1,906 meters). The Mer de Glace,
the icy ventricle running through
the Mont Blanc Massif, is dominated by the Grandes Jorasses
(13,806 feet / 4,208 meters).
To the right in the picture is the
"Giant's Tooth" (Dent du Géant).
Buried under the rubble lies the
Mer de Glace—a sad sight. One
hundred and fifty years ago, the
glacial tongue hung almost into
the Arve Valley. ▽ ▽

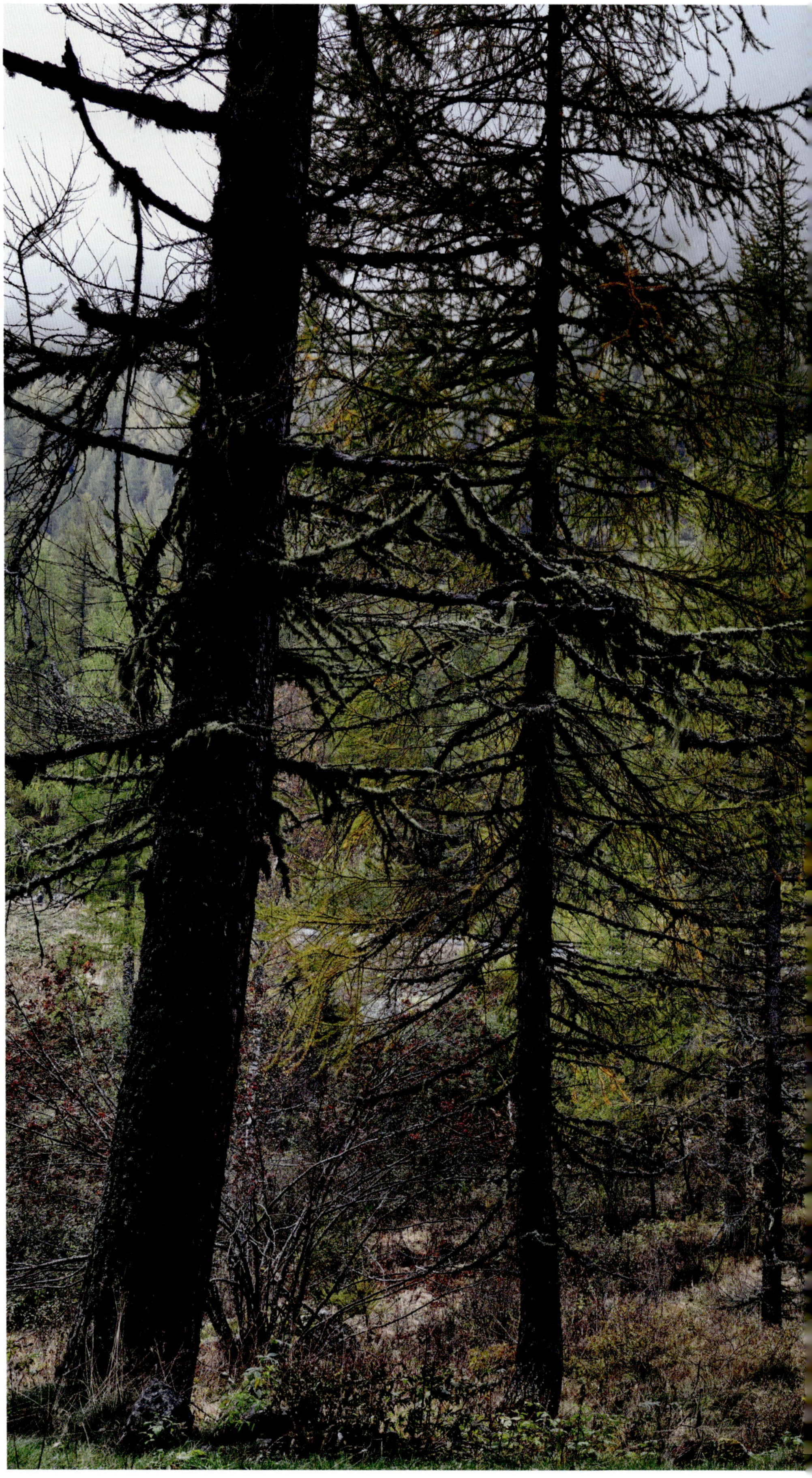

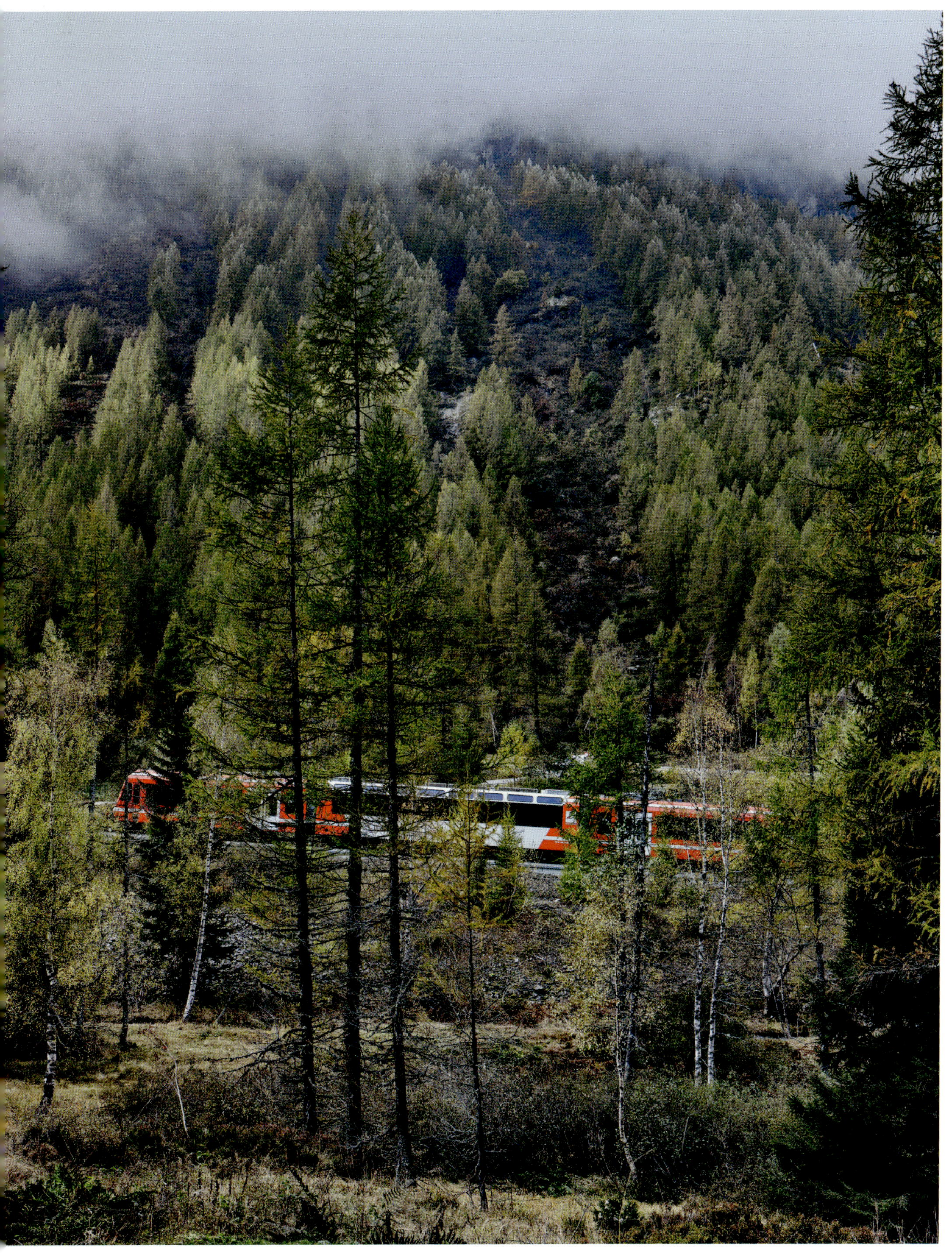

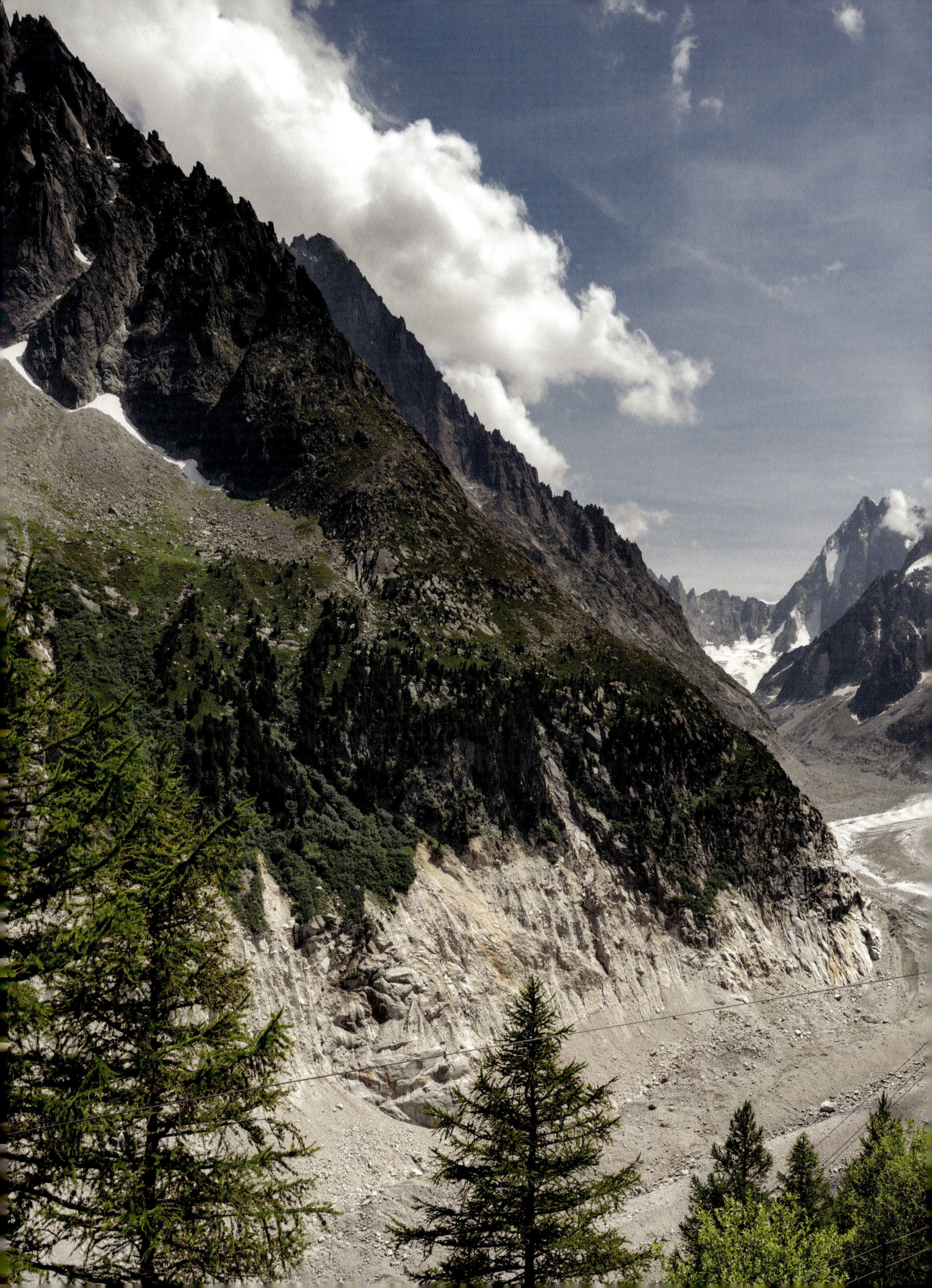

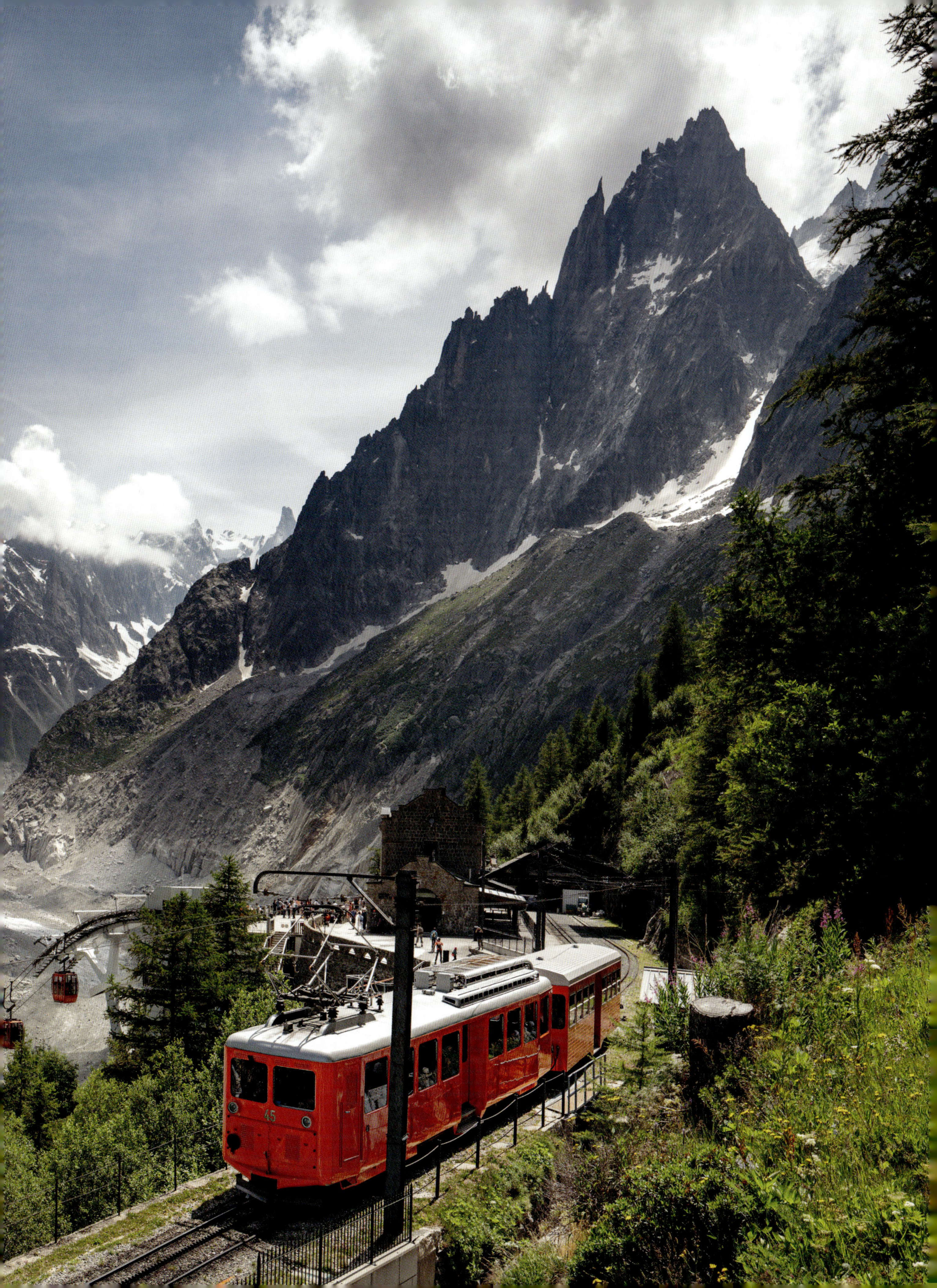

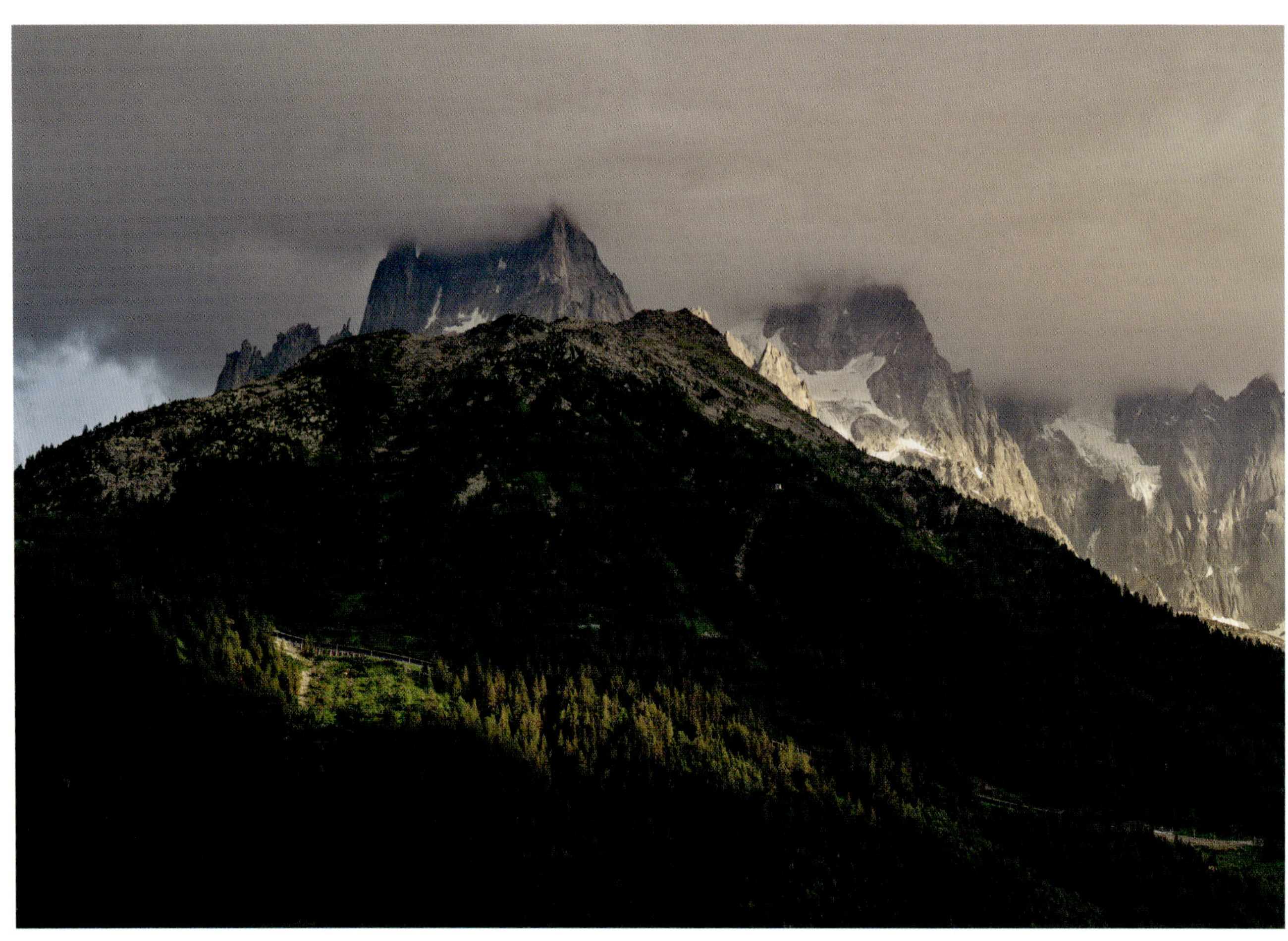

CHEMIN DE FER DU MONTENVERS

Galleries protect the cogwheel railway
route from Chamonix to Montenvers from
avalanches and mudslides.

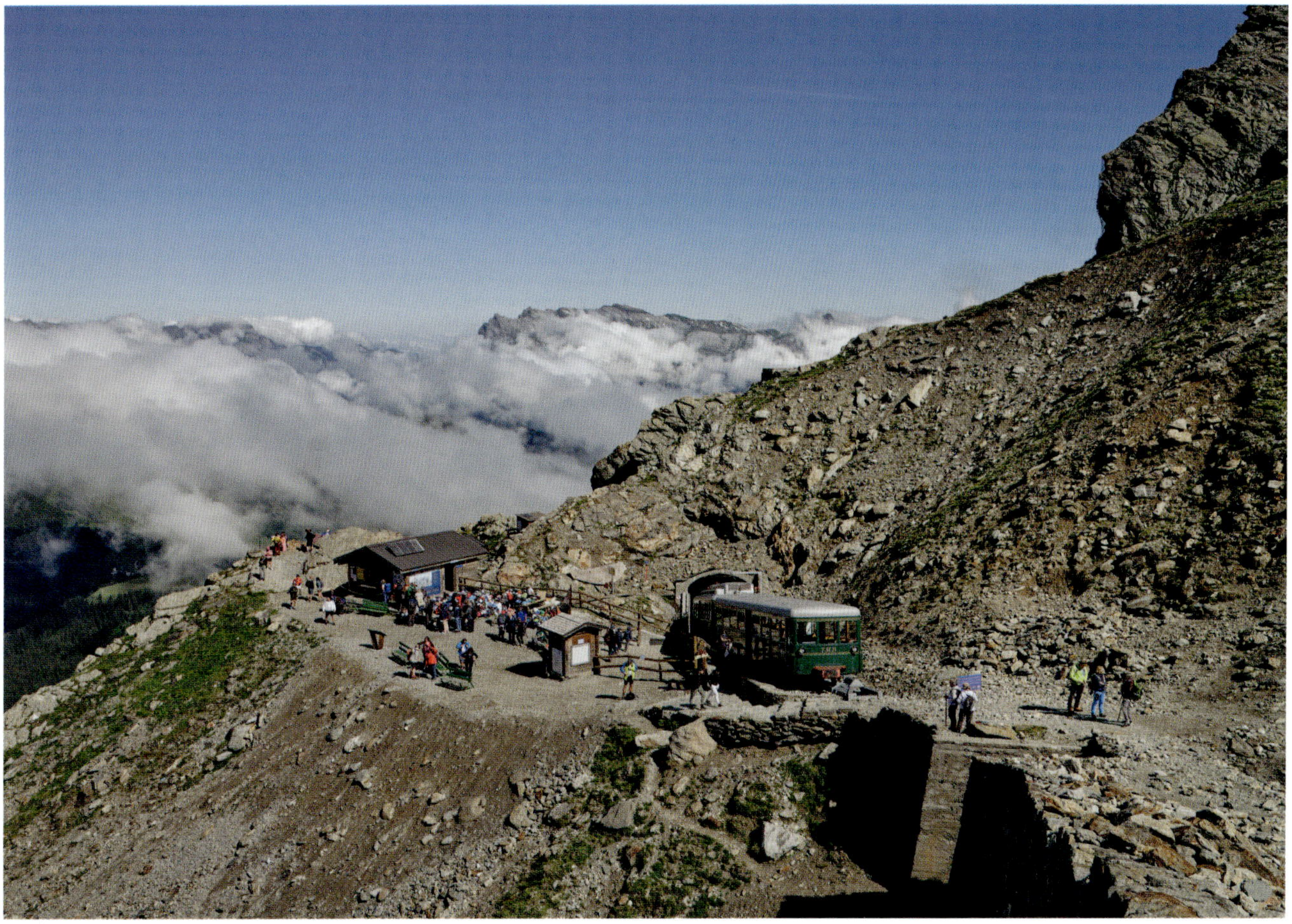

Last stop, "Eagle's Nest" (Nid d'Aigle, 7,782 feet / 2,372 meters). The cogwheel railway should have originally continued to Mont Blanc. This goal was obviously set too high.

The Tramway du Mont Blanc winds its way through increasingly stony terrain from the Col du Mont Lachat up to the Nid d'Aigle, an impressive viewing point on the southern flank of the Mont Blanc Massif.

▽ ▽

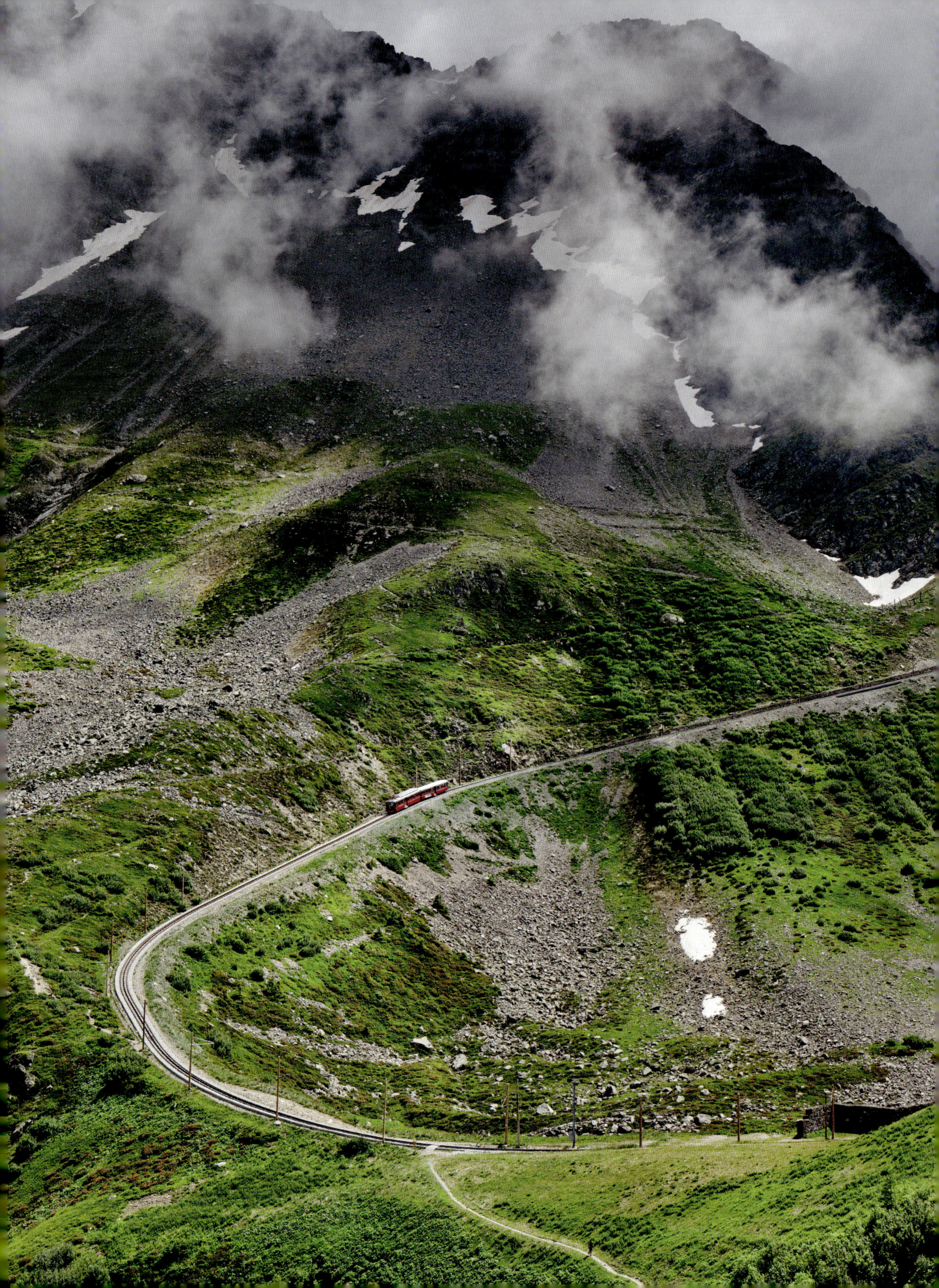

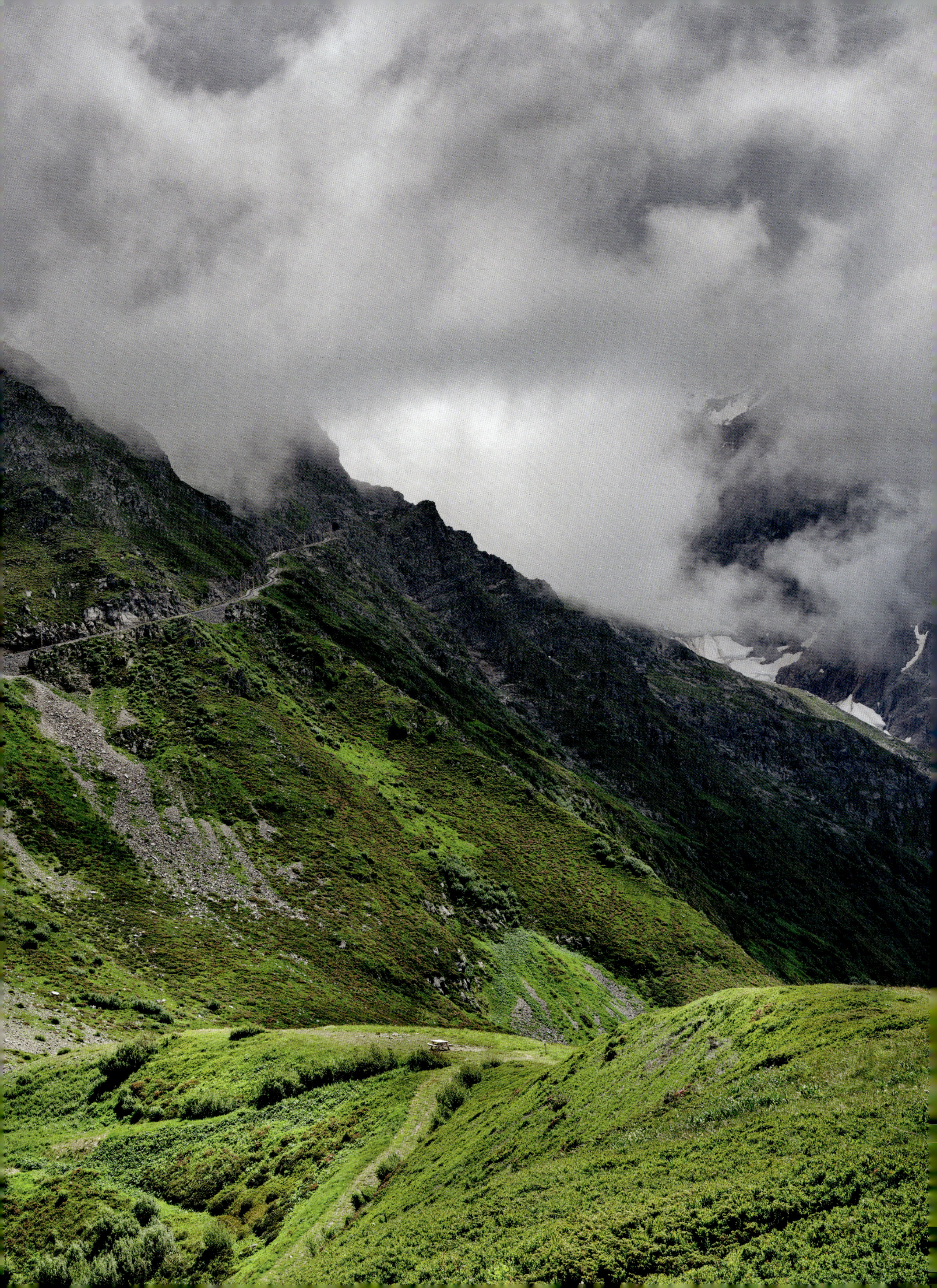

THE SWISS ALPS

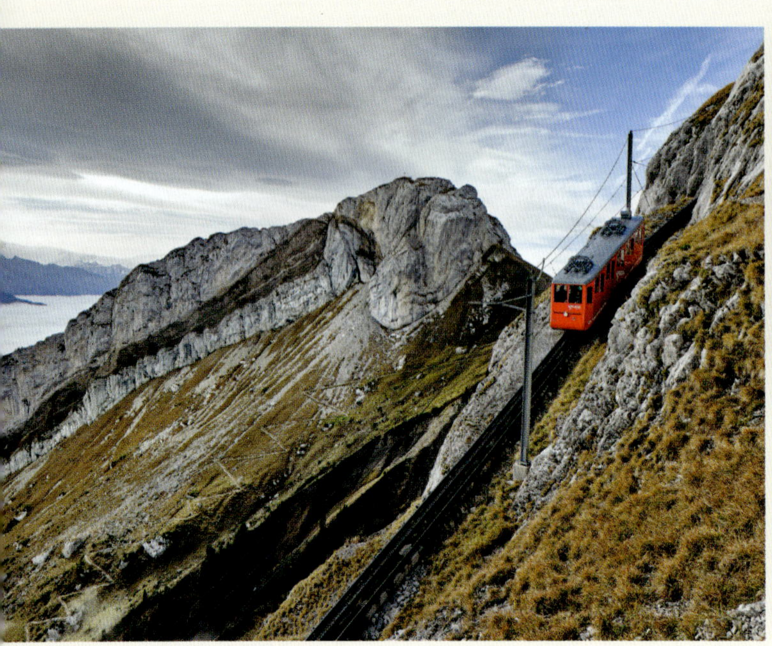

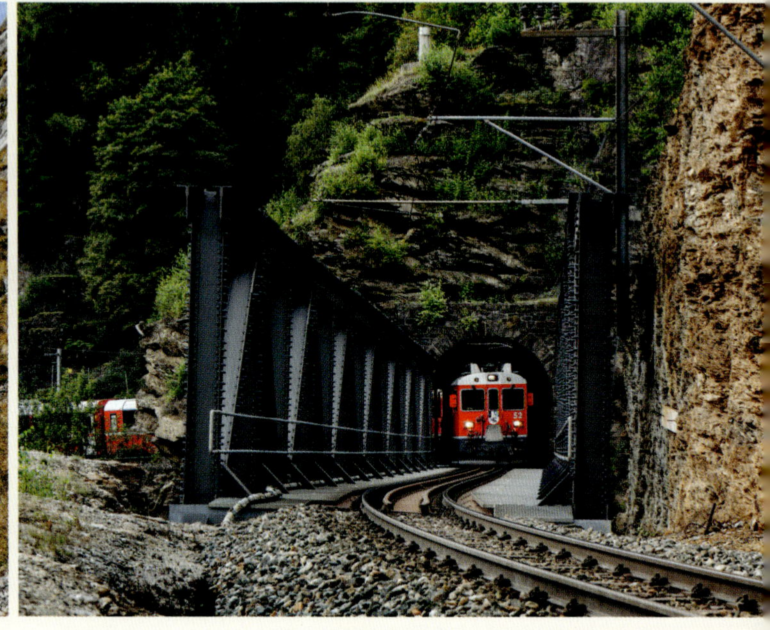

THE COUNTRY OF MOUNTAIN RAILWAYS—INTO THE HIGH MOUNTAINS ON THE TRACKS

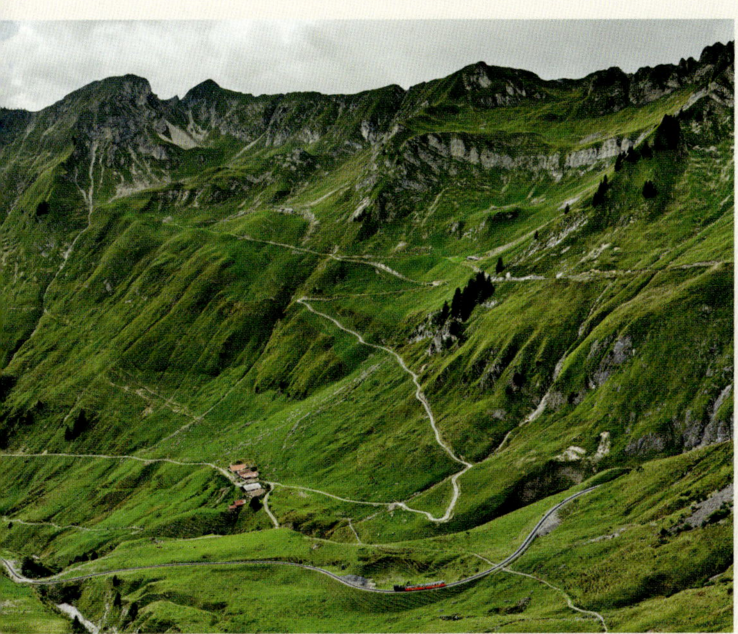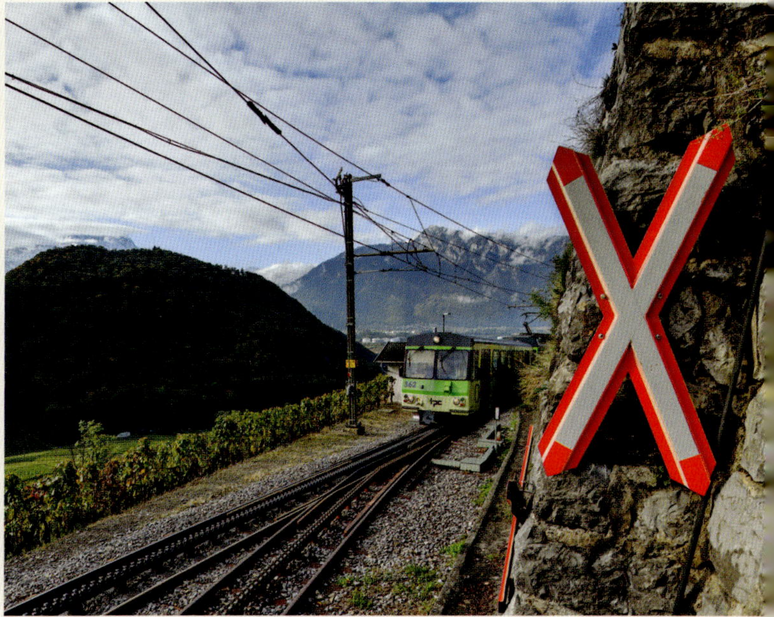

No question, the Swiss Confederation is without a doubt the country of mountain railways. This is not only because of its geographical location, which favored the construction of transit routes, but also because of tourism, which became a driving force early on. The invention of the cogwheel railway caused another construction boom, first in central Switzerland, the Bernese Highlands, and Lake Geneva, and later in Grisons as well. The value of this type of infrastructure was soon recognized, and it was maintained accordingly. The country's dense railway network even survived largely unscathed the triumph of the automobile after World War II.

PICTURESQUE SWITZERLAND: FROM THE BERNESE HIGHLANDS TO THE VAUD RIVIERA

Interlaken and Montreux are two tourist hotspots in Switzerland that have been popular since the Belle Époque era. The narrow-gauge *Montreux-Oberland Bernois Railway* is almost just as old as well, connecting both cities and running through a romantic Alpine landscape. Other narrow-gauge railways branch off to *Rochers de Naye, Leysin, Les Diablerets, Bertaye, Champéry*, and *Les Pléiades*, all using the rack-and-pinion system—and still running today. Typical Swiss rail country.

"Golden Pass" doesn't sound like Swiss German and definitely not French. More like an advertisement. Maybe those responsible for the Montreux-Oberland Bernois Railway (MOB) only wanted to avoid the so-called "Röschtigraben" (the cultural boundary between the German-speaking and French-speaking parts of Switzerland), but indeed their tracks do lead from French-speaking Switzerland (casual, French) to German-speaking Switzerland (hard-working, sober) and vice versa. Maybe that's why they decided to use a name that is Anglo-Saxon—in other words, linguistically neutral.

THE BELLE ÉPOQUE ERA'S BELIEF IN PROGRESS

This sort of nuanced linguistical problem tends to be foreign to train passengers, especially if they come from abroad. They are more interested in the natural world and the technology around them. A trip on the MOB shows that these two can be combined, and in the best possible way. The engineers from the turn of the nineteenth and twentieth centuries, contemporaries out of the Belle Époque era, laid the more than 43 miles (70 kilometers) of narrow-gauge track elegantly through the picturesque landscape between Lake Geneva (Lac Léman), Gruyères, and the Simmental. It's an area that's akin to a multifaceted, green-gray painting—fields, forest, and stone—with a few small villages in between: idyllic Switzerland. That's probably also how it was seen one hundred years ago on the largest Alpine lake and in Interlaken, where tourism started early on. Gstaad, today a home to the super-rich, was at that time an insignificant town, whose population of two hundred lived off milk and cheese. The railway was supposed to open a better future to them, running over two Swiss cantonal borders. This did not alleviate the situation, but in the end it was the strong belief in progress that finally caused the breakthrough. Construction began in 1907, and the route between Montreux to Zweisimmen was opened only four years later—electric from the start.

Even though the climate in Montreux has slightly Mediterranean features, the winter in the backcountry tends to last almost twice as long. On Rochers de Naye as well, which has an elevation of 6,699 feet (2,042 meters). A cogwheel railway from the year 1892 stretches a good 6 miles (10 kilometers) and runs from Montreux until slightly below the peak of the popular mountain.

From left to right: The Pilatus Railway, the steepest cogwheel in the world; at the southern ramp of the Bernina Railway; the Brienz-Rothorn Railway winds over steep grass flanks up to the famous lookout peak; crossing point of the cogwheel from Aigle to Leysin.

The Swiss shore of Lake Geneva experienced a true railway boom, set off by the connection to the international railway network (Simplon Railway). Lakes and mountains were an unbeatable attraction, even then. As a result, train routes were built to Leysin (which became popular at the end of the nineteenth century as a climatic spa), Villars-sur-Ollon, Les Diablerets, and Champéry, in addition to many trams around Montreux. A rack-and-pinion railway conquered the Col de Bretaye over Villars; funicular railways made Glion and Sonloup near Montreux easily accessible. Even Vevey, the neighboring western town on Lake Geneva (Lac Léman), also made rail connections: to Les Pléiades via a rack-and-pinion railway and to Mont Pelerin via a funicular railway. The route between Chamby and Blonay is in use today as a "Museum on Tracks"—an attraction (Chemin de Fer-Musée Blonay-Chamby) with a fantastic collection of decommissioned locomotives and wagons. An experience for railway fanatics!

The journey in one of the (gold-painted) train carriages from Interlaken to Montreux is also an experience. The pleasure lasts a good three hours, starting at Lake Thun and leading through the verdant Niedersimmental Valley with its magnificent farmhouses to Zweisimmen. Parallel to the Kleine Simme, the journey climbs to the Saanenmöser watershed. Descending to Gstaad, where perhaps more millionaires stay today than cows graze, a few striking peaks of the Fribourg Limestone Alps come into view, led by the Gummfluh. Between Saanen and Rougemont, the train crosses the border into the canton of Fribourg. Do you speak French?

Rossinière then boasts a special attraction: the Grand Chalet. It's truly enormous, with its 5,382 square feet (500 square meters) of floor space and an incredible 113 windows! It was built around the middle of the eighteenth century. Its prominent resident from 1976 until his death in 2001 was the painter Balthus.

AN AUSPICIOUS NAME: LE TRAIN DU CHOCOLAT

In Montbovon, you will find the Bulle Railway Line. Only a few miles farther north is Broc, which is serviced by the Train du Chocolat. This is no coincidence, since the Maison Callier has been here since 1898—it was the factory of the most profitable chocolate manufacturer in Switzerland at that time. Later, Cailler merged with two competitors, in the end becoming what we know now as Nestlé. Vevey, the birthplace of François-Louis Cailler (1796–1852), is where the headquarters of the largest food company in the world is today.

Back to Montbovon. This is where the climb to the Tunnel du Jaman begins, with a maximum gradient of an impressive 7.3 percent—without a rack-and-pinion system. Then you enter the darkness, until you finally emerge two minutes later at the western portal, and the landscape of Lake Geneva comes into view. What a finale! The lake, above which the Savoyard Chablais Alps run, is a picture that unfolds more and more beautifully on the descent. It's easy to see why the sunny side of upper Lake Geneva is called the Swiss Riviera by its visitors.

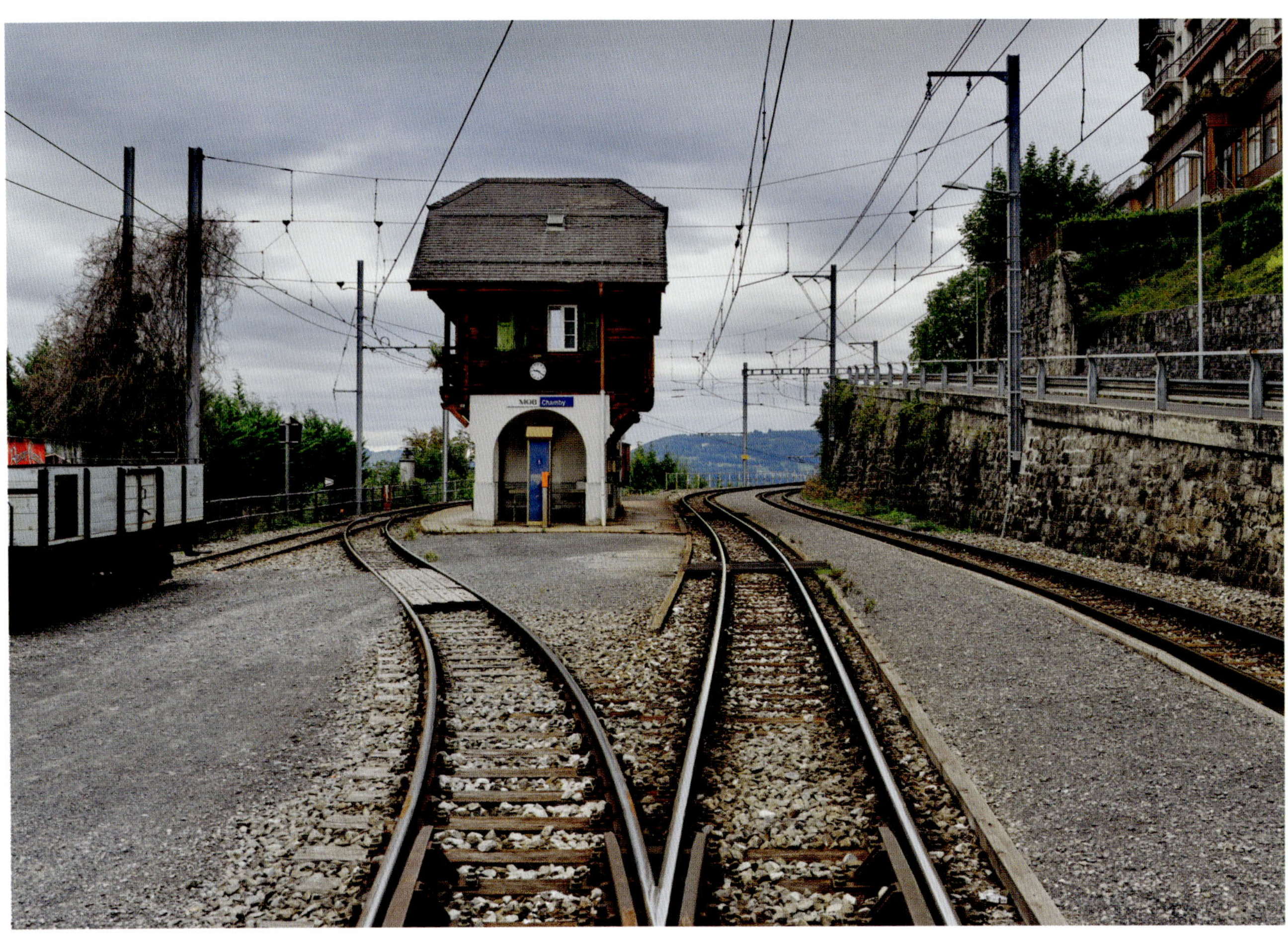

MONTREUX-OBERLAND BERNOIS RAILWAY

The small train station of Chamby shows its original
architecture. A tip for railroad fans is the historical
railway from Blonay to Chamby, with its sensational
collection of long-since-decommissioned locomotives
and railcars: a museum on tracks.

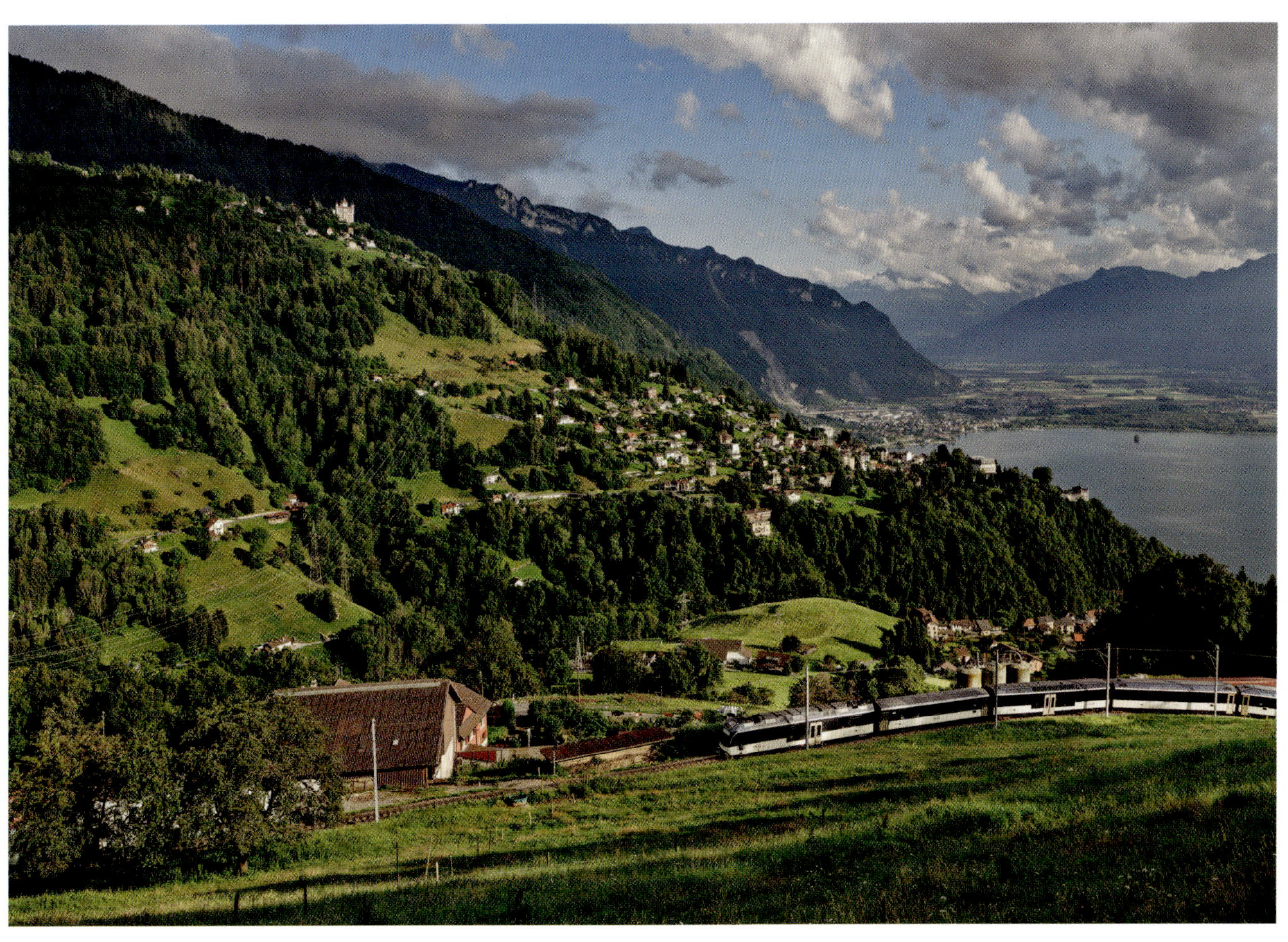

MONTREUX–OBERLAND BERNOIS RAILWAY

The ride down to Montreux offers views of the Vaud
Riviera, Lake Geneva, and the border mountains
with France.

The high valley of Hongrin under the Jaman Tunnel
of the MOB: lush meadows, rugged peaks, and a
famous cheese, Gruyère. To the left of the center
of the picture is the striking pyramid of the Dent de
Jaman (6,148 feet / 1,874 meters). ▽ ▽

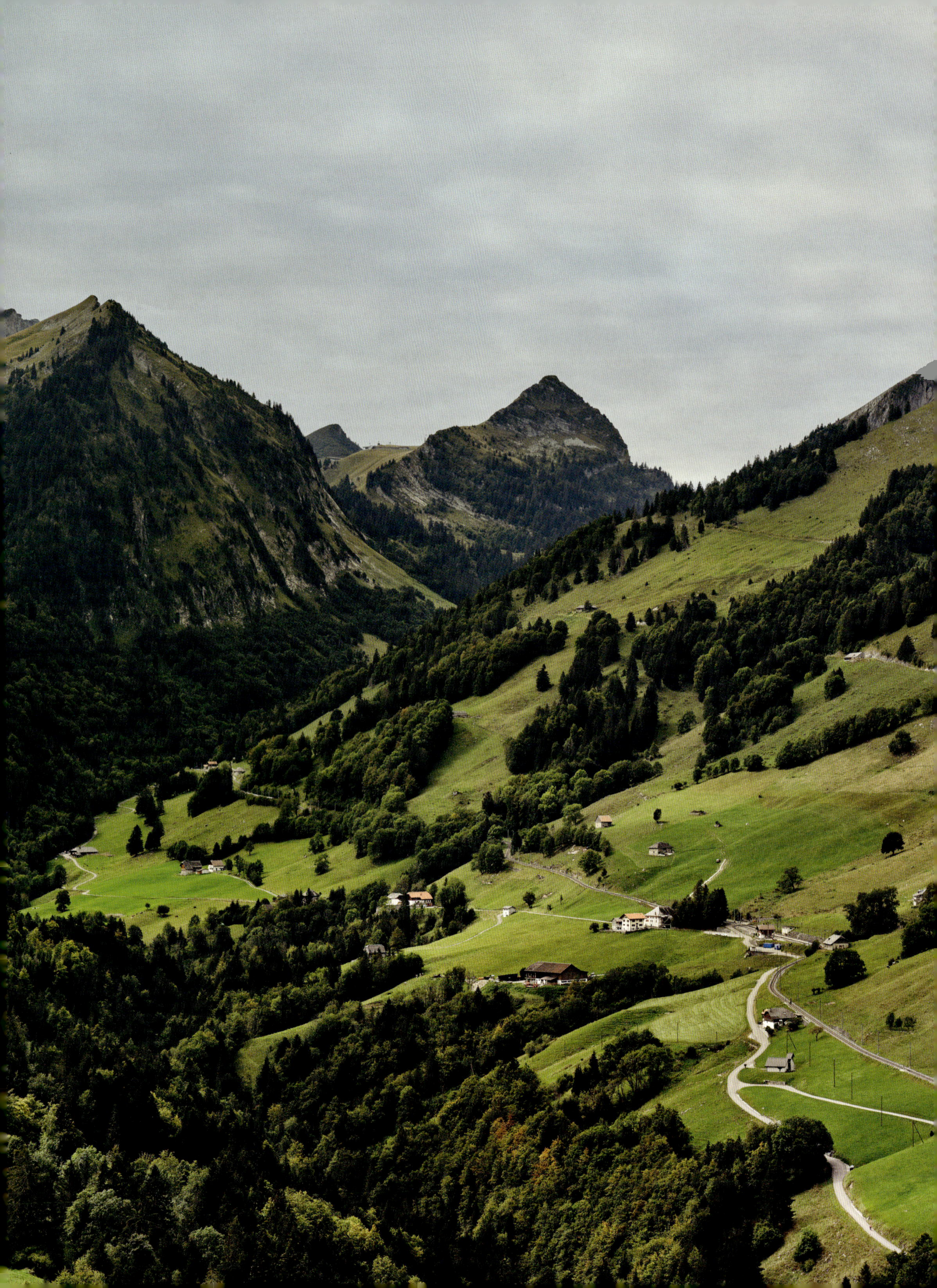

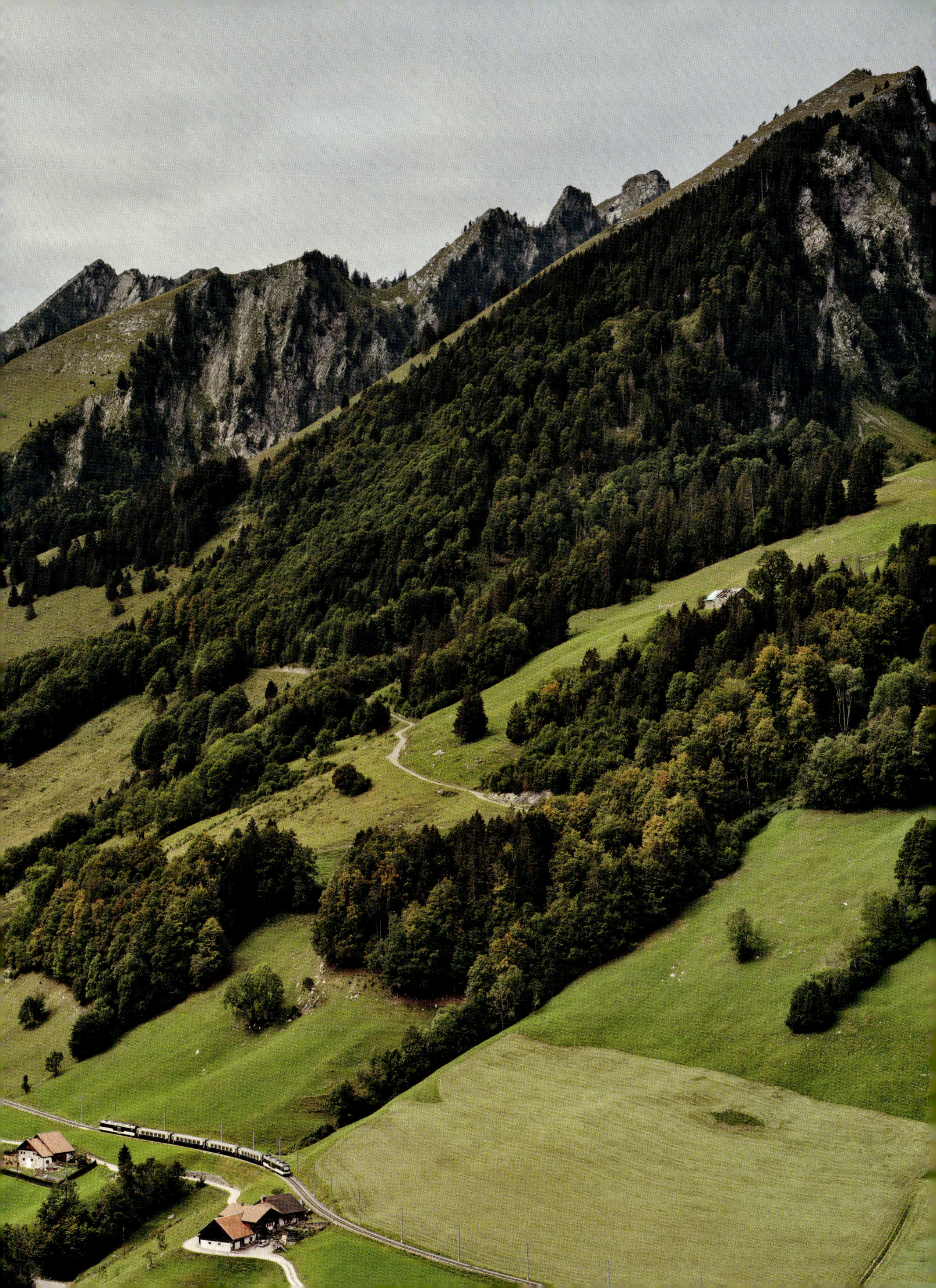

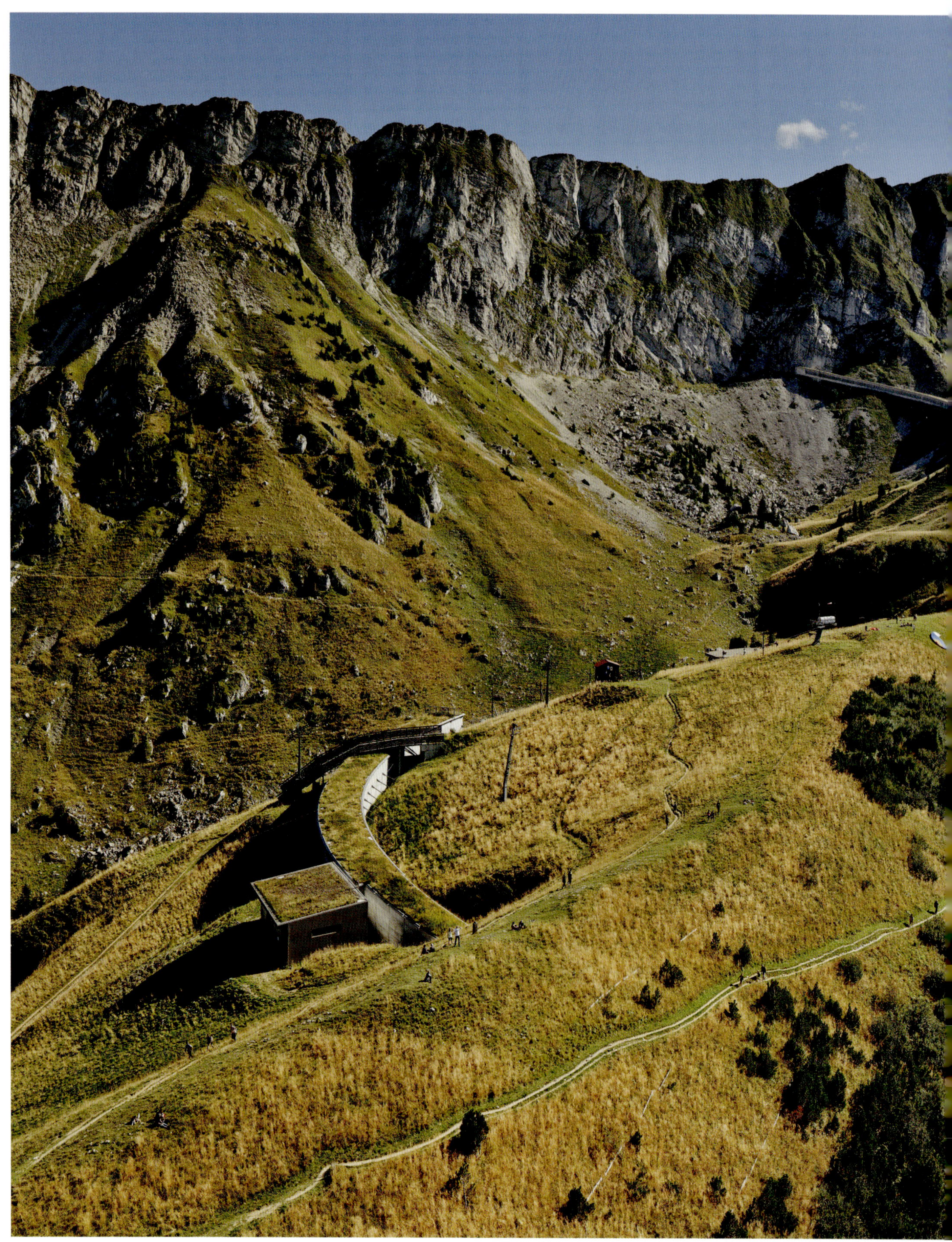

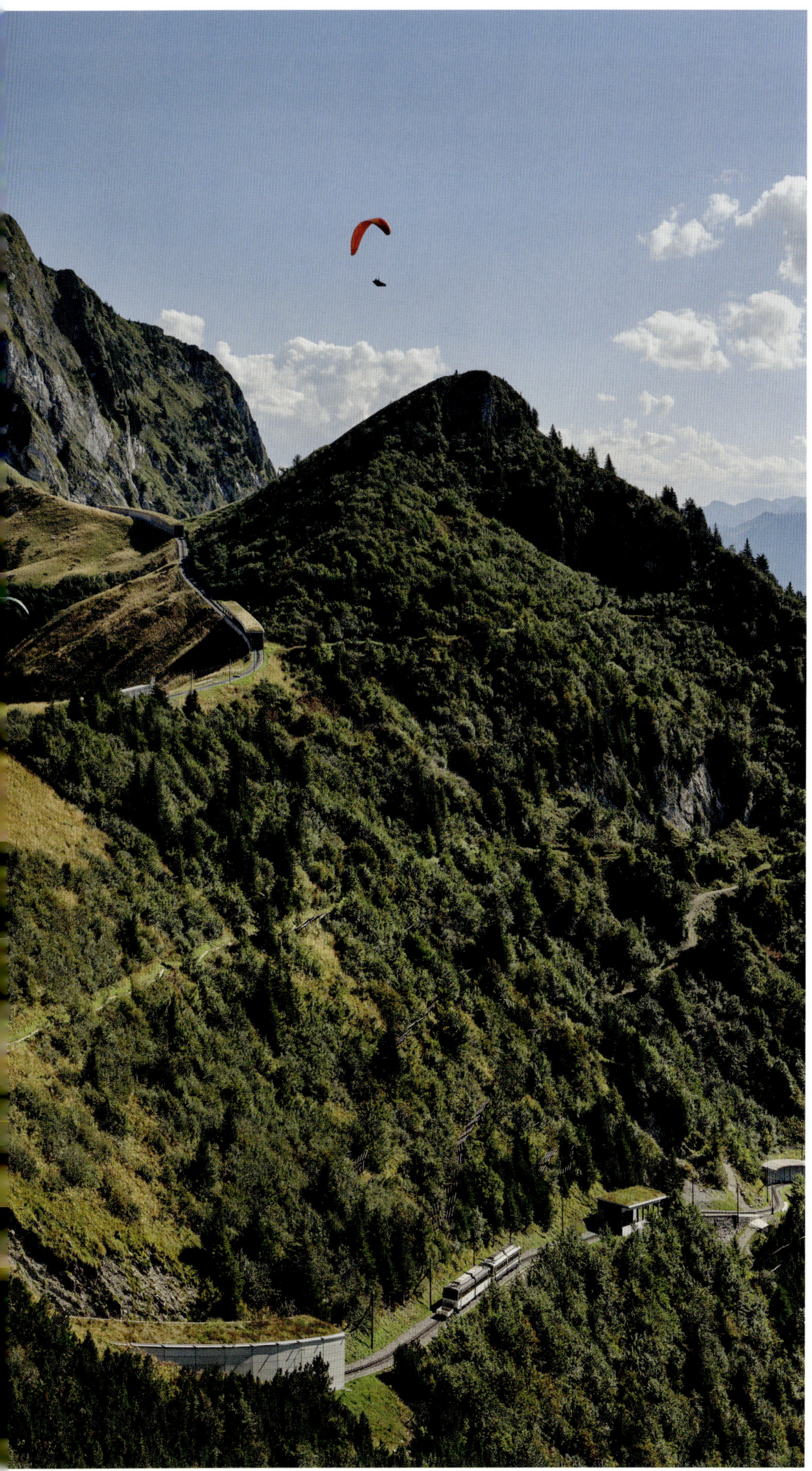

ROCHERS DE NAYE

The cogwheel railway, which was opened in 1892, winds its way in loops from Montreux via Caux up to the peak of Rochers de Naye (6,699 feet / 2,042 meters). On the upper section of the route, it passes by multiple avalanche protection galleries and through tunnels to reach the mountain station (6,453 feet / 1,967 meters). The portion between Jaman and the summit tunnel is especially spectacular.

At the Rochers de Naye summit, the view goes north over a few peaks of the Fribourg Pre-Alps to the midlands. The panorama is fantastic and includes a view to Lake Geneva. A travel tip to check out, especially for families: Marmot's Paradise. ▽ ▽

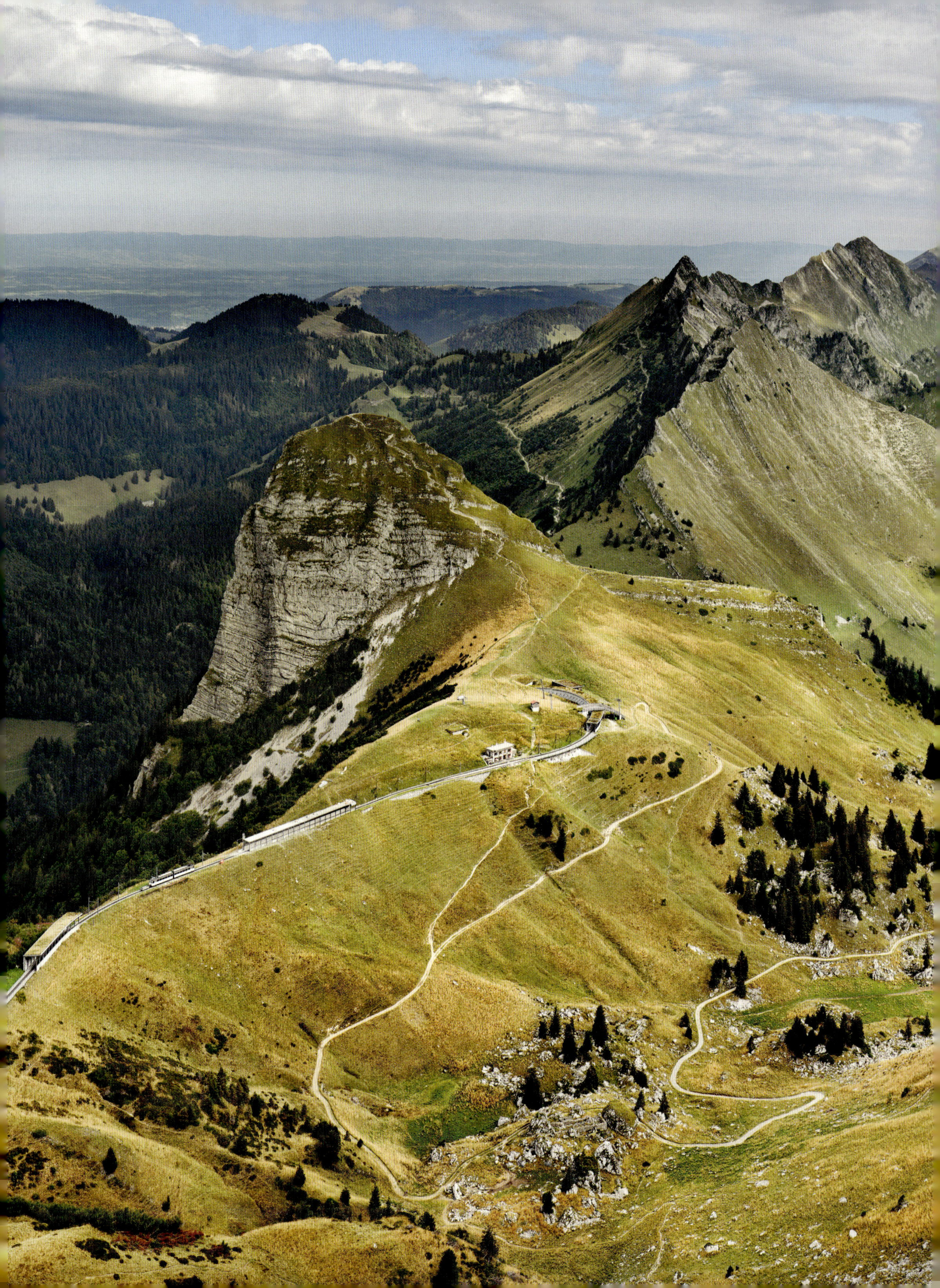

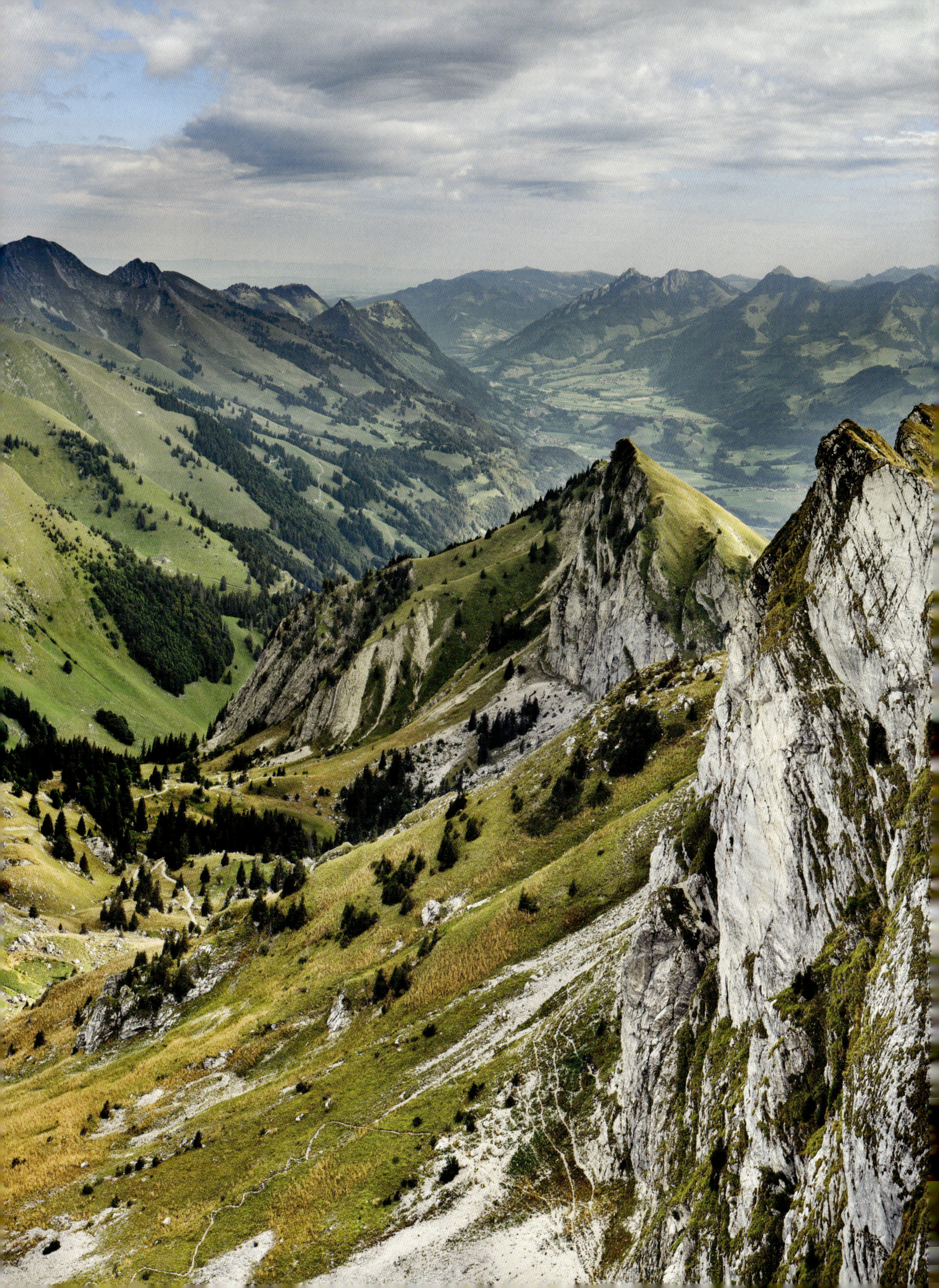

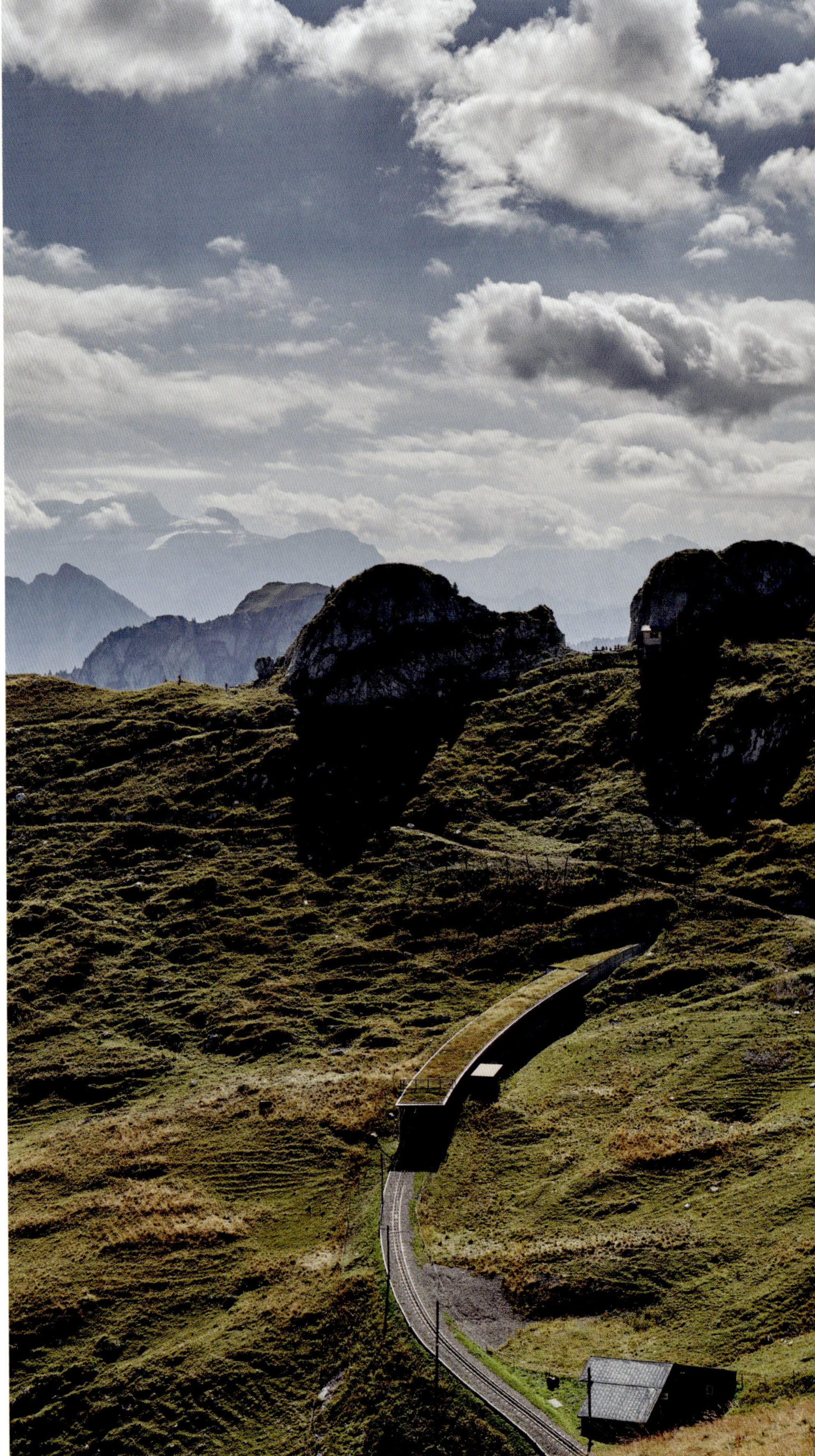

ROCHERS DE NAYE

In the Freiburg and Vaud Pre-Alps, there are a few very striking mountains such as the Tour de Mayen and the Tour d'Ai (*right*). On the ridge in the foreground, it blooms a hundredfold in the summer: in the botanical Alpine garden La Rambertia.

AIGLE–LES DIABLERETS RAILWAY

On the way to Les Diablerets behind Le Sépey, the limestone massif of the Diablerets (10,531 feet / 3,210 meters) comes into view.
▽ ▽

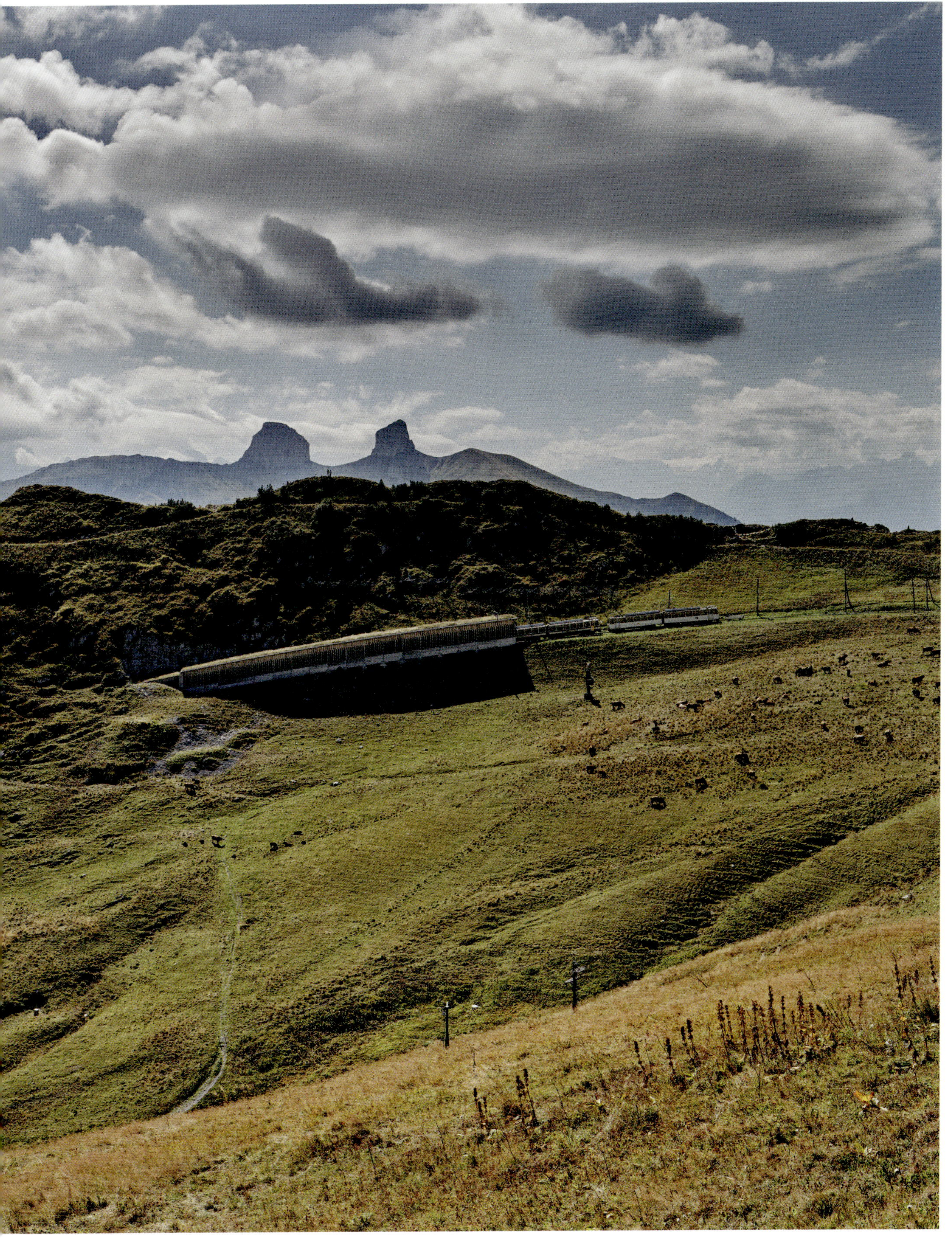

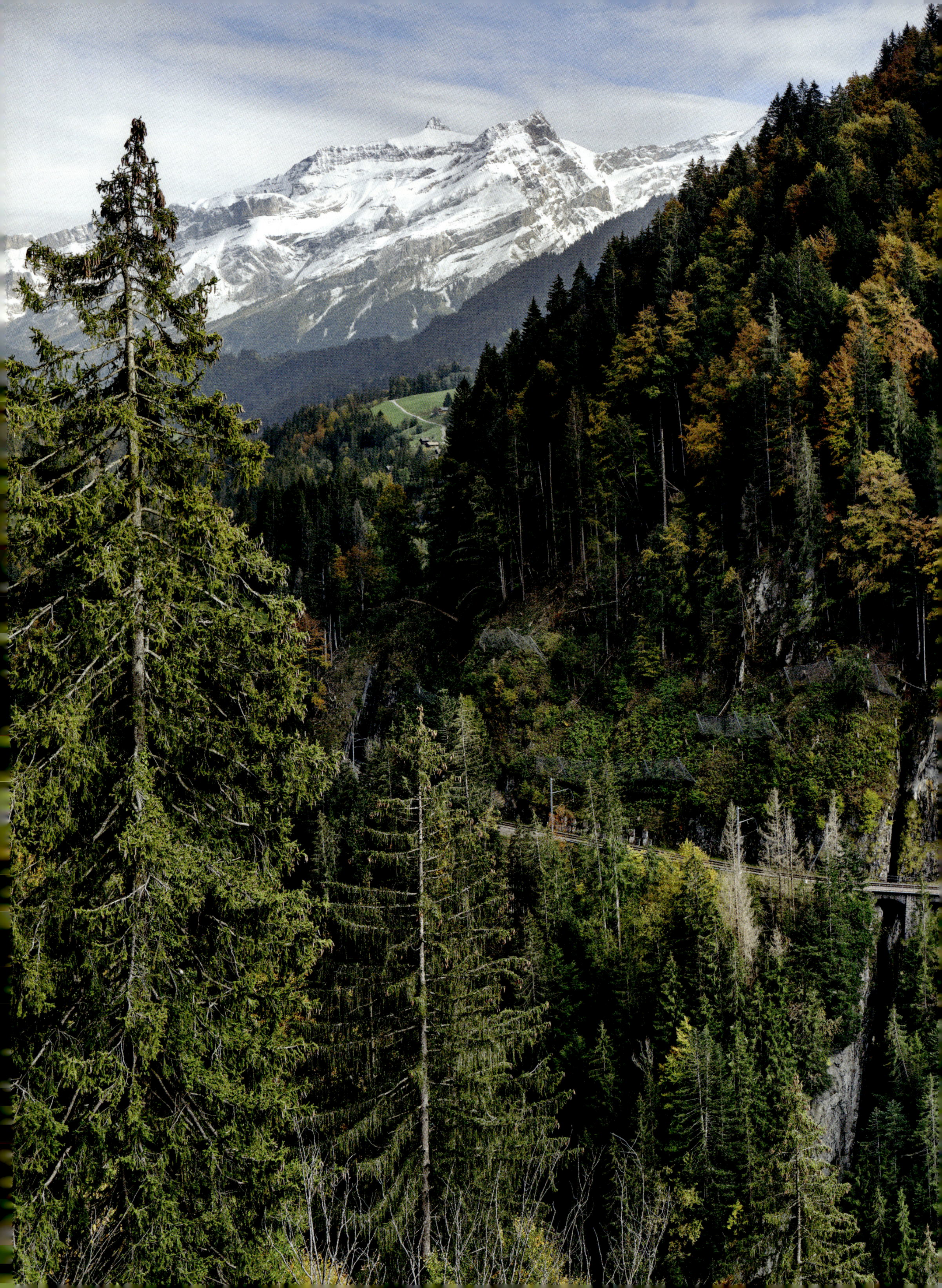

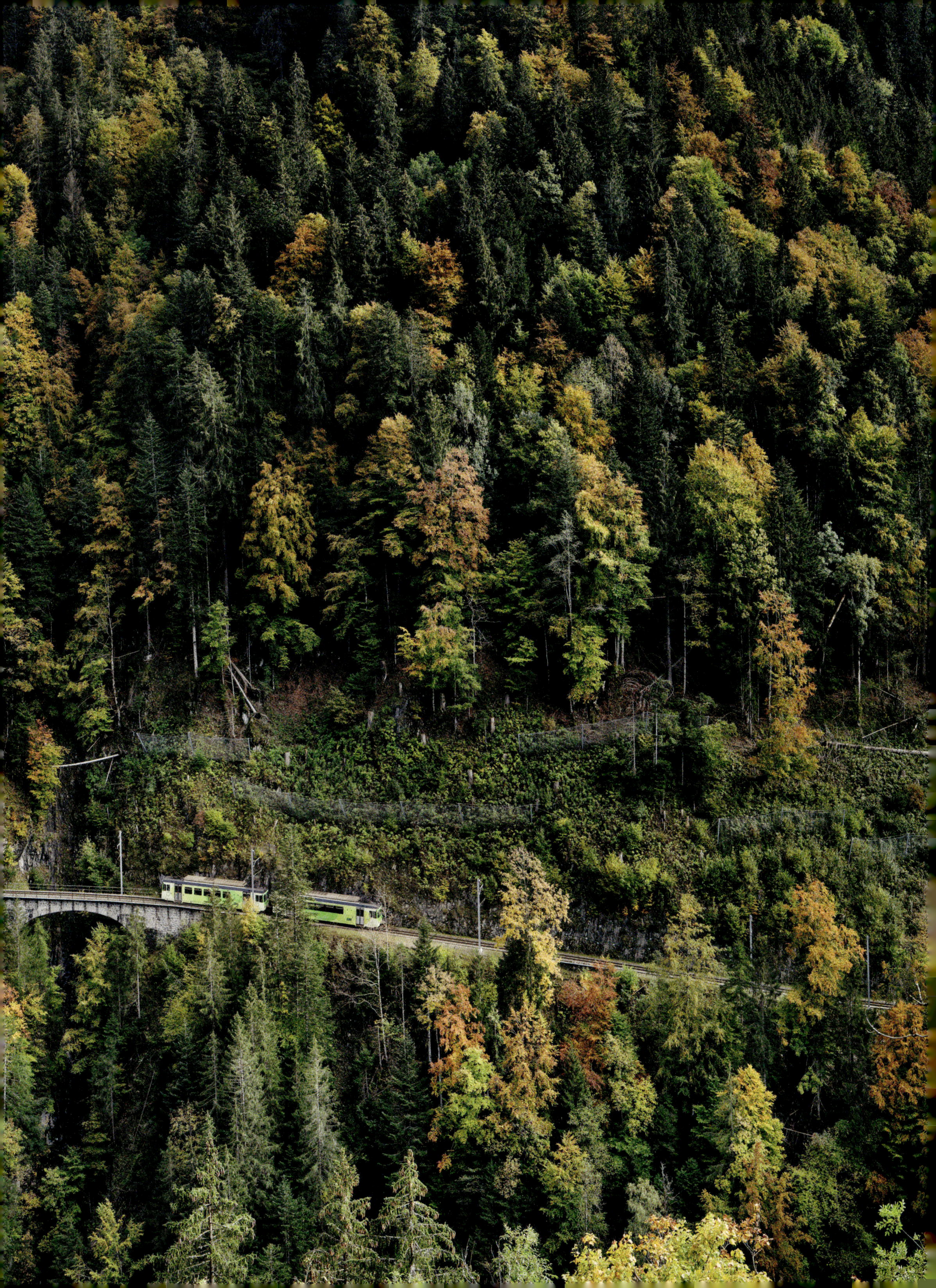

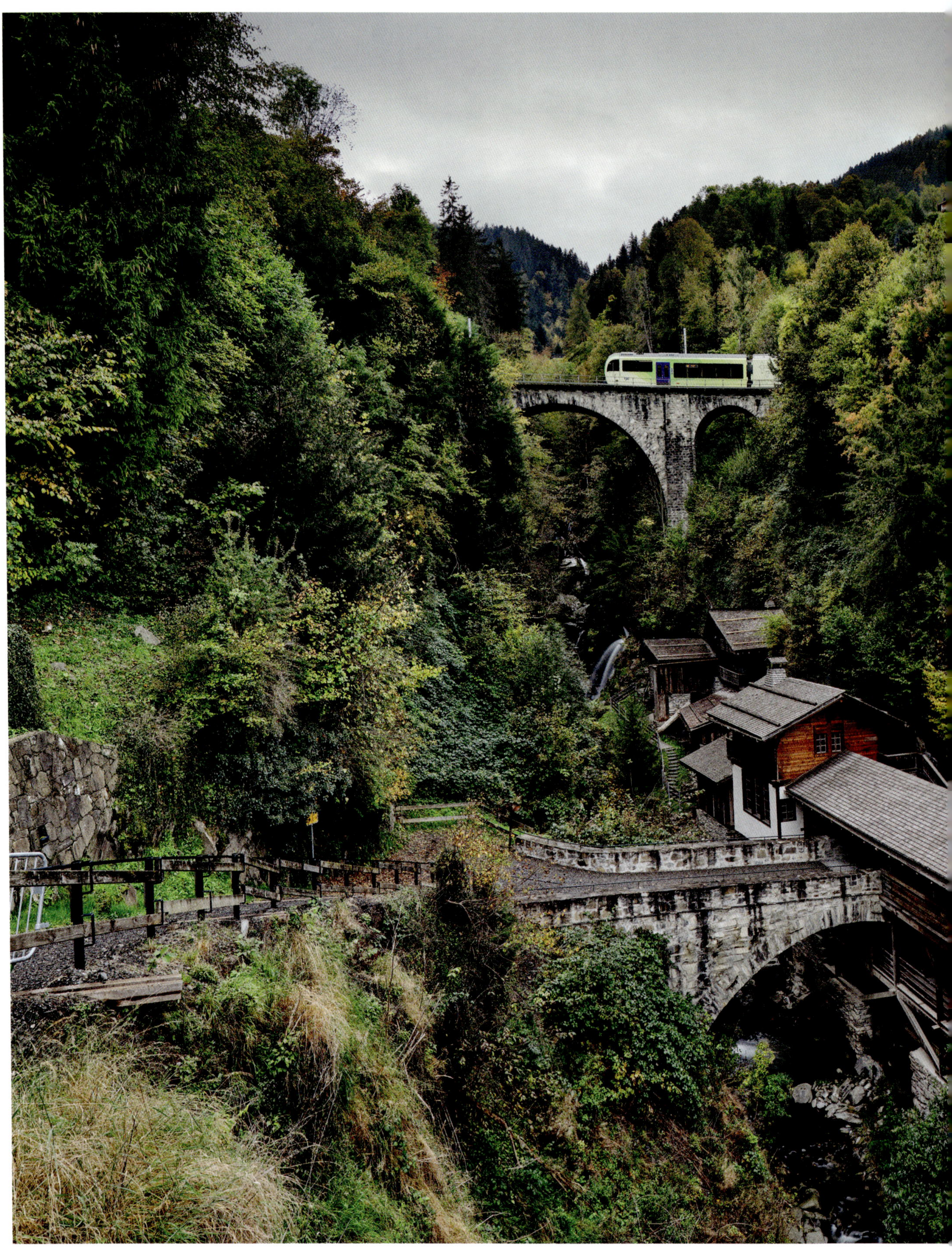

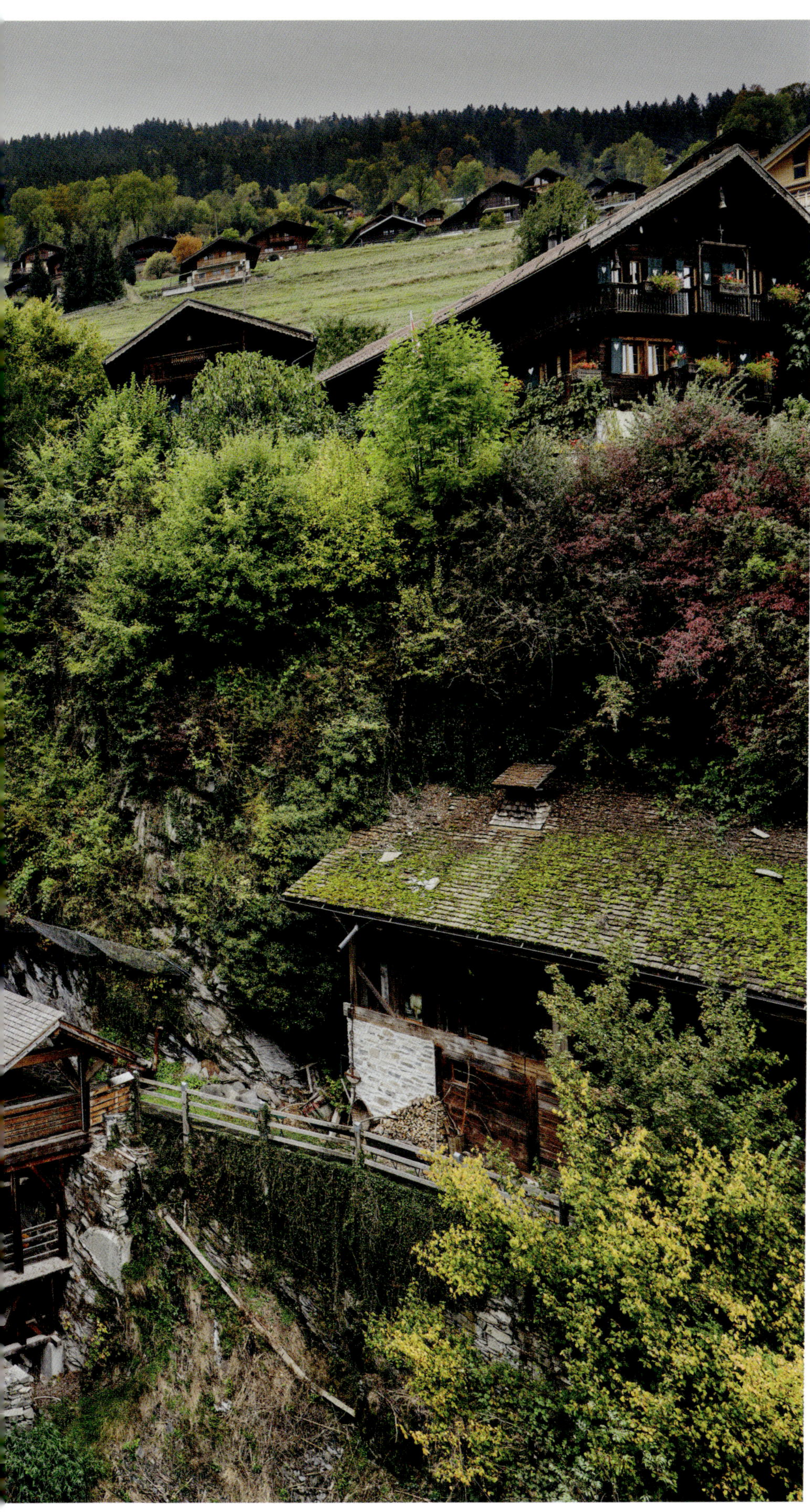

The railway line to Champéry crosses the Vieze de Morgins gorge at Troistorrents on a masonry viaduct. The picturesque ensemble of the historically protected mills of La Tine is visible only for a moment. They are proven through records to have existed back to the year 1401. The group of buildings can be visited with the Vimoti Museum.

LAKES, SUMMITS, AND A SMALL PASS—FROM LUCERNE TO INTERLAKEN

Lakes are the focal point of the ride with the *Zentralbahn* (Central Railway) from Lucerne to Interlaken via the Brünig Pass. Two summit railways offer sweeping Alpine panoramic views along the route: the *Pilatus Railway* and the *Brienz Rothorn Railway*. The latter is still being operated by water—using a steam engine.

There are plenty of railroad fans in Switzerland. And plenty of sensational things to see on railway tracks as well. When both come together, some historical, cultural, and industrial assets are preserved that would otherwise not be. For example, the Giswil and Meiringen train stations on the Brünig Line. They are located at the northern and southern points of the Brünig Pass, at the beginning of both cogwheel ramps. Steam engines ran here, which for technical reasons could not go backward downhill, until the route was electrified during World War II. Because of this, the trains had to be turned in the valley on a railroad wheelhouse. Finally, the trains could chug their way over the mountain again—up and down.

Later, they dutifully did the same on the nostalgic trips organized by the Ballenberg am Brünig Open-Air Museum—until the train stations were altered. The alterations threatened the popular events. In the end, a private initiative saved the two railroad wheelhouses, which simply needed to be moved a small distance and ended up staying in operation. The bill: a few hundred thousand francs. Cheers to the railway fans!

THE FIVE-LAKES RAIL RIDE

The Brünig Railway was opened in 1888, but only the stretch between Alpnachstad and Brienz. Connections for further travel could be found at Lake Lucerne and Lake Brienz, respectively: by water. Three decades later (1916) was the first time that the full, 46-mile (74-kilometer) route between Lucerne and Interlaken went into operation. With a track width of 3 feet (1 meter), it was the only narrow-gauge railway of the Swiss Federal Railways. In 2005 the Brünig Line was combined with the privately owned Lucerne-Engelberg Railway (LSE); both routes have since then been known as the ZB—short for Zentralbahn.

It takes about two hours to travel from central Switzerland to the Bernese Highlands. The Pilatus Railway travels much farther up—it is easy to transfer to its valley station in Alpnachstad from the LSE. It turns the climb up Lucerne's local mountain into a very special experience: 2.8 miles (4.5 kilometers) up, with an altitude gain of 5,364 feet (1,635 meters) and a maximum incline of 48 percent. A world record! The small trains complete the ride from the shore of Lake

Alpnach to the Alpine regions in a half hour—and to a grand view. On clear fall days or with Foehn winds, you can see from Säntis in the east to Wildhorn in the southwest. Real eye-catchers are the ice and stone giants of the Bernese Alps, led by Finsteraarhorn, Eiger, Mönch, and Jungfrau.

FROM BRIENZ TO ITS RED HORN (ROTHORN)

This ice-walled rock structure is even more impressive from the Brienz Rothorn. There, the four-thousanders are a good bit closer But first you must make your way up, which is both easy and comfortable with the cogwheel railway line. You need about an hour for the ride, including a stop to refill the water, for the 4.7-mile-long (7.6-kilometer-long) stretch from Brienz to the mountain station just below the well-known lookout peak. It's a ride leisurely enough to enjoy the increasingly beautiful unfolding views down to Lake Brienz. Eventually, the high peaks of the Bernese Alps with Schreckhorn and Finsteraarhorn enter the picture over the Schwarzhorn-Faulhorn chain, which lies in front. Wow!

A brisk breeze tends to blow up top, which is fortunate because it blows the smoke out of your clothes and hair. This is needed, because the Brienz Rothorn Railway is still run using steam in the twenty-first century. Nostalgists from all around the world are drawn to this railway due to the fact that it is the last steam railway in all of Switzerland.

The reason that this train still smokes and chugs and was never electrified is quite simple: lack of funding. The plans to modernize the over one-hundred-year-old equipment always failed, and now Brienz has a unique attraction. The oldest engines on the Brienz Rothorn Railway first went into operation in 1891 and continue to dutifully do their job. When the crowds are too large, additional diesel locomotives are also used.

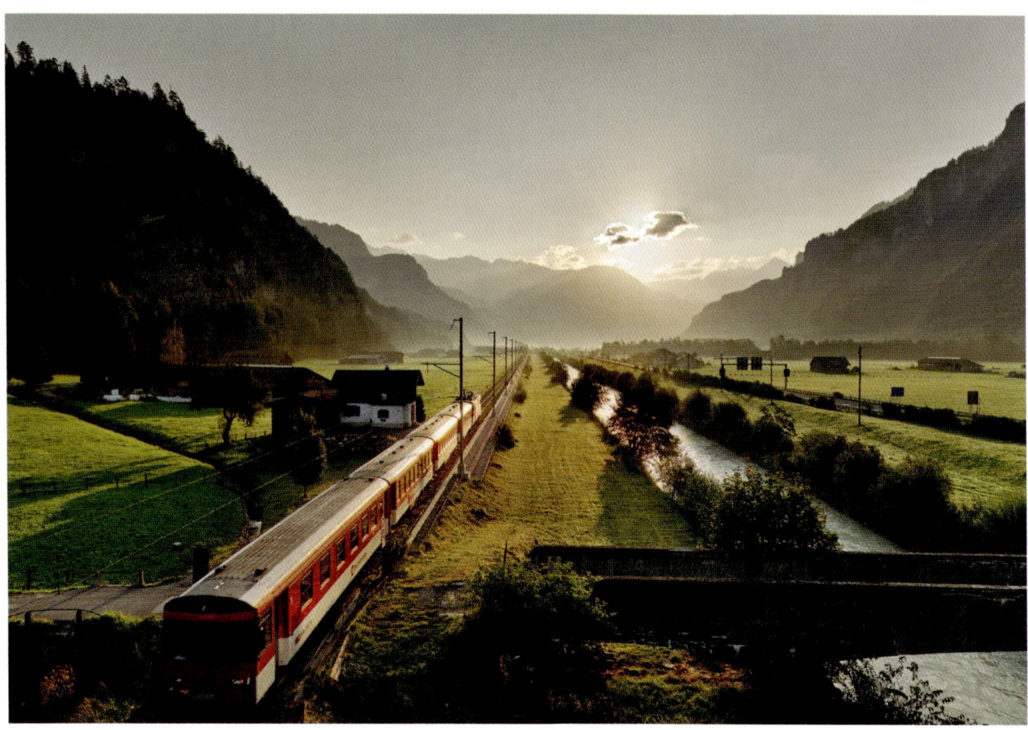

ZENTRALBAHN (CENTRAL RAILWAY)

Morning mood over the Aarboden. In the center of the picture are the canals of the Aare; to the right is the highway to Meiringen. And on the horizon, the peaks of the Uri Alps warm themselves in the sunlight of the early day. The even pyramid of the Mährenhorns is striking (9,593 feet / 2,924 meters). △

On two legs, on four legs, or on wheels: transportation in the twenty-first century. An idyllic country landscape on the Brünig Pass with the modern train composition of the Zentralbahn. It masters the steep routes on either side of the pass by using racks—just as it did one hundred years ago. ▷

BRIENZ ROTHORN RAILWAY

Up to the grand view! During the mountain ride to the Brienz Rothorn (7,703 feet / 2,348 meters), the giants of the Bernese High Alps come into view behind the mountain chain in front. There is an almost 2.5-mile (4-kilometer) differential in altitude between the reflections of Lake Brienz and the highest peak in the panorama, the Finsteraarhorn (14,022 feet / 4,274 meters). The Finsteraarhorn can be seen in the left half of the picture, right next to Lauteraarhorn and Schreckhorn. In the right half of the picture, Eiger, Mönch, and Jungfrau can be easily identified. ▽ ▽

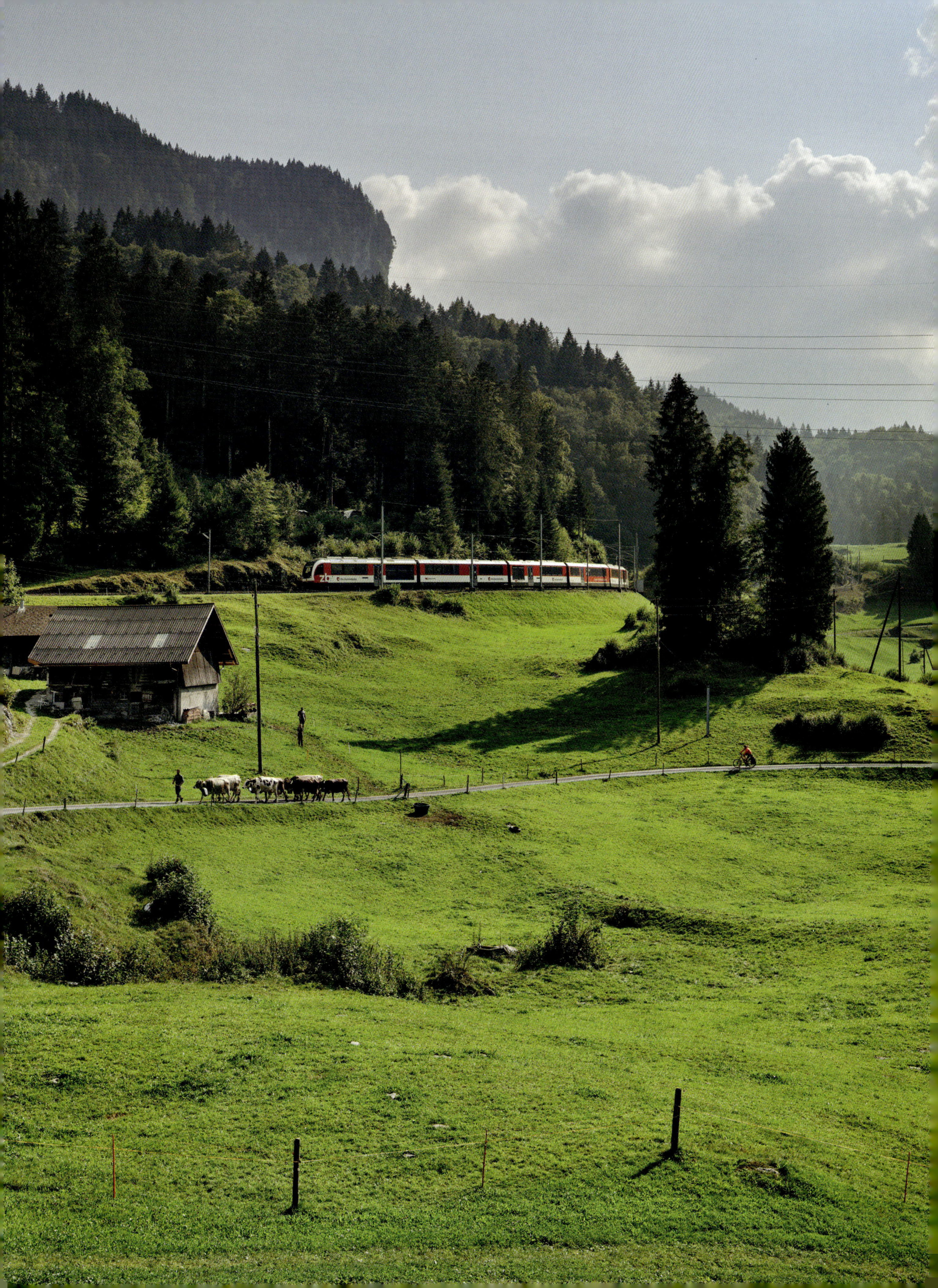

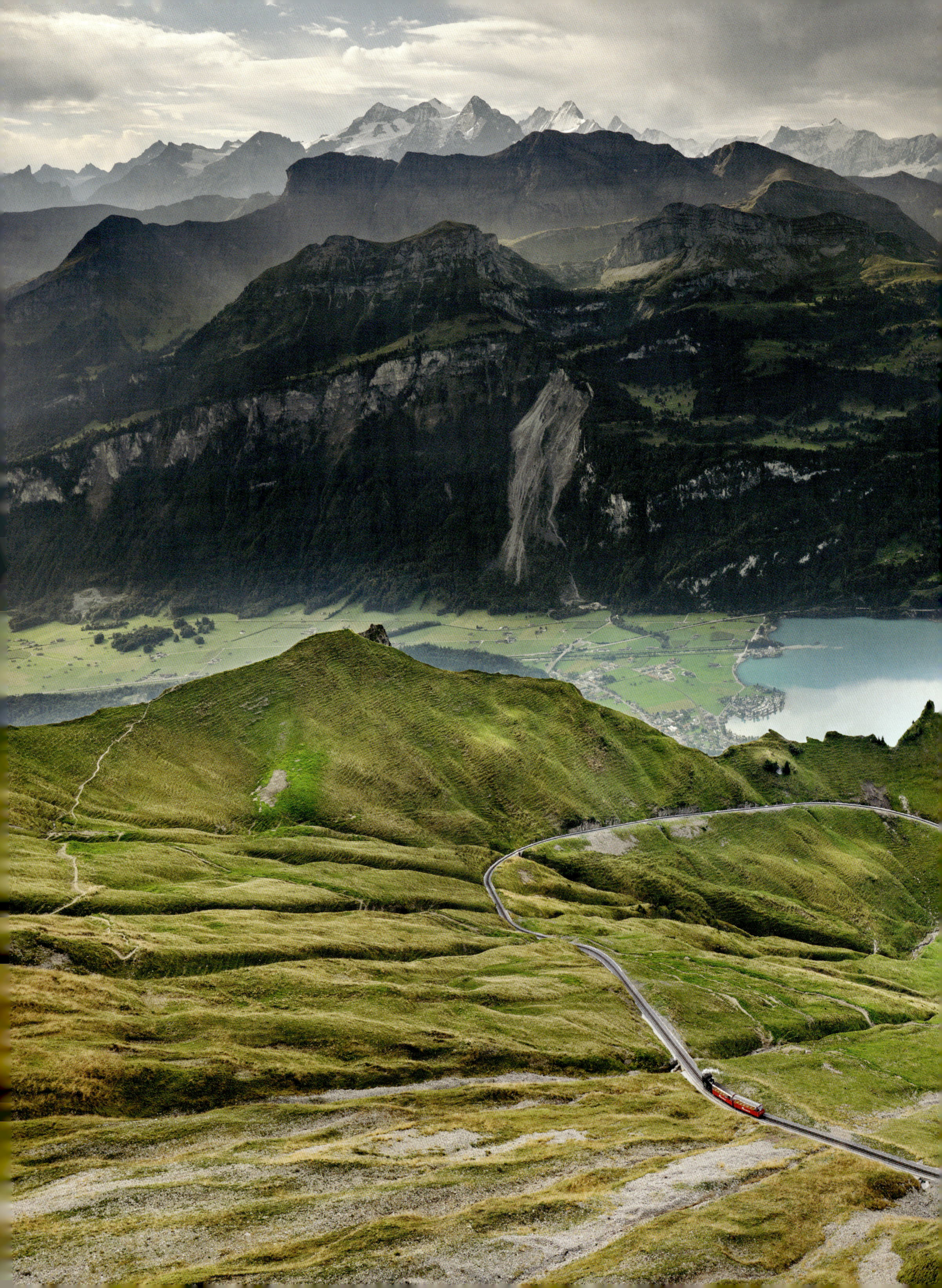

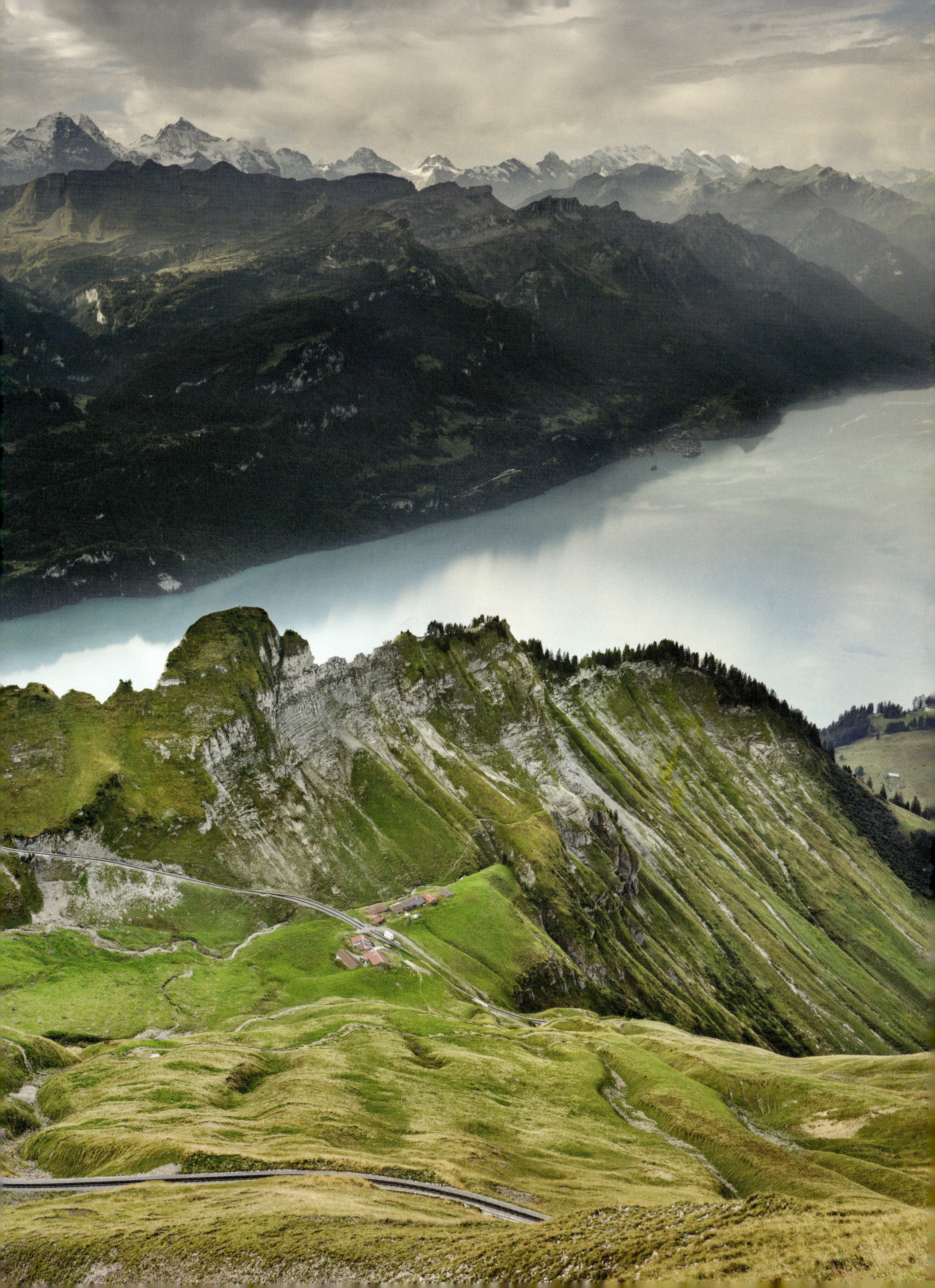

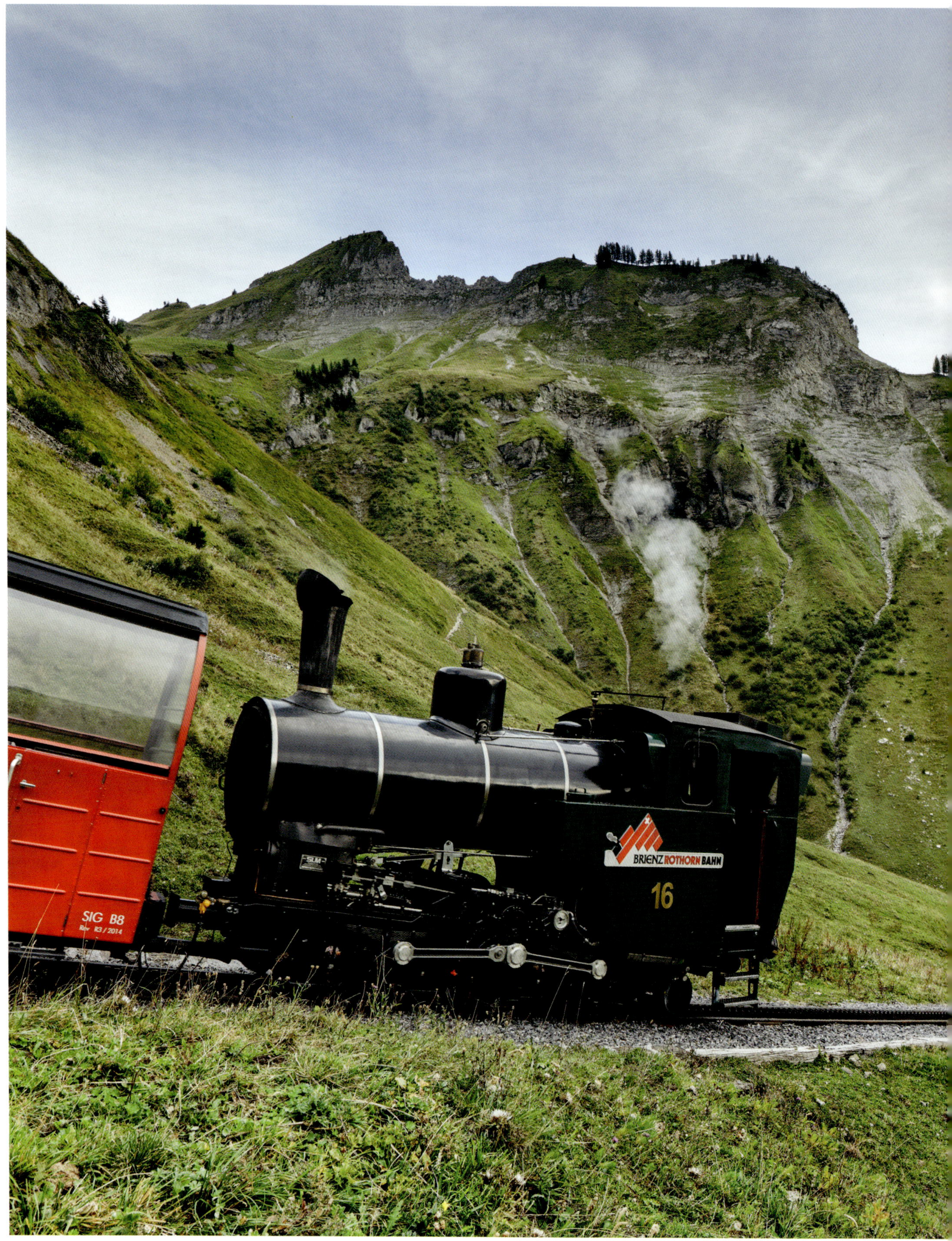
BRIENZ ROTHORN BAHN
16
SIG B8

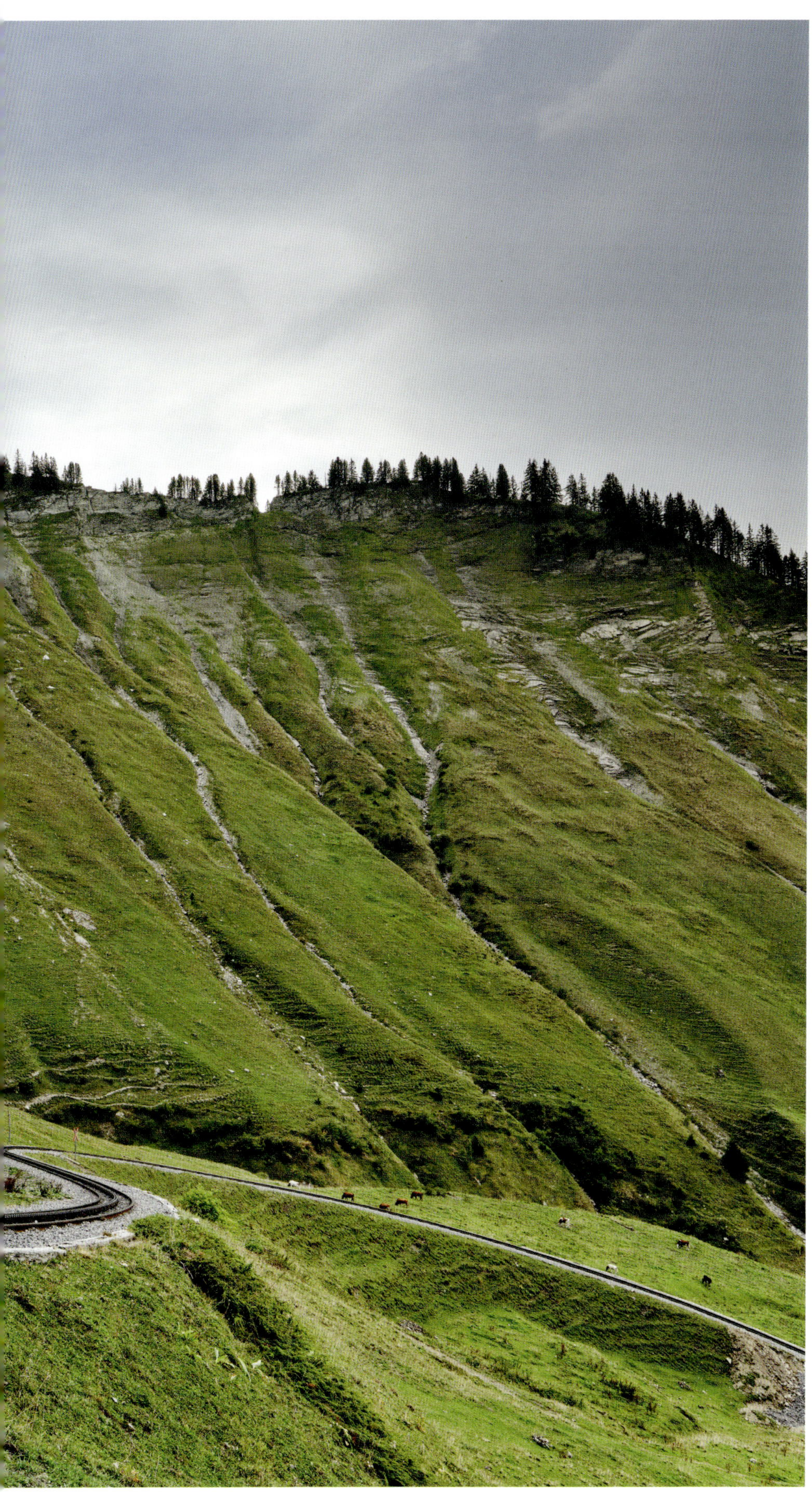

BRIENZ ROTHORN RAILWAY

There are only two engines still in operation that date back to the time the Brienz Rothorn Railway was constructed. Number 16 looks very similar to them but was actually built in 1992 and acquired by the Rochers de Naye Railway in 2005. In contrast to the original engines, it uses oil, not coal.

For almost 130 years, the Rothorn Railway has climbed from Brienz up to the well-known lookout point over the Lake Brienz. Even today, in our increasingly digital world, it is still run by steam just like on day one, starting on June 17, 1892. It's not surprising that a ride on the steam-powered cogwheel railway is a highlight for railway fans all around the world. ▽ ▽

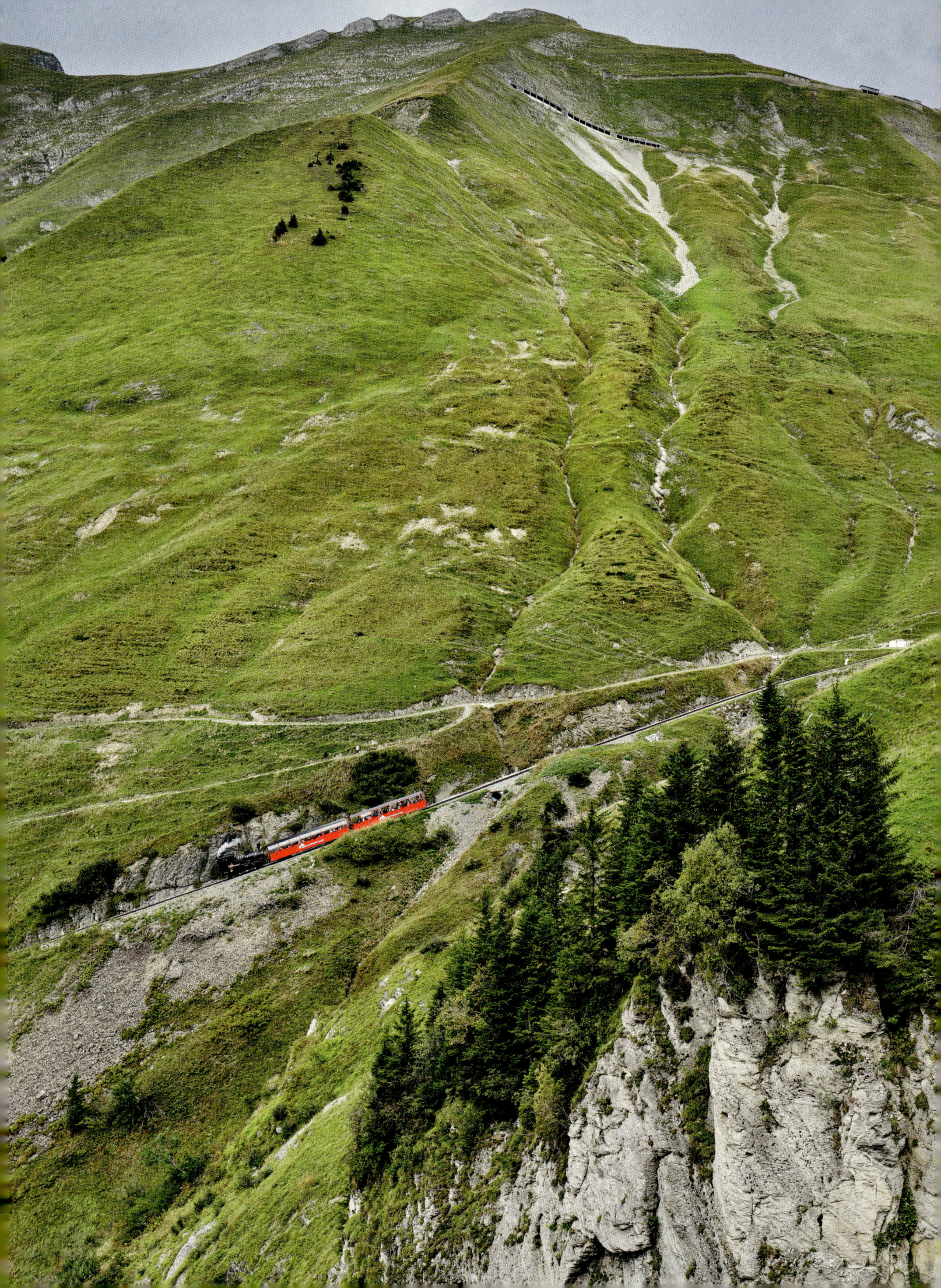

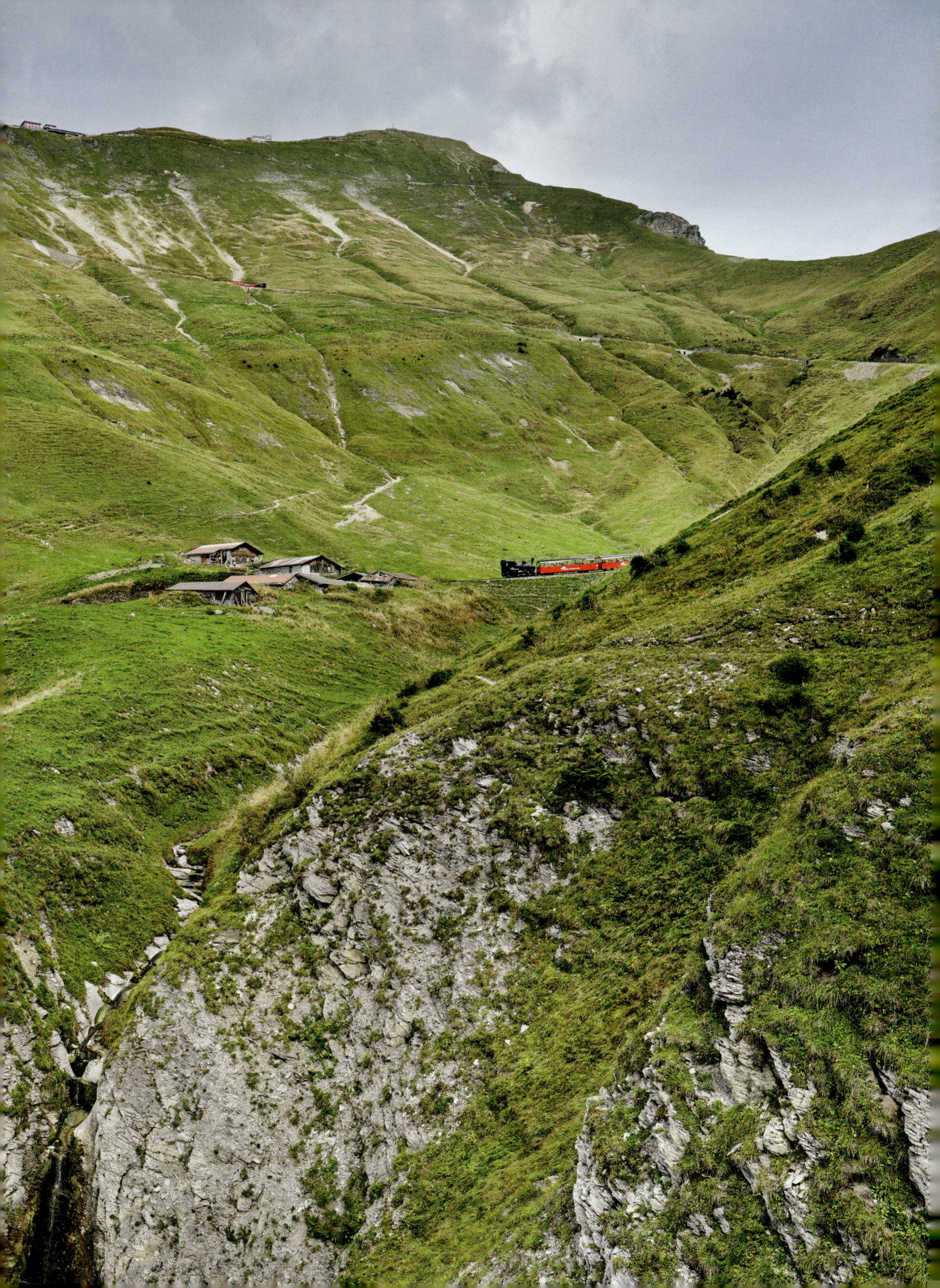

PILATUS RAILWAY

In the green village of Matt, in
a valley shaped by landslide
debris between the rock walls of
Chlingen and Mattstock, begins
the most spectacular track section
of the Pilatus Railway. Buckle your
seat belts!

Lake Lucerne lies under a thick
layer of fog—above it you can find
the peaks of the Glarus and Uri
Alps. The Pilatus Railway moves
along a rack from Matt up to the
mountain station. ▽ ▽

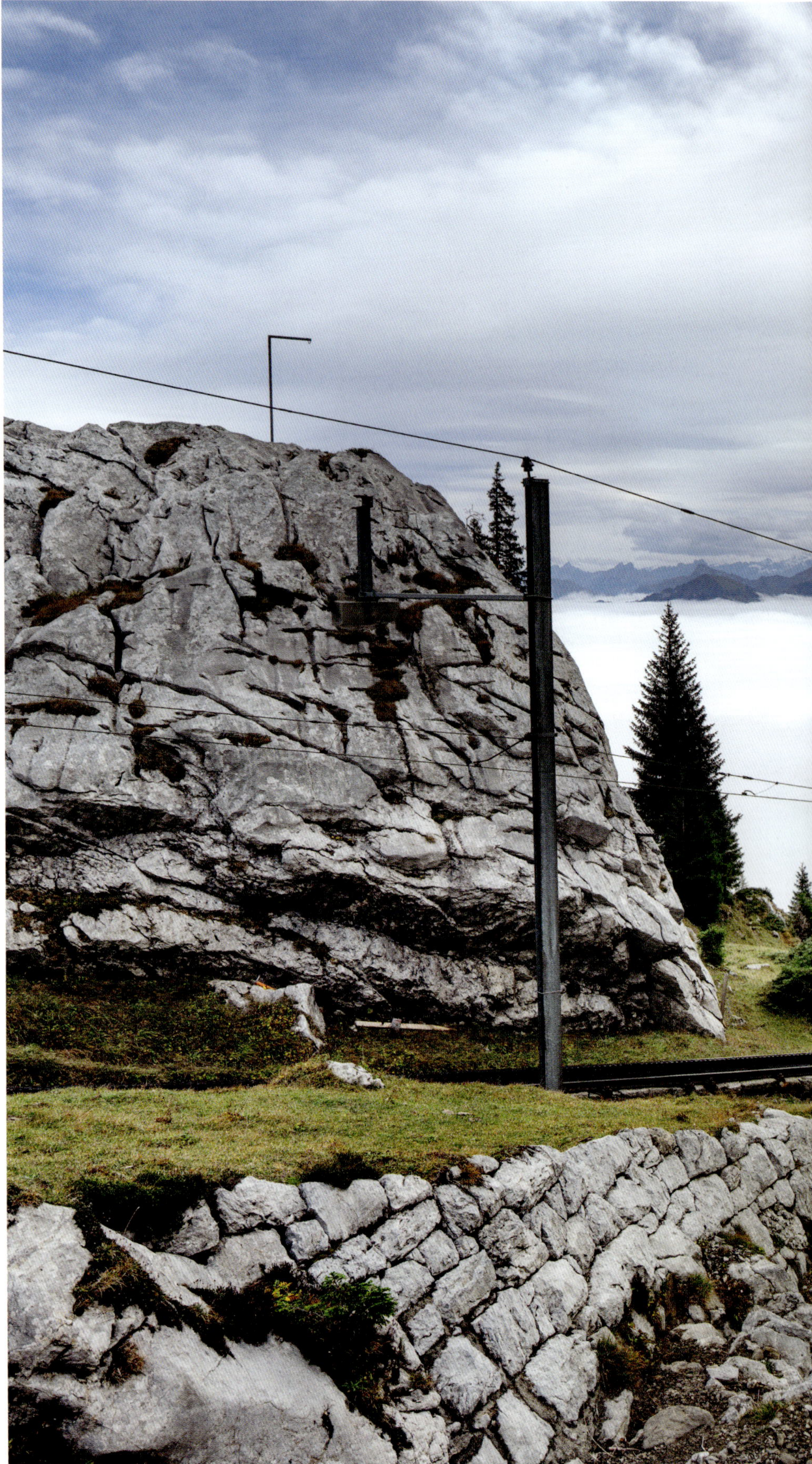

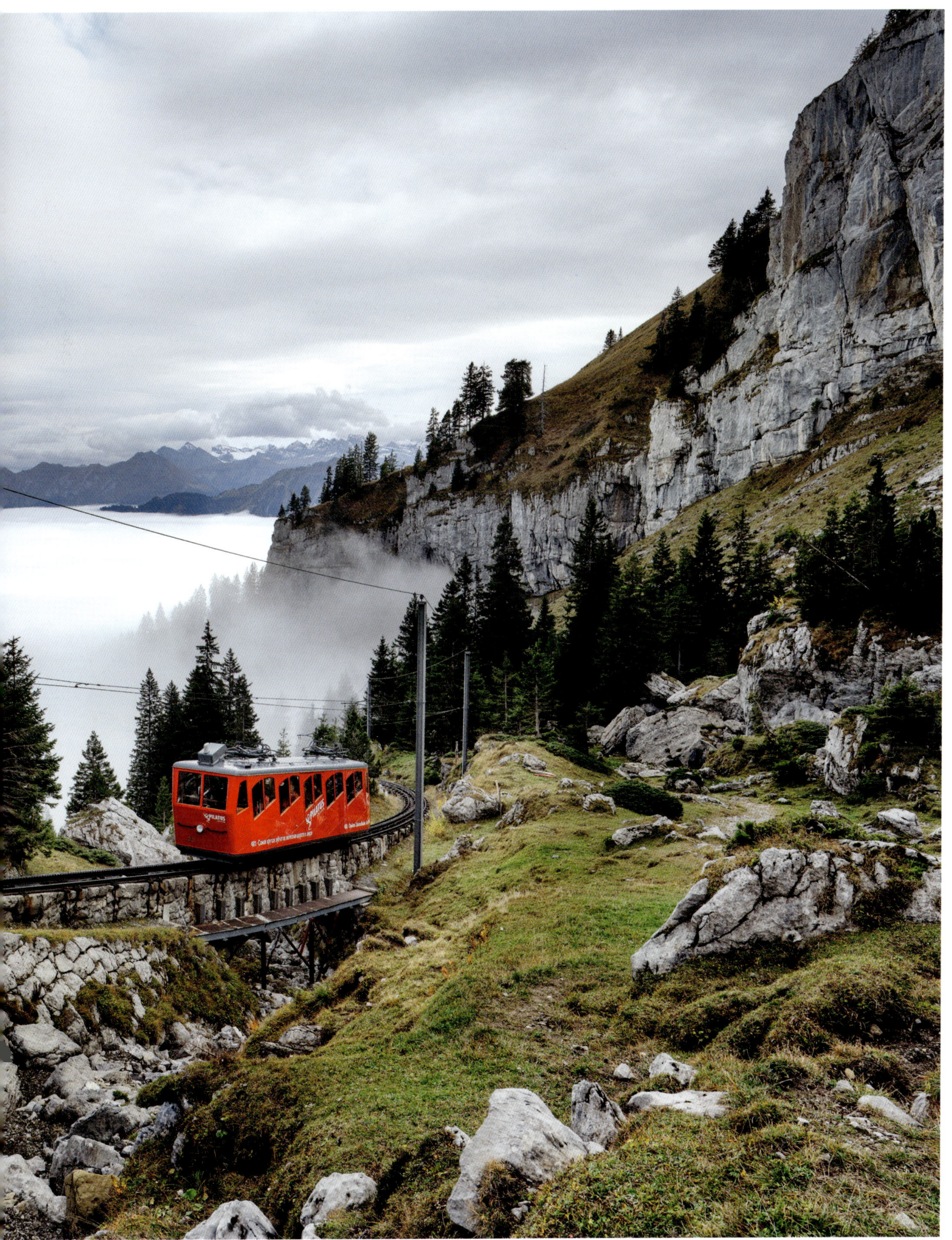

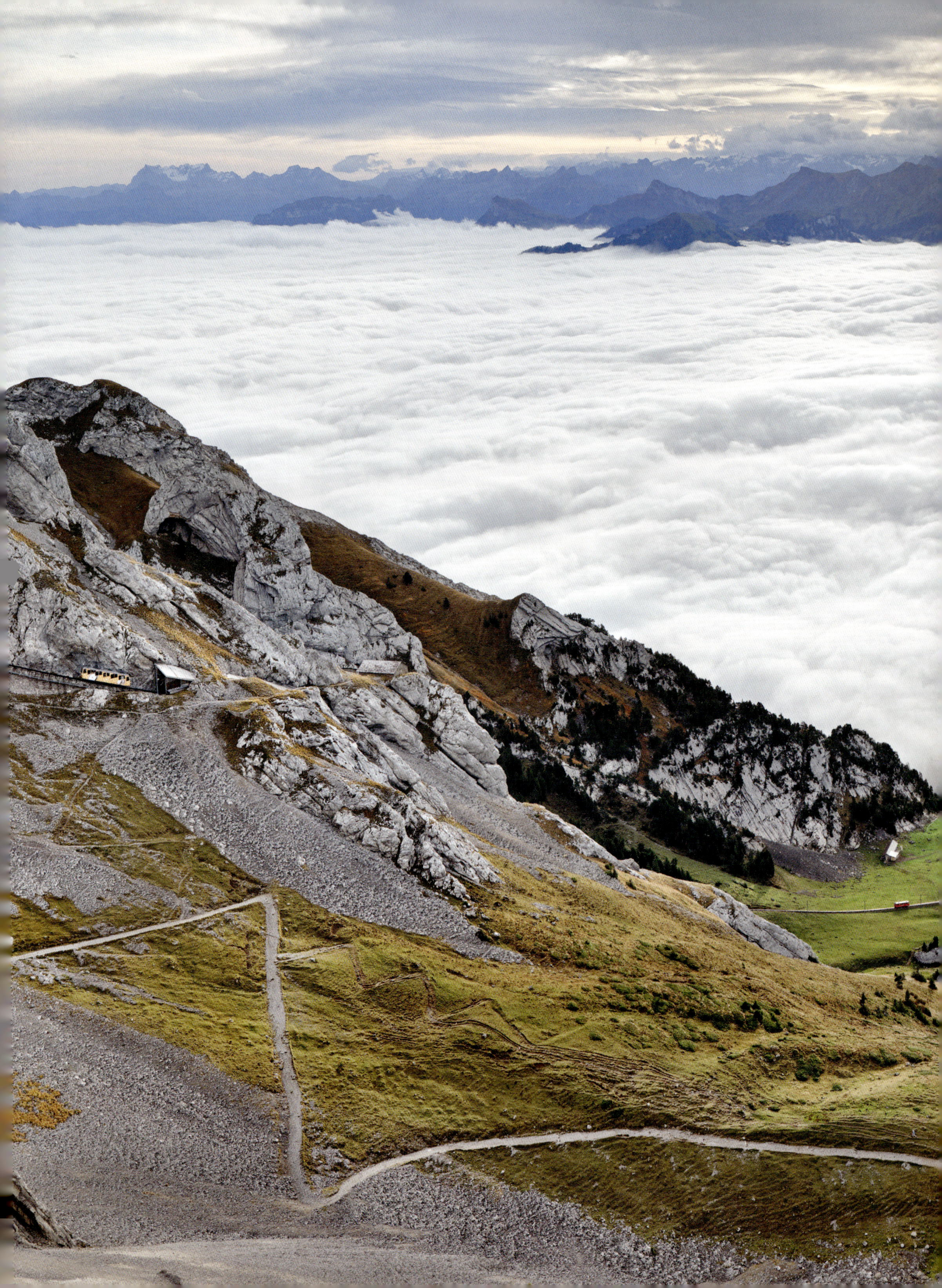

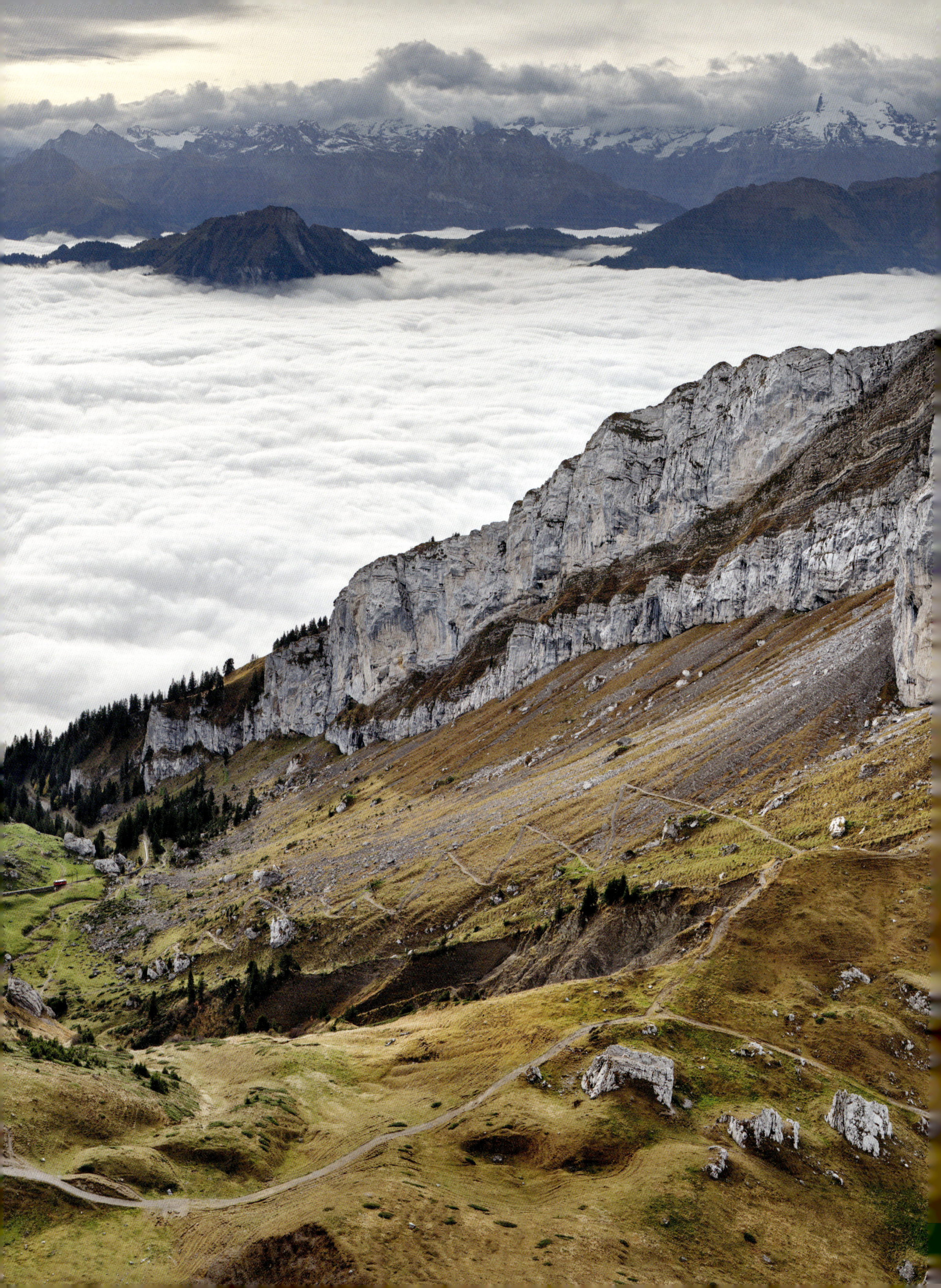

THE TUNNEL ROUTE—THROUGH THE MOUNTAIN TWICE

The second Swiss railway to traverse the Alps, the *Bern-Lötschberg-Simplon Railway* (BLS), breaks through the mountain walls two times: first at Lötschberg and again at Simplon. At Lötschberg, there are even two tunnels; in 2007, one century after the tunnel opening between Kandersteg and the Lötschental, the base tunnel went into operation.

Ritzibodo is the name of the place, and there's something special about it. It stands for something epochal, even though you would never know by looking at it. An ancient "suone," a type of water channel, on the rocky slopes babbles out of the Bietsch Valley and into the Rhone Valley. Water was flowing there when people were traveling by stagecoach along the bumpy paths over the Alps. Around 300 feet (100 meters) below the *bodo* (the Valais word for "ground"), miners drilled the Bietsch Valley Tunnel I in the rock, with modern trains today running 984 feet (300 meters) even deeper at a speed of more than 124 mph (200 kilometers per hour) with the Lötschberg Base Tunnel through the mountain: 21.5 miles (34.6 kilometers) in ten minutes!

Hikers who cross Lötschberg by foot, by contrast, need the whole day, even those who use the Lötschberg southern ramp trail. It is one of the classic hiking trains in Valais and was extended in 2013 from Eggerberg to Brig to an impressive total of 19 miles (31 kilometers). You move—gradually losing altitude—down the sunny side of the Rhone Valley and alternately enjoy the beautiful views of the four-thousanders of the Valais Alps and the goose-bump-inducing trails over the deep gorges that

need to be crossed. The double track of the Lötschberg Railway is never far, opened in 1913. Using spectacular viaducts, it crosses all the side valleys at their outlets.

IMPOSING ENGINEERED STRUCTURES

The Luogelkin Viaduct is the perfect photo op with its five wide arches every 66 feet (20 meters) near the Hohtenn train station at the beginning of the route. Engineering fans are not the only ones entranced by the steel construction of the Bietsch Valley Viaduct, which spans the gorge with one arch and originally was held together by 125,000 (!) rivets. For safety reasons, the rivets were partially replated by fitted bolts in the 1980s.

In addition, the northern ramp of the Lötschberg Railway also has some outstanding structures. It surmounts the altitude differential between Kandergrund and Kandersteg by using a double loop and two loop tunnels. The Kander Viaduct, with its eleven pillar arches, sets a distinctive accent in the Frutiger landscape. Here, too, there is an accompanying themed trail for hikers, the BLS adventure trail (Kandersteg–Frutigen).

The Simplon Tunnel opens the way into the south as a logical continuation of the Lötschberg route to Milan. Conversely, the Alpine railway provided a direct connection between northern Italy and France. In 1906 the first tunnel tube was opened in a joint venture between Switzerland and Italy. Half a century later, the Italian postal system celebrated this historic event with a 25-lire special stamp. The stamp, however, turned out to be quite unrealistic: In Italy, as in Switzerland, rail traffic runs on the left, not on the right. In addition, the "artist" took his inspiration for the stagecoach depiction quite shamelessly from the Swiss artist Rudolf Koller and his work *Die Gotthardpost.*

THE MAN WHO "DISCOVERED" THE SIMPLON PASS

The BLS never reached the same significance as the Gotthard Railway for crossing the Alps, not even after the base tunnel under Lötschberg was built. Only once in its history did the Simplon Pass surpass other Swiss Alpine crossings for a few decades, and that was during the lifetime of a man named Kaspar Stockalper (1609–91). He recognized the economic and strategic potential of the route. That turned out to be to his benefit, because during the Thirty Years' War, anarchy reigned across Europe, leading many trade routes to be unable to be used. Stockalper had the pass route expanded, built hospices and hostels, such as the "Taferna" and the "Alten Spittel" south under the top of the pass, and really cashed in because of it. In his palace, which literally casts a shadow over the small town of Brig, an un-Swiss luxury reigned: The "King of Simplon" surrounded himself with a whole court of servants. What a career.

Almost 100 feet (30 meters) above
the water, the two bridges cross
the Kander near Frutigen. The
869-foot (265-meter) viaduct, with
its eleven pier arches, went into
operation in 1913. When a later
expansion included a twin track
in 1981, a longer, more modern
concrete bridge was added.

A dizzying sight down to the
mouth of the Bietsch Valley. The
iron structure of the Bietsch Valley
bridge weighs around 1,400
tons and stretches lightly, almost
levitating, above the Bietschbach.
The sensational structure was
originally held together by
125,000 rivets. ▽ ▽

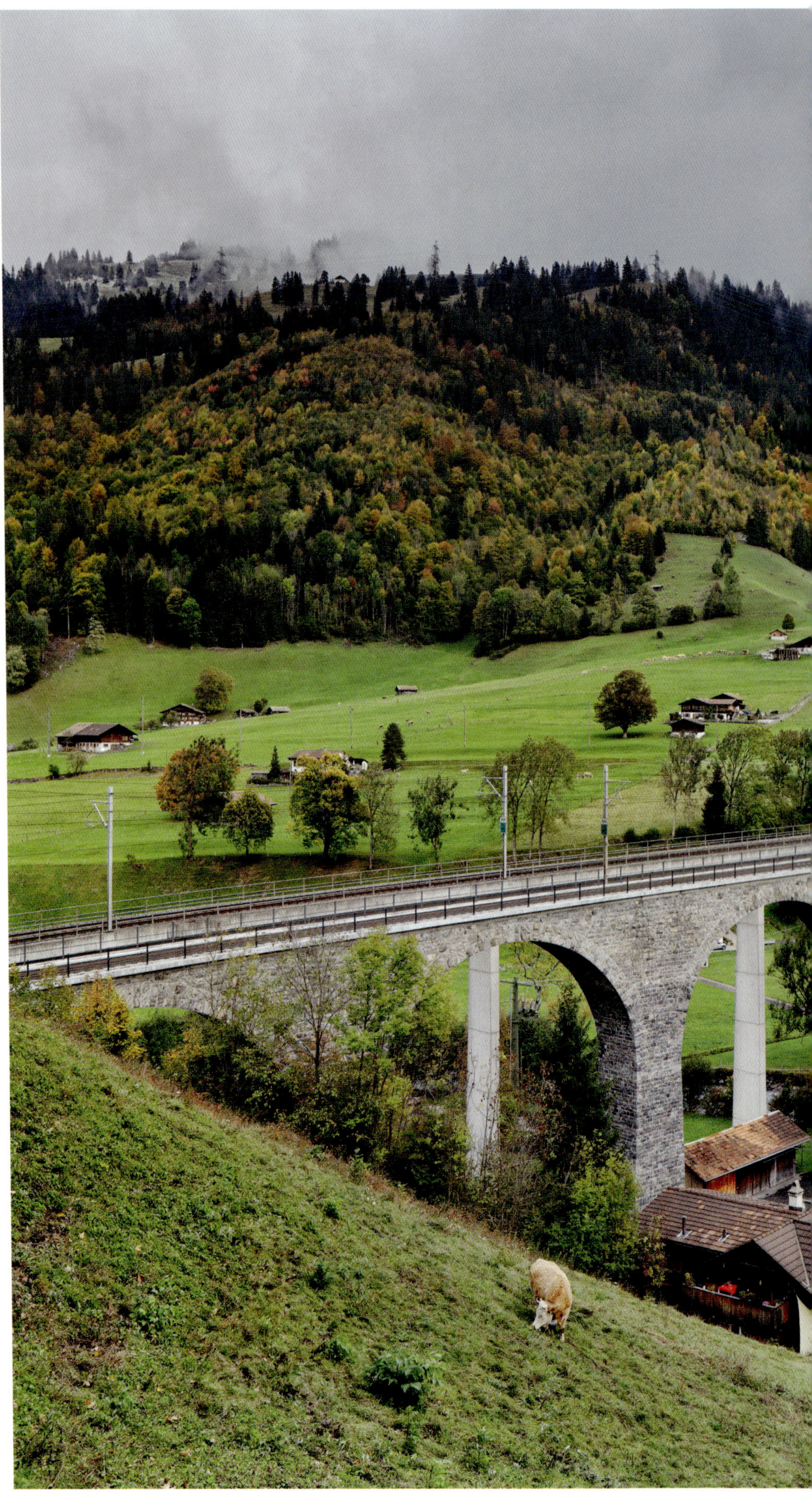

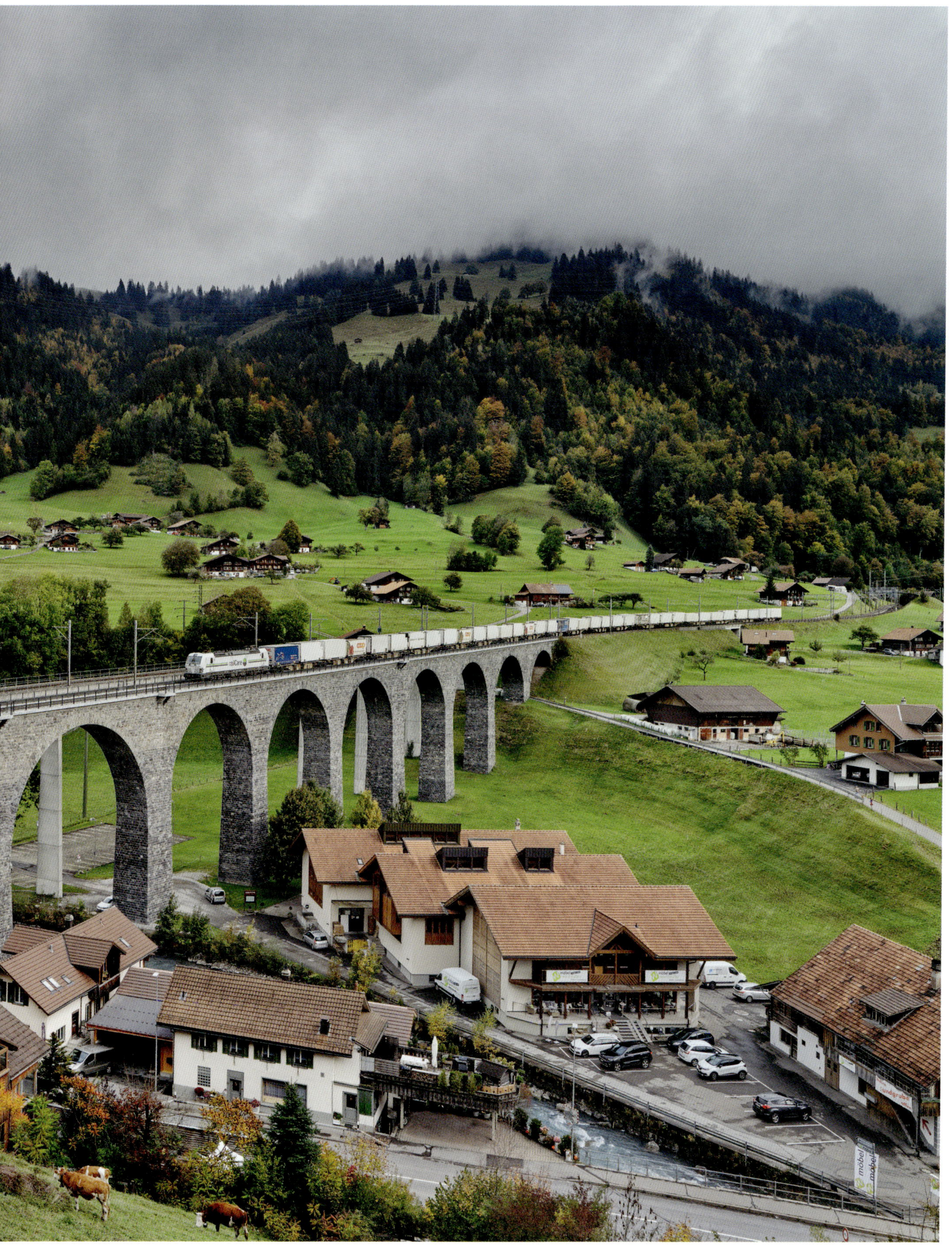

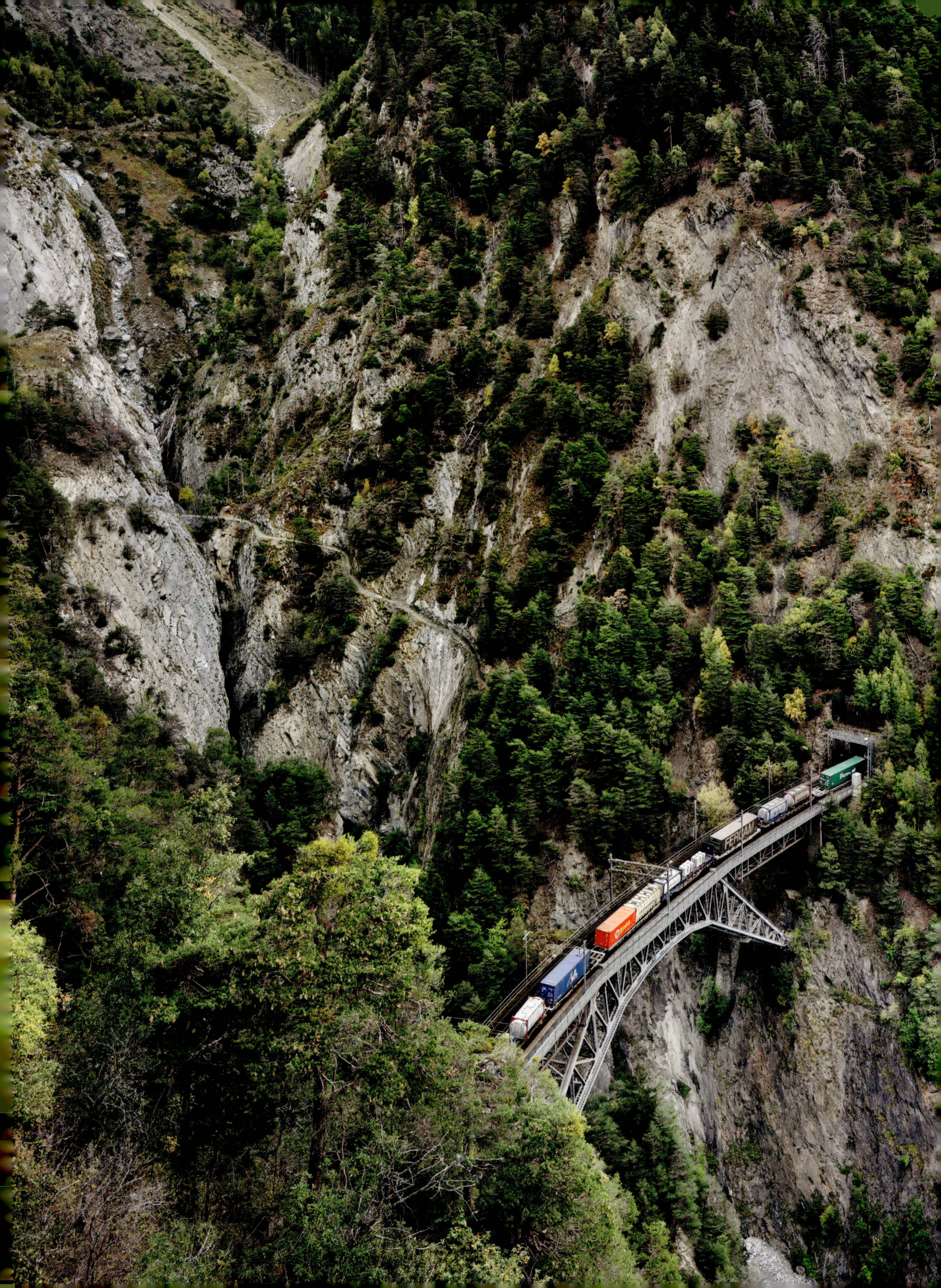

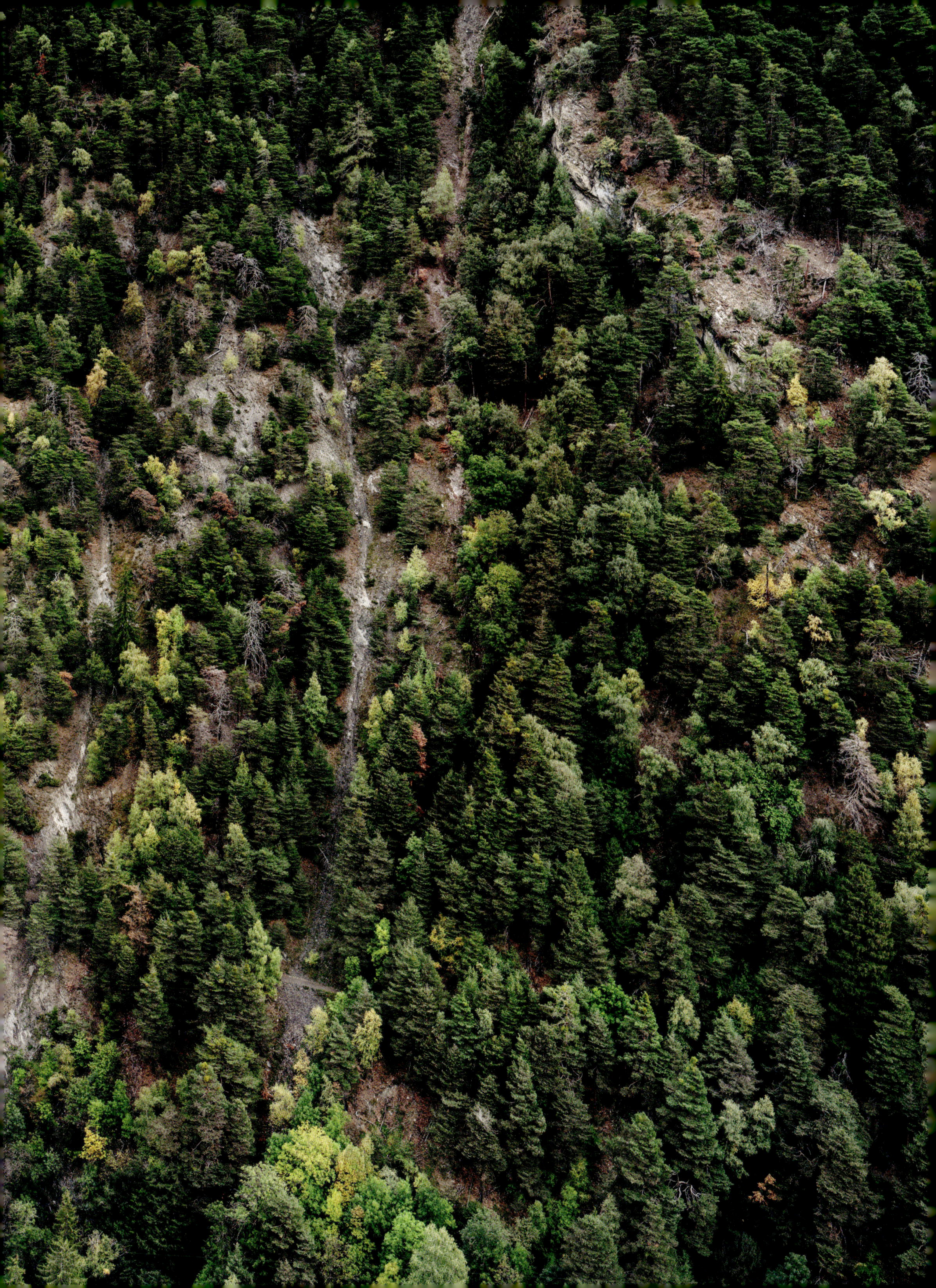

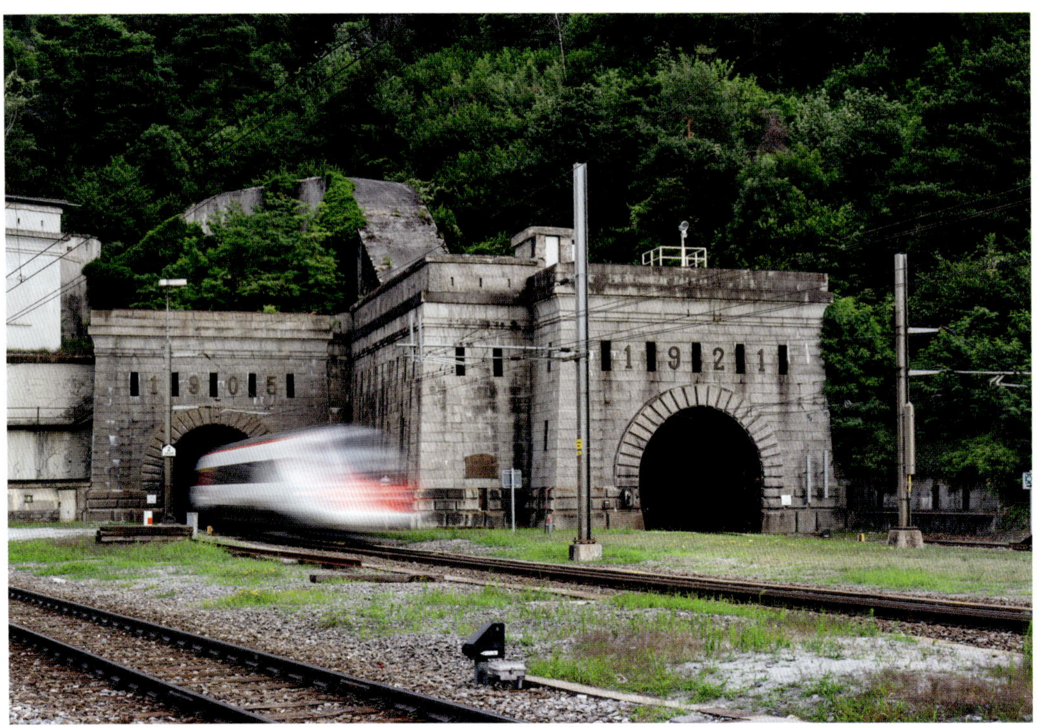

BERN-LÖTSCHBERG-SIMPLON RAILWAY

Tunnel entrance near Brig. The dates over the arches stand for the years when they went into operation: 1906 for the first tunnel, 1921 for the second. Up into 1982, the Simplon Tunnel was the longest tunnel in the world. △

Near Blausee-Mitholz, the tracks of the Lötschberg Railway make their way up the steep gradients to Kandersteg with the help of two long loops and multiple tunnels. On the way, views open up down to the green Kander Valley and the clear blue lake, one of the most popular destinations in the region. ▷

Since the opening of the Lötschberg Base Tunnel (21.5 miles / 34.6 kilometers), only regional trains still run along the old Lötschberg line. The journey along the southern ramp is still quite an experience. One of the most spectacular structures is the 417-foot-long (127-meter-long) Luogelkin Viaduct, with its five round arches. ▽▽

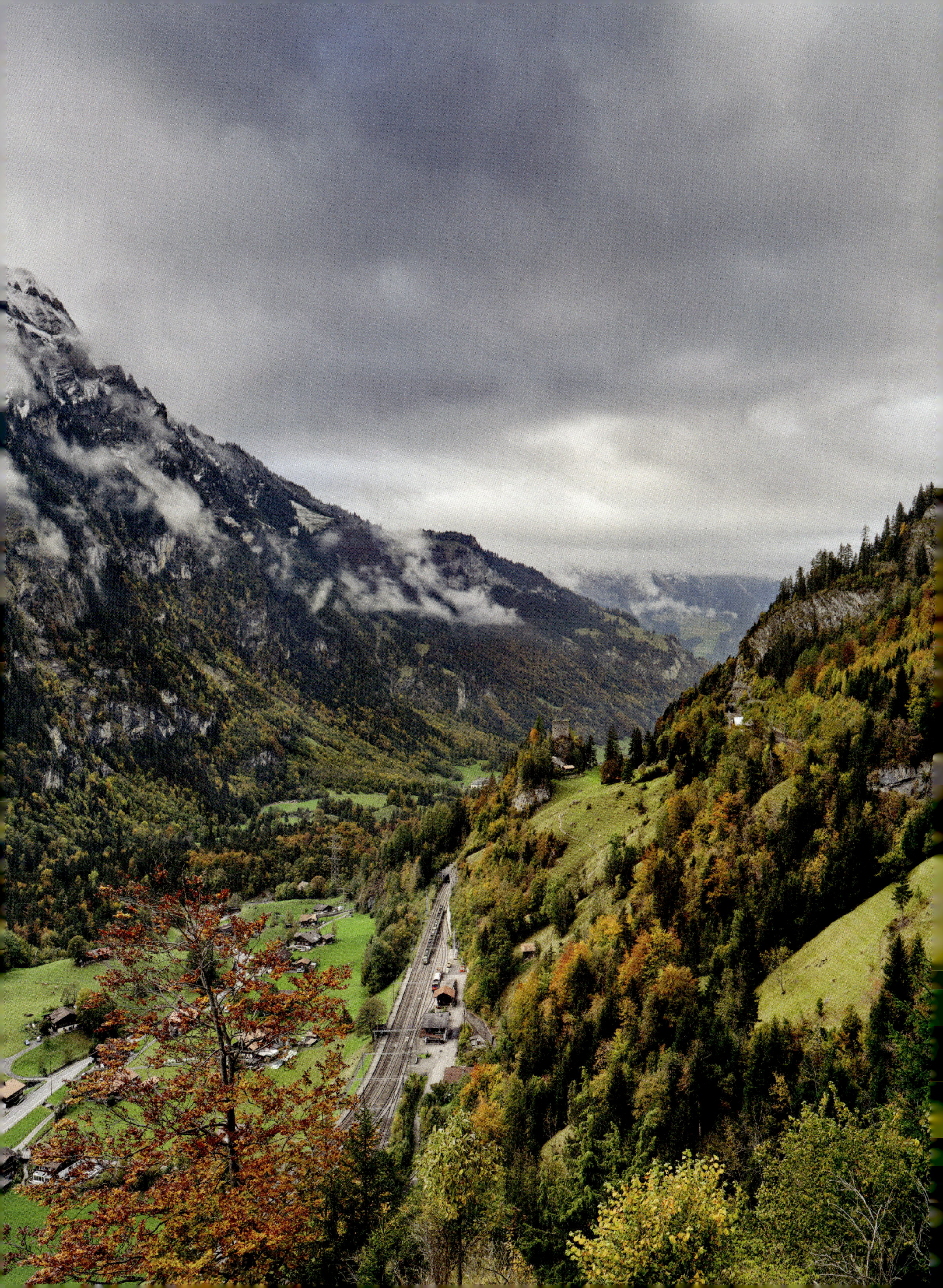

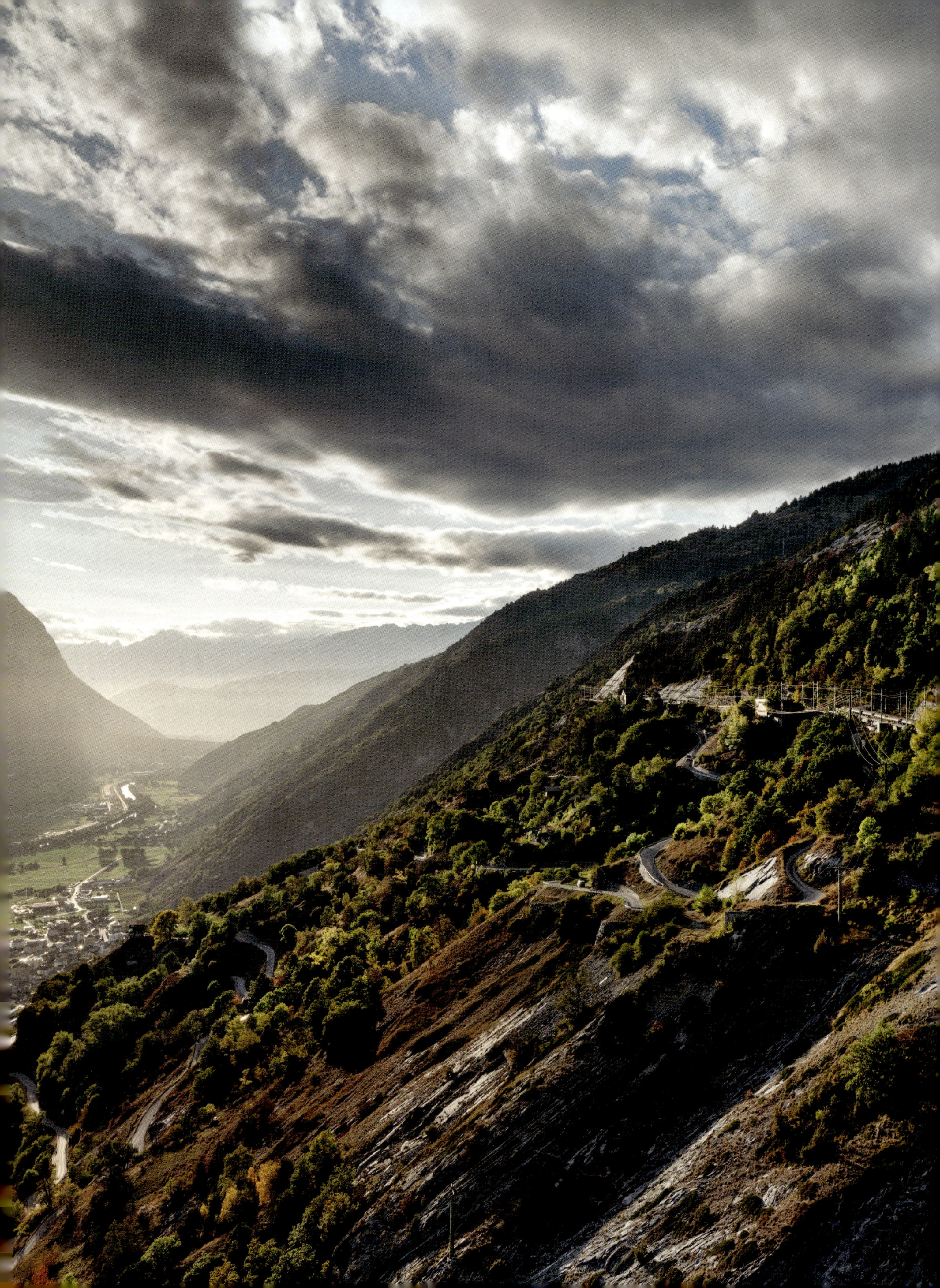

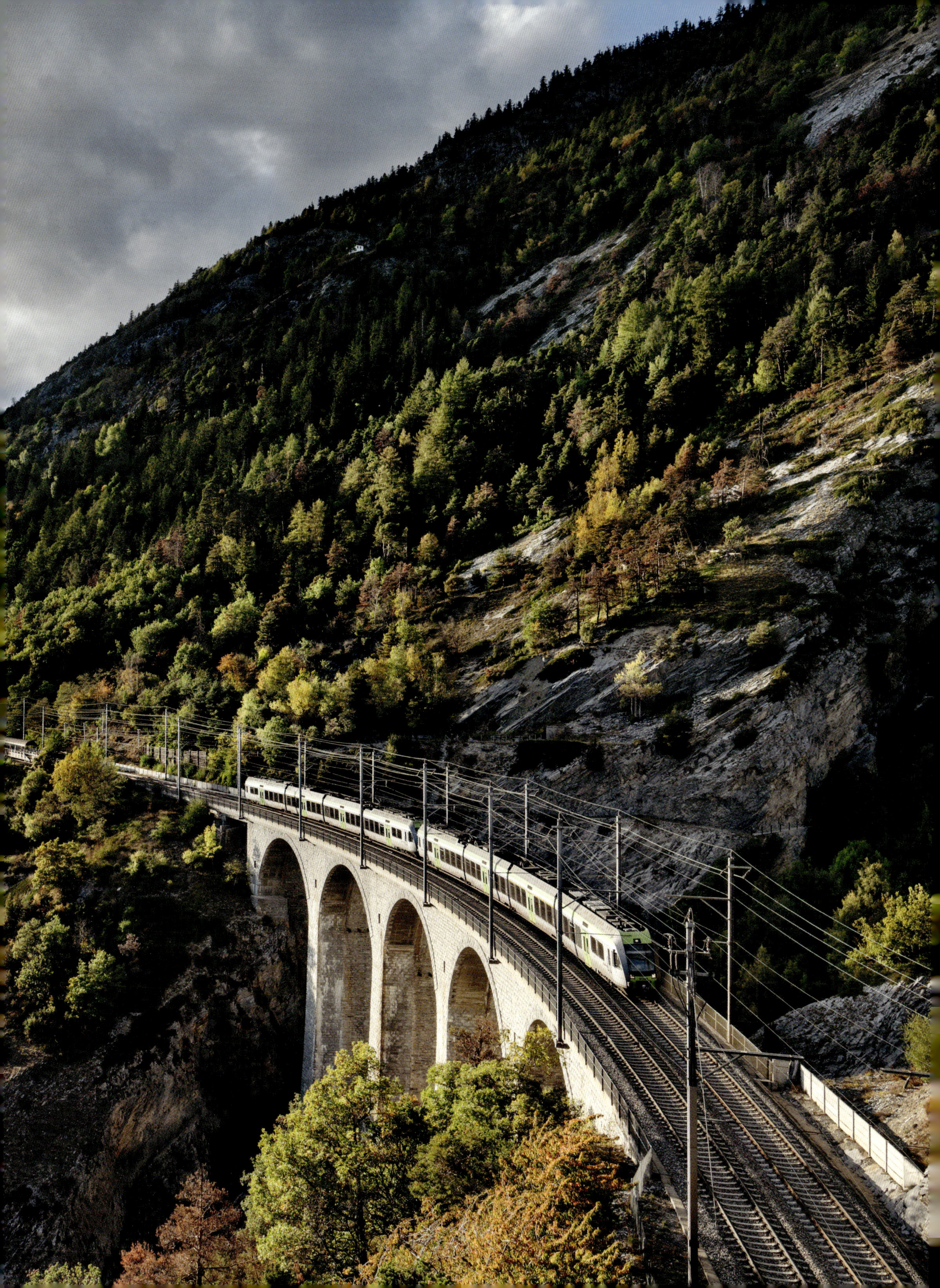

11,332 FEET (3,454 METERS)—THE TOP OF EUROPE

Eiger, Mönch, and Jungfrau: the famous trio of summits in the Bernese Highlands, including the northern face. A ride on the *Wengernalp Railway* to the Kleine Scheidegg offers a worm's-eye view of the monumental walls, while Eigerwand Station on the *Jungfrau Railway* allows a vertical view down into the green valley of Grindelwald.

Who invented it? Of course, it wasn't the company Ricola, but they were Swiss at any rate. And it was the Bernese, who are known for their measured cautiousness. This stereotype, however, doesn't apply in this case. In Grindelwald, the signs of the times could be seen early—namely, the age of travel was seen approaching. Goethe, Haller, and Rousseau planted the seeds: Nature was now "in," and the Alps were romantically glorified. The city of Bern quickly organized a huge open-air event in front of the grand backdrop of the high Alps. The Unspunnenfest of 1805 was a great success; visitors traveled across Lake Thun and delighted in the pastoral games, which were repeated three years later. In Paris and London the big newspapers reported about the country villagers who went about their daily work in the shadow of sky-high mountains.

A BREAKTHROUGH INTO THE FUTURE

The Bernese Highlands was the first travel destination in the Alps, which set off a construction boom. In the year 1832, it was already possible to spend the night in the mountain hotel on the Faulhorn, and a few years later, the first *Handbook for Travelers in Switzerland* appeared in London. Many routes were expanded—then the railroads conquered the mountains. Traveling became easier and much quicker. In 1859, Thun also gained a connection to the Swiss railway network, and soon after, connecting the two Lütschine River valleys with this modern mode of transportation was considered. In 1893 the first small locomotive steamed over the Kleine Scheidegg, over 11.9 miles (19.2 kilometers) of continuous track on the cog rail—a world record!

In the same year, the cogwheel railway up the Schynige Platte (6,453 feet / 1,967 meters) was opened. It is currently operated as a nostalgic railway—travel as it was one hundred years ago. It is a successful re-creation with rolling stock from the Belle Époque era, including wooden benches and train conductors in historical uniforms. The steam train makes its way over the 4.5-mile (7.3-kilometer) stretch four times during the summer. That's when Train H 2/3, built in the year 1894, can show what it can do.

Soon, the lofty visions went back up to the top, to the big summits. In the rampant Swiss mountain railway fever, fantastic projects blossomed, and the next target had to be the Jungfrau—at that point the most famous of the largest mountains in the Bernese Alps. Maurice Koechlin, who worked as an engineer for Gustave Eiffel (and the actual designer of the Eiffel Tower), planned a railway that would lead out of the Lauterbrunnen Valley to the summit in five sections. Eduard Locher's idea was particularly unusual, since it entailed driving railway cars through the mountain in two straight tunnel tubes, using compressed air.

THE JUNGFRAU RAILWAY—THE PROJECT OF THE CENTURY

Eventually, the project went to an entrepreneur of the name Adolf Guyer-Zeller. His electrically powered cogwheel railway was planned to start at Kleine Scheidegg and go— mostly through the mountain—to the Jungfraujoch and eventually reach just below the summit of the Jungfrau. He took the Wegnernalp Railway into account in his planning, which meant a significant reduction in distance. Construction started in 1896 and progressed slowly, with repeated funding difficulties. When Guyer-Zeller died in 1899 in Zurich, the continuation of the project was momentarily questioned. However, his heirs continued the project with perseverance, and on February 21, 1912, the tunnel workers arrived on the Jungfraujoch. "A magnificent work, a triumph of modern engineering, receives its consecration," cheered *Neue Zürcher Zeitung*. No one thought of continuing the line to the top of the mountain.

The railway went into operation in stages, first to Eigerwand Station (1903). When the first train drove to the Eismeer stop, the rush in demand was already huge. There were even fights at the ticket office, as the *Berliner Volkszeitung* reported: "The unexpected news about the planned morning opening on Tuesday, July 25, set the whole tourist world of Mürren, Wengen, and Grindelwald into motion. The Germans and English in particular fought over the first tickets, and it almost came to blows over the first ticket to the Eismeer between a towering American and a pithy Sachsen with resilient humor, who maintained that he was first in line."

The Jungfrau Railway, although incomplete, became a great commercial success; the passenger numbers exceeded all forecasts. In its opening year, almost eighty thousand people traveled up to the Jungfraujoch, the highest train station in Europe at 11,332 feet (3,454 meters). Before the coronavirus pandemic, there were around one million passengers per year. Enough? No—investment continues. The construction of a modern cable car (Eiger-Express) to the Eigergletscher Station should give Jungfrau tourism a push, which is the hope of some in Grindelwald, while others complain about the seemingly unending commercialization of nature. Where is beautiful Switzerland headed?

During the trip from Wengen over Wengernalp up to Kleine Scheidegg (6,762 feet / 2,061 meters), you have a clear view upon the massive northern face of Mönch, the Jungfraujoch (*center*), Jungfrau, and the fittingly named Silberhorn ("silver horn"). To the left are the tracks of the Jungfrau Railway. Behind Eigergletscher Station, the line disappears into the 4.5-mile-long (7.3-kilometer-long) tunnel to the Jungfraujoch.

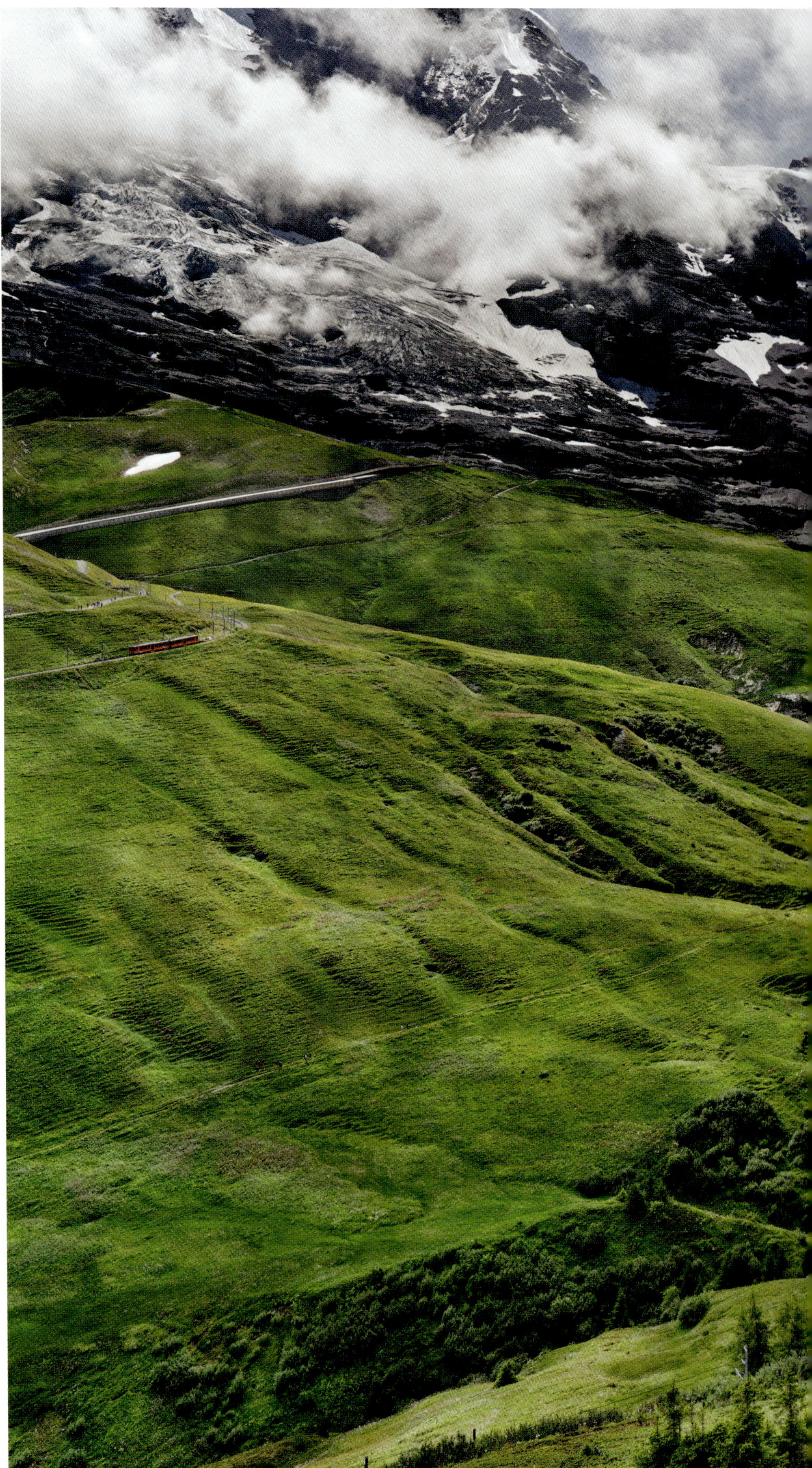

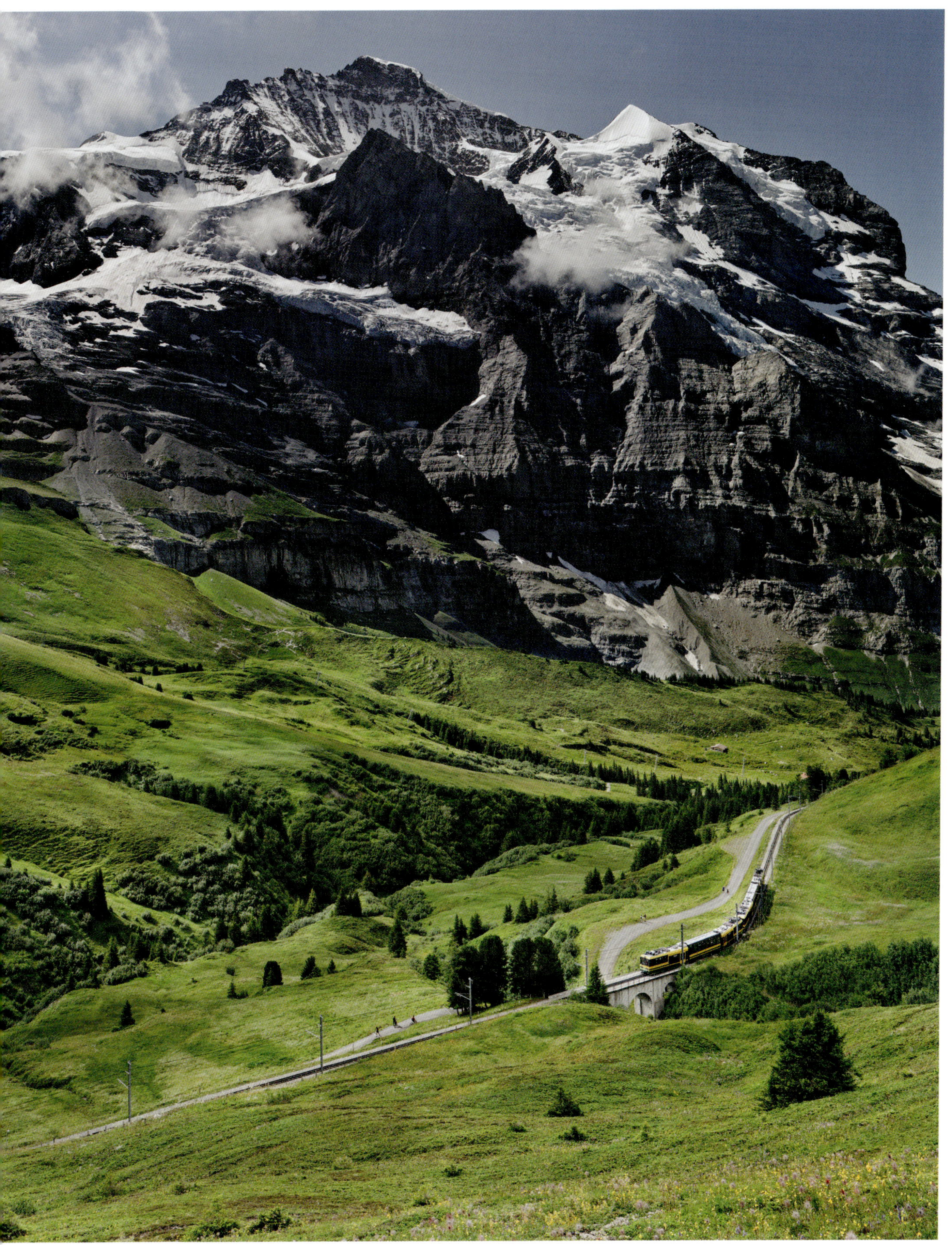

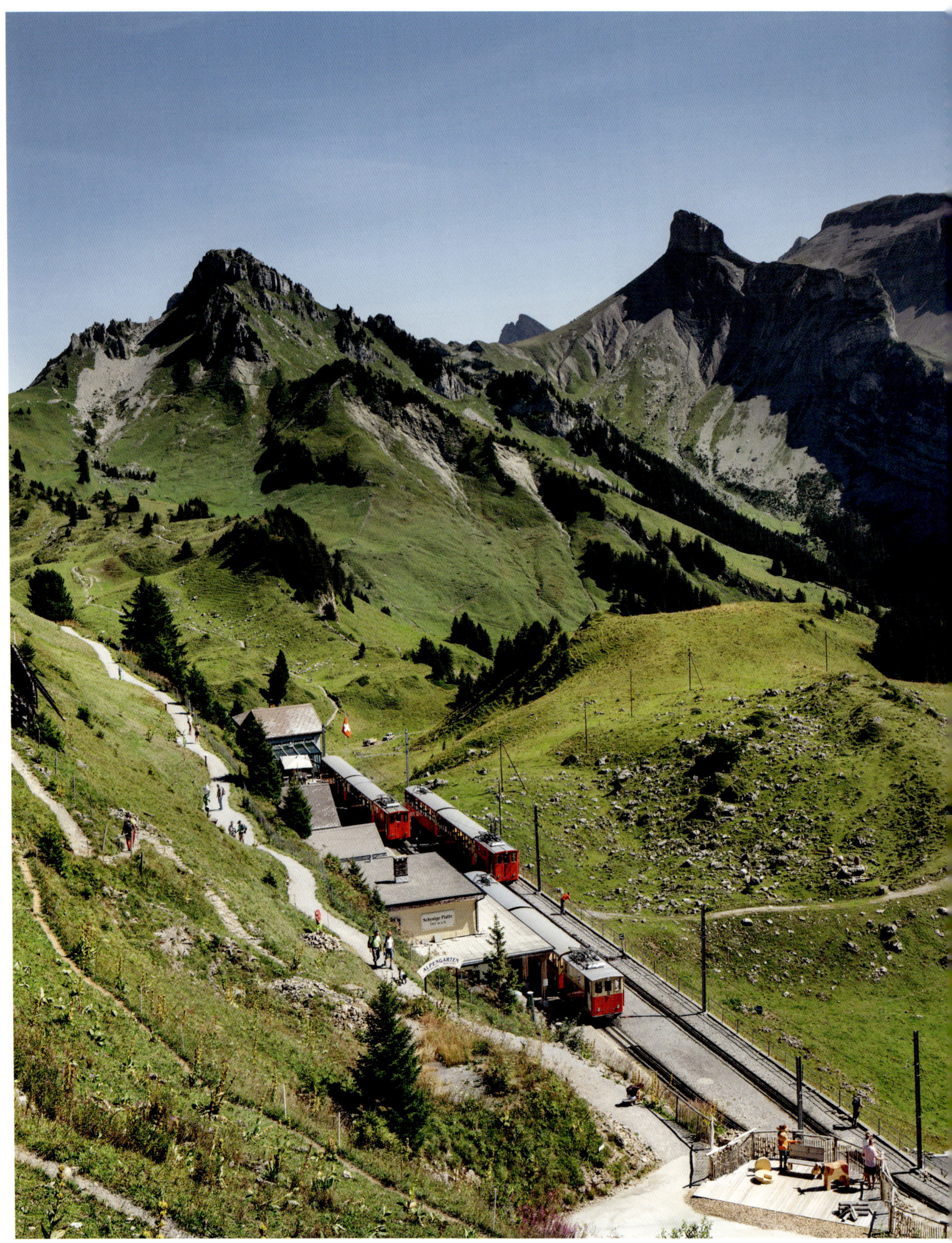

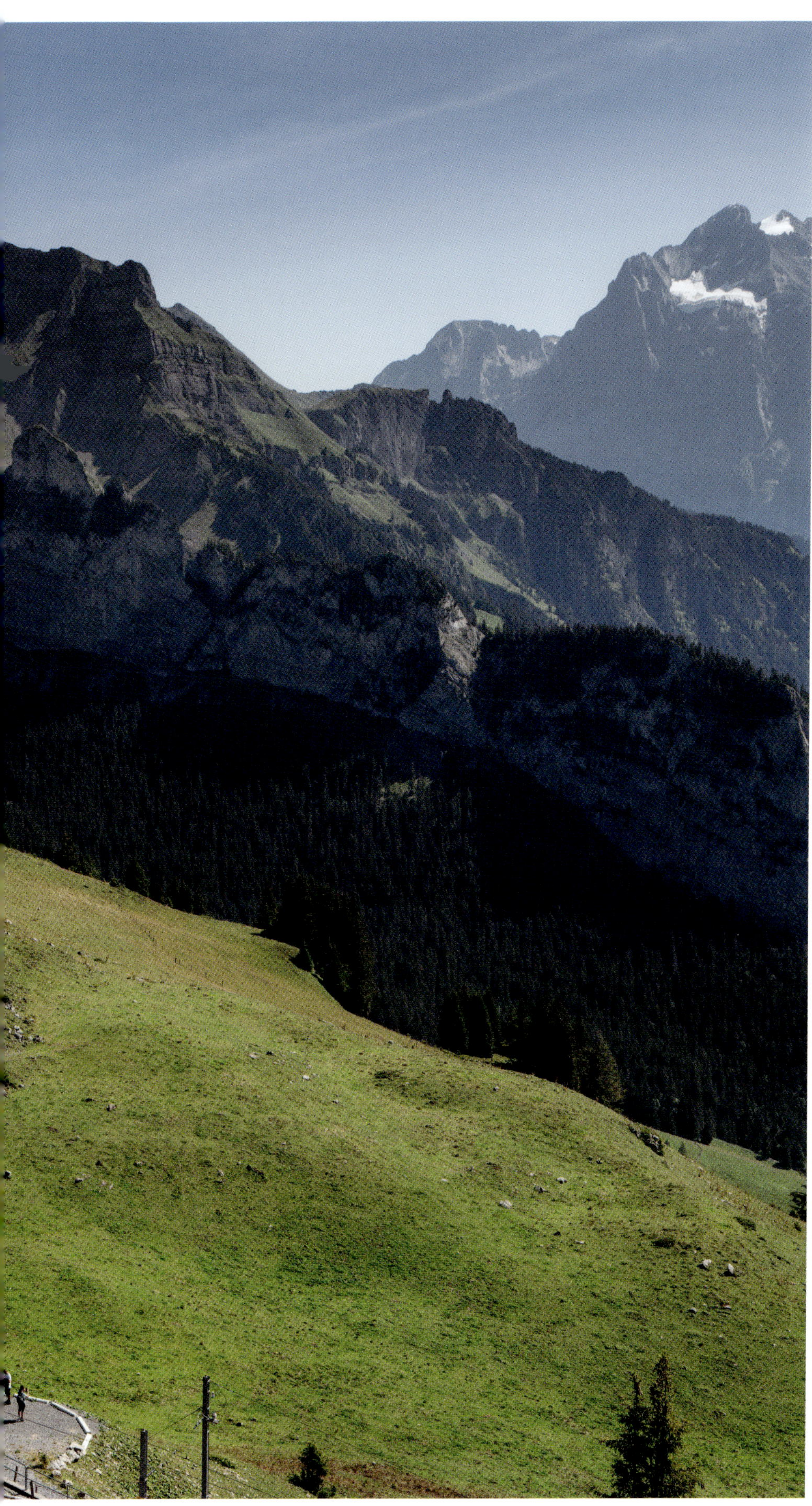

SCHYNIGE PLATTE RAILWAY

The Schynige Platte Railway opens up a first-class view to the high peaks of the Bernese Alps. There are many smaller sights to wonder at here during the summer: The mountain station is only a few steps away from the Alpine Garden. There, more than six hundred different types of plants reflect the diverse flora in the Swiss Alps.

The cliffs of the Schynigen Platte soar into the sky above Alp Bigelti, with the Gumihorn (6,886 feet / 2,099 meters) being the highest point. ▽ ▽

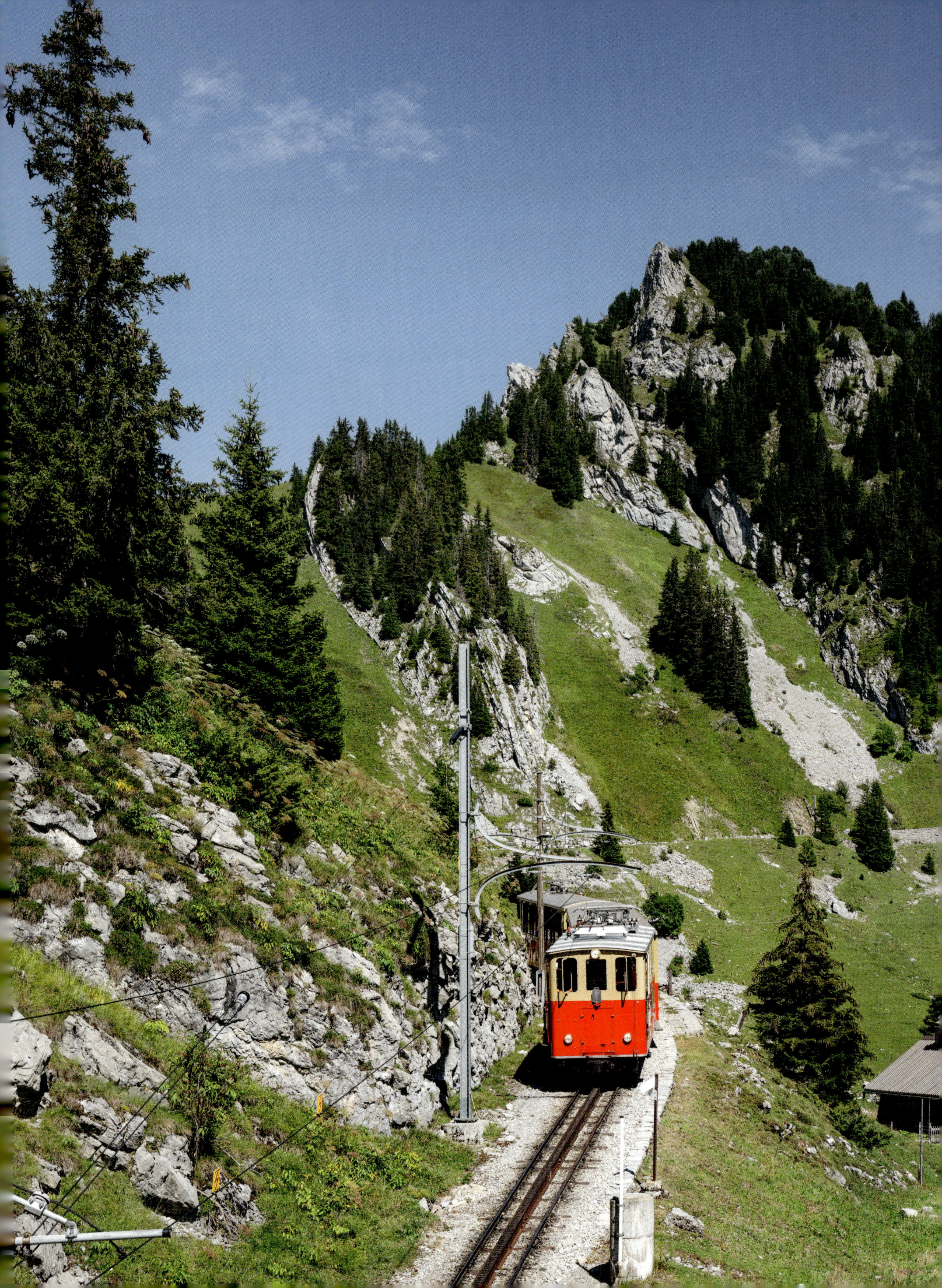

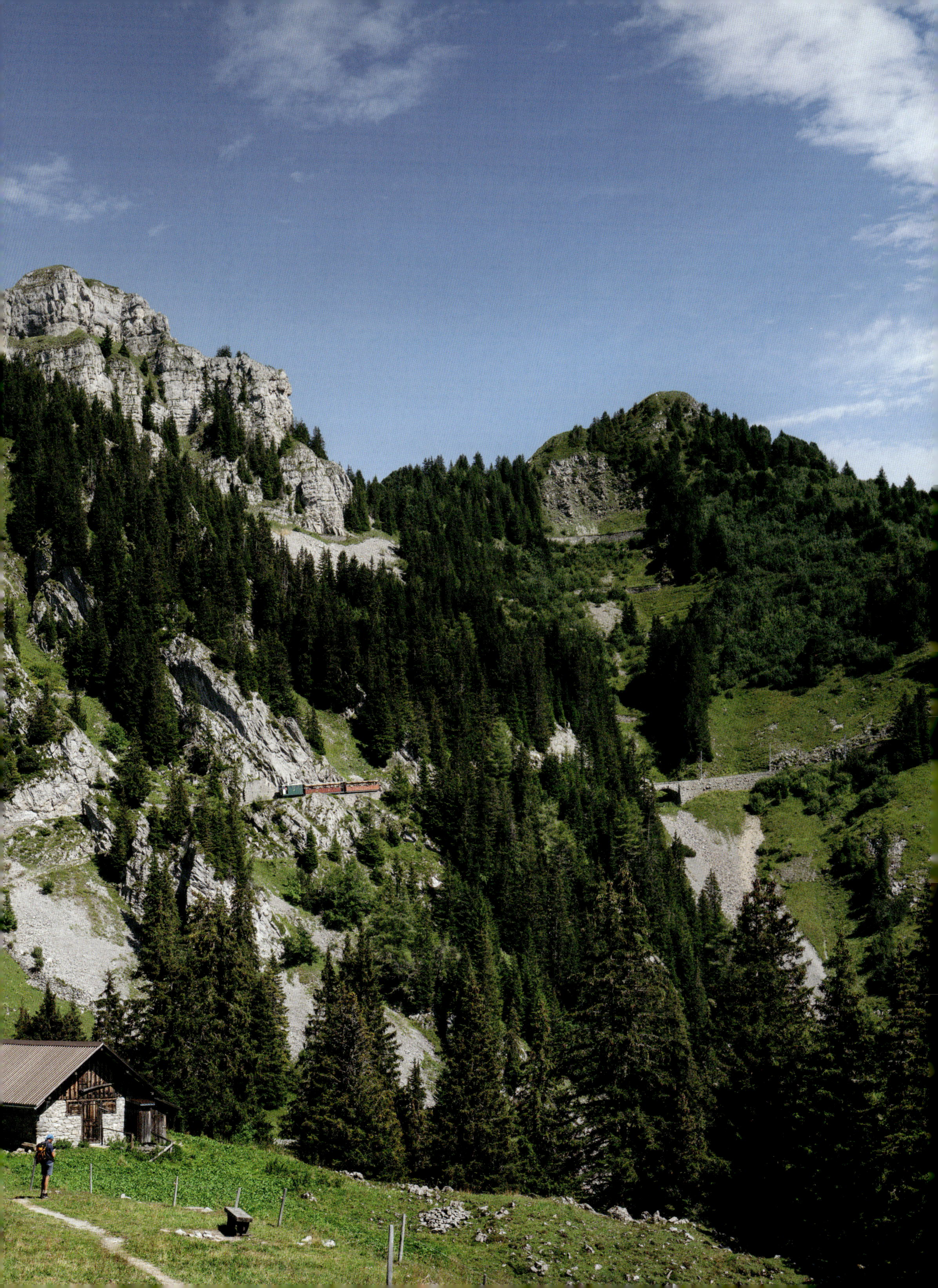

GOTTHARD RAILWAY

THE CLASSIC ROUTE INTO THE SOUTH

The famous *Gotthard Railway* is something like the north–south axis of Switzerland—a route of international importance. And a myth, a literal technical monument carved into stone. Going through the mountain was and is the name of the game, while going to the summit is possible, on the other hand, with the *Rigi Railways* and on the *Monte Generoso Railway*. The *Centovalli Railway* connects the Gotthard route with the Simplon route across national borders.

Myths. They are present all across the world, are anchored in people's souls, and, as a result, are easy to understand. Switzerland is no exception. Heidi represents an idyllic mountain farming world; Tell tells us about the desire for the freedom of the original Swiss. And Gotthard? Another myth, literally carved into stone and far more than just an Alpine crossing. Much of what makes up the essence of the Swiss Confederation can be found in it. The Gotthard Massif is regarded as Switzerland's moated castle; its largest rivers originate there: the Rhine, the Reuss and Aare, the Rhone, and the Ticino. But not only does Gotthard part water; it is also a cultural border: German in the north, Italian in the south, Romansch in the east. And the German Oberwalliser Rotten (Upper Valais Rhone) becomes the French Bas Valais Le Rhône (Lower Valley Rhone). A symbol of unity among all the diversity? When looking back into Swiss history, you find much strife and discord. However, the Swiss were united when it came to threats from abroad, most recently during World War II. Gotthard again became a symbol for Switzerland on guard, a myth. Fate spared the country from having to prove itself in this regard—luckily.

RAILWAY HISTORY

In the middle of the nineteenth century, Switzerland was still a developing country when it came to railroads. In 1847 only a single railway existed. It was economically not very prosperous, which probably was due to the high fare cost: eighty rappens—which at that time was a daily wage—for the 14-mile (23-kilometer) stretch from Zurich to Baden. In the vernacular, the train was soon called the "Spanish Brötli Railway" after a specialty pastry from Baden. Only once a national railway law was passed in 1852 did railway construction really begin. But a north–south connection through Switzerland was still missing. Everyone agreed upon the importance of an Alpine crossing (Germany–Italy), but the path it should take was more controversial. Splügenpass, Gotthard, or even Lötschberg?

Liberal business circles, led by the ubiquitous Zurich politician and entrepreneur Alfred Escher, finally pushed through the second option: the Gotthard line. The contract was awarded to the company of Louis Favre. His project envisaged a 9.3-mile (15-kilometer) summit tunnel between Göschenen and Airolo. The sometimes very difficult terrain on the access routes required many different structures, including several spiral and circular tunnels (Wassen, Leventina). Financial problems repeatedly delayed the construction, and a worker strike (mostly Italian) was brutally put down by force by the military. Louis Favre passed away during construction. In May 1882, ten years after construction began, the massive project was finally completed. The 35-mile-long (56-kilometer-long) new railroad tunnel went into operation 134 years later. Through the base instead of through the summit, as it is now said, the Gotthard obstacle has finally been moved out of the way.

It is still unclear if the historical route will meet its gradual end as a railway museum. The Swiss government rejected an attempt at adding it as a UNESCO World Heritage Site. The reason was that they did not want to guarantee the maintenance required to keep the route in operation. . . . The famous double loop near Wassen with its little church—lost to railway history? The two spiral tunnels between Lavorgo and Giornico, almost one on top of the other—just a memory?

THE RIGI RAILWAYS

Construction in the 1870s wasn't limited to Gotthard but also extended to Mount Rigi (5,896 feet / 1,797 meters). The famous scenic mountain in central Switzerland got not just one but two cogwheel railways. In 1871 the route originating in Vitznau on Lake Lucerne went into operation; four years later came the Arth-Rigi Railway. Three days after its maiden voyage, the Grandhotel Schreiber opened its doors on Rigi Kulm; according to the advertisement, it was an "architecturally magnificent building with three hundred beds, planned and executed by Mr. Ed. Davinet. Spacious,

elegant halls, restaurant." With the Rigi Railways, mass tourism also arrived at the top of the mountain. A gold rush sort of atmosphere spread, and with it came construction and investment. There was an abrupt stop with the outbreak of World War I, and all the much-too-large hotel boxes were later demolished. The Schweizer Heimatbund, traditionally conservative and looking for a return to the idyllic "Heidi" Switzerland, played a large role in this radical course of action. The high-altitude railway from Rigi Kaltbad to Scheidegg was also shut down; today, hikers and bikers make their way along the old tracks.

The hilly landscape between Lago Maggiore and Mendrisiotto was once a true railway country. Multiple lines connected cities and waterfront locations, such as Luino with Ponte Tresa (where you could connect to Lugano) or Varese with Porto Ceresio and Ponte Tresa. There is not much remaining; the funicular railway up to the local mountain of Varese, the Monte Campo dei Fiori (4,022 feet / 1,226 meters), was at least partially reactivated a few years ago.

There is a railway that still exists today that crosses national borders, the Centovalli Railway. The name says it all: one hundred valleys. However, gorges are probably a better characterization of the topography of the Melezza Valley between Intragna and Camedo. Behind the border you do find a valley, and on the ride to Domodossola, travelers have a clear view of the Valais Alps. What a contrast!

Between two tunnels, the upper Meienreuss Bridge spans across Wildbach. At the top of the picture is the Sustenstrasse.

The most interesting part of the route from a railway perspective is between Cavigliano and the Italian border, where the train passes through a total of twenty tunnels and over five longer bridges. The most beautiful structure: the 433-foot (132-meter) iron bridge near Intragna.

THE "RIGI OF TICINO"

The counterpart to Mount Rigi in central Switzerland lies in Ticino, also on the edge of the Alps, but in the south: Monte Generoso (5,581 feet / 1,701 meters). It is almost exactly as tall and offers a similarly impressive view—and a mountain railway. In contrast to the Rigi Railways, it was almost always in the red and went bankrupt on several occasions. The people of Ticino have Gottlieb Duttweiler, the legendary founder of the Migros Group, to thank for the fact that it is still running today. He bought the "Ferrovia Monte Generoso" after learning in 1941 that it would be discontinued. In 1954 the approximately 5.5-mile (9-kilometer) cogwheel railway, up to 22 percent steep, was switched to diesel, and in 1982 the route was electrified. Since 2017, the Fiore di Pietra, an octagonal glass-and-concrete building, has been a landmark next to the mountain station. Mario Botta, a world-renowned architect, was probably inspired by the unusually rich flora of the mountain massif when designing his "stone flower."

A hot tip: If you're feeling nostalgic, book a trip during the summer in an open car led by the steam engine from 1890. It's an unforgettable experience for true railway enthusiasts!

>> So always climbing, you come to the heights of
The Gotthard, where the eternal lakes are,
Which are filled by the streams of heaven themselves.
There you bid farewell to German soil,
And another stream leads you merrily down
To the land of Italy, the promised land to you. <<

From *William Tell* by Friedrich Schiller (1759–1805)

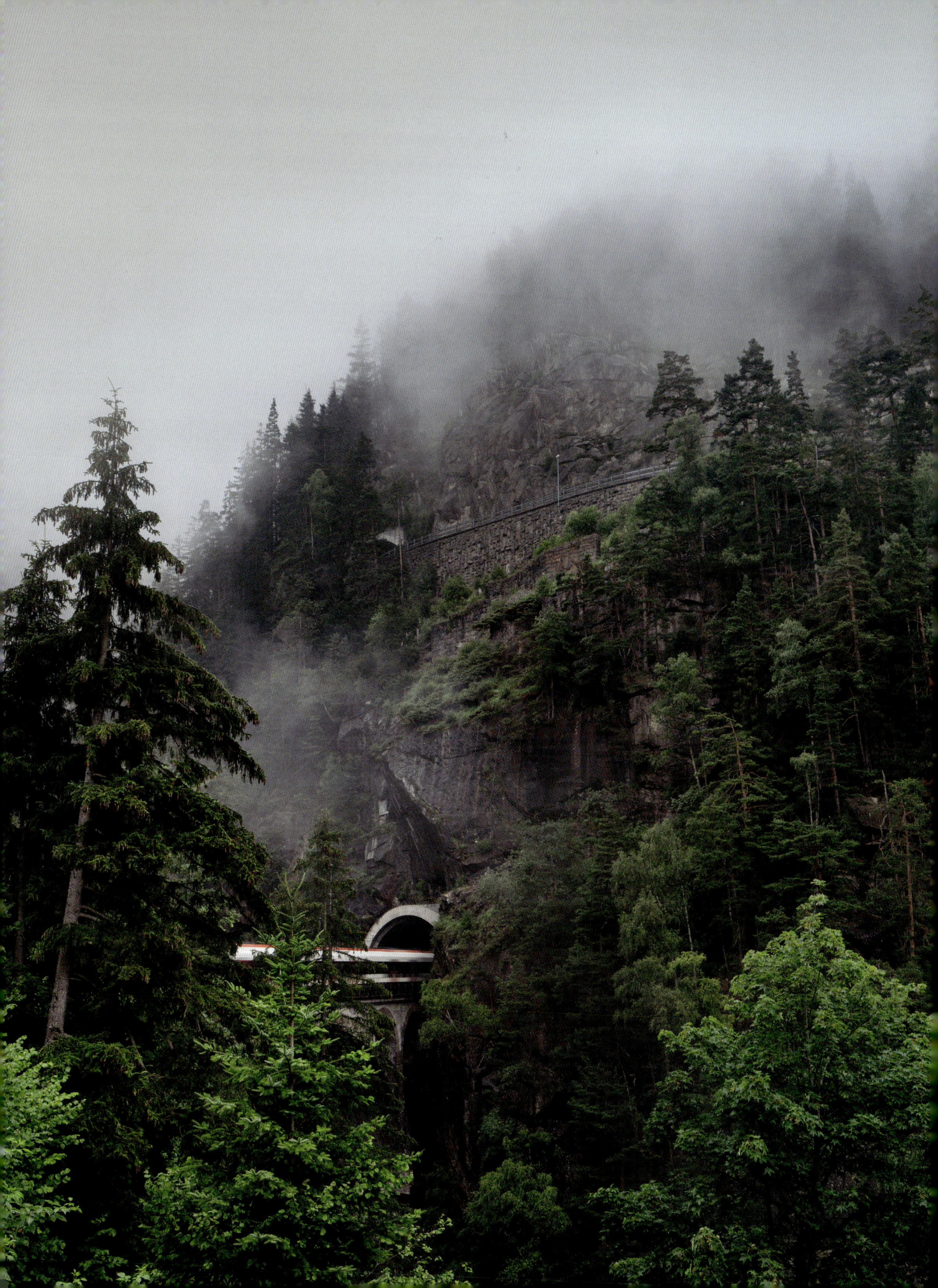

The Chärstelenbach Bridge is the longest bridge structure on the northern ramp of the Gotthard line, at 416.6 feet (127 meters). It crosses the Maderanertal at its outlet near Amsteg. The core of its construction dates to the 1870s, but it has since been remodeled many times. When the iron truss bridge was electrified, fish-bellied girders were installed for stability. In 1972 the bridge was replaced with an iron-and-concrete structure. ▷

You can find crocodiles not only in a Swiss zoo but also every now and then on the Gotthard Railway. However, they are made of iron and significantly larger than a Crocodilia—and much stronger. The Ce 6/8 II 14 253, built in 1919, brings an impressive 3,650 horse-power to the tracks. It is still in use today on the Gotthard line as the traction engine for the historical saloon wagons of the Swiss Federal Railways (Schweizerische Bundesbahnen, SBB), a special trip starting in Erstfeld. In the picture is the Intschi-Reussbrücke, which is the highest bridge at 253 feet (77 meters) between Lake Lucerne and Chiasso. ▽

Near Pfaffensprung, the Gotthard Railway gains altitude in an almost 1-mile-long (1.6-kilometer-long) spiral tunnel before heading for the north portal of the Gotthard Tunnel via two more loop tunnels near Wassen (3,002 feet / 915 meters). You can see the small church in Wassen three different times from very different perspec-tives—a famous view. ▽ ▽

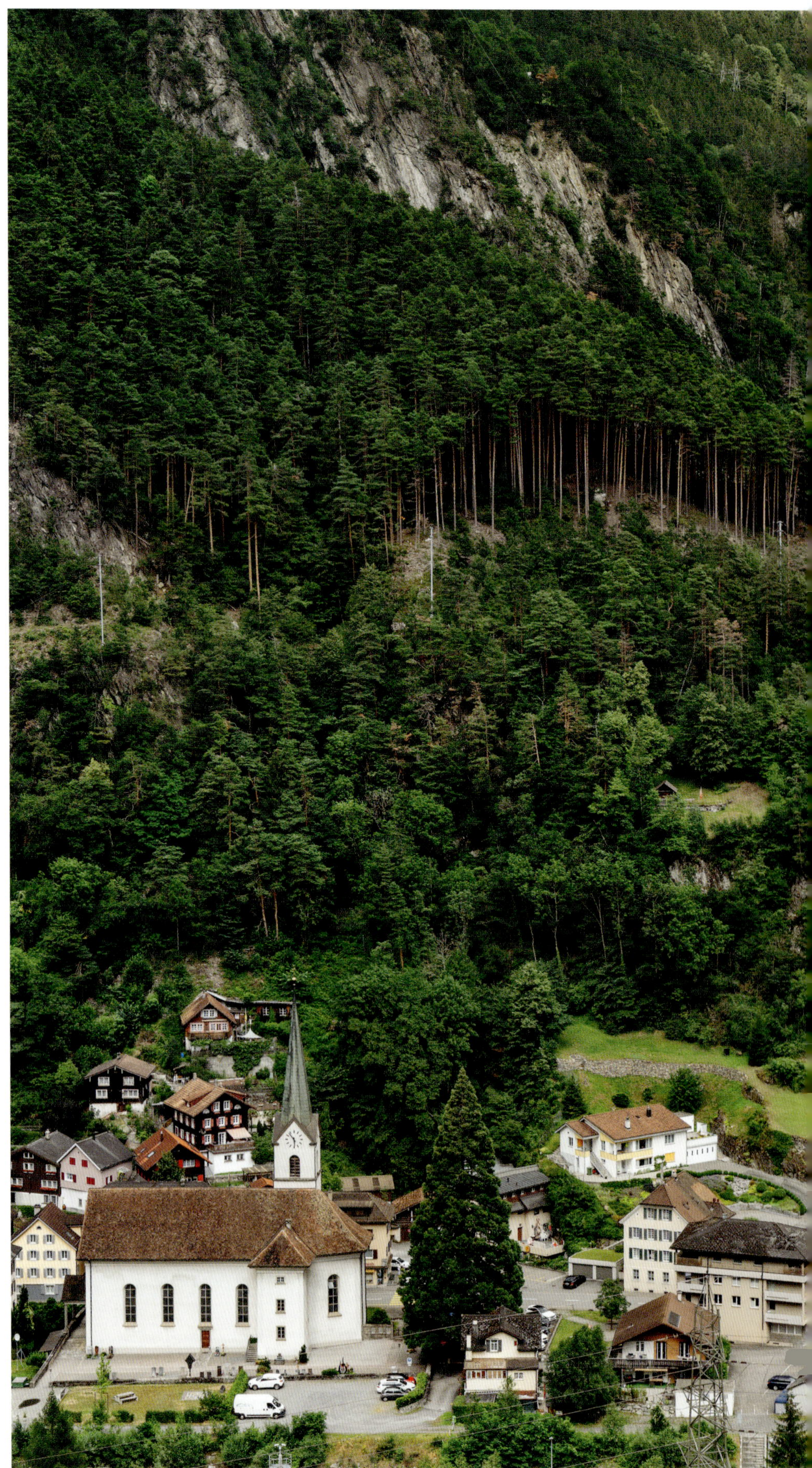

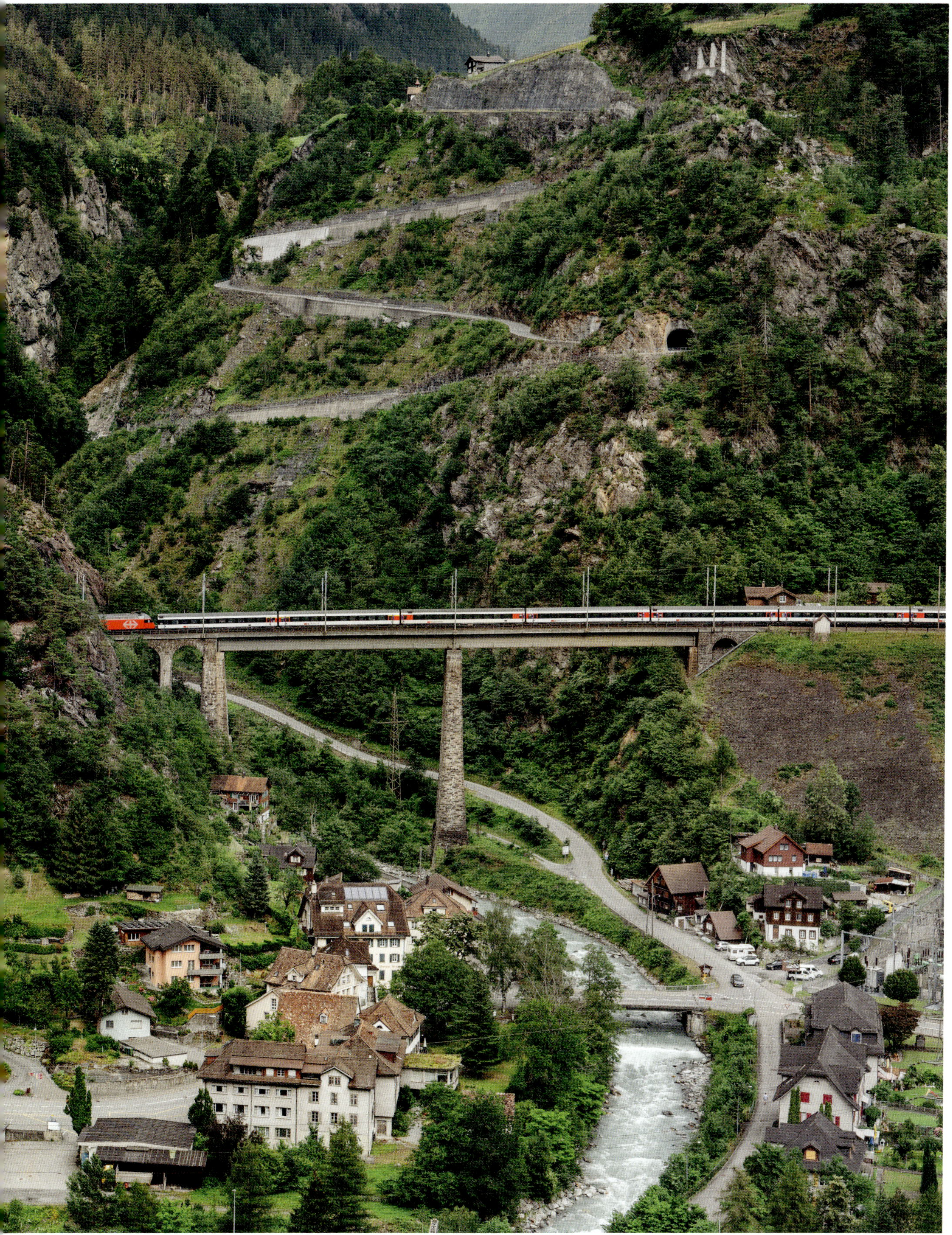

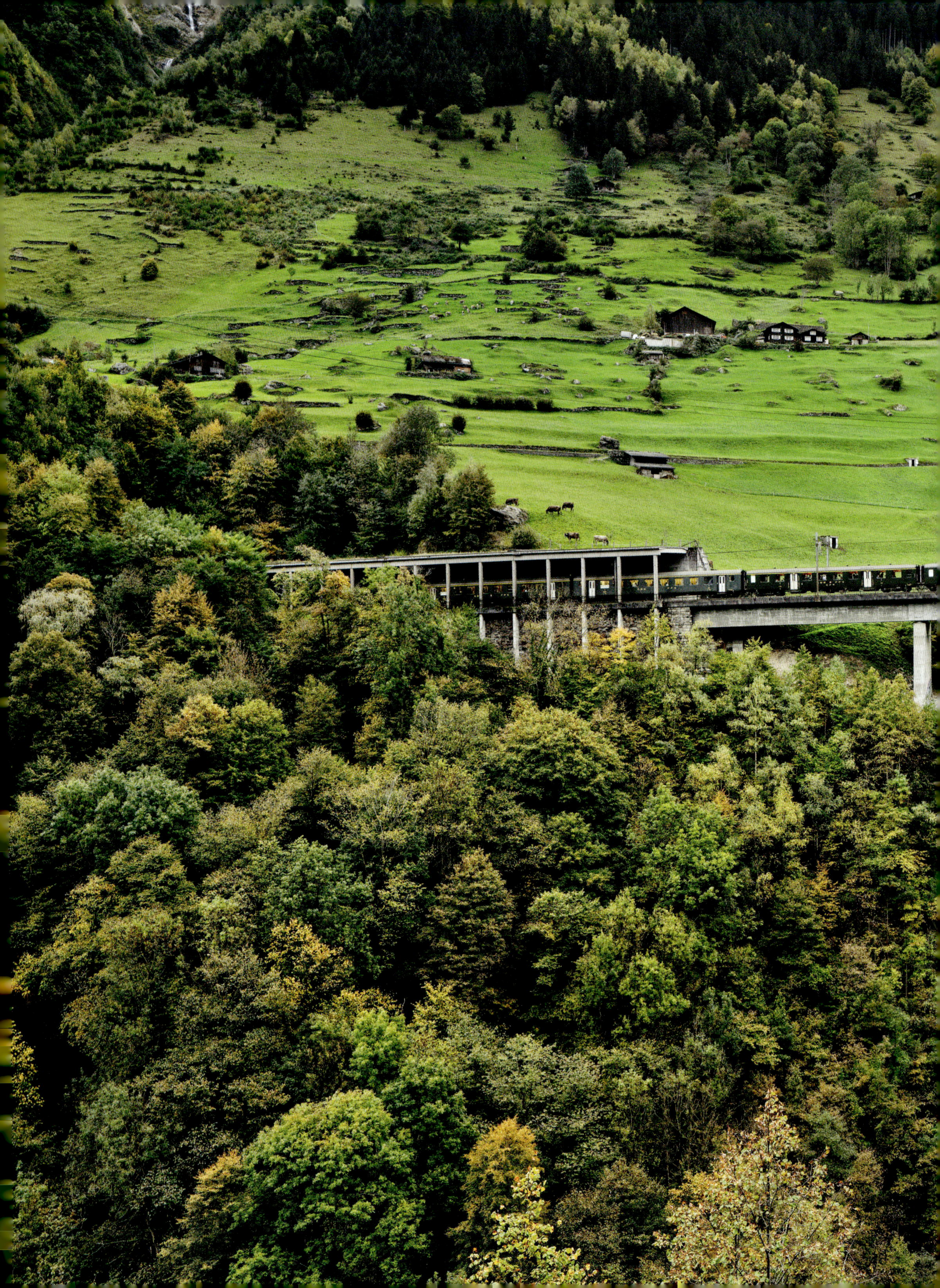

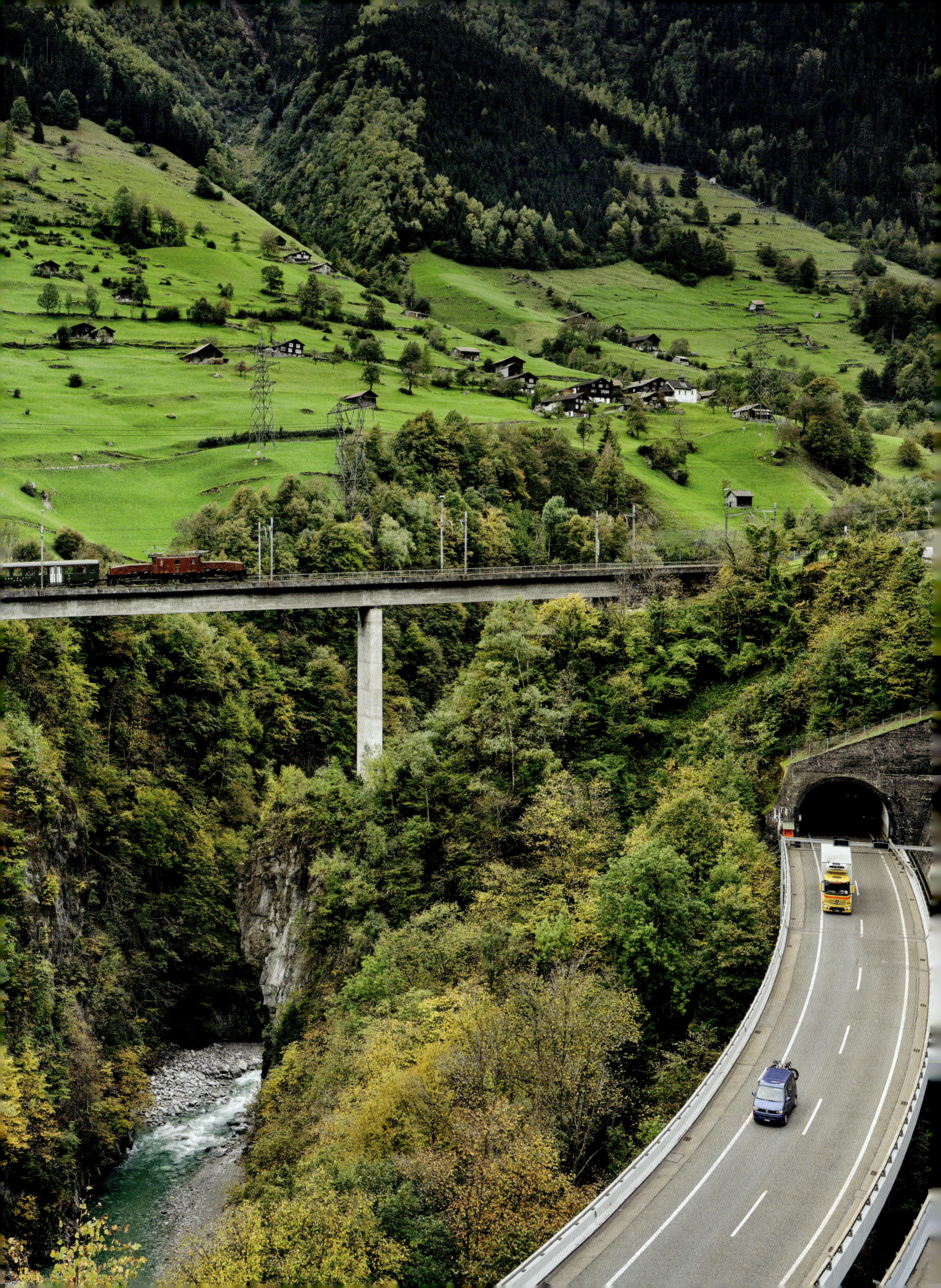

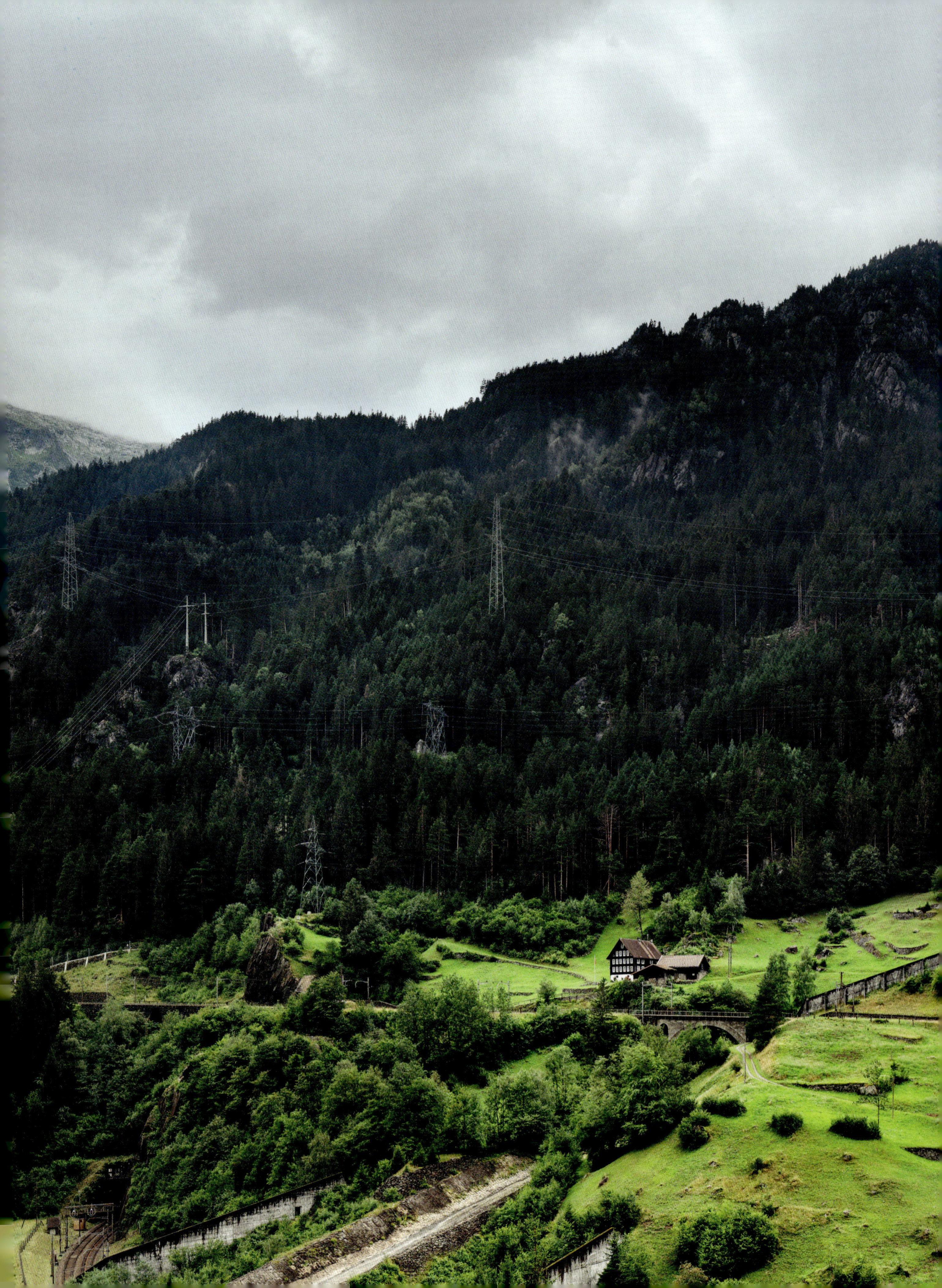

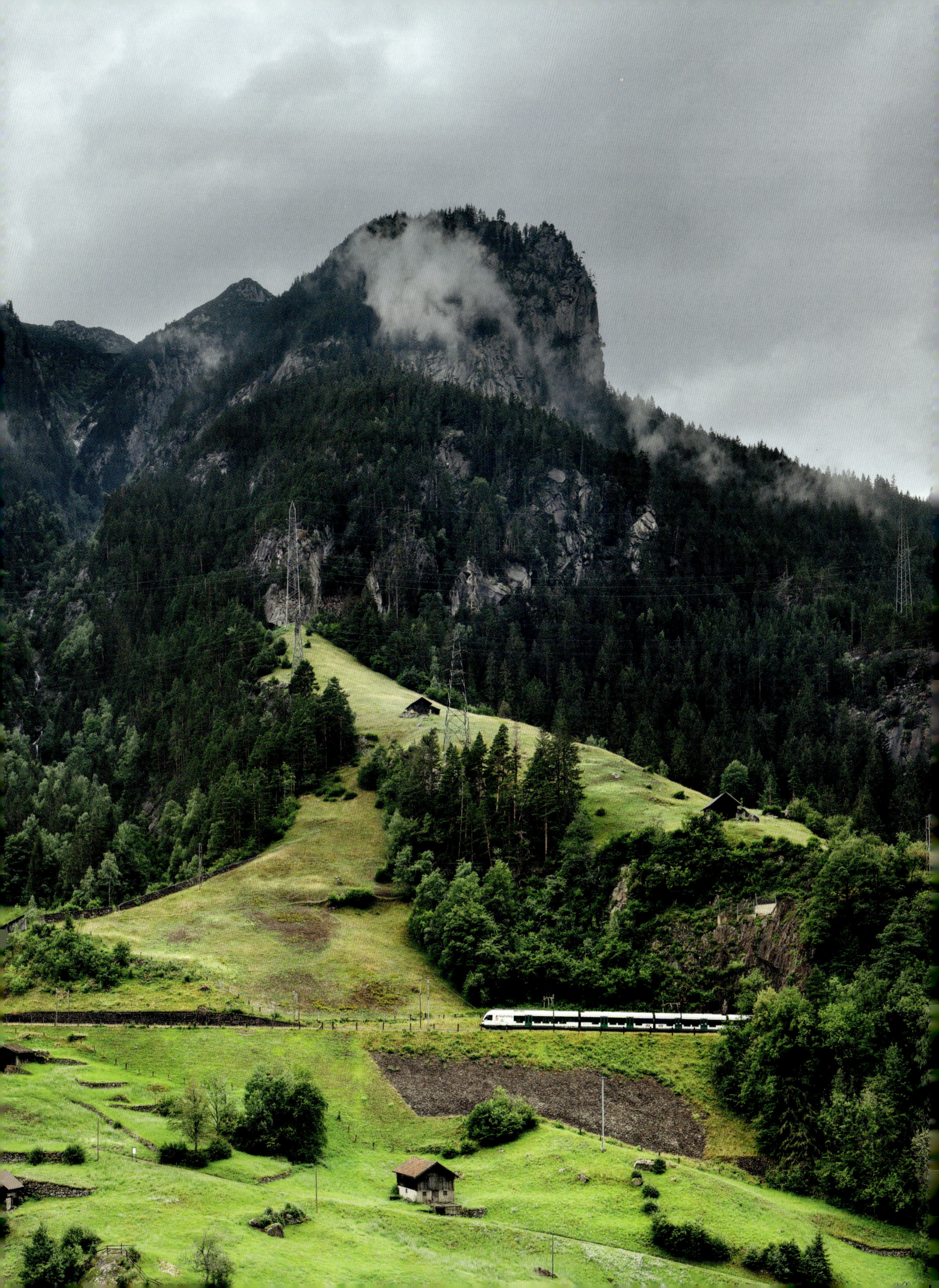

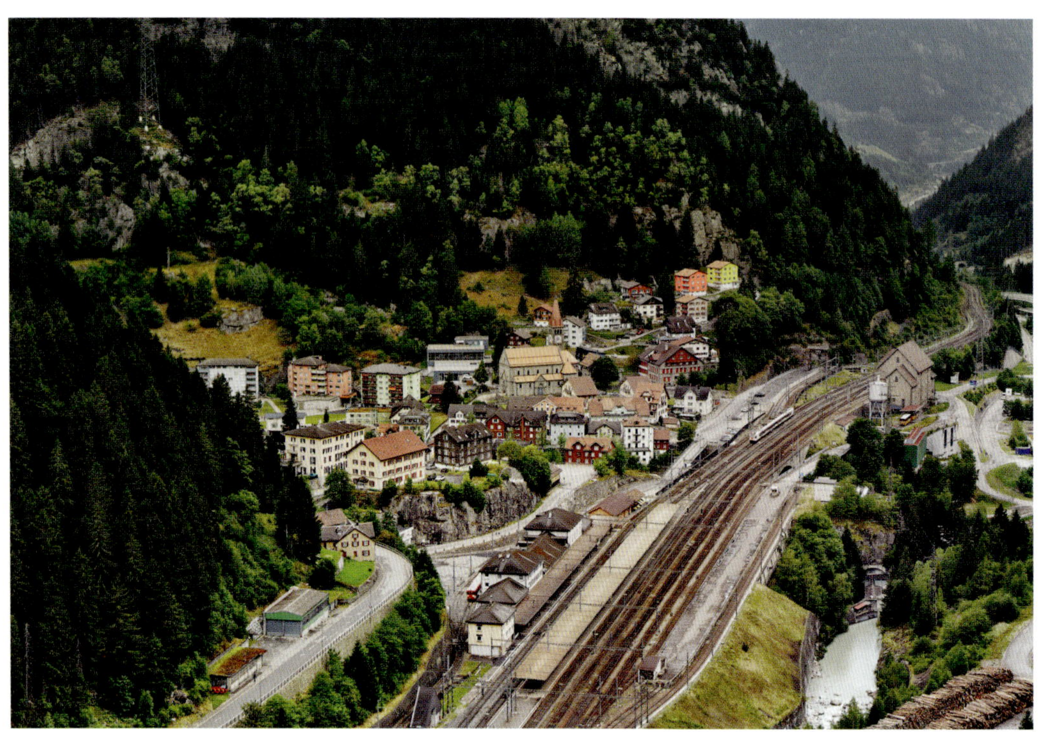

GOTTHARD RAILWAY

Göschenen has seen better days; since the opening of the Gotthard
Base Tunnel, long-distance trains have stopped traveling along the
old transit route. In the meantime, a part of the station tracks has been
dismantled. In the long term, it is possible that routine traffic through
the area could be stopped completely, and the "project of the century"
could simply become a nostalgic train. The Gotthard Railway of Louis
Favre—a victim of technological progress? △

The church in Wassen, an eye-catcher three times on the trip up to
Göschenen: before, between, and after the two looping tunnels of
Wattingen and Leggistein. ▷

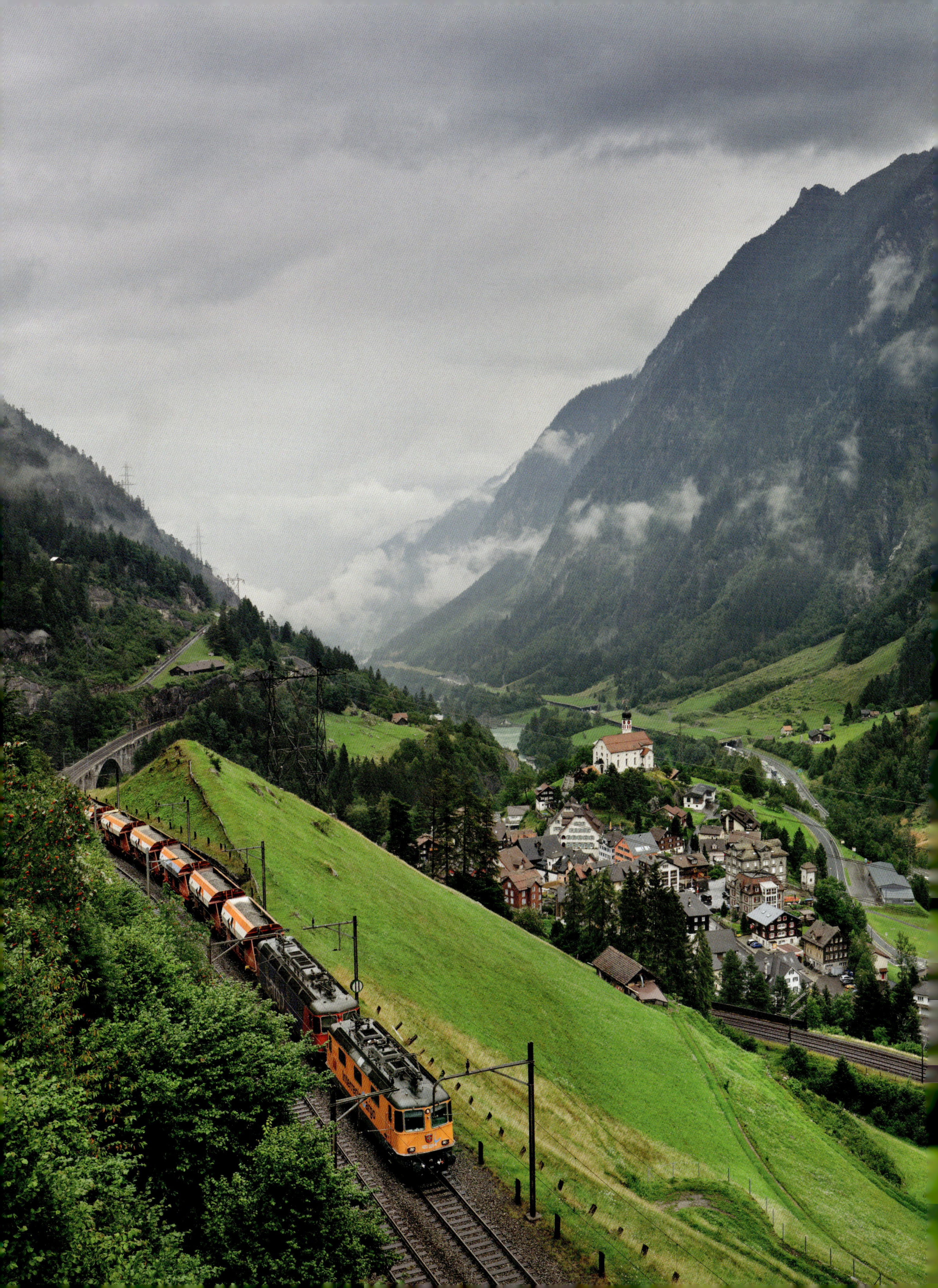

GOTTHARD RAILWAY

Streets and railways overcome
the striking valley slope (Piottino)
near Dazio Grande, the great
customs house, with impressively
engineered structures: the
roads with their tight bends and
the Gotthard line through the
1-mile-long (1.6-kilometer-long)
Freggio Tunnel.

One and a half centuries of transportation history at the Biaschina
Gorge in one picture: In 1830
the street through Leventina was
completed, in 1882 the Gotthard
Railway was opened, and in 1986
the last missing piece of the A2
highway was completed. The first
mail car drove over the pass in
1922, and today more than six
million passenger cars use the
Gotthard Road Tunnel each year.
▽ ▽

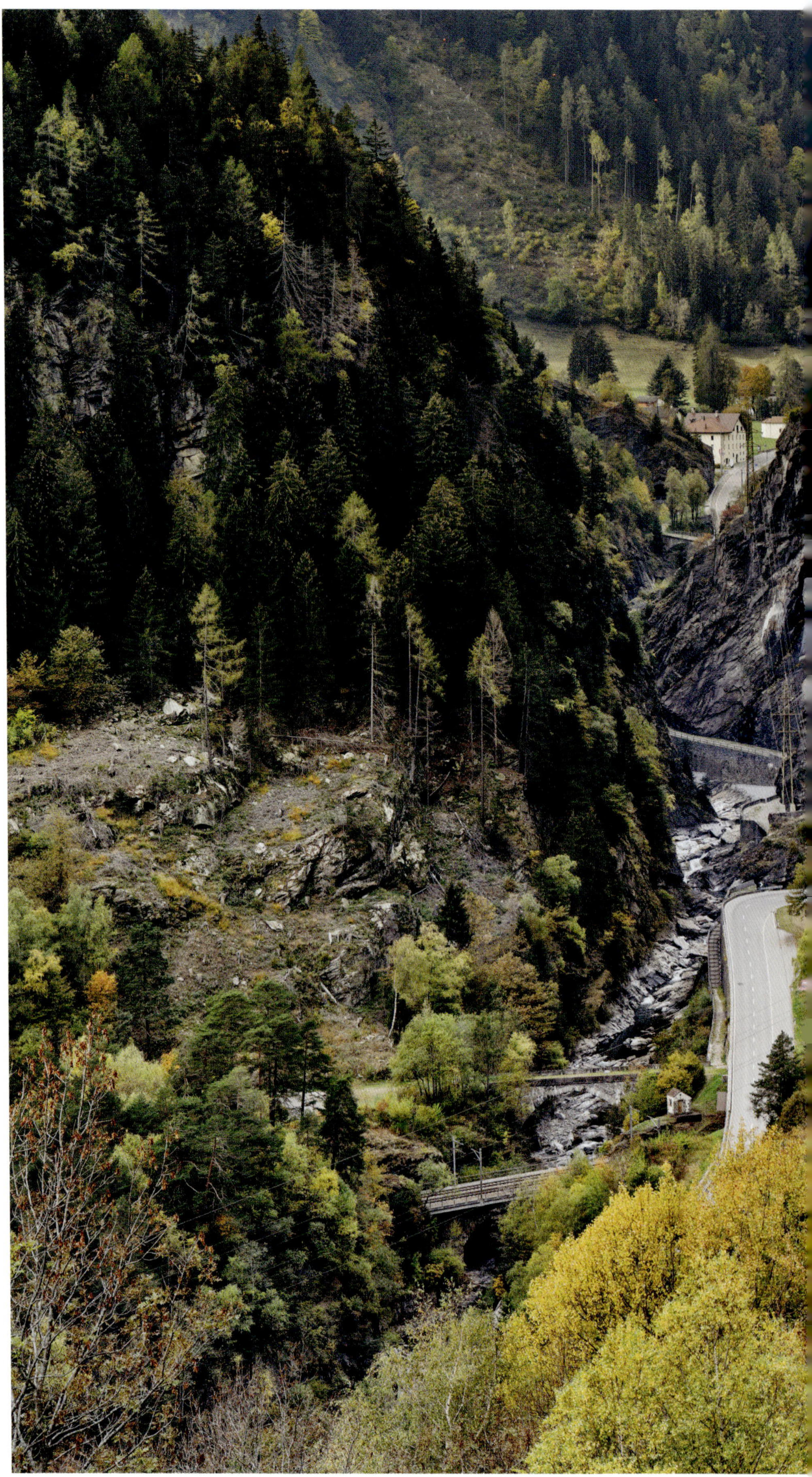

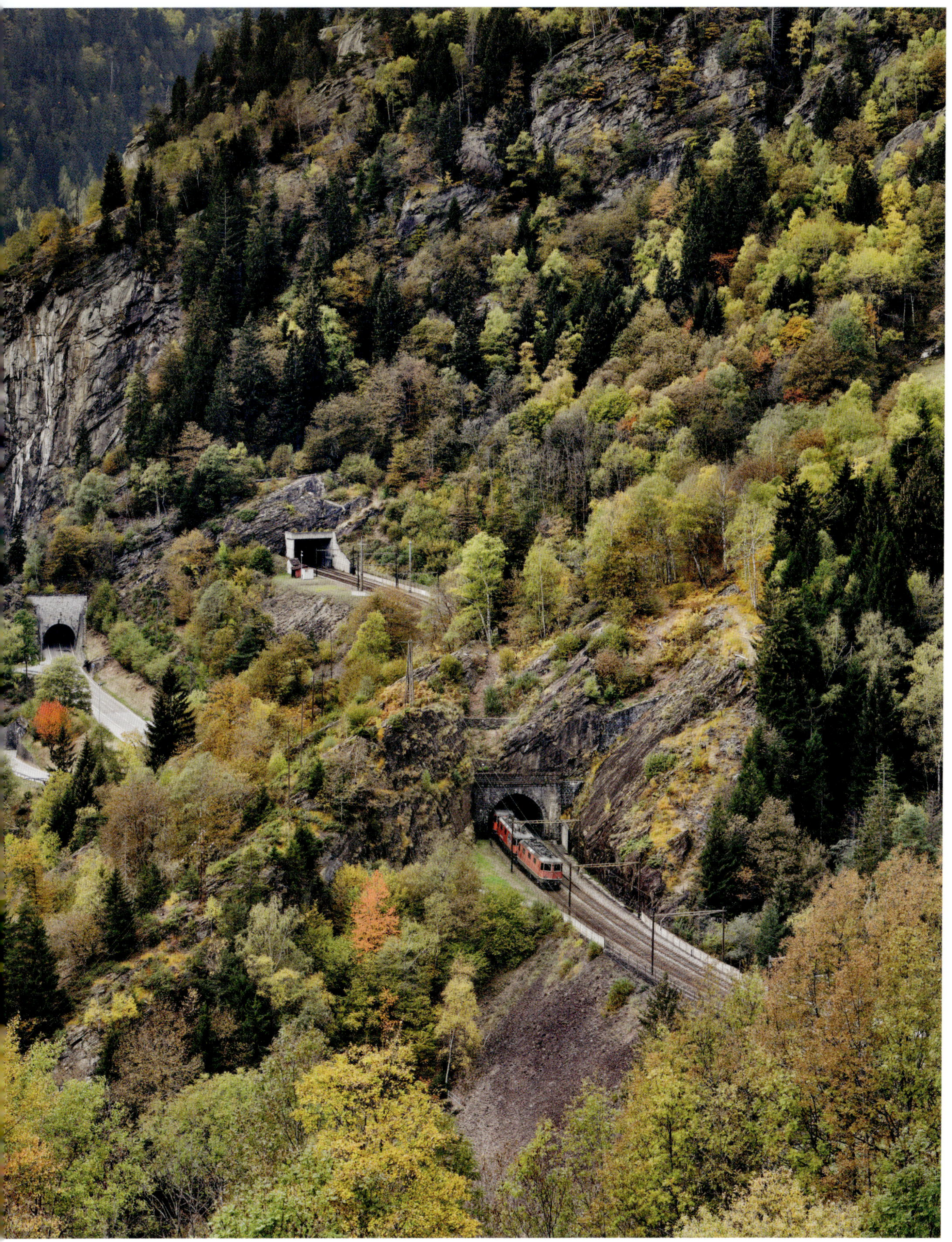

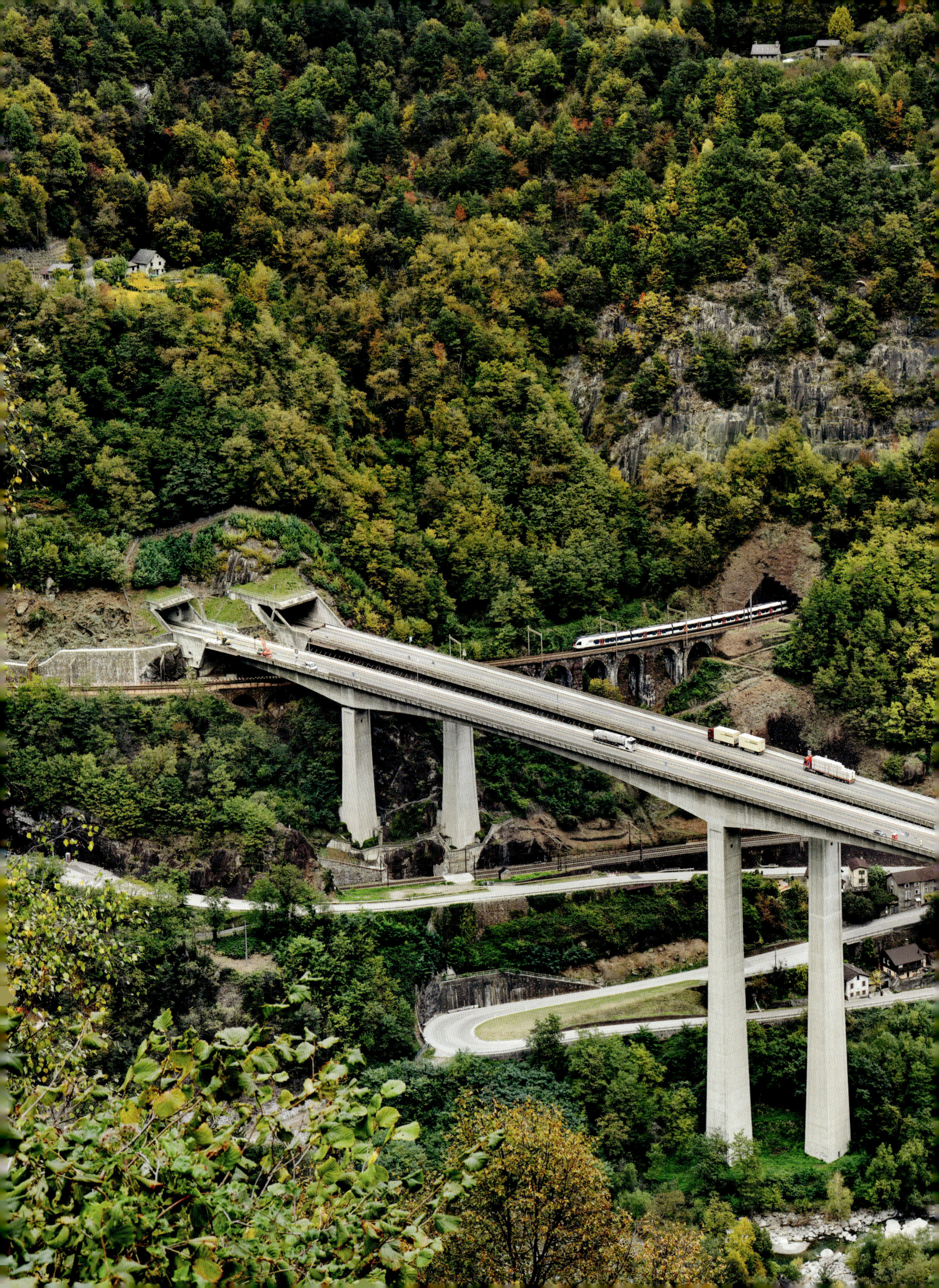

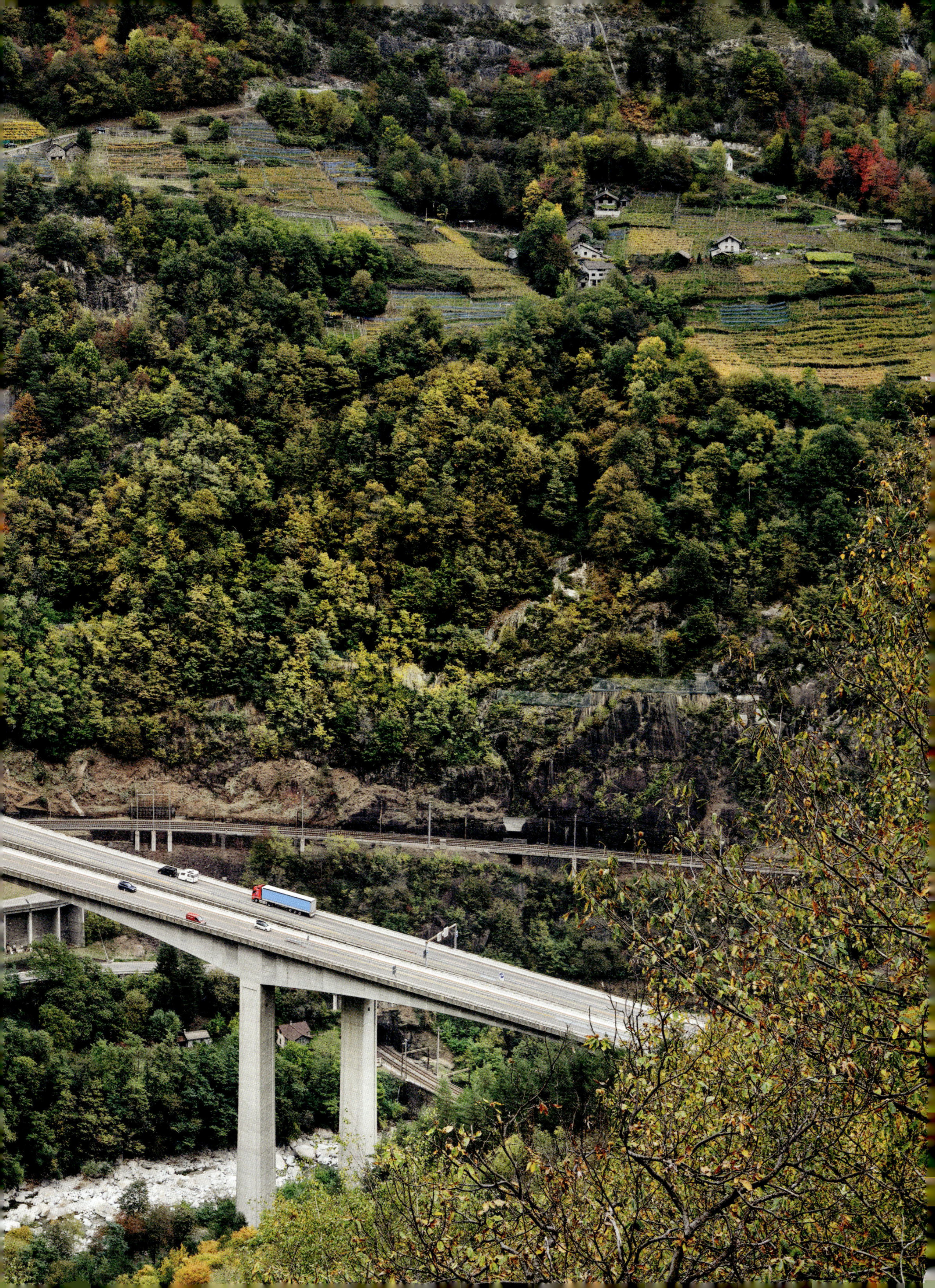

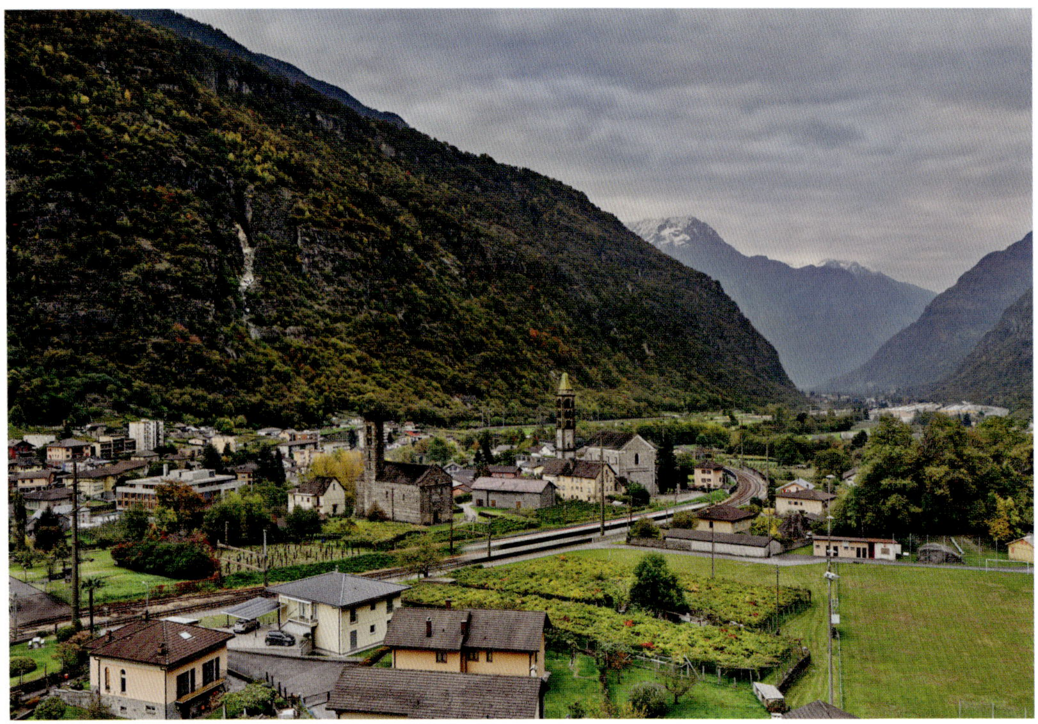

GOTTHARD RAILWAY

In Giornico, the mountain route of the Gotthard Railway comes to an end; the southern portal of the Gotthard Base Tunnel is in the neighboring town of Bodio. Long-distance trains spend only seventeen minutes in the 35-mile-long (57-kilometer-long) tunnel, when the same trip on the old route from Altdorf to Biasca would have taken an hour and a half. Trains don't stop in Giornico anymore, which is a shame because the little town would definitely be worth a visit. The San Nicolao church (*left*) is from the twelfth century and is considered the finest example of Lombard Romanesque in the Ticino. △

The Gotthard Railway and the A2 highway cross in the Leventina multiple times, at and inside the mountain. Here, they cross at the exit of the Piottino Gorge above Faido. ▷

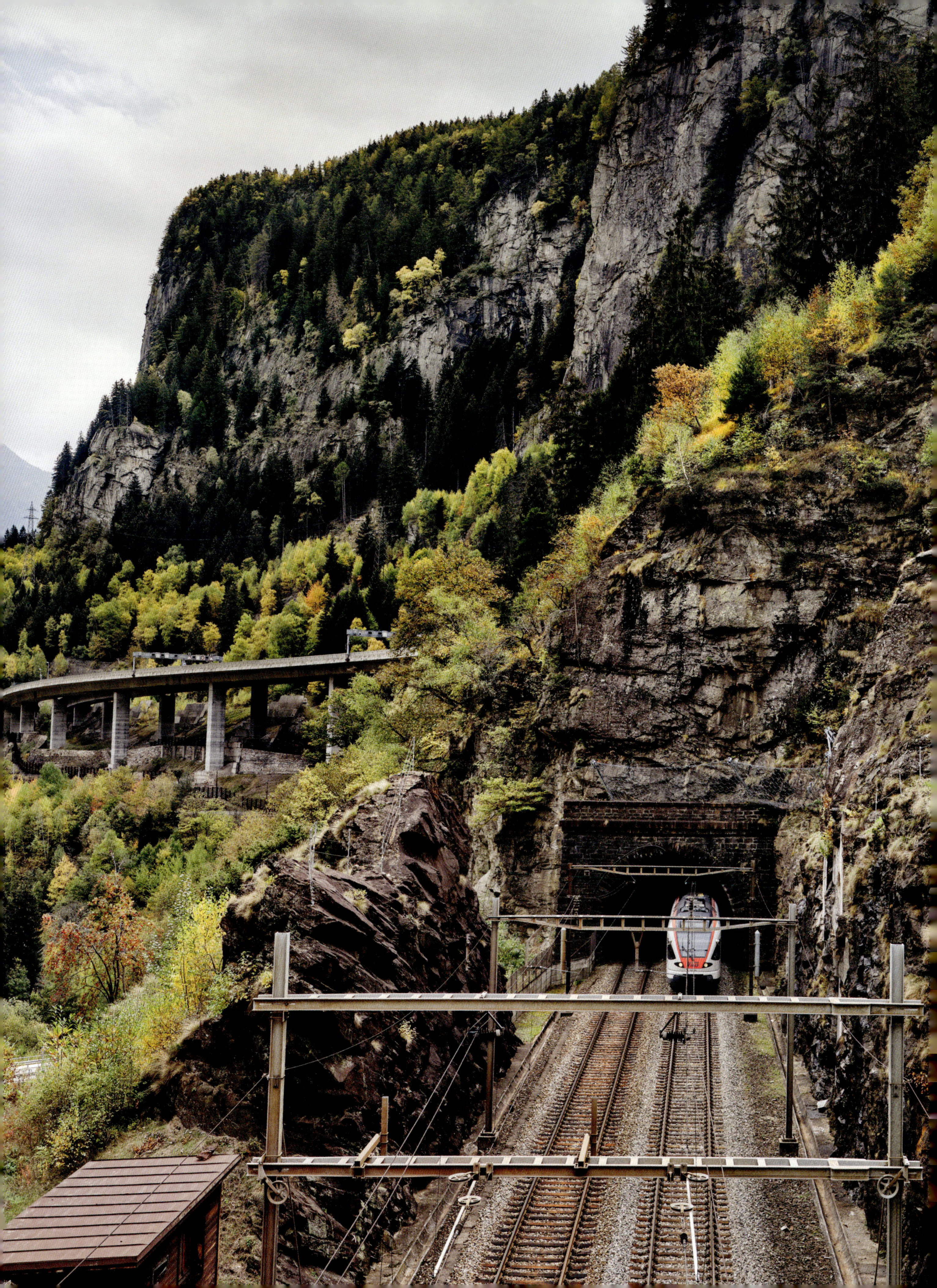

Red or blue? Both Rigi cogwheel railways, starting from Arth Goldau (blue) and Vitznau (red) make their way on separate tracks to the Rigi Kulm mountain station just under the peak of Mount Rigi (5,896 feet / 1,797 meters). Pedestrians take the comfortably developed Kulm Trail. Left upon the horizon is the Stanserhorn, and in the center is the Pilatus, both of which can also be reached by summit railways. To the right is Lake Lucerne with the Bay of Lucerne.

CENTOVALLI RAILWAY

The Ruinacci Viaduct is one of the most beautiful bridge structures of the Centovalli Railway. The 190-foot-long (58-meter-long) iron structure spans a rift high above the Palagnedra Reservoir. A little farther on, the train pulls into the border station of Camedo. ▽ ▽

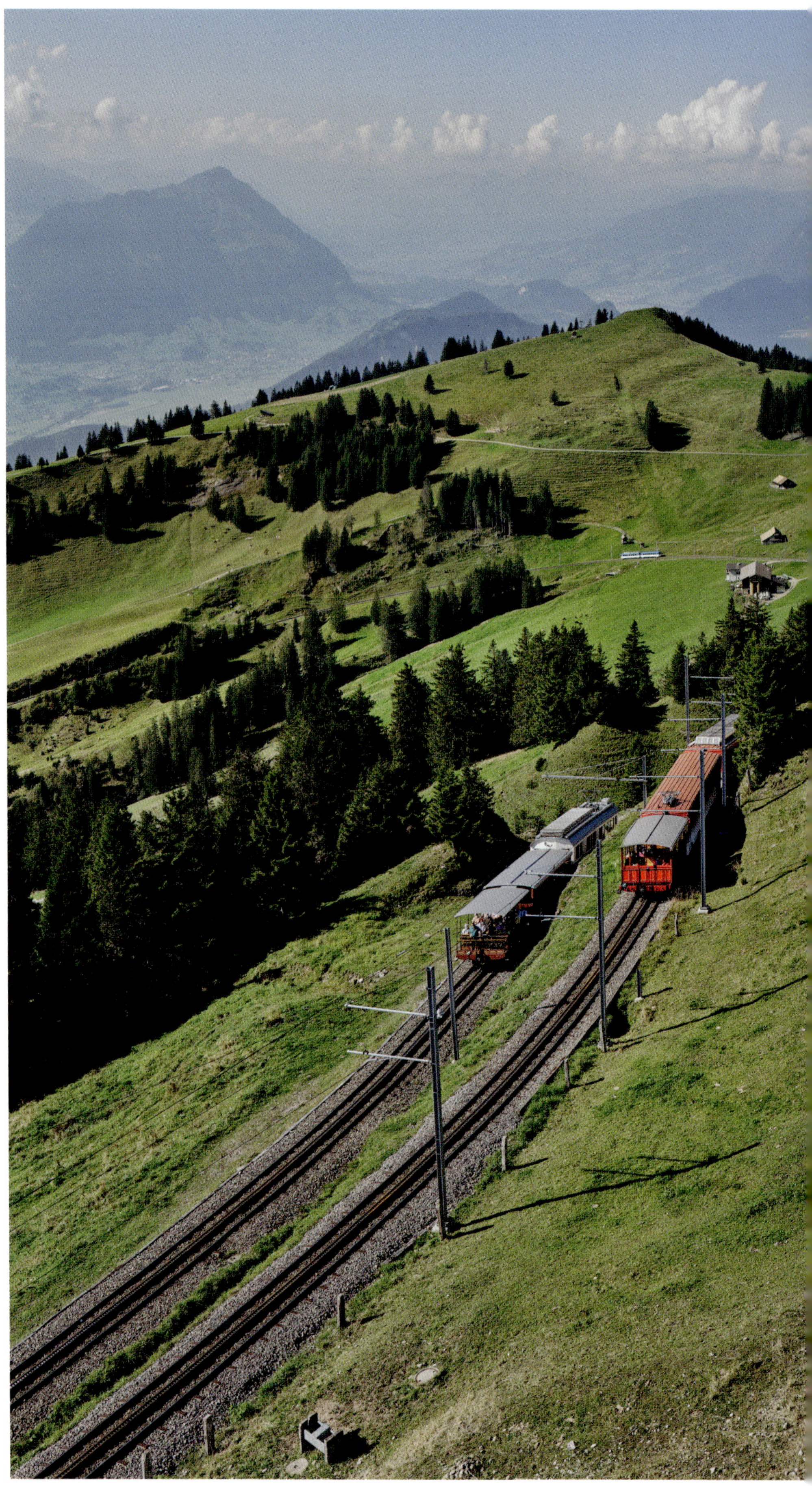

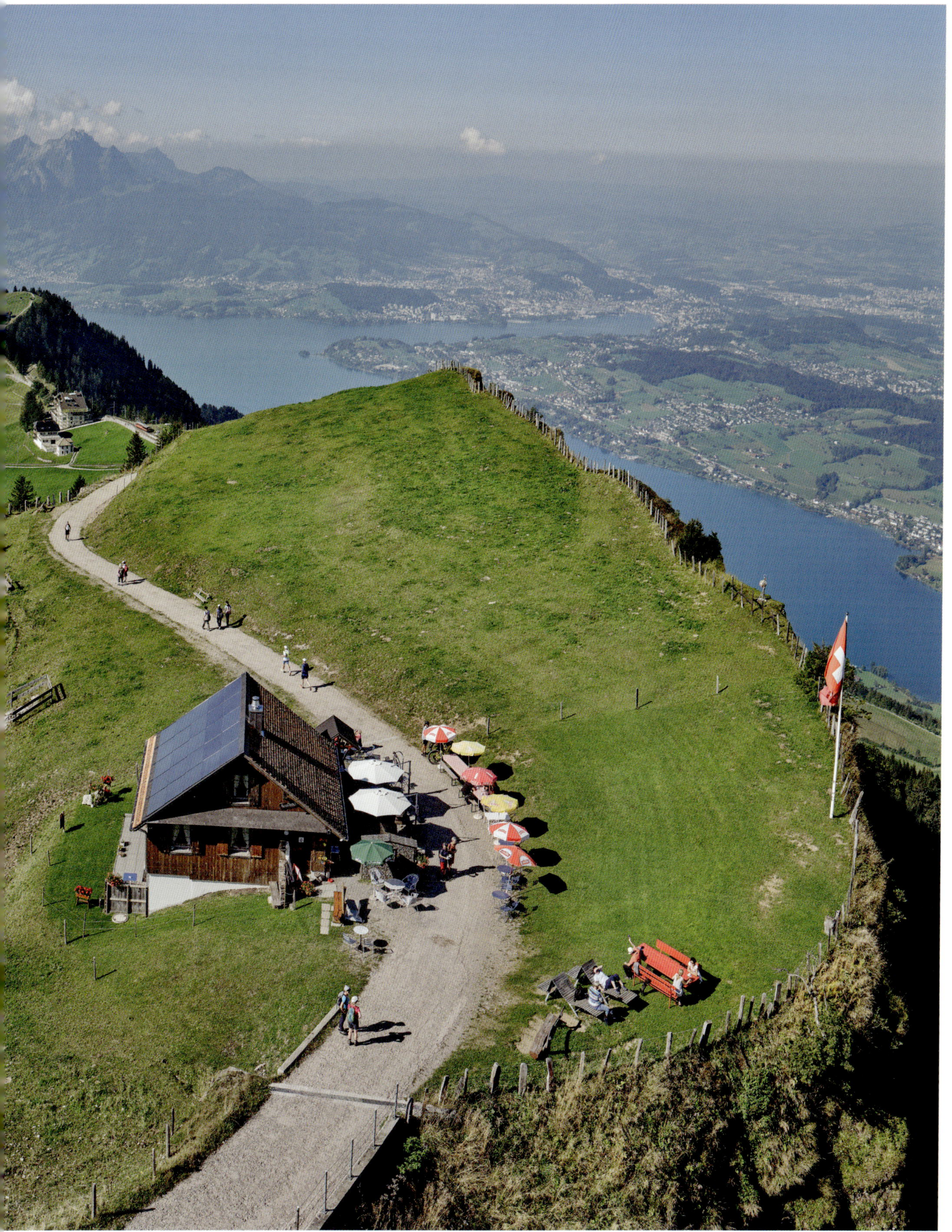

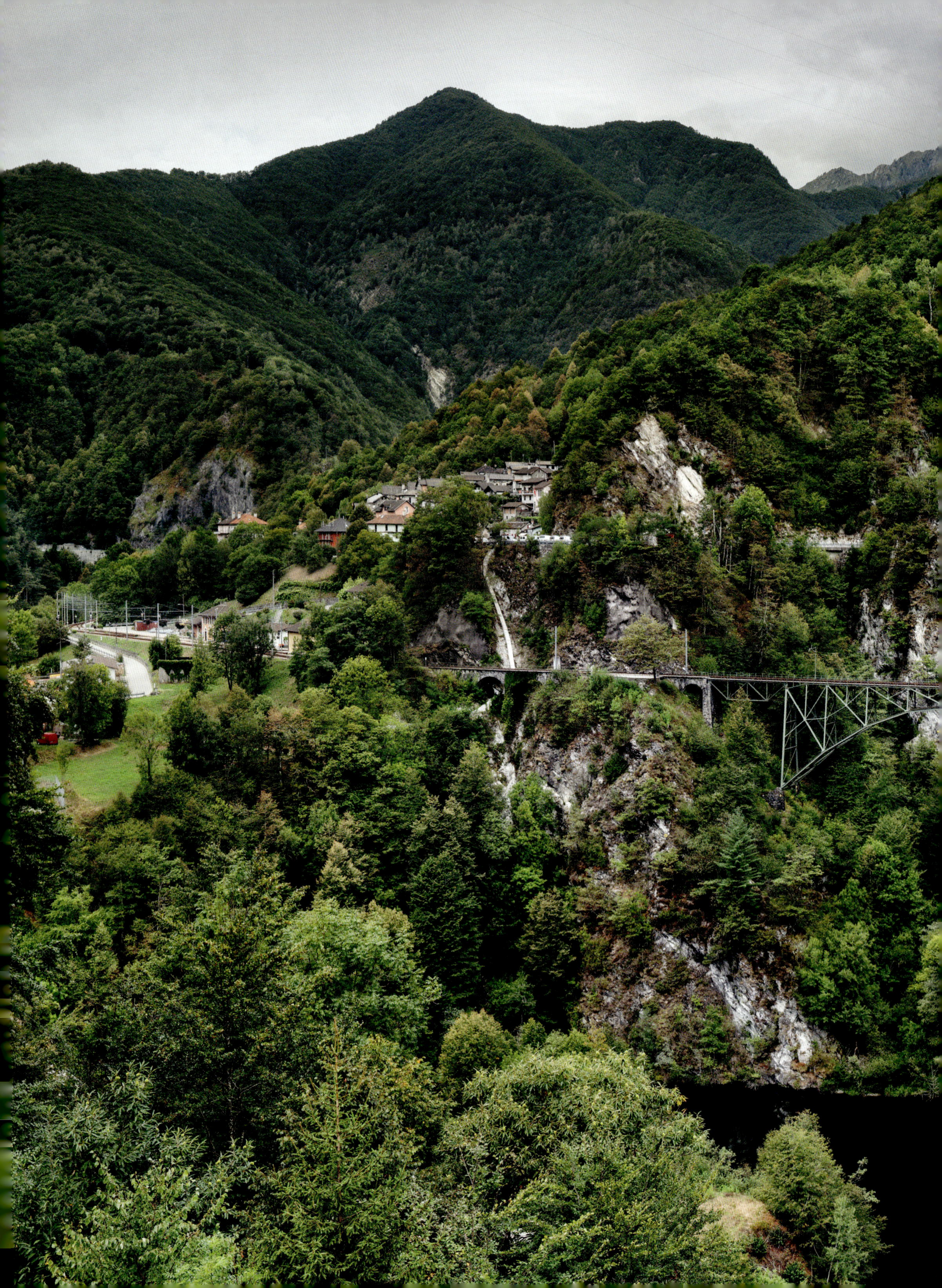

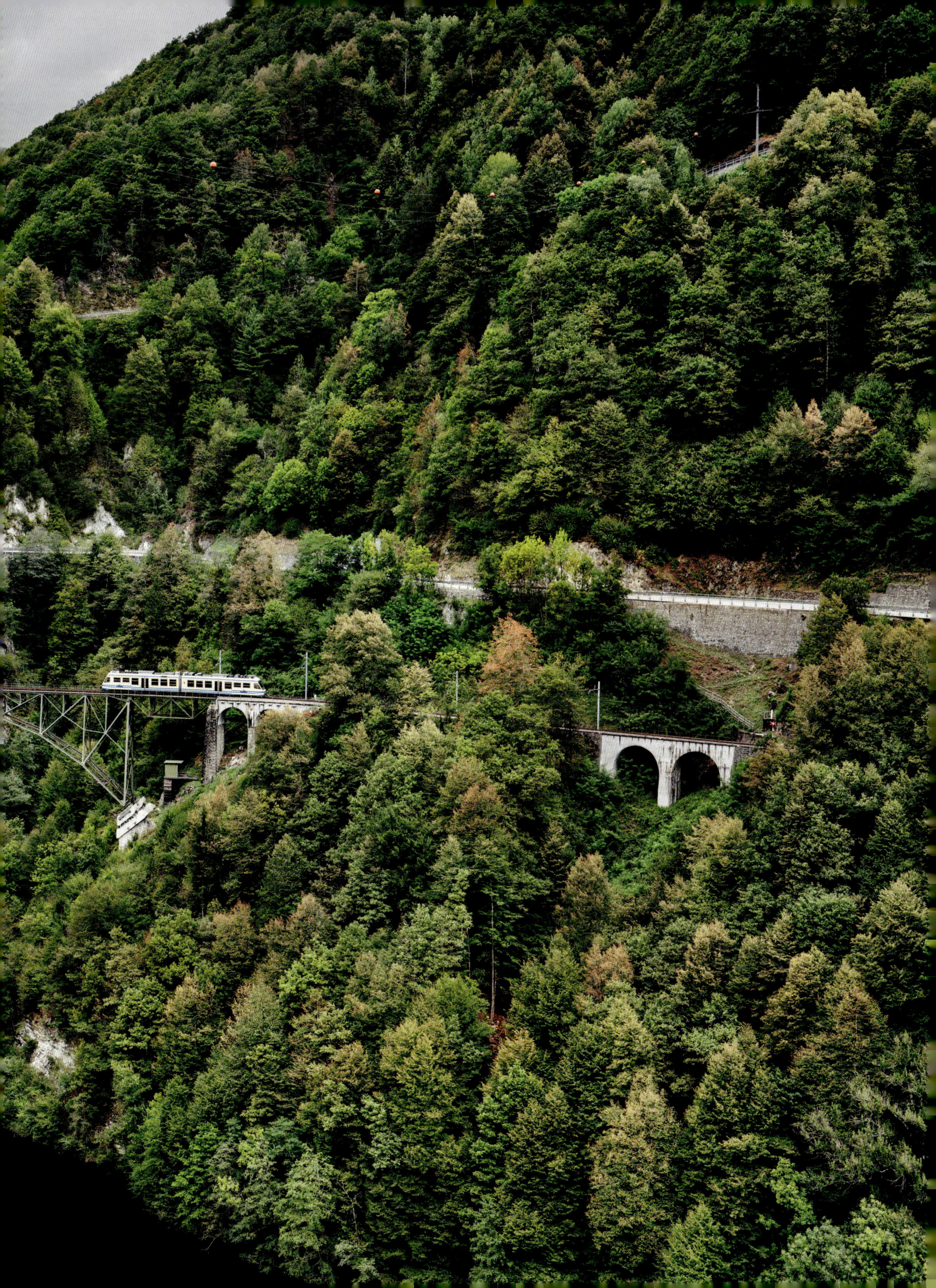

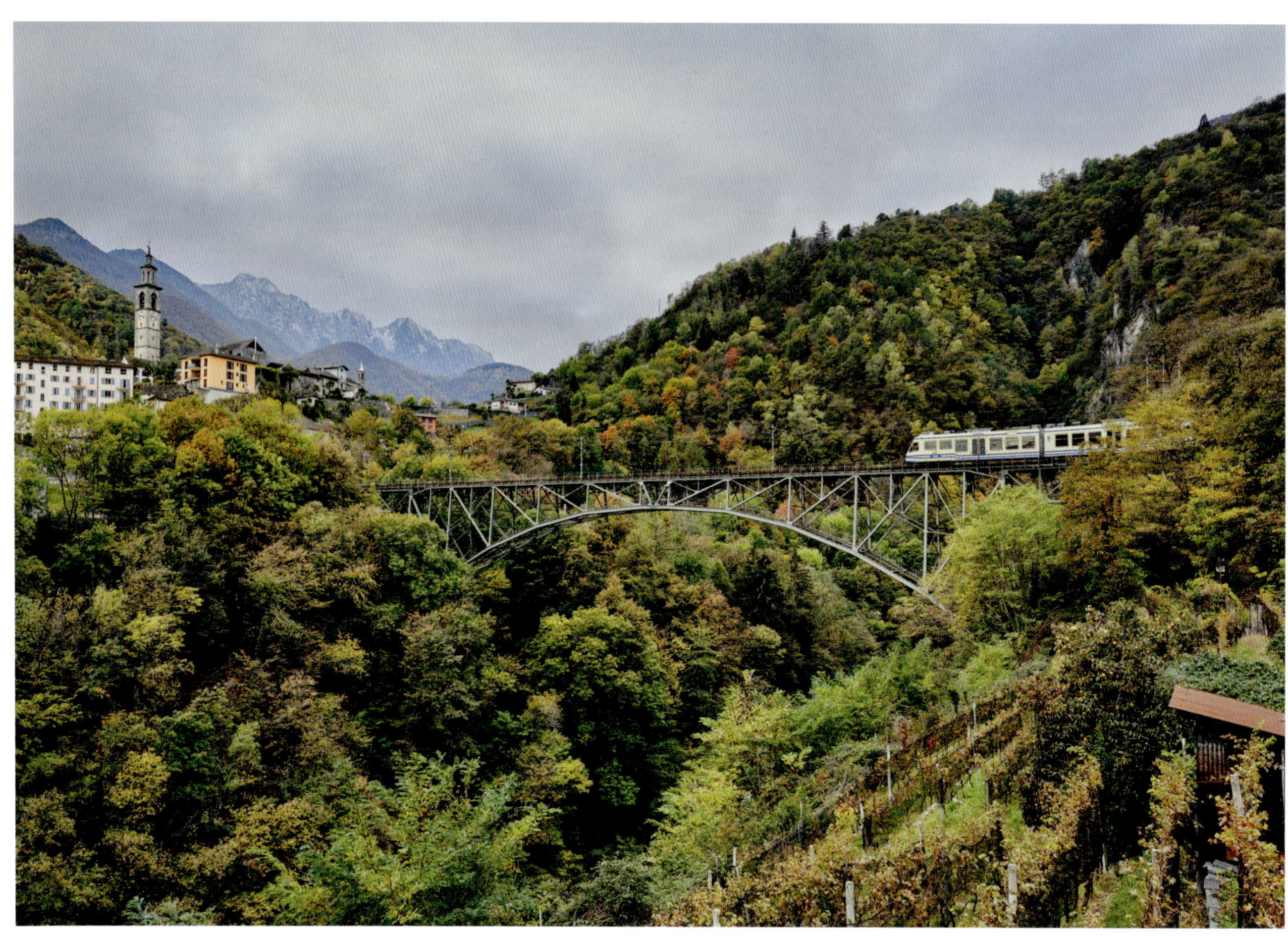

CENTOVALLI RAILWAY

Another elegant iron structure is the viaduct near
Intragna, which spans the Isorno Gorge in a broad arch.

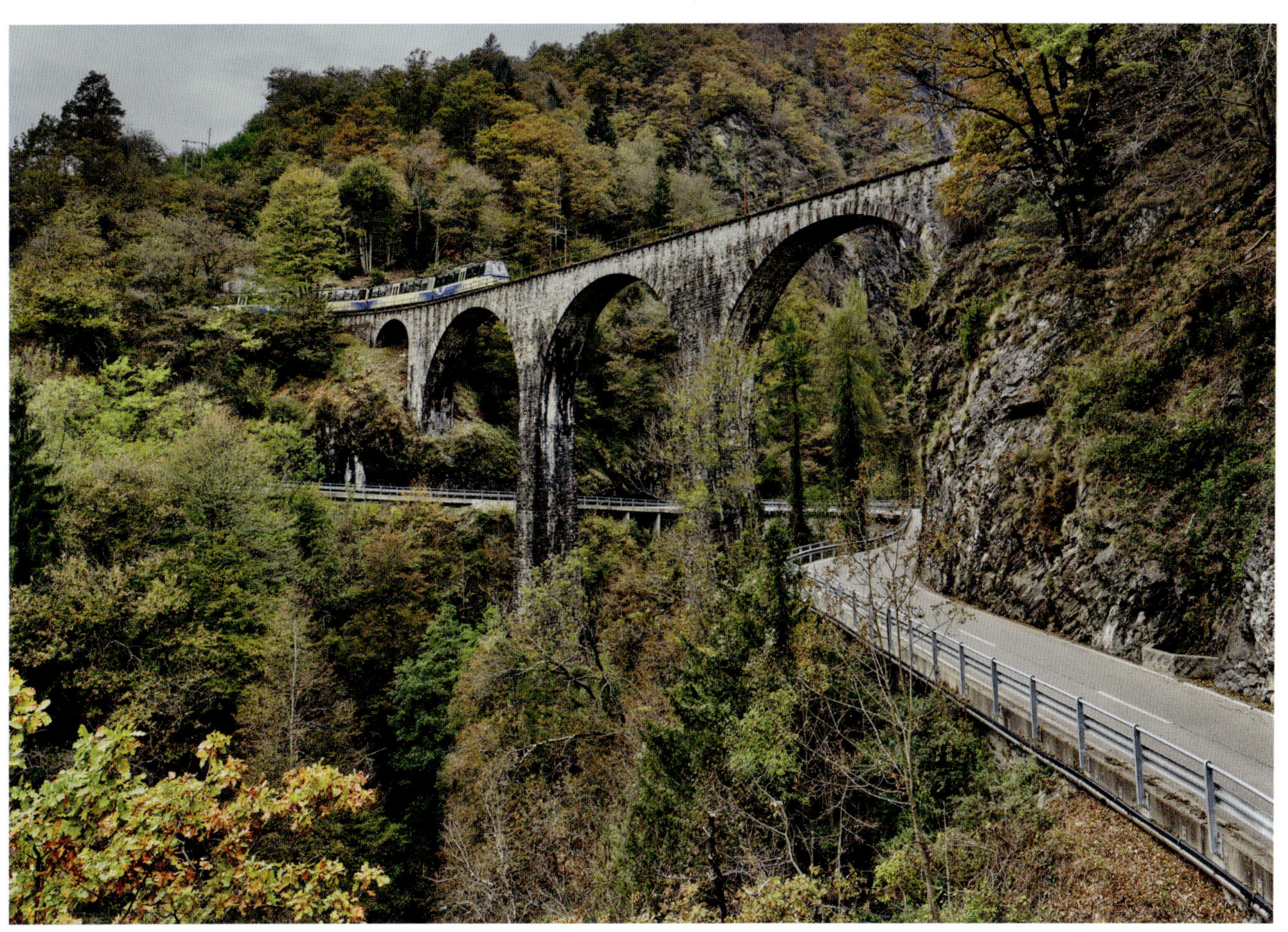

Masonry work: In the area around the Ingustria rift, road and railway cross twice. The railway viaduct is composed of five brick pier arches.

The Centovalli Railway doesn't have to cross a hundred gorges, but all the ones that it does have to cross are deep and rugged. Those building various paths in this landscape always struggled, but even so, farmers have managed to bring their wares out of the hundred valleys to the market in Locarno since the Middle Ages. It's much easier today, thanks to railways and streets. To the left in the picture is the train station in Palanedra; to the upper right is the village of Verdasio.

▽ ▽

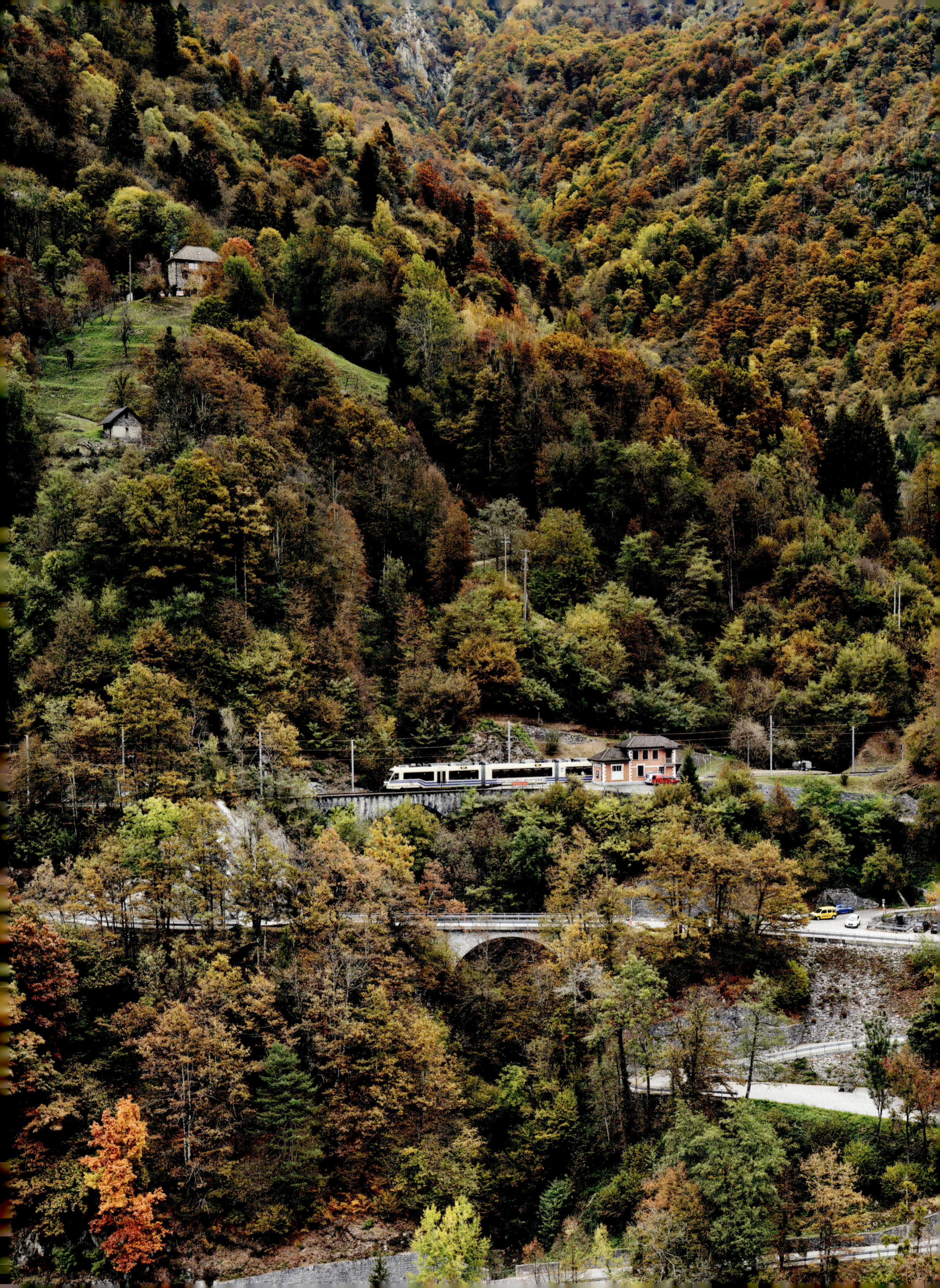

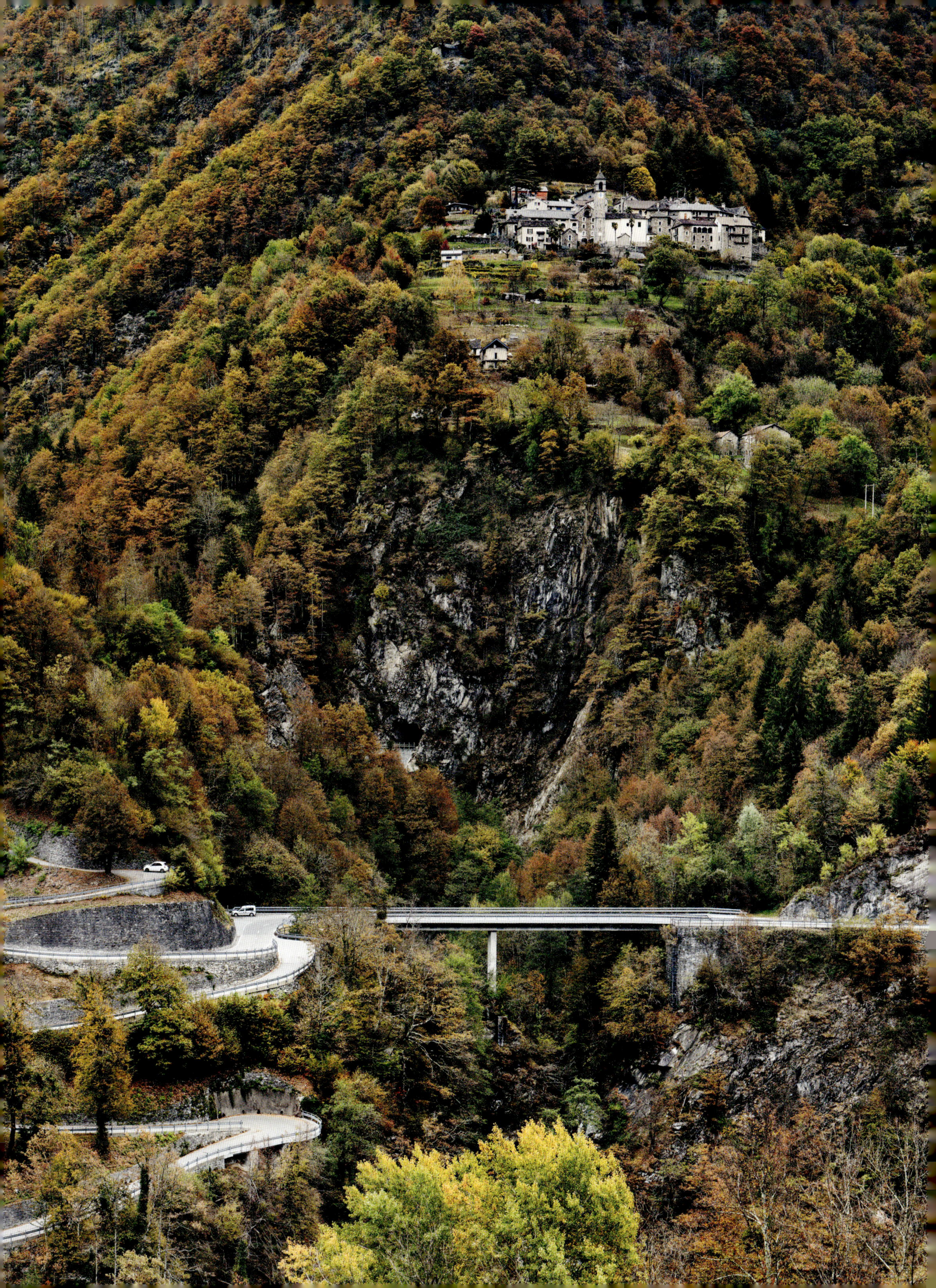

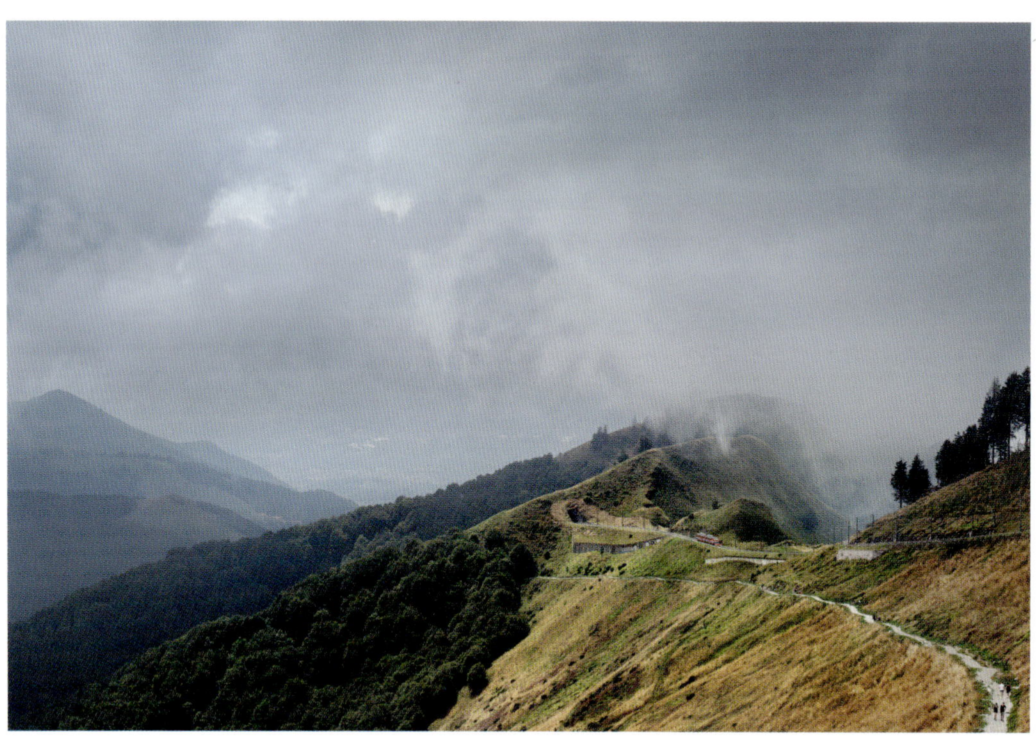

MONTE GENEROSO RAILWAY

No panoramic views today on the Monte Generoso.
Damp air from the Mediterranean enshrouds the
mountains in clouds; it will rain soon.

CENTOVALLI RAILWAY

Ponte Brolla—a word with a magical ring to it. The
canyon created by the Maggia enchants equally
with its bizarre rock formations and the crystal-clear,
turquoise water. Here you can meet sun worshipers
and rock climbers, even cliff divers. The Centovalli
Railway crosses the canyon in its lowest section. ▷

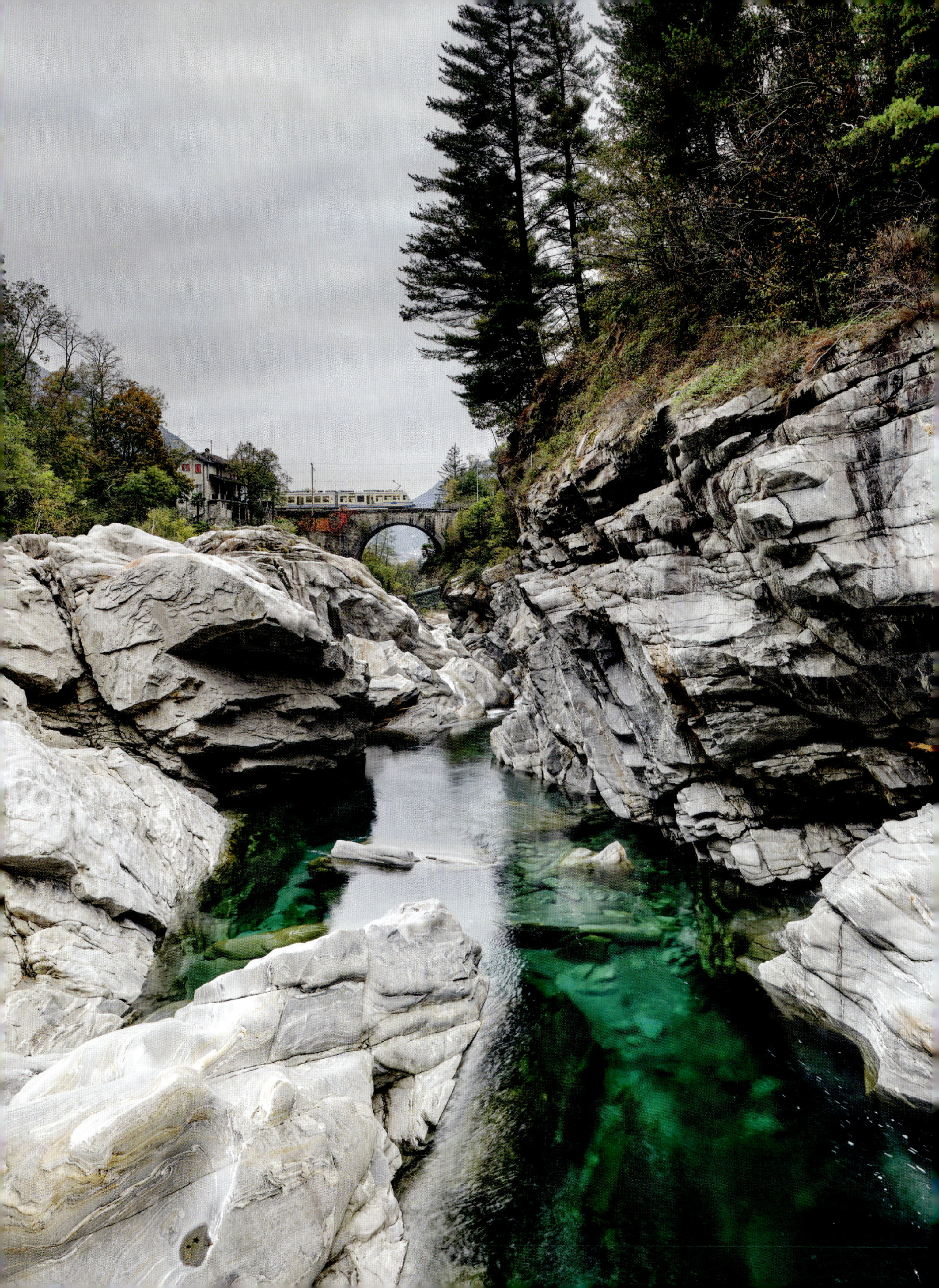

A RAILWAY, THIRTY-THREE FOUR-THOUSANDERS, AND MANY ADVENTURERS

Zermatt's most beautiful viewing platform has its railway as well: the *Gornergrat*. With it, even those feeling lazy can comfortably enjoy the unique four-thousander panoramas. Rather a curiosity: the *Riffelalp Tram*, still 2,215 feet (675 meters) long . . .

It is the most beautiful mountain, in the Alps at any rate, but perhaps even worldwide. Four ridges, four walls, above it the summit, slightly broken off. The Matterhorn, a unique, stony challenge for Alpinists and great business for Zermatt's mountain guides. It became suddenly famous in 1865 due to the tragic events of the successful first ascent of Edward Whymper with his six companies, of which four were involved in a deadly accident upon the descent. Alexander Seiler's hotel empire flourished, and everyone wanted to see the "mountain of all mountains," which can be seen in almost every room in Zermatt.

Many celebrities would travel to Zermatt in the summer; even the great humorist Mark Twain made a detour to Valais during his European trip in 1879. He left behind for his American readers the captivating account of his first ascent up the Riffelberg, a major expedition with 154 people and fifty-one animals. The equipment included not only two thousand cigars and 143 pairs of crutches but also two mosquito nets, ninety-seven ice picks, five boxes of dynamite, and 2 miles of hemp rope. By the way, the expedition was successful, the Riffelberg (8,474 feet / 2,583 meters) finally conquered! But was it?

THE MOST BEAUTIFUL LOOKOUT IN VALAIS

Two decades later, the Riffelberg was able to be "climbed" decidedly easier—while sitting—with the newly opened Gornergrat Railway. It runs from Zermatt right into the majesty of the high Alpine mountains of the Valais four-thousander and ends just beyond the three-thousander limit. The cogwheel railway was electrified from the beginning, as the first of its kind in Switzerland. It even had an energy recovery system, with which electricity flowed back into the grid during the descent—a technical pioneering achievement!

The project was led by Xaver Imfeld, a native of central Switzerland, engineer, and topographer. The undertaking was originally controversial because mountain guides and porters from the Matter Valley feared the competition of the modern mode of transportation. But it was built anyway, and after just three summers, the 6.2-mile-long (10-kilometer-long) mountain route went into operation in 1898. The route was already expanded toward the summit ten years later by just under 1,000 feet (300 meters). Starting in 1928, after the construction of an avalanche gallery at Riffelbord, the trains also ran during winter.

THE GLACIER MELTS

The view is impressive: a great four-thousander parade, led by the Monte Rosa, the Weisshorn, and, of course, the Matterhorn. However, a look around reveals things that are less positive: the ever-expanding development of tourism and the striking loss of glacier ice. Since Mark Twain's visit, the Gorner Glacier has lost almost a third of its size. In the meantime, the connection between the ice stream and its tributaries has been severed. Dying giants . . .

On Gornergrat there is a second railway line. The Riffelalp Tram may be only 2,215 feet (675 meters) long and narrow gauge, but it is Europe's highest tram railway, as it is self-promoted. It was built in 1899 as a connection from the Riffelalp station to the Grand Hôtel Riffelalp. After all, the clientele couldn't be expected to walk to such posh accommodations. . . . In 1961 the house burned down to the foundations. After the reconstruction, the tramway was also put back into operation.

>> Every night, do you understand, I see my comrades of the Matterhorn slipping on their backs, their arms outstretched, one after the other, in perfect order at equal distances—Croz the guide, first, then Hadow, then Hudson, and lastly Douglas. Yes, I shall always see them. <<

Edward Whymper (1840–1911)
on the first ascent of the Matterhorn and its tragic end

GORNERGRAT RAILWAY

The Matterhorn is the absolute showstopper in the great four-thousander panorama of Gornergrat. Only thirty-two years after the tragic first ascent did the first (electric!) train make its way up to the viewing point from Zermatt. At that time, the Gorner Glacier, with its south-facing tributaries, was still one huge mass of ice. There is not much of that remaining: With the exception of the Grenzgletscher Glacier, all ice feeders have lost contact with the Gorner Glacier, including the Lower Theodulgletscher Glacier (*on the left*).

Starting at the Riffelalp, the Gornergrat Railway has two-lane stretches, from Riffelberg to the mountain station continuously. This enables a tight timetable— every twenty-four minutes, a train leaves Zermatt on the tracks connected to the mountain. To the upper right in the picture is the Gornergrat Observatory, with its two towers. ▽ ▽

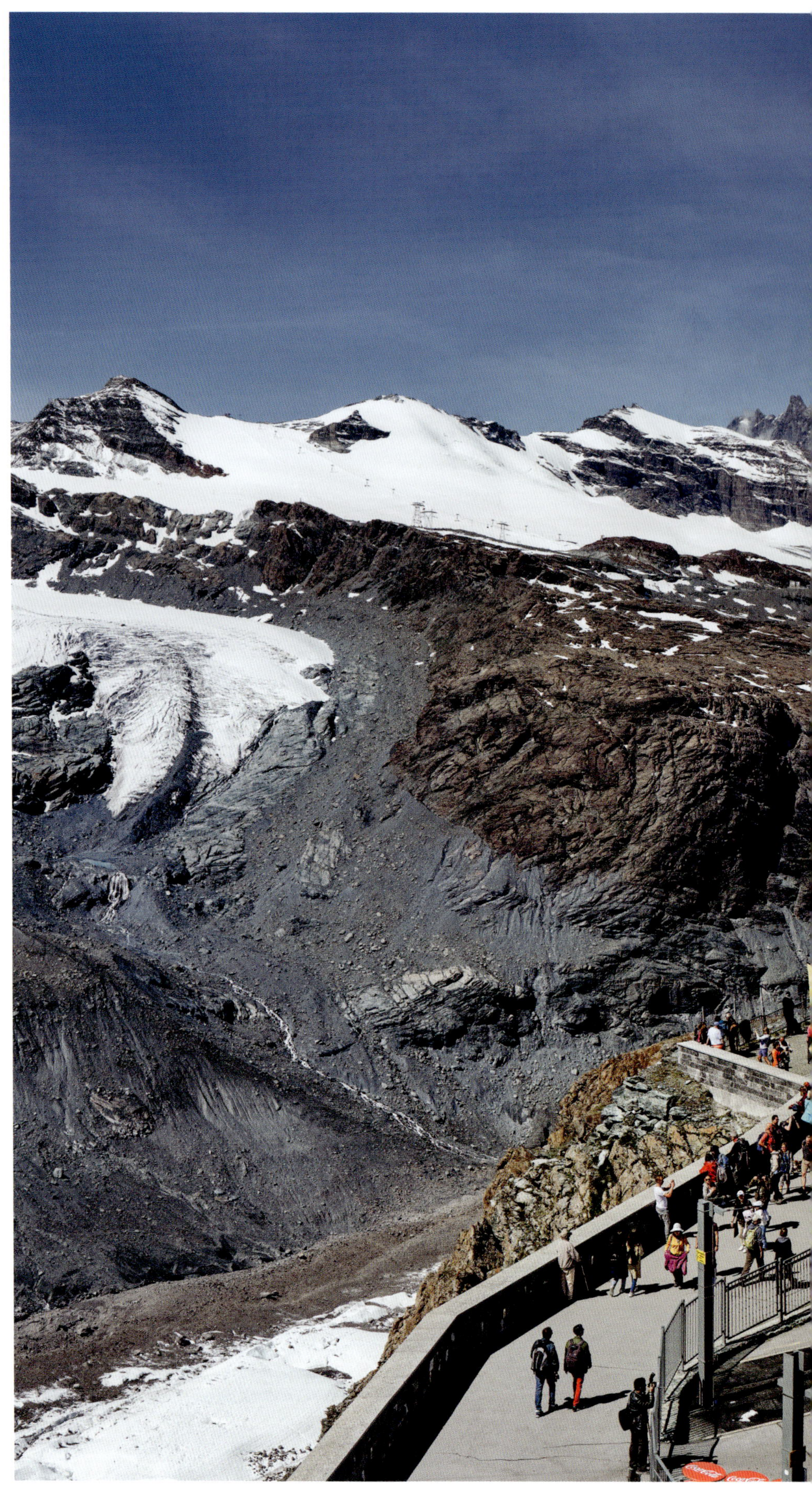

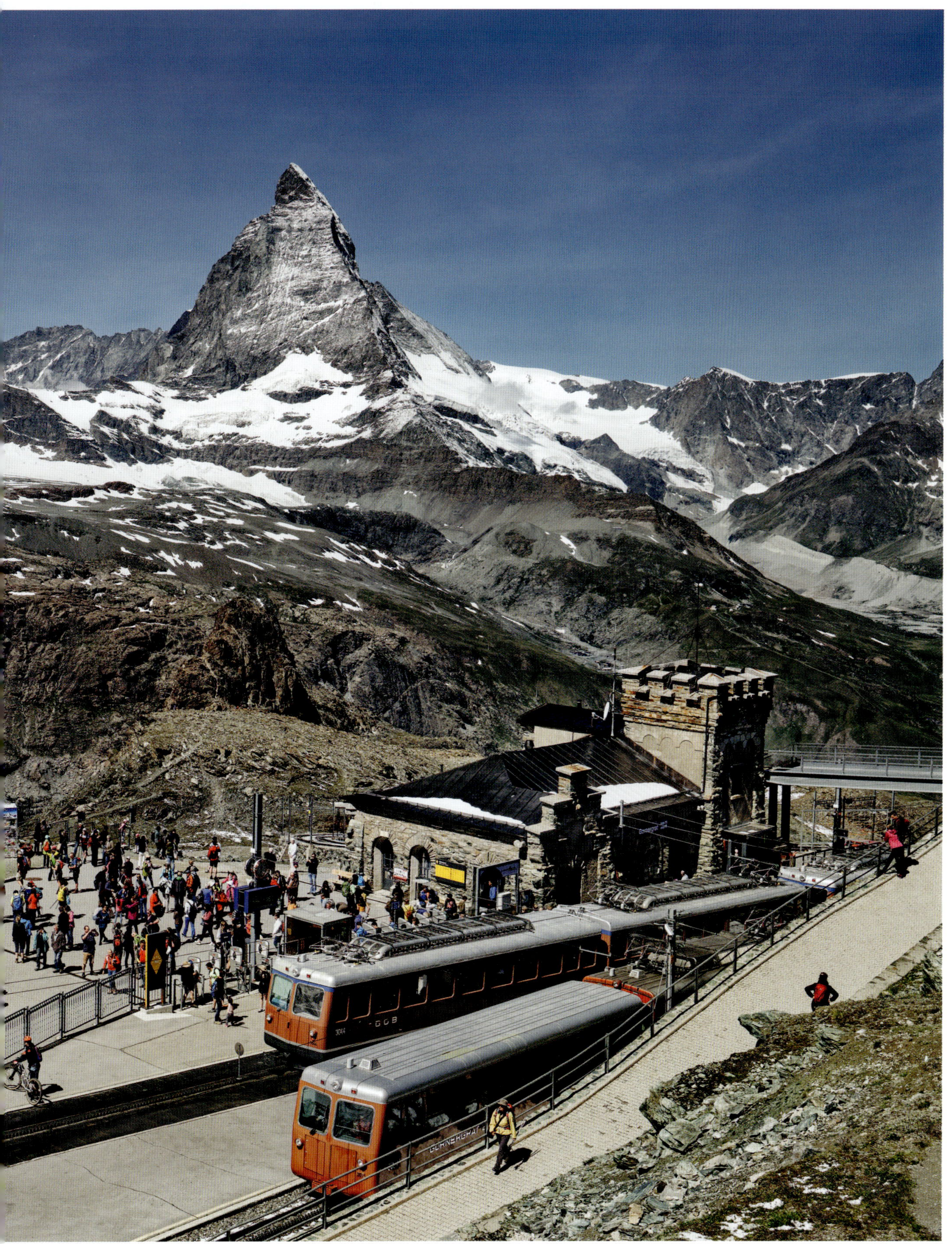

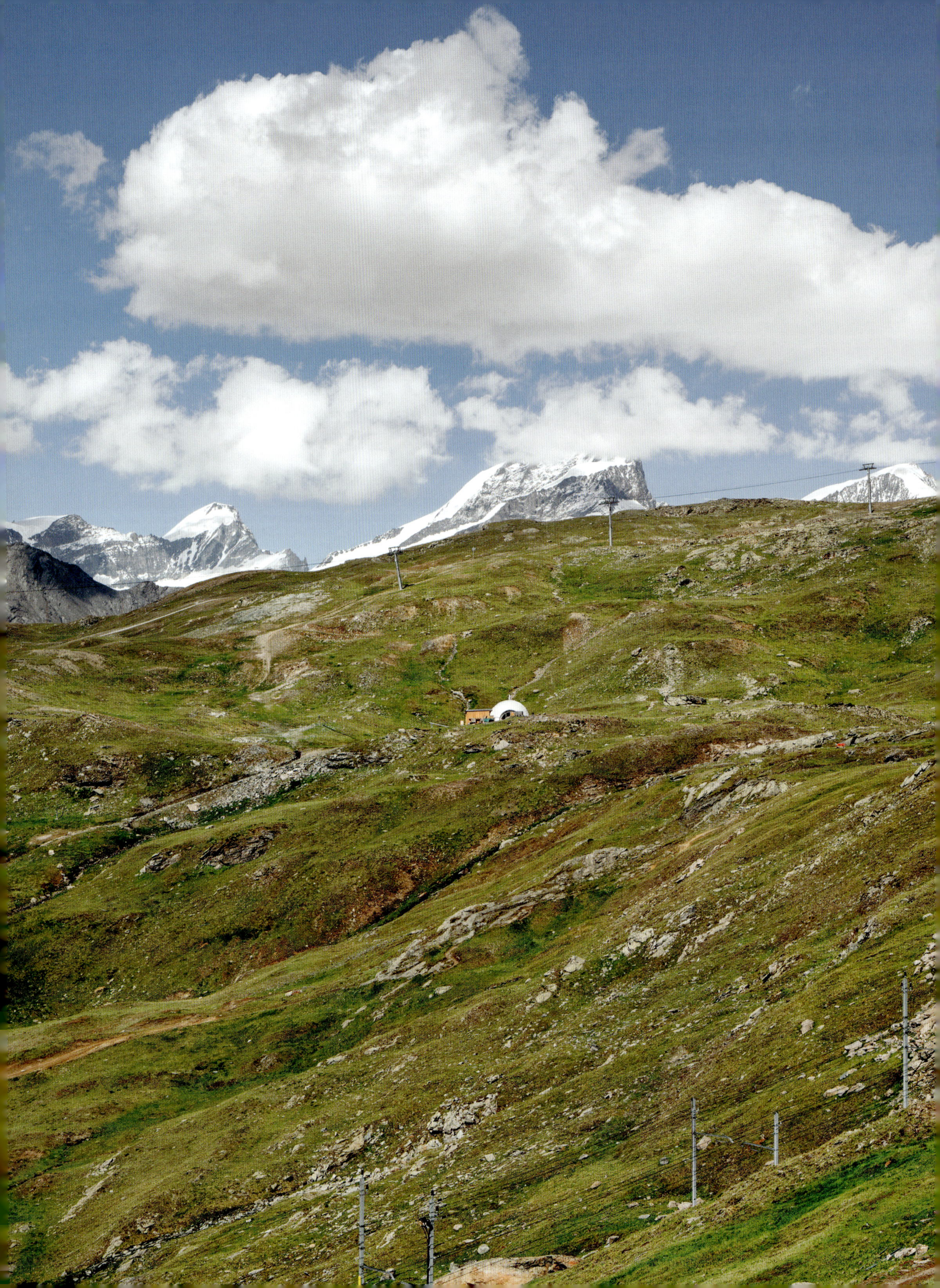

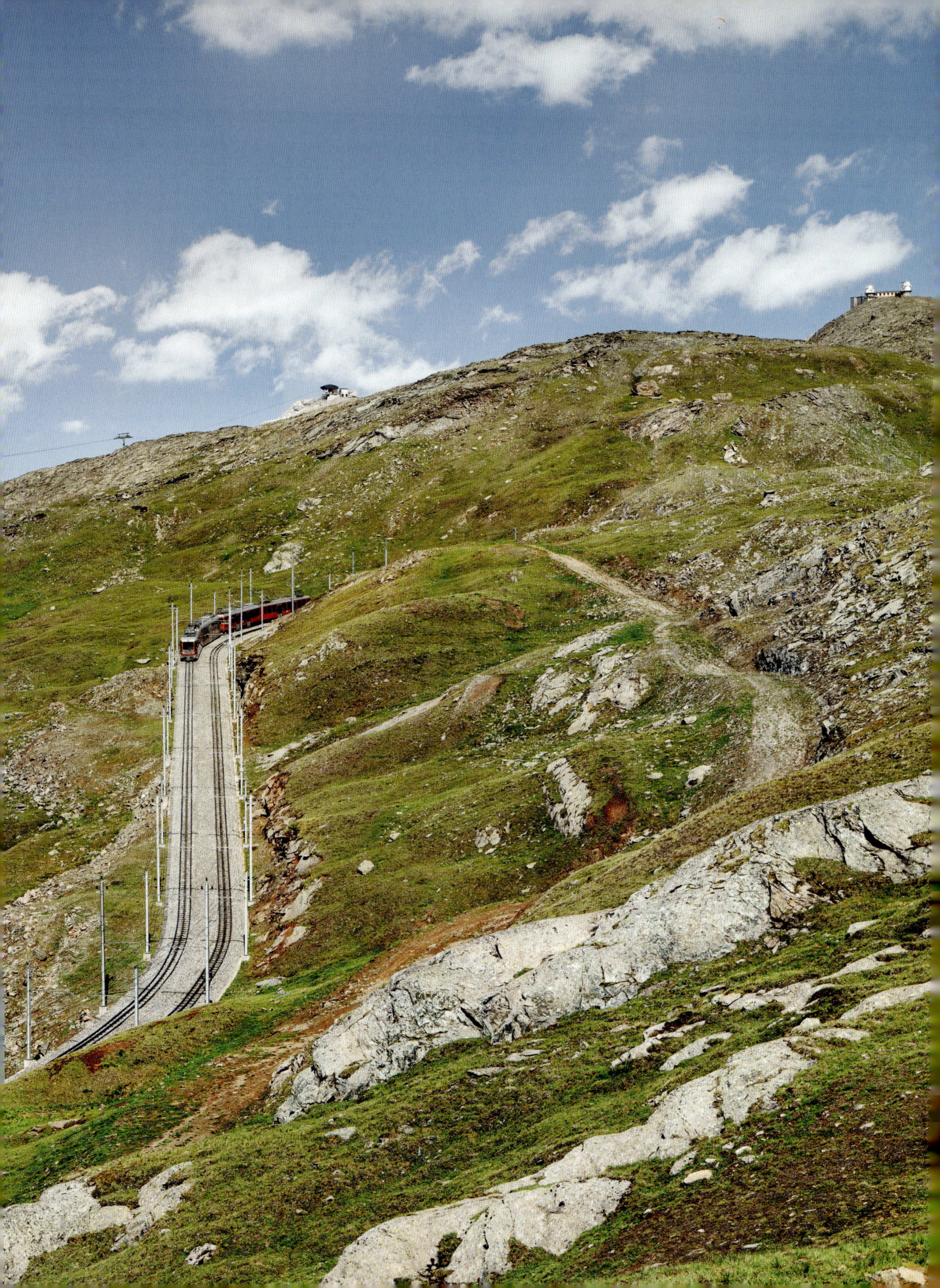

THE TRIP OF A LIFETIME ALONG THE SWISS ALPS

Not over but through the Alps: from Valais to the Swiss Engadin. The journey with the *Glacier Express* is an absolute highlight and offers beautiful mountain views. The *Rheinschlucht* (also known as the "Swiss Grand Canyon") is one of a kind, as are the *Albula Railway* and the *Davos Line*, both masterpieces in Swiss engineering. Nostalgists trundle over the pass during the summer on the historic Furka Railway. In Andermatt, you can transfer from the *Schöllenen Railway* to the Gotthard line.

When the first Glacier Express started its eleven-hour journey from Zermatt to St. Moritz on June 25, 1930, it was viewed as a breakthrough despite the rampant global economic crisis. The railway was once again a symbol of progress toward a better future. If you look back, almost one hundred years later, to the roots of "the Glacier," you will encounter a man with a vision: Alexander Seiler I. He is regarded as the founder of the Zermatt hotel industry, bought several hostels in the village, and finally built a Grand Hotel with 150 beds on the Riffelberg, where Mark Twain was a patron. Around the middle of the nineteenth century, Seiler bought land at the back of Goms around Gletsch. This is where the hotel Glacier du Rhône opened its doors, and soon a profitable tourism industry around the glacier developed. The multilingual guests of the elegant house feasted on the views of the mighty stream of ice, whose tongue stretched into the flat valley floor—a natural wonder.

OLD FURKA RAILWAY AND THE NEW FURKA BASE TUNNEL

Two generations later, "the Glacier" was launched as an express, with the ice formation being the name-giving sensation on the 181-mile (291-kilometer) stretch. It continued until 1982, the opening of the Furka Base Tunnel. Now, between Oberwald and Realp, the route went through the mountain. Goodbye to the "good old days" when trains climbed up the rack through the old summit tunnel under the pass to the highest point (7,096 feet / 2,163 meters) with a clear view of the jagged ice. The mountain route was shut down, and the end of the Glacier Express was rumored. It may have lost its glacier and glacial view, but it was still able to register a continually increasing number of travelers; currently there are around 250,000 passengers per year.

And the historic route? A private club ended up taking over the abandoned line. The 11.2-mile-long (18-kilometer-long) section was reactivated; steam locomotives and other rolling stock were purchased. Spectacularly, two type HG 4/4 locomotives, which were built in 1923 in Switzerland for use in French Indochina, were recovered from Vietnam and able to be repaired. They are in use from mid-June until the end of September over the pass, to the delight of countless railway fans from across the world.

Enthusiasm, personal commitment, and patience are what made the comeback of the old Furka route possible. However, railway nostalgists are powerless when it comes to climate change. The ice has been melting in the Alps for 150 years. The once-so-impressive Glacier du Rhône is no exception; nowadays its tongue has receded behind the distinctive terrain threshold at the altitude of Hotel Belvédere (one of Alexander Seiler's constructions).

A look at the map makes it clear that the Glacier Express has no counterpart in the Alps. In contrast to all other major mountain railways, it runs neither over nor through the Alps, but instead parallel to the main ridge—with a lot of ups and downs though. Vertically, the route profile ranges from the valleys of the Rhone and the Rhine to Alpine regions. The Oberalp Pass marks the highest point of the route, at 6,706 feet (2,044 meters). The different landscape impressions are just as diverse, like strings of pearls lined up one right after another. But in our case, strings of iron: rails, laid at a distance of exactly 1 meter and every now and then—when it gets really steep—with a rack-and-pinion system in between.

This support system for braking and climbing is first seen in the Matter Valley, then near Grengiols. Next, it flattens out a bit going into Goms, in the top section of the Rhone Valley. Near Oberwald, the mountain swallows the Express. Twenty minutes later it arrives in Realp, in the high valley of the Reuss: bare mountain flanks, high ridges. In Andermatt, the Glacier Express and the Gotthardstrasse (Gotthard Street) cross. The almost 2.5-mile-long (4-kilometer-long) Schöllenen Railway connects the former army village with the northern portal of the Gotthard Tunnel. On the short trip through the wild granite gorge, you can get very close to the rushing Reuss on the Teufelsbrücke (Devil's Tunnel)—fantastic!

INHERITED FROM THE ICE AGE

For the Glacier Express, once again, the motto is "up" in Andermatt. In a few wide loops, the rail track winds its way up the bare mountain flank of the Nätschen, then it heads gently uphill toward the watershed to the Bündner Oberland, the Oberalp Pass (6,706 feet / 2,044 meters). With the Vorderrhein it then goes down the valley via the monastery village of Disentis. The next sensation lies behind Ilanz: the Rheinschlucht. The "Rhaetian" follows the path of the Vorderrhein, while the road goes its own way toward Flims. As a result, railway passengers, hikers, and bikers stay among themselves, which does no harm to the nature, or to the experience. Ruinaulta is the local name of the 9.3-mile-long (15-kilometer-long) canyon, which can best be translated as "high rubble." And here we are actually dealing with rubble: 423,776 million cubic feet (12,000 million cubic meters) of rubble from a post–ice age rockslide off Flimserstein. This sealed off the valley and dammed the river to a huge lake. The Vorderrhein dug itself deeper and deeper into the "rubble" and ended up forming a fascinating rock formation.

At Bonaduz, the wide Domleschg Valley opens up from the south, known as Graubünden's Castle Paradise. Thusis lies at its upper end, towered over by the Hohenrätien ruins. This is where the Glacier Express turns into the wild Schin Gorge. Tunnels alternate with bridges, with the Albula rushing below. A few miles past Tiefencastel is where the most interesting stretch begins, from a railway perspective. It begins with the bridge over the Schmittner Tobel Valley, followed by a 446-foot-long (136-meter-long) viaduct, which swings over the Landwasser Gorge in an elegant right-hand curve in five semicircular arches. This is an example of nature combining with man to form a beautifully ideal scene. It's no surprise that this structure was deemed a UNESCO World Heritage Site as part of the Rhaetian Railway in 2008.

THE DAVOS LINE

The Davos Line of the Rhaetian Railway ends in Filisur: made up of even more bridges, fourteen tunnels, and the Zügenschlucht's wildly romantic backdrop. The structure that stands out the most is the 689-foot-long (210-meter-long) Wiesen Viaduct, which spans across the Landwasser at a height of 292 feet (89 meters). It inspired Ernst Ludwig Kirchner in his painting *Die Brücke bei Wiesen* (*The Bridge near Wiesen*) (1926). Today, visitors don't have easels but instead bring their much more convenient smartphones with them. The beautiful scene is saved in a millisecond to a chip, and from there it wanders into the wide world.

The Davos Line began regular operations in 1909. At that point, the climatic health resort already had a railway connection from Landquart in the Rhine Valley via Klosters. The initiator of this first "Rhaetian" railway was Willem Jan Hosboer, a Dutchman, who was looking for healing in Davos for his wife, who was suffering from lung disease. In 1890 the first train steamed through the Prättigau to Davos; five years later, the Landquart-Davos Railway (LD) was renamed the Rhaetian Railway and became a state railway.

GRAND ALBULA RAILWAY

The most spectacular stretch of the Glacier Express begins in Bergün. Even the *Baedeker* travel guide from 1920 is clearly impressed; it describes the ascent to Preda and to the western entrance of the almost 6-kilometer-long Albula Tunnel in detail:

"The direct distance from Bergün to Preda is 6 kilometers [3.7 miles], the altitude difference 416 meters [1,365 feet], which required a railway distance of 12.5 kilometers [7.8 miles] in order to overcome it (steepest gradient 3.5 percent). First in a large double loop upwards, with tunnels 486 meters [1,594 feet] and 262 meters [860 feet] in length; then on a 40-meter-high [131-foot-high] viaduct over the Tischbach. Continue along the mountain wall high above the Albulastrasse with a view of Piz Uertsch, Piz Rugnux, Piz Val Lunga, Piz Saltaras, back to Bergün and Latsch; through two short tunnels to the Muot viewing platform (1,580 meters [5,184 feet]). Through a tunnel, over the Albula and in the 66-meter-long [217-foot-long] Rugnux spiral tunnel uphill. Through rock cuts and on a double-arched viaduct back to the right bank of the river. In a large loop with two superimposed spiral tunnels 677 meters [2,221 feet] and 535 meters [1,755 feet] in length, the railway crosses the Albula twice. Preda (1,792 meters [5879 feet]), in a beautiful valley surrounded by partly snow-covered mountains on the Albula road."

Then you arrive at the "Roof of Europe" (an early Upper Engadine advertisement), in the wide and high mountain valley of Inn, with its sparse larch forests, high summits, and—another natural wonder!—the lakes, former hollows of the Inn glacier, which stretch from the forest of Staz to the Maloja Pass watershed. The longest and most beautiful train ride in the Alps ends in St. Moritz. Whoever has the desire (and who wouldn't?) can continue the trip the next day with the Bernina Express over the pass of the same name into the Italian Valtellina, maybe with a detour up to Muottas Muragl. There you can find the most beautiful view over the Upper Engadine.

>> The best education for a clever person is found in travel. <<

Johann Wolfgang von Goethe (1749–1832)

The dream journey through the
Swiss Alps begins with a descent.
It goes into the Matter Valley from
Zermatt down into Visp or Brigg
(or both!) in the Rhone Valley.
The stretch between Zermatt
and Täsch is largely protected
from rockslides and avalanches
by galleries. In the picture you
can see the 2,090-foot-long
(637-meter-long) Täschwang
Gallery.

Wild, untamed mountain nature.
Deep in the ravine—locals refer to
it as the "snake pit" (Schlangen-
gruebe)—the Matter Vispa River
roars and sprays. The train keeps
its distance from the bottom of the
gorge. ▽ ▽

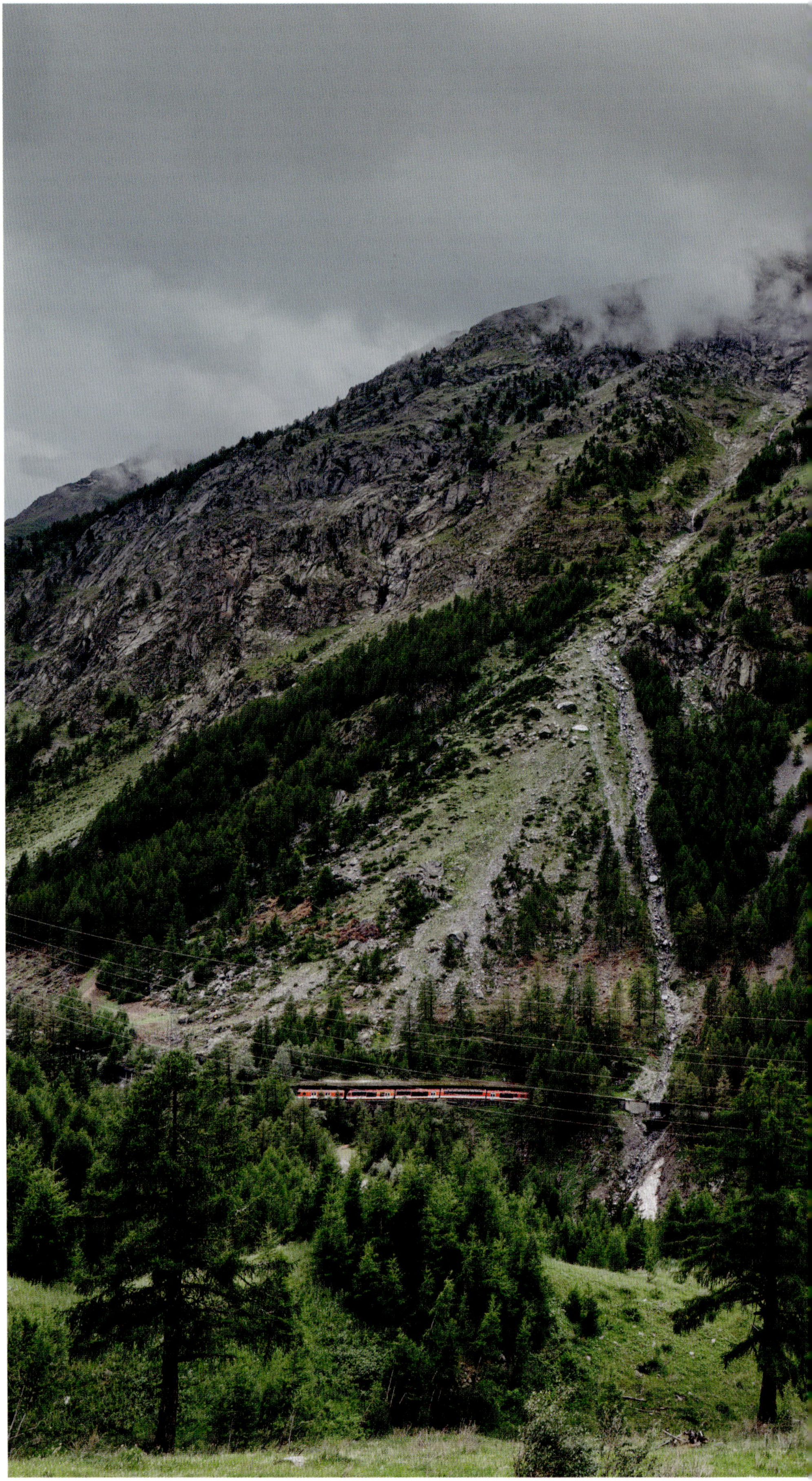

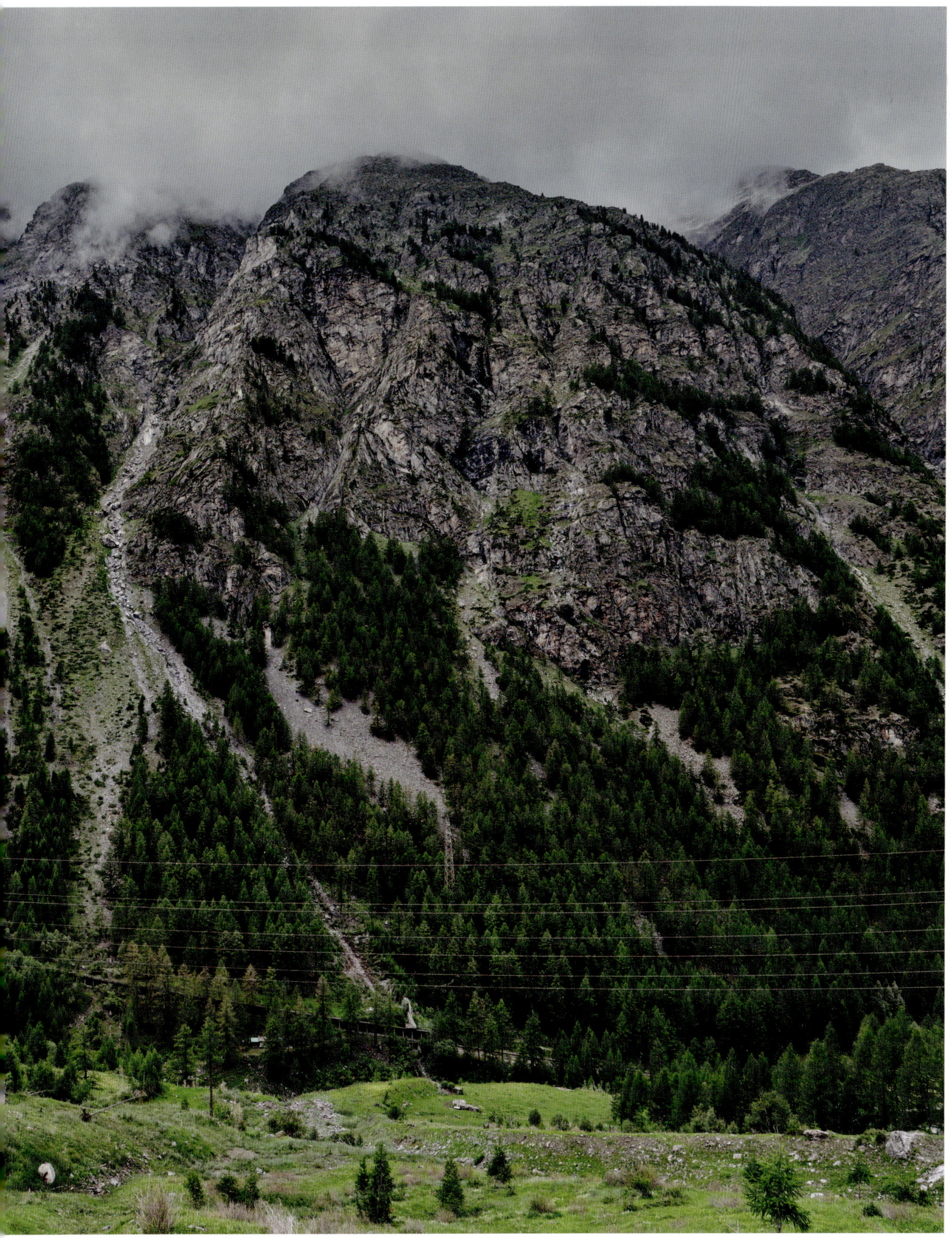

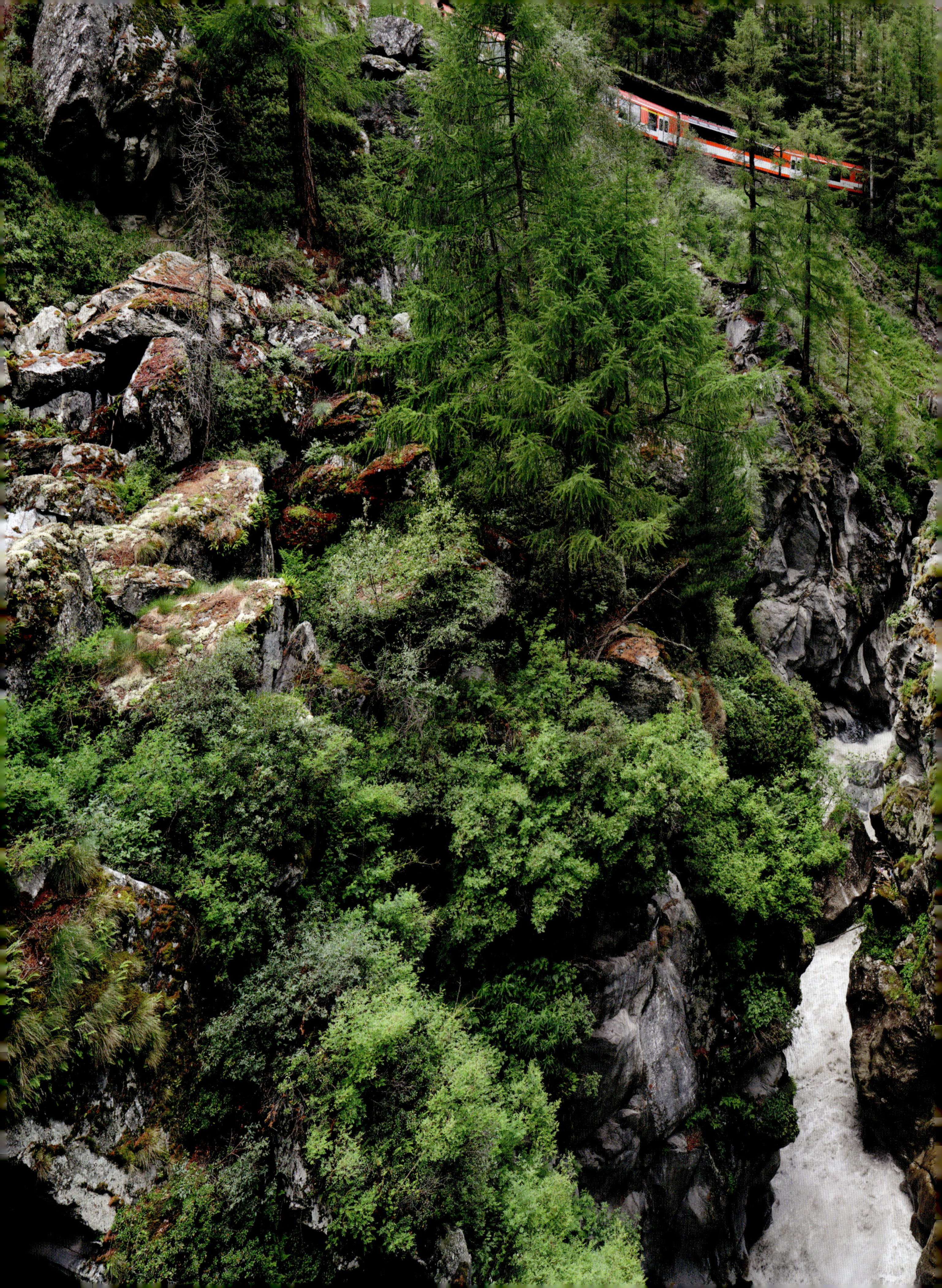

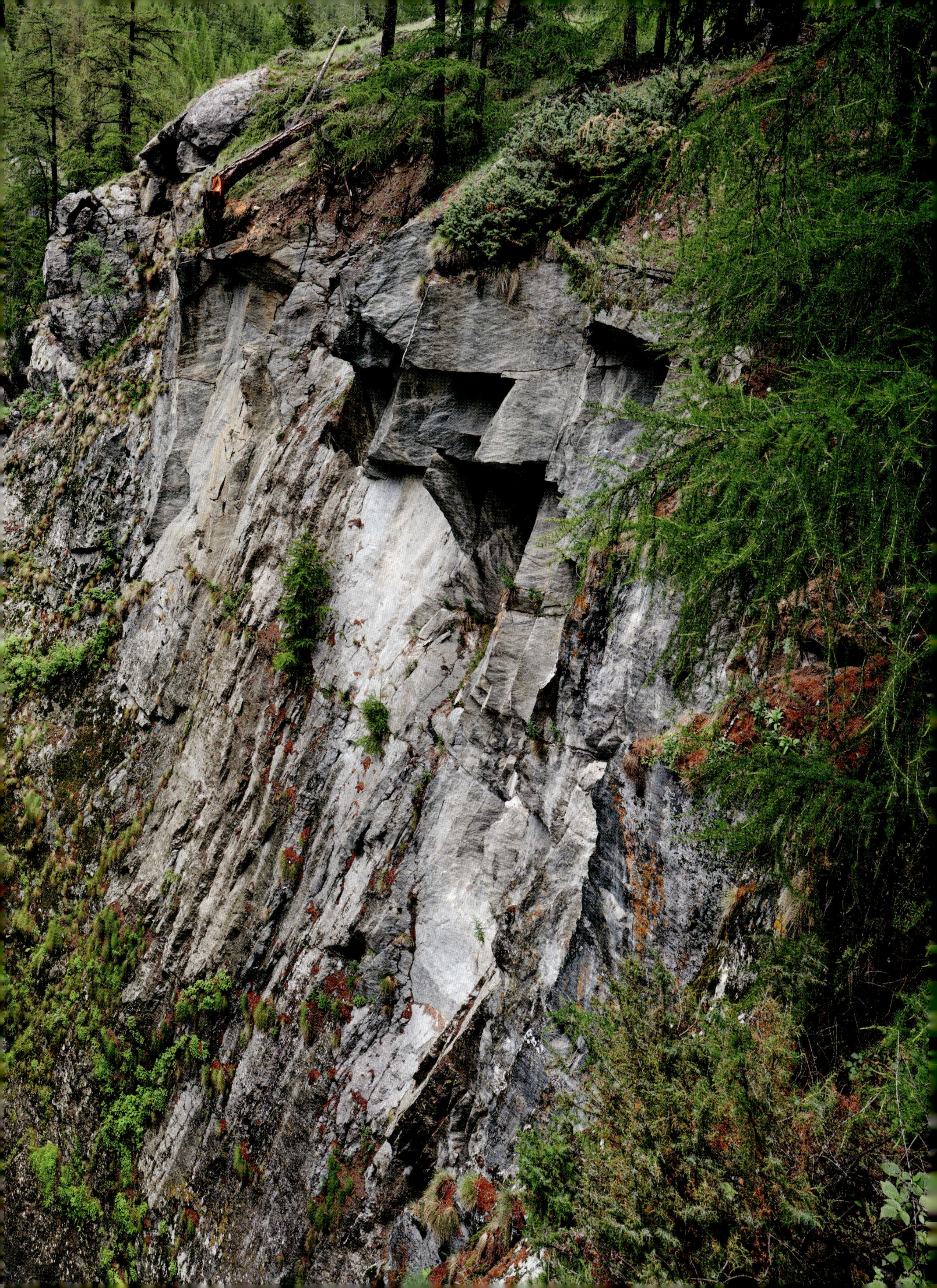

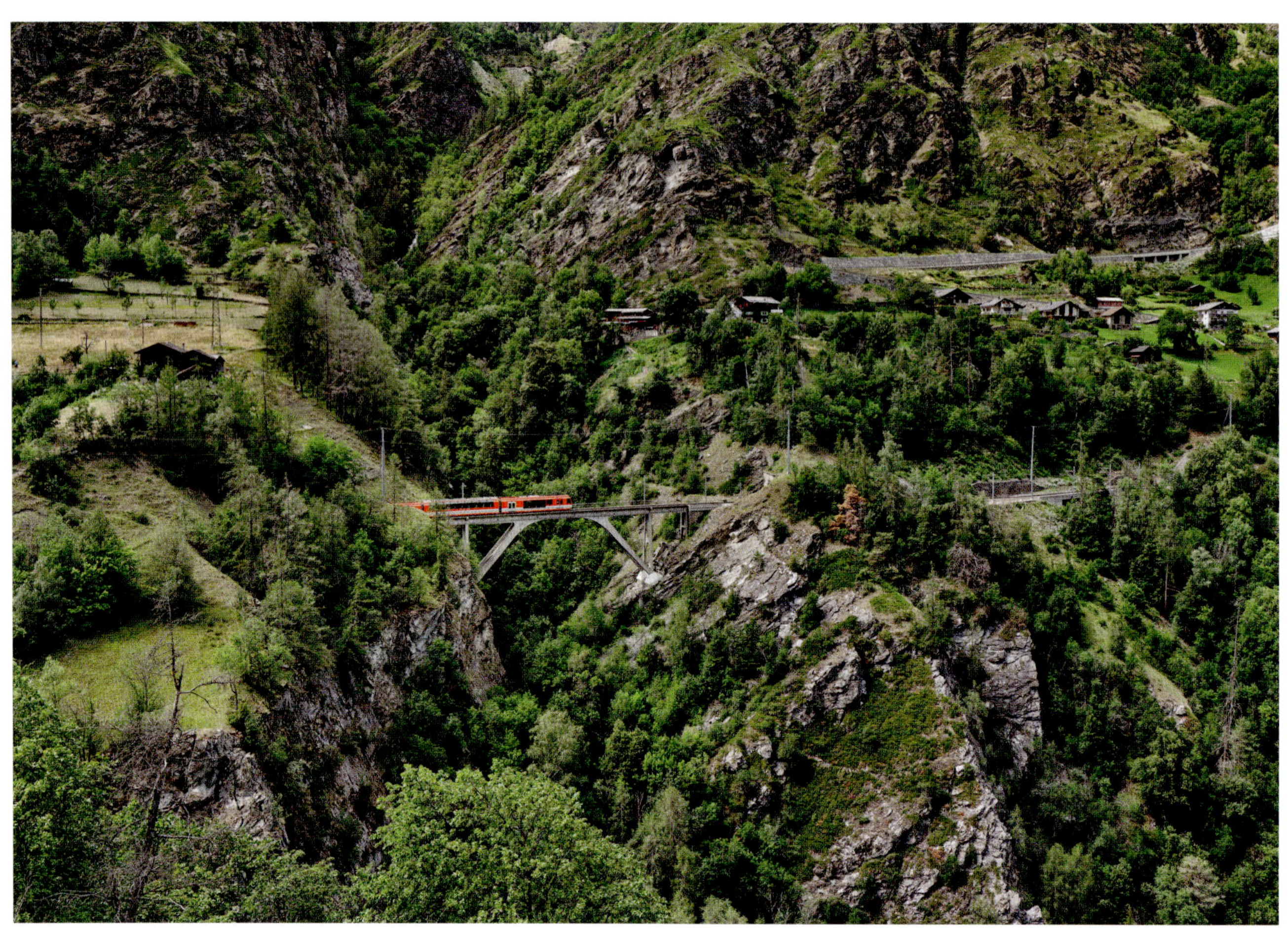

Between Stalden and Kalpetran, the Mühlebach
Viaduct spans across the gorge of the same name. The
prestressed concrete arch bridge was opened in 1959
and replaced the old iron bridge.

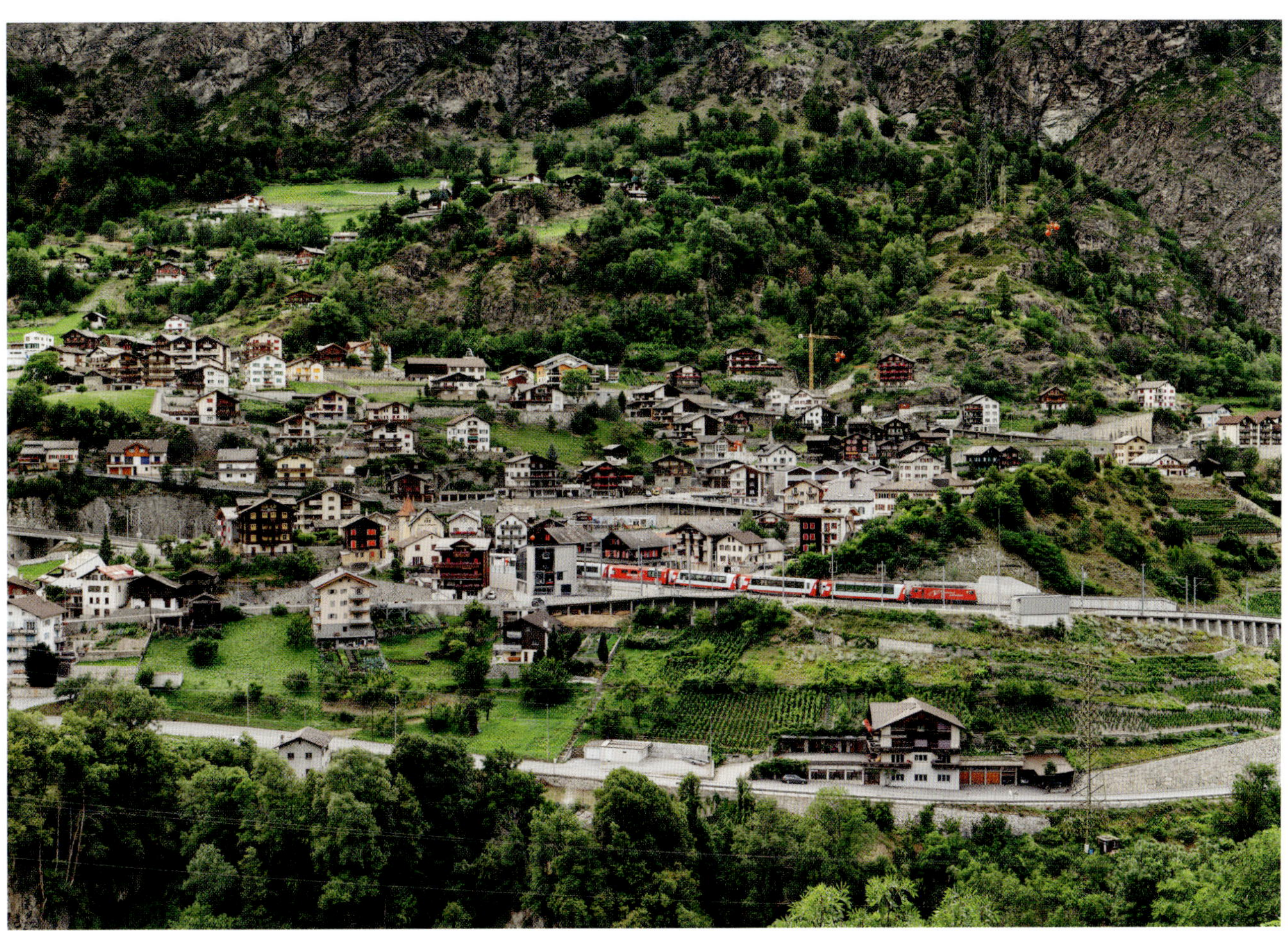

The valley forks in Stalden, about 6 miles (10 kilometers) south of Visp. If you want to continue to Saas-Fee, you must transfer into a postbus. The narrow-gauge railway, completed in 1891, continues to Zermatt via Sankt Niklaus. Near Randa, the great cone of debris of the Grossgufer comes into view. In the spring of 1991, 1,695 million cubic feet (48 million cubic meters) of stone broke off the Längenflueberg and thundered down the valley. No one was injured by the event—a miracle!

GLACIER EXPRESS

By using a rack and a spiral tunnel,
the regional train near Grengiols
is able to overcome the valley step
to Goms, the highest part of the
Rhone Valley.

OLD FURKA MOUNTAIN LINE

Travel as they did in days past.
Since 2010, the old Furka summit
route is back in operation, from
Realp to Oberwald, of course
also with historical rolling stock.
Everything is authentic, including
the uniform of the engine driver.
The train is about to enter a spiral
tunnel near Gletsch. Above in the
picture are the serpentine curves
of the Grimsel Pass Road. ▽ ▽

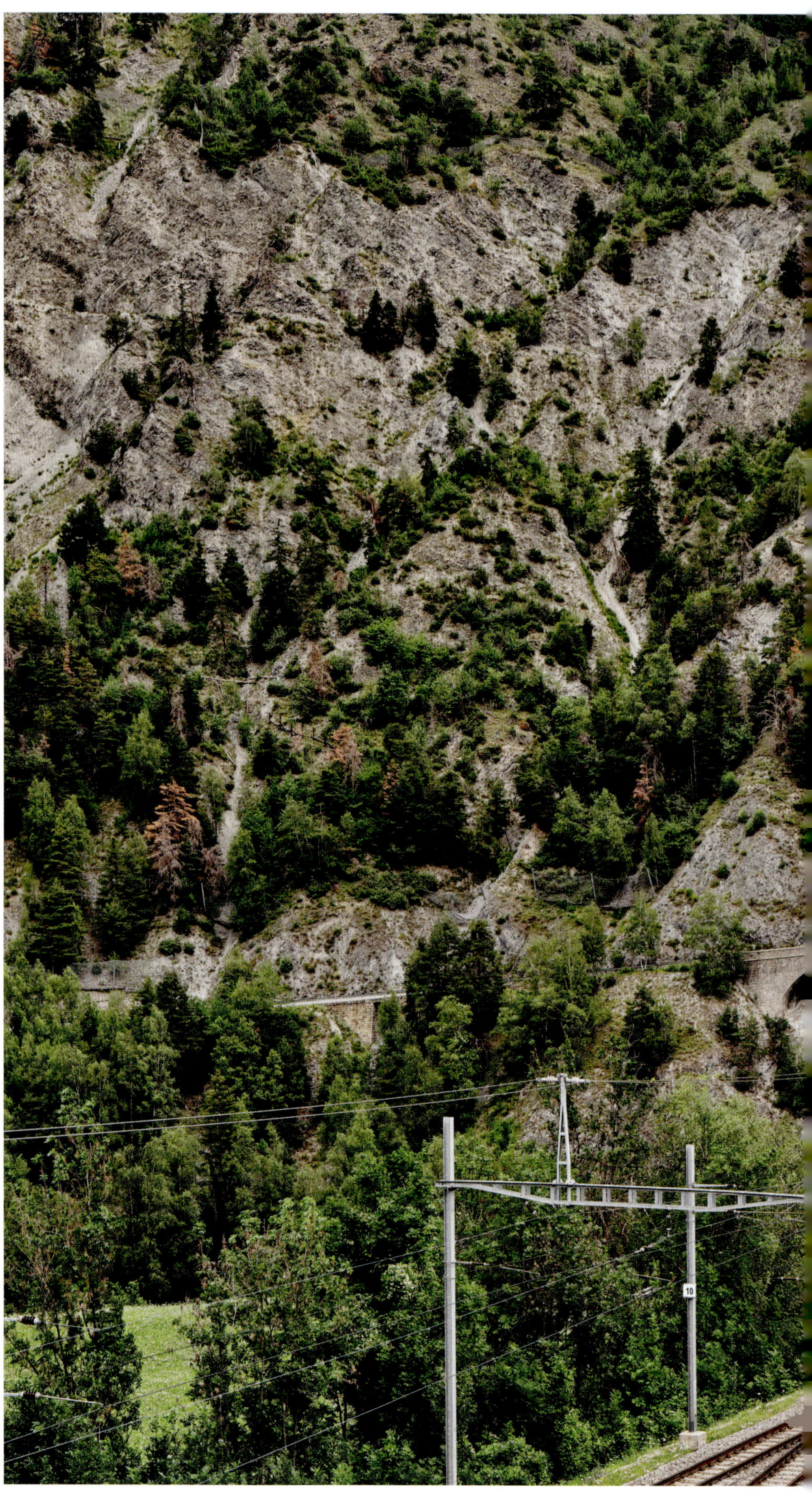

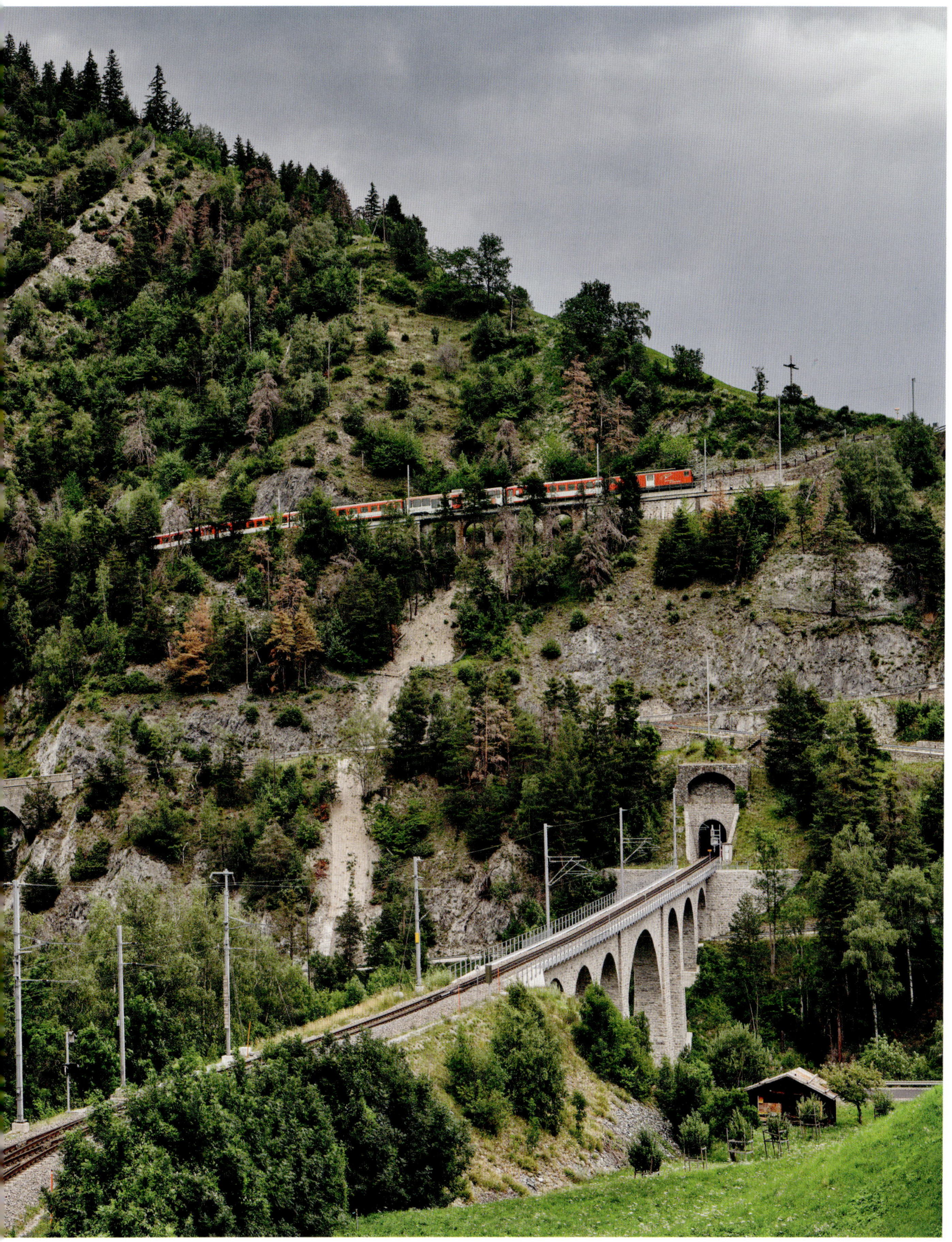

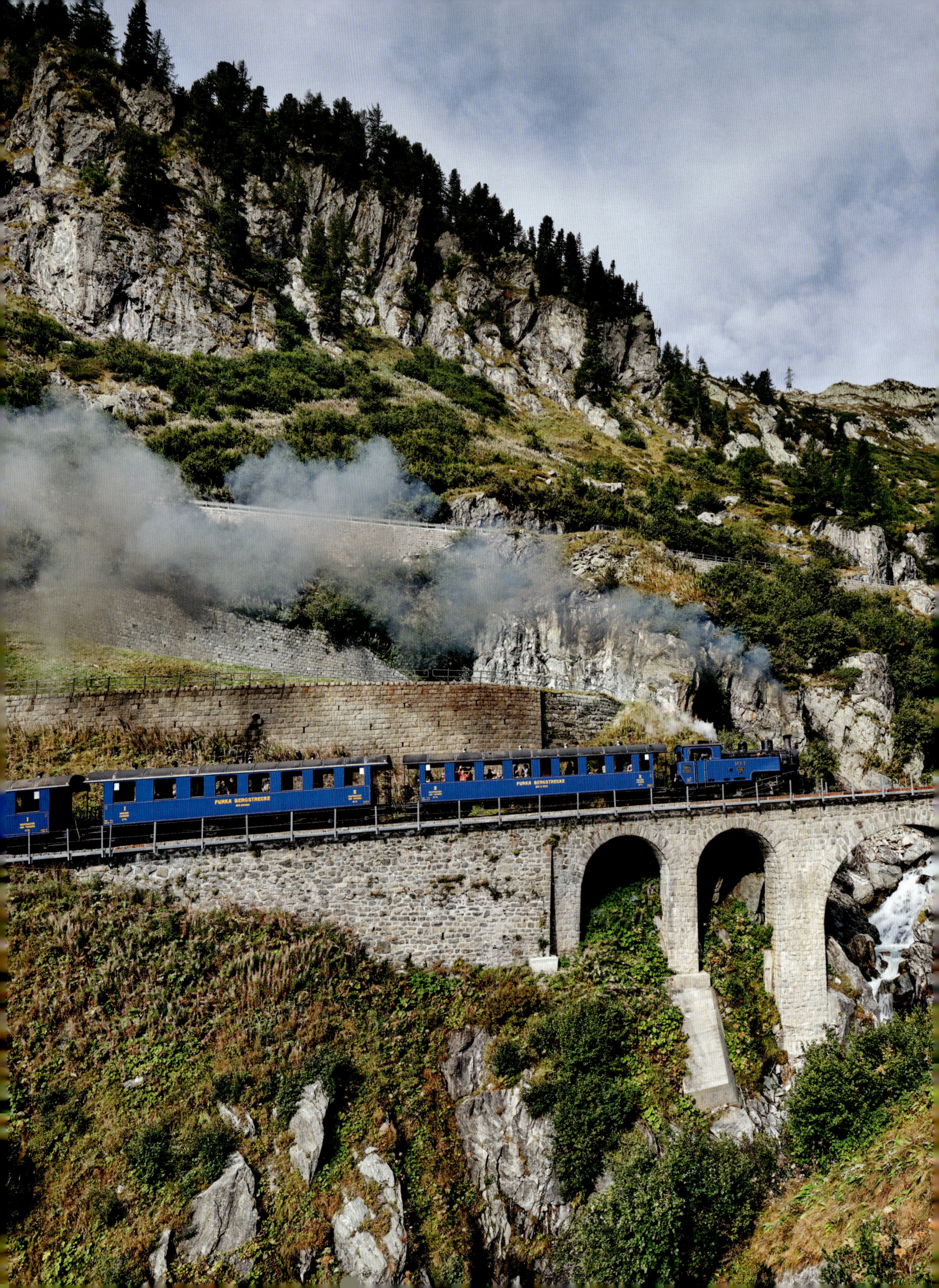

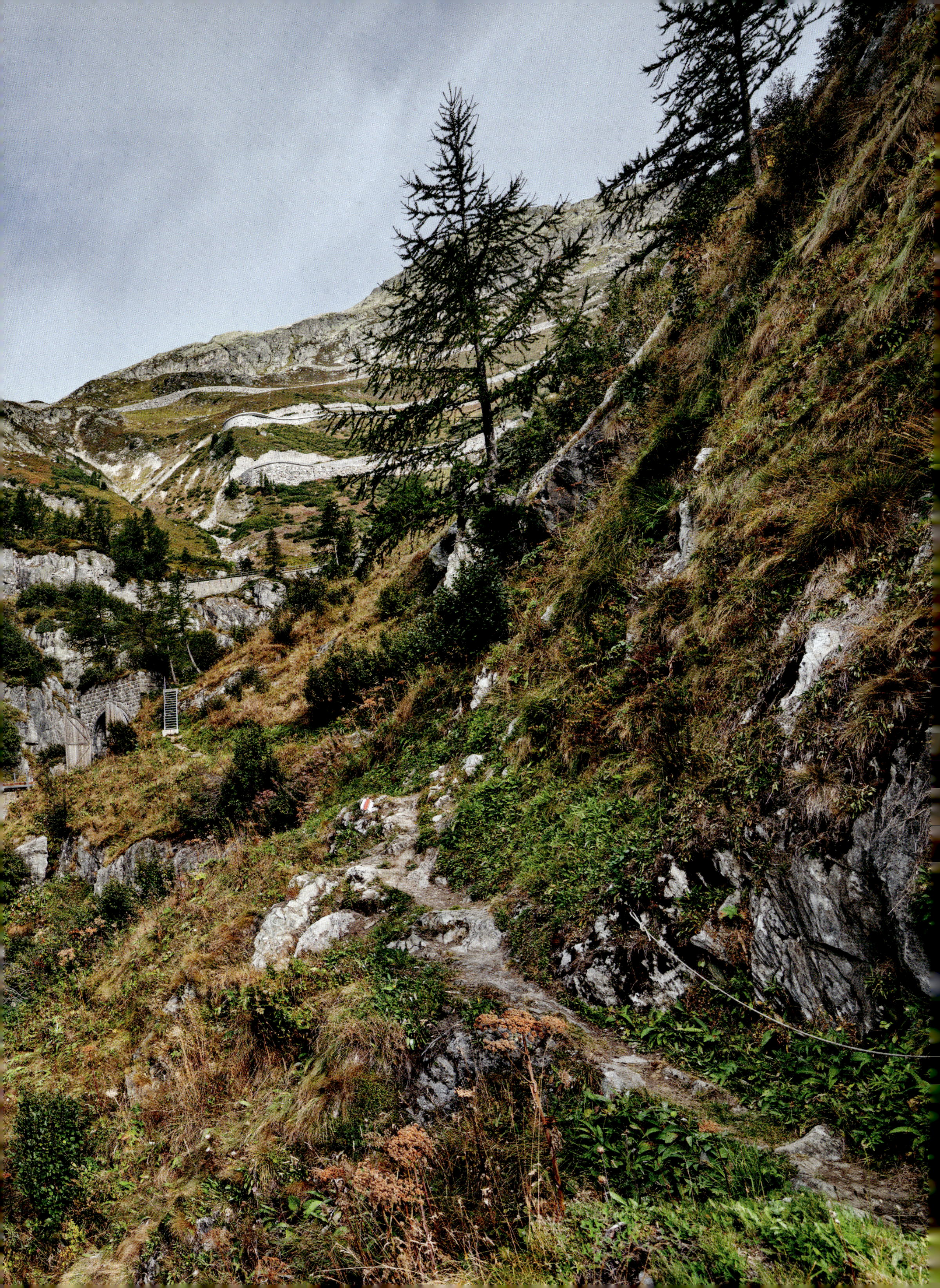

OLD FURKA MOUNTAIN LINE

Fall colors along the Furka Pass. In the center of the picture is the Steinstafel Viaduct; above is the summit height of Furka. The name of the pass can be traced to the Latin word *furca*, which more or less means "fork" and can also be found in Italian (*forcella*).

GLACIER EXPRESS

A regional train of the Matterhorn-Gotthard Railway is underway in the Urseren Valley, between Hospental and Realp. The Rossmettlengrat with the Spitzberg (9,623 feet / 2,933 meters) towers over the autumn-brown ridge. ▽ ▽

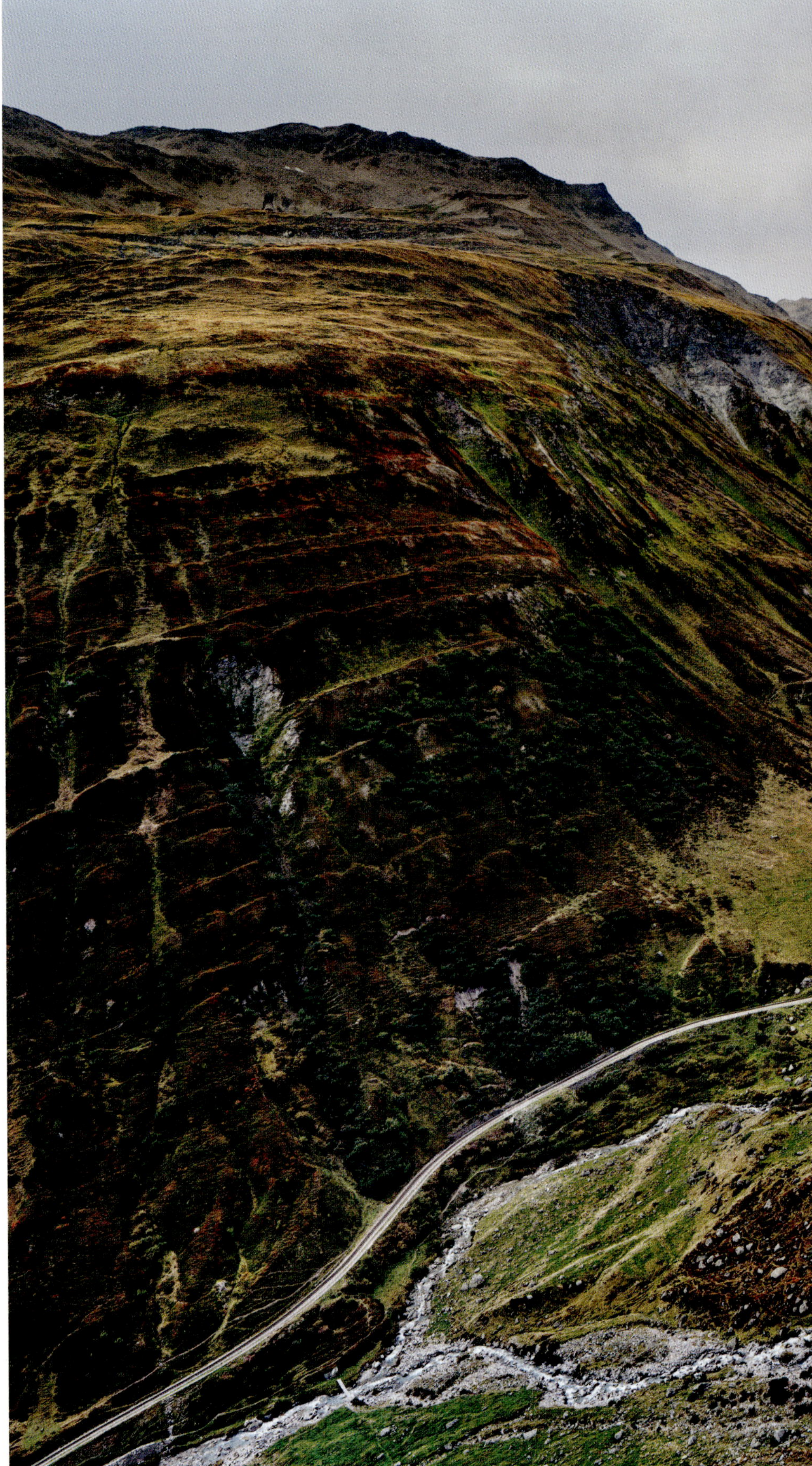

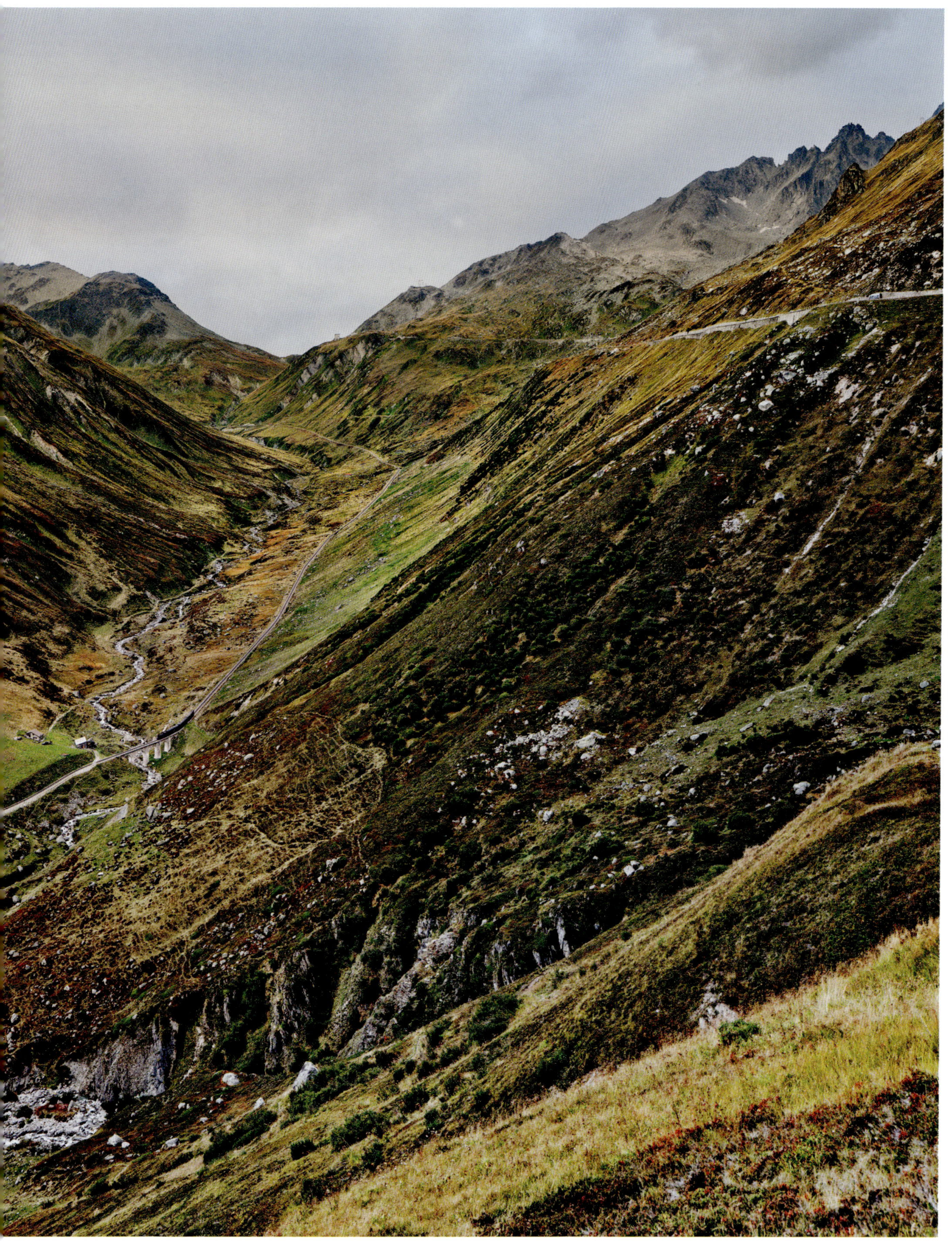

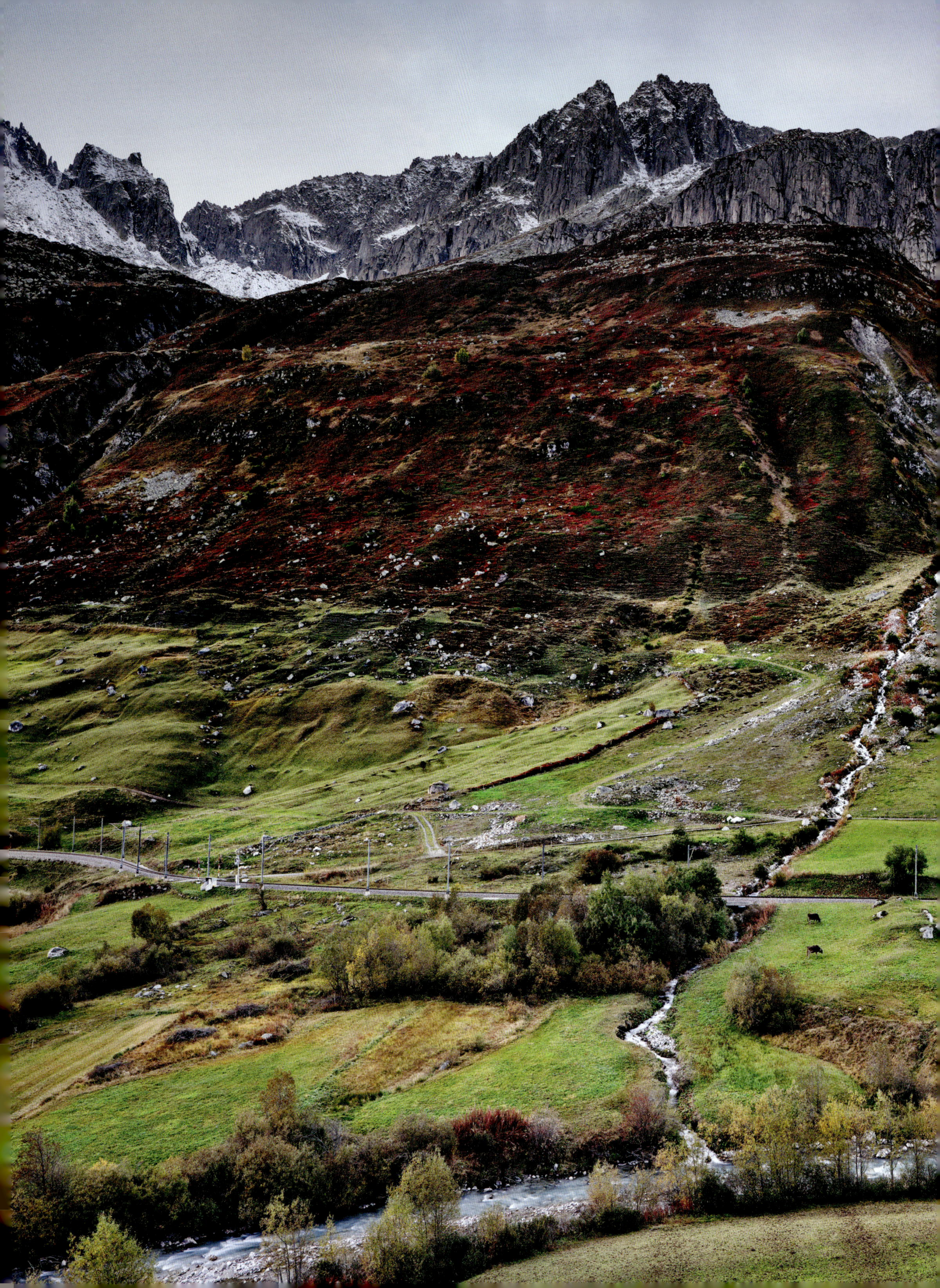

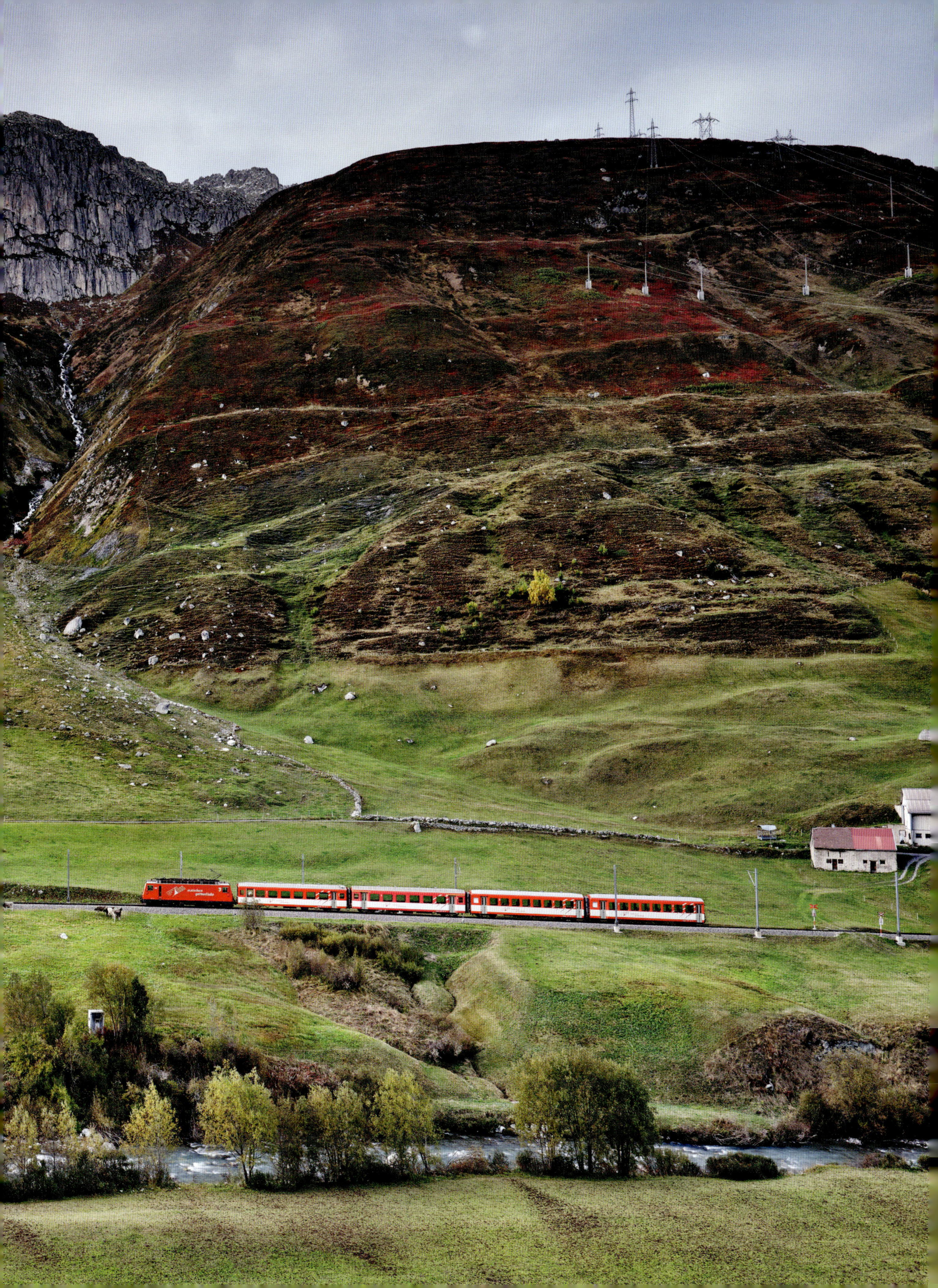

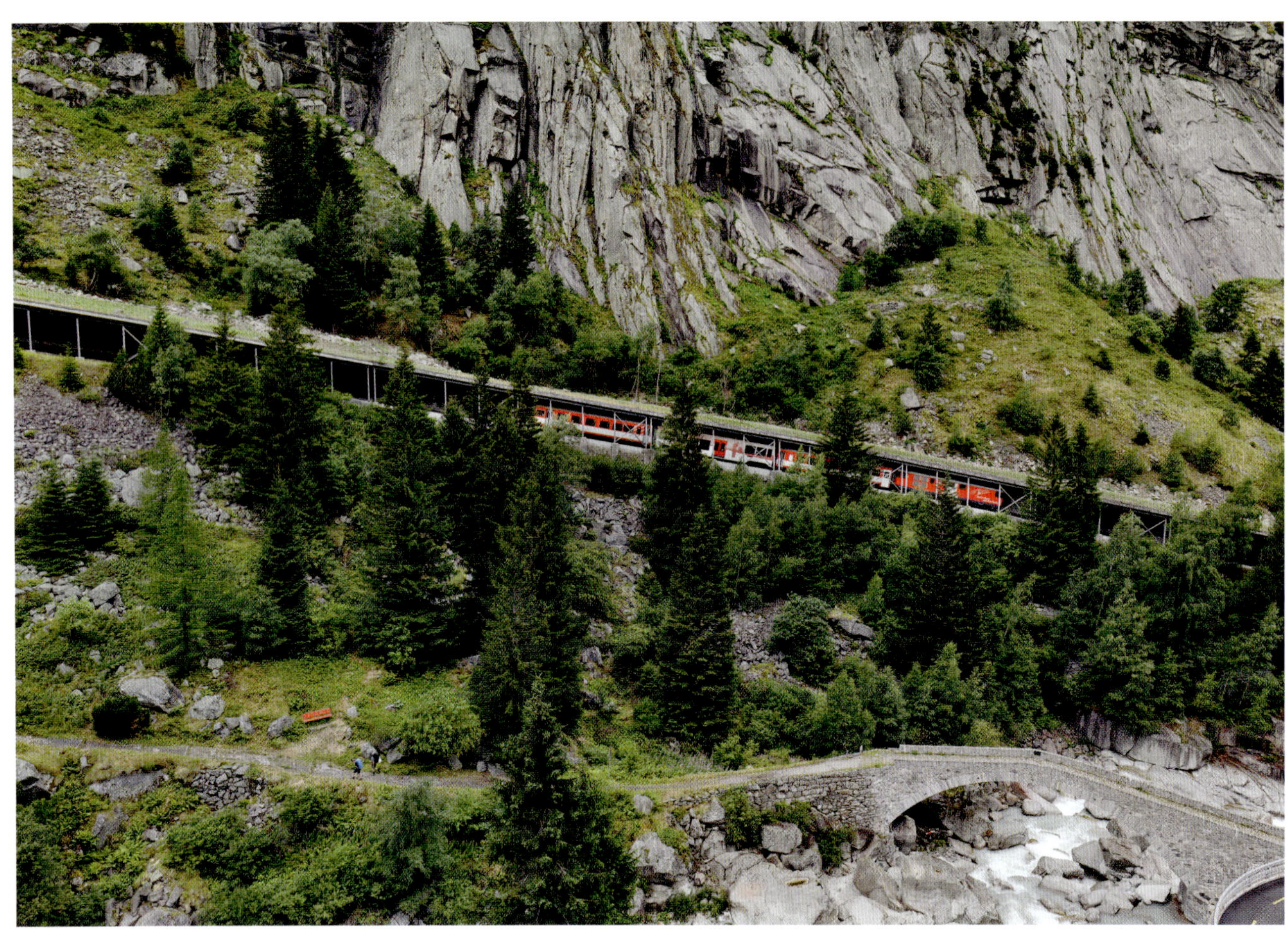

SCHÖLLENEN RAILWAY

The Schöllenen Gorge was once a real obstacle along
the Gotthard route. Below in the picture is the old
mule track with the Häderlisbrücke bridge from the
seventeenth century (destroyed by flooding in 1987 but
authentically reconstructed); above is a gallery of the
Schöllenen Railway.

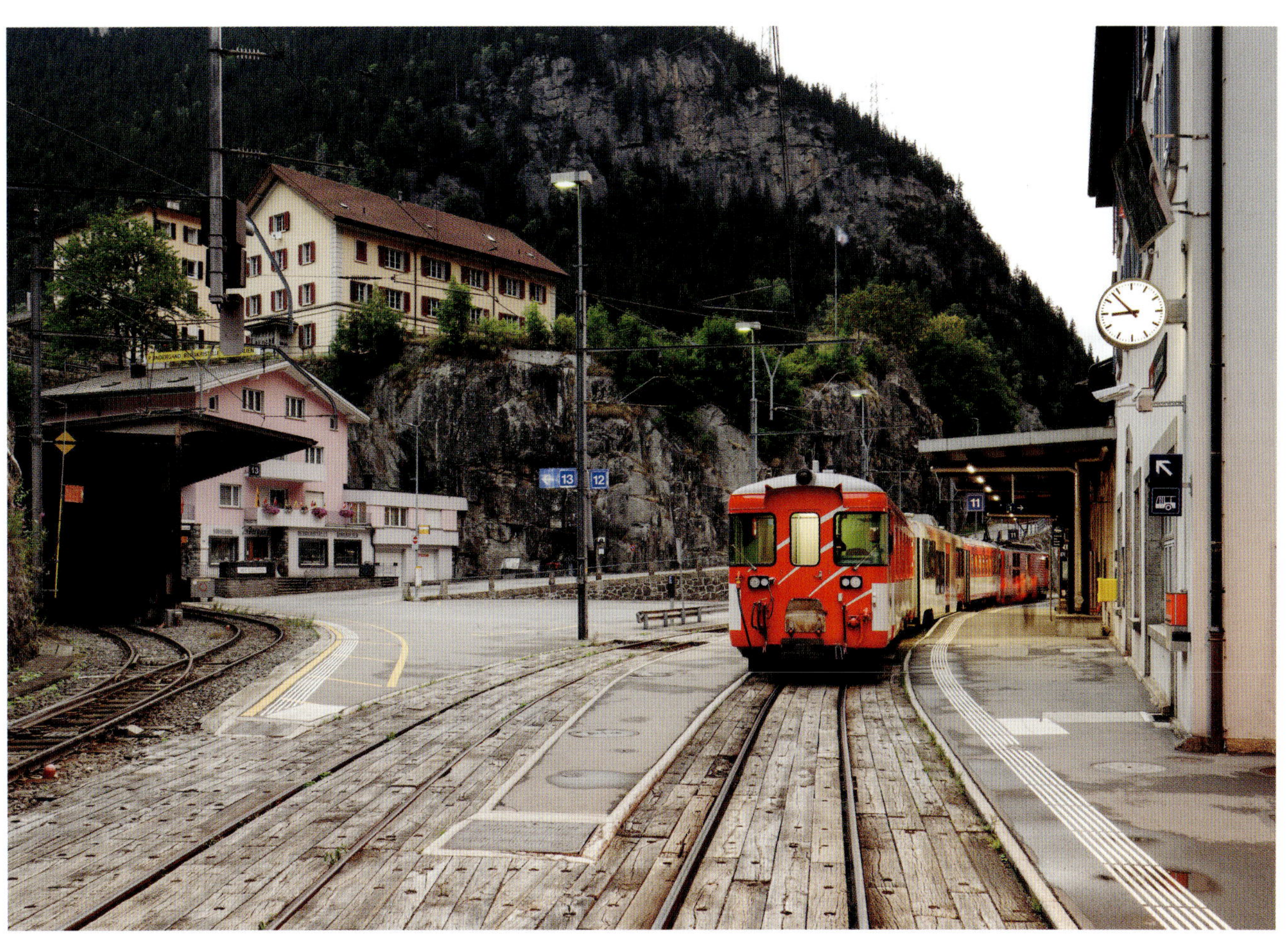

SCHÖLLENEN RAILWAY

In Göschenen, the train has left the station—
almost. The town at Gotthard has, for the most
part, lost its traffic significance.

GLACIER EXPRESS

The Oberalp Railway climbs in many loops
from Andermatt up to the pass of the same
name, the transition from the Urseren to the
Vorderrhein Valley. ▽ ▽

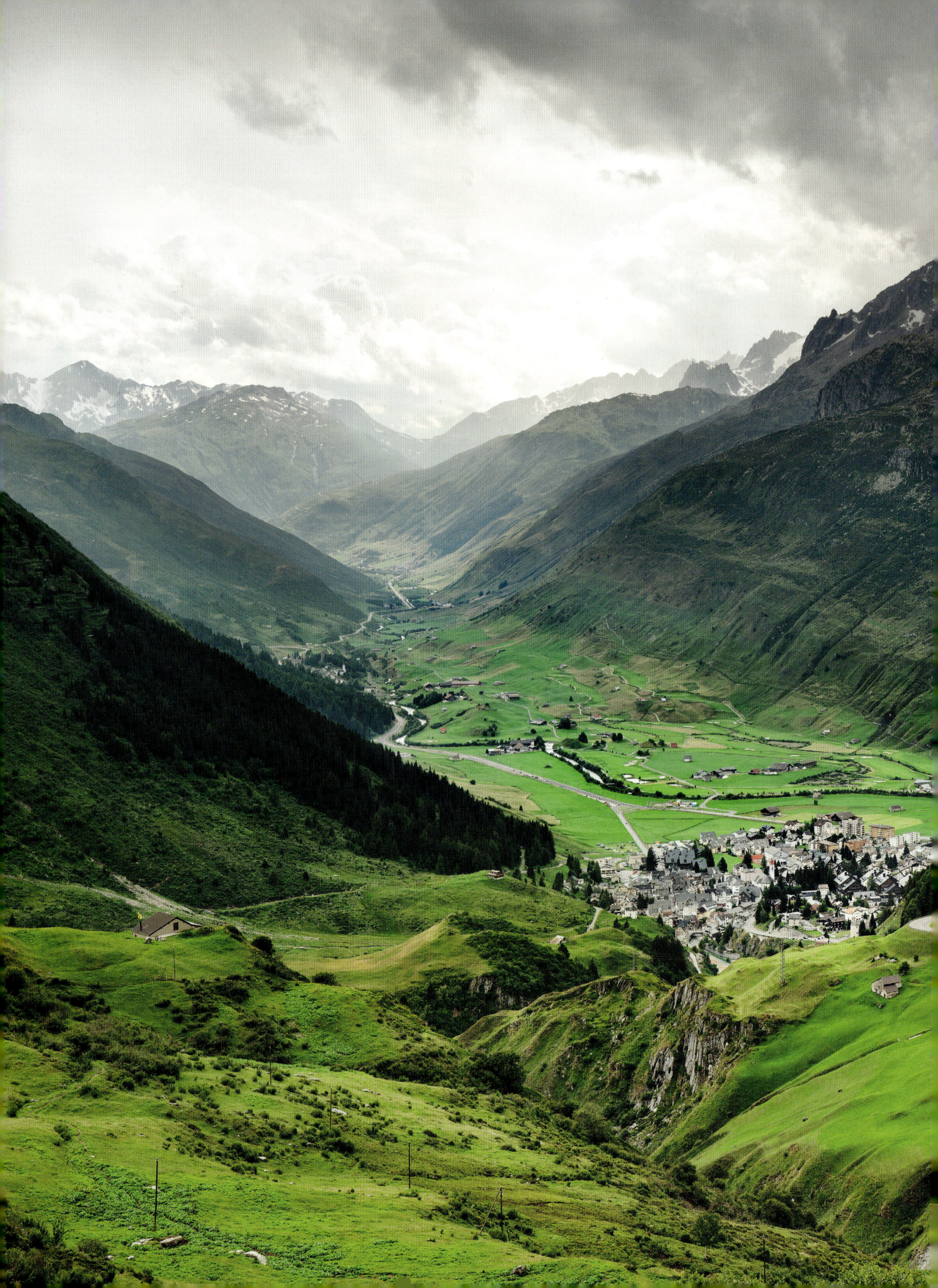

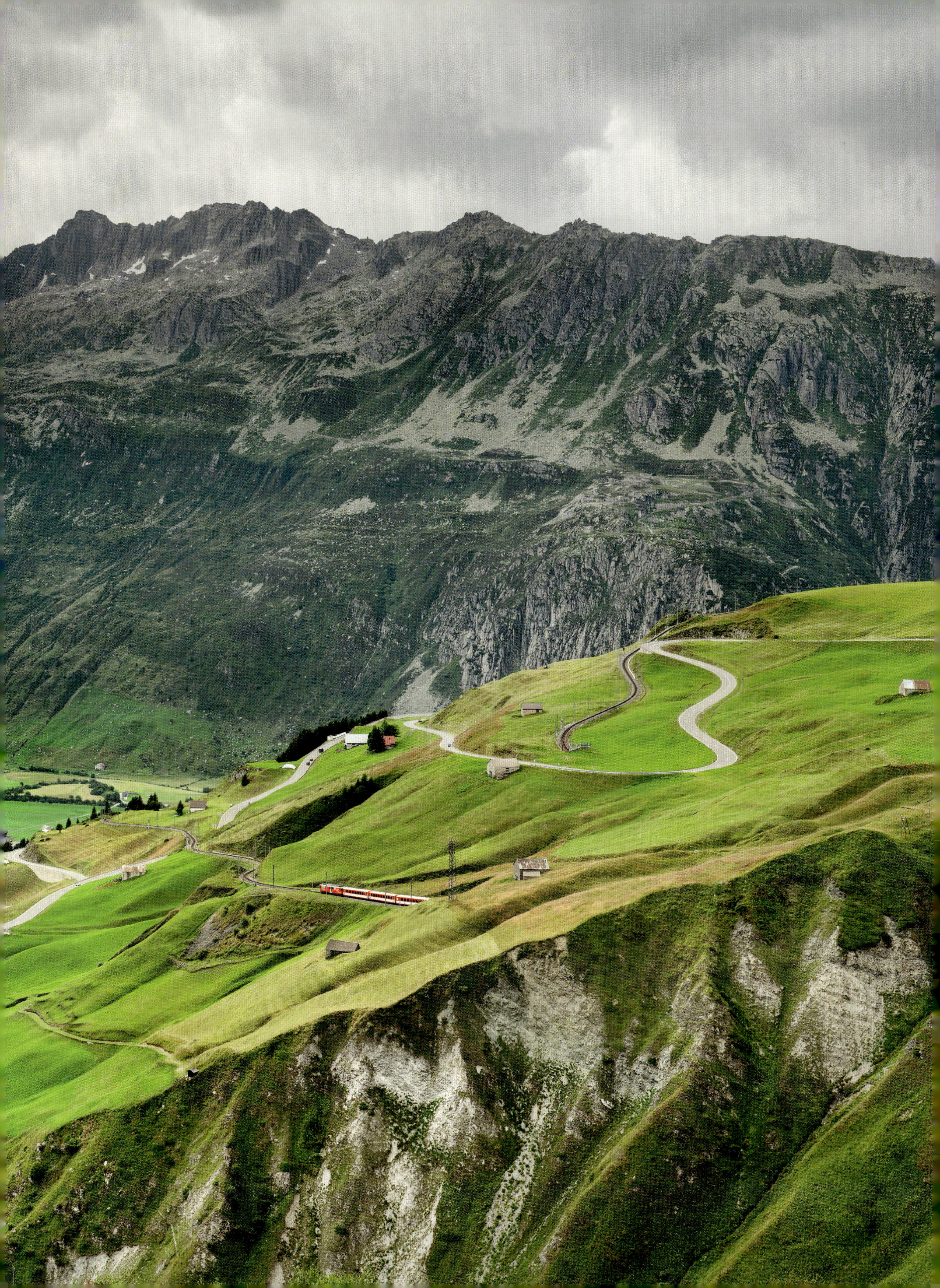

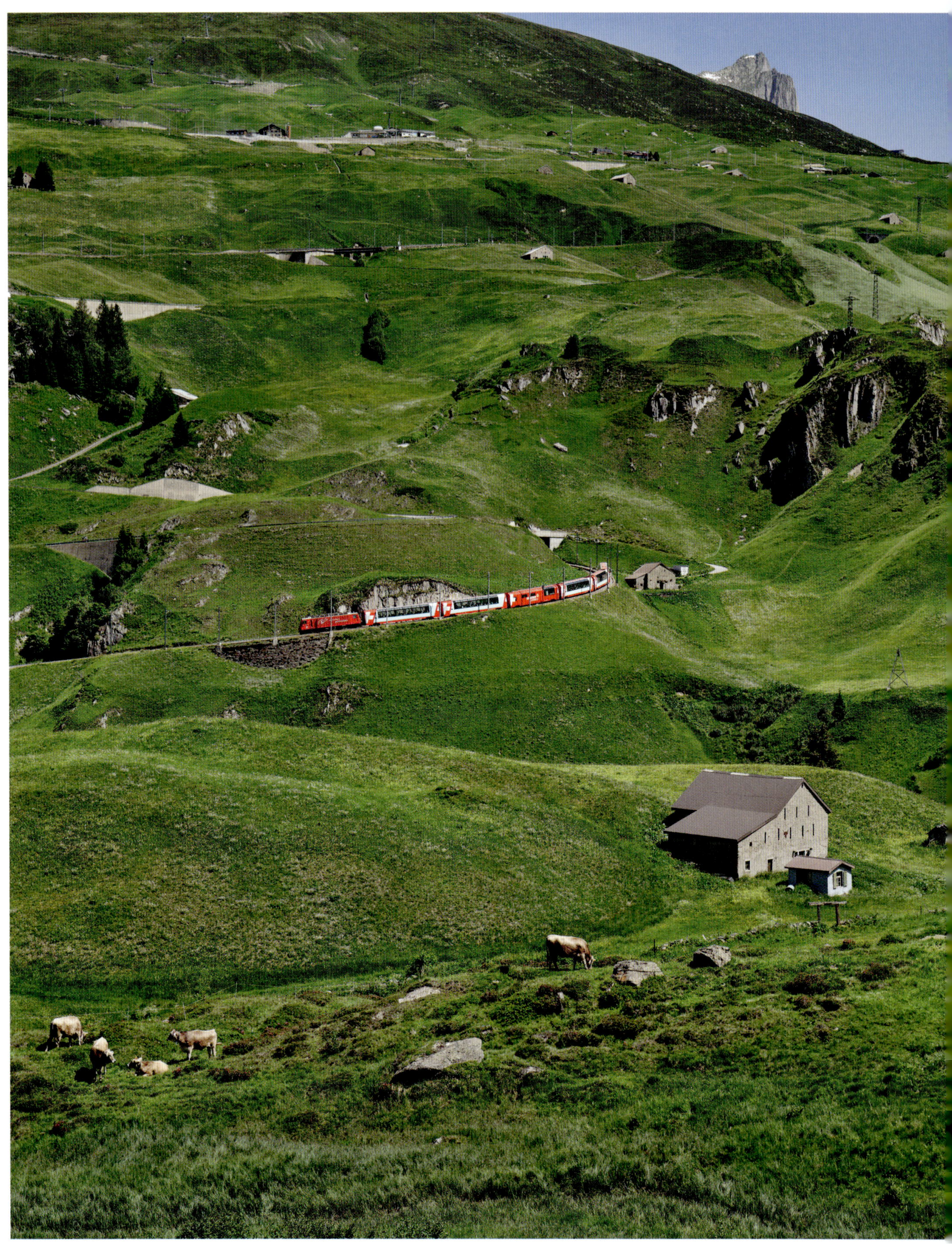

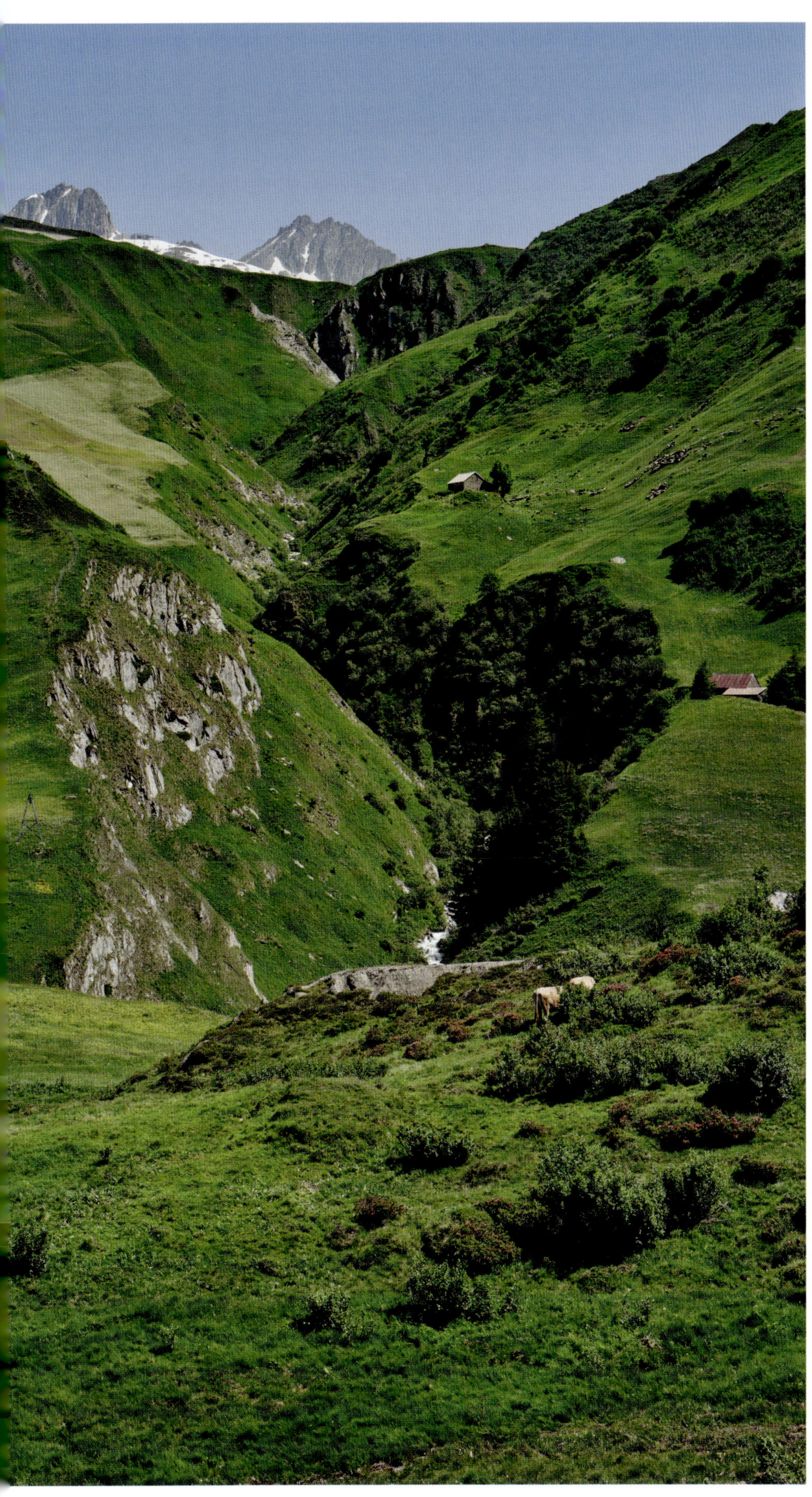

GLACIER EXPRESS

In elegant loops running with the
contours of the landscape, the
railway from Andermatt winds
its way to the long valley basin of
Oberalp. Above the green, three
peaks jut into the picture, one with
the name Unghürstöckli.

Autumn at the Oberalp Pass.
Winter is approaching, and the
summits are already covered with
the first snow. ▽ ▽

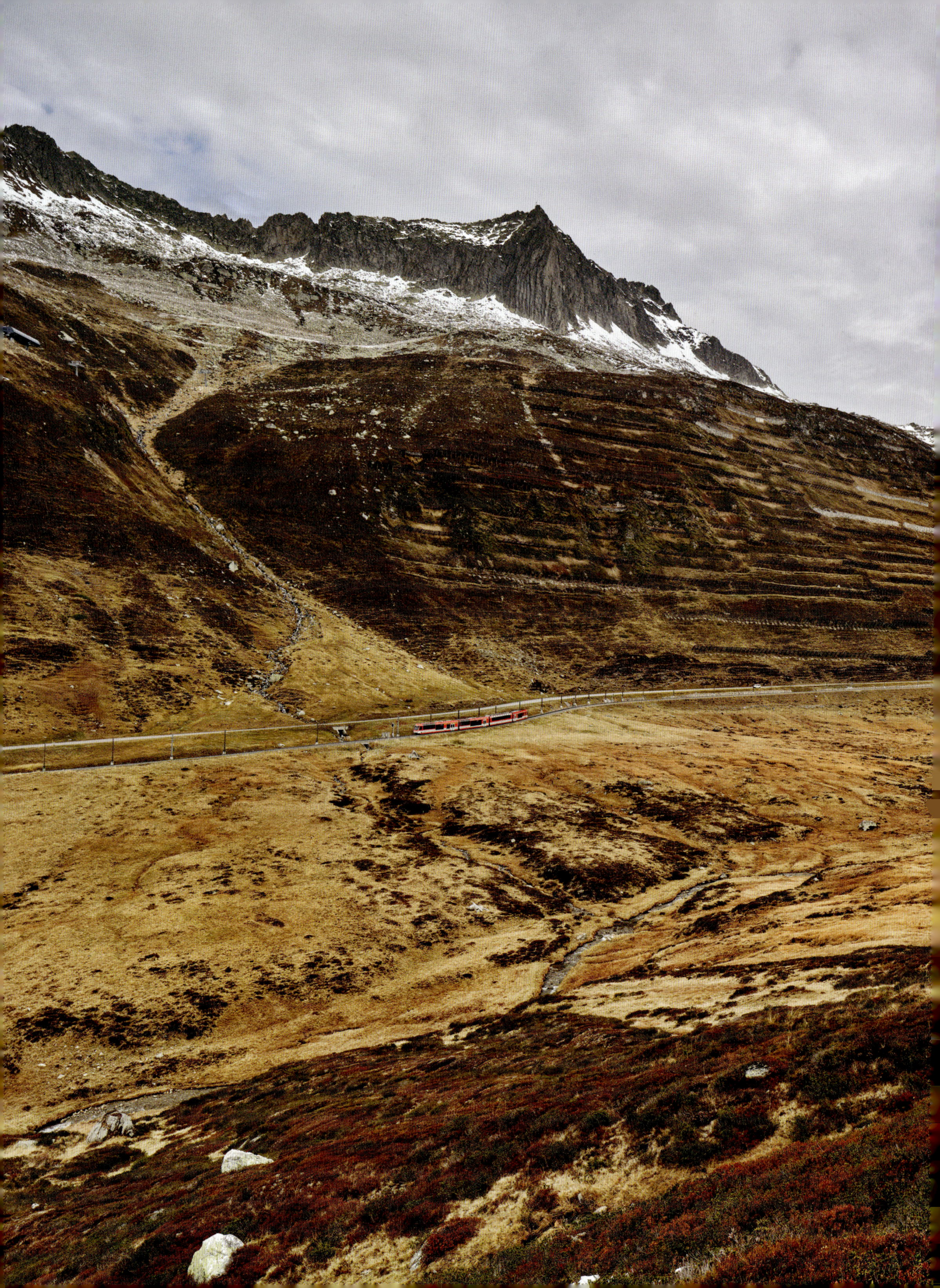

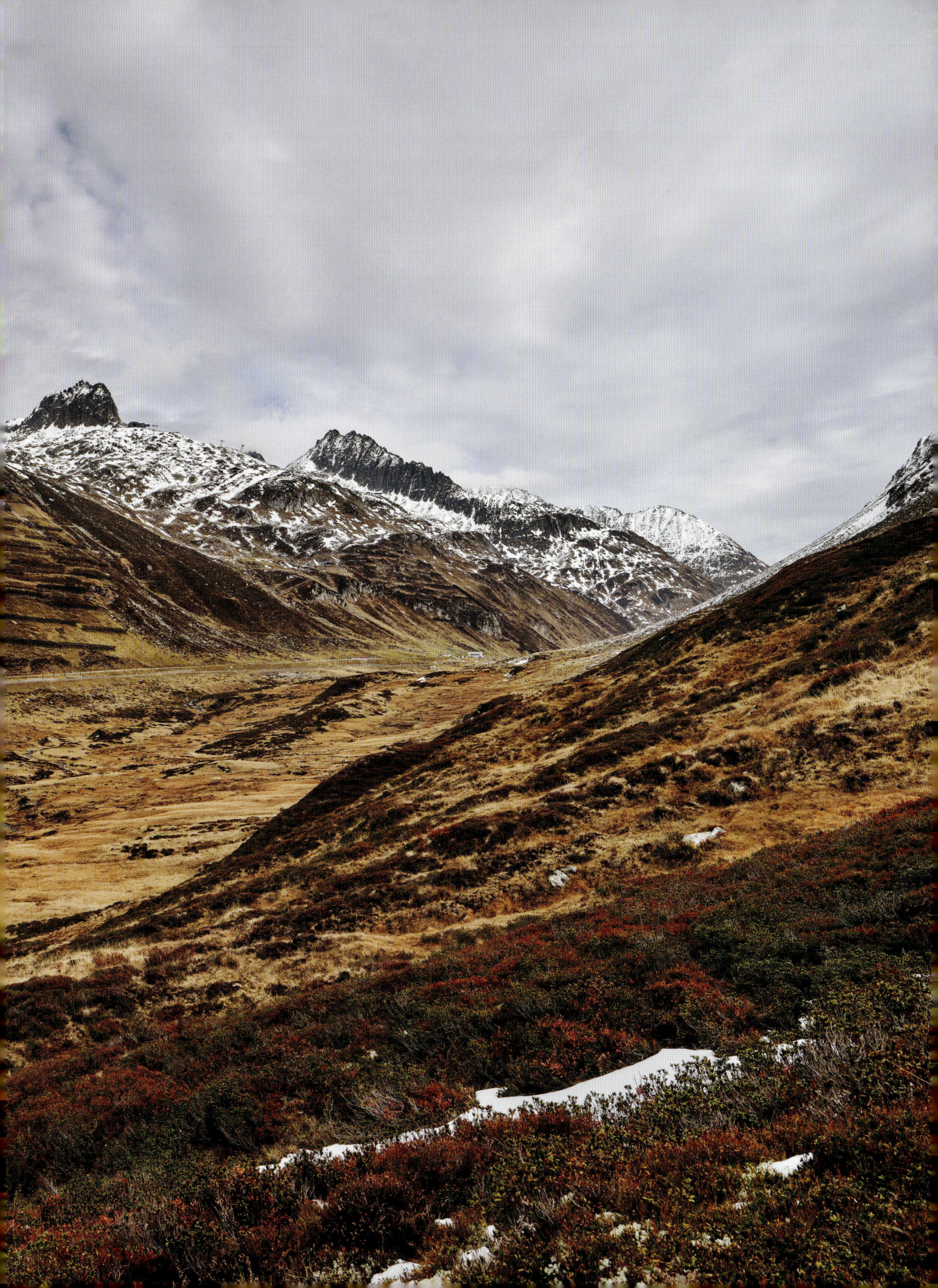

Although the streets through the pass are no longer cleared during the winter months, trains pass through during the whole year. A long avalanche gallery secures the railway near the Oberalpsee. It freezes completely during winter and hides under a thick blanket of snow.

Tunnels and galleries also protect the tracks of the Furka-Oberalp Railway near the Calmut mountain from avalanches. This allows the trains to run during the whole year, thanks to the Furka Base Tunnel from Valais to the Surselva region, continuing to Chur. ▽ ▽

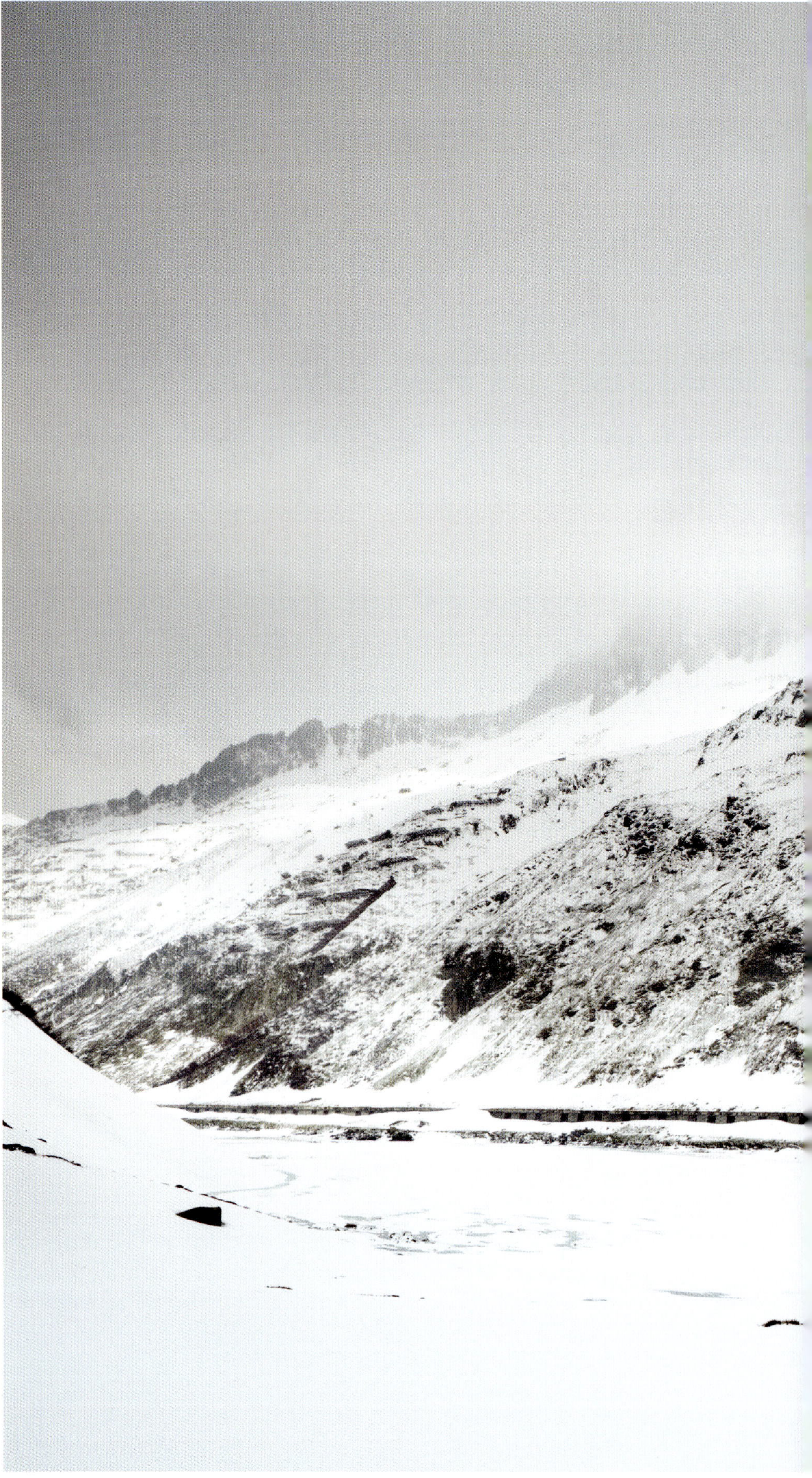

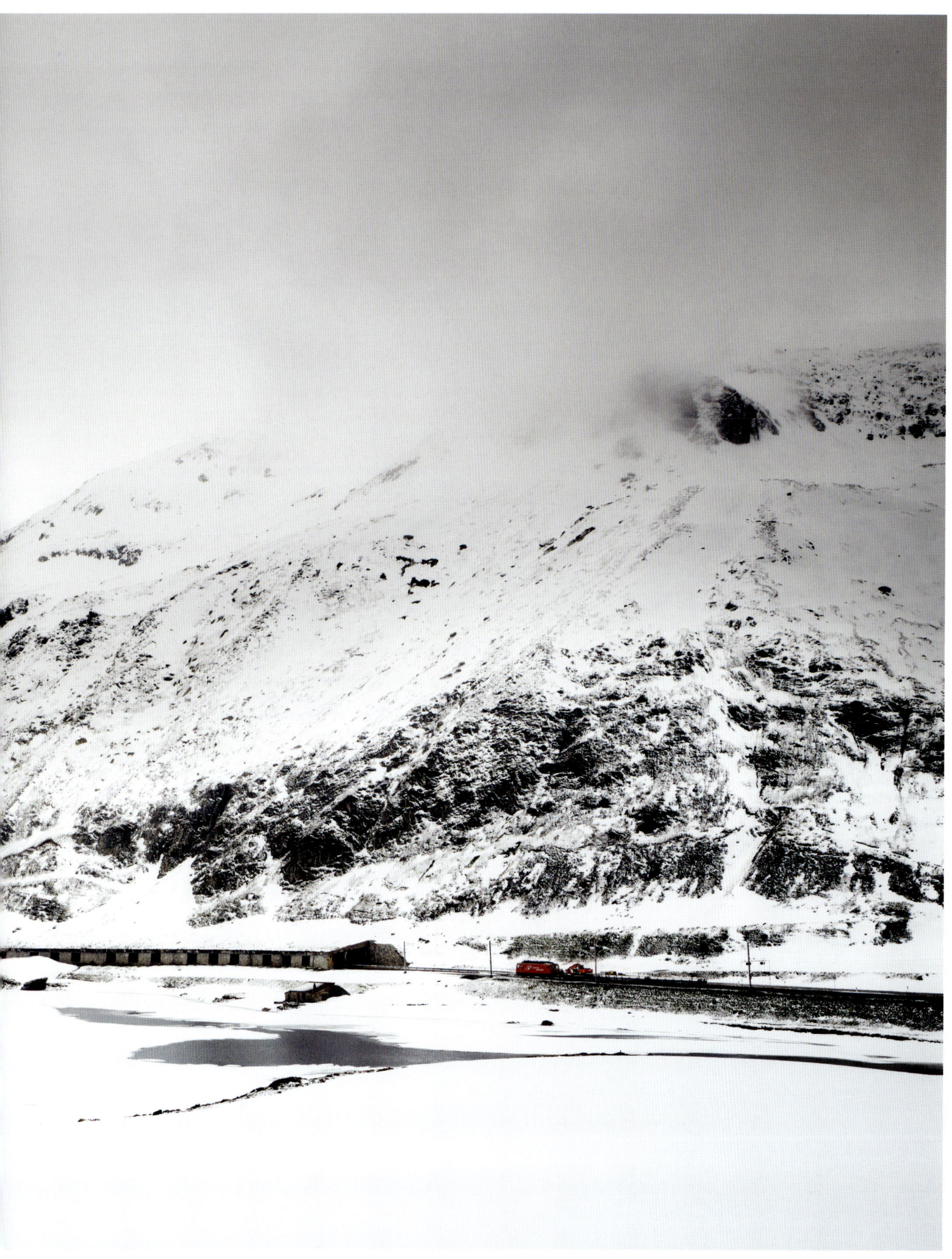

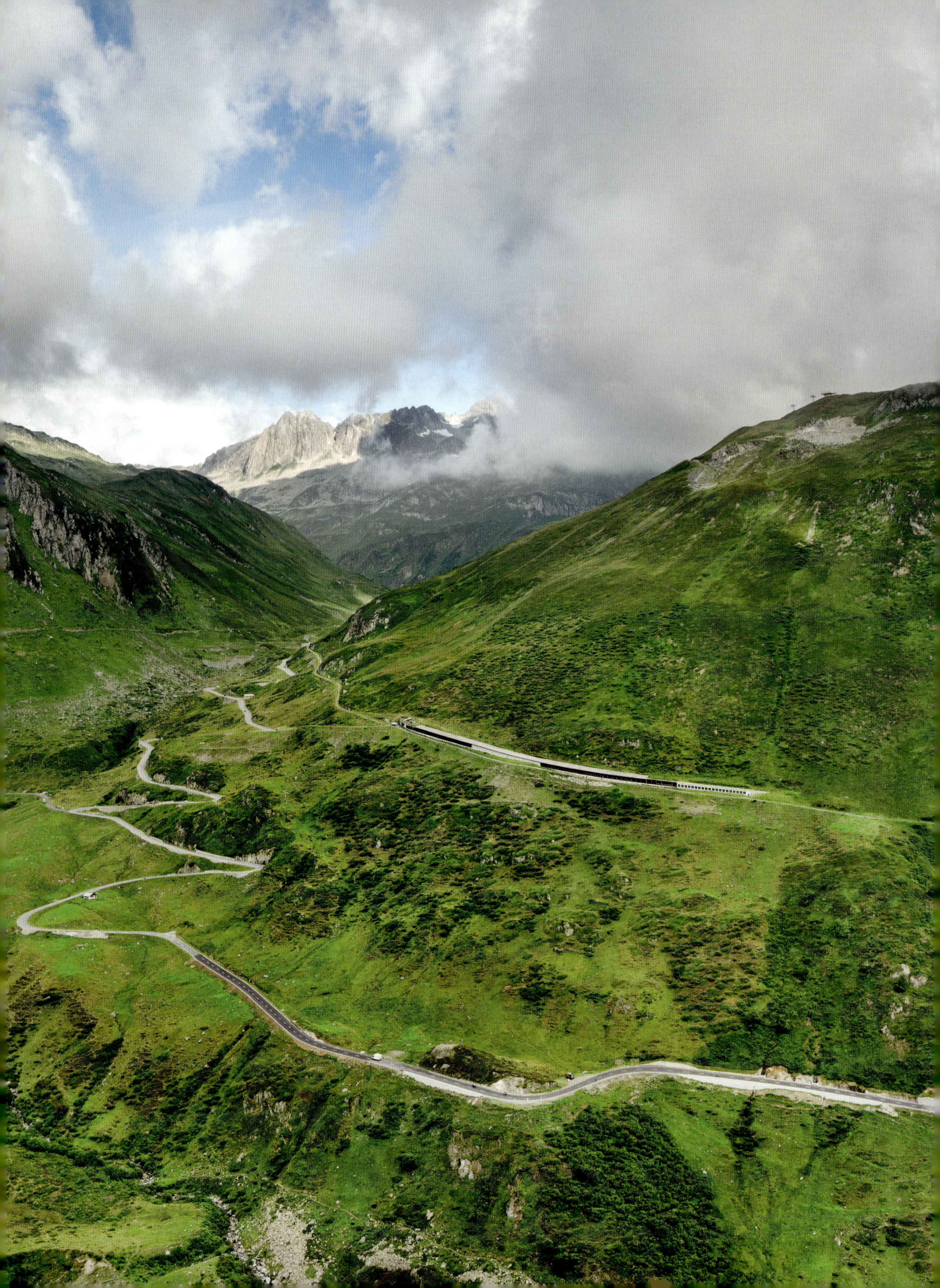

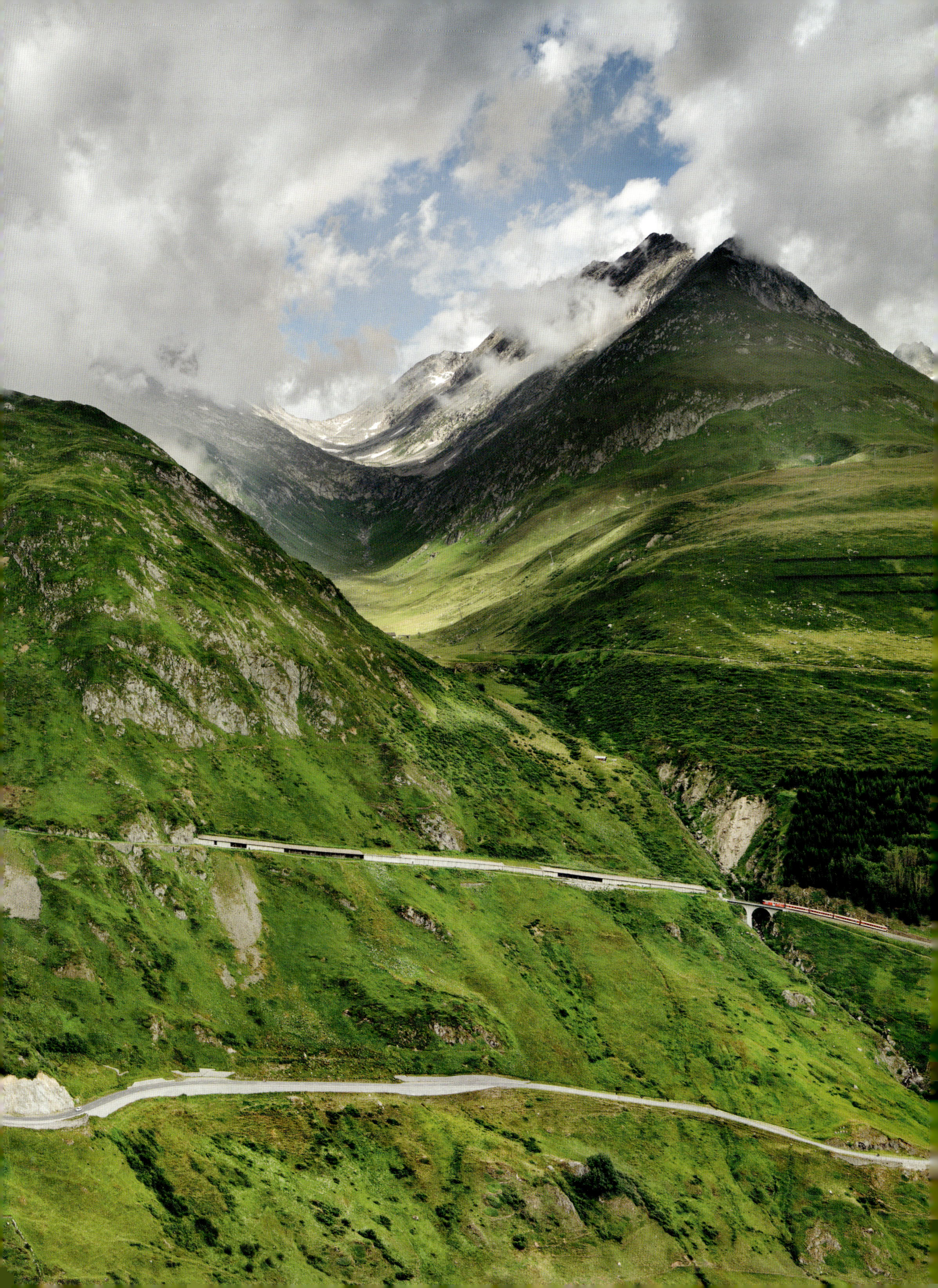

One of the largest natural wonders of Grisons: Ruinaulta. The "Bündner Grand Canyon" can best be experienced by foot—or with the Rhaetian Railway. It follows the path of the Vorderrhein from Castrisch to Bonaduz over about 15.5 miles (25 kilometers).

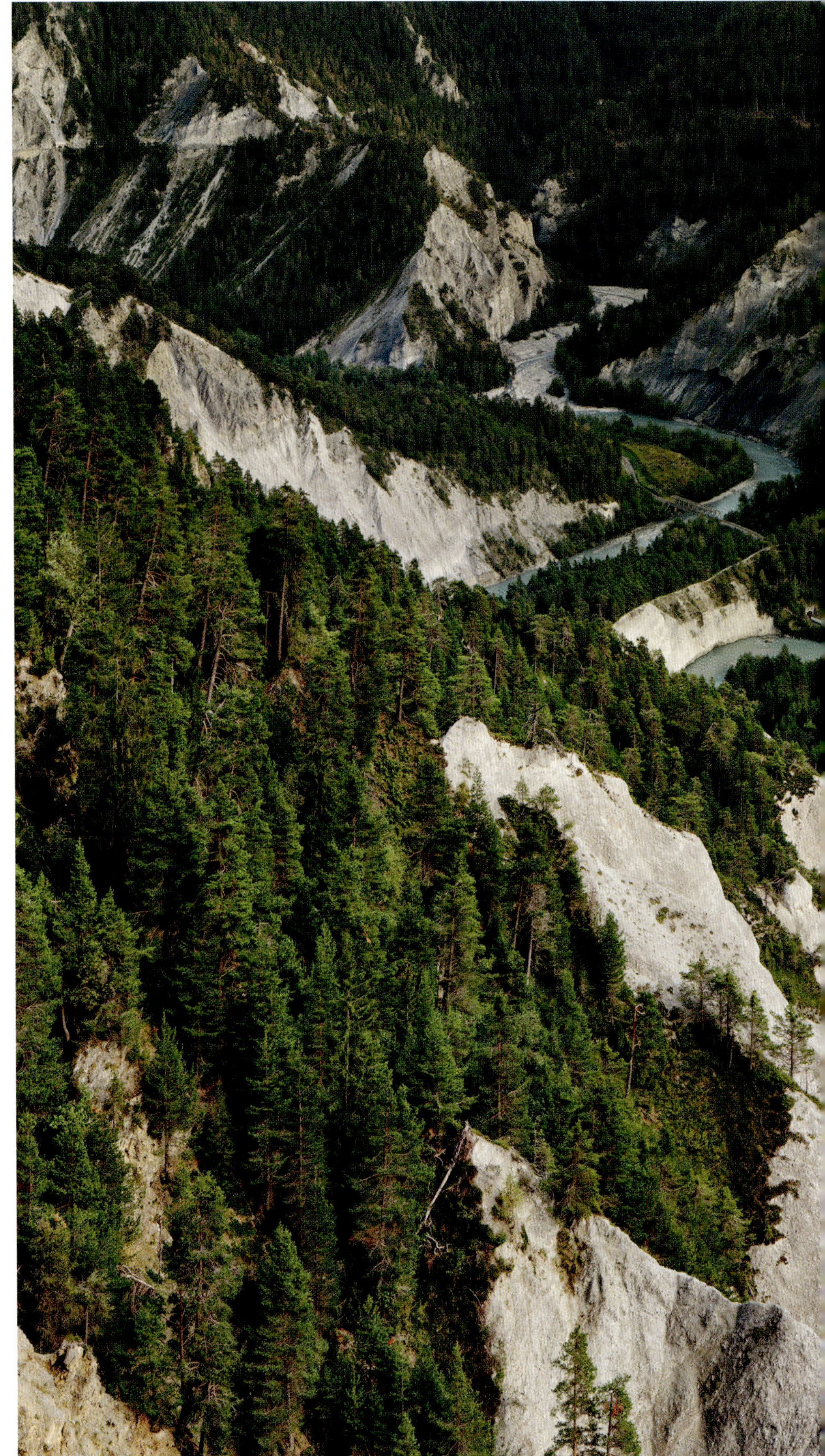

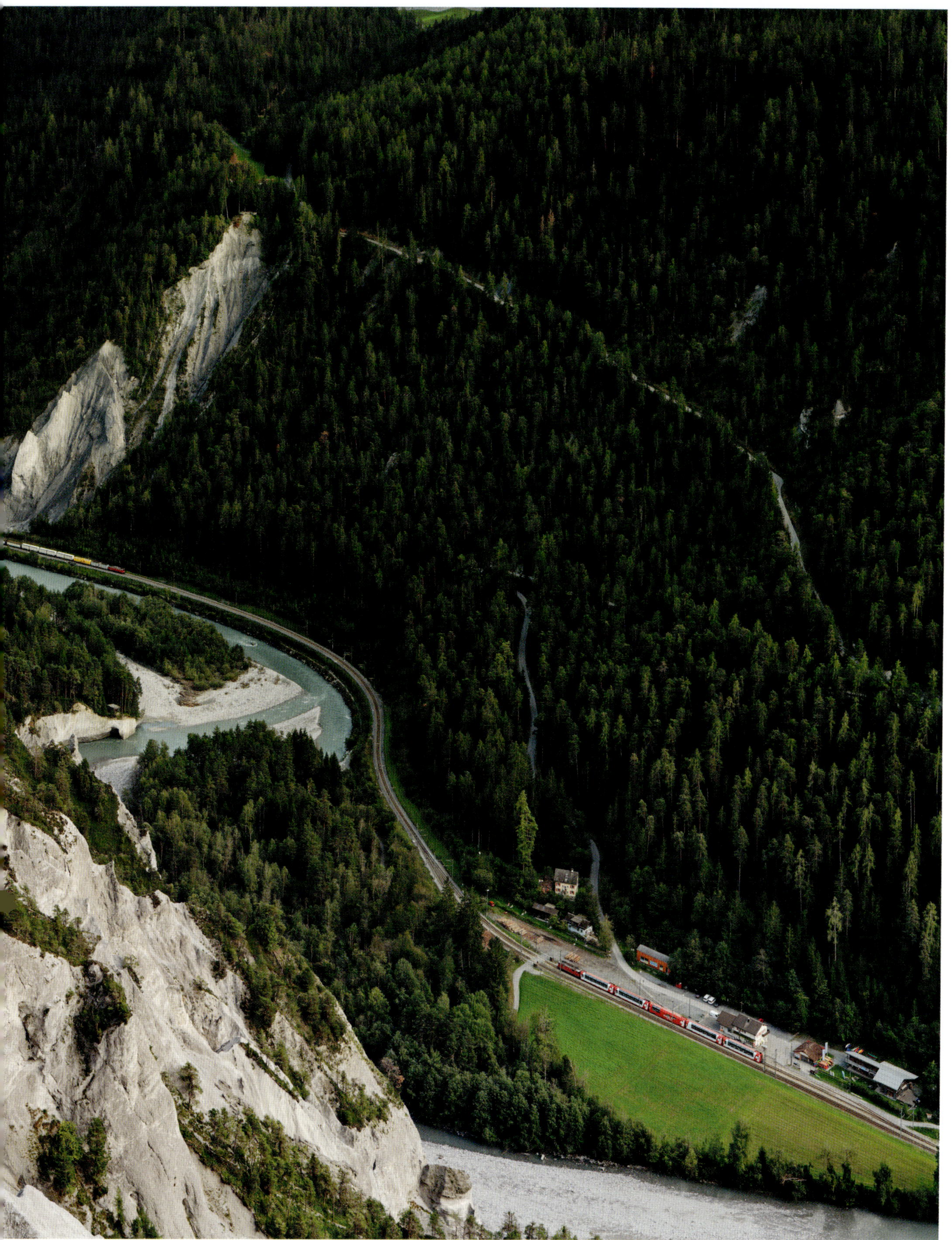

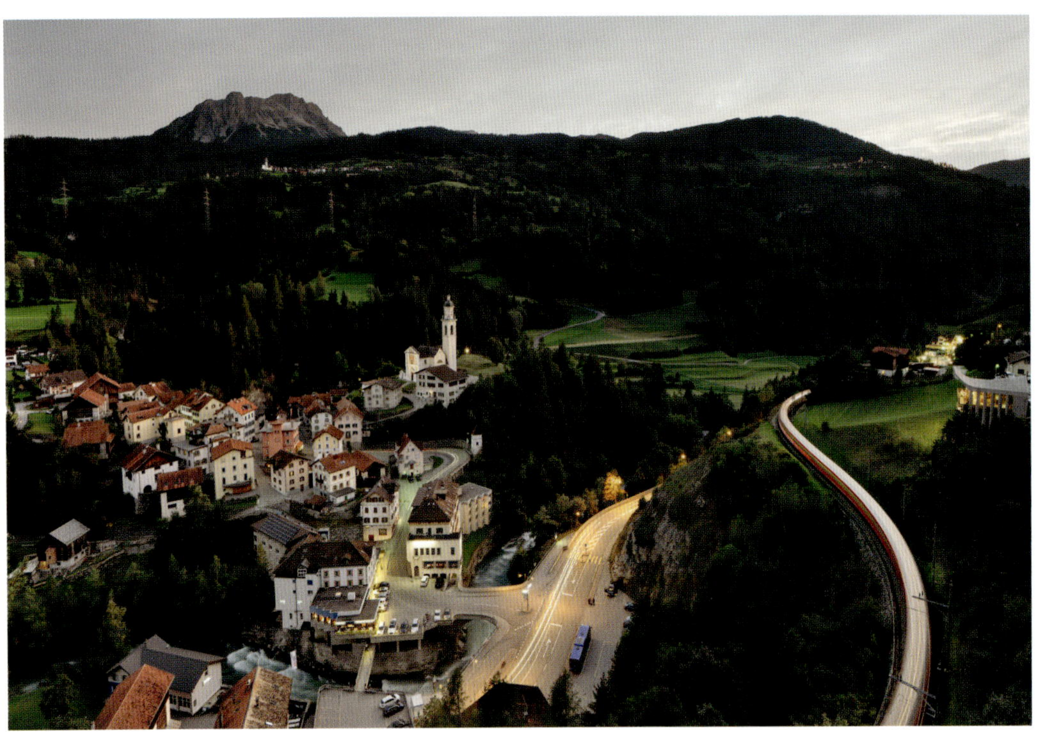

GLACIER EXPRESS

Traffic junction in Tiefencastel: This is where the streets of Chur
to the Julier Pass via Lenzerheide cross the Albula Railway. △

Between Solis and Alvaschein, the road and the Albula Railway
cross the deep, rocky Schin Gorge. The construction of the beautiful stone viaduct from 1903 cost 125,000 francs at that time. ▷

The most popular photo shot of the Rhaetian Railway: the
Landwasser Viaduct on the Albula route, which spans 65 meters
(213 feet) over the ditch of the mountain river with six arches. Its
construction in 1903 cost 280,000 francs. A century later, the
bridge was renovated while staying in operation, including
injections into the masonry. Cost: 4.6 million francs. ▽ ▽

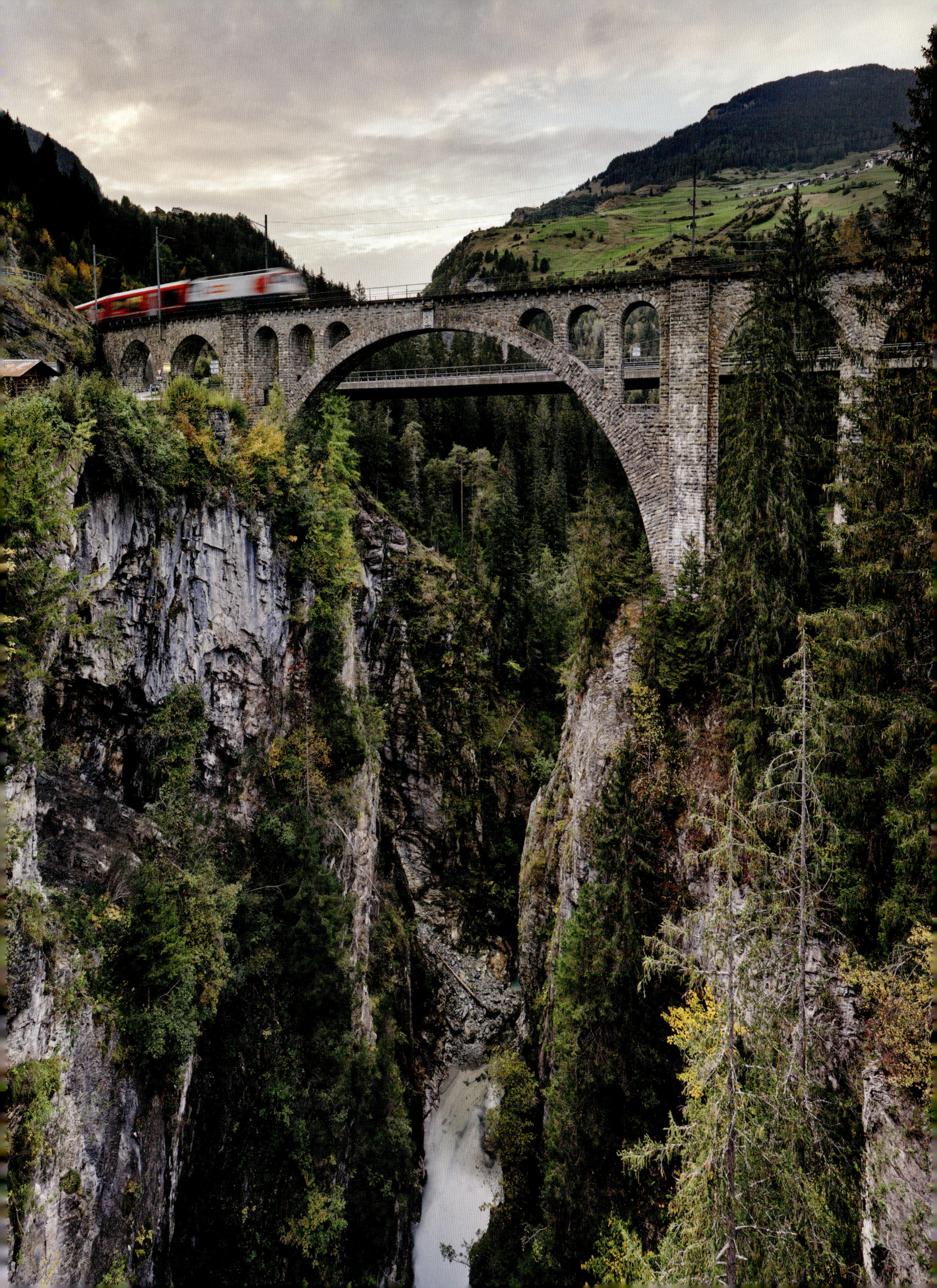

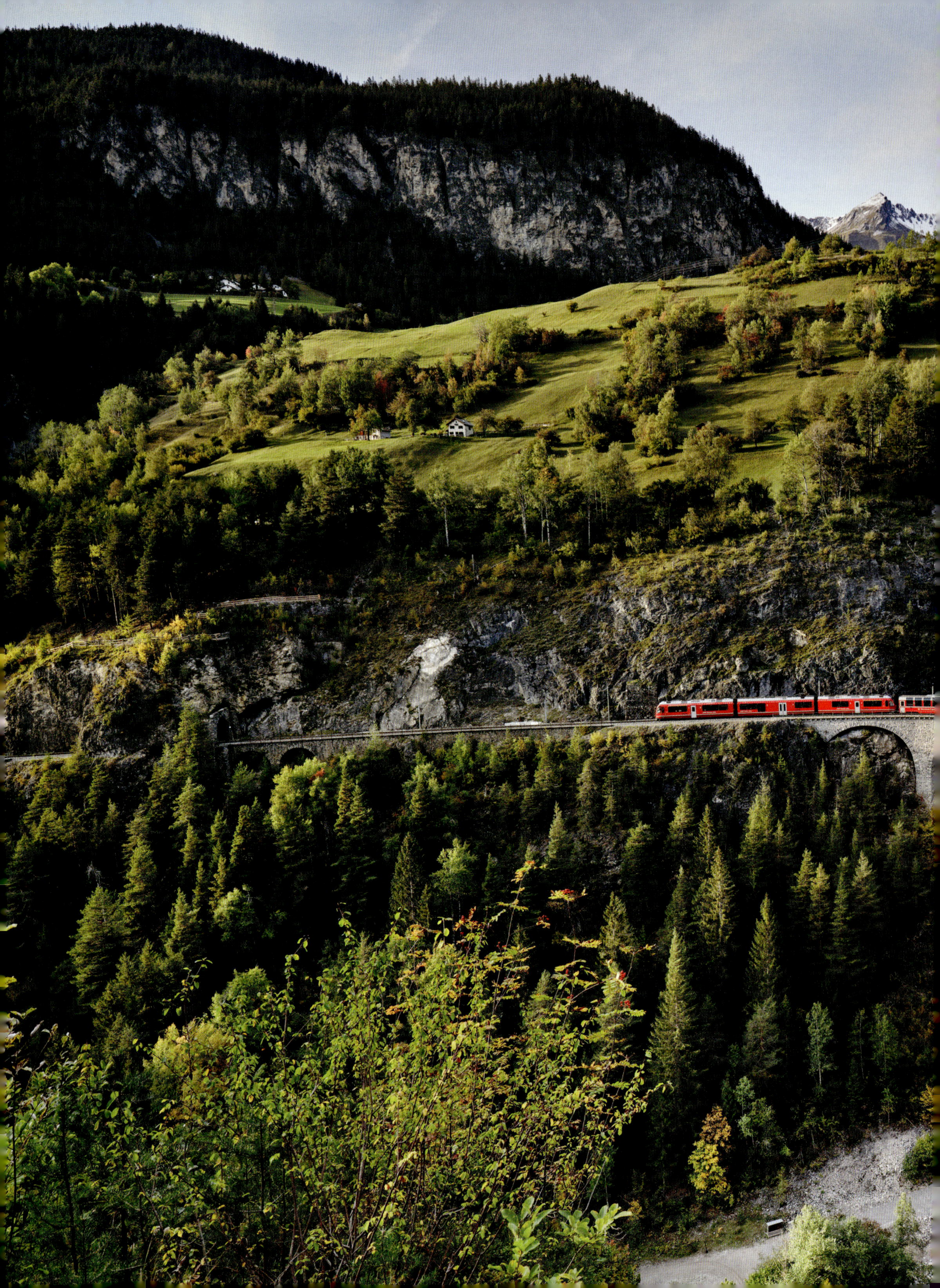

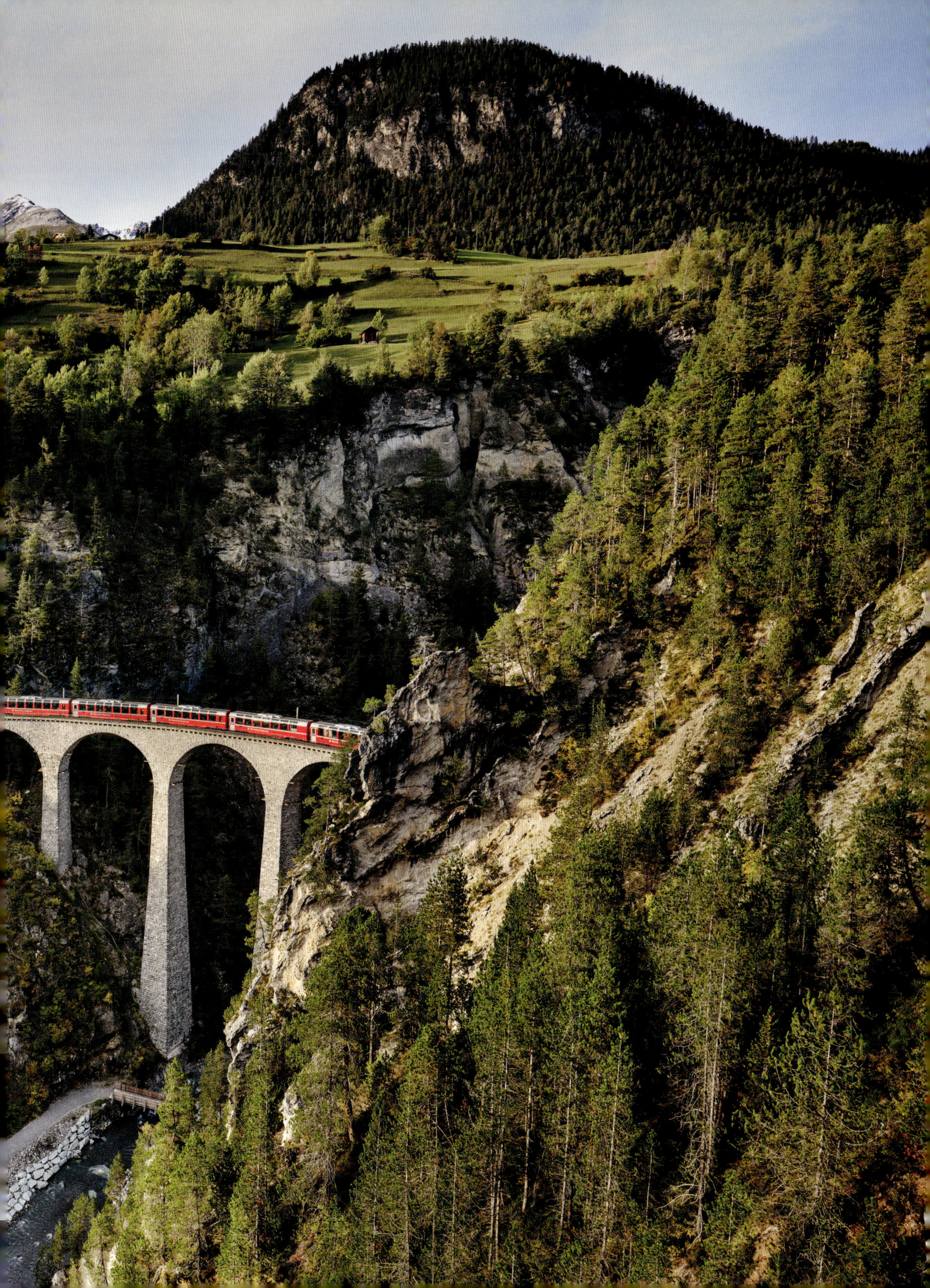

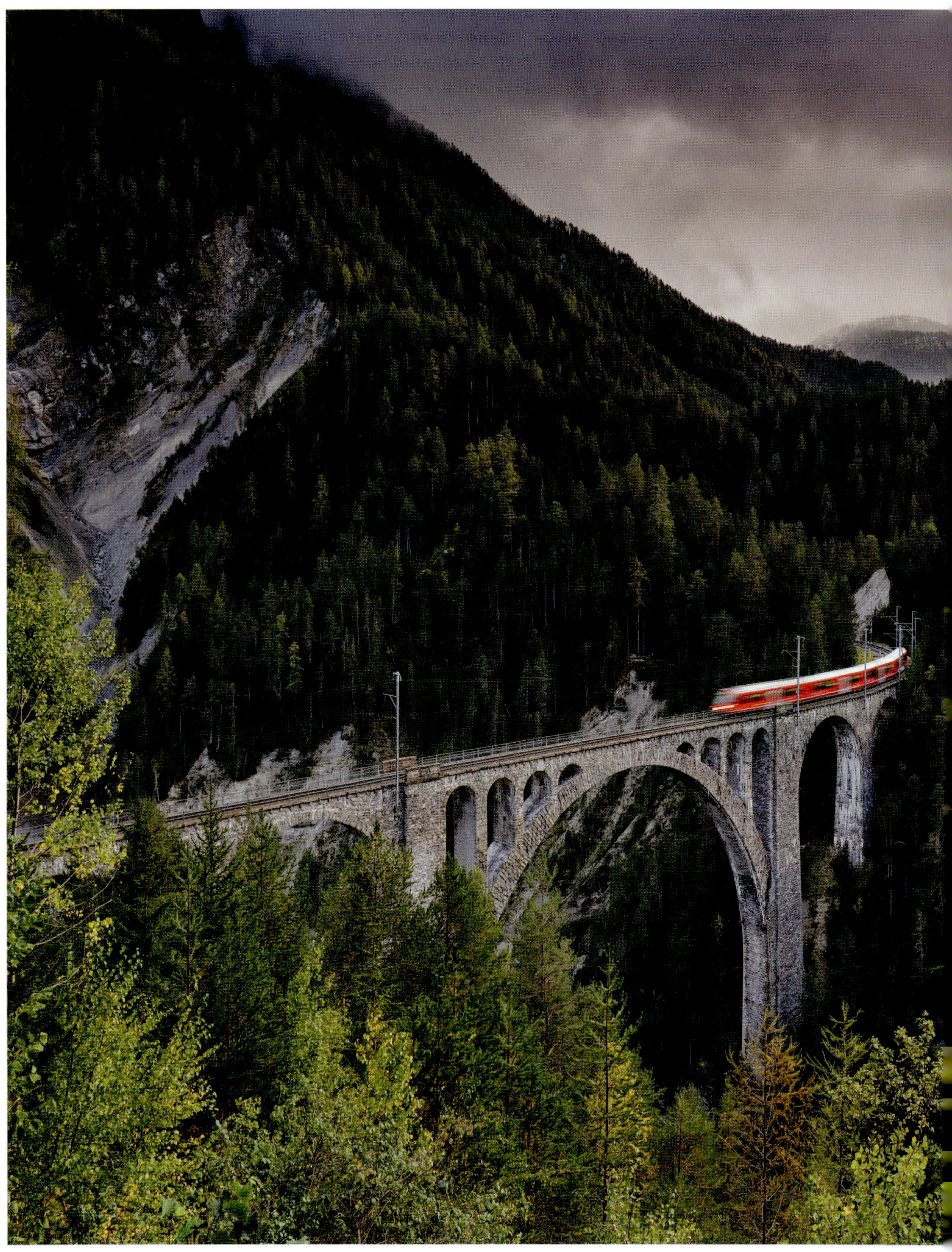

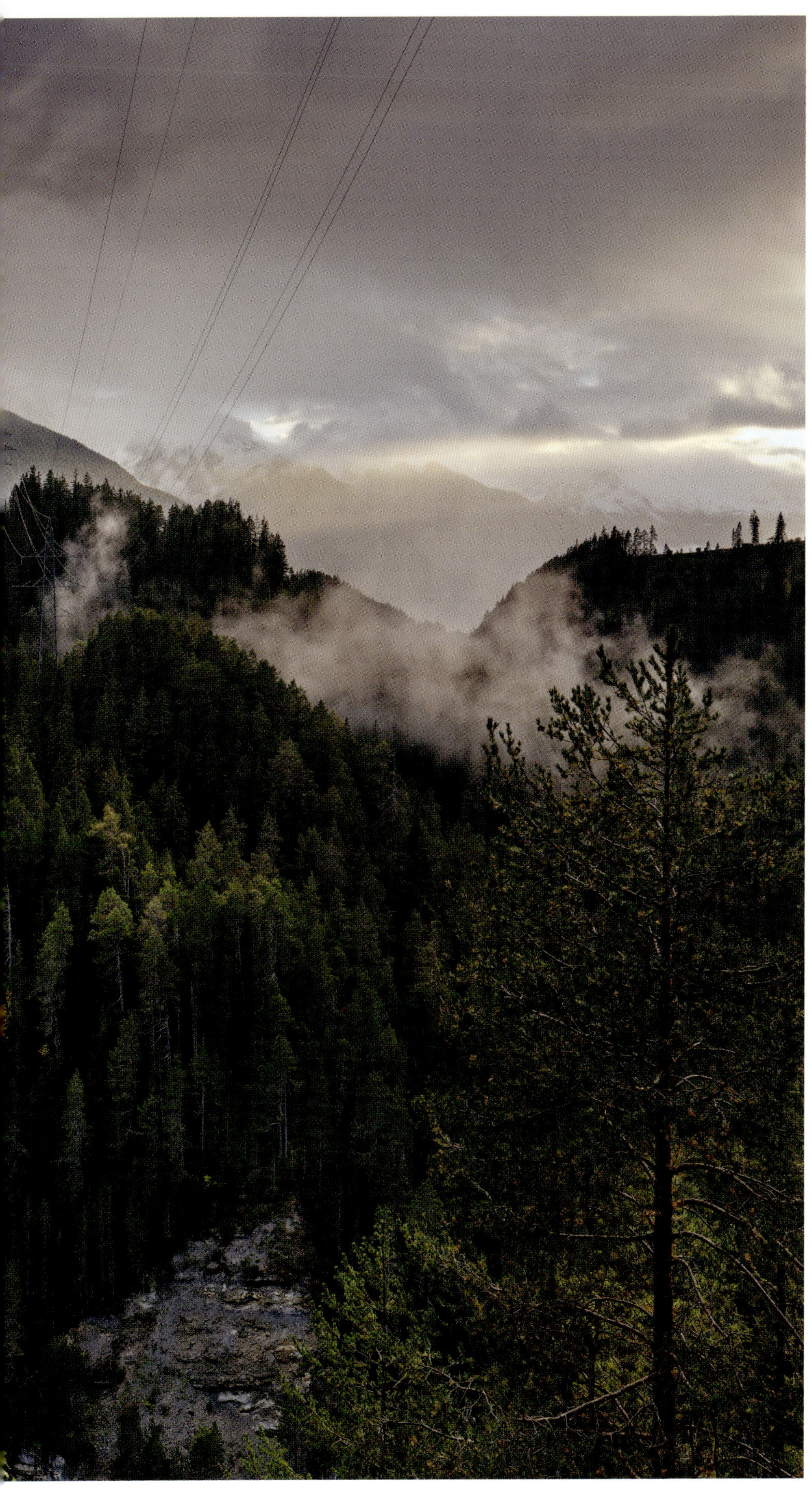

DAVOS RAILWAY

The most spectacular structure of the Davos–Filisur railway line is the Wiesen Viaduct, the highest viaduct of the Rhaetian Railway (291.7 feet / 88.9 meters). Ernst Ludwig Kirchner, who lived in Davos, was inspired to paint his picture *Die Brücke bei Wiesen* (*The Bridge near Wiesen*). A detail for insiders: On the left side of the picture, you can see a Hipp tuning-disc signal next to the track. The railway signal was created by Swiss inventor Matthias Hipp in 1860. It still stands without function on the bridge today.

GLACIER EXPRESS / ALBULA RAILWAY

Curves galore: With four looping and spiral tunnels (Rugnux, Toua, Maliera, and Zuondra), the Rhaetian Railway overcomes the altitude differential between Bergün und Preda: 1,368 feet (417 meters) over a distance of 7.8 miles (12.5 kilometers). It also passes over four viaducts along the same stretch. ▽

Albula Viaducts III and IV, between them the Maliera Gallery. View to Piz Ela (10,955 feet / 3,339 meters) and Piz Rugnux. ▽ ▽

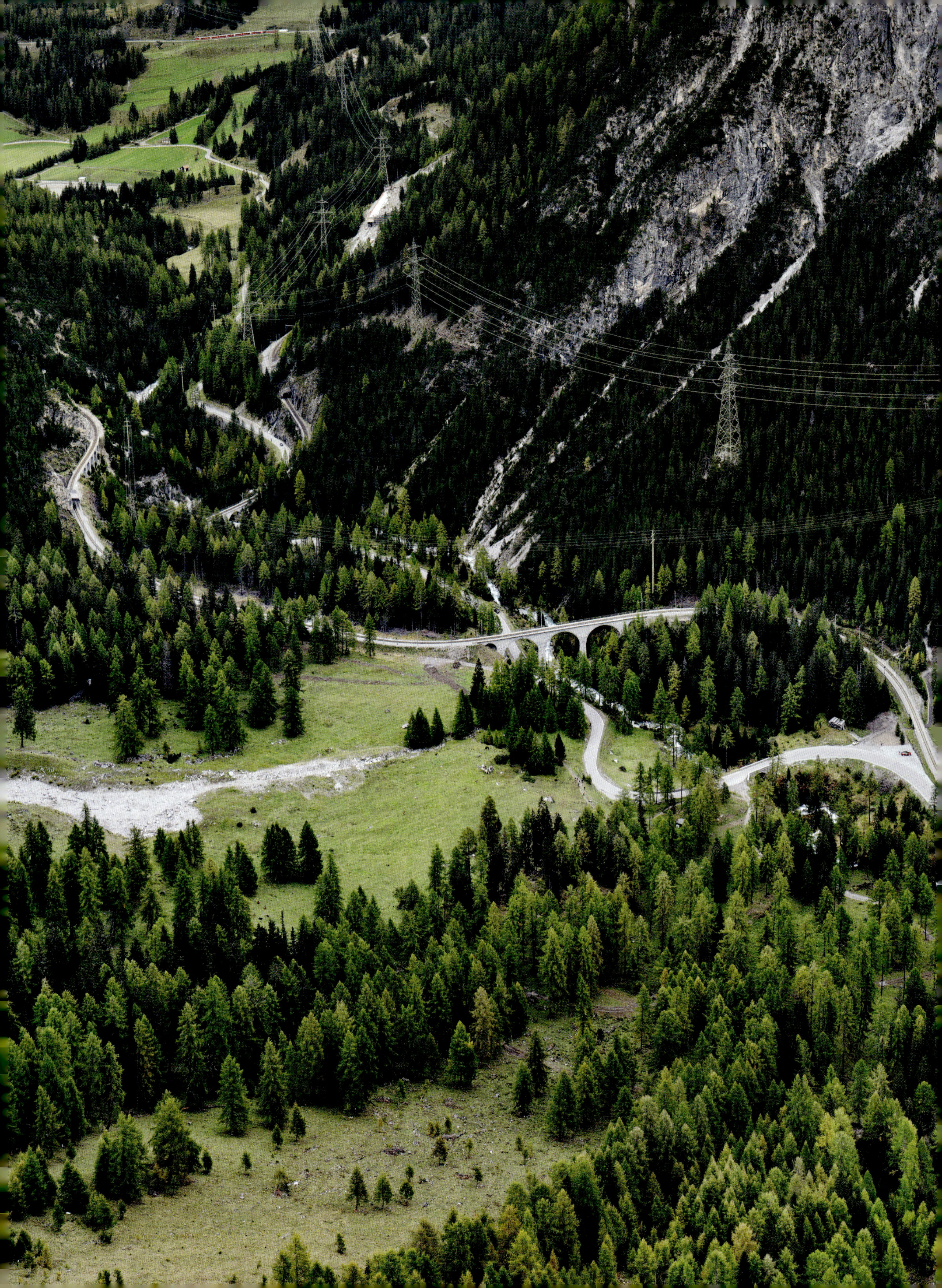

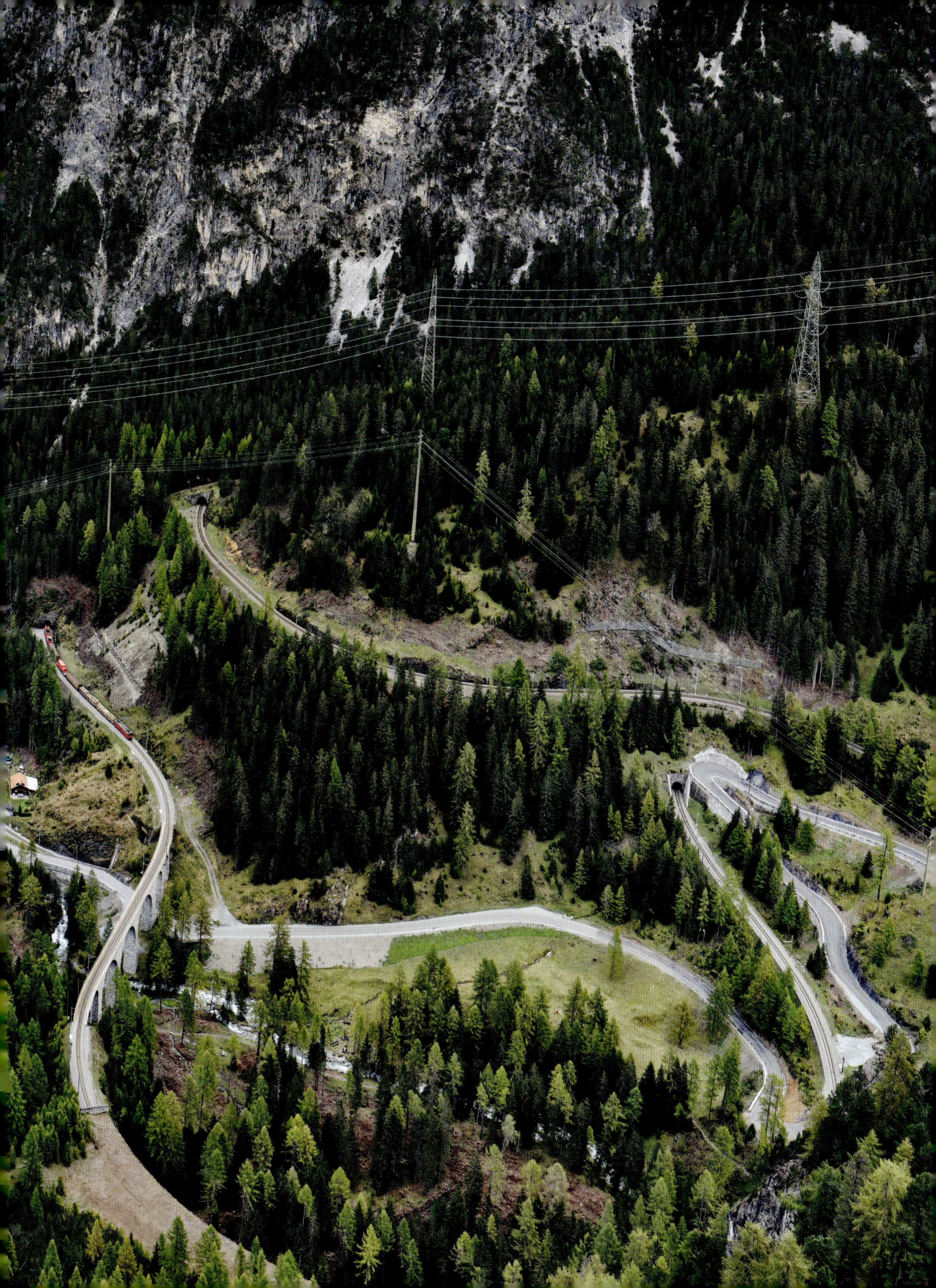

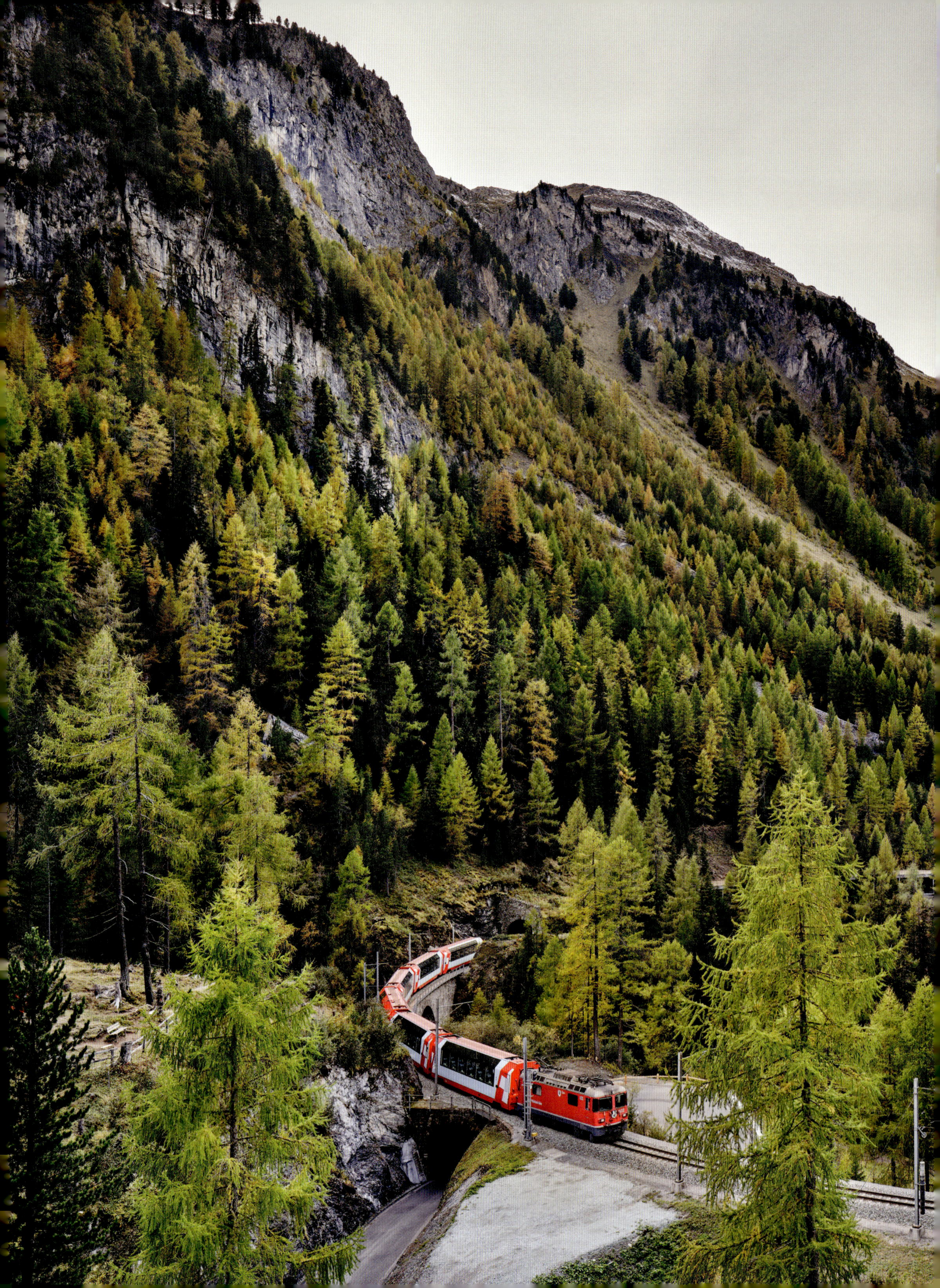

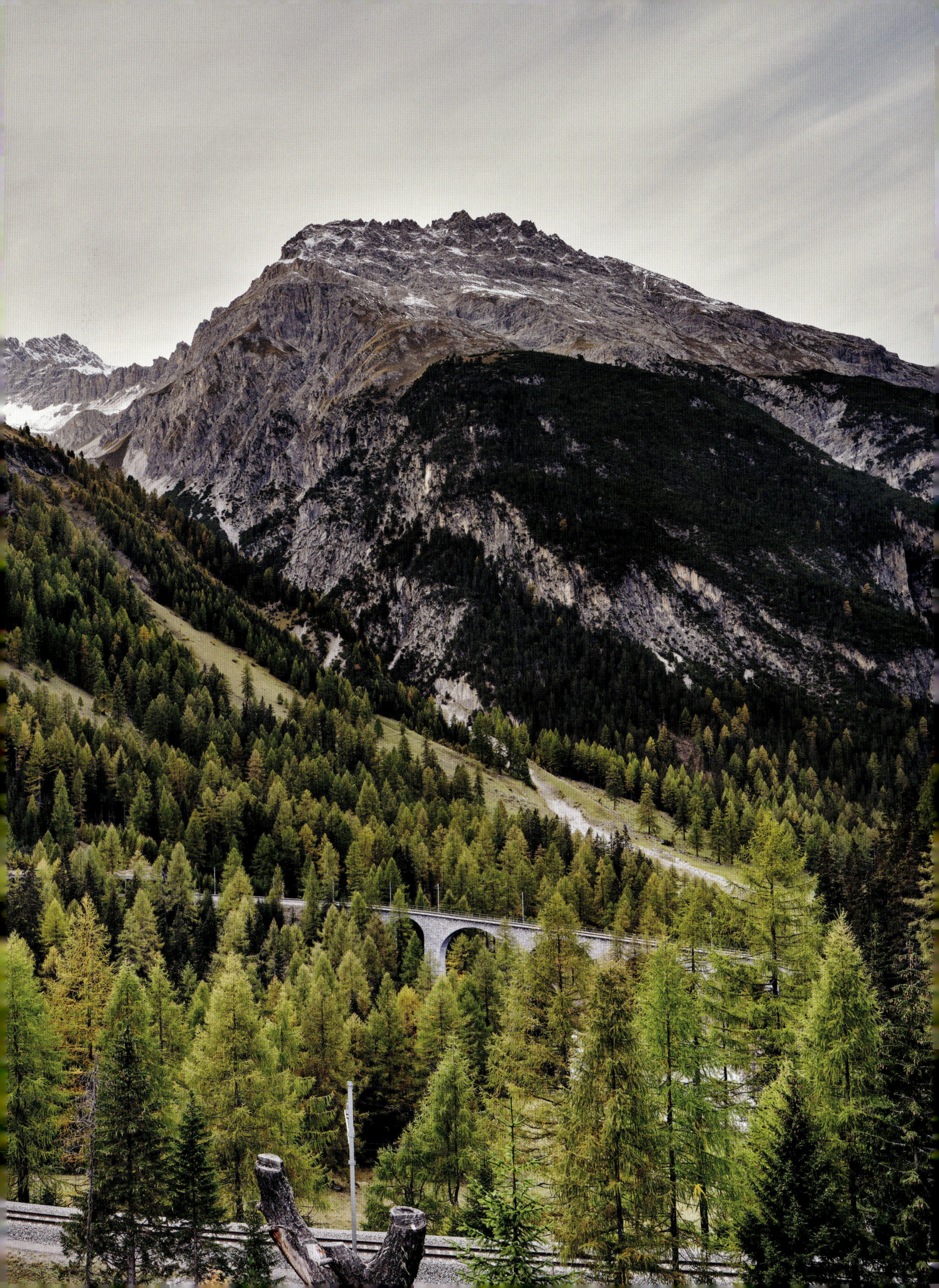

FROM THE GLACIAL ICE OF BERNINA TO THE VINEYARDS OF VALTELLINA

Puschlav is the only one of the southern valleys of Grisons to be connected by a rail line with the rest of the largest Swiss canton. The *Bernina Express* runs from the Upper Engadine down to Valtellina, where it connects with the Italian rail network. The *Engadine Line*, which also starts in St. Moritz, ends right before the border in Scuol; it is connected to the Davos Line via the *Vereina Tunnel*.

The name should make it successful. That's what they probably thought in Chur, where the Rhaetian Railway (RhB) has its headquarters, when they created the Bernina Express in 1973 out of the Bernina Railway. The red trains did not run much faster because of it, which isn't a bother, considering there are sensational things to see along the 37-mile (60-kilometer) route (travel time: two and a half hours). The highest adhesion railway of the Alps climbs from St. Moritz to the Bernina Pass (7,392 feet / 2,253 meters) and then descends in wide loops with a maximum slope of 7 percent in Puschlav (Val Poschiavo).

The Bernina Railway was built at the start of the twentieth century by a private company. The goal was to connect St. Moritz with Tirano and the Italian rail network. After a series of partial openings, the whole stretch went into operation in 1910. It didn't bring too much to the investors except losses. In the middle of World War II, the line was taken over by the Rhaetian Railway. This takeover proved to be worth it, but only in the long run. Rail travel became increasingly popular as a travel experience of a different kind and allowed people to pass through the mountain landscape of Grisons stress-free.

THE ICE UP CLOSE

The Montebello bend behind Pontresina offers the first highlight with a clear view to the Bernina Massif and the Morteratsch Glacier. However, it has been severely affected by climate change, losing 1.2 miles (2 kilometers) in length. But even so, the Vadret da Morteratsch, with an ice volume of more than 0.2 cubic miles (1 cubic kilometer), is still the most massive glacier of the eastern Alps.

A few kilometers farther down the mountain, the Diavolezza cable car offers a comfortable option to get closer to the icy world of Bernina. Diavolezza means female devil, but you don't have to be afraid of this viewing point. The view of Piz Palü is simply heavenly, even more beautiful when you have already stood on the summit . . .

DOWN INTO THE VAL POSCHIAVO

The Lago Bianco marks the divide between the Mediterranean and the Black Sea, between Engadin and Puschlav. The lake, dammed by southern and northern walls, forms the apex of the pass. The Bernina Pass is the only one in the Alps whose height varies a few meters during the year. In the winter, the water freezes, and if it's not snowing at that time, black ice will form. It's a fascinating, rare natural phenomenon.

The descent into Puschlav occurs in wide loops and allows for many new perspectives. From Alp Grüm you have a first view of Poschiavo; even more impressive is the jagged Palü Glacier. Poschiavo, the valley's main town, has a heavy Italian influence. In Le Prese, the streets and the train use the same tracks; the express becomes a tramway, which can cause confusion among travelers who are unfamiliar with the area.

The last valley step then has another engineering sensation in store: the circular viaduct of Brusio. Tirano is the last station of the Bernina Express; on the tracks of the Ferrovia statale you can continue through Valtellina to Comer Lake and to Lecco. Scuol in the Lower Engadine is the end of the Engadine Line that begins in St. Moritz, but it doesn't have a rail connection toward Tyrol. This is because the extension that was originally planned to Landeck never came to fruition. The focus today is on a connection between the Lower Engadine and Mals in the South Tyrolean Vinschgau. Together with the 12-mile-long (19-kilometer-long) Vereina Tunnel, which was opened in 1999, this would create a new connection between eastern Switzerland and southern Tyrol, which would be interesting for tourism.

Even a connection to the Glacier Express would be possible. From Bolzano to the Matterhorn via St. Moritz by train—how sensational! Or will it remain a fantasy?

The Montebello bend offers an impressive view to the Bernina Massiv and the Morteratsch Glacier. You can't overlook the dramatic reduction of the ice; in the last century, the glacier lost about 1.3 miles (2.5 kilometers) in length and much of its volume. ▽ ▽

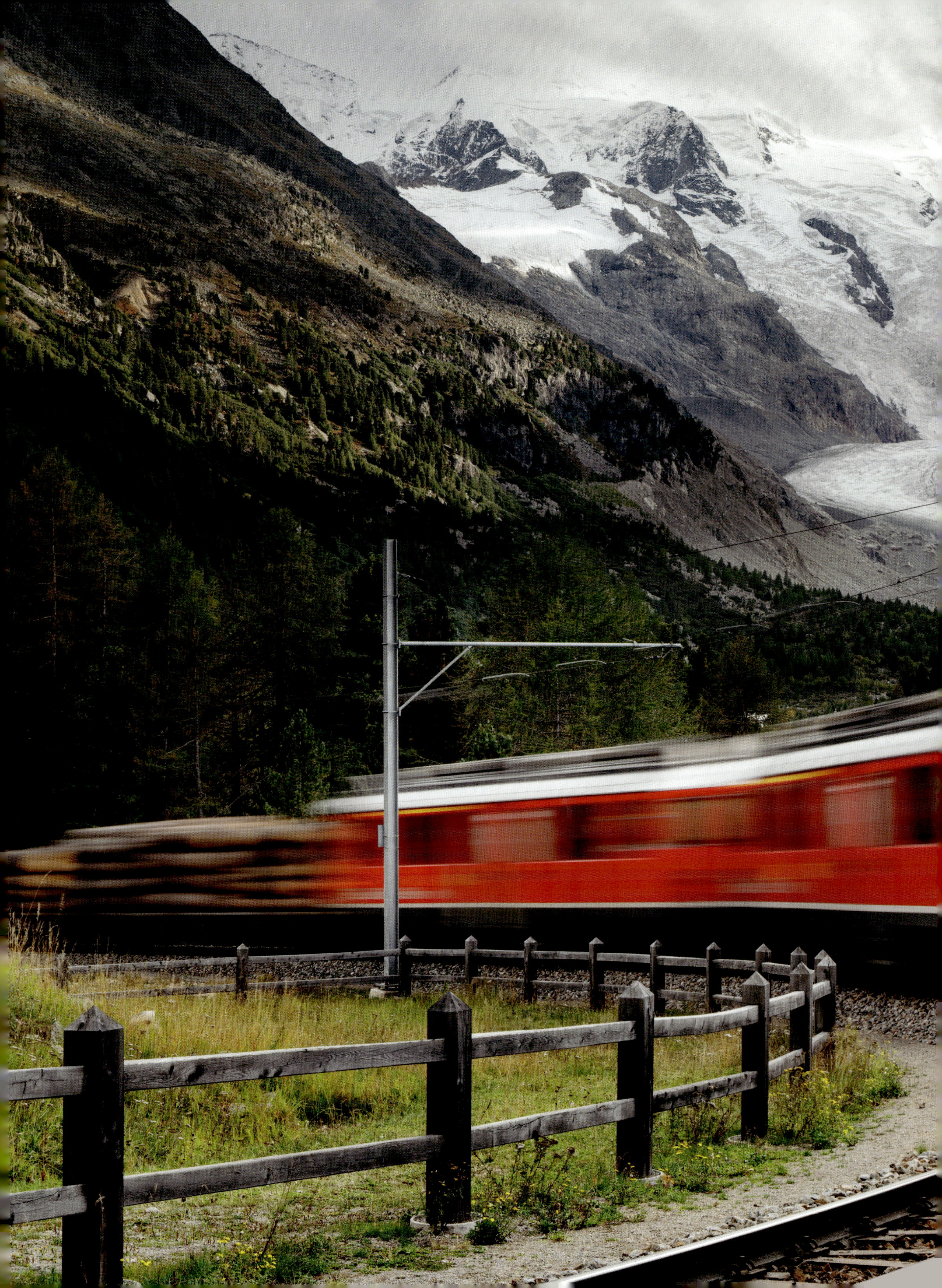

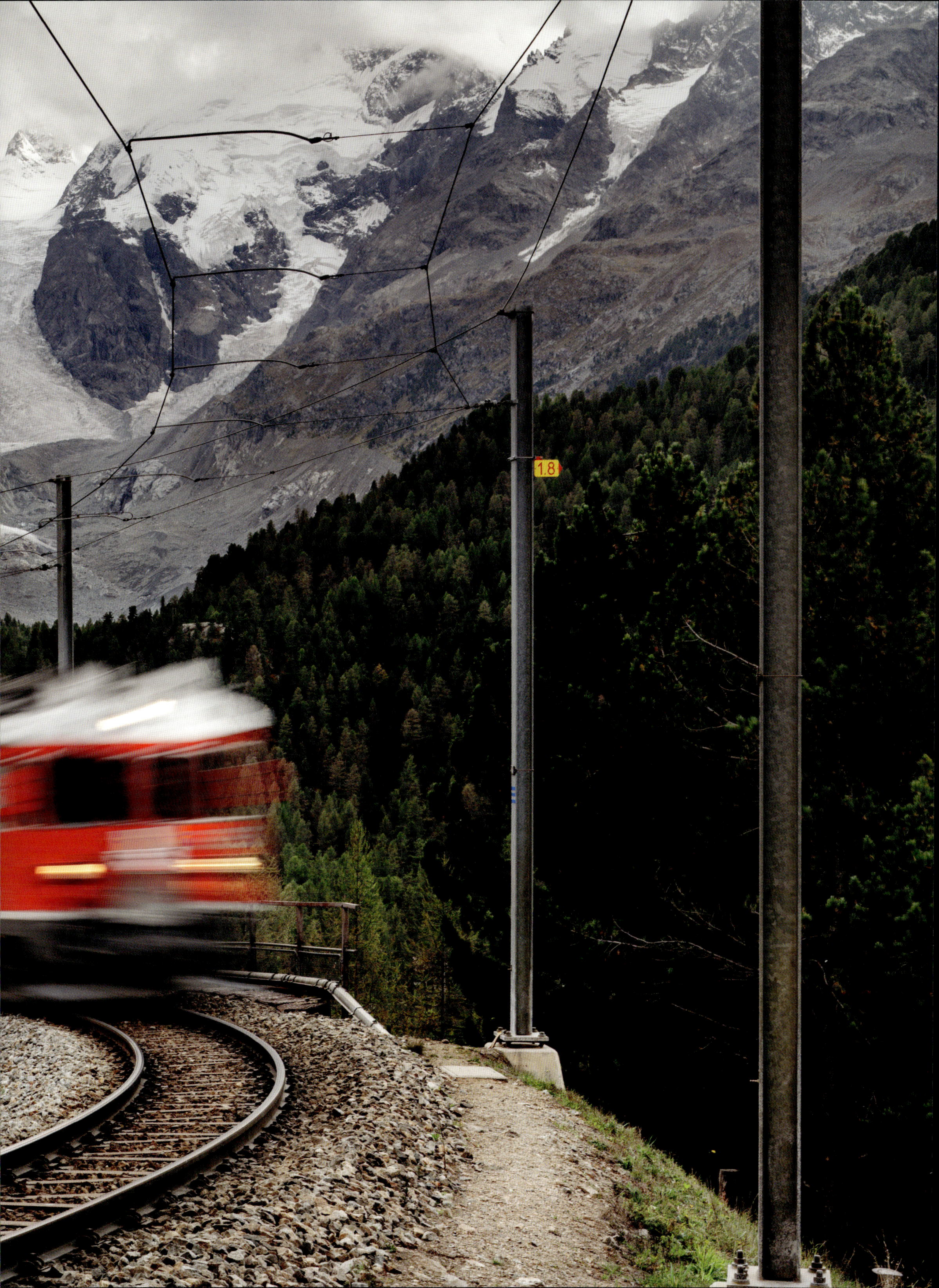

BERNINA EXPRESS

On the last few miles to the summit,
the train passes the Alp da Buond.
In the center of the picture, the
Sassal Mason (9,944 feet / 3,031
meters) can be seen.

Underway with the Allegra
multiple-unit train on the Bernina
Pass. In the center of the picture
is the Lago Bianco (7,329 feet /
2,234 meters); above it is the ice
and stone of the Bernina Group.
Starting from the left: Sassal
Mason, Piz Caral, Piz Cambrena
(11,831 feet / 3,606 meters), Piz
d'Arlas, and Piz Trovat.
▽ ▽

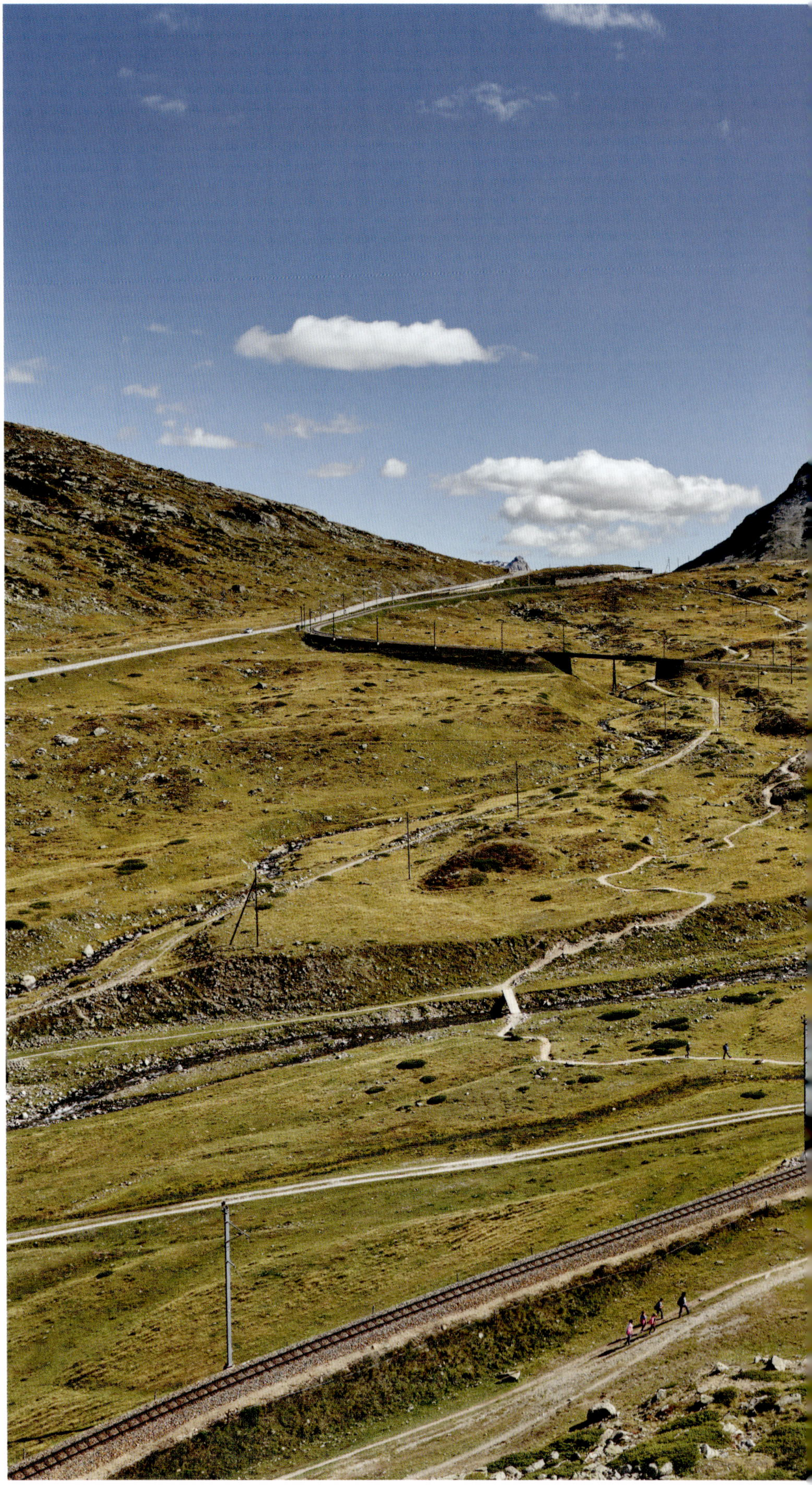

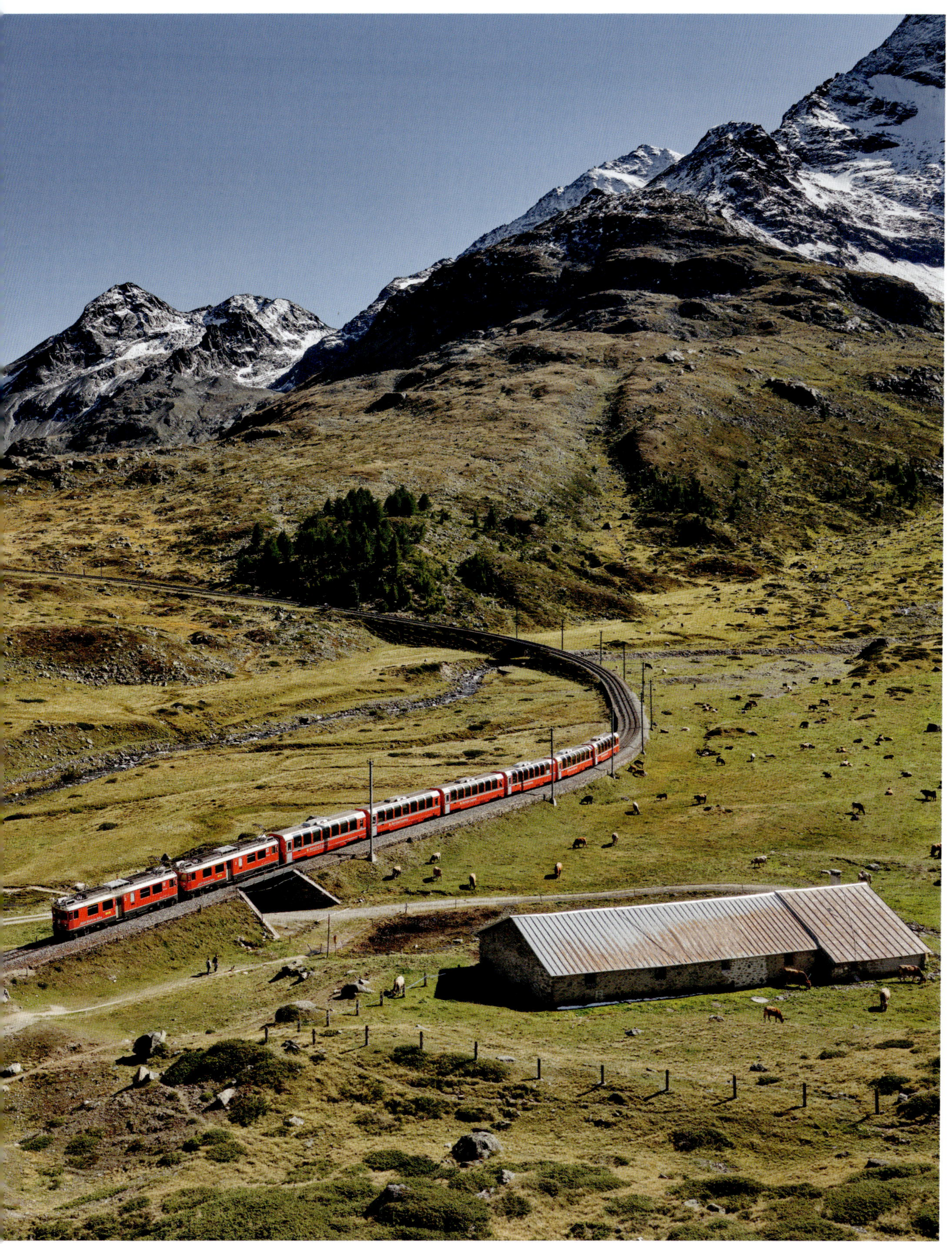

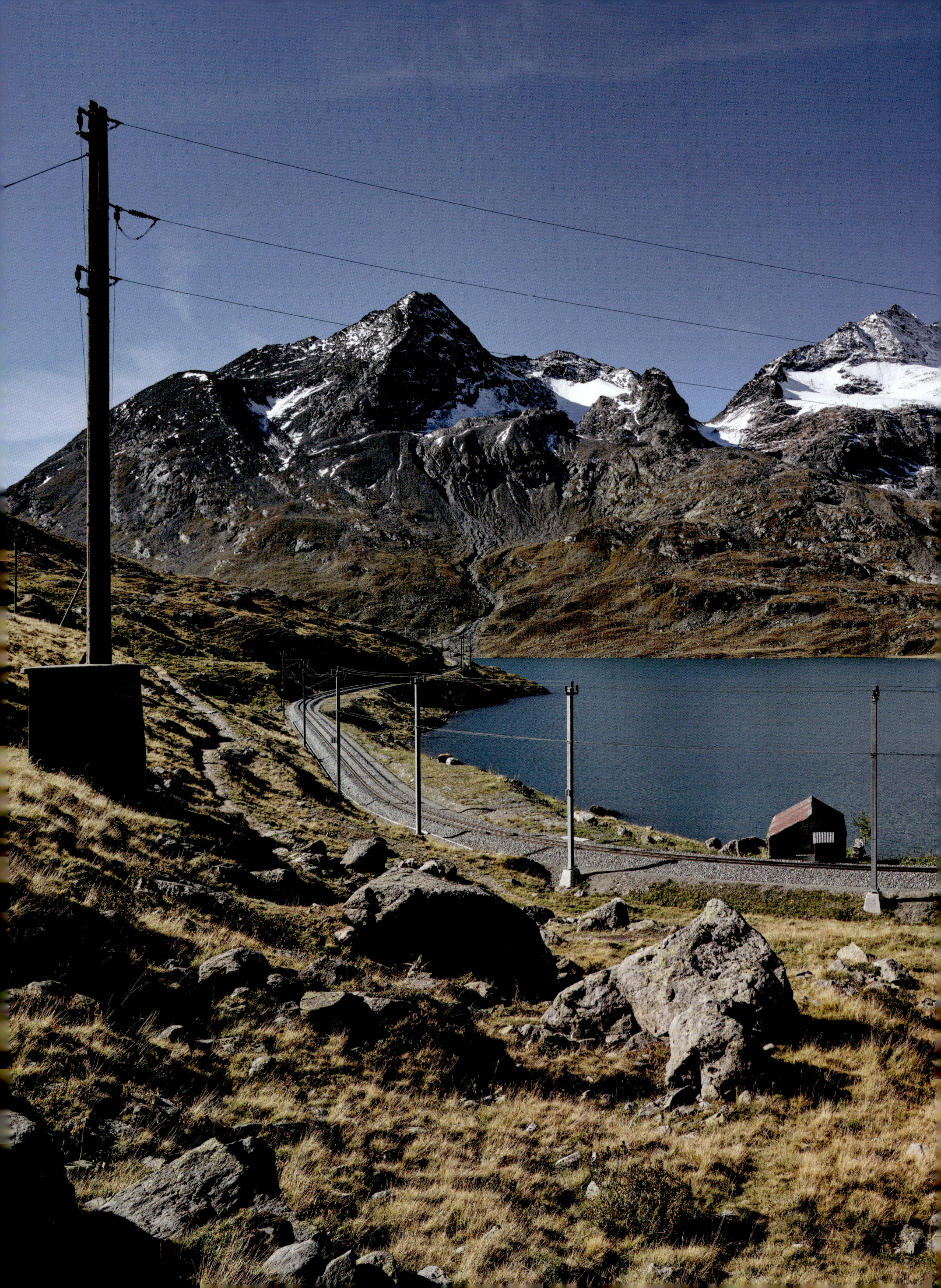

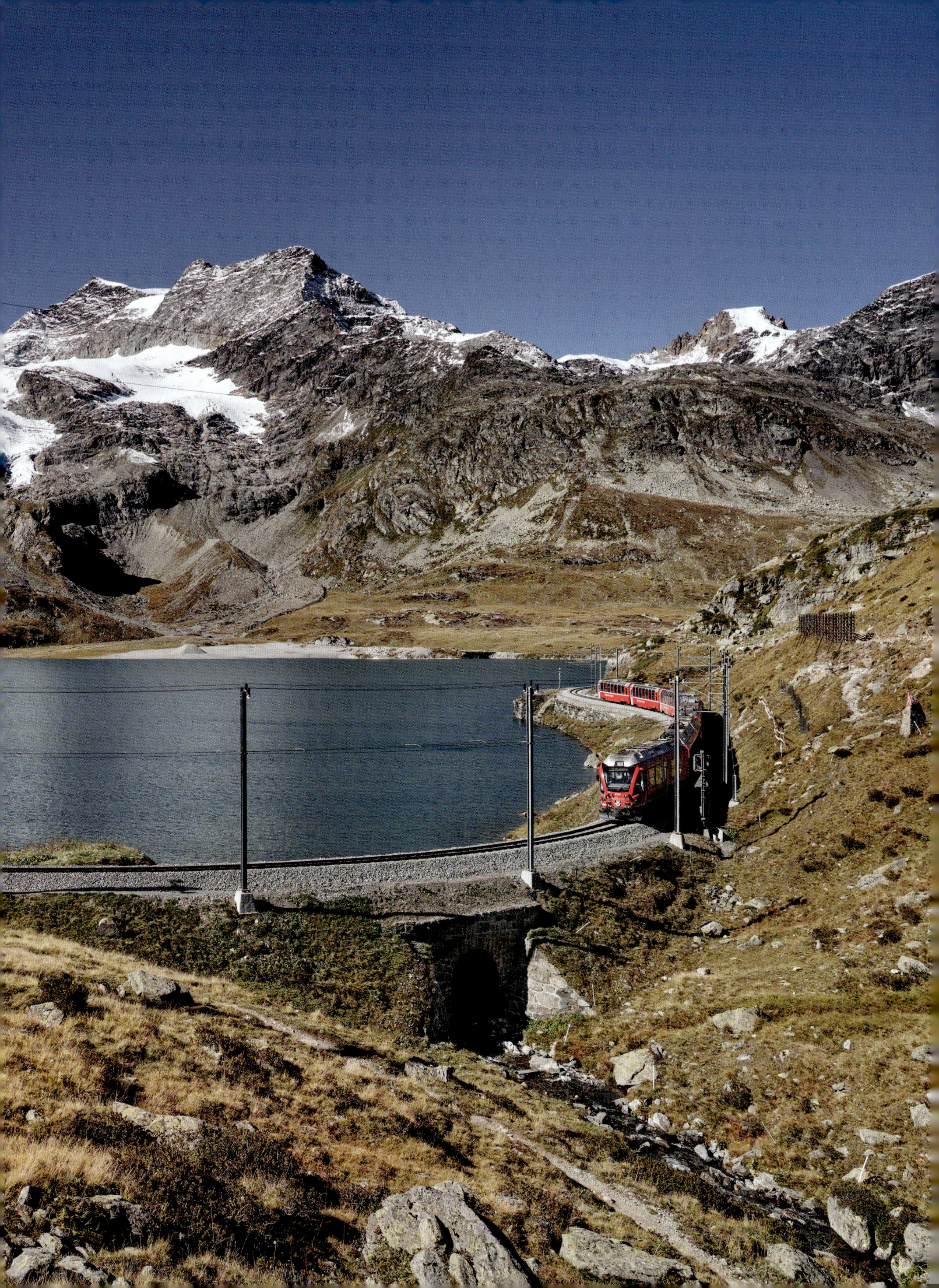

The ensemble of the Bernina-Hospiz train station was designed—like other buildings along the Rhaetian Railway—by the Engadin architect Nicolaus Hartmann. In addition to the train station building, it includes a residential building and a train depot with an integrated turntable (1912).

The long descent out of the high mountain region into the valley begins with the Scala Gallery at the Bernina Pass, goes down into Puschlav, and continues into Valtellina. ▽

South of the Lago Bianco, the remains of a railroad embankment, the Scala Loop, are a reminder of the original tracks, which fell victim to a straightening of the route in 1924. This stretch was exposed to heavy snowdrifts in the winter, which was the basis for the route correction. The train is just entering the Galleria Lunga, consisting of the Scala and Pozza del Drago tunnels as well as the Sassal–Mason Gallery II, the longest along the Bernina route, with a length of 1,142 feet (348 meters). ▽ ▽

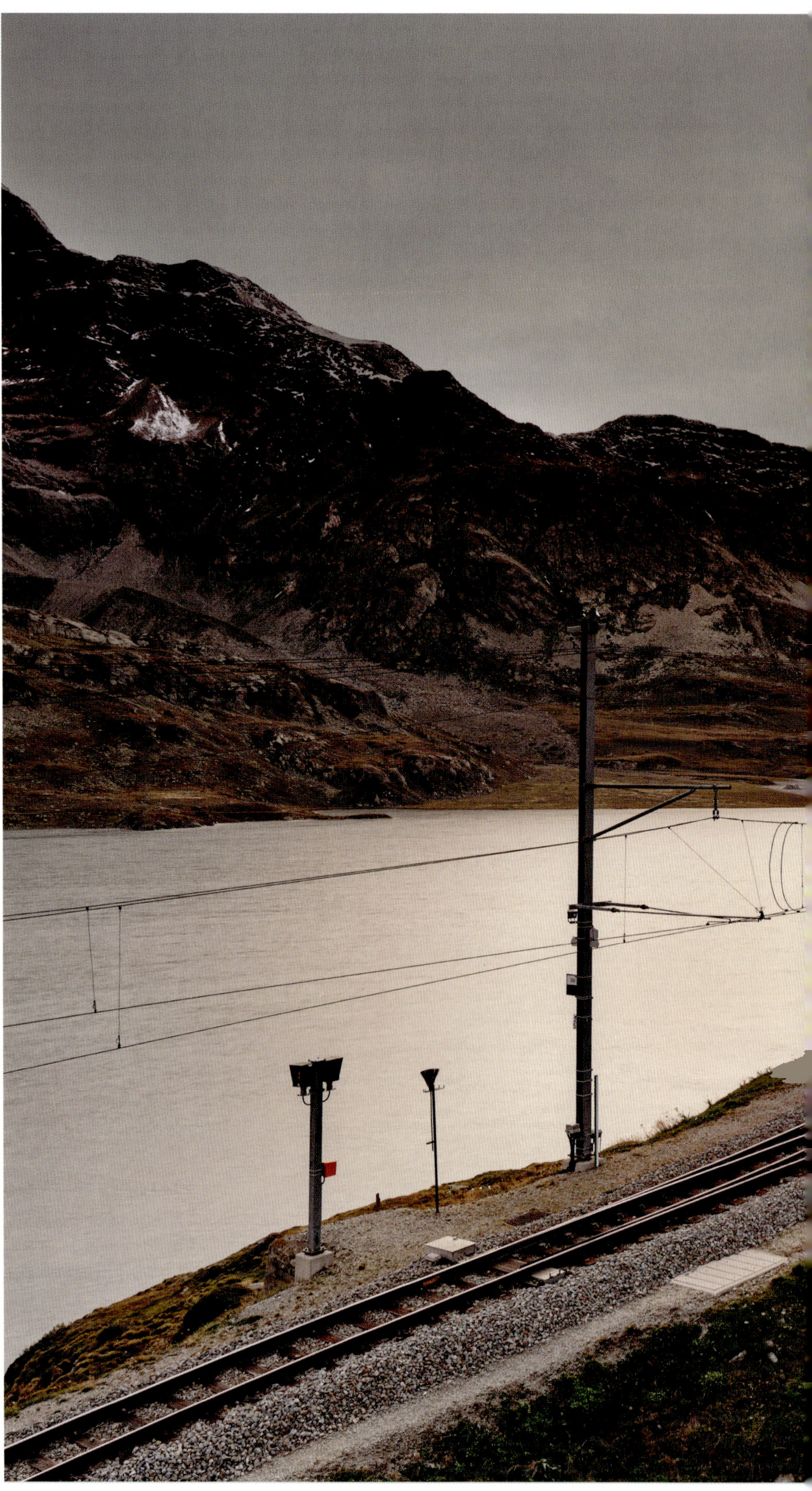

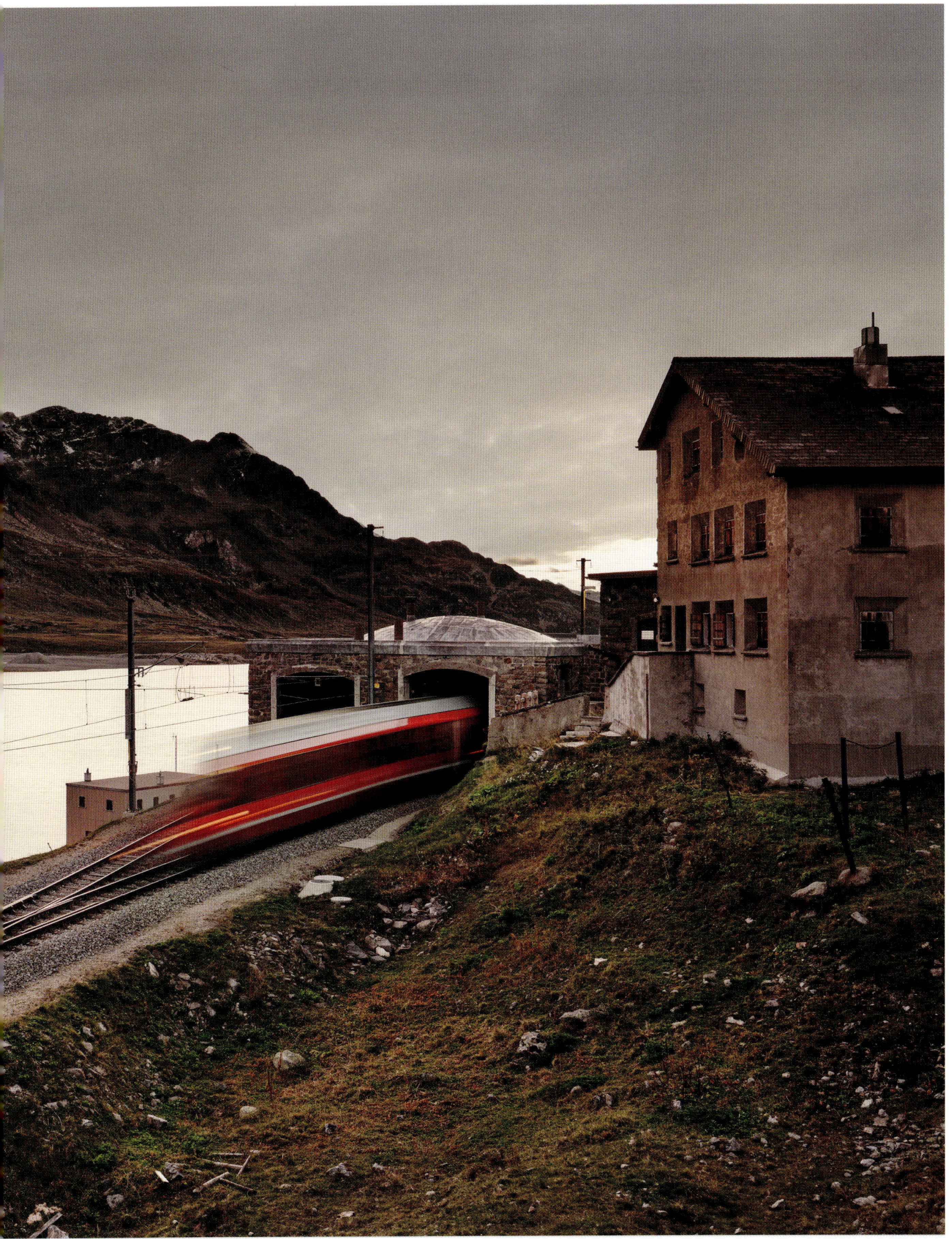

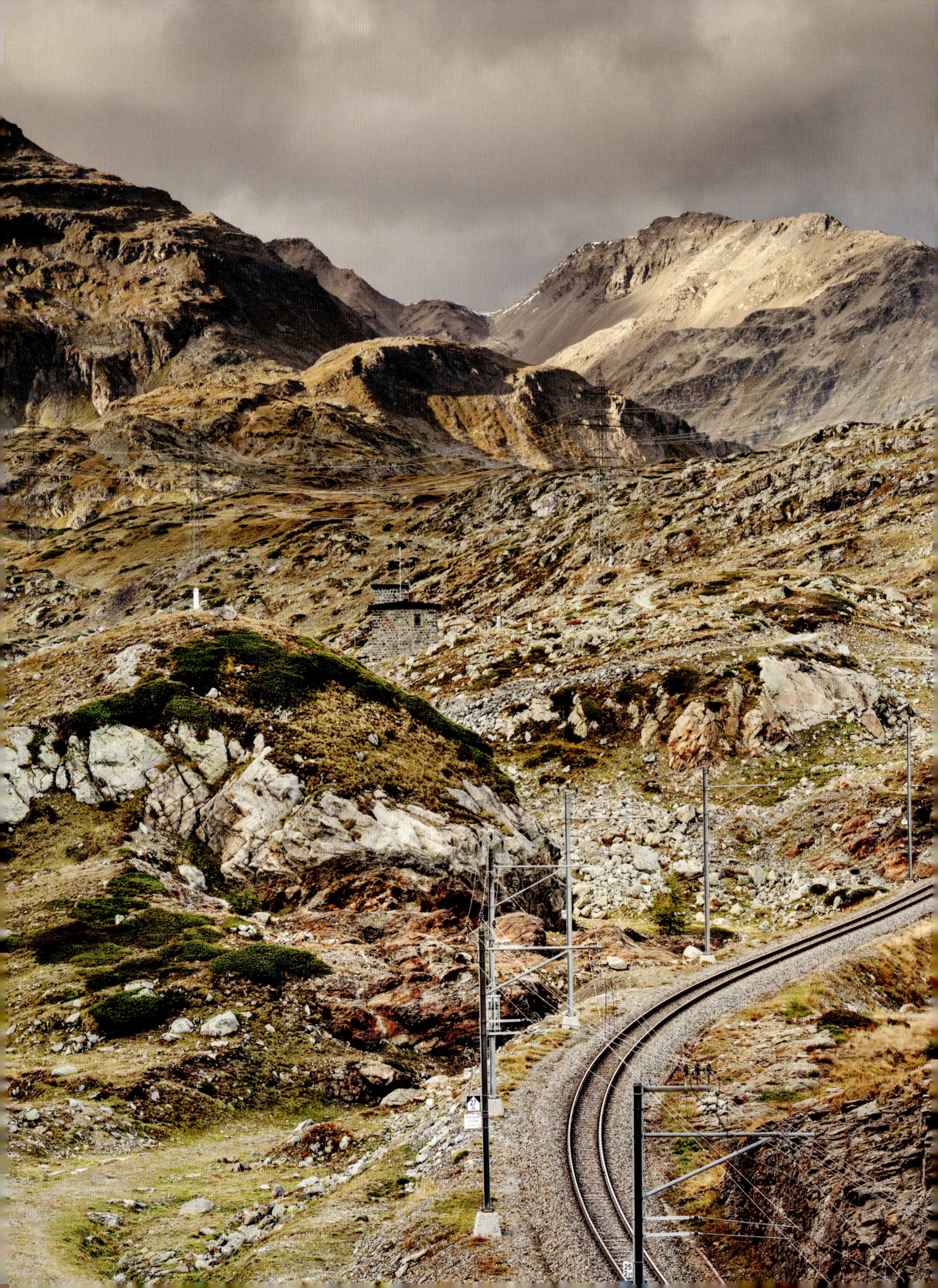

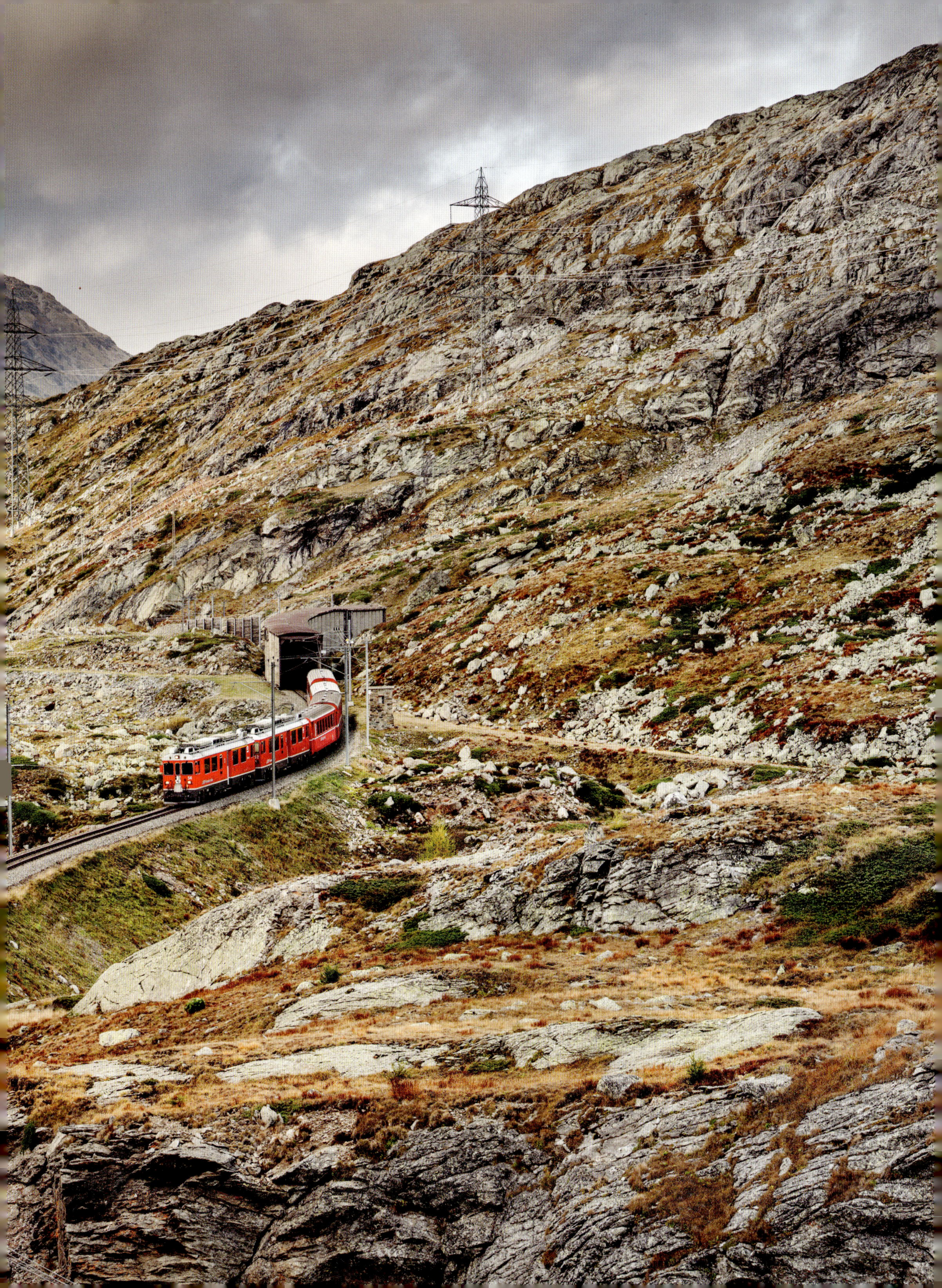

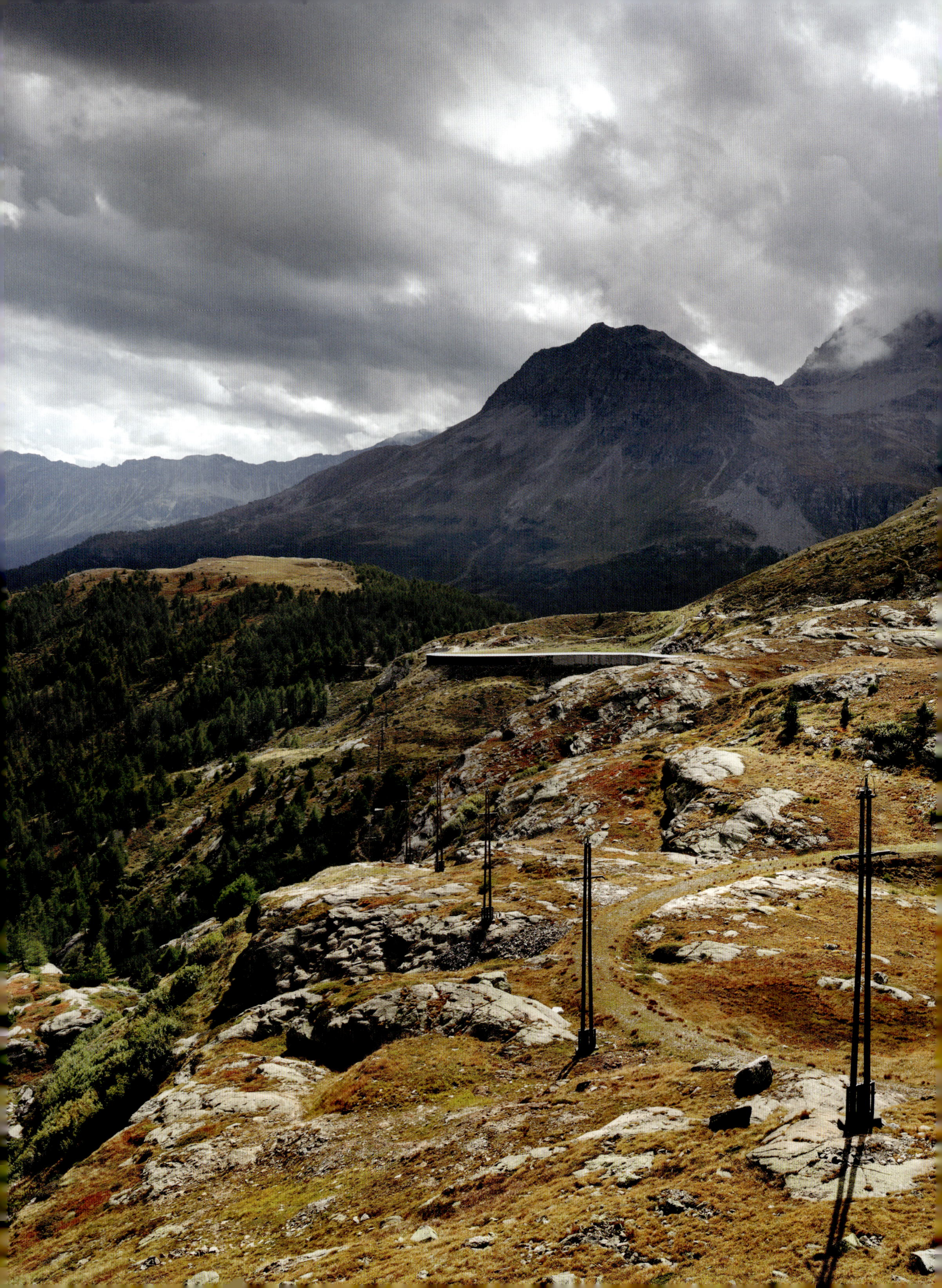

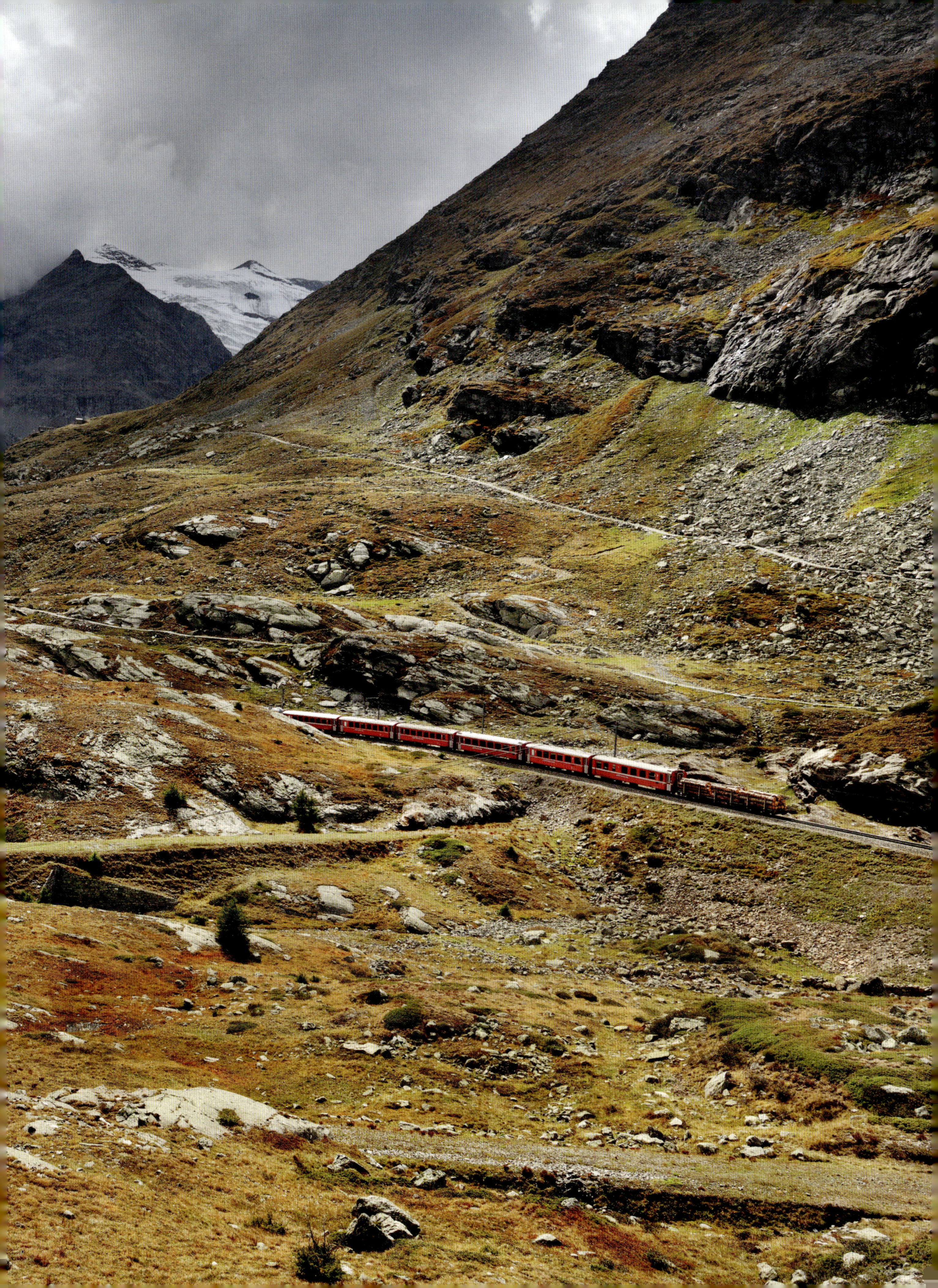

BERNINA EXPRESS

What a view! Looking down from the Alp Grüm over the Stablini curve to the flat floor of Cavaglia. It's not a long way by foot from the train station there to Giardino dei Ghiacciai (Cavaglia Glacier Garden) with its mill. ▷

In order to winterize the Bernina Line, long galleries and elaborate avalanche protection structures were necessary between Alp Grüm and Cavaglia. At the intersection near Stablini, the train continues down the valley through the Val-Pila spiral tunnel. The entry and exit are additionally protected by galleries. In the background, the Palü Glacier; to the left of it, Hotel Belvedere. ▽

Famous structure of the Rhaetian Railway: the circular viaduct at Brusio, near the Italian border. The specs: length of 466 feet (142 meters), height of 23 to 56 feet (7 to 17 meters), nine stone arches, rail radius of 230 feet (70 meters), and slope of 7 percent. A replica of it has been around for a good twenty years—in Central America. The mountain railroad was planned for a farmer on Lake Geneva but was never approved. So, the track and equipment traveled to Costa Rica in 1999, where the emigrated Swiss hotelier transformed them into his own private 2.2-mile-long (3.5-kilometer-long) mountain railroad with two tunnels, a bridge, a switchback, and the circular viaduct. ▽ ▽

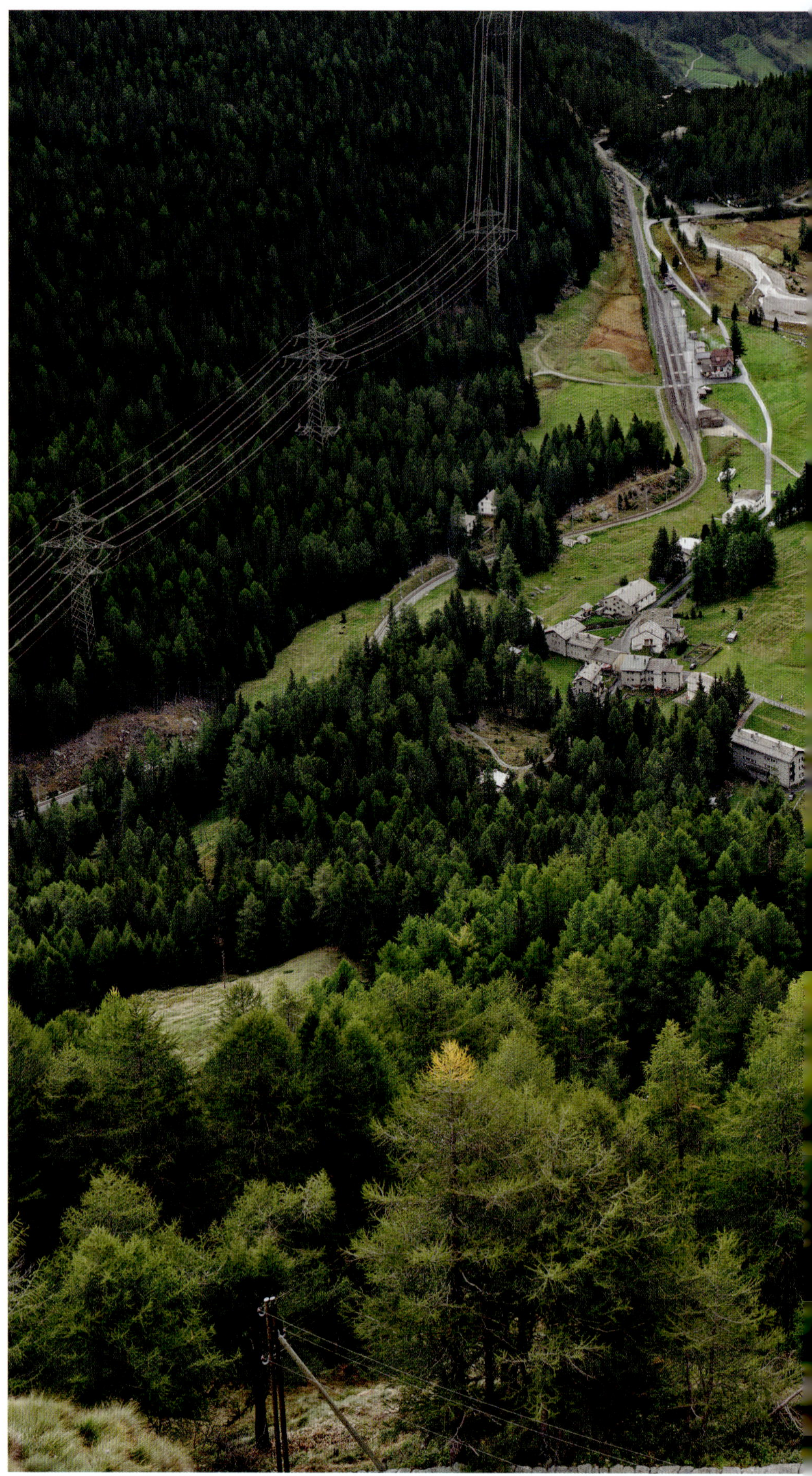

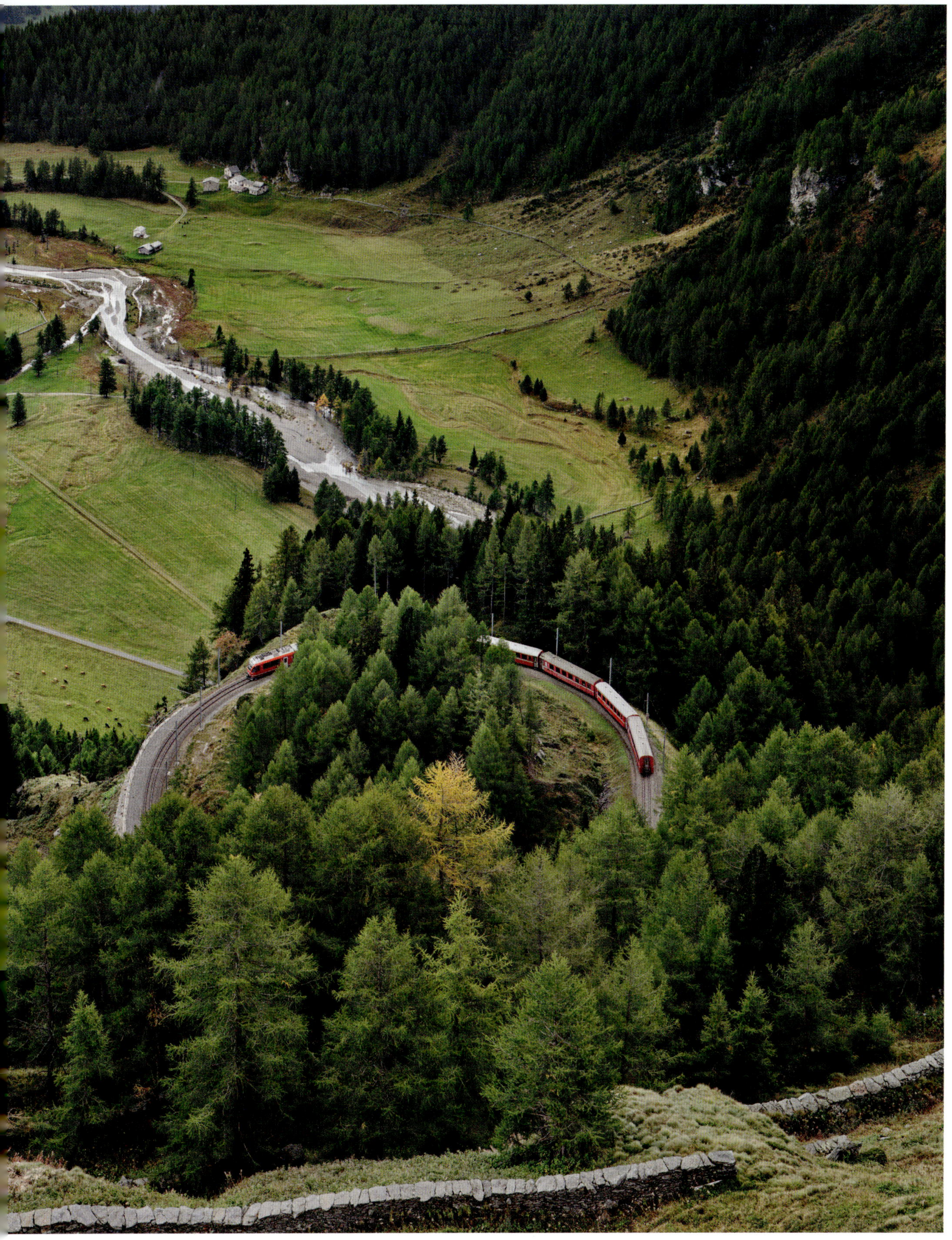

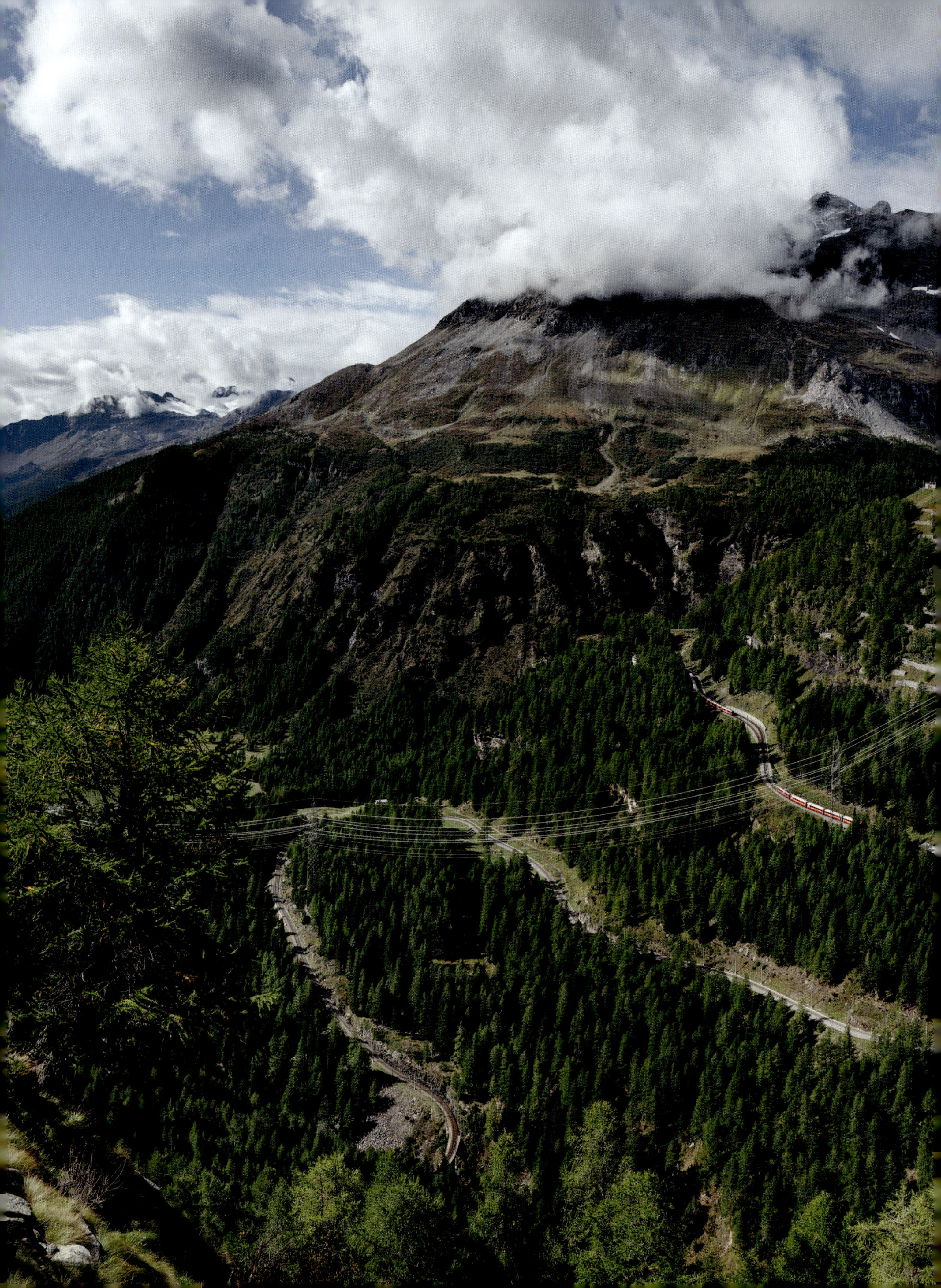

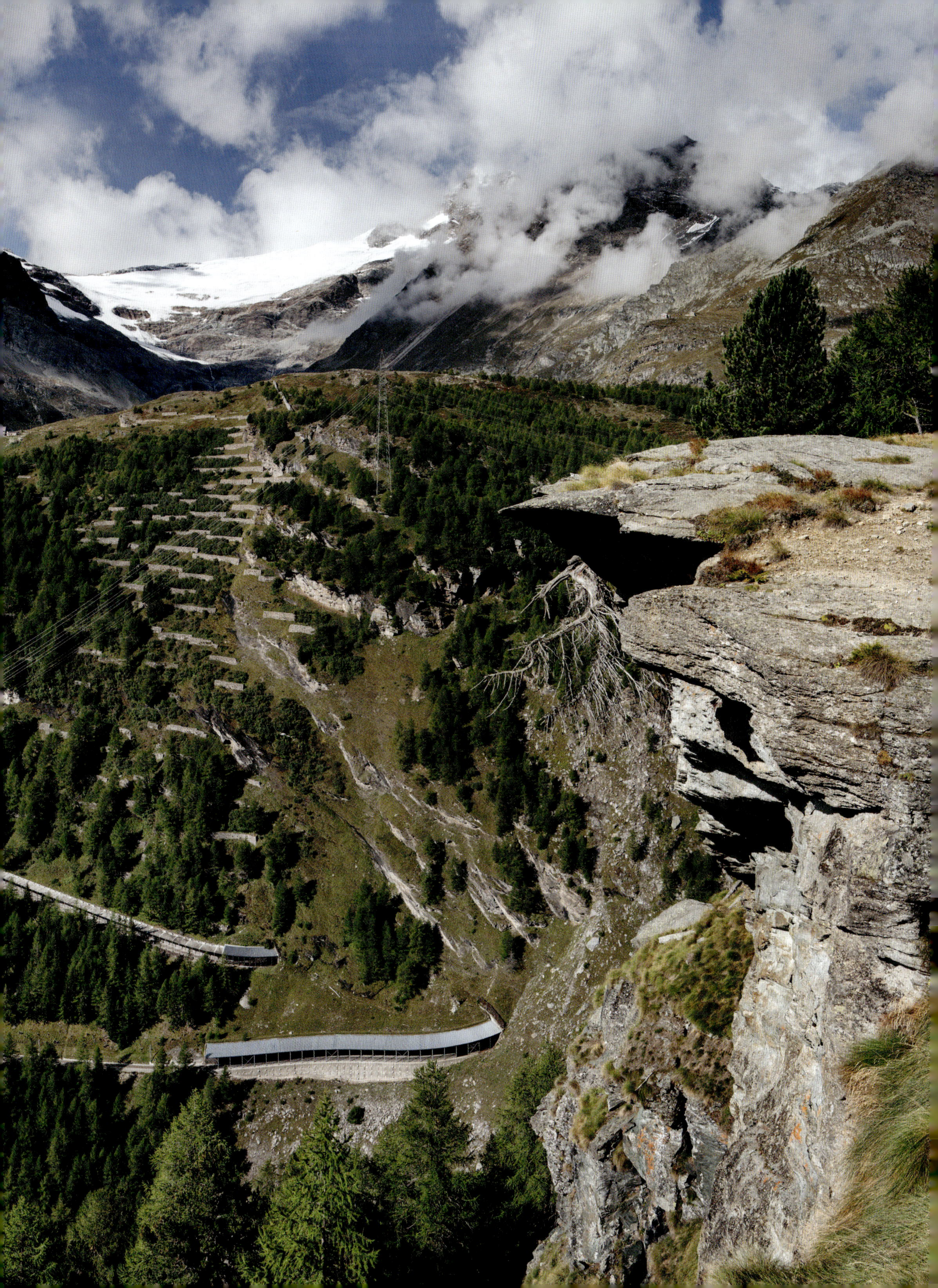

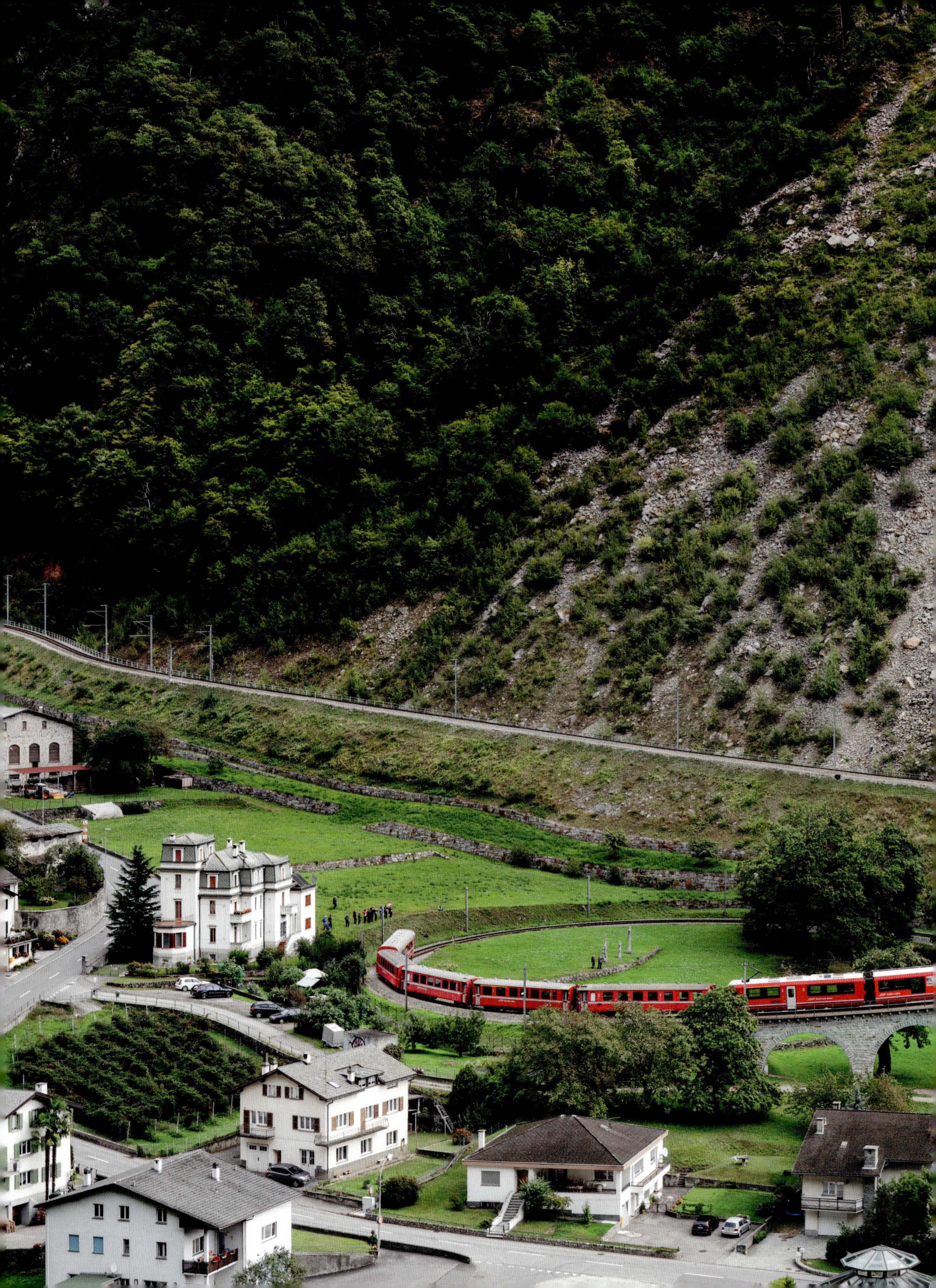

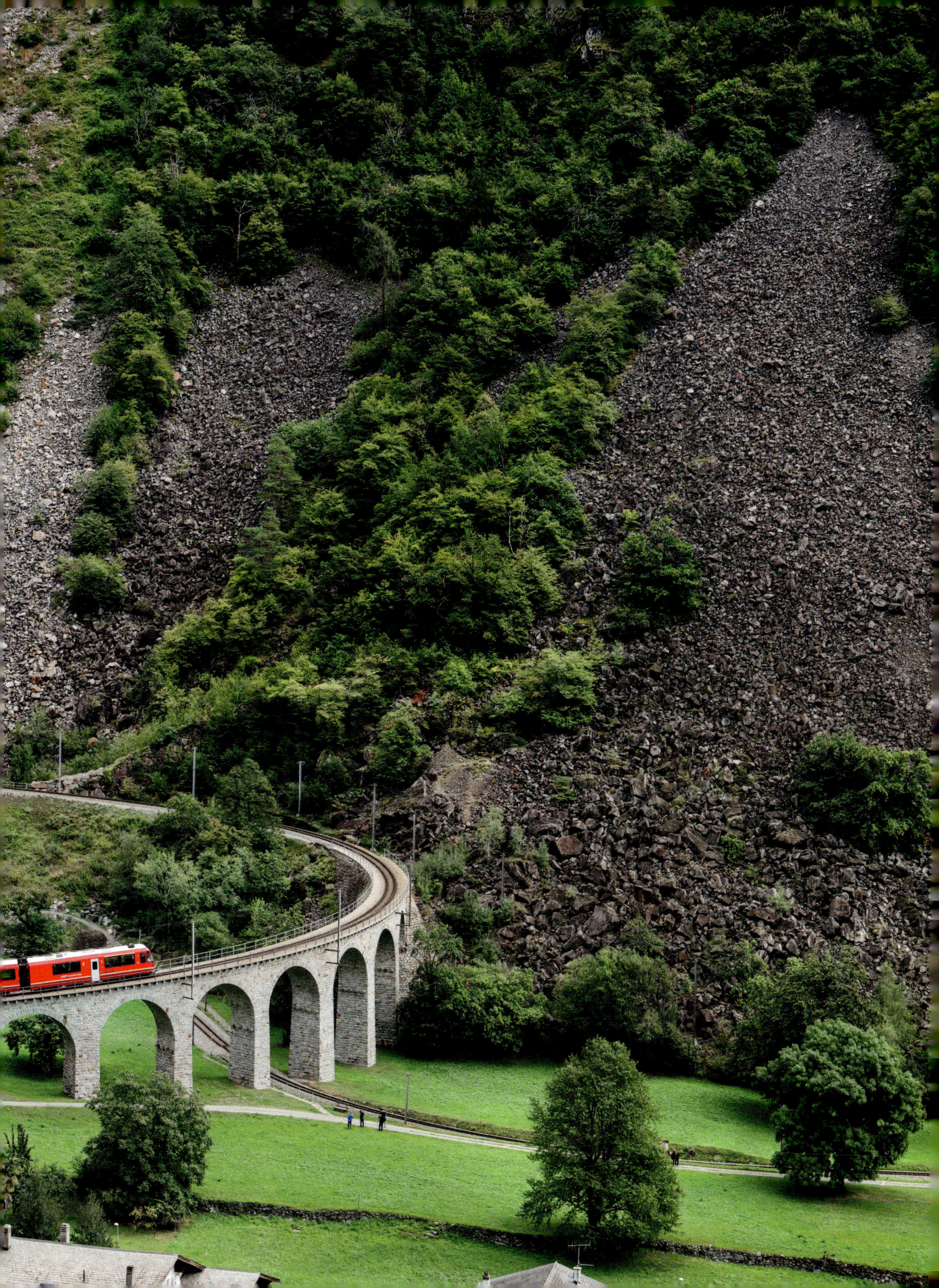

The journey on the Bernina Express ends in the middle of Tirano. From here, you can connect to the Italian railway network (Sondrio–Lecco–Mailand).

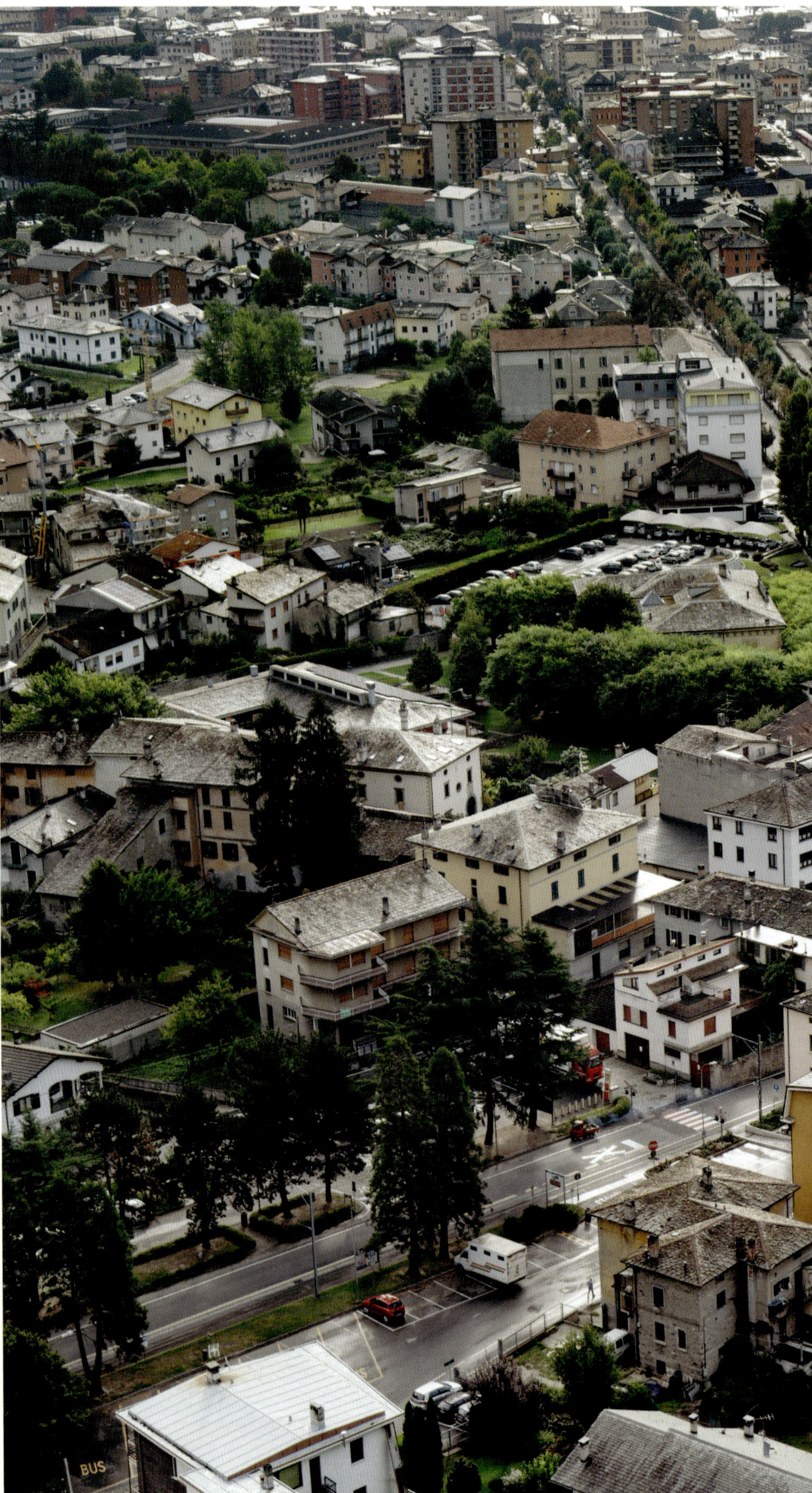

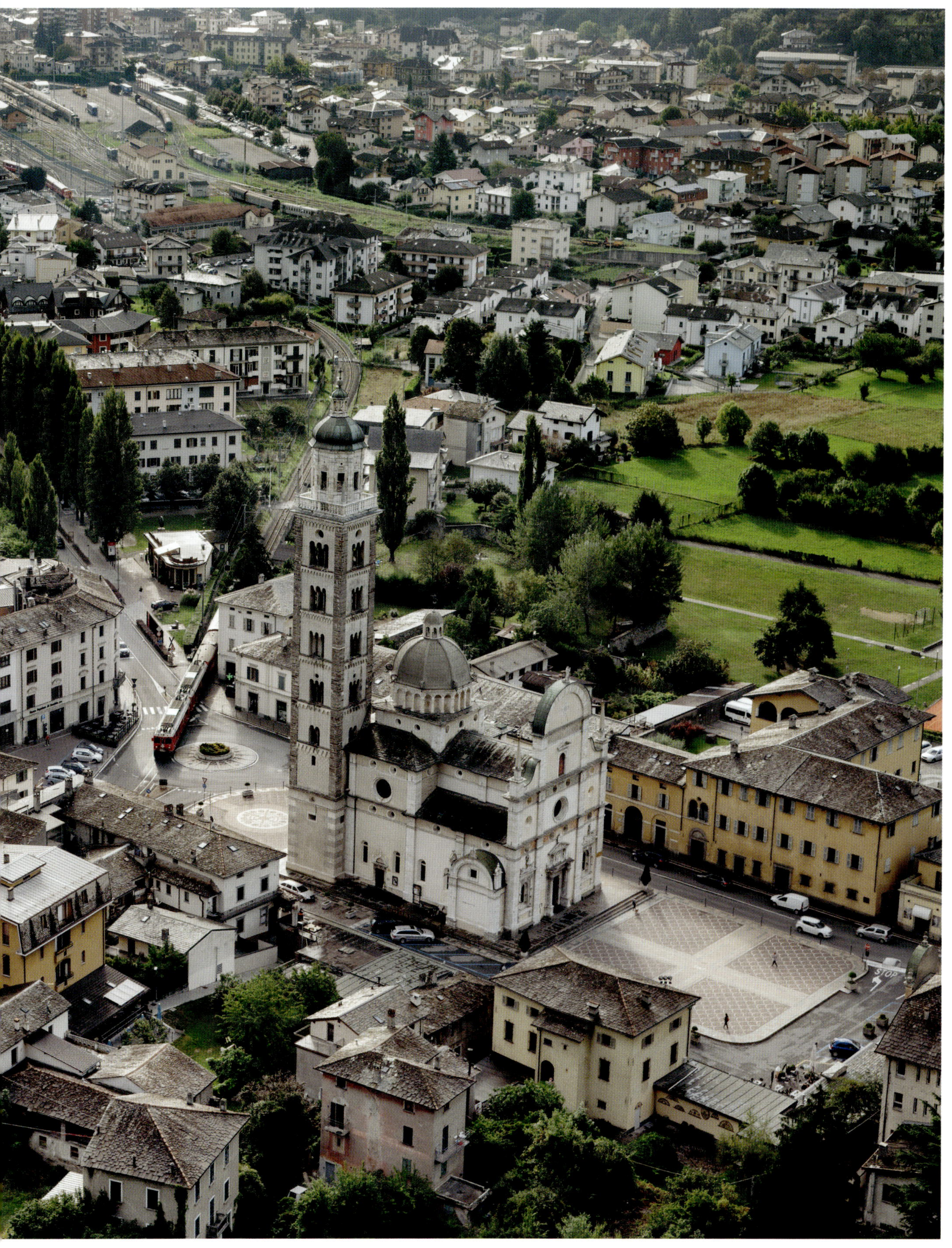

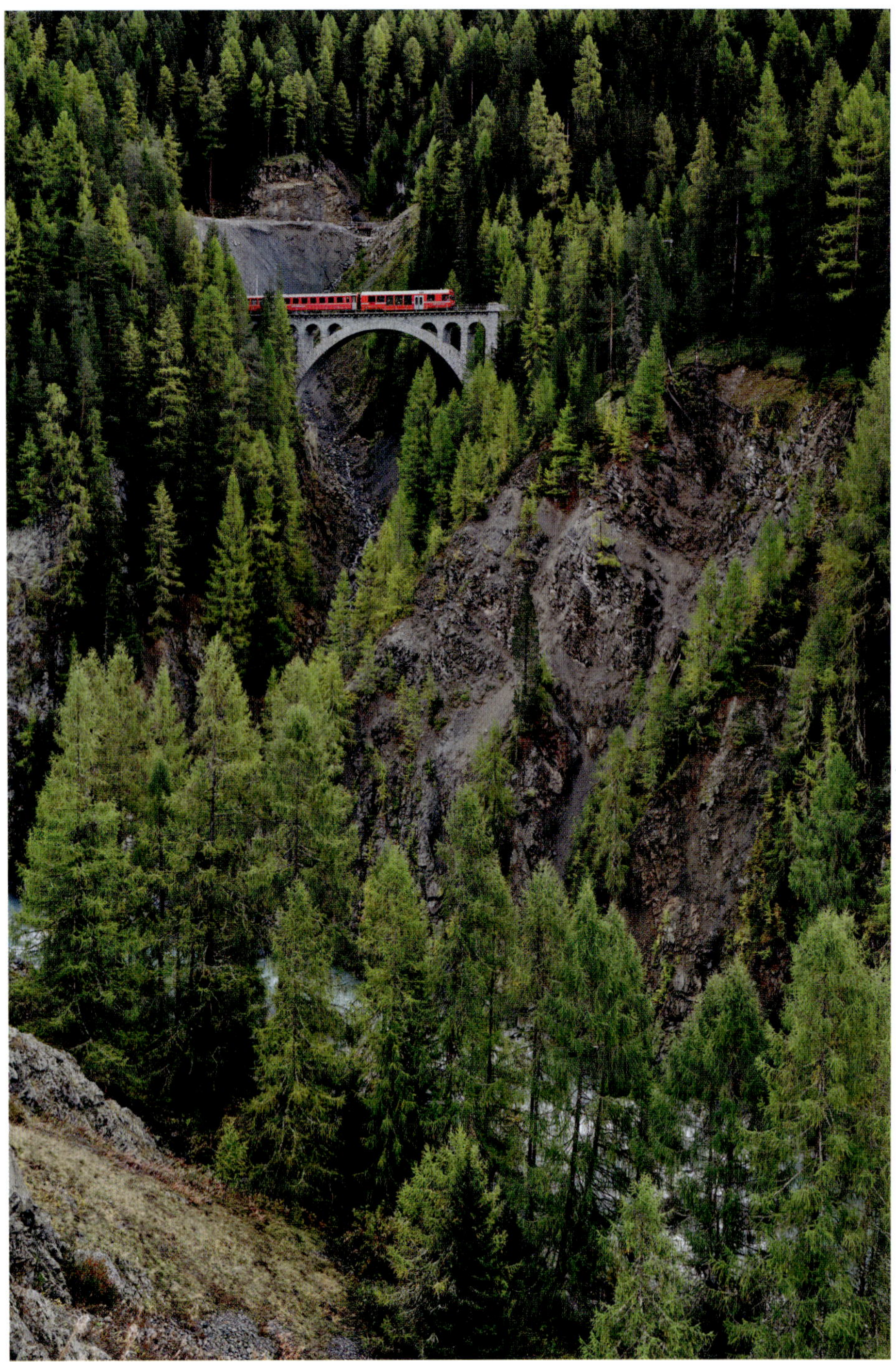

Near Brail, a viaduct of the Engadine Railway spans over the deep Val Mela at its opening. △

The Lower Engadine village of Ardez is visually dominated by the ruins of the Steinsberg Castle. It dates to the twelfth century. In the Swabian war of 1499, it was destroyed and then only partially restored. ▷

Below Ftan, the Engadine Railway crosses the mouth of the Val Püzza gorge. ▽ ▽

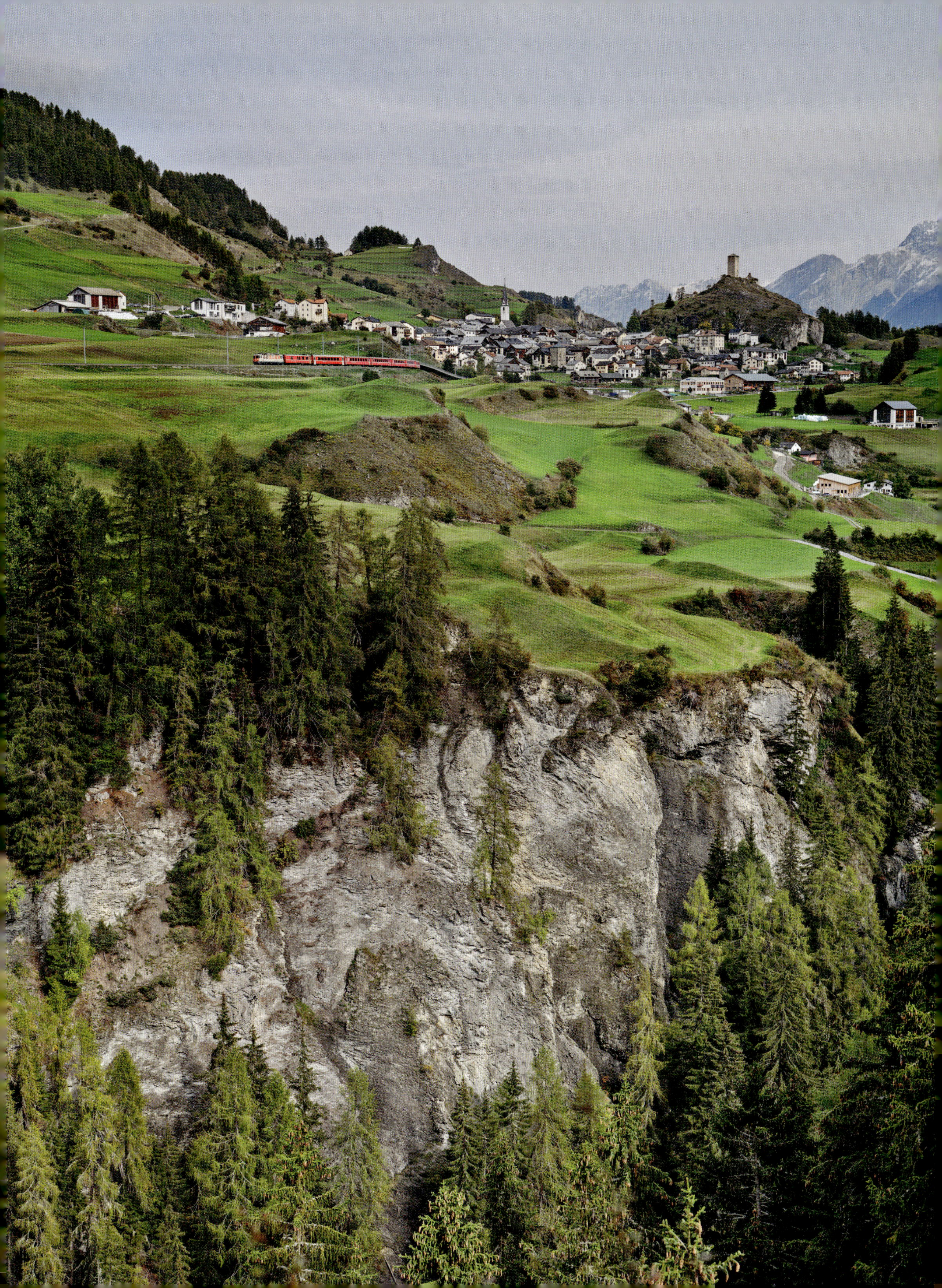

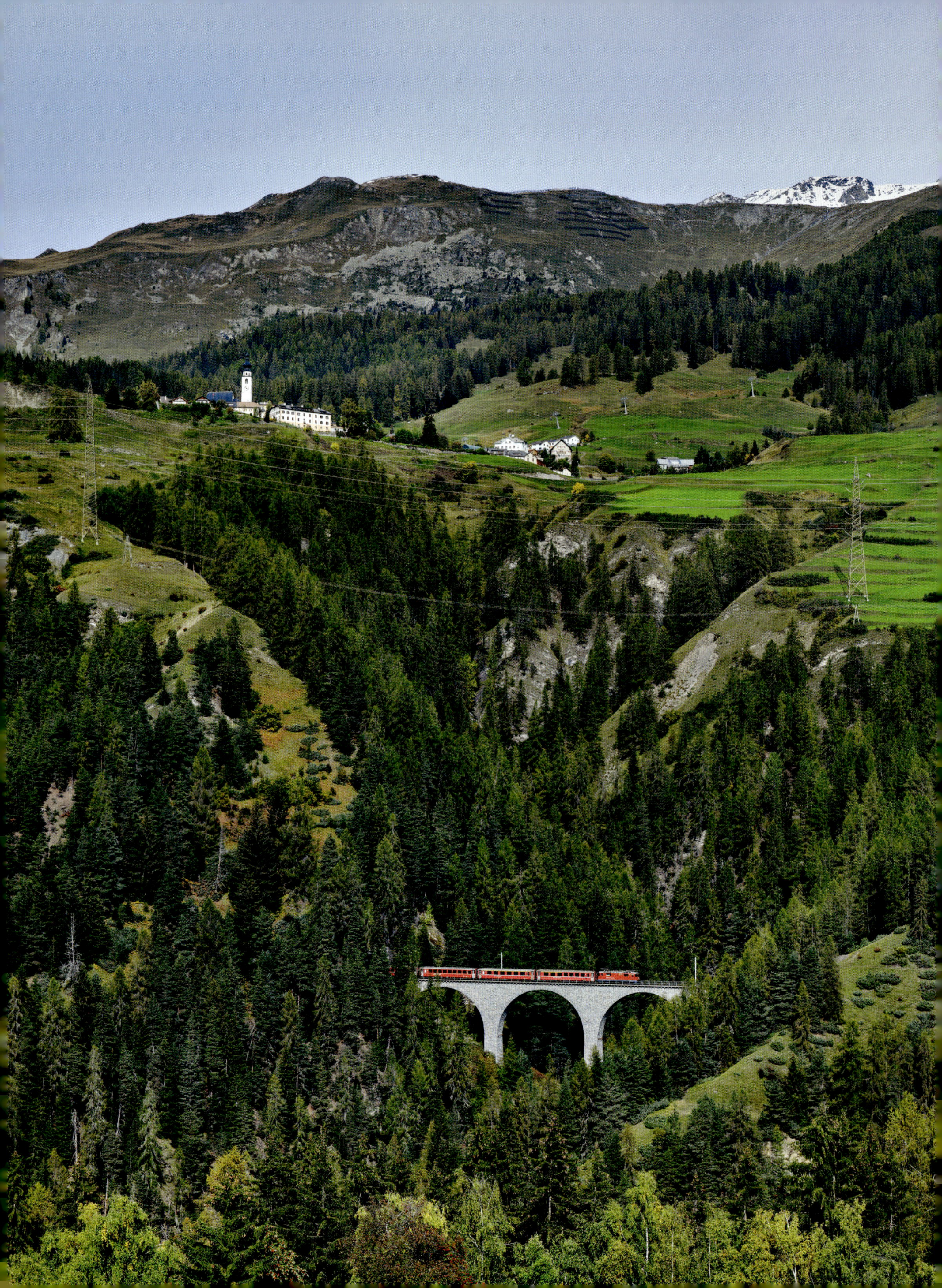

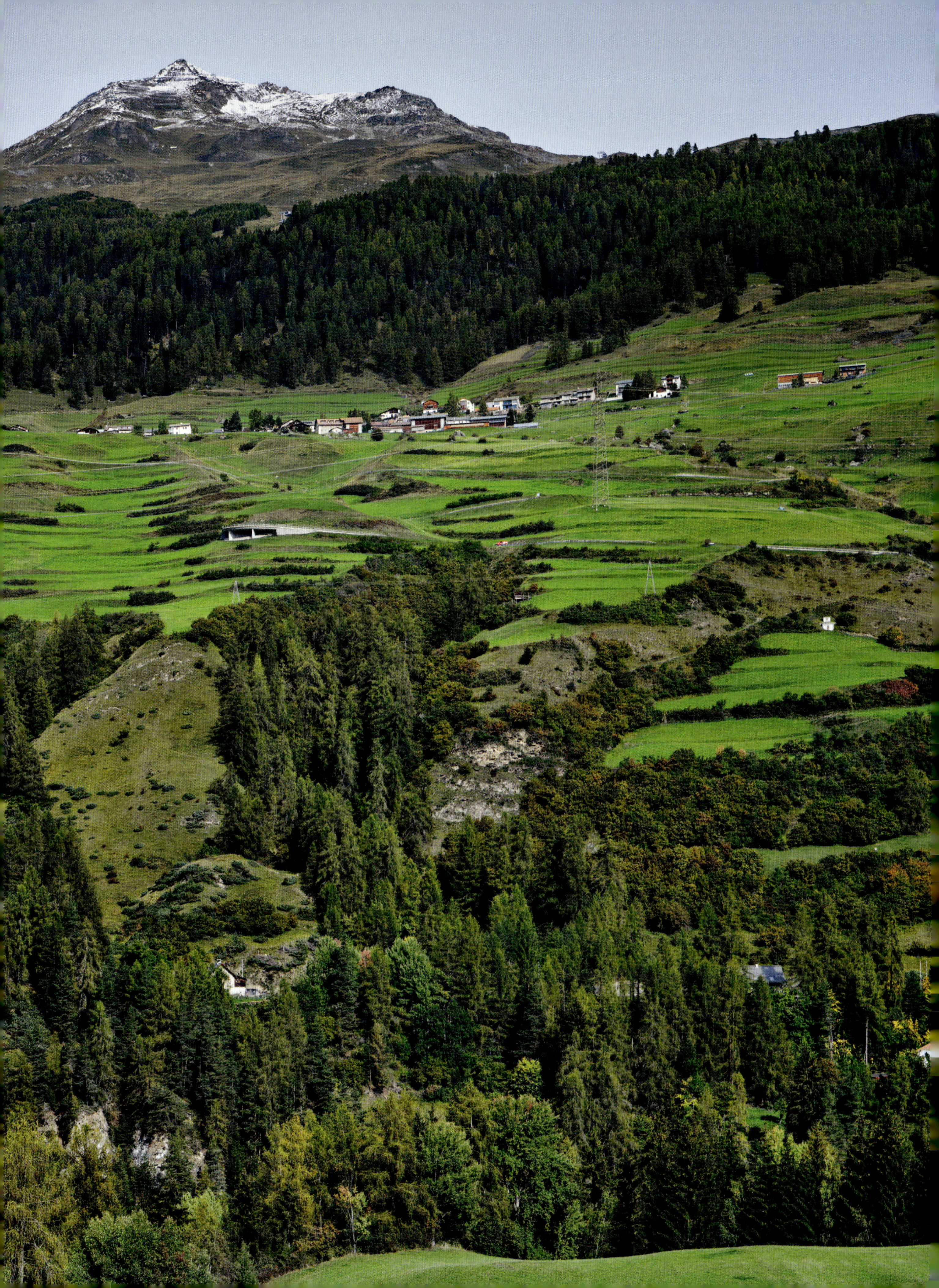

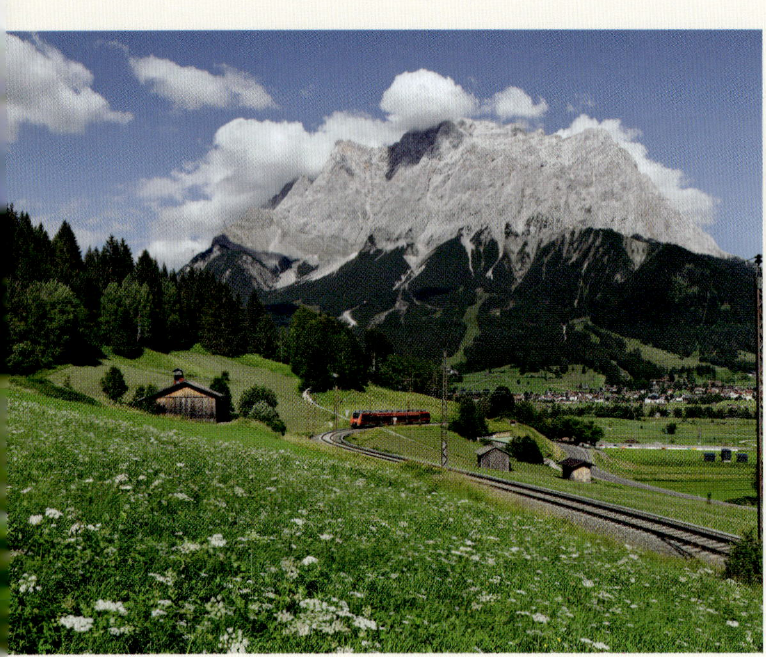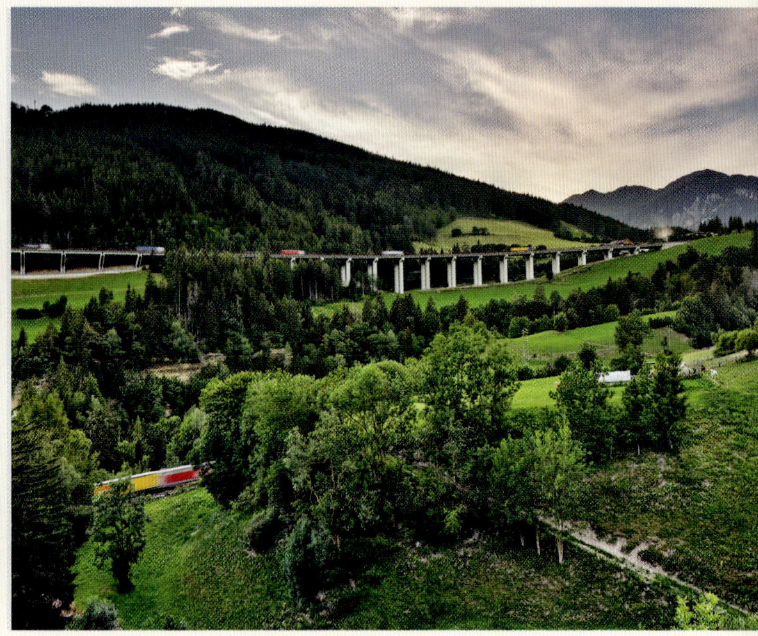

INHERITED FROM A MONARCHY—THE RAILROADS OF EMPEROR FRANZ JOSEPH

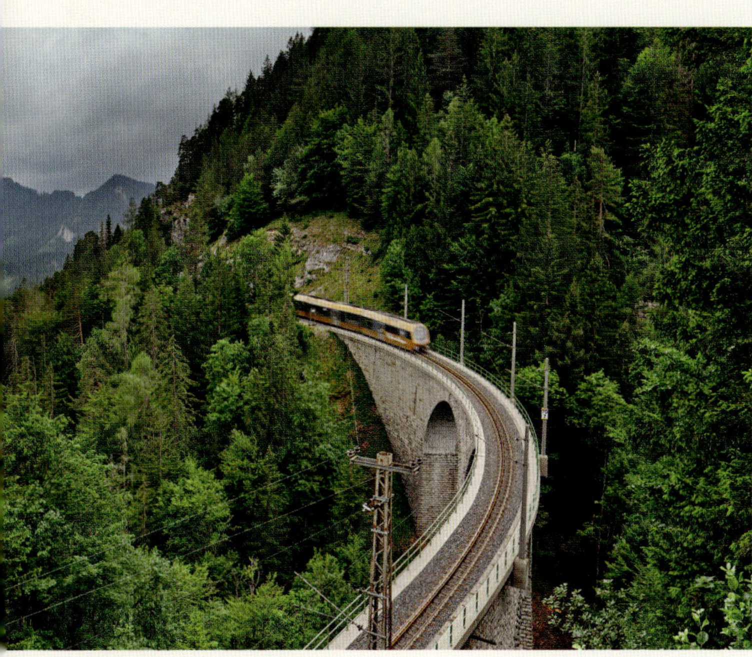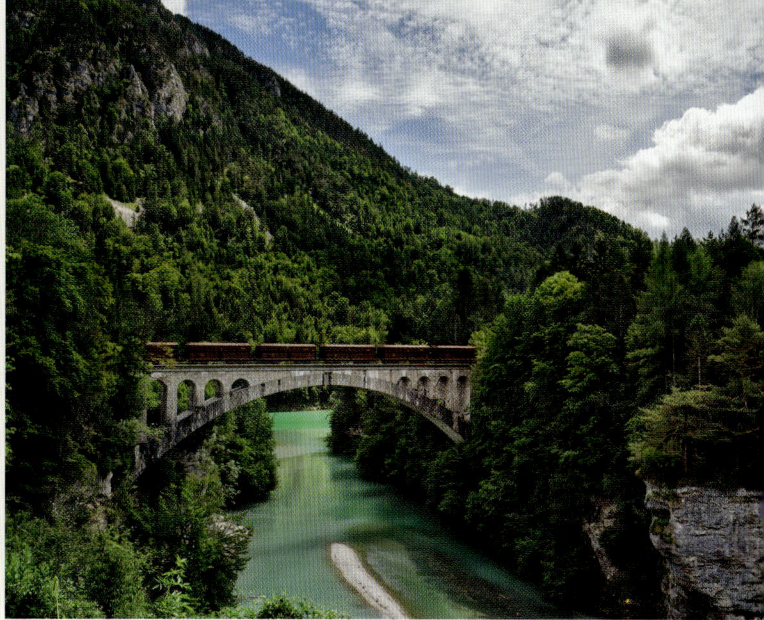

In the nineteenth century, the eastern Alps were mostly Imperial and Royal sovereign territory. Early on, around the middle of the nineteenth century, the first mountain railroads were built at Semmering, far in the east of the Alpine arch. The Arlberg Railway and the Brenner Railway followed. The strategic military importance of the new mode of transportation was soon recognized in Vienna, the center of the large empire. Thus, at the beginning of the twentieth century, Alpine railroads were built on the Pyhrn, in the Tauern, on the Karawanks ridge, and as a connection to the Adriatic port of Trieste, named the Bohinj Railway. Connections to the top of Alpine peaks, using cogwheel railways, were limited, similar to neighboring Bavaria.

ZUGSPITZE RAILWAY AND MITTENWALD RAILWAY

FROM THE HIGHEST MOUNTAIN IN GERMANY TO THE CAPITAL OF TYROL

The shortest rail connection between Munich and Innsbruck does not run through the Inntal but through Mittenwald to the capital of Tyrol. The Mittenwald Railway *is only of regional importance, however, as is the* Ausserfern Railway. *On the other hand, the* Zugspitz Railway, *which leads to Germany's highest mountain peak, became a hit.*

How did the Swiss Jungfraujoch come to Bavaria? As an idea, as something to aspire to. That cogwheel railway, which had already been opened in 1905 as far as the Eismeer station (10,364 feet / 3,159 meters) and runs mostly in the interior of the mountain, proved that connections to the high Alpine regions are not pipe dreams but realistic possibilities.

The German engineer Wolfgang A. Müller wrote in the same year in *Die Erbauung einer elektrischen Bahn auf die Zugspitze* (*The Construction of an Electric Railway to the Zugspitze*): "Although our German Alps are sought out each year from hundreds of thousands of people for the relaxation of their bodies and souls, the transportation options of these northern Alpine regions leave much to be desired in many areas. . . . Switzerland has been leading by example in this area for the last thirty years through the construction of one mountain railway after the other." He found the idea of a cogwheel railway up to the Zugspitze a good one: "Closer investigations soon proved that the economic conditions for such an enterprise are particularly favorable, and there should be no major difficulties with the technology involved."

TO THE ZUGSPITZE ON THE RACK

It should have taken more than two decades for the Bavarian Zugspitze Railway to go into operation. However, after the opening of the aerial cableway in Tyrol (1926), it went very quickly. Of course, they didn't want to leave the peak solely to their Austrian neighbors. In June 1928 the *Münchner Neusten Nachrichten* (*Munich's Latest News*) shared the happy news about the start of construction. Two years later, the railway (with the bishop's blessing) could already be opened. Up through the end of 2019, the railroad had transported exactly 16,295,933 passengers up the mountain. The first rider was Karl Hauck, who is also the undisputed record holder with a total of 10,025 trips.

You can reach Garmisch-Partenkirchen comfortably with the train in about one hour from Munich. The journey after is also possible by rail, to the west through the Ausserfern and to Innsbruck via Mittenwald and Seefeld. The connection with the Tyrolean capital was opened in 1912 as an electric local railway with a construction time of only two years. The *Naturfreund* (*Nature Lover*) from 1910 praised the new line as

From left: the Ausserfern Railway near Ehrwald in front of the Zugspitze massif; the Brenner Railway and motorway in the Eisack Valley in South Tyrol; the 381-foot-long (116-meter-long), curved Saugraben Viaduct of the Mariazell Railway; the Steyrling Bridge of the Pyhrn Railway

"one of Austria's most daring mountain railroads, especially on the Innsbruck–Reith stretches," with its numerous engineered structures. The longest tunnel is the one at the Martinswand. "The tunnel breaks through the cliff almost parallel to its front and at a very respectable height. At its exit, the track is 258 meters [846 feet] above the road (850 meters [2,789 feet] above sea level), which is about 50 meters [164 feet] higher than the famous grotto that Emperor Maximilian I climbed during the chamois hunt. . . . The nice idea to build a lookout station similar to the 'Eismeer' station of the Jungfrau Railway must unfortunately be abandoned due to technical reasons."

The tunnel ended up being longer and cutting deeper into the mountain. As a result, rail passengers do not get an awe-inspiring view of the Martinswand. Today it is a popular climbing area, but it cannot be ruled out that once in a while someone fails during the trek to the top. An angel helped Maximilian out of his predicament almost half a millennium ago.

THROUGH THE AUSSERFERN

The Mittenwald Railway project also included the connection between Garmisch-Partenkirchen and Kempten. It was built between the years 1895 and 1913 but never gained any more than a regional significance. This was also because the almost 62-mile (100-kilometer) stretch crosses the German-Austrian border twice. Electrification also progressed only in stages. In the end, the line was threatened to be shut down. Plans to build a railroad over the Fernpass into the Inntal, or at least to connect to the DB (Deutsche Bahn— German Railway) in Füssen, never made it past the project stage. It wasn't until 2019 that a Swiss study about a new Alpine railway between the Allgäu and southern Tyrol was presented, including a "rolling road" at the Fernpass. This is considered to be the worst bottleneck in Tyrolean road traffic, with up to thirty thousand vehicles a day. Back to the railroad—and on track into the future?

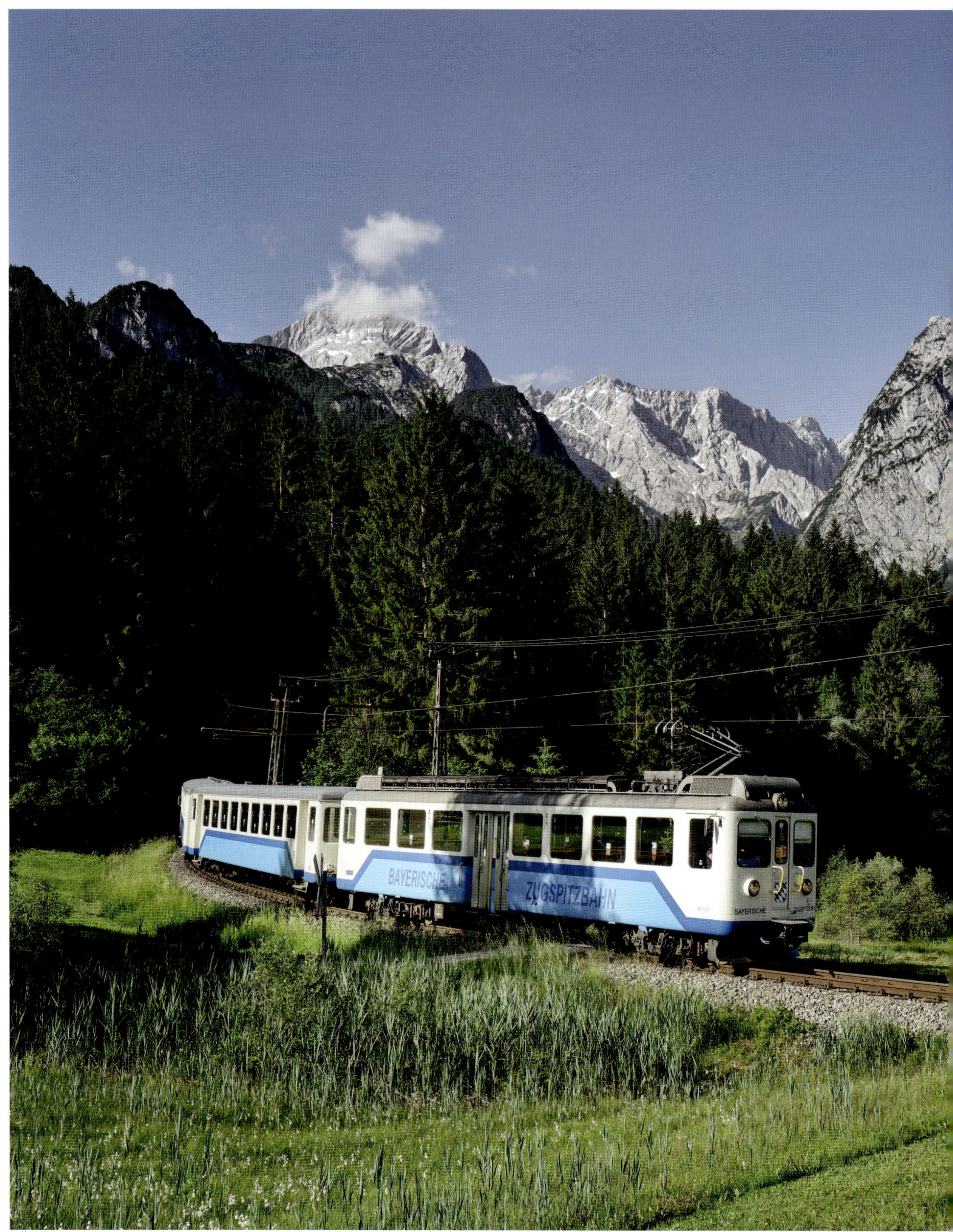

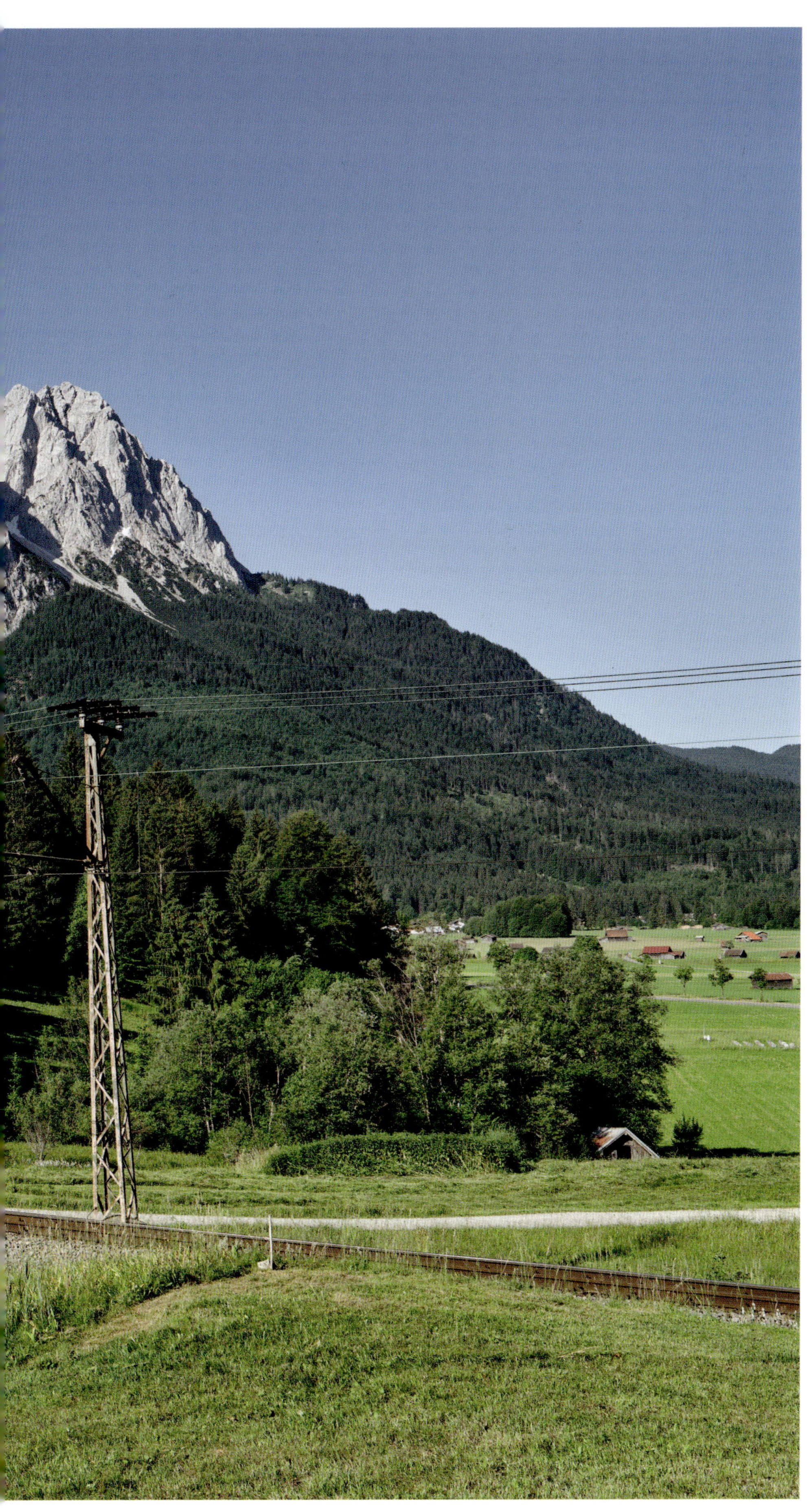

ZUGSPITZ RAILWAY

A gradual approach. The journey
to Germany's highest point, the
summit of the Zugspitz (9,718
feet / 2,962 meters) begins in
Partenkirchen and leads along the
base of the Wetterstein Massif
westward to Grainhau, where
the cogwheel route begins. View
of Alpsitze, Jubiläumsgrat, and
Waxenstein.

AUSSERFERN RAILWAY

With its three castles and the spectacular 1,312-foot-long (400-meter-long) suspension bridge, the Ehrenberger Klause is a hotspot in Ausserfern tourism. Roads and railways squeeze through the narrow valleys, watched over by the ruins of Ehrenberg Castle.

MITTENWALD RAILWAY

At a lofty height, the steel, 217-foot-long (66-meter-long) arched truss bridge of the Mitten-wald Railway spans the deep Schlossbach gorge above Zirl.
▽ ▽

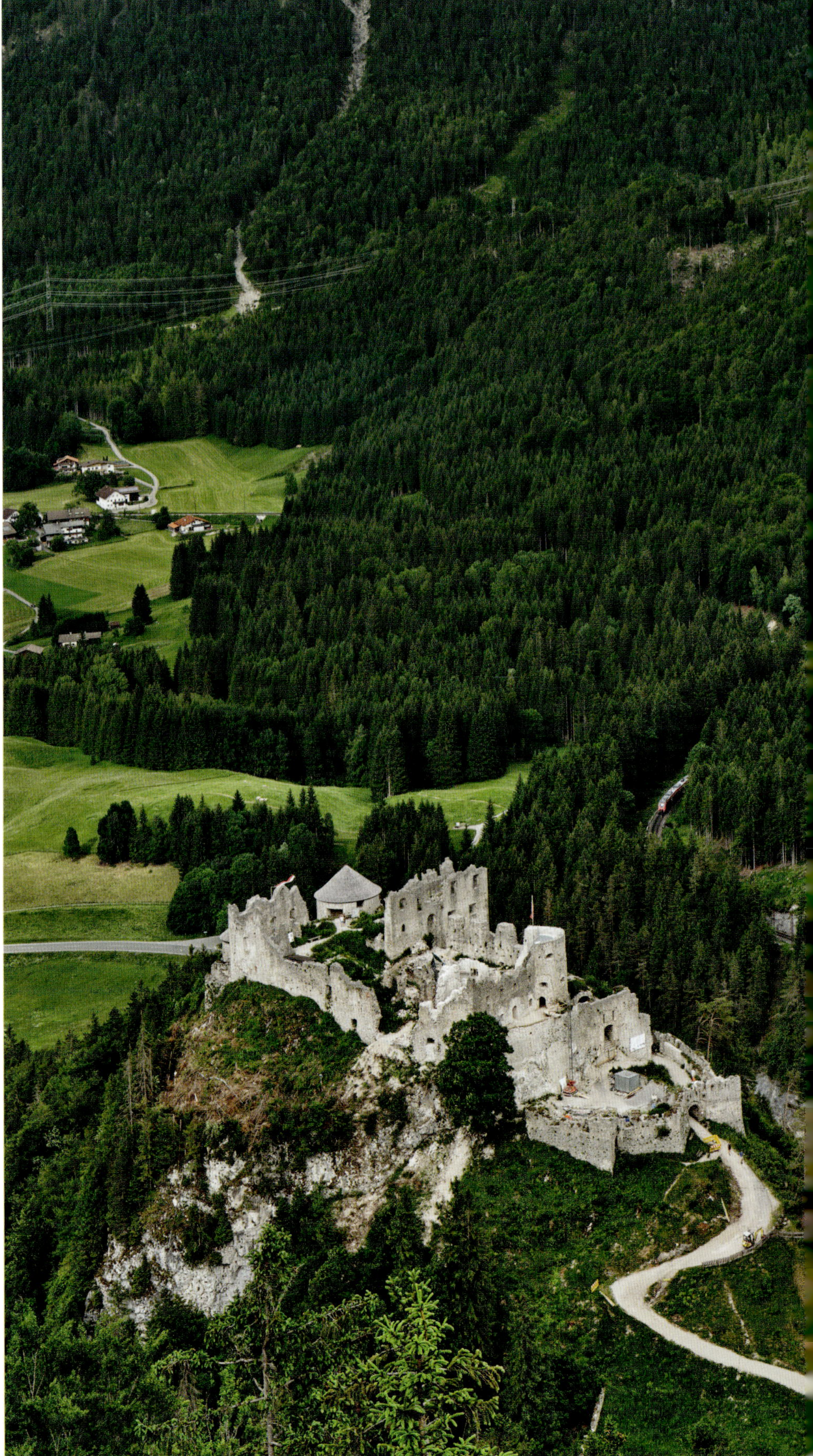

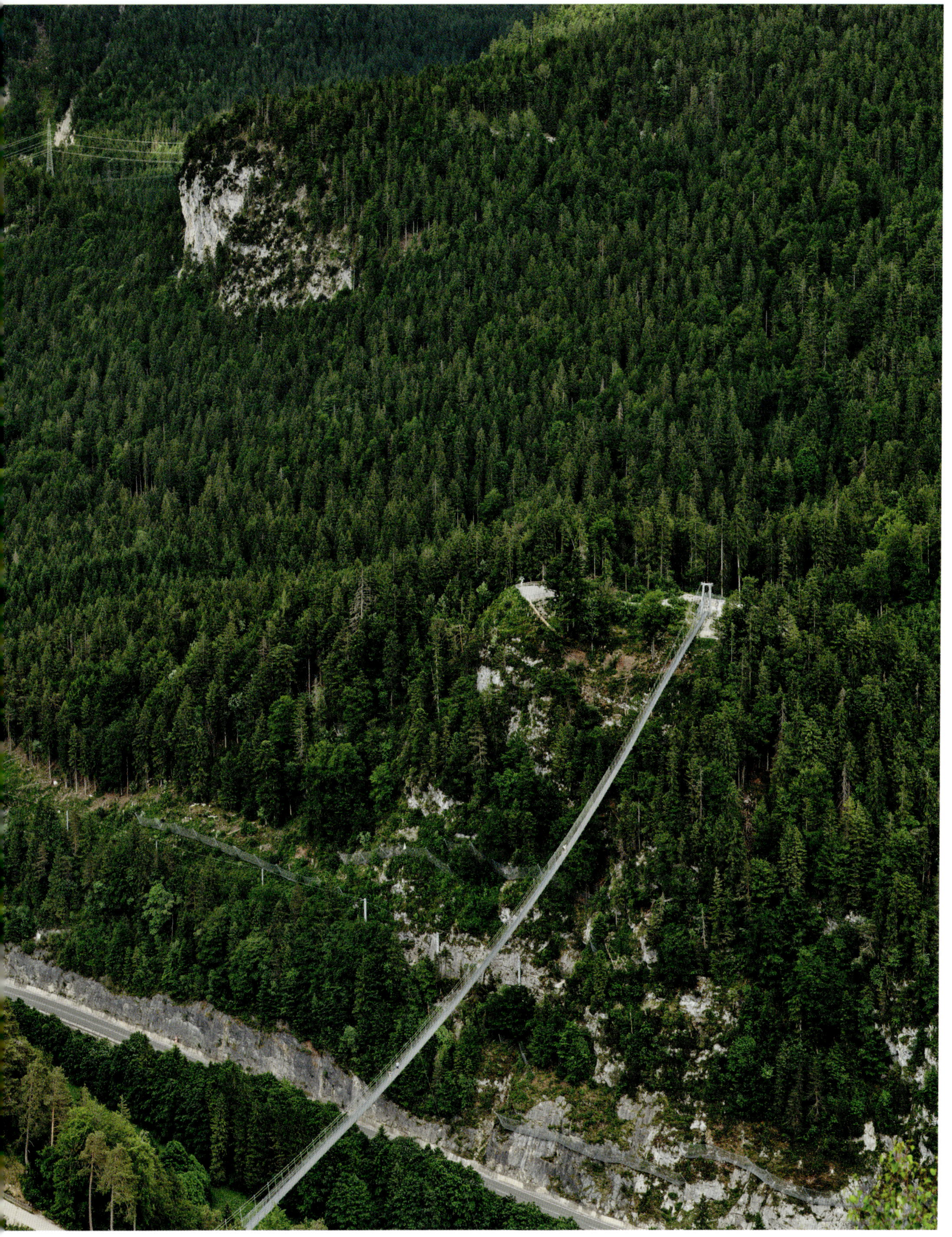

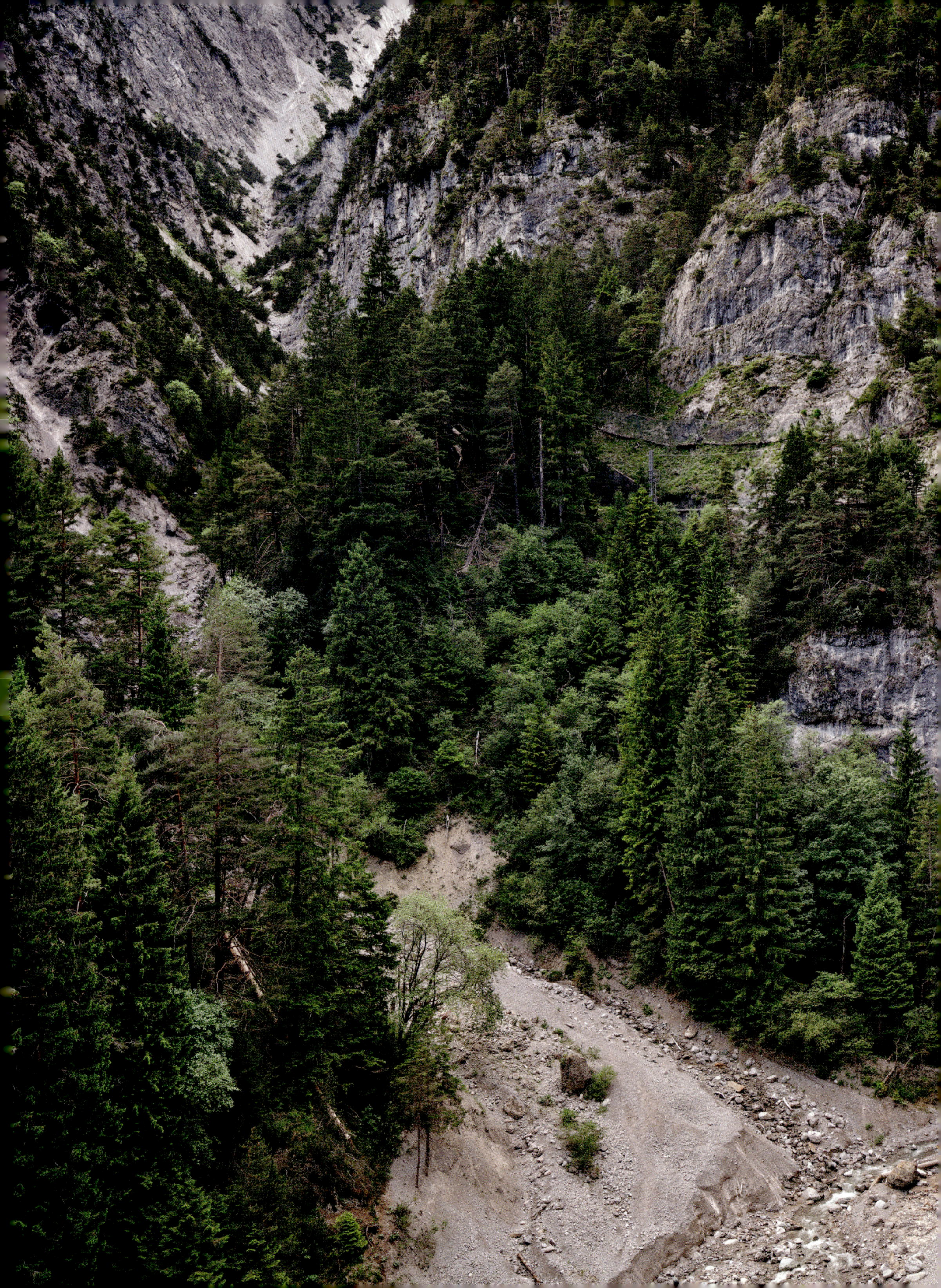

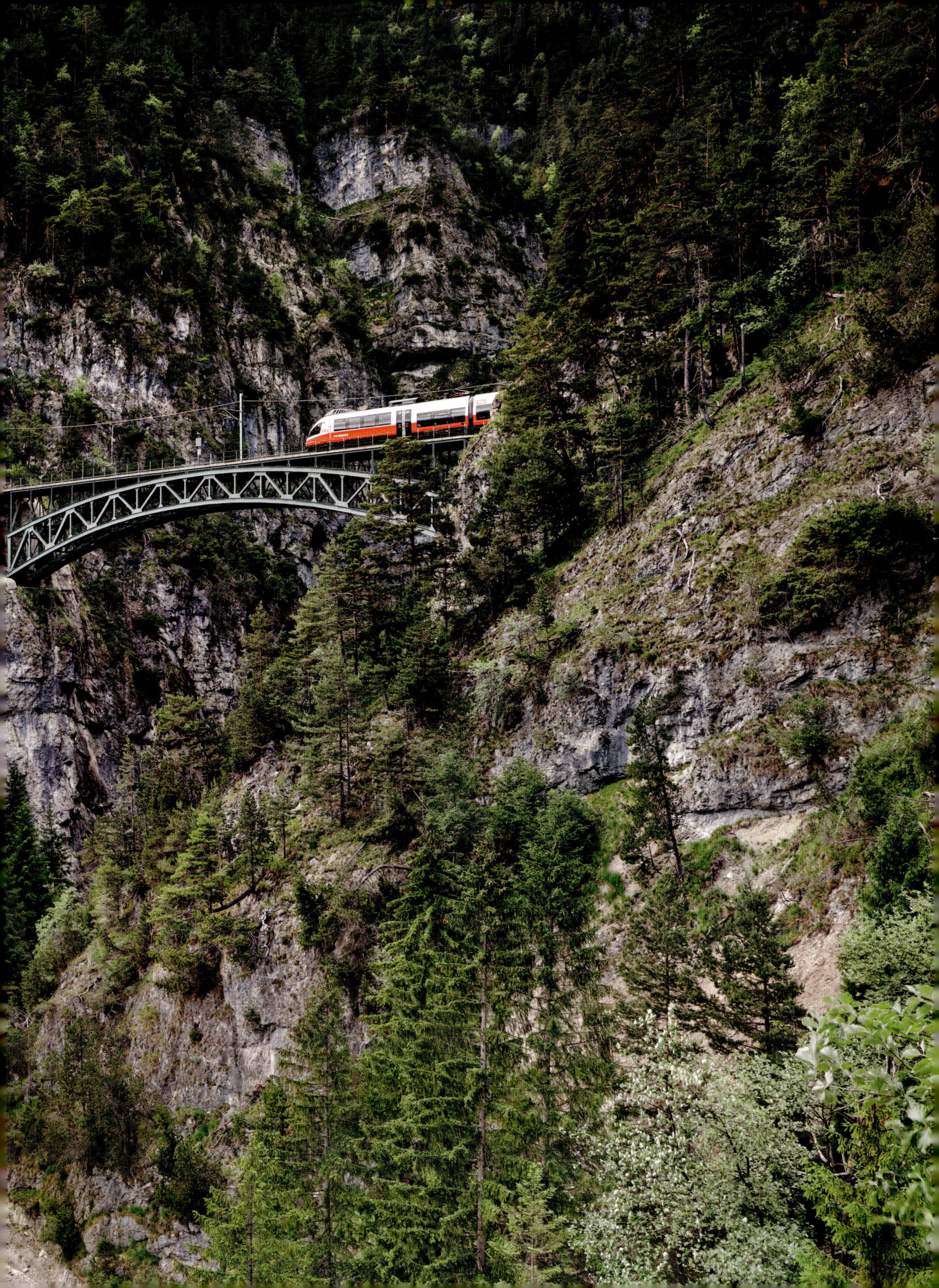

THE MOUNTAIN OF OTTO VON STEINBEIS

The most beautiful peak in the Mangfall Mountains? Of course, it's the striking pyramid of the Wendelstein, an eye-catcher on every trip over the Irschen mountain highway. And it's the only one with a railway—the *Wendelstein Railway* already has over a century under its belt.

"59°F or more (15°C), no clouds, good visibility," reports the weather service on this autumn day in gray, overcast Munich. On the Wendelstein, the sun is shining, and the railways are expecting an onslaught. While the cabins of the cable cars are swinging almost silently along their thick wire ropes, the cogwheel railway rattles along its iron rack up to the station below the summit. The Wendelstein is 6,030 feet (1,838 meters) high and finely decorated. Whoever is out and about in their car on the Irschenberg (or standing in traffic) cannot overlook the elegant stone pyramid—or that humans have decorated it with all kinds of ornaments. It wears them with dignity, the spike high antenna as well as the dome of the observatory, a few additions, and a lookout terrace.

It is not known who first climbed the summit at the edge of the Alps. The first prominent visitor was King Maximillian II in the summer of 1858, on the occasion of his grand tour of the Alpine foothills. The royal visit was, of course, a festive occasion in Bayrischzell, and the village teacher Johann Hager wrote and composed something fitting: "Wendelstein Song" ("Lied vom Wendelstein").

AN IDEA BECOMES REALITY

Two generations later, the future began on the lookout mountain: "The train is coming!" The initiator, planner, head of construction, and financer of the groundbreaking undertaking was the industrialist Otto von Steinbeis. He had built a large-scale forest management system in Bosnia, including 250 miles (400 kilometers) of narrow-gauge railroad. He then sold the company to the Imperial and Royal monarchy and used the money to realize his great dream of building the first cogwheel summit railroad in Bavaria. The 6.2-mile-long (10-kilometer-long) mountain line was operated electrically from the beginning—still a pioneering achievement.

The meter-gauge railroad overcomes a height difference of 4,101 feet (1,250 meters), three-quarters of which is done on the rack. It has seven tunnels, eight galleries, and twelve bridges; its crossing of the nearly vertical Soinwand cliff with six short tunnels is especially spectacular. About eight hundred workers—mainly from Bosnia—blasted and shoveled the route free. The railroad went into operation on May 25, 1912. Exactly 37,722 people "climbed" the Wendelstein that same year.

The last 111 meters between the mountain station and the summit platform can be done on foot along a wide and winding path. With some luck (and good weather), there is an immense panorama waiting at the top, which looks deep into the Alps and far into the flat countryside.

EVENTFUL HISTORY

The Wendelstein had the house on its summit long before the railroad came. It was opened in 1883 but soon proved to be too small. After only four years, a new building was erected, which in turn had to make way for a hotel after the opening of the railroad.

The Wendelstein Railway did not become a big hit originally. Two world wars and the economic crisis repeatedly brought the company to the brink of bankruptcy. In 1961 the valley station was relocated to the Waching district of Brannenburg, shortening the overall route by more than a mile (a good 2 kilometers). When the cable cars were also installed on the mountain (starting in Bayrischzell-Osterhofen), the fate of the cogwheel railway seemed to be sealed. The fact that it still is in operation today doesn't please just railroad enthusiasts, since the work of Mr. Steinbeis is a high-ranking cultural monument. And the ride up from the Inntal is always quite an experience—as it was a hundred years ago.

» Believe me, that I often consider
About my Wendelstein
There is no other place,
It is my greatest treasure.
There the king is at home,
He looks out upon the mountain often,
He should come back someday.
He won't be sorry! «

From "Wendelstein Song" ("Lied vom Wendelstein") by Johannes Hager (1822–98)

Along the highest part of the
route, the train runs mainly
through galleries and tunnels. The
Wendelstein Church is to the left
of the center of the image.

The Wendelstein Railway slightly
above the Zeller Sharte. On the
left is the summit path; in the
center is the green backside of the
Soinwand cliff. ▽ ▽

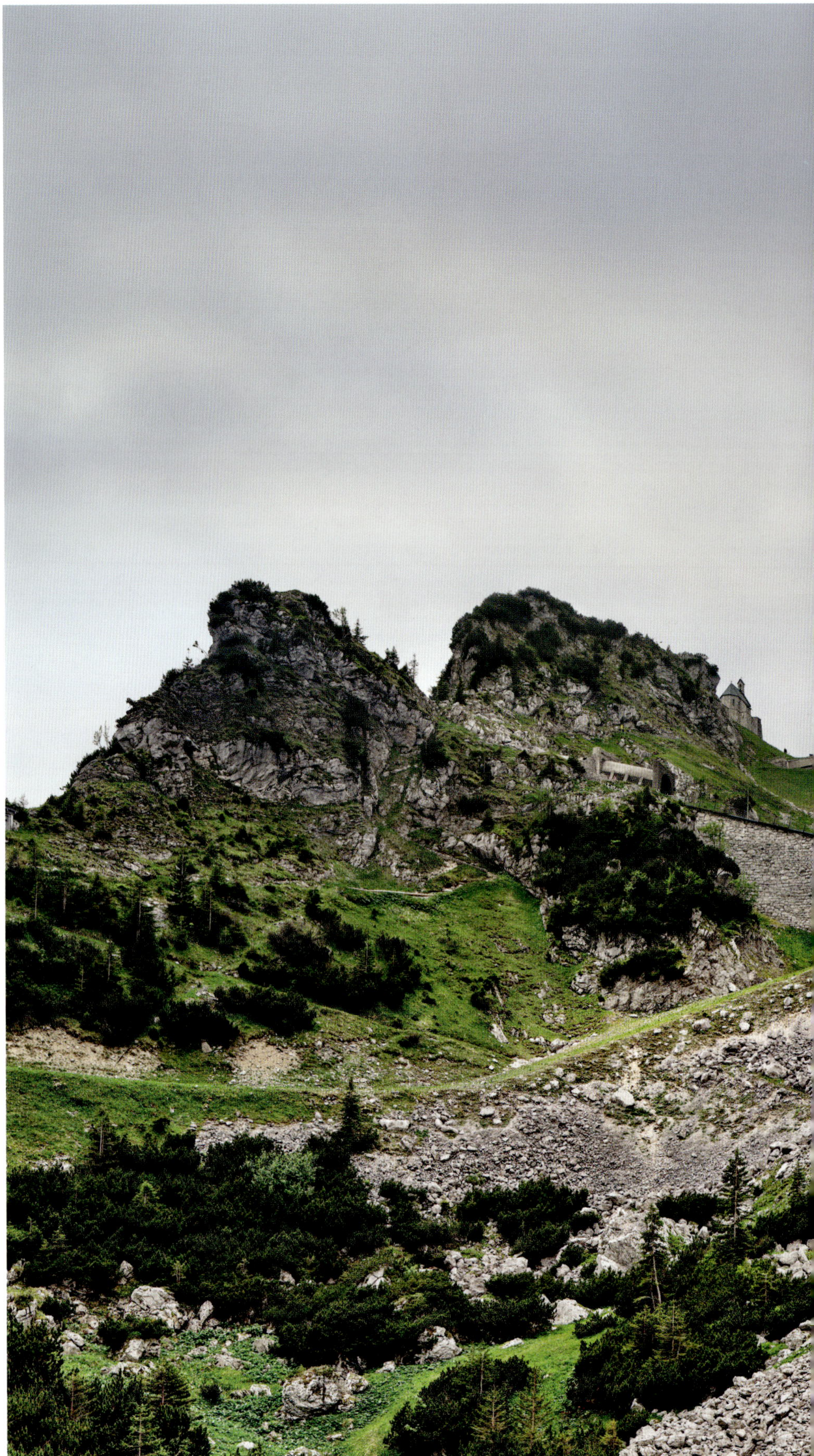

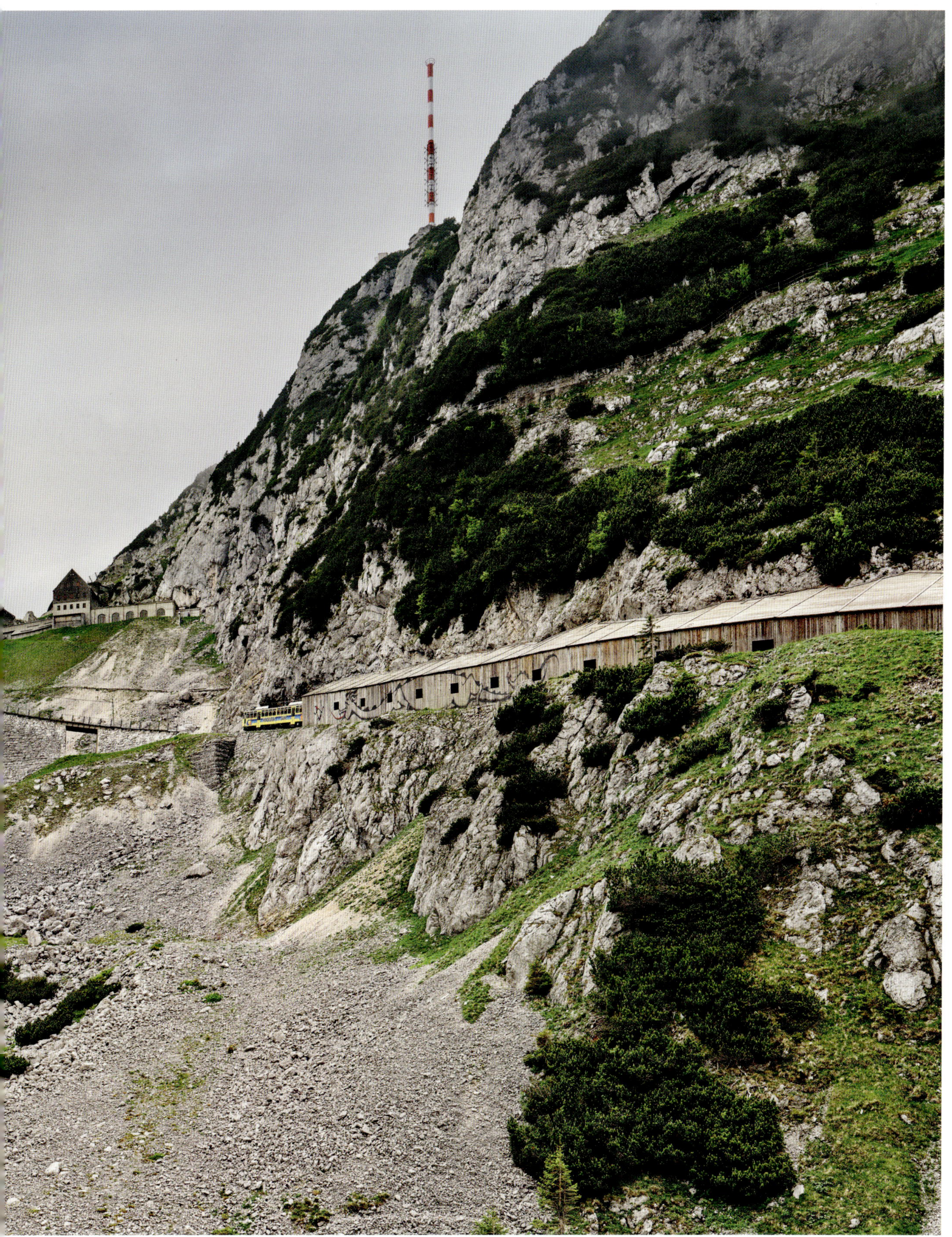

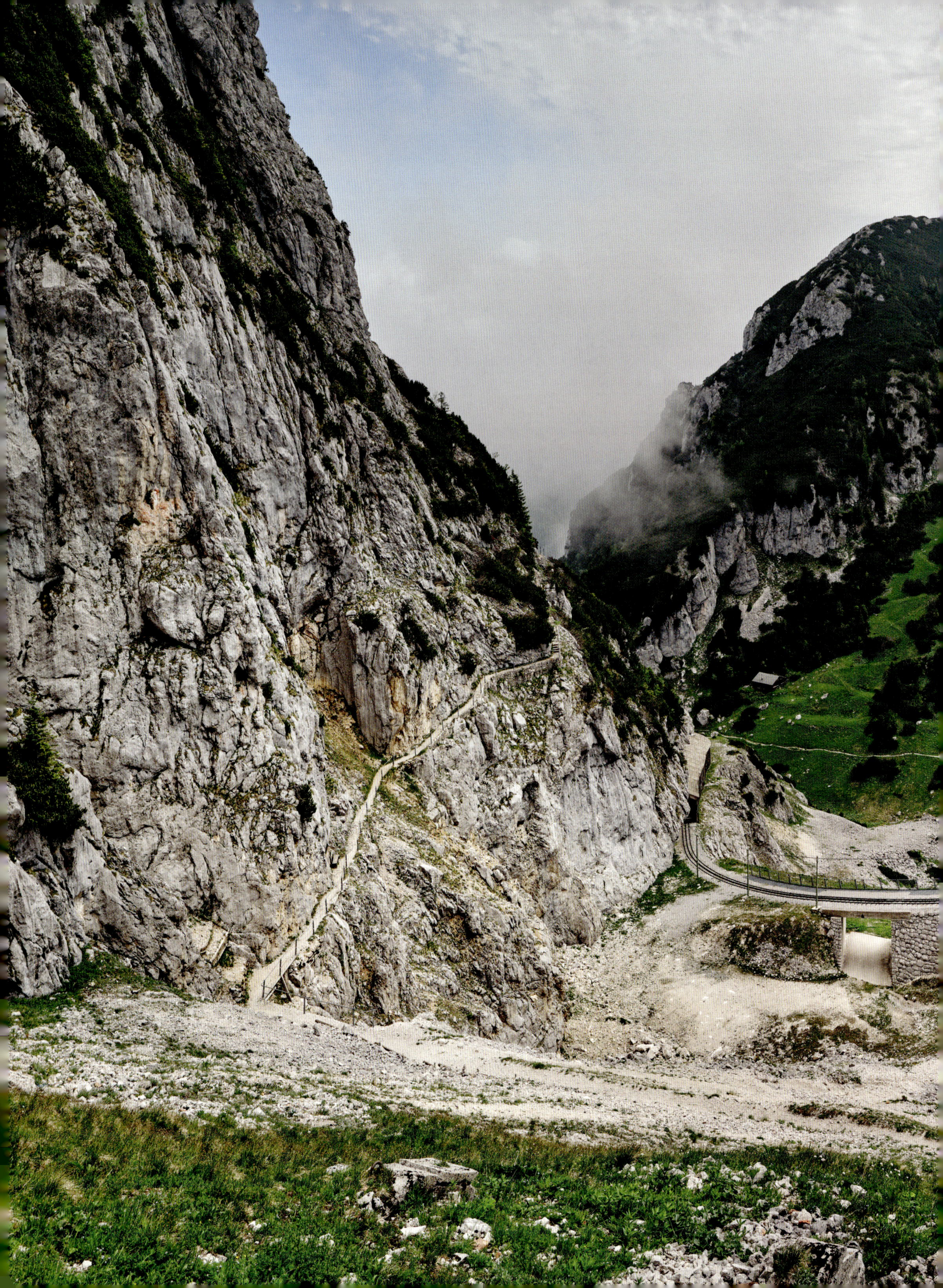

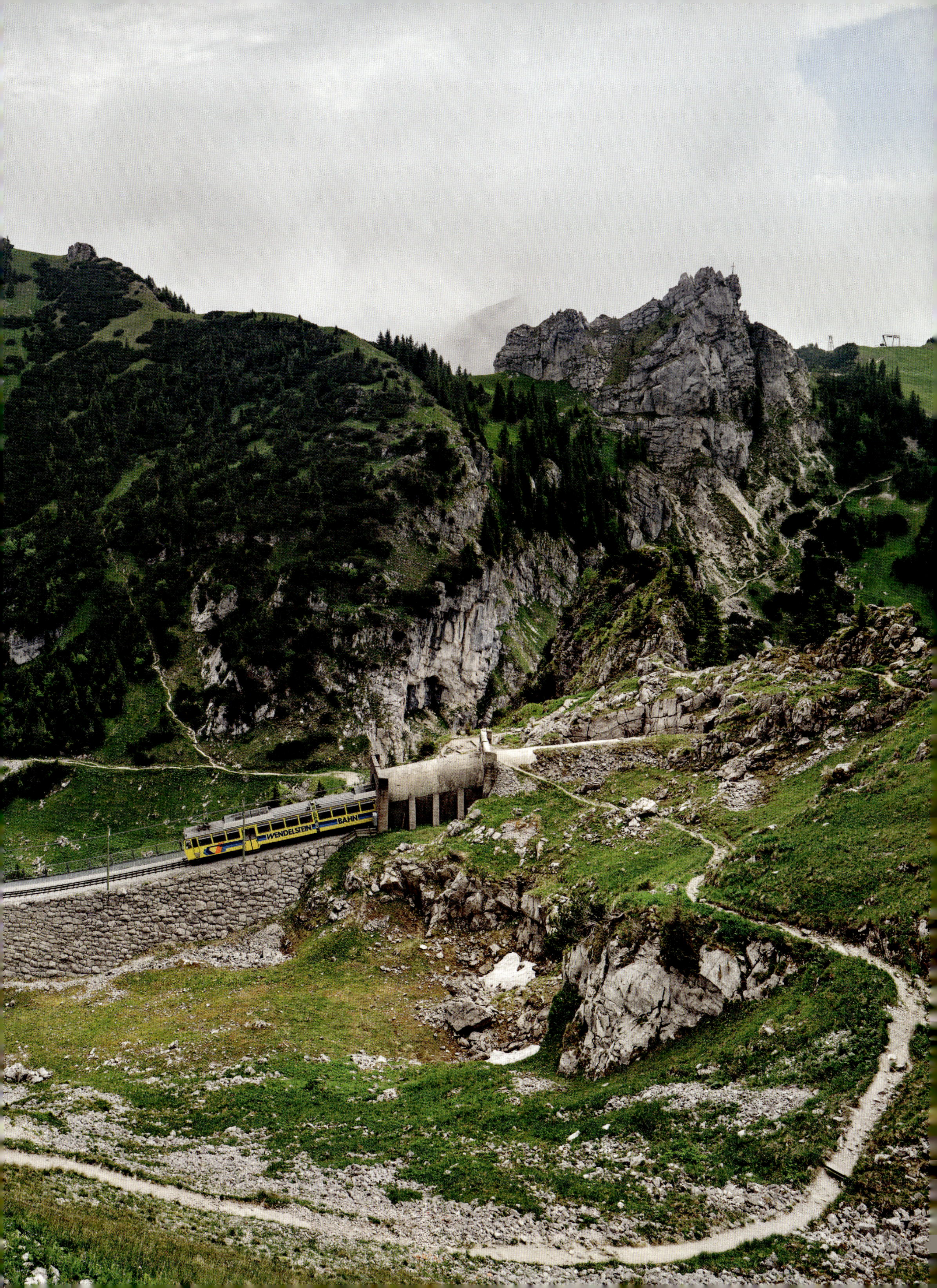

WENDELSTEIN BAHN

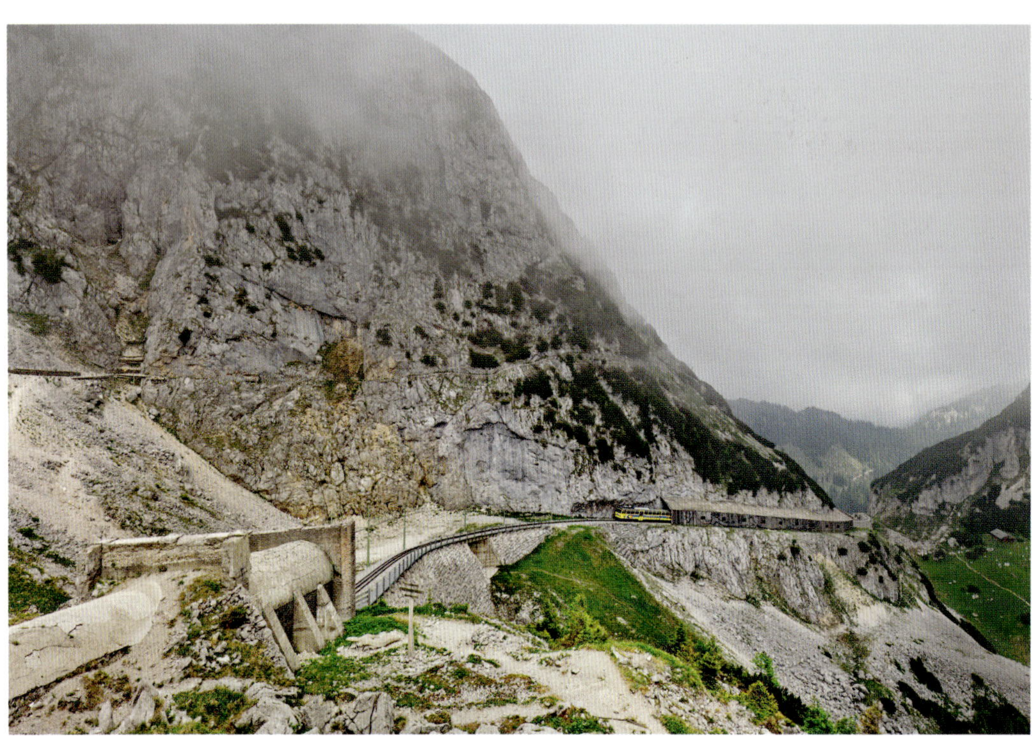

WENDELSTEIN RAILWAY

It's not the right weather for a great panorama; the summit is
hiding among the clouds. That means it's a great day to visit
the Wendelstein caves. Sensational! △

The highest church in Bavaria reigns on a rocky peak only a few
steps from the mountain station of the cogwheel railway. ▷

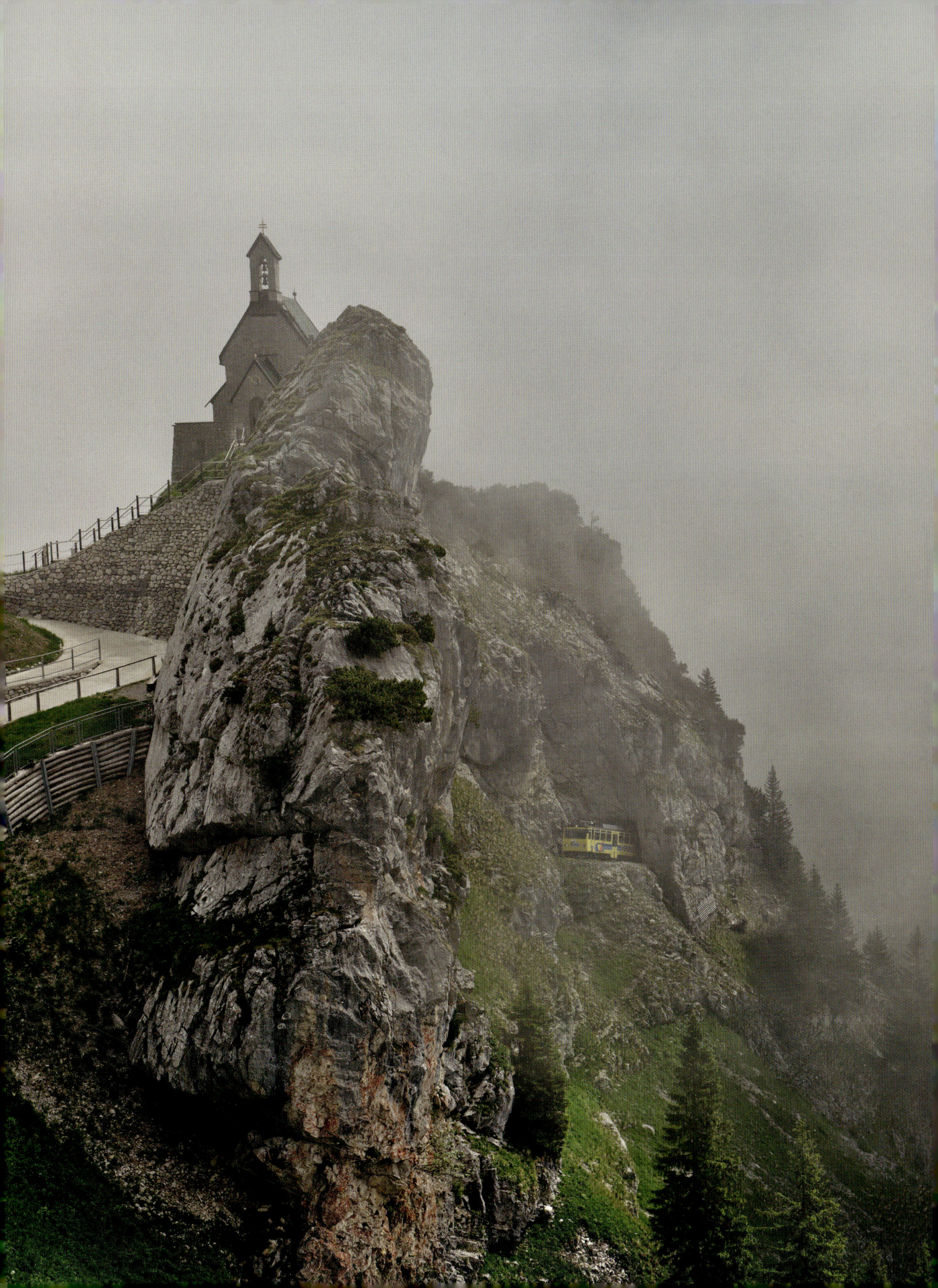

WHERE THE ORIENT EXPRESS ONCE RAN

A rail line with a big history. The Arlberg Orient Express used to run along the Arlberg Railway around a hundred years ago: in a luxury train from London to Bucharest, through the longest railroad tunnel in Austria at that time.

The Balkans begin behind the Arlberg. You hear that quite often in the "Ländle," as the Voralbergers like to call their homeland. Historically, the Alemanni people feel closer to their relatives in the west than to Vienna: efficiency instead of sloppiness, no nepotism. And one could also think that nature is of the same opinion: It is open to the Rhine and barricaded at the Alberg. Business was preferably done with the Swiss and the neighbors in southern Germany. After the outbreak of the Franco-Prussian War (1870), there was—a result of a secret treaty between Vienna and Paris—a trade embargo imposed on Austria. This hit Voralberg hard and simultaneously made clear how isolated the "Ländle" was. The borders to the west were closed and the Arlberg was to the east, but there were no transportation connections with Tyrol and the rest of the monarchy.

In Bregenz, people had been calling for a connection by rail for a long time—in vain. Only the war in France prompted the government to act. With rather unusual haste, the Viennese civil service was put into motion.

Work began on June 20, 1880, and the tunnel was excavated shortly after. The tunnel breakthrough occurred by 1883, and—after the ceremonial opening by Emperor Franz Joseph I—regular operation could begin in the fall of 1884, one year earlier than planned. The most prominent train of the 1920s and 1930s was the luxurious Arlberg Orient Express, which ran from London to Bucharest, from which elegant winter sports enthusiasts disembarked in Sankt Anton.

TUNNEL CONSTRUCTION WITH PROBLEMS

Up to five thousand men were employed in the construction of the 6.4-mile-long (10.25-kilometer-long) tunnel. This led not only to logistical problems but also to considerable tensions between the locals and the workers from all parts of the Austrian monarchy. As the priest of St. Jakob, Paul Bernhard, noted: "For the simple valley people, the four years of tunnel construction brought many hard trials. For men, the dangers lay with hedonism, particularly the drunkenness in the thirty-four taverns, the violation of fasting days, and the desecration of Sundays. For the females, especially the maidens, the seduction of moral corruption was extremely great, and thirteen girls in the village had bear the heavy fate of single motherhood."

The terrain also proved to be problematic, especially on the tunnel access road on the western side. Franz Kreuter wrote in the *Zeitschrift des Deutschen und Österreichischen Alpenvereins* (*Journal of the German and Austrian Alpine*

Club) in 1884: "The 10-kilometer [6.2-mile] stretch from Langen to Braz, where the greatest construction difficulties were encountered, has, in addition to enormous retaining walls, fifteen large bridges and viaducts with a total clearance of 402 meters [1,319 feet], two aqueducts, nine tunnels and galleries with a total of 896 meters [2,940 feet], and about 200 meters [656 feet] of protective roofs against avalanches. The sharpest curves on the mountain section have a radius of only 250 meters [820 feet] and the largest gradient on the eastern side is 2.64 percent, on the western side 3.14 percent." The culmination point of the railroad line is the summit tunnel at 4,301 feet (1,311 meters).

THE SPECTACULAR TRISANNA BRIDGE

The most striking structure along the 85-mile-long (137-kilometer-long) Alberg Line between Bludenz and Innsbruck is the Trisanna Bridge—still a popular photo motif today, along with the Wiesberg Castle. With a total length of 755 feet (230 meters), it crosses the Trisanna with a deck height of 285 feet (87 meters). Between the two highest piers, the main span of the steel construction is a sensational 394 feet (120 meters). For safety reasons, the center section of the bridge was later reinforced with a so-called fish-bellied girder. In 1964 the entire steel structure was replaced in an elaborate undertaking: 1,600 tons of iron had to be moved laterally. The duration of the dismantling and rebuilding was ten hours and twenty minutes!

》 You are full up tonight, I hear? 《

》 It is incredible, Monsieur. All the world elects to travel tonight. 《

From *Murder on the Orient Express* by Agatha Christie (1934), filmed several times,
including in 1974 with Albert Finney as detective Hercule Poirot (directed by Sidney Lumet)

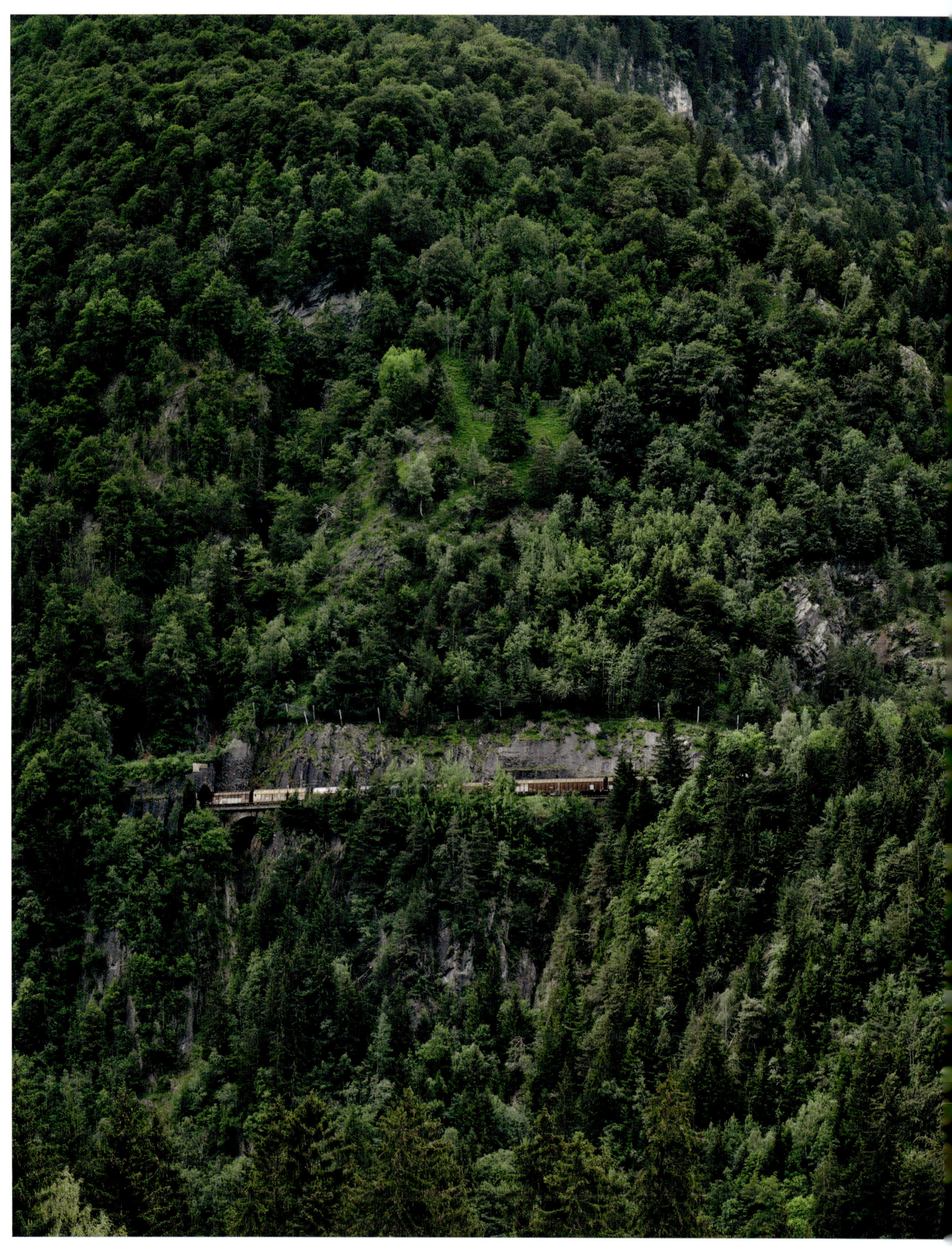

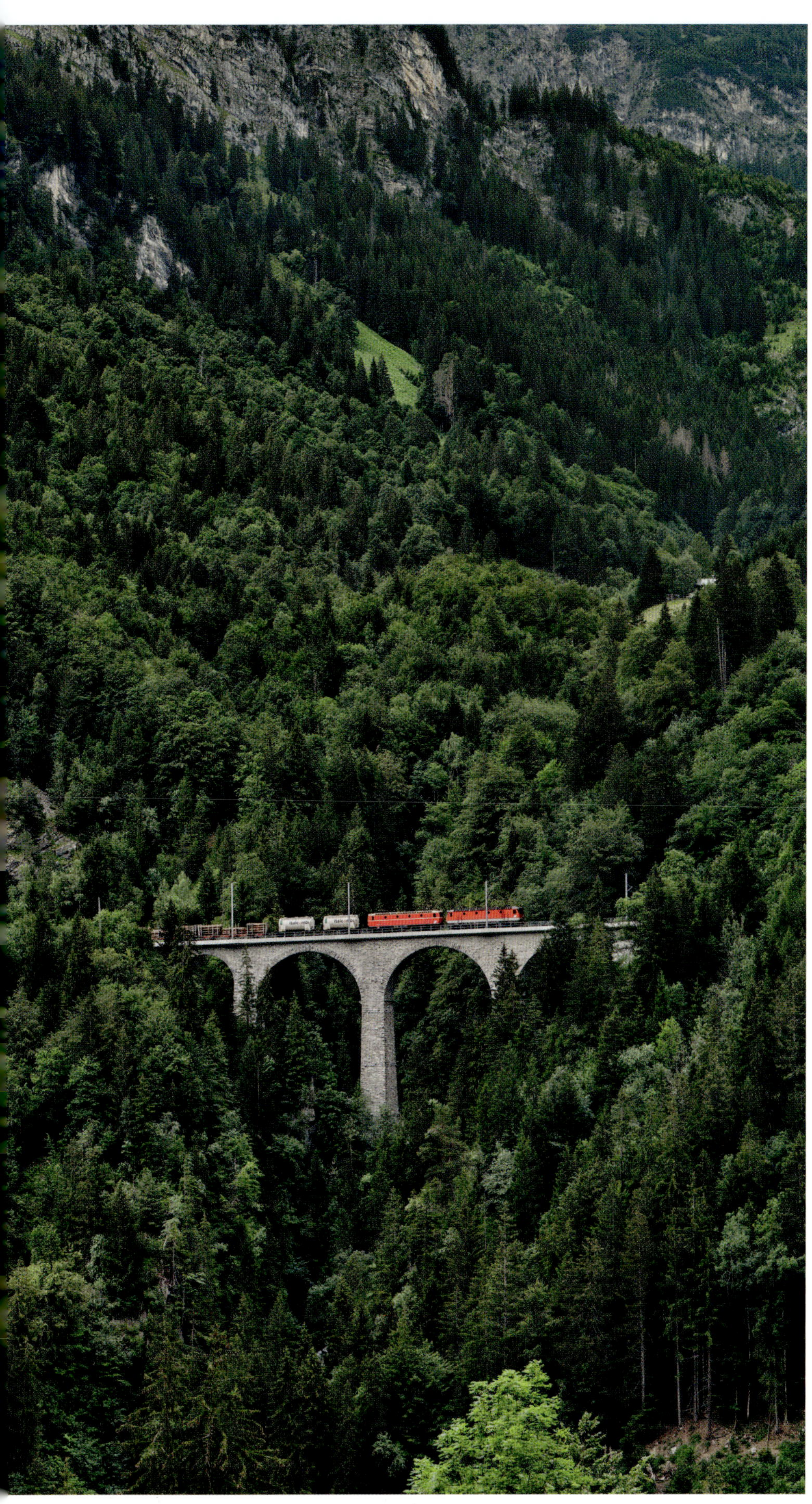

ALBERG RAILWAY

A train transporting goods along the 394-foot-long (120-meter-long) Schmiedtobel Bridge near Dalaas. In total, there are fifty-nine short and seventeen long bridges along the mountain route.

The Alberg Railway's climb to the western portal of the summit tunnel begins with the Braz Arch. The view to the west goes to the Bludenz Valley basin and to the rim elevations of the Rätikon mountain range. ▽ ▽

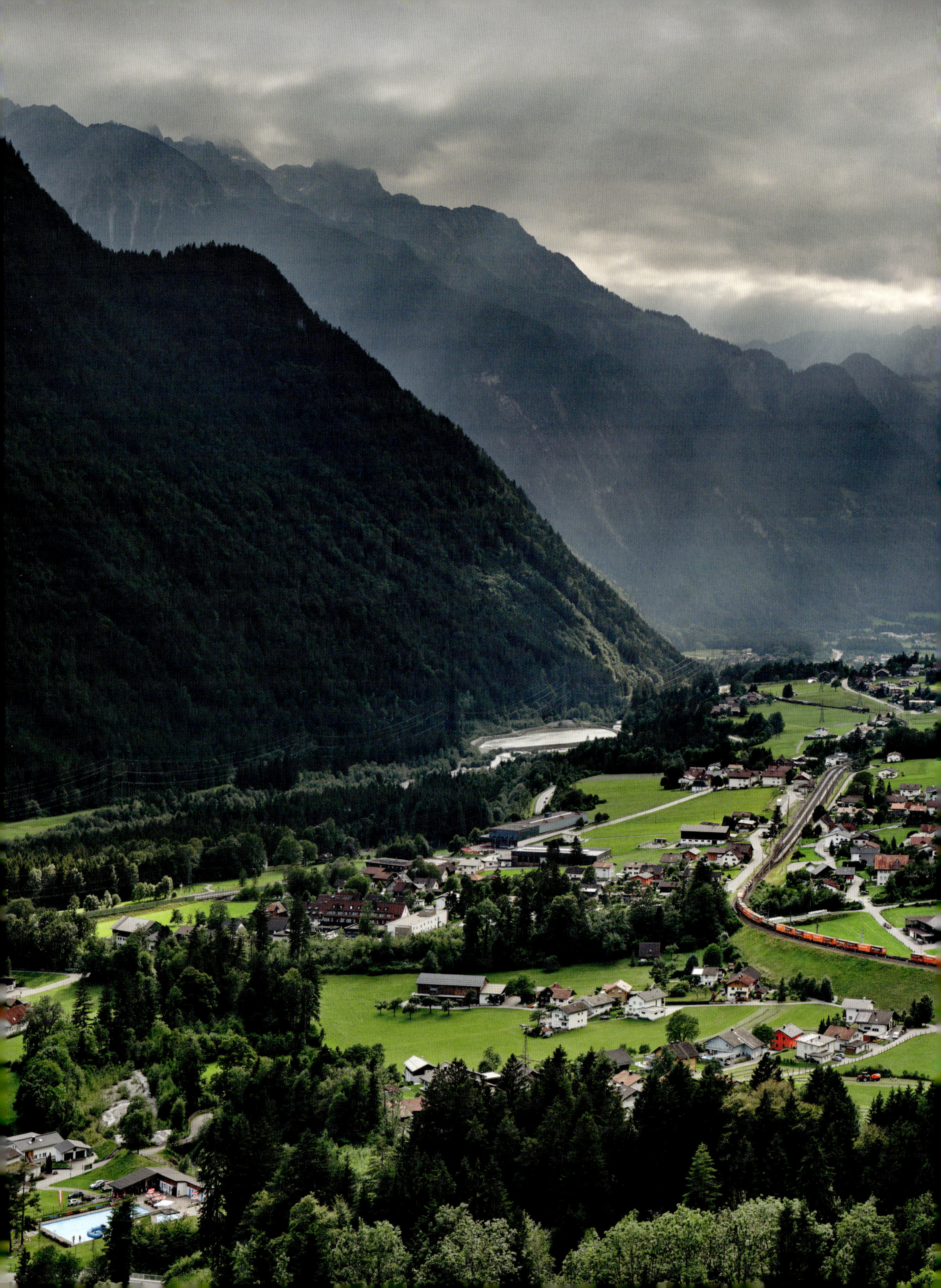

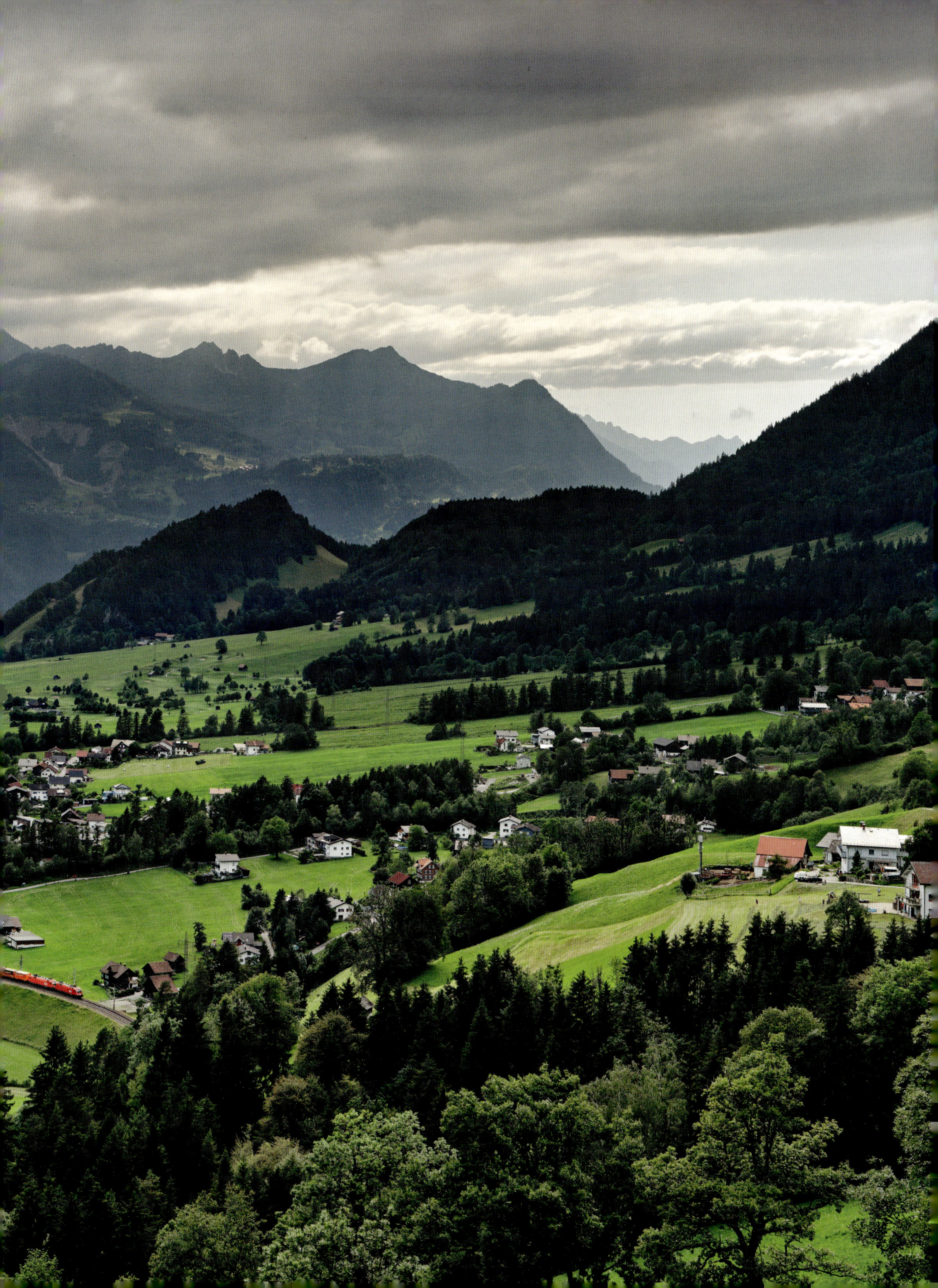

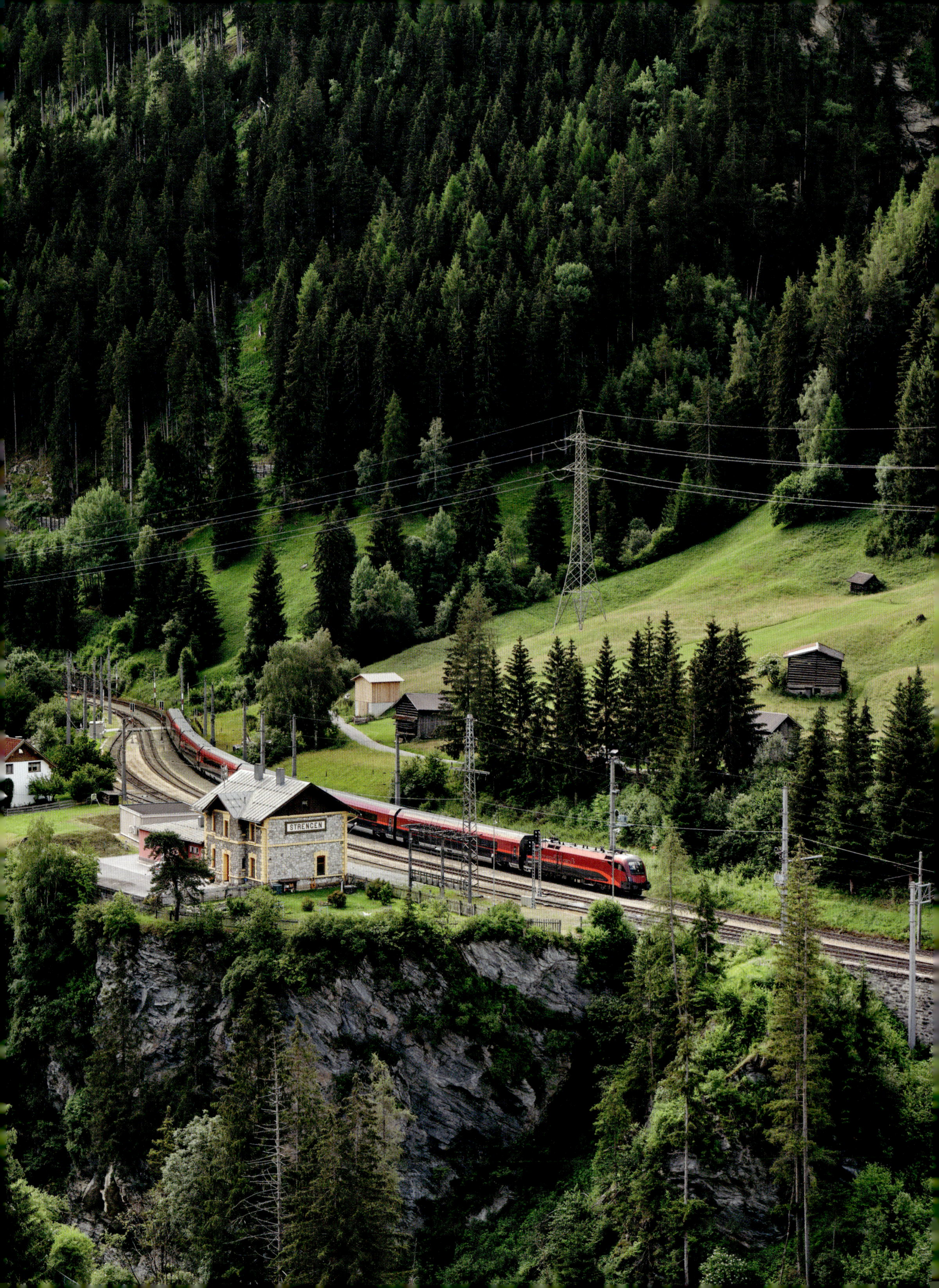
STRENGEN

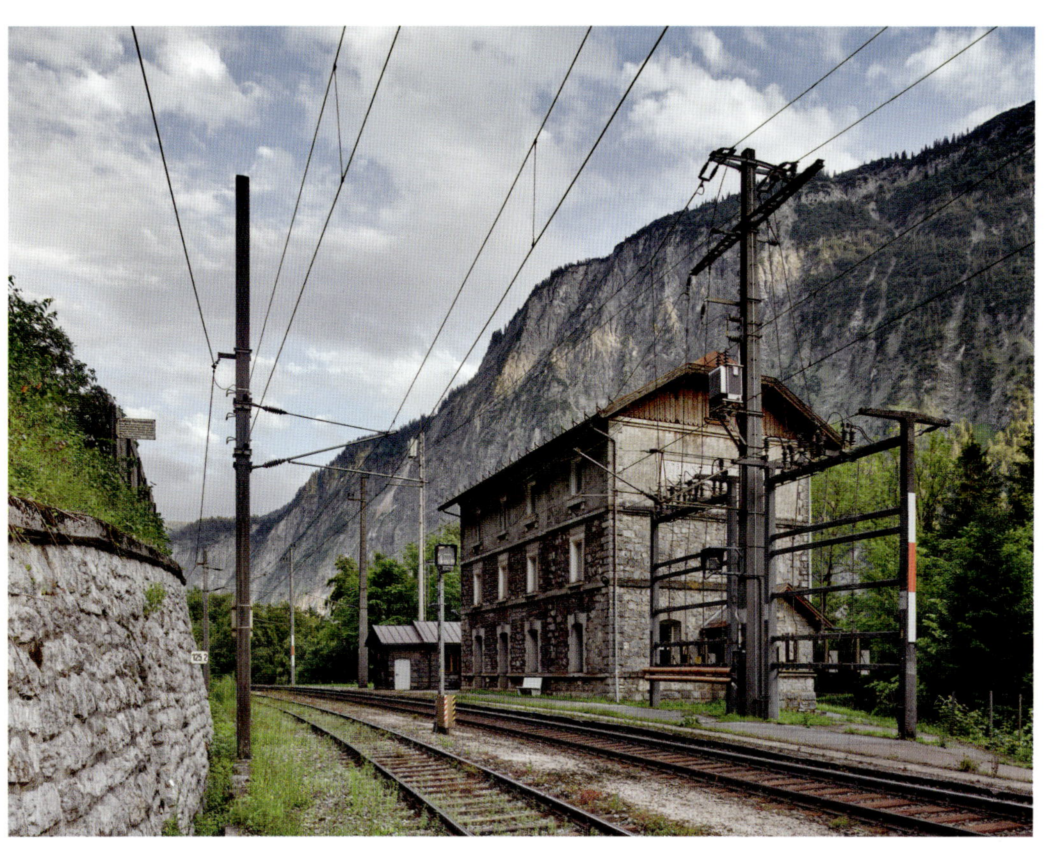

ALBERG RAILWAY

Trains don't stop at these train stations anymore. With the exception of Sankt Anton and Langen, all stations on the Arlberg Line were shut down, even the Strengen ones in the Stanz Valley and Hintergasse in the Kostertal Valley. △

The photo motif of the Arlberg Line par excellence: the Trisanna Bridge with the Wiesberg Castle. The main span of the steel construction between the two main piers is 394 feet (120 meters). ▽ ▽

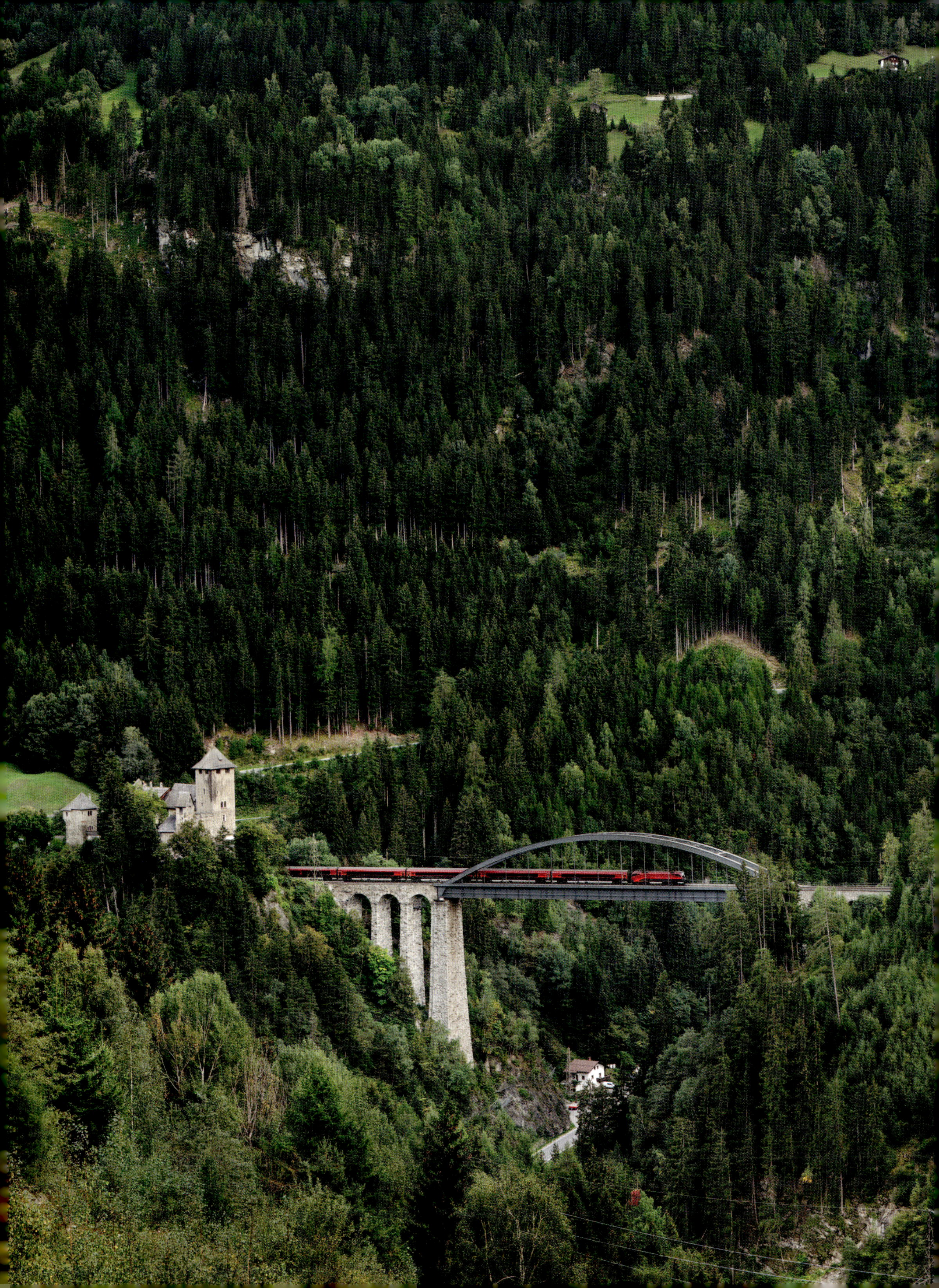

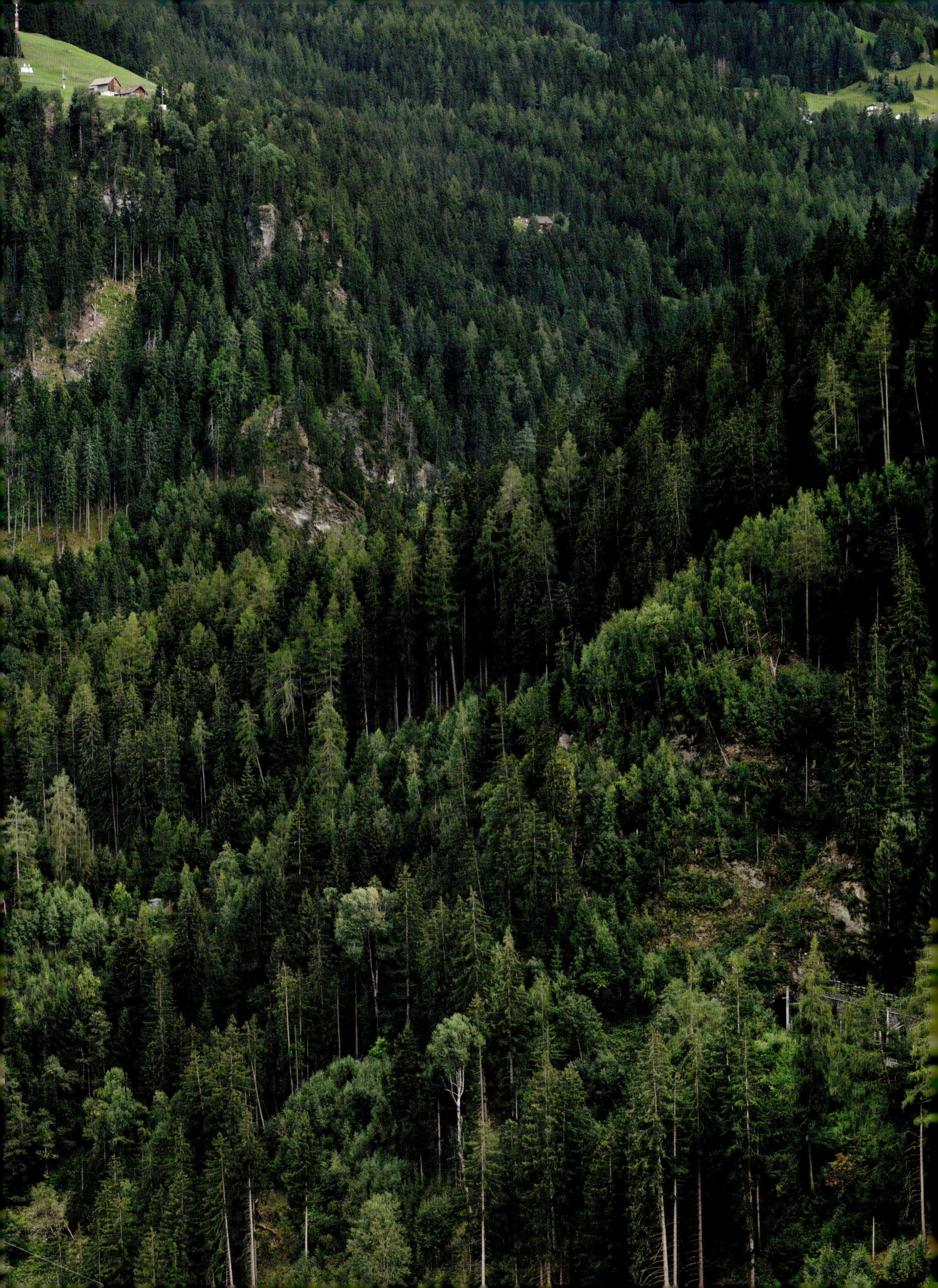

BRENNER RAILWAY

CIAO, BELLA ITALIA!

The *Brenner Railway* is the only line to cross the main ridge of the Alps without a tunnel—no wonder, since the culmination point has a height of only 4,495 feet (1,370 meters). It connects North Tyrol, South Tyrol, and the historical Welsch Tyrol (today Trentino). Of the numerous branching lines from the Imperial and Royal period, only three have survived the Italian automobile boom: the *Vinschgau, Ritten,* and *Non Valley Railways.*

People from all around the world travel over the Brenner Pass. By car. From Bavaria to Innsbruck, over the border pass, into the south of Tyrol, and on to Lake Garda. To Italy, that is. Since 1919, Italy's territory has begun at the top of the Alpine watershed, but the "real" Italy begins at Lake Garda. It offers everything that a vacationer could desire: 143 square miles (370 square kilometers) of water, framed by high mountains, perfect tourism infrastructure, and a population accustomed to speaking with visitors from the north. Ciao, bella Italia!

It is not possible to travel exclusively by train to the great lake. Not anymore. That's because the railroad line between Rovereto and Riva del Garda, opened in 1891, was shut down in the 1930s—a warning sign of the troubled times ahead for railroads after World War II. While the double-headed eagle of the Imperial and Royal monarchy still ruled in South Tyrol and Trentino (Welsh Tyrol), you could still reach Val Gardena through the Vinschgau Valley by rail, as well as the Val di Fiemme, the Val di Sole from Trento, and the Mendel Pass. The military was also involved in some of these projects for strategic reasons; the prosperous tourism of the fin de siècle opened the door for innovations as well.

In the vicinity of Bolzano, the Ritten Railway (whose rack-and-pinion stretch was later replaced by a cable car) and the Überetscher Railway were built. Today, it has been discussed if the short line (Bolzano–Kaltern) that was shut down in 1961 should be renewed and reopened. Many an excursionist would have been glad to have had the opportunity to take a trip into the South Tyrolean wine paradise and not have to sit behind a steering wheel.

VINSCHGAU RAILWAY

And what about the upper road to the Reschen Pass, part of the Via Claudia Augusta in Roman times and the most important transit route across the Alps? At the beginning of the twentieth century, a private company built the railroad line from Merano through the Vinschgau Valley to Mals. The planning included a continuation over the Reschen Pass to Landeck. However, nothing came of this Alpine crossing. There were doubts about the profitability of such a line, also in light of the competition from the Brenner Line. Then came the war: South Tyrol fell to Italy, and the Vinschgau Railway was taken over by the state railway. They showed little interest in the "unfinished" line. The (temporary) end came in the summer of 1990.

A decade later, the existing infrastructure went to the province of South Tyrol. Here, people thought regionally, recognizing the potential of the rail line for commuters as well as for tourism. After renovation measures, the first Stadler Rail train ran on the renovated line in 2005. This marked the beginning of a real success story, with the predicted passenger numbers being far surpassed. The railroad soon reached its capacity limits, which is why Bolzano decided to electrify the line. From 2023 onward, new, more powerful train compositions will run every half hour in Vinschgau with a direct connection to Bolzano.

THE GATE TO THE SOUTH—BRENNER PASS

The fact that tracks were built through the Brenner Pass relatively late, although it's the deepest dip in the main Alpine ride and the shortest connection between Innsbruck and Bolzano, had both a political and military background. First, at that time, Vienna was the absolute center of a major European power; Tyrol was far away in comparison. A train connection to the port of Trieste seemed much more important than a regional railroad in Andreas Hofer's farming country. Only the blatant misjudgments of the Imperial and Royal generals and the associated territorial losses (Lombardy) turned the attention of the army leadership to the southwestern flank of the empire. Then, however, things moved quite quickly: In 1864 the construction crews arrived, and regular traffic started as early as 1867. There were only limited difficulties due to the terrain, and a summit tunnel as in the case of the other major Alpine transit lines was not required.

It's not necessary to know that the "Nonsberger Kuh" is a railroad, and a mountain railroad at that. It connects Trento with the Nonsberg, the largest apple-producing area in the province, and then continues a little farther into the Val di Sole. Around the same time, a branch route was built from Dermulo via Fondo up to the Mendel Pass. That route has been history for a while, unlike the Vacca della Val di Non. In 2003, it was even extended 6.2 miles (10 kilometers)—a real miracle in this car-crazed country. Maybe there still is a future for the railroad?

The future is also being tinkered with hundreds of feet below the Brenner Pass: at the base tunnel. The main purpose of this tunnel is to transfer the growing volume of freight traffic to the railways. On the other hand, up until just a few years ago at the top of the pass, you could look back in time. Here, travelers were allowed to view the rather dusty buildings, a lot of rolling stock, and a bit of mountain nature for a half hour at a time while standing still. Only then did they move on. The reason behind this: Austria's trains run on alternating current (AC), while those in Italy run on direct current (DC); the trains drive on the right in Austria but on the left in Italy. A united Europe? The base tunnel will make travel much easier, for people and goods. The 35-mile-long (56-kilometer-long) tunnel is slated to be completed in 2032, provided the deadlines are met and the access routes are completed. Austria and South Tyrol are working on this, while Bavaria is really taking its time—slightly worrisome, if you think about the prolonged German projects such as the Berlin Brandenburg Airport or the "Stuttgart 21" urban development plan.

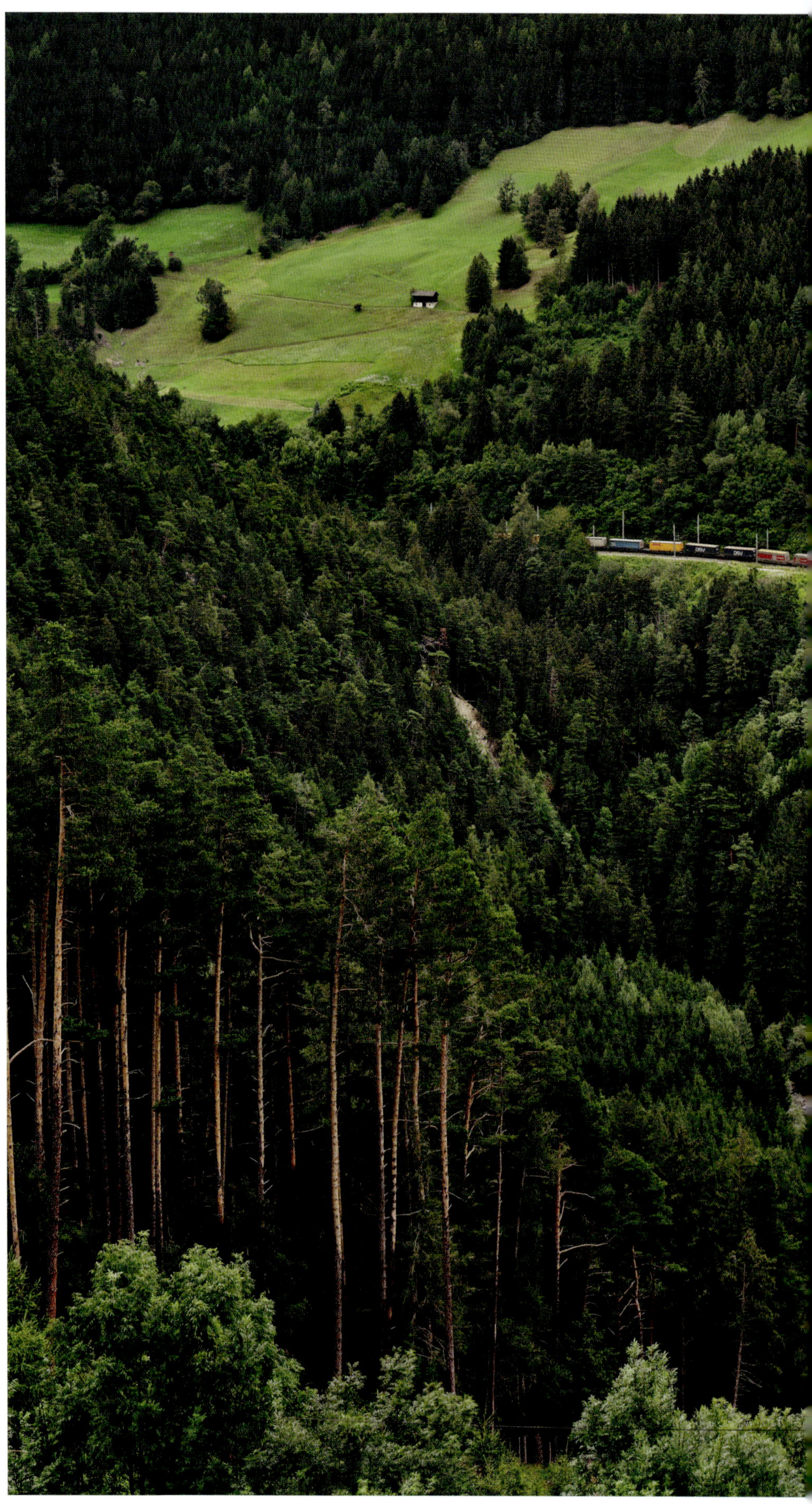

BRENNER RAILWAY

A standard freight train in the Tyrolean Wipp Valley. Trains from the "Rollenden Landstrasse" (ROLA) also make their way along the Brenner Line. The contents of about 180,000 tractor trailers went along it in 2020—an environmentally friendly alternative to the road.

Gossensass, the first village south of the Brenner Pass, ducks under the monumental viaduct of the highway. The railroad descends into the 4.5-mile-long (7.3-kilometer-long) Pflerscher Tunnel into the valley of the same name. The picture was taken from the old, abandoned track with a branch tunnel. ▽

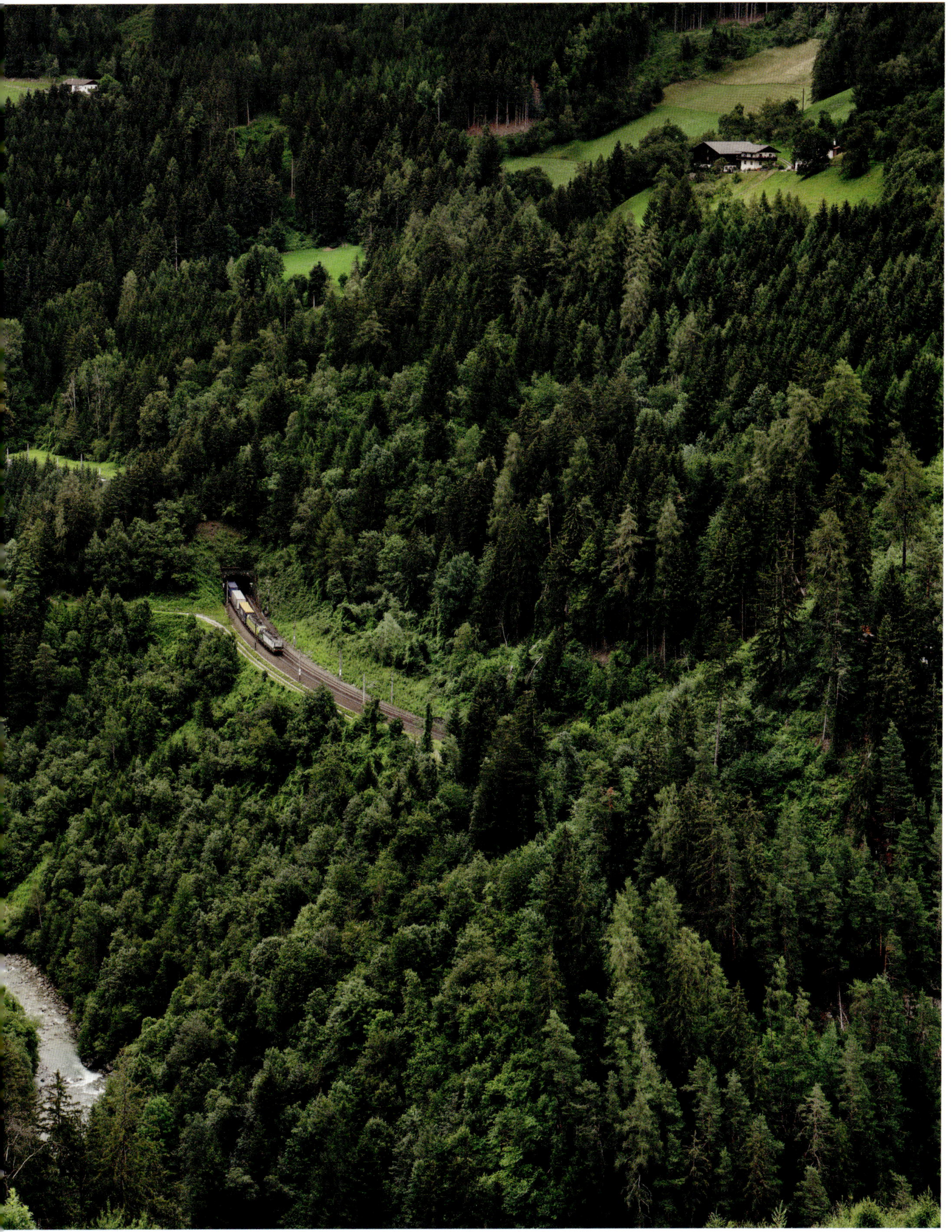

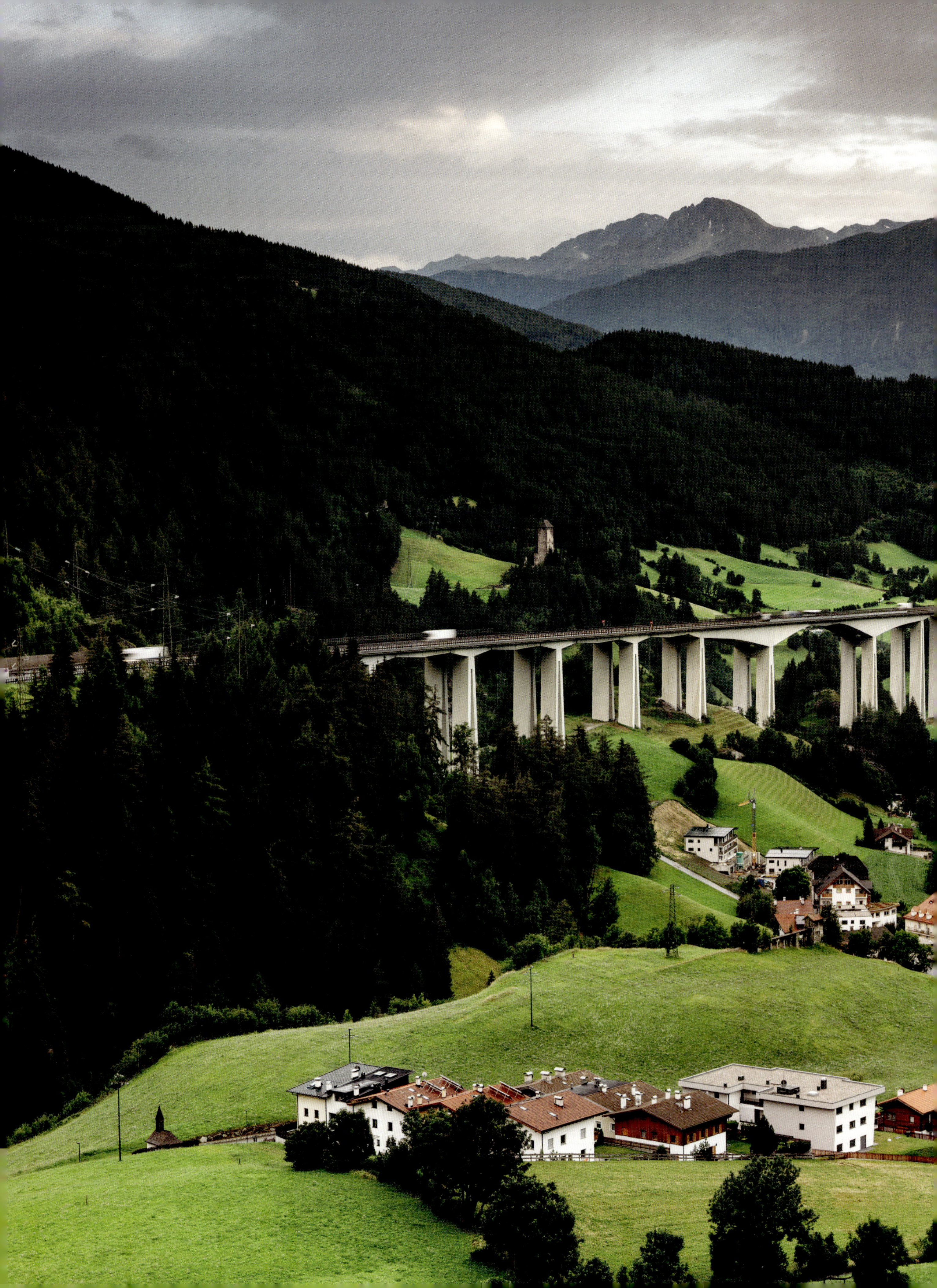

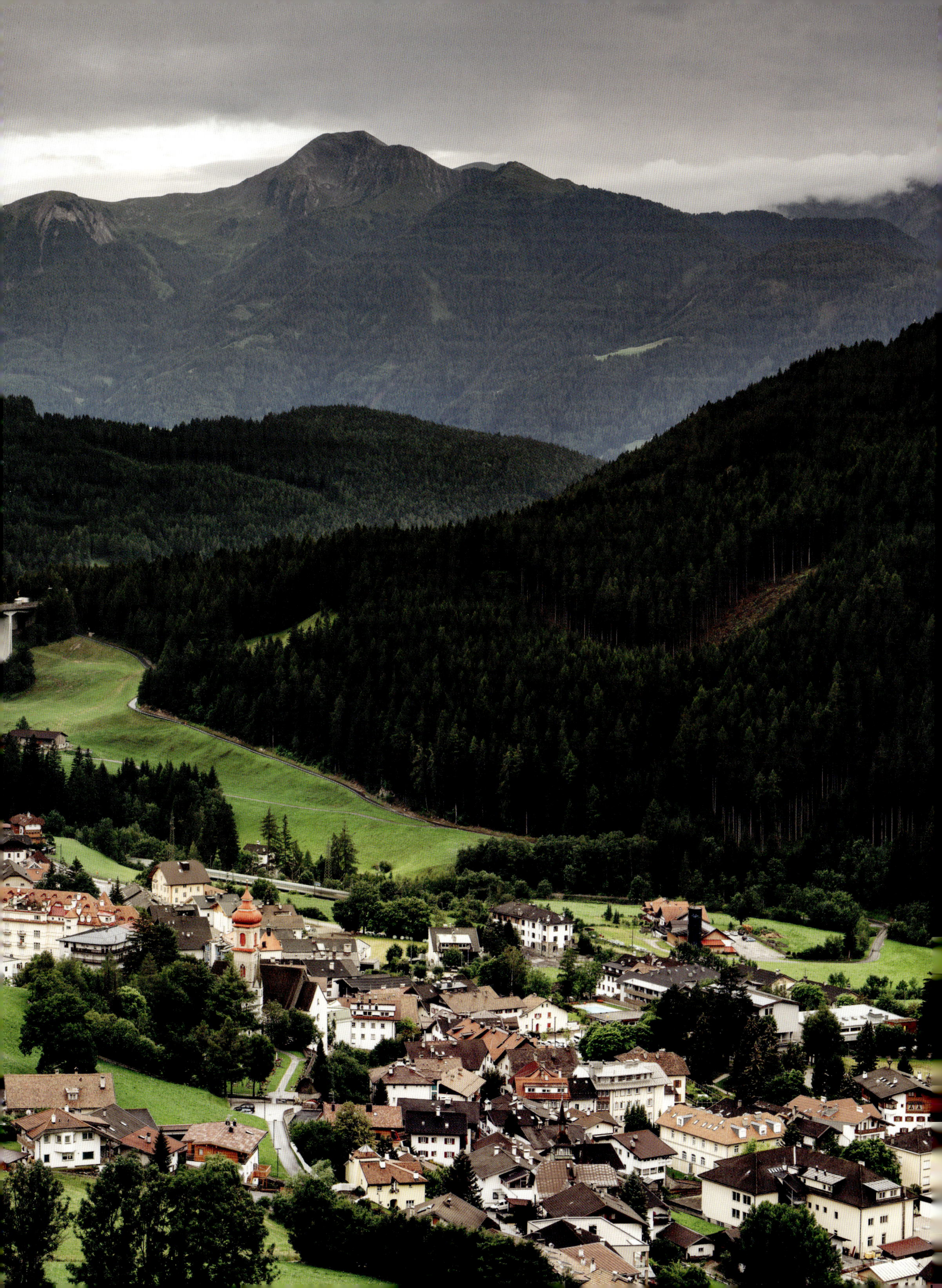

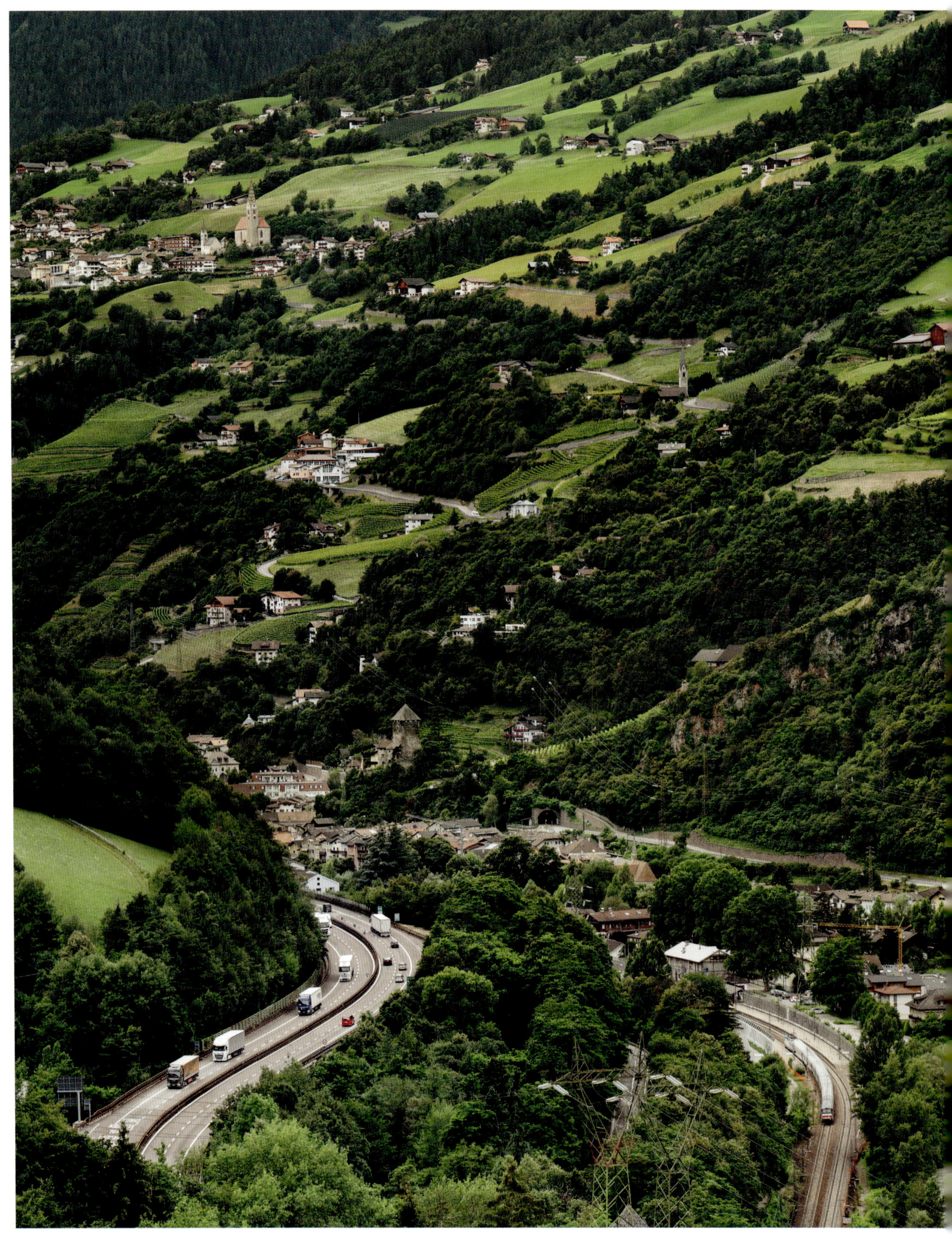

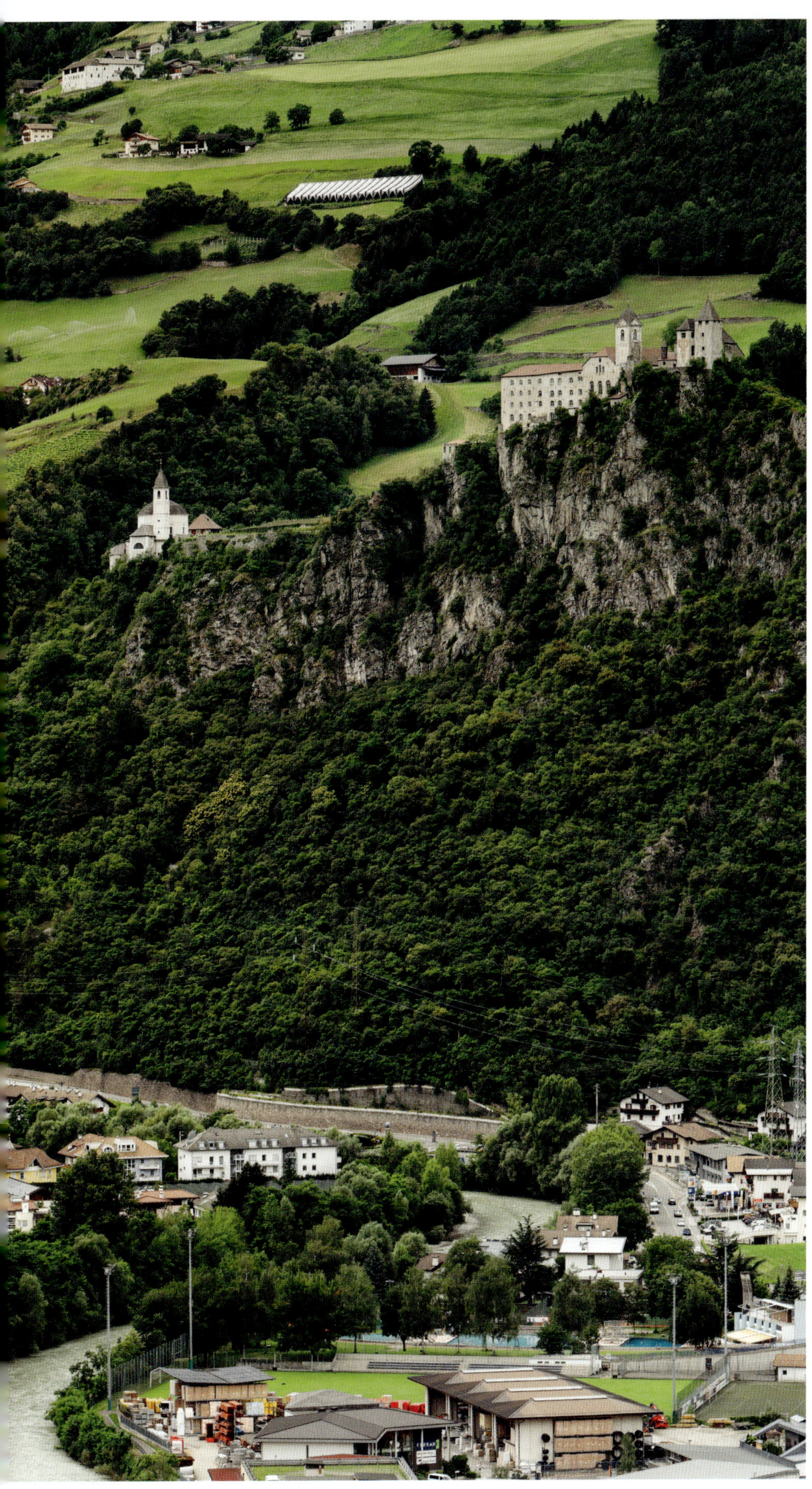

BRENNER RAILWAY

Old walls, new traffic routes: For many centuries, Säben, Tyrol's oldest bishop's seat (until 990), which was later expanded into a fortress, has looked down into the Eisack Valley. The railroad has been running there for 150 years, and the highway A22 has been in operation for half a century.

PUSTER VALLEY RAILWAY

The massive Franzensfeste, consisting of three forts, was built between 1833 and 1838 and is considered the largest historical building in South Tyrol, now being used as a museum. The expensive complex was never involved in military conflicts. The Pustar Valley Railway runs through the middle of the extensive complex, which was opened in 1871. ▽▽

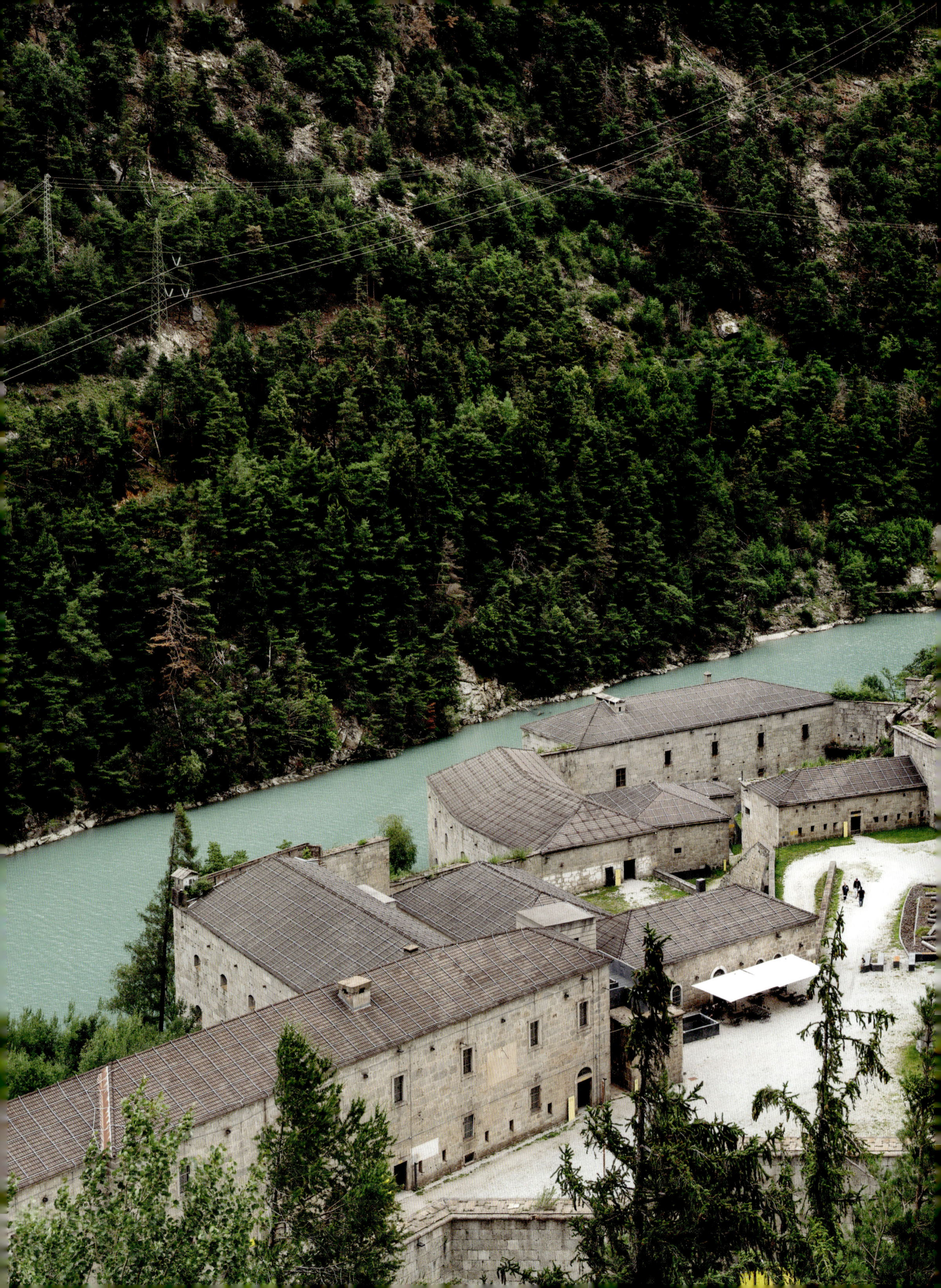

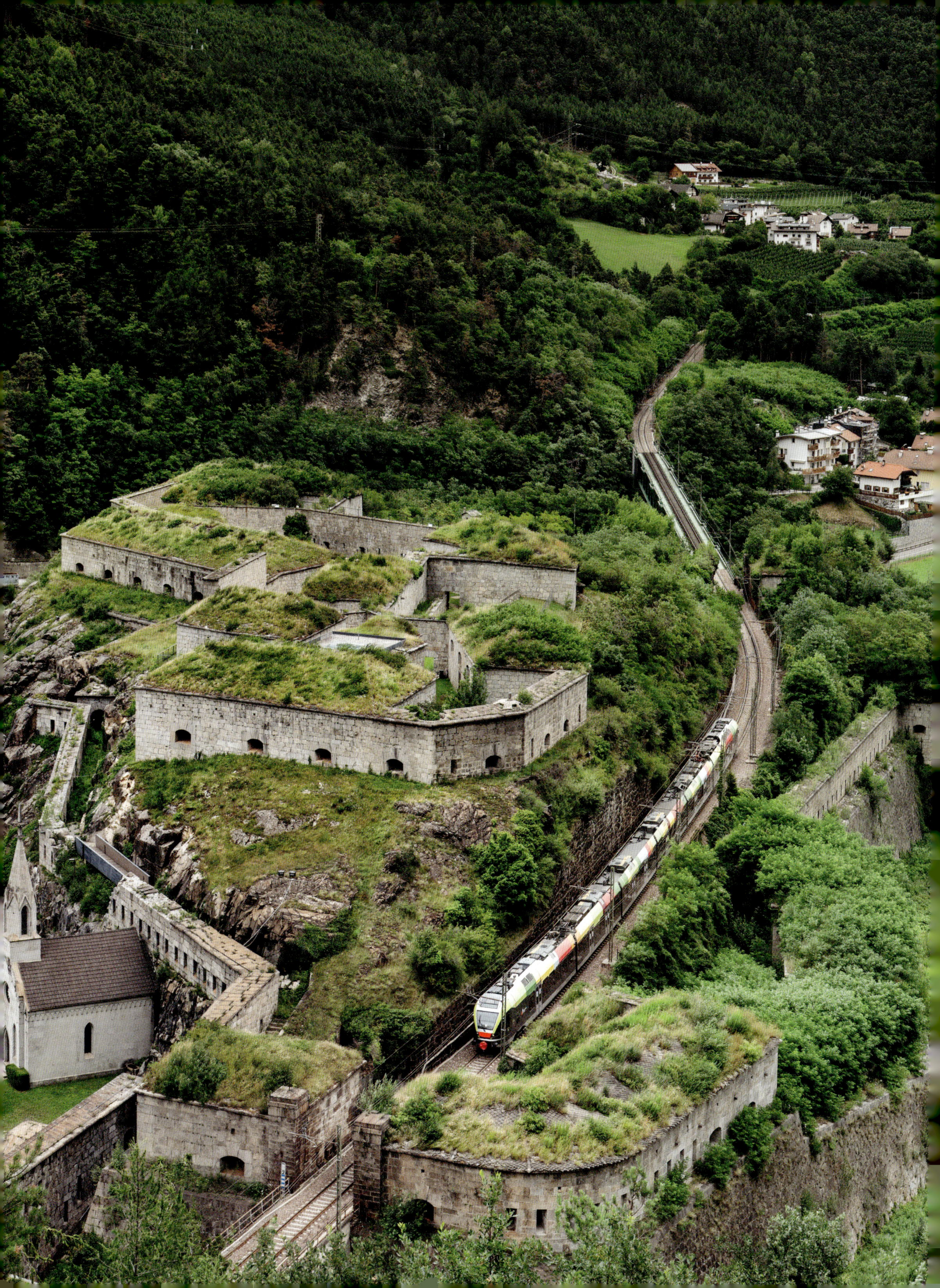

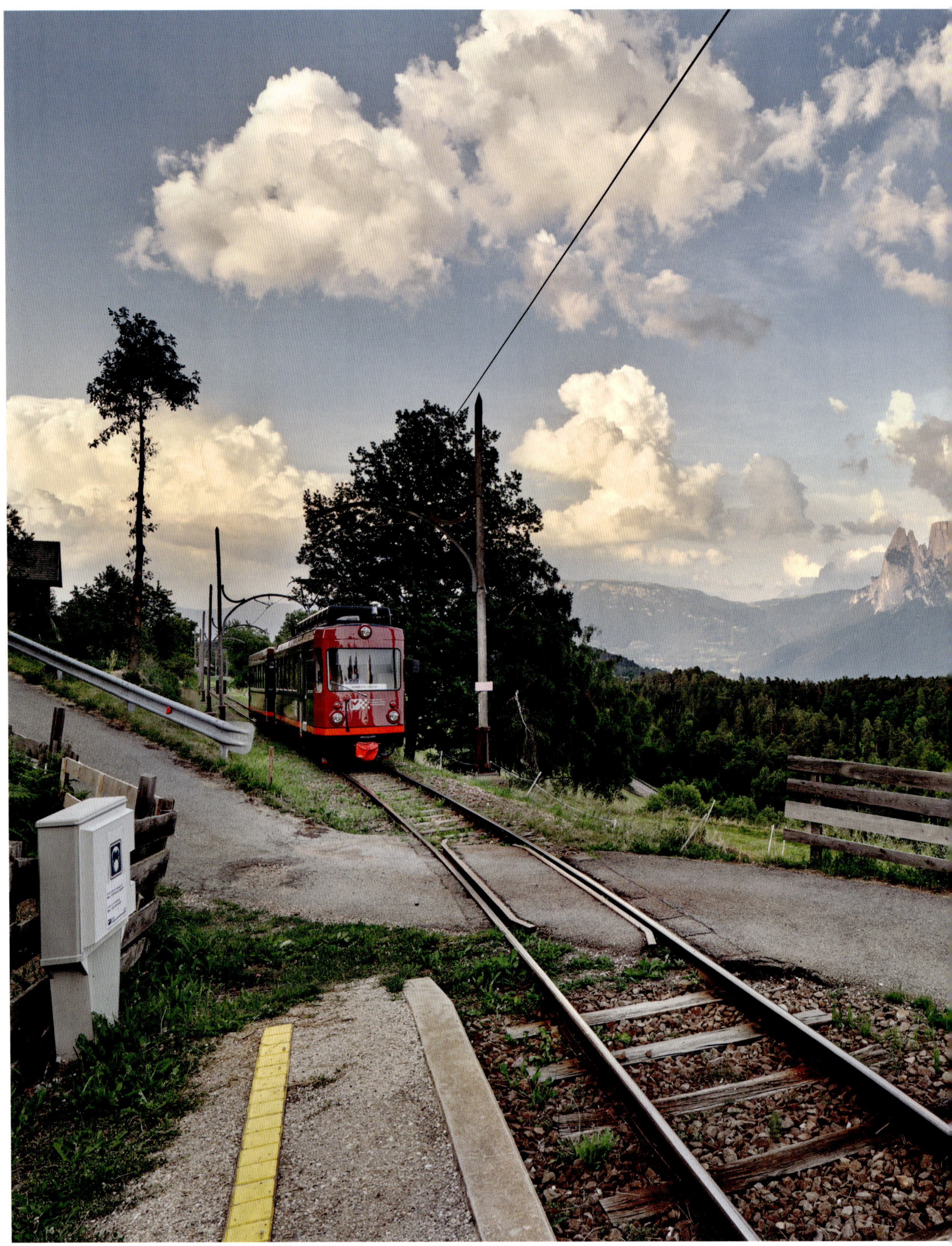

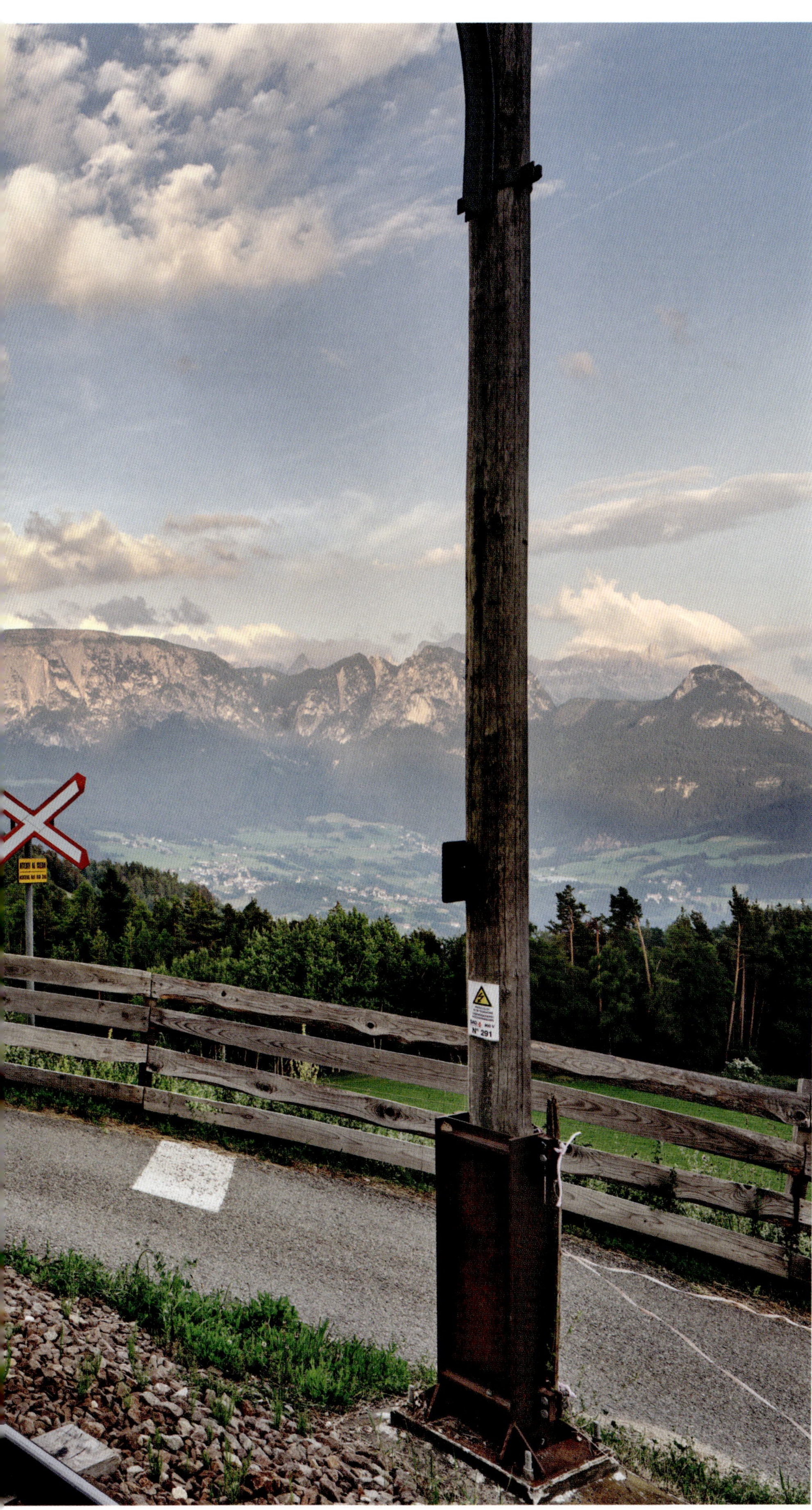

RITTEN RAILWAY

The Ritten Railway connects Maria Himmelfahrt with Kloben- stein over 3.7 miles (6 kilometers). It is a meter-gauge adhesion railroad. Originally, it consisted of three sections: a city railway in Bolzano, a cogwheel railway up to the Ritten plateau, and the section that is still in operation today. The tramway in the city was disman- tled, and the cogwheel railroad was replaced by aerial cable cars. The ride to Klobenstein offers magnificent views of the Schlern Massif beyond the Eisack Valley.

VINSCHGAU RAILWAY

There they all stand: apple orchards near Tschengls in central Vinschgau. ▽ ▽

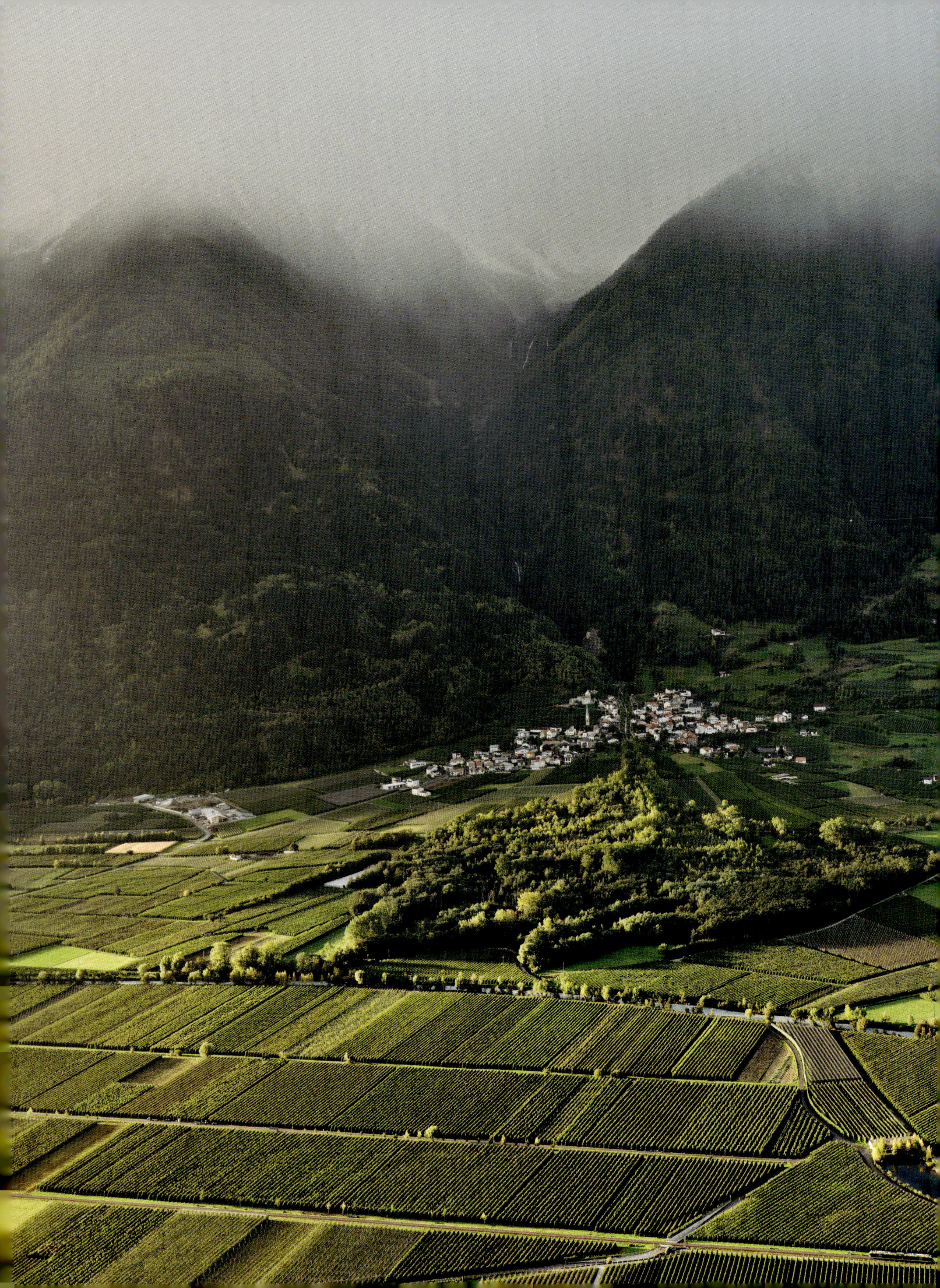

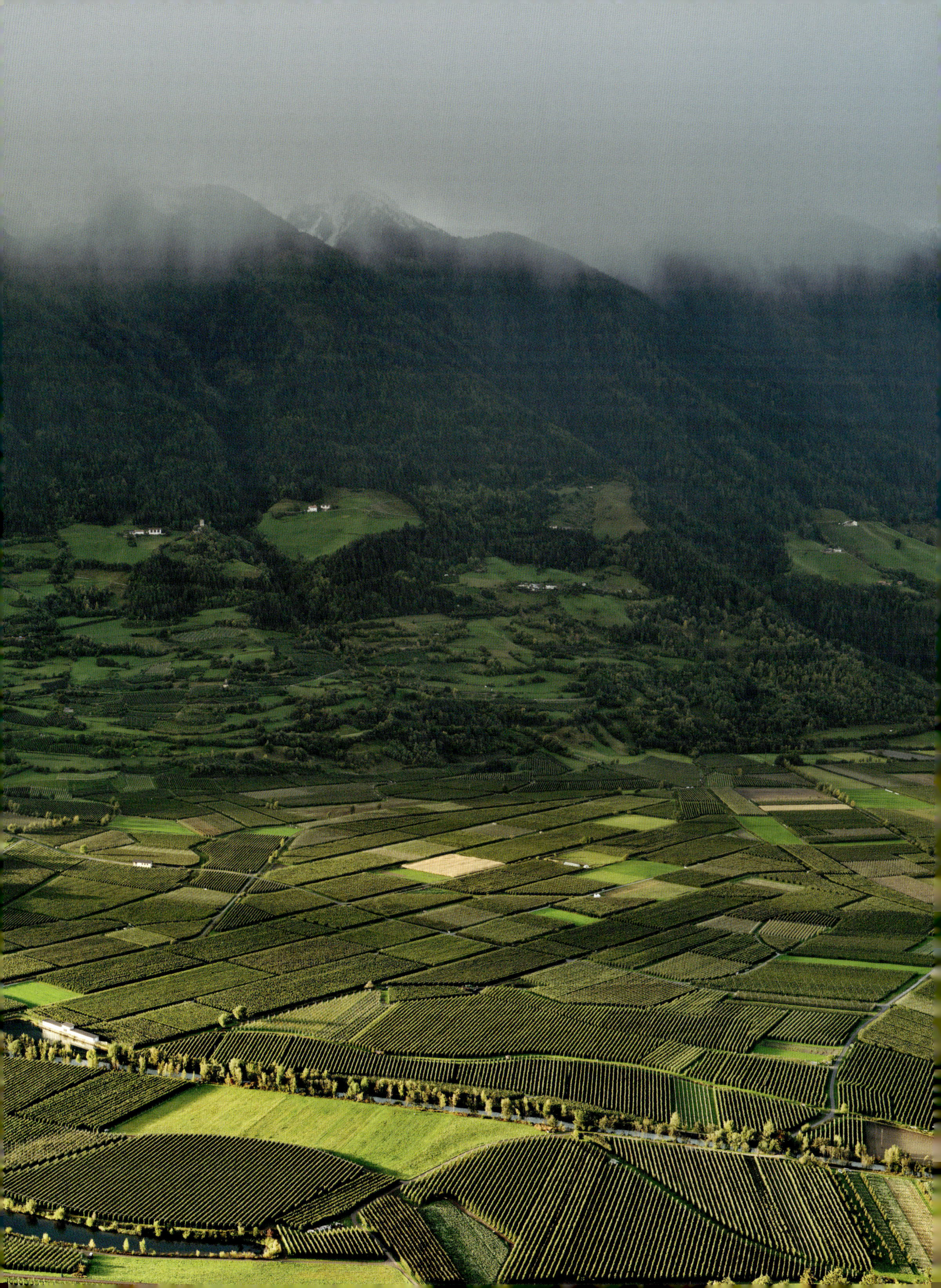

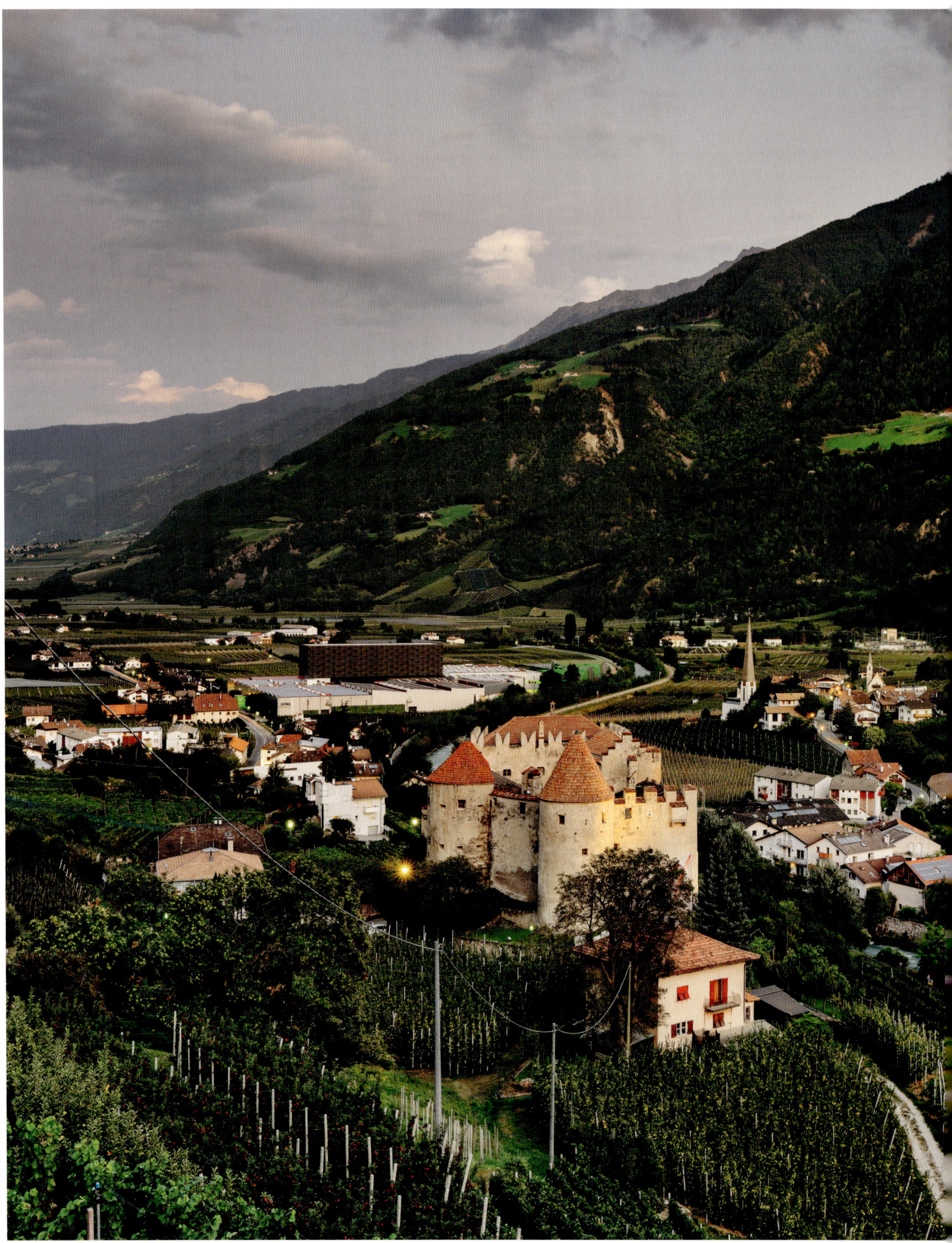

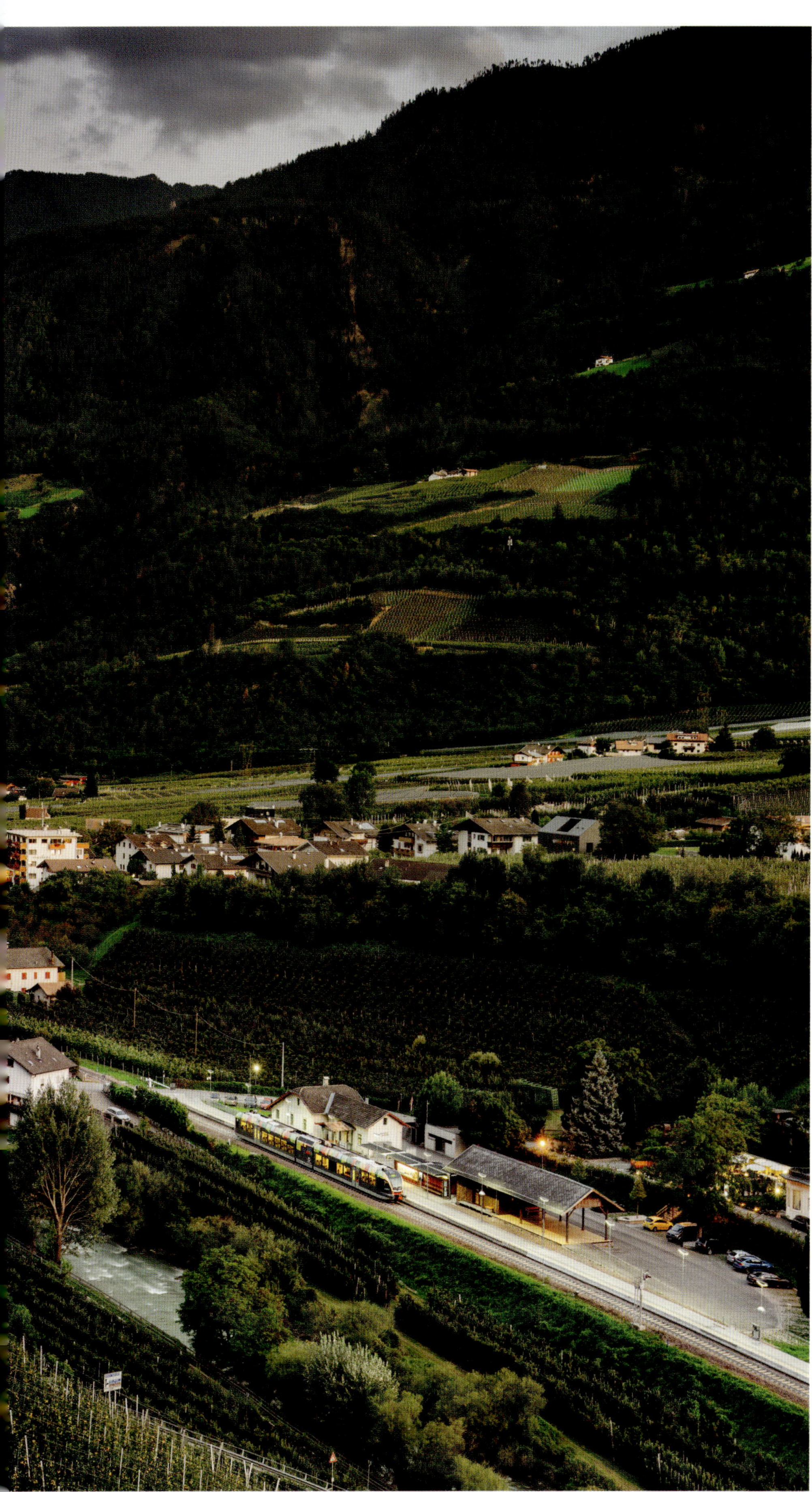

VINSCHGAU RAILWAY

The reactivated Vinschgau
Railway has become a real
success story since it was put
back into service in 2005, to the
appreciation of locals and tourists
alike. Kastelbell, with its landmark
castle, is one stop on the 37-mile
(60-kilometer) route between
Meran and Mals.

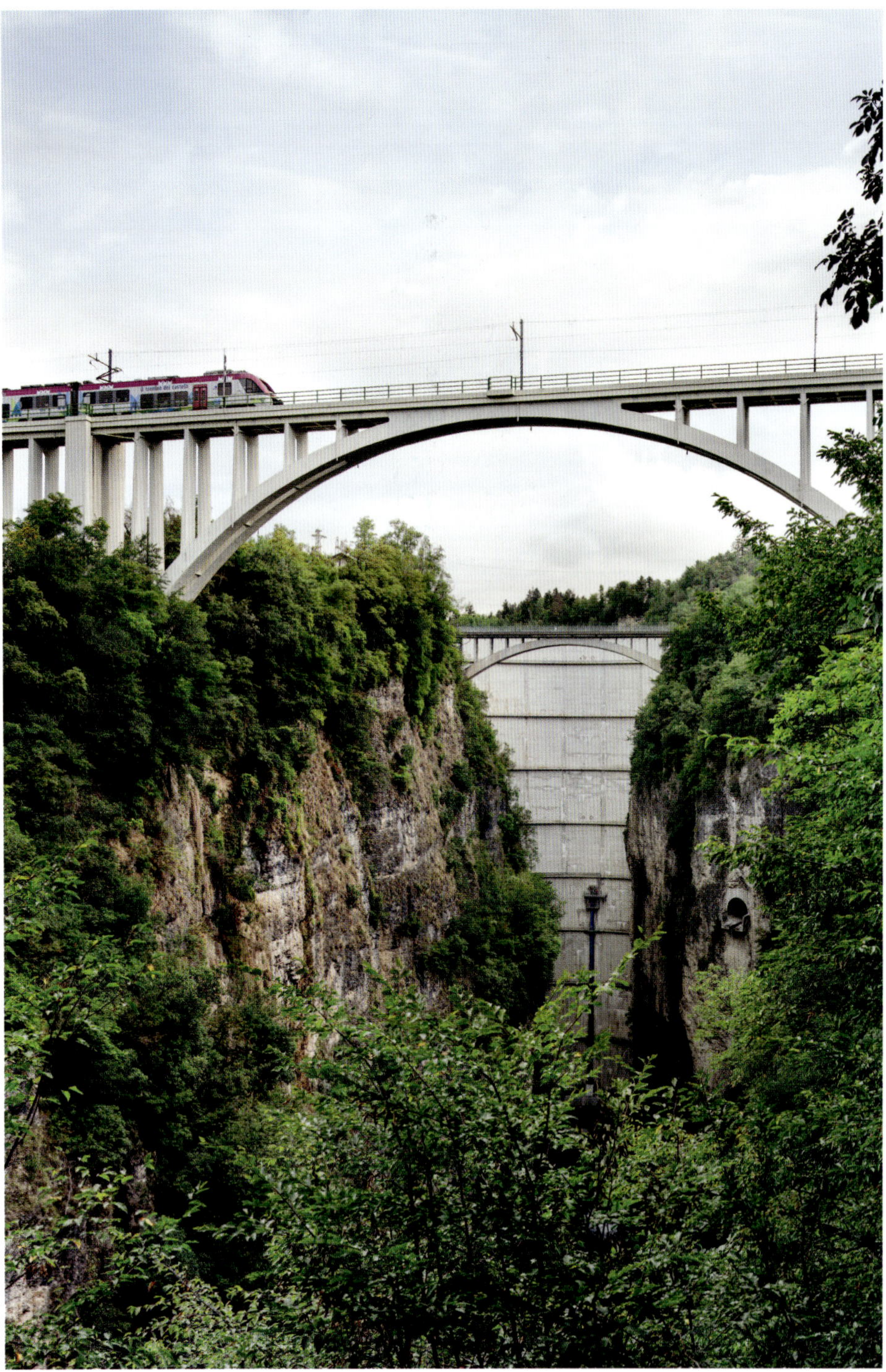

NON VALLEY RAILWAY

The topography of the Non Valley is characterized by many deep gorges. As a result, there are numerous bridges on the railroad line to Val di Sole. Inaugurated in 1959, the Santa Giustina Viaduct, in front of the dam of the lake of the same name, is particularly spectacular. It crosses the Noce at a height of 459 feet (140 meters); when it was built, it was considered the highest railroad bridge in the world.

Just above Lago di Santa Giustina, the Non Valley Railway crosses the Noce a second time at the Ponte Mostizzolo. ▽▽

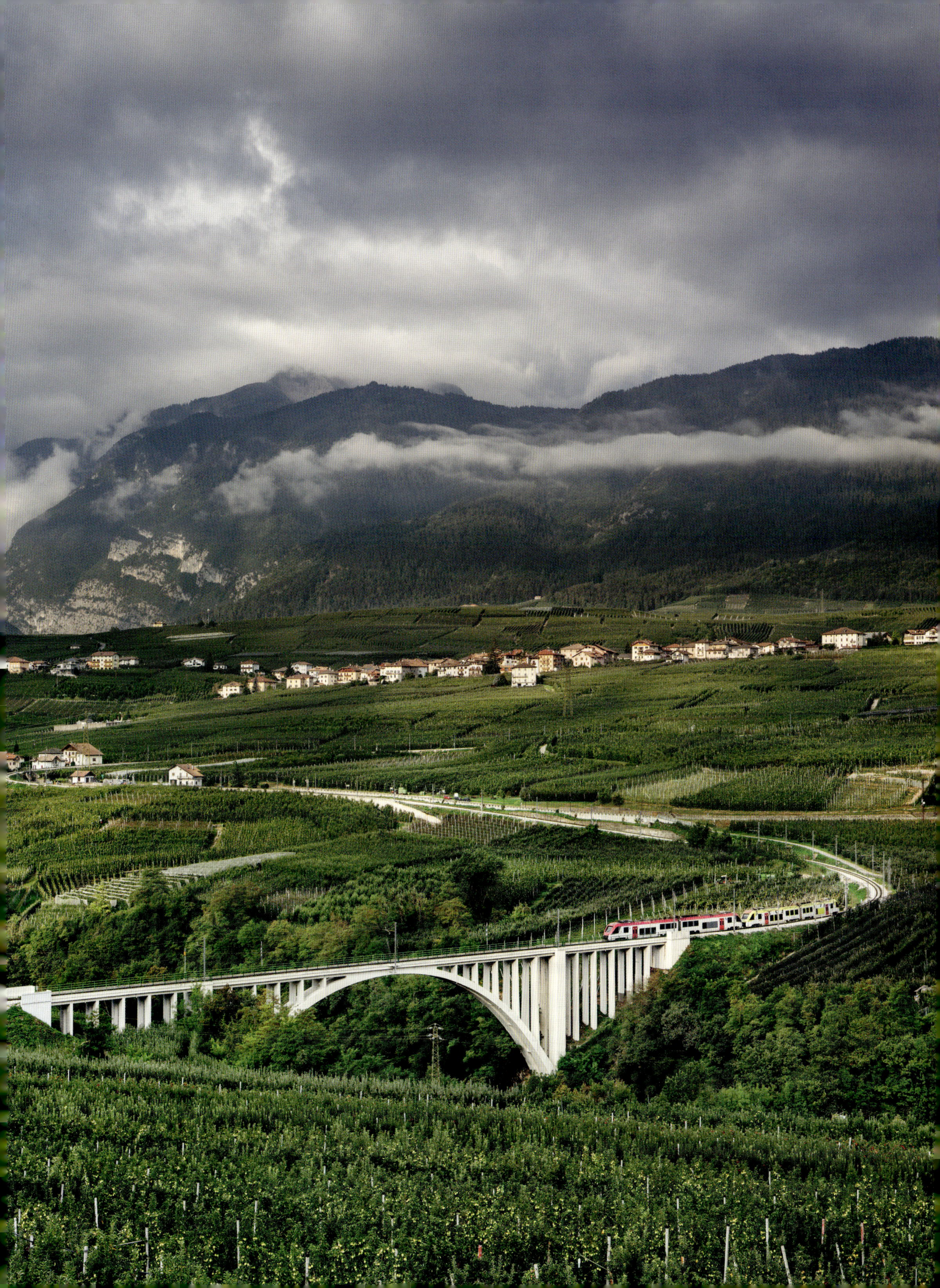

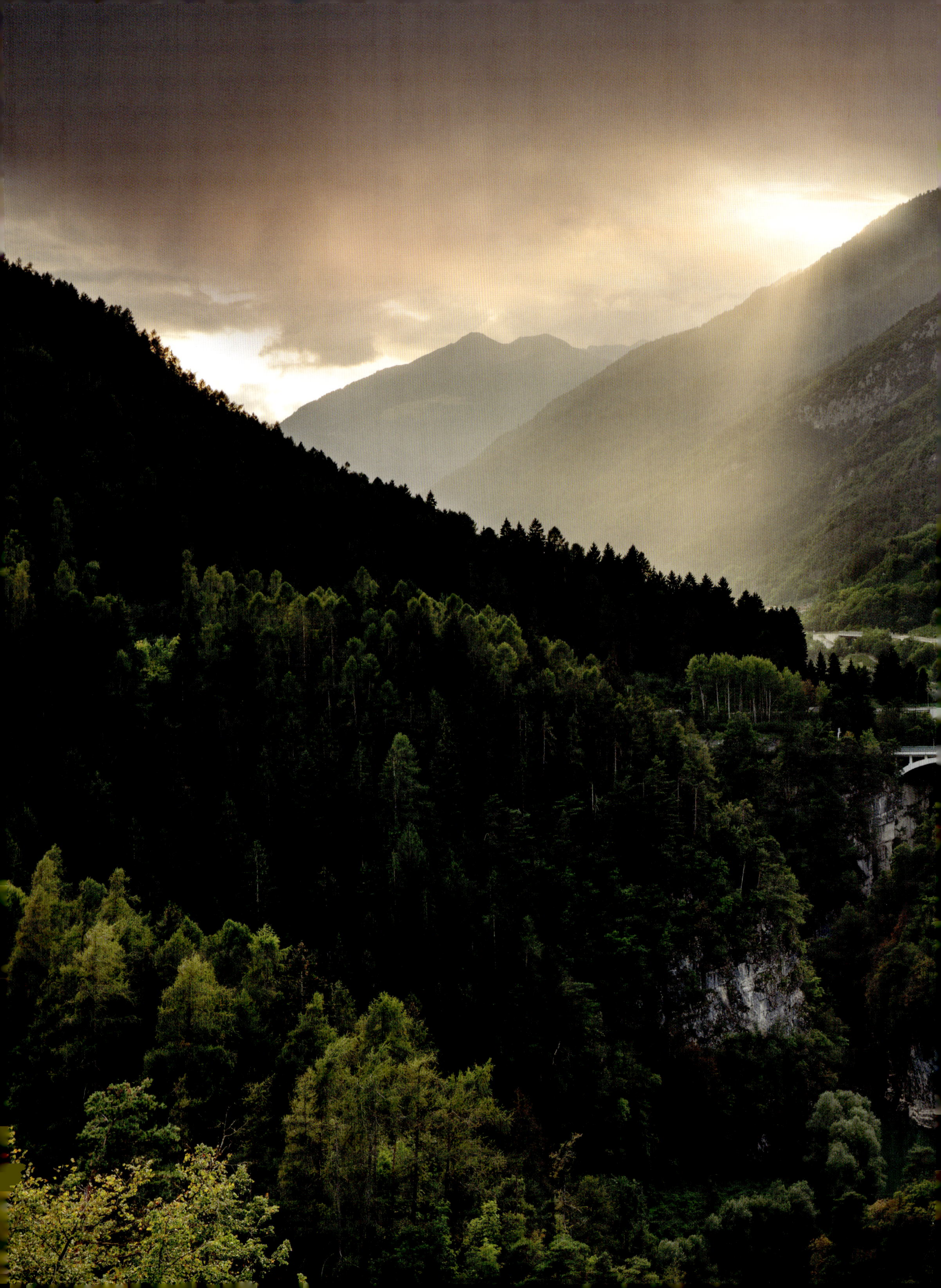

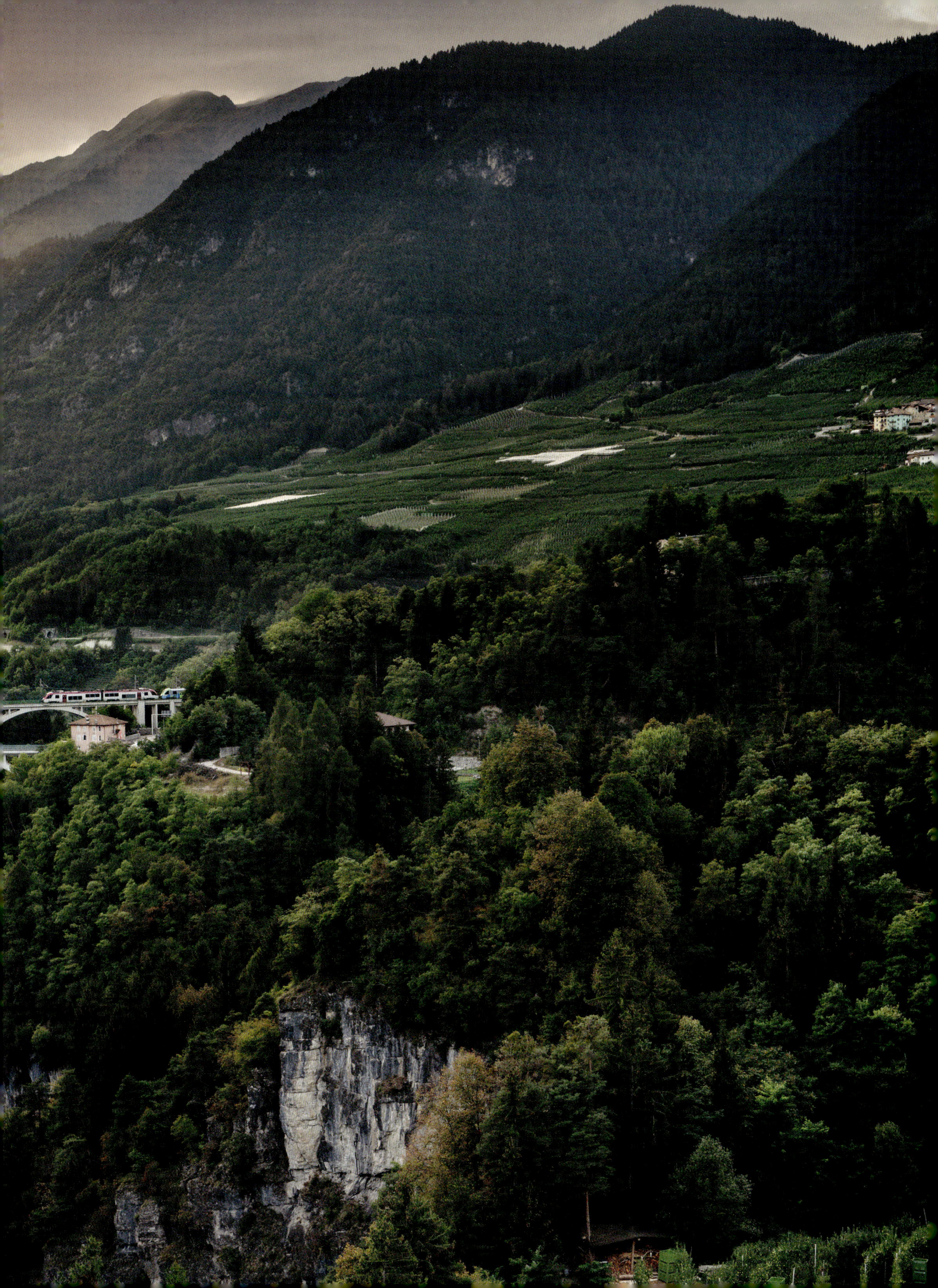

LAKES, MOUNTAINS, AND A TOUCH OF NOSTALGIA

The Salzkammergut Local Railway has long been history; the Salzkammergut Railway of the ÖBB is now only of regional importance. Sankt Wolfgang, the starting point of the Schafberg Railway, has not been reached by train, either from Salzburg or from Bad Ischl, since 1957, when the last local train ran.

"Today I drive for the last time through the beautiful, green valley. My dear mountains and lakes, goodbye."
It was raining. It was nothing unusual for Salzburg, but it was fitting for this September 30 in 1957, because at 7:30 p.m., the passenger train with the number 6527 started on its last trip to Bad Ischl. That was finally the end of the narrow-gauge railroad opened in 1893. Passenger numbers had fallen steadily after a brief postwar peak—the automobile began its triumphant march as a means of transportation suitable for the masses. Since then, a gradual change in thinking has taken place, and the value of a regional railroad is being recognized—not only for commuters but also for tourism, offering travelers the opportunity to enjoy the magnificent lake and mountain scenery on the northern edge of the Alps stress-free, highlighted with a touch of nostalgia. Salzburg, Mondsee, Wolfgang Lake, Bad Ischl—the history of the Imperial and Royal monarchy at its finest. In the second half of the nineteenth century, the Salzkammergut was a favorite of Vienna's high society; Bad Ischl even served as a summer residence for Franz Joseph I, the eternal emperor of this monarchy, until the outbreak of World War I.

THE DAWN OF A NEW ERA

In 1877 the village got its railroad connection, not (yet) from Salzburg, but from the north, from the Hausruckviertel. The

Neue Freie Presse (*New Free Press*) honored the event with a short article: "Today, at 7:15 in the morning—as we are informed by telegraph—the first scheduled passenger train of the Salzkammergut Railway with the locomotive 'Hallstatt' passed the Gmunden train station. From Ischl, we received the following telegram: 'The inaugural train of the Salzkammergut Railway, led by chief inspector Mahr, in connection with the Westbahn, left Attnang this morning. A large crowd of people waited at all stations to greet the train sympathetically. The station in Ebensee was decorated with triumphant banners and flags. The train was greeted with fireworks, as was the case in Traunkirchen, where the municipal representatives and corporations appeared with a musical band."

The future had begun—thanks to salt production, because the construction of the Salzkammergut Railway was primarily about salt, not about special imperial wishes or passenger transport. The salt works in Ebensee, Bad Ischl, and Bad Aussee consumed immense amounts of fuel, and since wood was gradually becoming scarce, substitutes were sought and found in the rich coal deposits of the Hausruckviertel. Thus, the "black gold" traveled south, with the white salt traveling in the opposite direction.

Salzburg was still waiting for a connection to the Salzkammergut region. It was not until 1893 that the time had come: The Salzkammergut Local Railway began scheduled service. It connected Bad Ischl with Salzburg and ran through the Salzkammergut region without major inclines, passing Lake Wolfgang and the Mondsee lake. The "Weisse Rössl" in St. Wolfgang was already a well-known hotel at that time—the emperor paid his respects with his wife, Sisi, and Viennese society of course happily followed. As early as the 1860s, Wolfgang Grömmer, owner of the hotel, built Austria's first mountain inn on the summit of the Schafberg (5,846 feet / 1,782 meters) and later also a horseback trail—to make the ascent easier for visitors.

RECORD-BREAKING: THE SCHAFBERG RACK RAILWAY

Starting in 1983, the Schafberg cogwheel railway made the journey even more comfortable. It took just under an hour to cover the approximately 3.7-mile (6-kilometer) route, with a maximum gradient of 25.5 percent. That is still a record in Austria today. An interesting fact: Anyone arriving on the Salzkammergut Local Train first needed to cross the water before he could start the ascent. St. Wolfgang lies on the northern shore of its lake, while the train runs along the southern shore. Thanks to the masses of rock that the Zinkenbach carries into its considerable delta, the 5-square-mile (13-square-kilometer) body of water is only about 656 feet (200 meters) wide at this point. In 1930 the operetta by Ralph Benatzky, which was later filmed several times with a well-known cast, gave the "Weissen Rössl" an additional boost in popularity. Yes, yes, "in the Salzkammergut, you can be funny there!"

This "funny" corner of Austria also includes the area around Bad Aussee, although it is located on land in the state of Styria. The high society of Vienna, however, made no distinction; lakes and mountains were the same here as there. And the high nobility provided diligent support. In Bad Aussee, Archduke Johann, half brother of the emperor, met the postmaster's fifteen-year-old daughter, Anna Plochl, who later became his wife. The monarchy has long been history; the hereditary and moneyed nobility have disappeared. Instead, other new "gentlemen" appeared who are not so fondly remembered today: Nazis from Germany. They disappeared again but left a rumor behind that did not, about a legendary gold treasure, which is said to have been sunk in Lake Toplitz at the end of the war.

The last section of the Salzkammergut Railway leads over two gentle, barely noticeable watersheds down into the Enns Valley, where it ends not far from Liezen after almost 62 miles (100 kilometers). It's a rail journey full of impressionable moments, characterized by lakes and mountains. At the top of the list is the Hohe Dachstein, where—upon its summit—the borders of Salzburg, Upper Austria, and Styria converge. What a magnificent stretch of land! It's a pity that you can no longer experience the journey from Salzburg to Bad Ischl by train. The S 12 locomotive, which took its last trip in September 1957, is now in service with the Lungau Taurach Railway—on a nostalgic ride (Tamsweg–Mauterndorf). But maybe one day it will return to the beautiful Salzkammergut, maybe on a restored route?

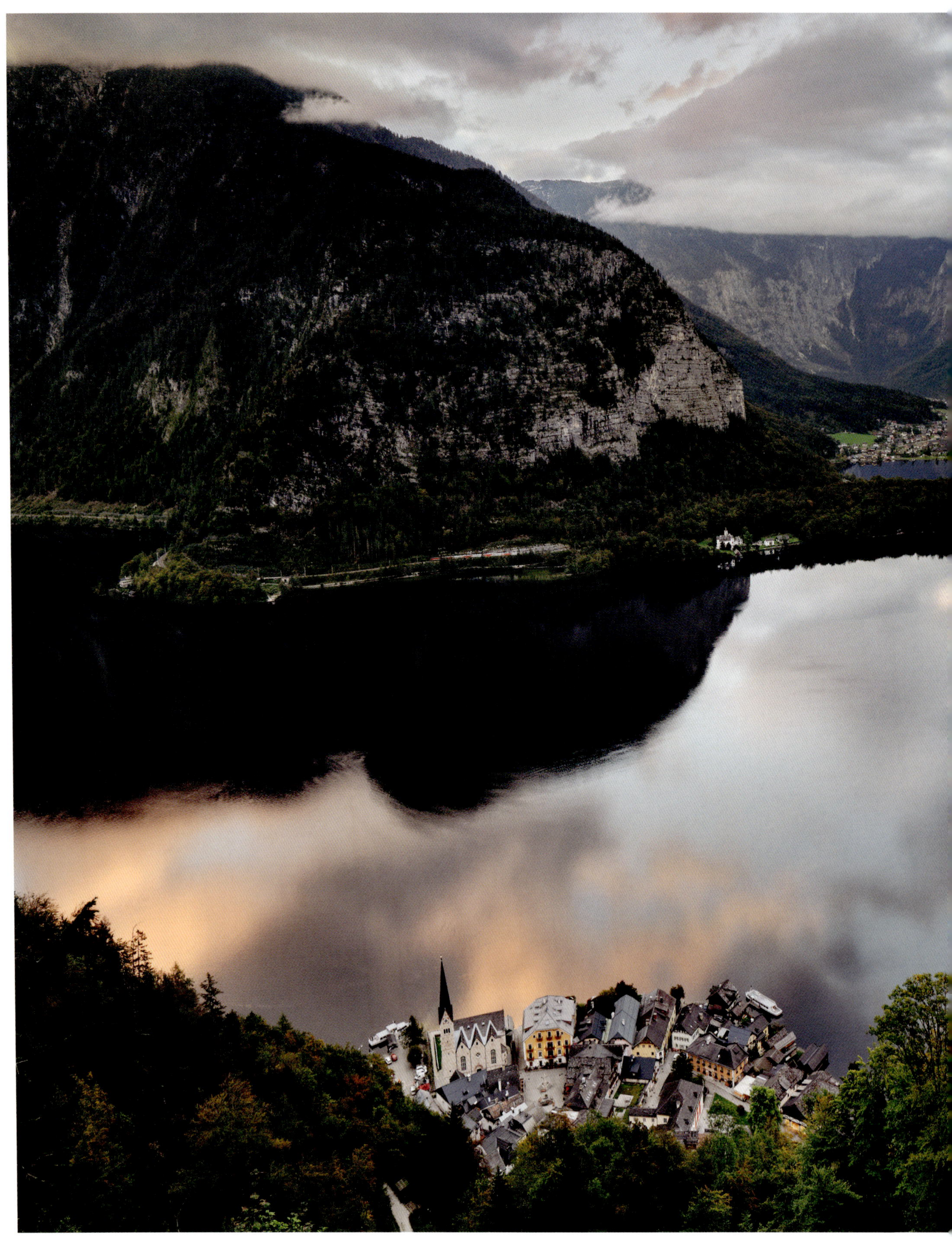

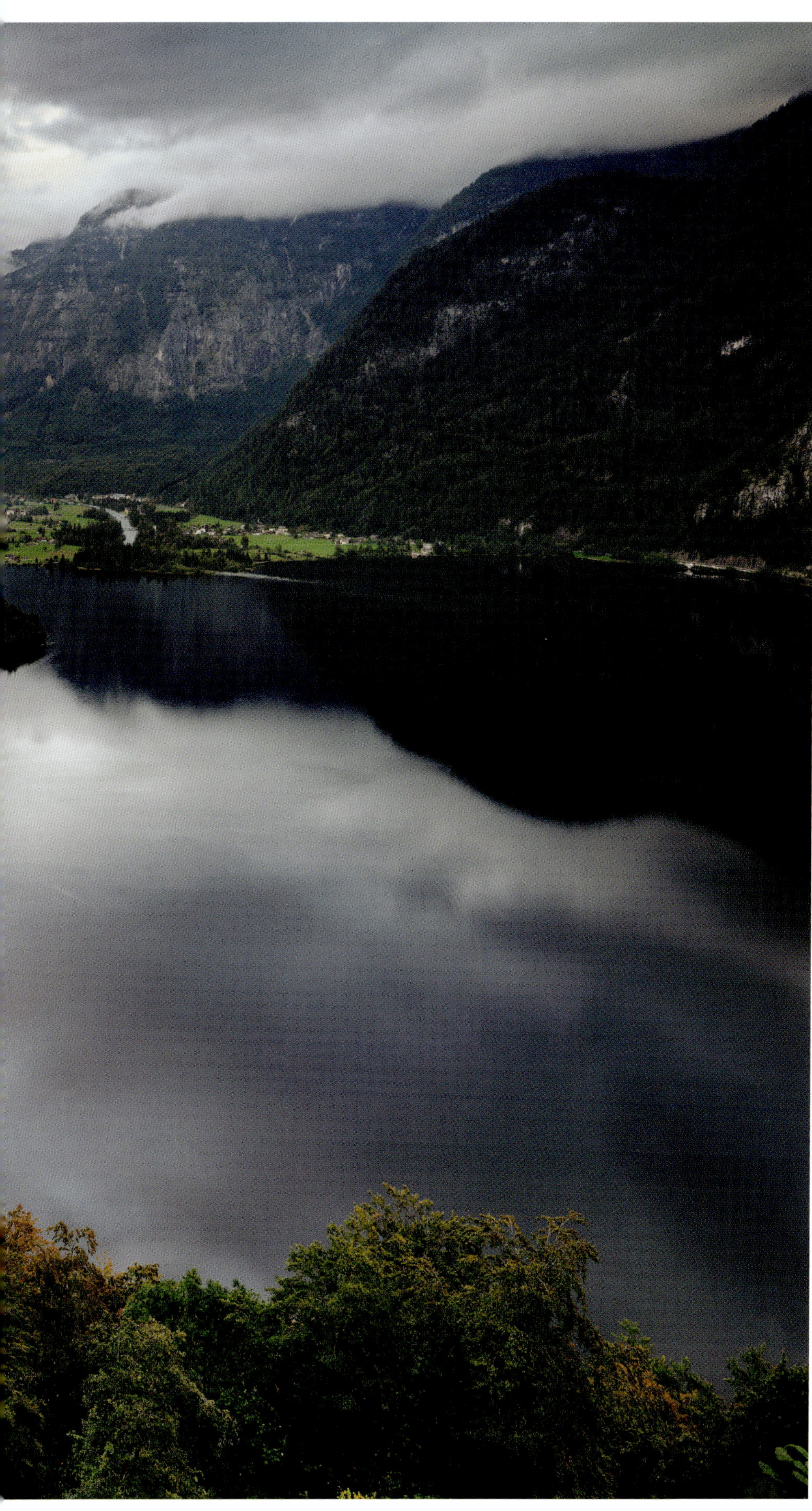

SALZKAMMERGUT RAILWAY

Small town, big purpose: Hallstatt, the overrun gem on its lake. On the opposite shore, the Salzkammergut line leads to Obertraun. The tops of the Dachstein Massif are hidden in the clouds.

SCHAFBERG RAILWAY

Will we get the big panorama? Fog billows around the summit of the Schafberg in the Salzkammergut. ▽ ▽

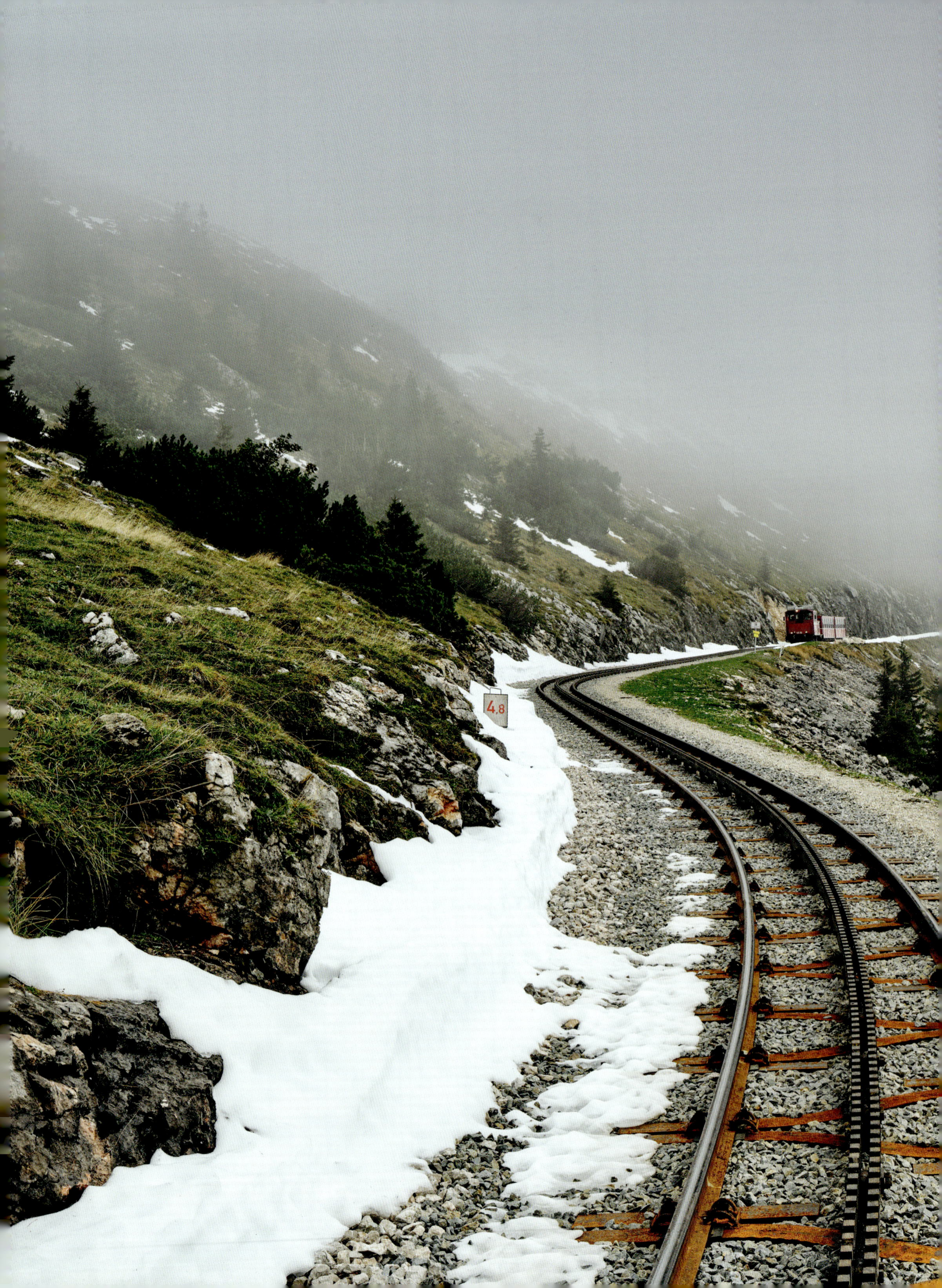

4,8

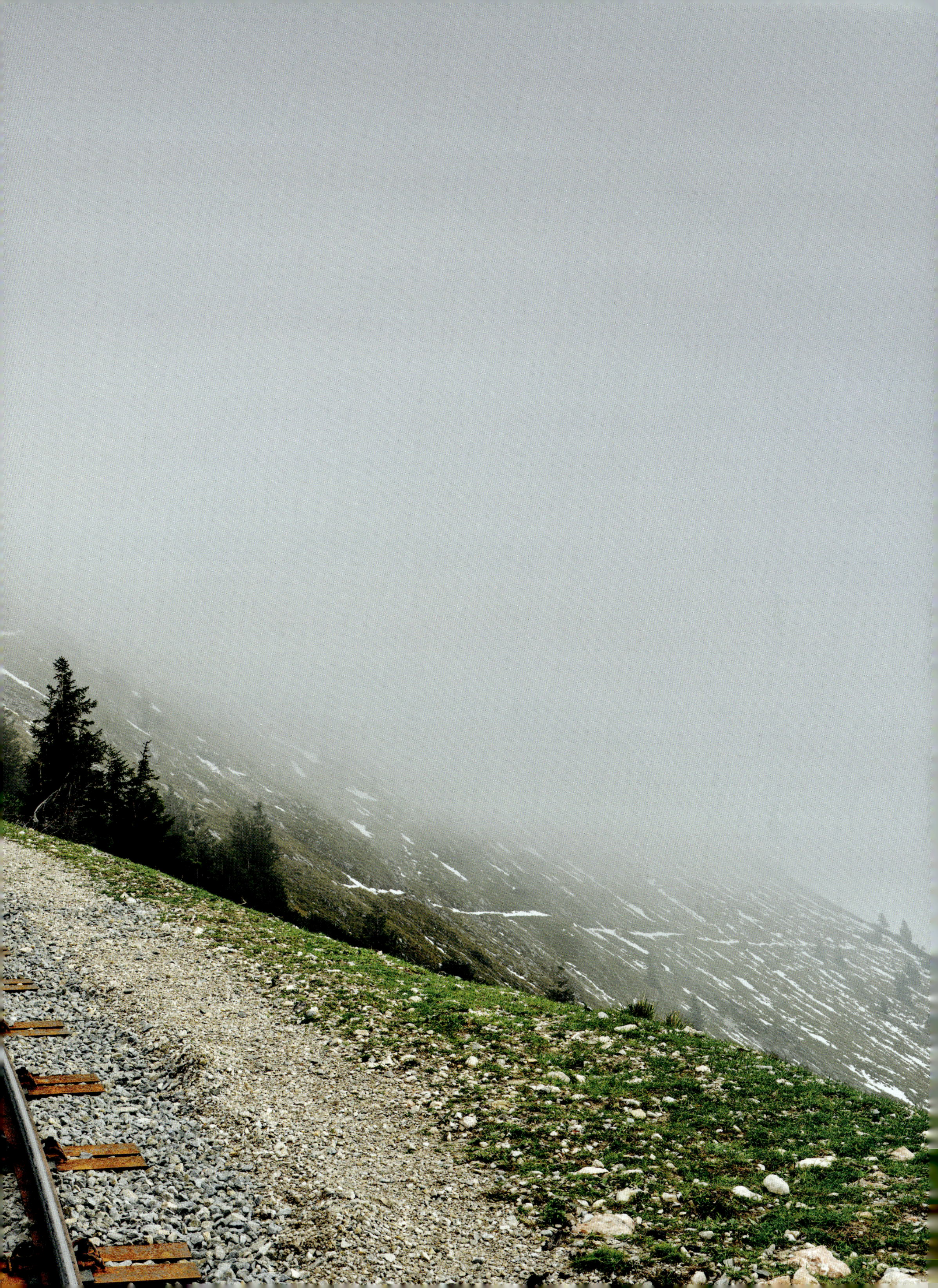

THE IMPERIAL AND ROYAL ALPINE RAILWAYS

THE VIENNESE DREAM OF THE MEDITERRANEAN SEA

The largest railway project in the eastern part of the Alpine range stretched from Vienna to the Adriatic port of Trieste. The project at the beginning of the twentieth century resulted in the *Tauern, Pyhrn, Karawanks,* and *Bohinj Railways,* all with longer tunnel sections.

"At 12:25 p.m., roaring cheers announced the approach of the royal train. After the announcement was made, the archduke left the carriage, whereupon the governor of Carniola and the railroad minister addressed the archduke, who replied. Thereupon the introductions took place. The archduke then went to the court tent. The archbishop handed him the aspergill and then consecrated the railroad tracks and the garlanded locomotives according to the Roman Ritual. During this rite, the archduke knelt on the prayer stool.

After this, he walked along the fronts of the associations that had been set up, distinguished several personalities by means of speeches, and boarded the court salon carriage. The schoolchildren sang the national anthem, the sound of which the train steamed off to at 1:25 p.m. to Trieste." —*Freie Presse Wien* (*Free Press Vienna*), July 19, 1906

What was celebrated in Assling (today Jesenice) in July 1906, in the presence of the heir to the Austrian throne, was the opening of a section of the new Alpine railroads. They were intended to better connect Trieste, the Adriatic port of the monarchy, to Vienna. It was an unprecedented financial feat. Large tunnels were planned at the Pyhrn Pass, in the Hohe Tauern, the Karawanks, and in the Bohinj, including their feeder lines. In 1906, most of the new lines were opened for operation, including the Karawanks Tunnel in the fall.

BOHINJ RAILWAY AND TAUERN TUNNEL

One of the guests of honor at its opening in October 1906 was Karn Wurmb, who had rendered outstanding services to the Imperial and Royal Alpine Railways but had resigned after quarrels with parliament. He oversaw the Bohinj Railway until 1905. The most striking structure of this mountain line with its thirty-five tunnels is, along with the 3.9-mile-long (6.3-kilometer-long) Bohinj Tunnel, the Solkan Bridge (Slovenian: Solkanski most), which is considered the largest masonry arch bridge in the world. The span of the main arch is an incredible 279 feet (85 meters)!

The central structure of the new railroad lines was the 5.3-mile-long (8.5-kilometer-long) Tauern Tunnel, the completion of which, however, was delayed by about three years due to geological and construction problems (opening in 1909). Workers and engineers also had to contend with massive geological problems at the Bosruck Tunnel.

BIG PROJECTS—SMALL EFFECTS?

With the completion of the Alpine railroads, the expansion of the Austrian railroad network came to an end. There were and still are very different opinions about the military and economic value of the new connection to Trieste, because, after all, there was already a line between the capital and the Adriatic port; however, it was not operated by the state railroads, but by the private Südbahn. Undisputed is the importance of the Bohinj Railroad in World War I in supplying the troops on the Isonzo front.

Many interests were taken into account in the planning of the new Alpine railways. Triest lobbied after its importance greatly increased after the opening of the Suez Canal in 1869. Giacomo Ceconi, a native of the Carnic Alps, showed special interest in the mammoth project. He was a gifted self-made man who had also been involved in the construction of the Arlberg Tunnel and wanted to profitably use the resources he had freed up after the completion of the project. As a result, he had the project for the Tauern Railroad, including a summit tunnel already drawn up as early as 1884.

After the end of the war, the Dual Monarchy lost its most important access to the Mediterranean. The great power became a small state, its area shrinking to one-eighth of what it had been in Imperial and Royal times. Shattered dreams.

The entire railway network of the Austro-Hungarian Dual Monarchy had a total length of around 28,583 miles (46,000 kilometers) before the outbreak of World War I. At that time, around fifty-six million people lived under Imperial and Royal rule.

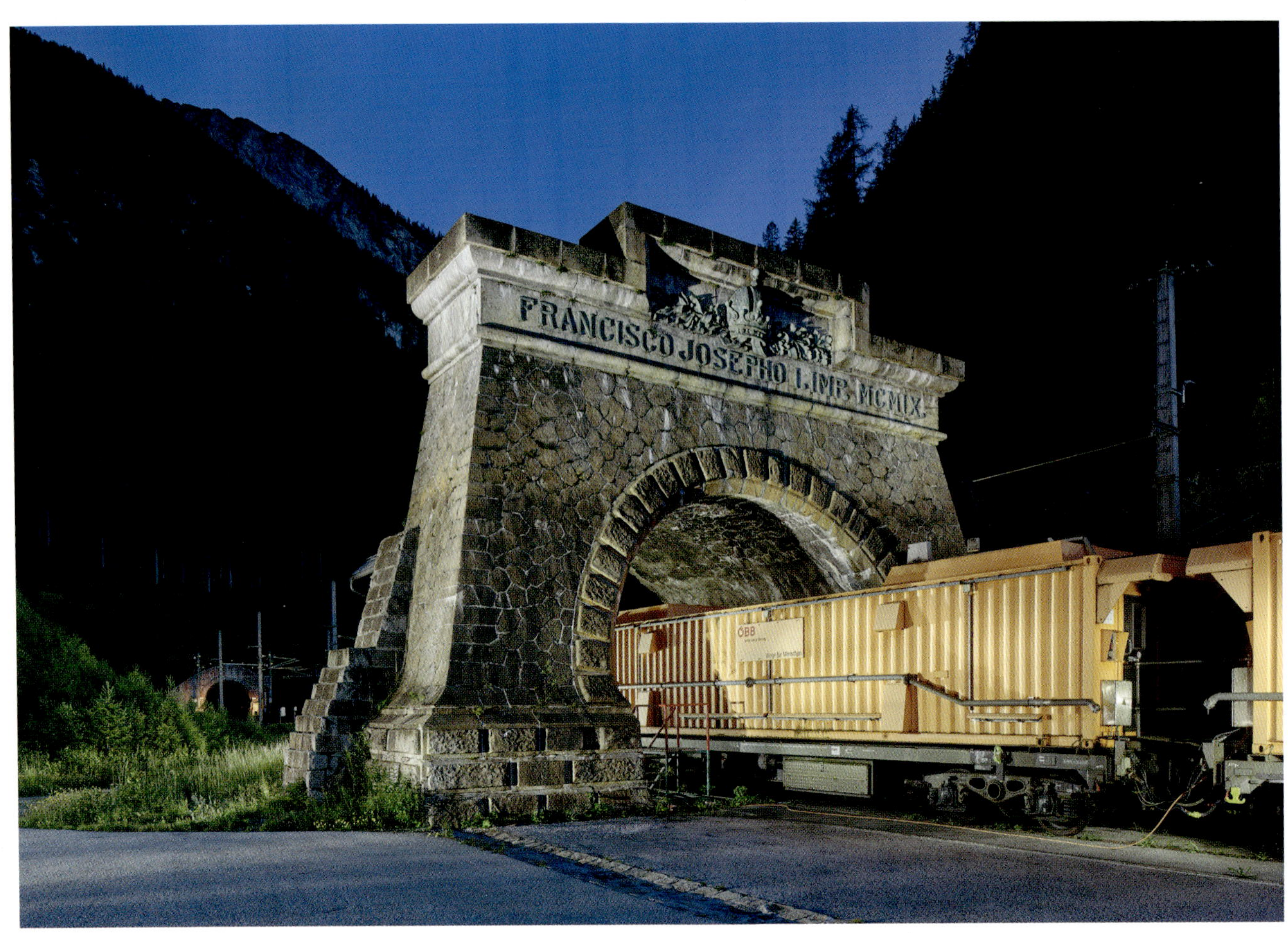

TAUERN RAILWAY

Imperial posturing carved in stone: the old north
portal of the Tauern Tunnel. It was built during the
reign of Franz Joseph I.

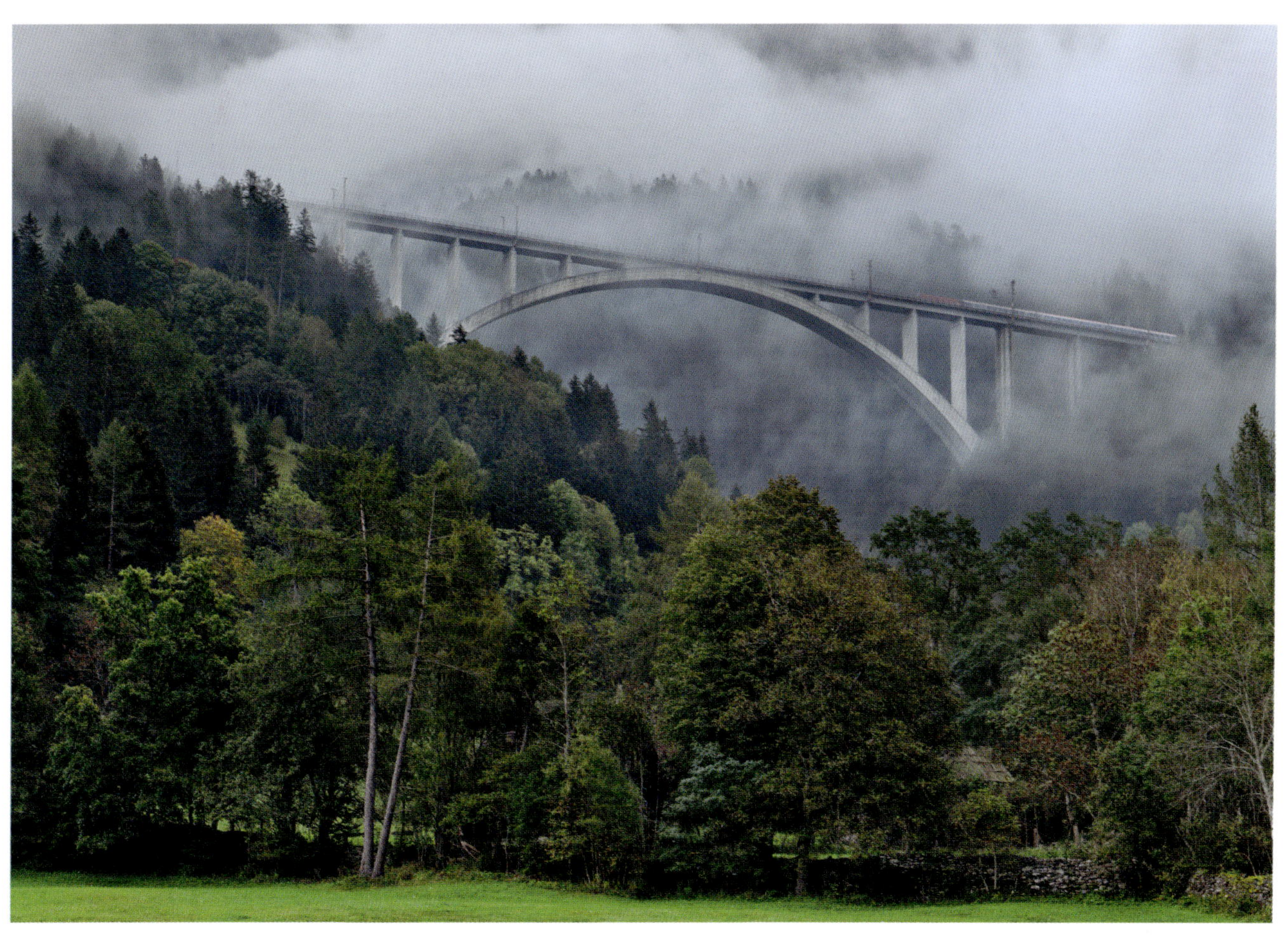

With the double-track expansion of the southern ramp of the Tauern Railway, several new bridges were built in the early 1970s, including the 1,237-foot-long (377-meter-long) Pfaffenberg Viaduct. At the time of its inauguration, it was the longest reinforced concrete arch bridge for rail traffic in Europe.

TAUERN RAILWAY

The Falkenstein Bridge is even longer, at 1,299 feet (396 meters). It takes its name from the castle complex, which consists of two buildings. Niederfalkenstein, originally just an outbuilding, was rebuilt and extended in its historical style at the beginning of the twentieth century.

KARAWANKS RAILWAY

The train passes the Feistritz Reservoir in the Rosental on a long bridge along the stretch from Klagenfurt to the Karawanks Tunnel. ▽ ▽

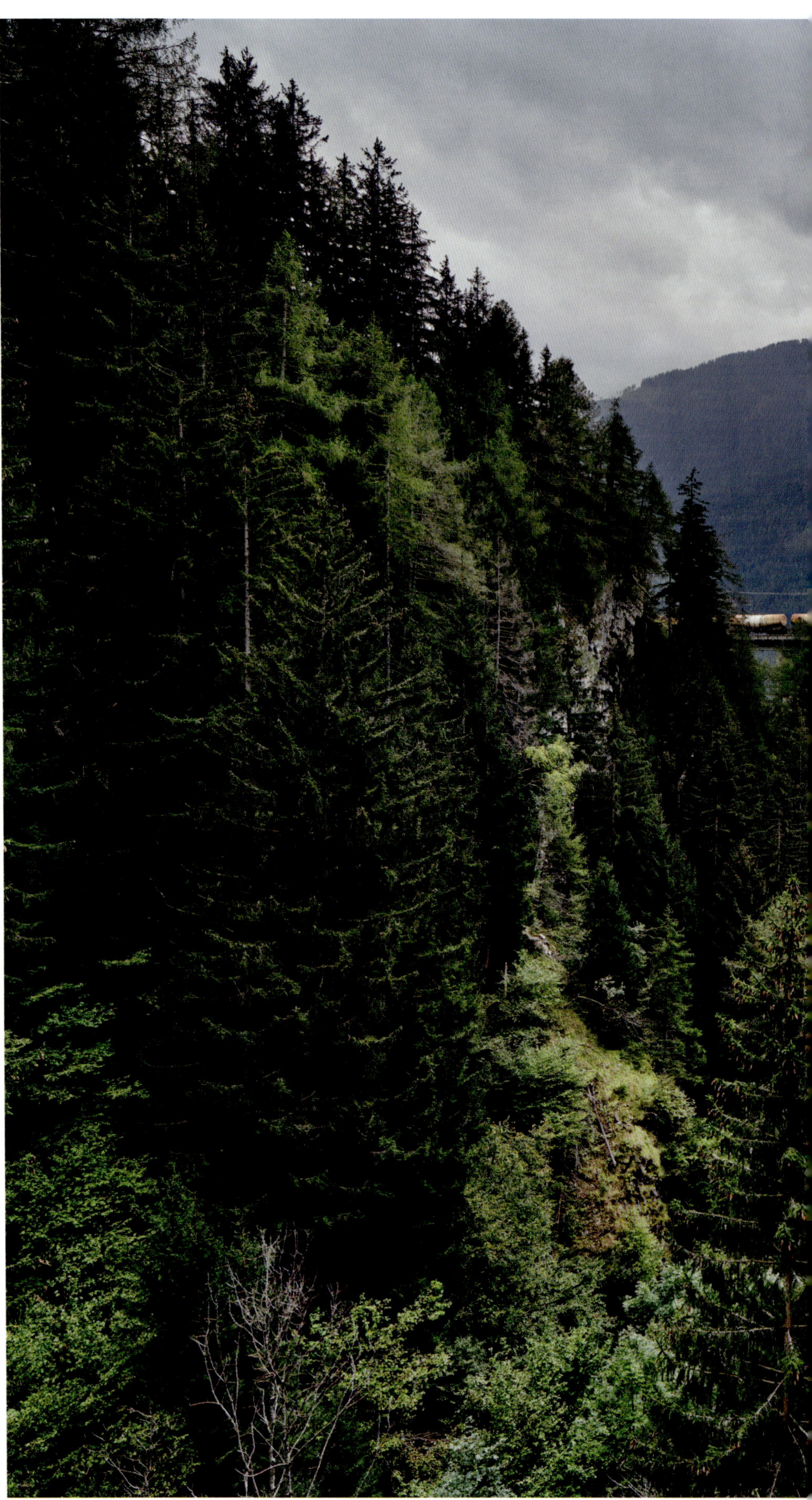

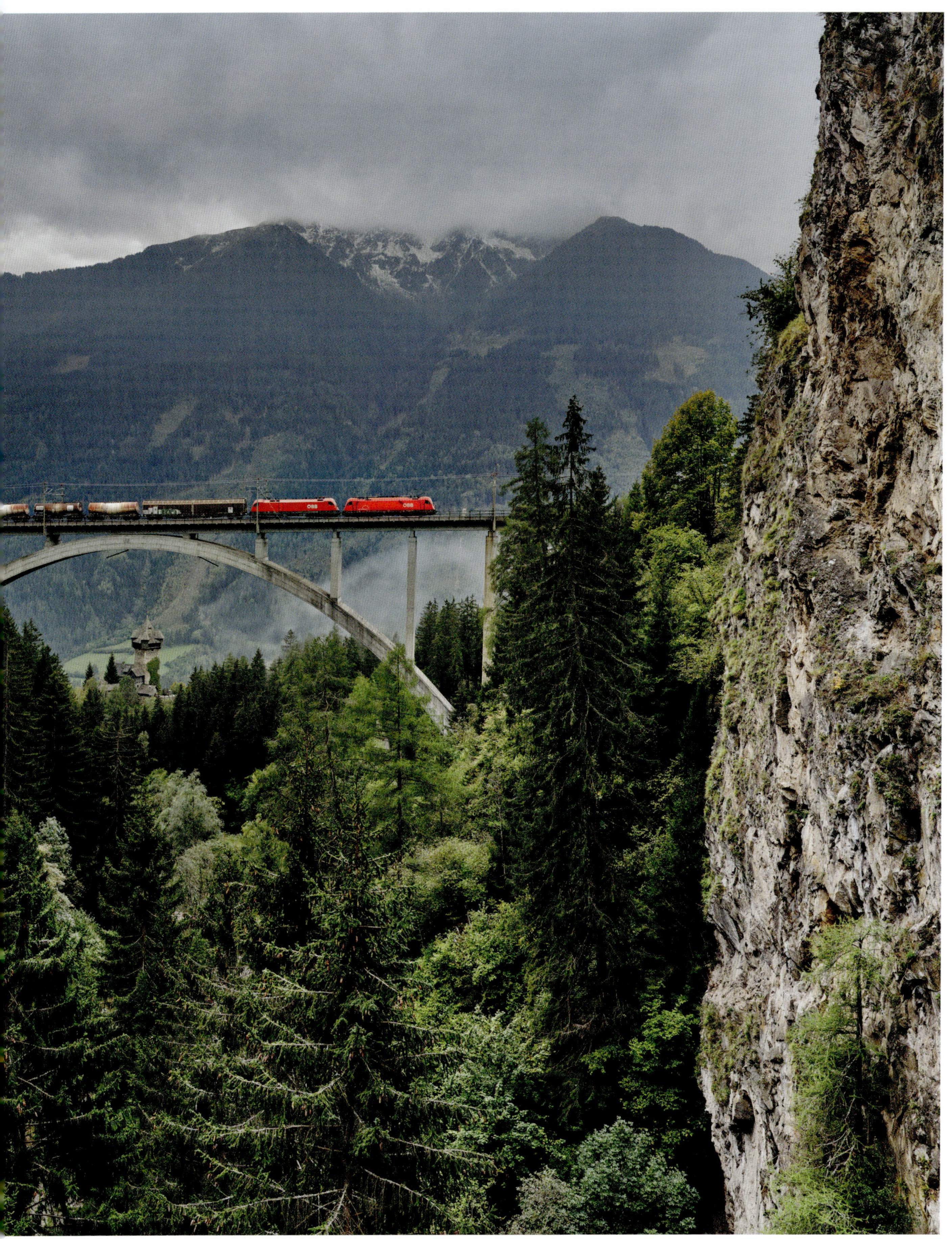

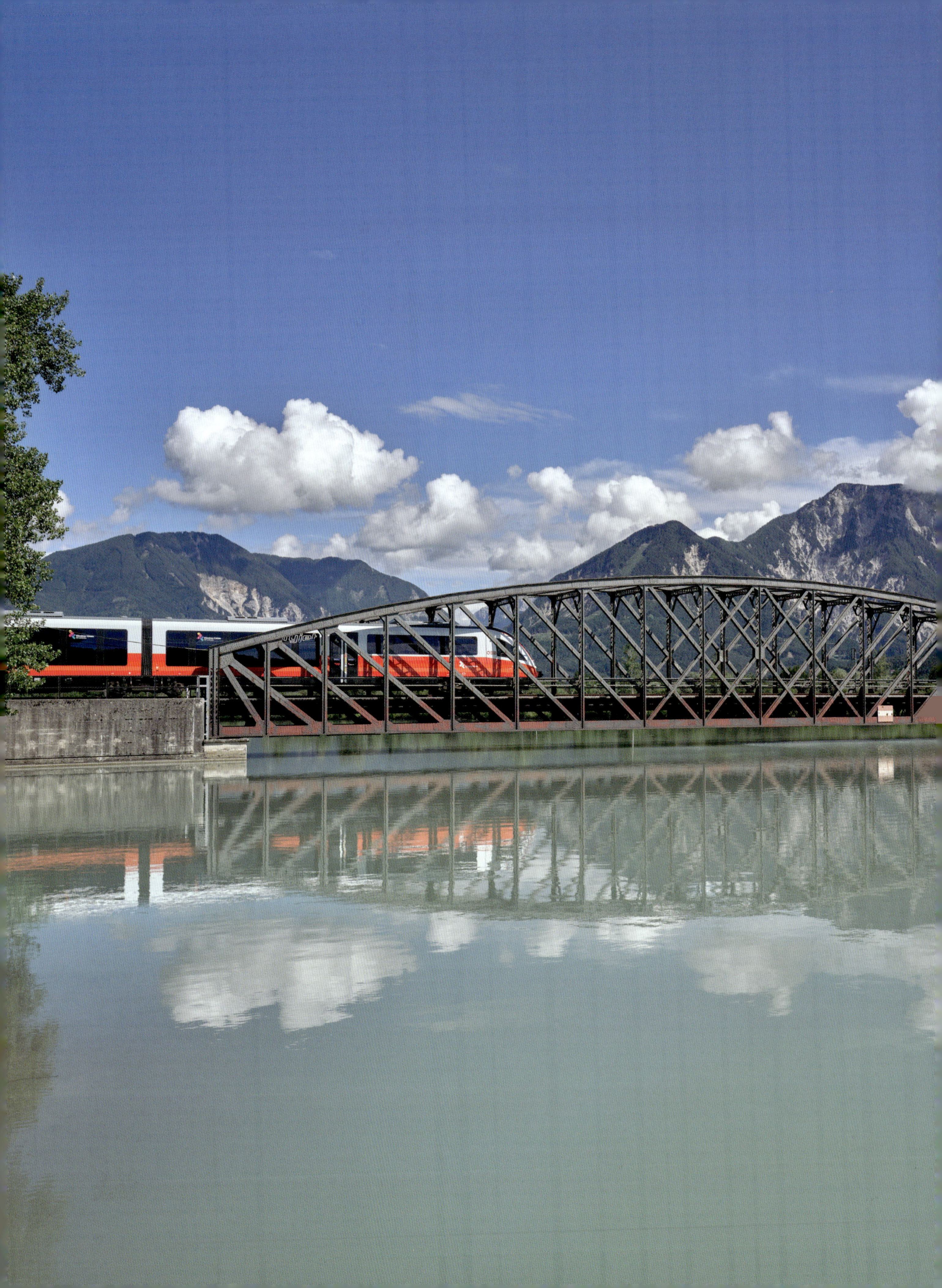

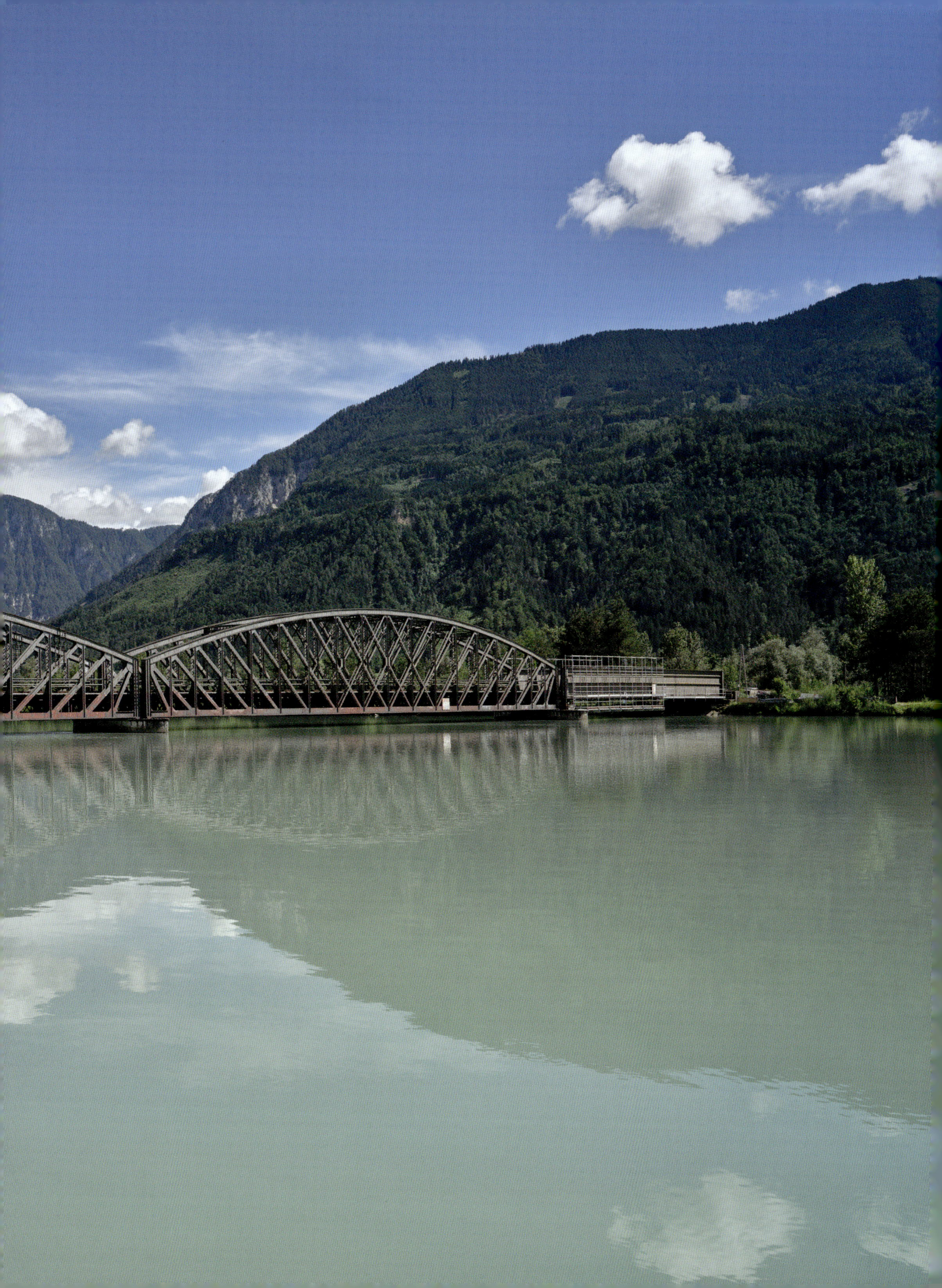

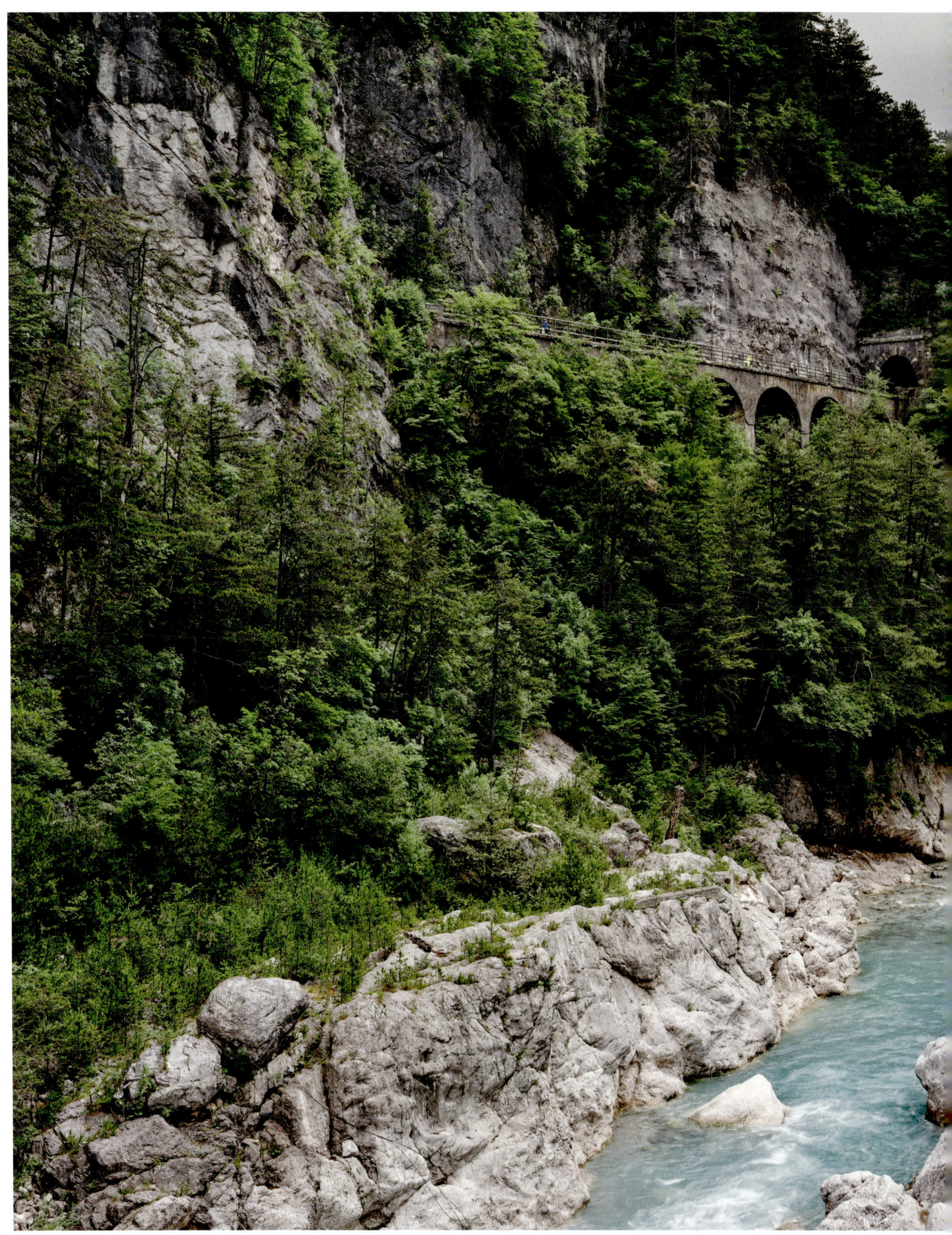

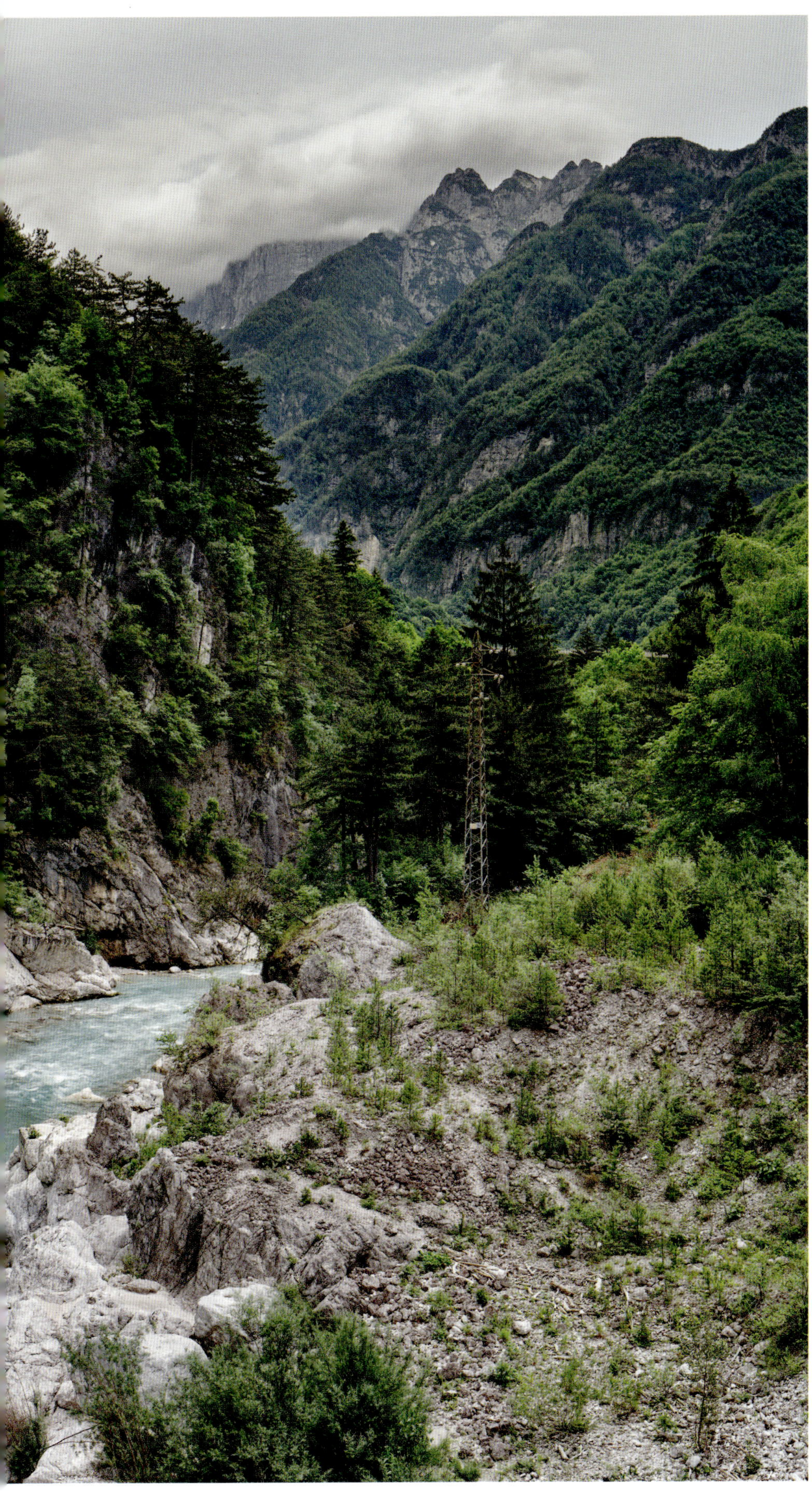

TARVISIO-UDINE RAILWAY

Thin tires instead of heavy iron wheels: The Tarvisio-Udine Railway (Pontebbana) has been converted into a bike path and is part of the "Ciclovia Alpe Adria." The new rail line runs between Tarvisio and the Canal del Ferro mostly in tunnels.

BOHINJ RAILWAY

Near the border town of Nova Gorica, the Solkan Bridge crosses the Soča (Isonzo). Opened in 1906, it is still considered the largest masonry arch bridge in the world. A few hundred yards later, the train enters the train station of Gorizia / Nova Gorica. The border between East and West, between Tito's Yugoslavia and Italy, used to run straight through the city and the train station. Now that's a thing of the past, thanks to the EU. ▽ ▽

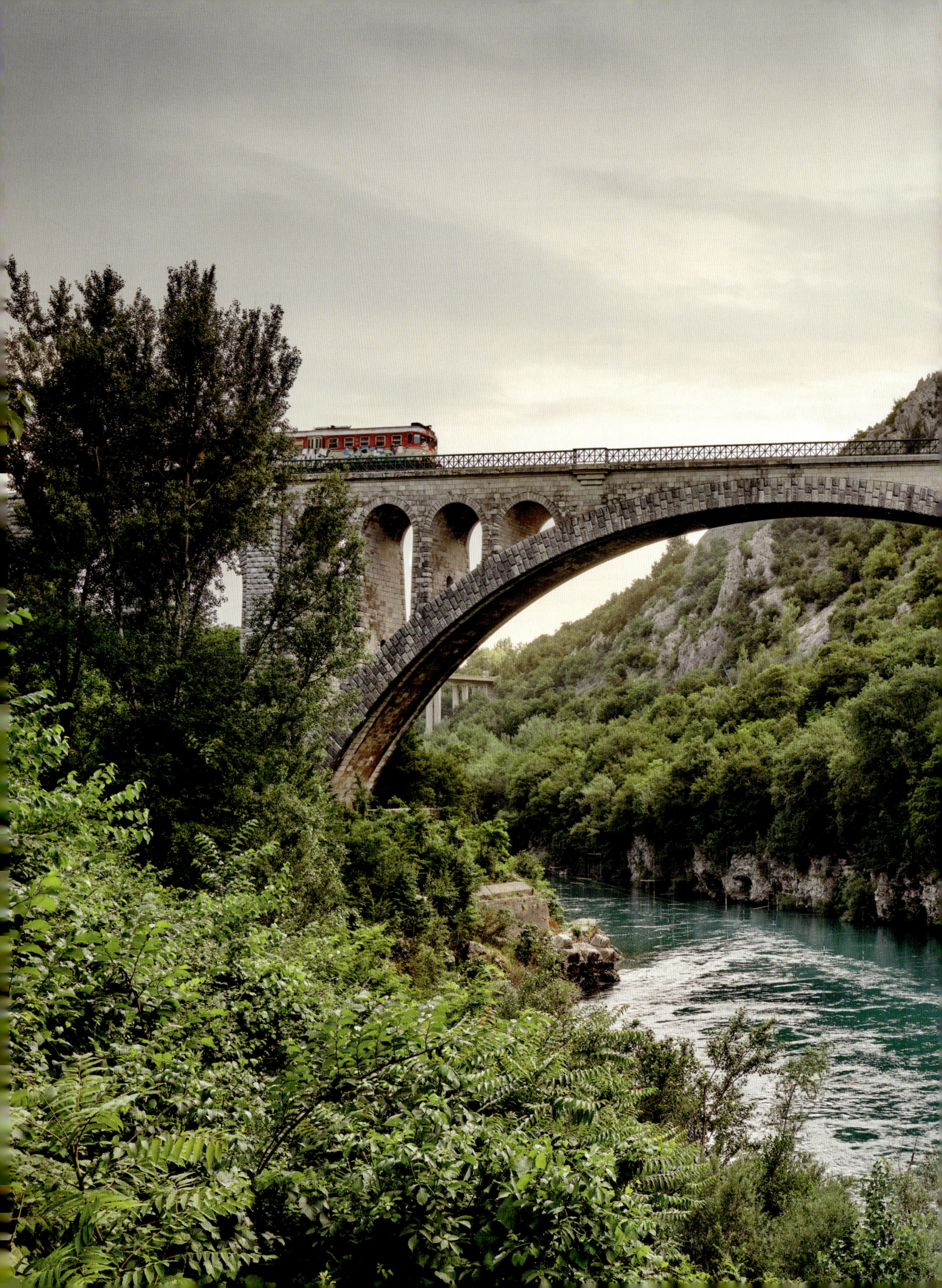

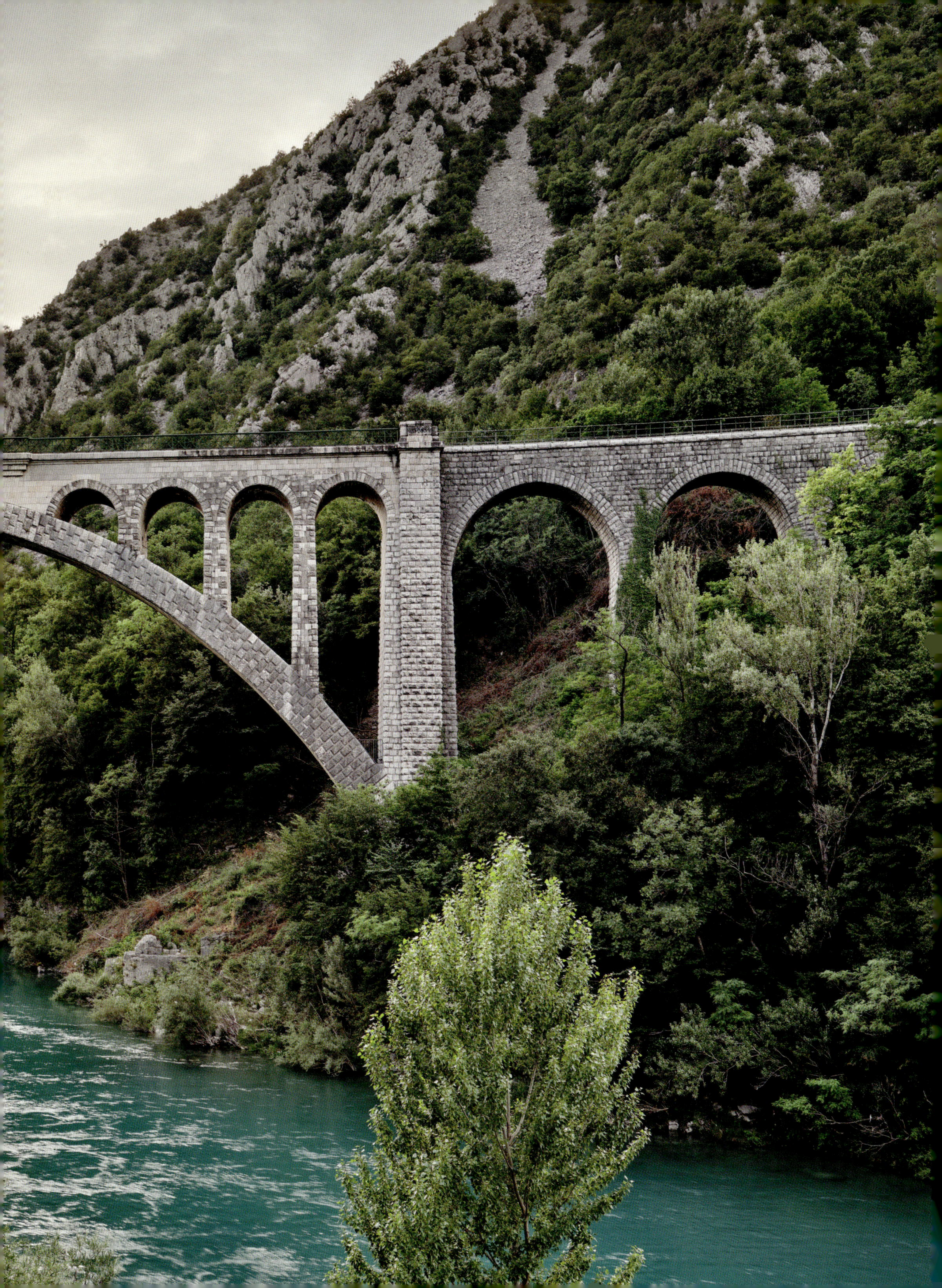

A LOAF OF BREAD MADE OF ORE AND A RUSHING RIVER

Here, (almost) everything revolves around iron. Stone is quarried at Erzberg and smelted in the industrial districts of Linz and Leoben. In earlier times, the ore was transported by rail, via the *Rudolf Railway* and the *Erzberg Railway*. The *Reichraming Forest Railway* owes its—rather short—life to another raw material of the region: wood.

If you want to go from Liezen to Leoben and are in a hurry, take the A9, which leads almost straight as an arrow over the Schober Pass into the industrial region on the Mur. However, the detour via the Gesäuse, Eisenerz, and Präbichl is much more rewarding. Not only does the route lead through the wildest gorge in Upper Styria—the Gesäuse—and past the Erzberg; it also immerses you in the history of this region.

It is closely connected to the Erzberg ("ore mountain"). For centuries, man has been working his way through it, literally, since it supplies extremely high-quality iron ore. The ore was first mined underground; later it was mined in open pits, which gave the "Styrian loaf of bread" its unmistakable appearance. However, the ore had to be not only mined but also transported to the furnaces in Linz and Leoben. This led to the construction of several train lines in the nineteenth century. As early as the 1870s, the Rudolf Railway was put into operation, leading from Hieflau on the Enn River to within a few miles of the Erzberg. In 1873, Vordernberg was connected, and Eisernz (from Leoben) a year later, but then it took awhile for the gap to be closed.

OVER THE PRÄBICHL—WITH OR WITHOUT THE RACK

It was decided—also for cost reasons—to use a combination of adhesion and cogwheel railroads. The mountain line was opened in 1891. The maximum gradients were 2.6 percent and 7.1 percent. During the construction of the summit tunnel on the Präbichl (4,022 feet / 1,226 meters), "a large rib was found 35 meters [115 feet] below the terrain, which some dying great beast might have deposited there for posterity during primeval times," according to *Mitteilungen des Deutschen und Österreichischen Alpenvereins* (*Announcements of the German and Austrian Alpine Club*). Dinosaurs at the Präbichl? Later, "primeval lizards" made of iron steamed over the pass for almost a century. It was not until the 1970s that they were gradually replaced by diesel locomotives that were more powerful and could handle the inclines without a rack. This brought the line a record: It became the steepest adhesion standard-gauge railroad in Europe! With the shift of freight transport from rail to road, the Erzberg Railway lost its importance. After a mudslide in 1988, operations between Vordernberg and Eisenerz were discontinued. A private group acquired the mountain route and now organizes museum trips over the pass, with vintage railcars from Vordernberg to Erzberg and back. What an experience!

THROUGH THE GESÄUSE

This is also conveyed by the journey through the Gesäuse, which since 2002 has been at the heart of the 43-square-mile (111-square-kilometer) national park of the same name. Engineers were also active here in the century before last. They laid iron rails along the Enns, which forces its way through a narrow gorge between Hieflau and Admont. This gorge did not get its name from the river but from the unmistakable roar of the high water coming from the sky-high rock faces.

In 2009, passenger traffic on the scenic route was discontinued. The Gstatterboden train station in the middle of the Gesäuse, once a base camp for many mountaineers, is deserted—no more whistles of approaching trains can be heard. Is the end of an era creeping in, which was once one to lead into the future?

FOREST RAILWAY (WALDBAHN)

Ore was not the only thing mined in the region; the Reichramiger Hintergebirge (mountain range) was an important supplier of wood for centuries. The raw material was transported to the customers by water, a cost-efficient but rather dangerous method.

With the dawn of modern times, log driving came to a standstill. The iron processing plants switched to coal firing, and the wood, which was usually badly damaged by the rough transport, could no longer be sold elsewhere. When a devastating winter storm felled more than 35 million cubic feet (1 million cubic meters) of timber during World War I, they decided in Reichramig to build a railroad to ensure the removal of the beetle-infested trees. The first section went into operation in 1920; just two years later, the line was extended and finally was expanded to a total length of almost 25 miles (41 kilometers)—with nineteen tunnels—by 1951. Even passenger cars ran on the lines at times. In 1971 the line was shut down due to a lack of profitability. Then the bulldozers arrived. Soon a branched network of wide forest tracks went through the Hintergebirge. Today, it is part of the Kalkalpen National Park—protecting nature instead of using it.

The "Bread Loaf of Styria"—a mountain with deep wounds. Each year, up to 3 million tons of ore are extracted. To the right of the center of the picture you can see the former loading station, the Erzberg train station, and the tunnel entrance. ▽ ▽

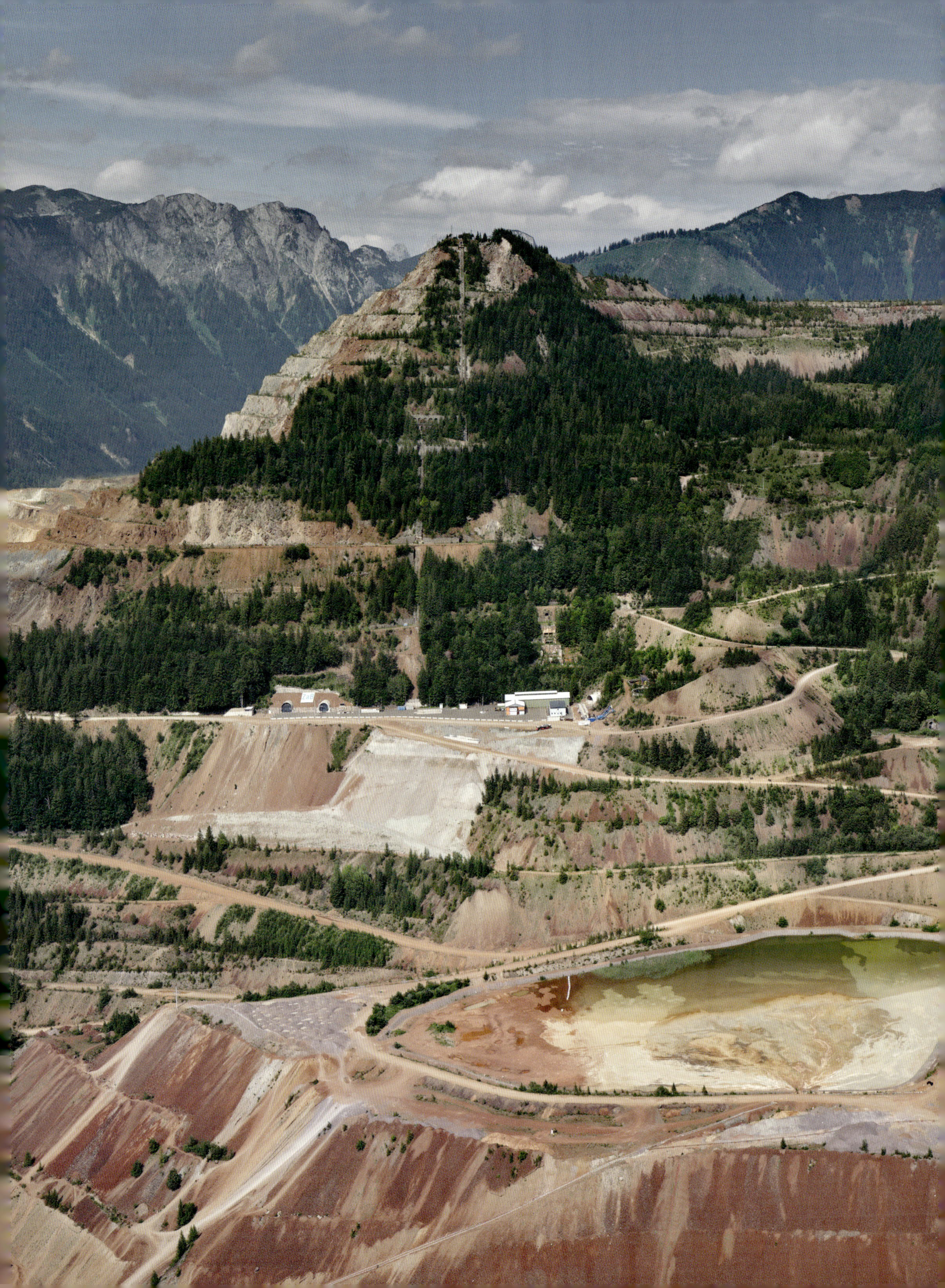

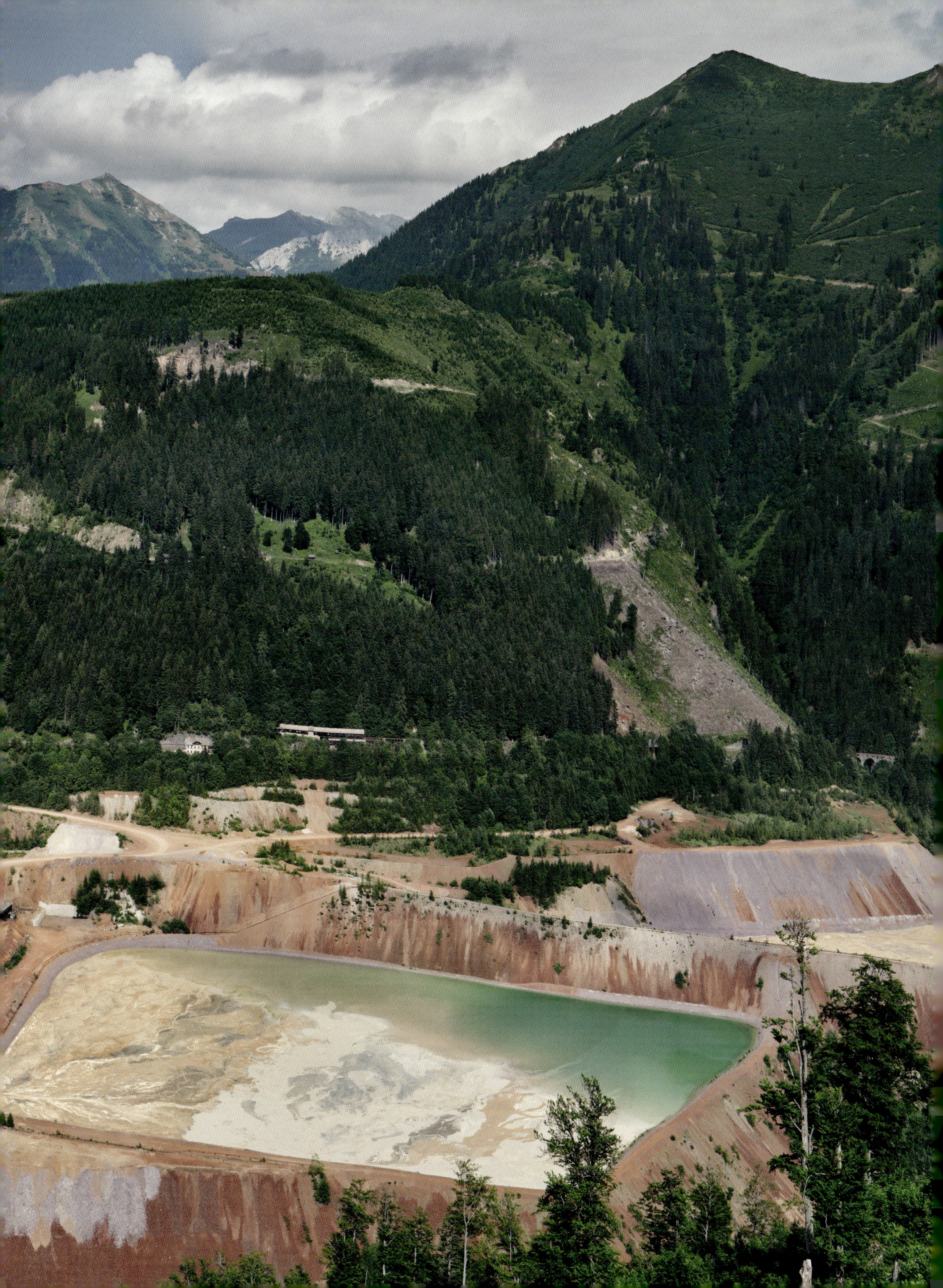

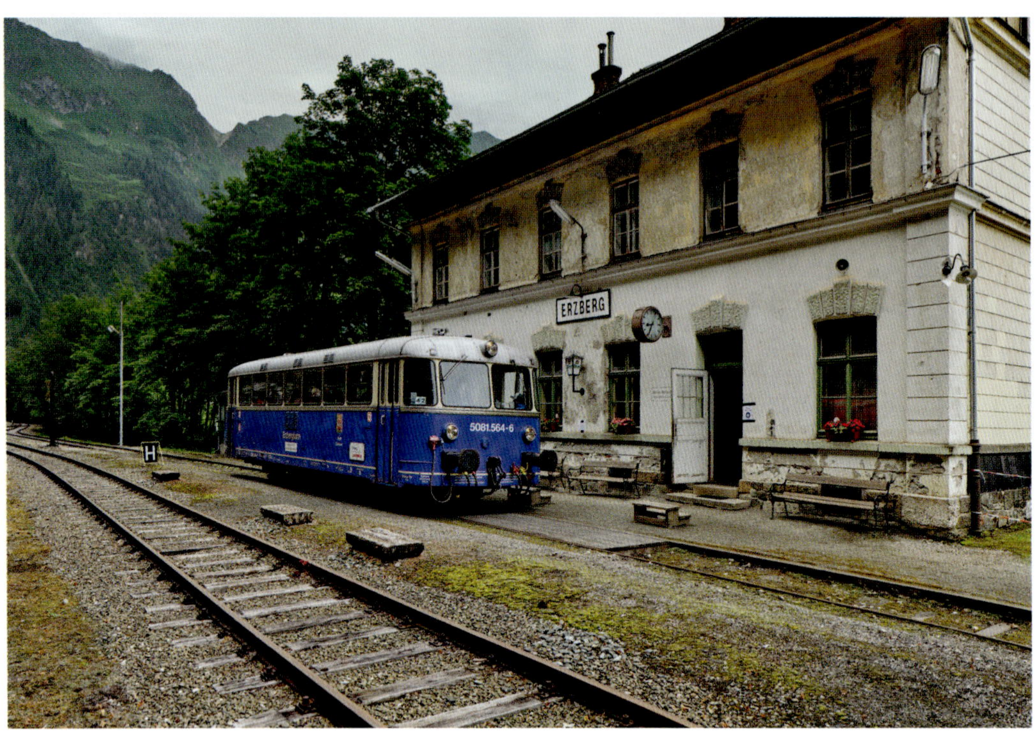

ERZBERG RAILWAY

A step back into the 1970s—train station and railcar
as they were in the past, all original. The rail bus of the
5081 series runs as a museum train over the Präbichl.

GESÄUSE RAILWAY

The Enns "rushes" at the entrance to the Gesäuse. The
mighty gorge surrounded by peaks was declared a
national park in 2002. ▷

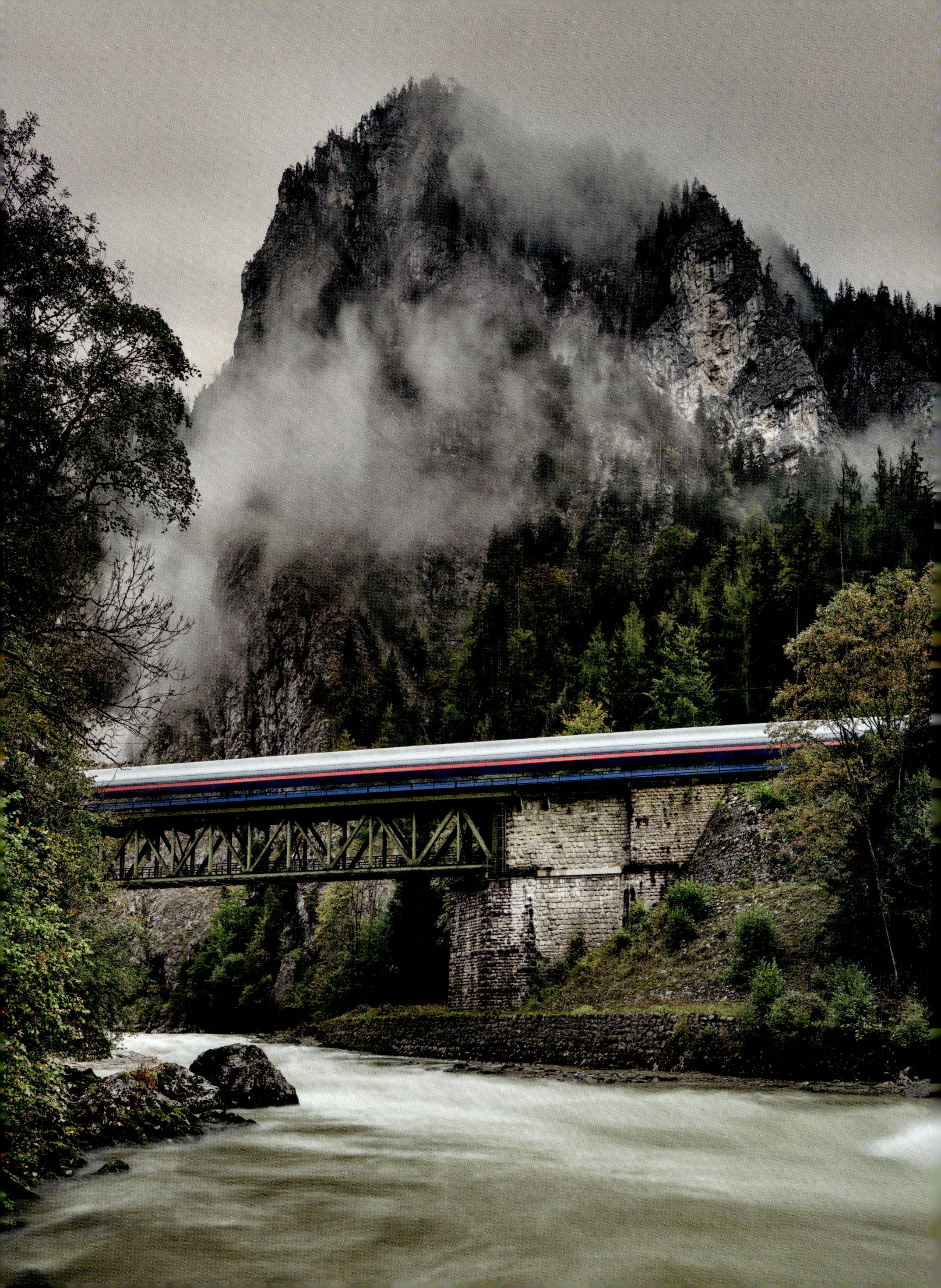

THE TECHNICAL GENIUS CARL VON GHEGA

In the far east of the wide Alpine range, almost at Vienna's doorstep, the *Semmering Railway* winds its way up to the spa town of the same name. Its crest lies just below the thousand-meter mark. You can go significantly higher a little to the north with the *Schneeberg Railway*. Austria's most popular place of pilgrimage also has a rail connection: from St. Pölten through a hundred curves with the *Mariazell Railway*.

Carl Ritter von Ghega is undoubtedly one of the most outstanding figures of the Imperial and Royal monarchy in the nineteenth century. It was a time of technical upheaval, also in transportation. And Carl von Ghega, born in Venice to Albanian parents, soon found a place there thanks to his pronounced talent for mathematics. He was educated at an almost breathtaking pace, first at the Vienna Military College, then at the famous University of Padua, where he graduated as doctor of mathematics at the tender age of seventeen!

His professional career began with road and canal projects in Veneto; Ghega was also involved in the construction of the Strada d'Alemagna (Treviso–Cortina d'Ampezzo). However, he became increasingly interested in the mode of transportation that would become the future: the railway. When he was assigned a project management role for the future rail network throughout the southern part of the monarchy, he promptly traveled to the United States for further training. The insights gained there ultimately flowed into his most famous construction: the Semmering Railway. His idea of an adhesion railway with a summit tunnel was dismissed by many contemporaries as nonsense. Carl von Ghega, knighted in 1851, confidently refuted it.

ONCE RIDICULED, TODAY A WORLD HERITAGE SITE

In 1854 the railroad line went into operation. It was a technological triumph, entirely to the taste of Ghega. His likeness adored the front of the twenty-schilling banknote of 1966. Since 1996, the Semmering Railway has been a UNESCO World Heritage Site. Despite its modest summit height of 2,946 feet (898 meters), it can certainly be called a mountain railroad. Between Gloggnitz and Mürzzuschlag, there are no fewer than fifteen tunnels and sixteen viaducts, several of which are double-decker, such has the 479-foot-long (146-meter-long) Kalte-Rinne Viaduct.

With all these structures, it is easy to forget the twenty thousand (!) workers who toiled along the line for six years, living in inhuman conditions in barracks camps. There were repeated outbreaks of typhoid and cholera. "In the vicinity of Klamm, cholera is beginning to spread terribly among the workers there, and there are already so many corpses each day, that the local cemetery will . . . not be able to accommodate them in a few days." (Johann Robert Pap, UNESCO World Heritage Semmering Railway, 2017). The price of progress?

Nevertheless, it could not be stopped; technology also took hold of the mountains. Tourism proved to be the driving force. As early as the 1870s, the first plans for a mountain railroad to the Schneeberg emerged, and before the end of the century, the first little train steamed up the mountain on the rack. Even before the construction of the railroad, the easternmost 6,560-foot (2,000-meter) peak in the Alps was a popular excursion destination for the Viennese, especially because of the phenomenal view. In the summer, you can even climb the Schneeberg at sunrise, with the help of an early train (departure at 4:00 or 4:45 a.m.). It's an experience you'll never forget.

THE PILGRIMAGE TO MARIAZELL

Even more popular with the public is the pilgrimage site of Mariazell. With up to one and a half million visitors a year, it even outshines the "Steffl" in Vienna. It is therefore not surprising that the idea for a railway to the pilgrimage site emerged very early on in order to channel the rush of pilgrims.

Today it is called "the stairway to heaven." But will a trip on the narrow-gauge railroad from St. Pölten to Mariazell really bring pilgrims closer to heaven? Nature lovers will probably answer in the affirmative, in light of the picturesque scenery in the shadow of the Ötscher mountain and its mighty valleys. The almost 53-mile (85-kilometer) stretch opened in 1907 and was electrified just two decades later. It repeatedly comes close to the canyon and offers an unobstructed view of what is probably the most famous mountain in Lower Austria.

The ride, as winding as it is leisurely, ends within sight of Mariazell's basilica. Mountain enthusiasts who have become hungry during the two-and-a-half-hour ride head for one of the many inns. The others visit the church. The church welcomes its visitors with three towers. The middle one is unmistakably from the Gothic period; it is supported by two more towers to the left and the right built in the early baroque style by the Grisons architect Domenico Sciassia in the seventeenth century. A success?

Incidentally, there are three legends surrounding the Mariazell pilgrimage. The oldest tells of the miracle of a statue of the Virgin Mary (around 1550); more recent is the legend of a miraculous healing. The last one was the victory of the Hungarian king Ludwig I against a numerically far superior Turkish army.

A tip: The hike through the Ötscher Canyon can be combined very well with a train ride. The walking time from the Erlaufklause stop to Gösing along the Mariazell railroad is about six hours.

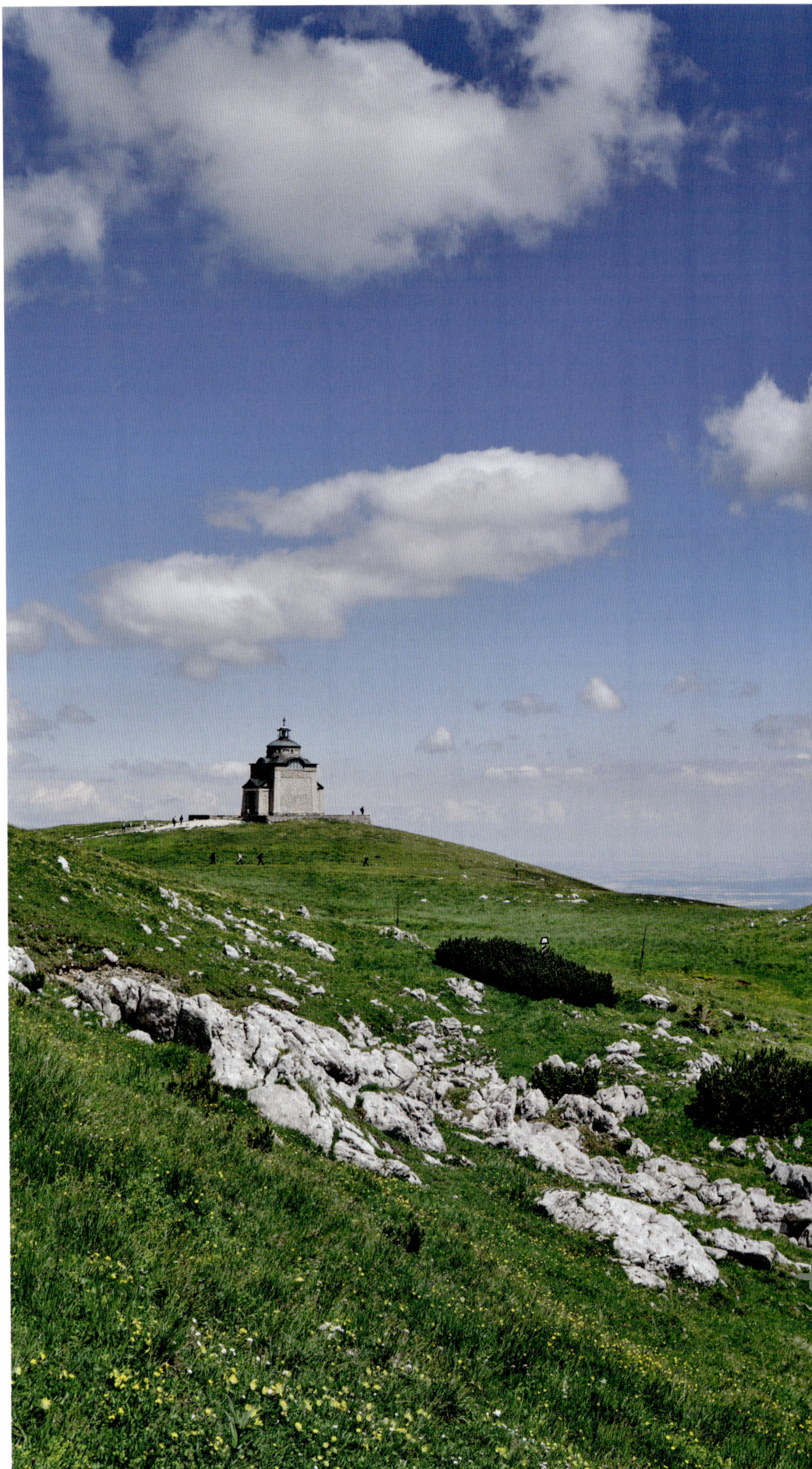

A "salamander car" of the
Schneeberg Railway entering the
mountain station (5,892 feet /
1,796 meters). Then you are only
a few steps away to the Elisabeth-
kircherl. Emperor Franz Joseph
I had the art nouveau building
built in 1901 in memory of his wife,
who was murdered in Geneva.
From the green hillside terrace,
the view extends far out into the
flat countryside.

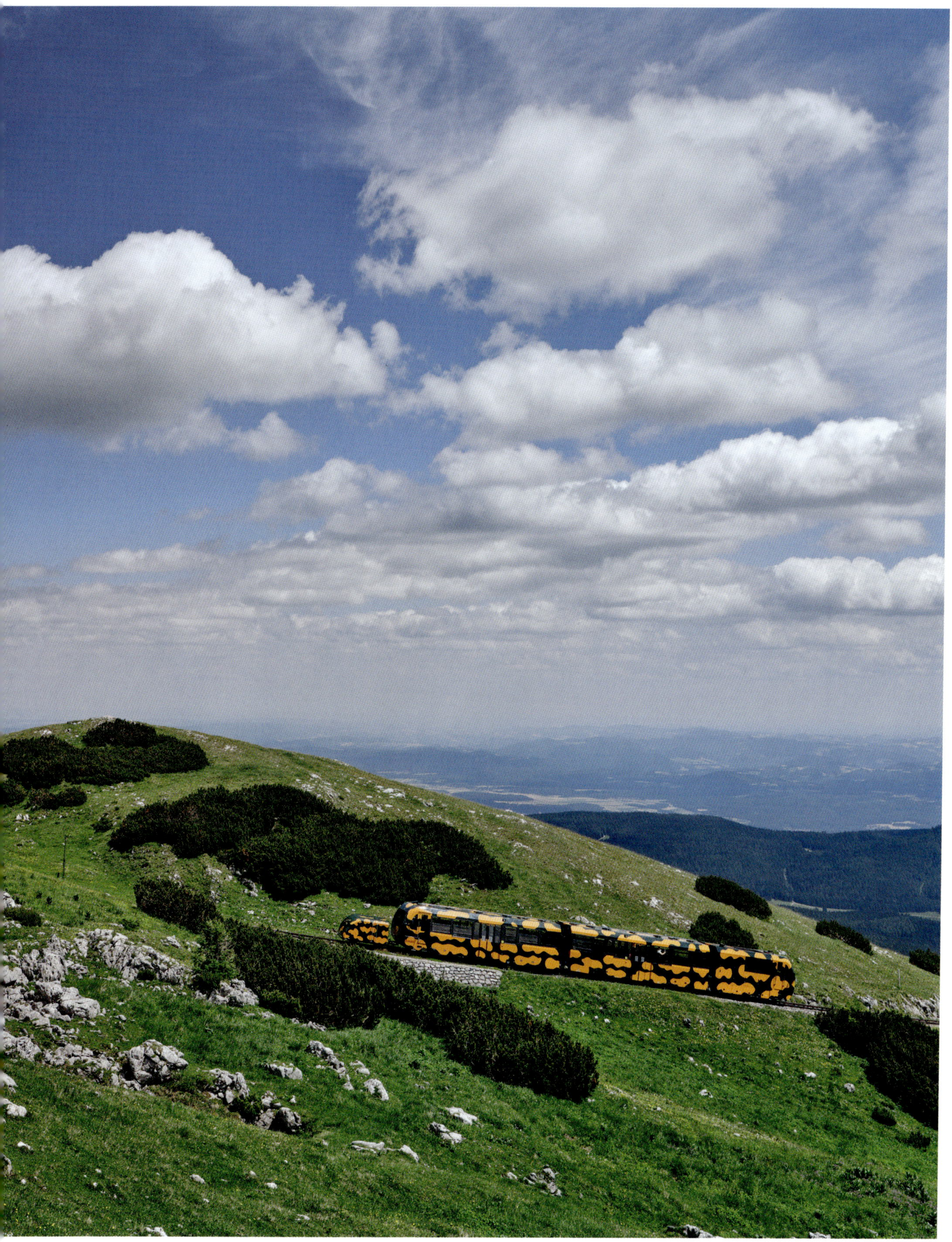

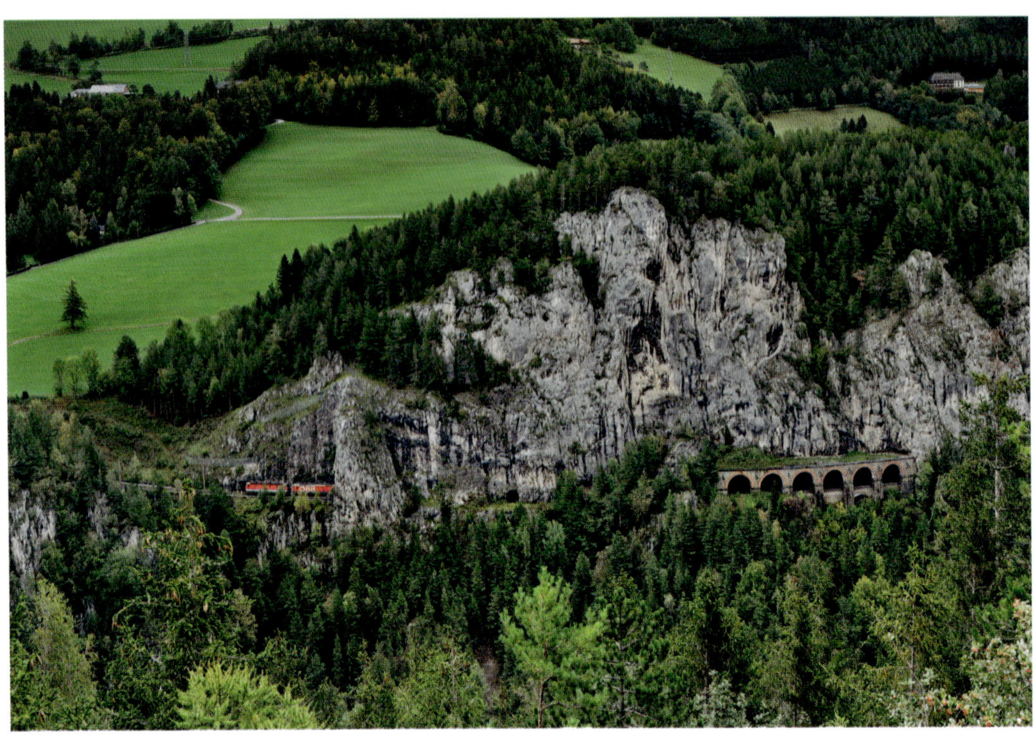

SEMMERING RAILWAY

The Semmering Railway passes through the vertical drop of the Weinzettelwand in three tunnels and two galleries with a total length of about 2,297 feet (700 meters). △

The Semmering Railway at the Klamm-Schottwein station. In the foreground is an overhead control station, which makes it possible to switch tracks in the event of disruptions or accidents. In this case, trains run in both directions on one track. ▷

A particularly beautiful view of the Semmering Railway, especially of the double-decker Kalte-Rinne Viaduct, is offered by the "twenty-schilling view" on the Wolfsbergkogel. The famous structure was depicted on the twenty-schilling banknote; hence the name. On the right under the Polleroswand is the Krauselklause Viaduct. ▽ ▽

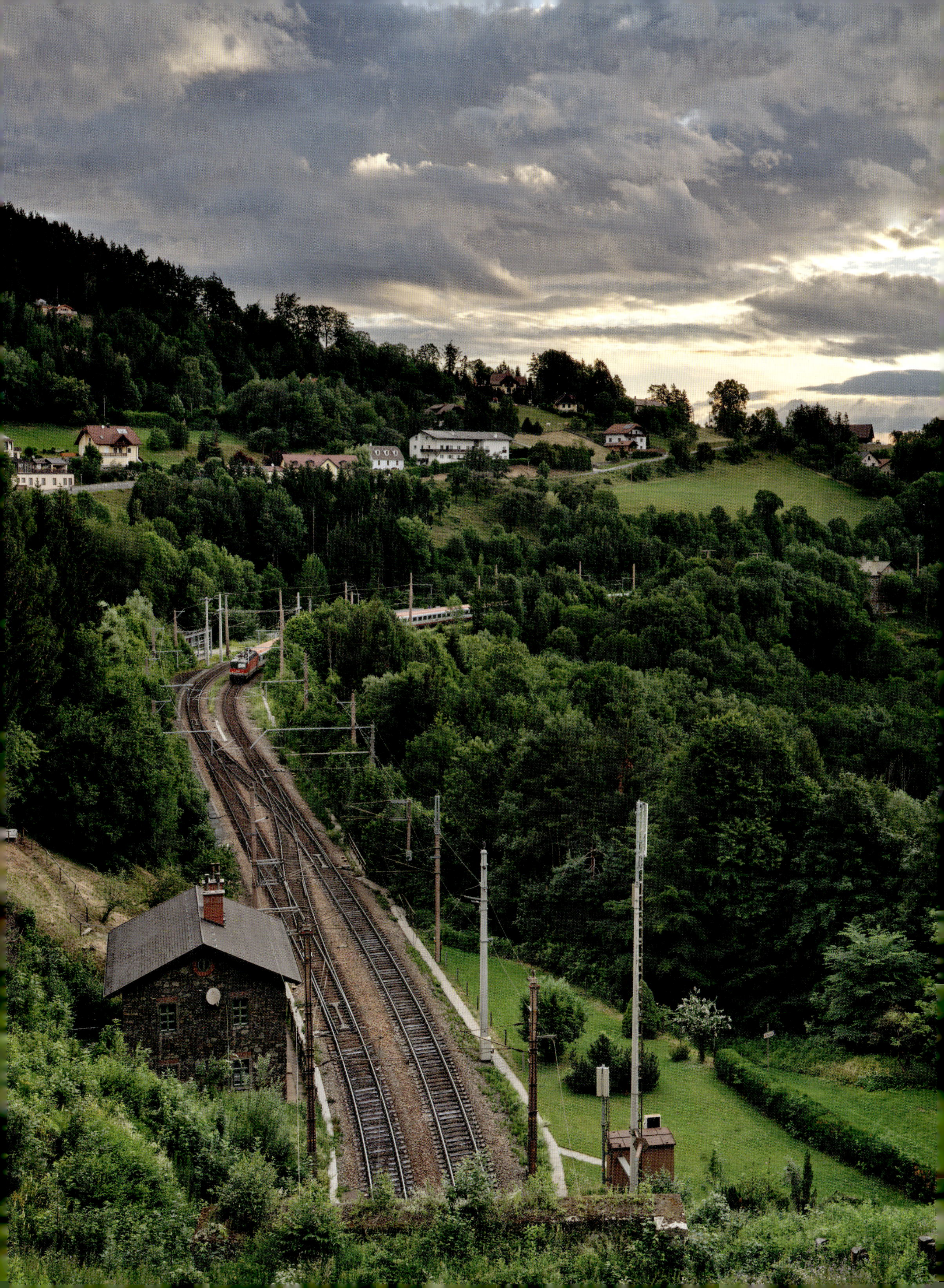

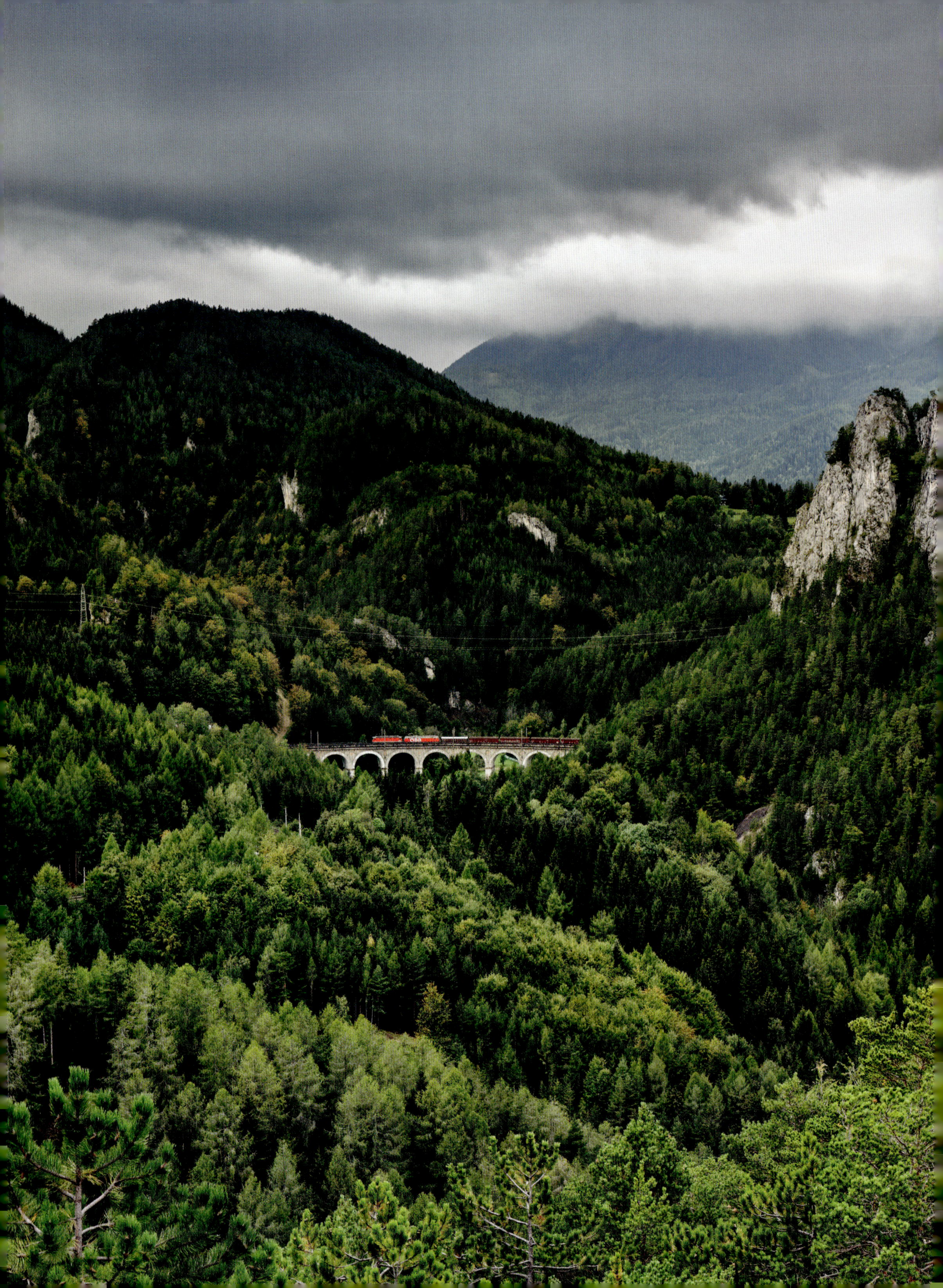